Making Software

Making Software

What Really Works, and Why We Believe It

Edited by Andy Oram and Greg Wilson

O'REILLY®

Beijing · Cambridge · Farnham · Köln · Sebastopol · Tokyo

Making Software
Edited by Andy Oram and Greg Wilson

Copyright © 2011 O'Reilly Media, Inc.. All rights reserved.
Printed in the United States of America.

Published by O'Reilly Media, Inc., 1005 Gravenstein Highway North, Sebastopol, CA 95472.

O'Reilly books may be purchased for educational, business, or sales promotional use. Online editions are also available for most titles (*http://my.safaribooksonline.com*). For more information, contact our corporate/institutional sales department: (800) 998-9938 or *corporate@oreilly.com*.

Editors: Andy Oram and Mary Treseler	**Indexer:** Lucie Haskins
Production Editor: Kristen Borg	**Cover Designer:** Mark Paglietti
Copyeditor: Genevieve d'Entremont	**Interior Designer:** David Futato
Proofreader: Kristen Borg	**Illustrator:** Robert Romano

Printing History:

October 2010:   First Edition.

ISBN: 978-0-596-80832-7

[M]

1286812050

CONTENTS

Preface

Does the MMR vaccine cause autism? Does watching violence on TV make children more violent? Are some programming languages better than others? People argue about these questions every day. Every serious attempt to answer the first two questions relies on the scientific method: careful collection of evidence, and impartial evaluation of its implications. Until recently, though, only a few people have tried to apply these techniques to the third. When it comes to computing, it often seems that a couple glasses of beer and an anecdote about a startup in Warsaw are all the "evidence" most programmers expect.

That is changing, thanks in part to the work of the contributors to this book. Drawing on fields as diverse as data mining, cognitive psychology, and sociology, they and their colleagues are creating an evidence-based approach to software engineering. By gathering evidence drawn from a myriad of primary sources and analyzing the results, they are shedding new light onto some vexing questions of software development. What do most programmers get wrong in their first job? Does test-driven development lead to better code? What about pair programming, or code reviews? Is it possible to predict the likely number of bugs in a piece of code before it's released? If so, how?

The essays in this book will present answers to some of these questions, and explain why the jury is still out on others. Just as importantly, they will show you how to find and evaluate evidence yourself, both quantitatively and qualitatively. Every programmer is unique, and no two programs are exactly the same, but if you are careful, patient, and open-minded, they *can* be persuaded to give up their secrets.

We hope the questions and answers in this book will change how you think about software development. We also hope these essays will persuade you to say, "Citation, please," the next time someone claims that one way of laying out braces in C or Java is better than another. And as with *Beautiful Code* (Andy and Greg's previous collaboration for O'Reilly), all author royalties will be donated to Amnesty International, which has been demanding answers to much more difficult questions than these for almost 50 years.

Organization of This Book

Each chapter of this book was written by a different contributor or team. The order is not particularly important, but we've started the book with several chapters that look at the topics of research, validity, and meaning at a rather high level. We think that reading Part I, "General Principles of Searching For and Using Evidence," will give you a stronger background for understanding Part II, "Specific Topics in Software Engineering."

Part I consists of the following contributions:

Chapter 1, *The Quest for Convincing Evidence*, by Tim Menzies and Forrest Shull.

Chapter 2, *Credibility, or Why Should I Insist on Being Convinced?*, by Lutz Prechelt and Marian Petre.

Chapter 3, *What We Can Learn from Systematic Reviews*, by Barbara Kitchenham.

Chapter 4, *Understanding Software Engineering Through Qualitative Methods*, by Andrew Ko.

Chapter 5, *Learning Through Application: The Maturing of the QIP in the SEL*, by Victor R. Basili.

Chapter 6, *Personality, Intelligence, and Expertise: Impacts on Software Development*, by Jo E. Hannay.

Chapter 7, *Why Is It So Hard to Learn to Program?*, by Mark Guzdial.

Chapter 8, *Beyond Lines of Code: Do We Need More Complexity Metrics?*, by Israel Herraiz and Ahmed E. Hassan.

Part II consists of the following contributions:

Chapter 9, *An Automated Fault Prediction System*, by Elaine J. Weyuker and Thomas J. Ostrand.

Chapter 10, *Architecting: How Much and When?*, by Barry Boehm.

Chapter 11, *Conway's Corollary*, by Christian Bird.

Chapter 12, *How Effective Is Test-Driven Development?*, by Burak Turhan, Lucas Layman, Madeline Diep, Hakan Erdogmus, and Forrest Shull.

Chapter 13, *Why Aren't More Women in Computer Science?*, by Michele A. Whitecraft and Wendy M. Williams.

Chapter 14, *Two Comparisons of Programming Languages*, by Lutz Prechelt.

Chapter 15, *Quality Wars: Open Source Versus Proprietary Software*, by Diomidis Spinellis.

Chapter 16, *Code Talkers*, by Robert DeLine.

Chapter 17, *Pair Programming*, by Laurie Williams.

Chapter 18, *Modern Code Review*, by Jason Cohen.

Chapter 19, *A Communal Workshop or Doors That Close?*, by Jorge Aranda.

Chapter 20, *Identifying and Managing Dependencies in Global Software Development* by Marcelo Cataldo.

Chapter 21, *How Effective Is Modularization?*, by Neil Thomas and Gail Murphy.

Chapter 22, *The Evidence for Design Patterns*, Walter Tichy.

Chapter 23, *Evidence-Based Failure Prediction*, by Nachiappan Nagappan and Thomas Ball.

Chapter 24, *The Art of Collecting Bug Reports*, by Rahul Premraj and Thomas Zimmermann.

Chapter 25, *Where Do Most Software Flaws Come From?*, by Dewayne Perry.

Chapter 26, *Novice Professionals: Recent Graduates in a First Software Engineering Job*, by Andrew Begel and Beth Simon.

Chapter 27, *Mining Your Own Evidence*, by Kim Sebastian Herzig and Andreas Zeller.

Chapter 28, *Copy-Paste as a Principled Engineering Tool*, by Michael Godfrey and Cory Kapser.

Chapter 29, *How Usable Are Your APIs?*, by Steven Clarke.

Chapter 30, *What Does 10x Mean? Measuring Variations in Programmer Productivity*, by Steve McConnell.

Conventions Used in This Book

The following typographical conventions are used in this book:

Italic
    Indicates new terms, URLs, email addresses, filenames, and file extensions.

`Constant width`
    Used for program listings, as well as within paragraphs to refer to program elements such as variable or function names.

`Constant width italic`
    Shows text that should be replaced with user-supplied values or values determined by context.

Safari® Books Online

 Safari Books Online is an on-demand digital library that lets you easily search over 7,500 technology and creative reference books and videos to find the answers you need quickly.

With a subscription, you can read any page and watch any video from our library online. Read books on your cell phone and mobile devices. Access new titles before they are available for print, and get exclusive access to manuscripts in development and post feedback for the authors. Copy and paste code samples, organize your favorites, download chapters, bookmark key sections, create notes, print out pages, and benefit from tons of other time-saving features.

O'Reilly Media has uploaded this book to the Safari Books Online service. To have full digital access to this book and others on similar topics from O'Reilly and other publishers, sign up for free at *http://my.safaribooksonline.com*.

Using Code Examples

This book is here to help you get your job done. In general, you may use the code in this book in your programs and documentation. You do not need to contact us for permission unless you're reproducing a significant portion of the code. For example, writing a program that uses several chunks of code from this book does not require permission. Selling or distributing a CD-ROM of examples from O'Reilly books *does* require permission. Answering a question by citing this book and quoting example code does not require permission. Incorporating a significant amount of example code from this book into your product's documentation *does* require permission.

We appreciate, but do not require, attribution. An attribution usually includes the title, author, publisher, and ISBN. For example: "*Making Software* edited by Andy Oram and Greg Wilson. Copyright 2011 O'Reilly Media, Inc., 978-0-596-80832-7."

If you feel your use of code examples falls outside fair use or the permission given above, feel free to contact us at *permissions@oreilly.com*.

How to Contact Us

Please address comments and questions concerning this book to the publisher:

> O'Reilly Media, Inc.
> 1005 Gravenstein Highway North
> Sebastopol, CA 95472
> 800-998-9938 (in the United States or Canada)
> 707-829-0515 (international or local)
> 707-829-0104 (fax)

We have a web page for this book, where we list errata, examples, and any additional information. You can access this page at:

> *http://www.oreilly.com/catalog/9780596808327*

To comment or ask technical questions about this book, send email to:

> *bookquestions@oreilly.com*

For more information about our books, conferences, Resource Centers, and the O'Reilly Network, see our website at:

> *http://www.oreilly.com*

## PART I

General Principles of Searching For and Using Evidence

When researchers investigate programmer behavior, a messy area involving human factors, their methods must become ever more sophisticated. Above all, we must be aware of how much we can learn and where we must accept limits to our knowledge. Therefore, this section discusses the principles that help us find software engineering data we can trust and apply it with appropriate caution to new situations. The chapters touch on some applications of the data, but focus on broader lessons that you can take to other contentious issues in software engineering.

## CHAPTER ONE

The Quest for Convincing Evidence

Tim Menzies
Forrest Shull

What makes evidence elegant, valid, useful, and convincing? This is the question the authors of this chapter have been pursuing for the past two decades. Between us, we have published over 200 papers on empirical software engineering and organized seemingly countless panel discussions, workshops, conferences, and special journal issues about the topic.

In this article, we want to reflect a little. We review the progress in software engineering so far and ask, what's it all good for? And where do we go from here? Our findings were that:

- The quest for convincing evidence is much, much harder than we first thought.
- Software engineering researchers need to work together more as a community to share more of our evidence.
- We need to acknowledge that evidence has a context-specific component. Evidence that is convincing to us might not be convincing to you. Accordingly, we need to be armed and ready to reinterpret and reanalyze, if ever the audience changes.

In the Beginning

Decades ago, when asked what we thought was "beautiful evidence," we would have laid out some combination of the following traits:

Elegance of studies

Many studies in software engineering include human factors, because the effectiveness of many software technologies depends heavily on the people who are using them.[*] But dealing with human variability is a very challenging task. Studies with sophisticated designs that minimize these confounding aspects can be a source of admiration for other researchers. For example, a study by Basili and Selby [Basili and Selby 1987] used a fractional factorial design, in which every developer used every technique under examination, and every technique was used on every program snippet in the experiment.

Statistical strength

As mathematical sophistication grows, so too does an emphasis on statistically significant results, so that researchers can be confident that their theory has some real-world effect that can be picked out from random background noise.

Replicability of results

Results are far more convincing when they're found again and again in many different contexts—i.e., not limited to one context or set of experimental conditions. In other sciences, replication builds confidence, and for this reason much effort has been expended to make software engineering experiments easy to rerun by other researchers in other contexts [Basili et al. 1999]. As an example of replicability, Turhan showed that software defect predictors learned at other sites could be successfully applied at a new site [Turhan et al. 2009].

The State of Evidence Today

Looking back, we now realize how naive our definitions of convincing evidence were. Elegant, statistically strong, replicated evidence turns out to be harder to find than we ever thought, and moreover, often doesn't satisfy the more relevant goals we have for our research.

Challenges to the Elegance of Studies

We've found that elegant studies may be persuasive to those with sufficient training in research, but can be hard to explain to practitioners because they generally introduce constraints and simplifications that make the context less representative of real development environments. For example, the Basili and Selby study applied the techniques under study only to "toy" problems, none more than 400 lines of code, in an artificial environment. This

---

[*] After studying 161 projects, Boehm [Boehm et al. 2000] found that the best project personnel are 3.5 times more productive than the worst.

study is often cited, and although it has been the subject of many replications, it does not seem that any of them used substantially larger or more representative applications [Runeson et al. 2006]. Although this elegant study has made a strong contribution to our understanding of the strengths and weaknesses of different approaches for removing defects from code, it is perhaps not ideal for a substantial part of our thinking on this subject to come from relatively small code segments.

Challenges to Statistical Strength

There is surprisingly little consensus about what constitutes "strong" statistics for real-world problems. First, there is the issue of external validity: whether the measures that are being tested adequately reflect the real-world phenomena of interest. Showing statistical significance is of no help when the measures are meaningless. For example, Foss et al. show that commonly used assessment measures for effort estimation are fundamentally broken [Foss et al. 2003]. Worse, they argue that there is no single fix:

> [I]t is futile to search for the Holy Grail: a single, simple-to-use, universal goodness-of-fit kind of metric, which can be applied with ease to compare (different methods).

Moreover, different authors apply very different statistical analyses, and no one method is generally accepted as "strongest" by a broad community:

- Demsar documents the enormous range of statistical methods seen at one prominent international conference focusing on learning lessons from data [Demsar 2006].

- Cohen discusses the use of standard statistical hypothesis testing for making scientific conclusions. He scathingly describes such testing as a "potent but sterile intellectual rake who leaves...no viable scientific offspring" [Cohen 1988].

In support of Cohen's thesis, we offer the following salutary lesson. Writing in the field of marketing, Armstrong [Armstrong 2007] reviews one study that, using significance testing, concludes that estimates generated from multiple sources do no better than those generated from a single source. He then demolishes this conclusion by listing 31 studies where multiple source prediction consistently out-performs single source prediction by 3.4% to 23.4% (average = 12.5%). In every study surveyed by Armstrong, these improvements are the exact opposite of what would be predicted from the significance test results.

Based on these discoveries, we have changed our views on statistical analysis. Now, as far as possible, we use succinct visualizations to make some point (and demote statistical significance tests to the role of a "reasonableness test" for the conclusions drawn from the visualizations).†

---

† But we still reject about two journal submissions per month because they report only mean value results, with no statistical or visual representation of the variance around that mean. At the very least, we recommend a Mann-Whitney or Wilcoxon test (for unpaired and pair results, respectively) to demonstrate that apparently different results might actually be different.

Challenges to Replicability of Results

Replicability has proved to be a very elusive goal. On certain topics, there is little evidence that results from one project have been, or can be, generalized to others:

- Zimmermann studied 629 pairs of software development projects [Zimmermann 2009]. In only 4% of cases was a defect prediction model learned from one project useful on its pair.

- A survey by Kitchenham et al. claims that one project's data is useful for effort estimation on a second one [Kitchenham et al. 2007]. They found the existing evidence inconclusive and even contradictory.

On other topics, we can find evidence that a certain effect holds across a number of different contexts—e.g., that a mature technique such as software inspections can find a significant amount of the extant defects in a software work product [Shull 2002]. However, if a new study reports evidence to the contrary, it is still difficult to determine whether the new (or old) study was somehow flawed or whether the study was in fact run in a unique environment. Given the wide variation in the contexts in which software development is done, both conclusions are often equally plausible.

Indeed, it would seem that despite the intuitive appeal of replicable results, there are either very few such studies related to a specific software engineering question or the studies are incomplete.

As an example of a lack of studies, Menzies studied 100 software quality assurance methods proposed by various groups (such as IEEE1017 and the internal NASA IV&V standards) and found no experiments showing that any method is more cost-effective than any other [Menzies et al. 2008].

As examples in which available studies were incomplete:

- Zannier et al. studied a randomly selected subset of 5% of the papers ever published at ICSE, the self-described premier software engineering conference [Zannier et al. 2006]. They found that of the papers that claim to be "empirical," very few of them (2%) compare methods from multiple researchers.

- Neto et al. reported a survey of the literature on Model-Based Testing (MBT) approaches [Neto et al. 2008]. They found 85 papers that described 71 distinct MBT approaches, and a very small minority of studies with any experimental component, indicating an overall tendency for researchers to continue innovating and reporting on new approaches rather than understanding the comparable practical benefits of existing ones.

To check whether these papers were isolated reports or part of a more general pattern, we reviewed all presentations made at the PROMISE‡ conference on repeatable software engineering experiments. Since 2005, at the PROMISE conference:

- There have been 68 presentations, 48 of which either tried a new analysis on old data or made reports in the style of [Zannier 2006]: i.e., that a new method worked for one particular project.
- Nine papers raised questions about the validity of prior results (e.g., [Menzies 2009a]).
- Four papers argued that the generality of software engineering models was unlikely or impossible (e.g., [Briand 2006]).
- Only rarely (7 out of 68 presentations) did researchers report generalizations from one project to other projects:
  — Four papers reported that a software quality predictor learned from one project was usefully applied to a new project (e.g., [Weyuker et al. 2008] and [Tosun et al. 2009]).
  — Three papers made a partial case that such generality was possible (e.g., [Boehm 2009]).

Somewhat alarmed at these findings, we discussed them with leading empirical software engineering researchers in the United States and Europe. Our conversations can be summarized as follows:

- Vic Basili pioneered empirical software engineering (SE) for over 30 years. After asserting that empirical software engineering is healthier now than in the 1980s, he acknowledged that (a) results thus far are incomplete, and (b) there are few examples of methods that are demonstrably useful on multiple projects [Basili 2009].
- David Budgen, along with Barbara Kitchenham, is a leading European advocate of "evidence-based software engineering" (EBSE). In EBSE, the practices of software engineers should be based on methods with well-founded support in the literature. Budgen and Kitchenham ask, "Is evidence-based software engineering mature enough for practice and policy?" Their answer is "no, not yet": the software engineering field needs to significantly restructure itself before we can show that results can be replicated in different projects [Budgen et al. 2009]. They argue for different reporting standards in software engineering, specifically, the use of "structured abstracts" to simplify the large-scale analysis of the SE literature.

‡ See *http://promisedata.org*.

Change We Can Believe In

To date, we have not realized our dream of evidence that is elegant, statistically sound, and replicable. And where we have found evidence in each of these categories, it has not always had the impact we hoped for. Perhaps we need to revisit our definitions of "convincing evidence." Given the feedback in the previous section, is there a more practical definition of convincing evidence that should be motivating researchers?

A more feasible (if humble) definition is this: convincing evidence *motivates change*. We suspect that many of the authors in this book began their hunt for convincing evidence when they saw firsthand the problems and difficulties in real-world software development. The Holy Grail for such researchers tends to be the research results that can create real-world improvement.

To motivate change, some influential audience has to trust the evidence. One way to deal with the lack of rigor in experience reports or case studies might be to assign a "confidence rating" to each piece of evidence. The rating would attempt to reflect where each report fit on a spectrum that ranges from anecdotal or problematic evidence to very trustworthy evidence. Such evaluations are an essential part of the process proposed by Kitchenham for systematic reviews and aggregations of software engineering studies [Kitchenham 2004]. A simple scale aimed at helping to communicate confidence levels to practitioners can be found in a paper by Feldmann [Feldmann et al. 2006].

Generating truly convincing bodies of evidence would also require a shift in the way results are disseminated. It may well be that scientific publications are not the only technology required to convey evidence. Among other problems, these publications usually don't make raw data available for other researchers to reanalyze, reinterpret, and verify. Also, although the authors of such publications try very hard to be exhaustive in their description of context, it is almost impossible to list every possible factor that could be relevant.

What may hold more promise is the creation of software engineering data repositories that contain results across different research environments (or at least across projects) and from which analyses can be undertaken. For example:

The University of Nebraska's Software-artifact Infrastructure Research (SIR) site[§]
> This repository stores software-related artifacts that researchers can use in rigorous controlled experimentation with program analysis and software testing techniques, and that educators can use to train students in controlled experimentation. The repository contains many Java and C software systems, in multiple versions, together with supporting artifacts such as test suites, fault data, and scripts. The artifacts in this repository have been used in hundreds of publications.

[§] *http://sir.unl.edu/*

The NASA Software Engineering Laboratory (SEL)

The NASA laboratory (described in Chapter 5) was a great success; its impact was large, and its data and results continue to be cited. One important lesson concerned its context: the leaders of the laboratory required researchers who wanted to use their data to spend time in the lab, so that they could understand the context correctly and not misinterpret results from their analyses.

CeBASE

This was an NSF-funded effort to create repositories of data and lessons learned that could be shared and reanalyzed by other researchers. We leveraged experiences from the SEL to explore ways of contextualizing the data with less overhead, such as by tagging all data sets with a rich set of metadata that described from where the data was drawn. These experiences in turn provided the underpinnings for a "lessons learned" repository maintained by the U.S. Defense Department's Defense Acquisition University,‖ which allows end users to specify their own context according to variables such as size of the project, criticality, or domain, and find practices with evidence from similar environments.

The PROMISE project

Another active software engineering repository comes from the PROMISE project, cited earlier in this chapter. PROMISE seeks repeatable software engineering experiments. The project has three parts:

- An online repository of public-domain data.# At the time of this writing, the repository has 91 data sets. Half refer to defect prediction, and the remainder explore effort prediction, model-based SE, text mining of SE data, and other issues.

- An annual conference where authors are strongly encouraged not only to publish papers, but also to contribute to the repository the data they used to make their conclusions.

- Special journal issues to publish the best papers from the conference [Menzies 2008].

Repositories are especially useful when they provide a link back to the contributors of the data. We need to recognize that data can seldom stand alone; authors should expect as a norm rather than an anomaly to have to answer questions and get involved in a dialogue with those trying to interpret their work. Such contacts are very important to learn the context from which the data was drawn, and possibly help users navigate to the data that is most relevant for their question or their own context. For example, Gunes Koru at University of Maryland, Baltimore County (UMBC) found a systematic error in some of the PROMISE data sets. Using the blogging software associated with the PROMISE repository, he was able to publicize the error. Further,

‖ See *https://bpch.dau.mil*.

See *http://promisedata.org/data*.

through the PROMISE blog,* he contacted the original data generators who offered extensive comments on the source of those errors and how to avoid them.

The Effect of Context

While a necessary element of the solution, repositories such as PROMISE are only a part of the solution to finding motivating and convincing evidence. We described in the previous section how the gathering of evidence is always somewhat context-specific. Recently we have come to appreciate how much interpreting the evidence is also context-specific, even audience-specific. To appreciate that, we need to digress quickly to discuss a little theory.

Many software engineering problems live in a space of solutions that twists and turns like a blanket hastily thrown onto the floor. Imagine an ant searching the hills and valleys of this blanket, looking for the lowest point where, say, the software development effort and the number of defects are at a minimum.

If the problem is complex enough (and software design and software process decisions can be very complex indeed), there is no best way to find this best solution. Rather, our ant might get stuck in the wrong valley, thinking it the lowest when in fact it is not (e.g., if some ridge obscures its view of a lower neighboring valley).

Optimization and Artificial Intelligence (AI) algorithms use various heuristics to explore this space of options. One heuristic is to model the context of the problem, according to the goals of a particular audience, and then nudge the search in a particular direction. Imagine that the ant is on a leash and the leash is being gently pulled by the goal heuristic.

Now, here's the kicker. These search heuristics, although useful, impose a bias on the search results. If you change the context and change the heuristic bias, these algorithms find different "best" solutions. For example, in experiments with AI searches over software process models, Green et al. used two different goal functions [Green et al. 2009]. One goal represented a safety-critical government project where we tried to reduce both the development effort and the number of defects in the delivered software. Another goal represented a more standard business situation where we were rushing software to market, all the while trying not to inject too many defects. That study examined four different projects using an AI optimizer. Each search was repeated for each goal. A striking feature of the results was that *the recommendations generated using one goal were usually rejected by the other*. For example, an AI search using one goal recommended *increasing* the time to delivery, whereas the other recommended *decreasing* it.

This result has major implications for any researcher trying to find evidence that convinces an audience to change the process or tools used to develop software. Rather than assume that all evidence will convince all audiences, *we need to tune the evidence to the audience*. It is not enough to stand on the stage and pull seemingly impressive evidence out of a hat. Even statistically

---

* See *http://promisedata.org/?p=30#comments*.

strong, repeated evidence from elegant studies will not prompt any change if the evidence is about issues that are irrelevant to the audience. Put another way, we have to respect the *business bias* of the audience who may be asking themselves, "But what's it all good for?"

Looking Toward the Future

Despite the decades of software engineering research, so far we have seen relatively few examples of convincing evidence that have actually led to changes in how people run software projects. We speculate that this is due to the context problem: researchers have been generating evidence about A, and the audience cares about B, C, D, and so on. We recommend a little more humility among researchers exploring evidence about software engineering, at least as things stand now, and a willingness to mingle with and listen to software practitioners who can help us better figure out what B, C, and D actually are. We think our field may need to retire, at least for a time, the goal of seeking evidence about results that hold for all projects in all cases; finding local results that make a difference tends to be challenging enough.

Endres and Rombach proposed a view of how knowledge gets built about software and systems engineering [Endres and Rombach 2003]:

- *Observations* of what actually happens during development in a specific context can happen all the time. ("Observation" in this case is defined to comprise both hard facts and subjective impressions.)

- Recurring observations lead to *laws* that help understand how things are likely to occur in the future.

- Laws are explained by *theories* that explain why those events happen.

Given the complexity of the issues currently being tackled by empirical research, we'd like to slow the rush to theory-building. A more productive model of knowledge-building based on all the data and studies we're currently seeing would be a two-tiered approach of "observations" and "laws" (to use Endres's terminology), supported by the repositories that we described earlier.

For the first tier, a researcher would model the goals of the local audience, and then collect evidence focused on those goals. The ready availability of modern data mining tools† can help engineers to learn such local lessons.

On the second tier, where we abstract conclusions across projects and/or contexts, we may have to be content for now to abstract the important factors or basic principles in an area, not to provide "the" solution that will work across some subset of contexts.

For example, Hall et al. tried to answer the question of what motivates software developers [Hall et al. 2008]. They looked across 92 studies that had examined this question, each in a

† Weka: *http://www.cs.waikato.ac.nz/ml/weka/*; R: *http://www.r-project.org/*; YALE: *http://rapid-i.com/*.

different context. In trying to wrestle with all of the studies and their various results, the researchers took the approach of looking for which factors seem to motivate developers, even though it wasn't feasible to quantify *how much* those factors contribute. Thus, factors that were found to contribute to motivation in multiple studies could be included in this model with some confidence.

The end result was not a predictive model that said factor X was twice as important as factor Y; rather, it was a checklist of important factors that managers could use in their own context to make sure they hadn't neglected or forgotten something. Maybe the best we can do on many questions is to arm practitioners who have questions with the factors they need to consider in finding their own solutions.

To do this, we need to broaden the definition of what "evidence" is acceptable for the first tier of observations. Some researchers have long argued that software engineering research shows a bias toward quantitative data and analysis, but that qualitative work can be just as rigorous and can provide useful answers to relevant questions [Seaman 2007]. A start toward building more robust collections of evidence would be to truly broaden the definition of acceptable evidence to incorporate qualitative as well as quantitative sources—that is, more textual or graphical data about *why* technologies do or don't work, in addition to quantitative data that measures *what* the technologies' effects are.

However, truly convincing bodies of evidence would go even further and accept different types of evidence entirely—not just research studies that try to find statistical significance, but also reports of investigators' experience that can provide more information about the practical application of technologies. Such experience reports are currently underrated because they suffer from being less rigorous than much of the existing literature. For example, it is not always possible to have confidence that aspects of interest have been measured precisely, that confounding factors have been excluded, or that process conformance issues have been avoided. However, such reports should be an explicit part of the "evidence trail" of any software development technology.

As Endres indicated by defining "observations" broadly enough to include subjective impressions, even less rigorous forms of input can help point us to valid conclusions—if they are tagged as such so that we don't create laws with an unwarranted sense of confidence. Applying a confidence rating to these sources of evidence is important so that those methodological issues can be highlighted. (Of course, even the most rigorous research study is unlikely to be *completely* free of any methodological issues.)

Experience reports can keep research grounded by demonstrating that what is achieved under practical constraints may not always match our expectations for a given technology. Just as importantly, they provide insights about how technologies need to be tailored or adapted to meet the practical constraints of day-to-day software development. In the area of tech transfer, we often find that a single good case study that recounts positive experiences with a technology in practice can be more valuable to practitioners than a multitude of additional research reports.

Such convincing bodies of evidence can also help drive change by providing evidence that can reach different types of users. Rogers proposed an oft-cited model that characterized consumers of some innovation (say, research results) along a bell curve: the leftmost tail comprises the innovators, the "bulge" of the bell represents the majority who adopt somewhere in the middle curve, as the idea has increasingly caught on, and the rightmost tail contains the "laggards" who resist change [Rogers 1962]. Researchers who know their audience can select appropriate subsets of data from a truly robust set in order to make their case:

- Early adopters may find a small set of relatively low-confidence feasibility studies, or one or two "elegant" research studies, sufficient for them to adopt a change for themselves—especially if the context of those studies shows that the evidence was gathered in an environment somewhat like their own.

- The majority of adopters may need to see a mix of studies from different contexts to convince themselves that a research idea has merit, has been proven feasible in more than just a niche environment, and has started to become part of the accepted way of doing things.

- Laggards or late adopters may require overwhelming evidence, which may comprise more than a handful of high-confidence studies and a wide range of contexts in which beneficial results have been obtained.

Some ways that such different types of evidence can be combined have been proposed [Shull et al. 2001]. But what matters most is the interplay of having both types: qualitative reports as well as quantitative data. We have often seen that practitioners do respond better to data sets that have mixes of different types of data. For example, having a rich set of both hard data and positive experiences from real teams helped software inspection technologies diffuse across multiple centers of NASA [Shull and Seaman 2008].

Evidence from well-designed empirical studies can help a finding reach statistical significance but can still be impractical to implement or too slow at delivering timely answers (especially in an area of rapid technological change, such as software engineering). Evidence from application in practice can be more convincing of the benefits but is typically less rigorous. Often it is a combination of evidence from both sources—where one corroborates the other—that is ultimately convincing.

References

[Armstrong 2007] Armstrong, J.S. 2007. Significance tests harm progress in forecasting. *International Journal of Forecasting* 23(2): 321–327.

[Basili 2009] Basili, V. 2009. Personal communication, September.

[Basili and Selby 1987] Basili, V., and R. Selby. 1987. Comparing the Effectiveness of Software Testing Strategies. *IEEE Transactions on Software Engineering* 13(12): 1278–1296.

[Basili et al. 1999] Basili, V.R., F. Shull, and F. Lanubile. 1999. Building Knowledge Through Families of Experiments. *IEEE Transactions on Software Engineering* 25(4): 456–473.

[Boehm 2009] Boehm, B. 2009. Future Challenges for Software Data Collection and Analysis. Keynote address presented at the International Conference on Predictor Models in Software Engineering (PROMISE09), May 18–19, in Vancouver, Canada.

[Boehm et al. 2000] Boehm, B.W., C. Abts, A.W. Brown, S. Chulani, B.K. Clark, E. Horowitz, R. Madachy, D. Reifer, and B. Steece. 2000. *Software Cost Estimation with Cocomo II*. Upper Saddle River, NJ: Prentice Hall PTR.

[Briand 2006] Briand, L. 2006. Predictive Models in Software Engineering: State-of-the-Art, Needs, and Changes. Keynote address, PROMISE workshop, IEEE ICSM, September 24, in Ottawa, Canada.

[Budgen et al. 2009] Budgen, D., B. Kitchenham, and P. Brereton. 2009. Is Evidence Based Software Engineering Mature Enough for Practice & Policy? Paper presented at the 33rd Annual IEEE Software Engineering Workshop (SEW-33), October 13–15, in Skövde, Sweden.

[Carver et al. 2008] Carver, J., Juristo, N., Shull, F., and Vegas, S. 2008. The Role of Replications in Empirical Software Engineering. *Empirical Software Engineering: An International Journal* 13(2): 211–218.

[Cohen 1988] Cohen, J. 1988. The earth is round (p < .05). *American Psychologist* 49: 997–1003.

[Demsar 2006] Demsar, J. 2006. Statistical Comparisons of Classifiers over Multiple Data Sets. *Journal of Machine Learning Research* 7: 1–30.

[Endres and Rombach 2003] Endres, A., and H.D. Rombach. 2003. *A Handbook of Software and Systems Engineering*. Boston: Addison-Wesley.

[Feldmann et al. 2006] Feldmann, R., F. Shull, and M. Shaw. 2006. Building Decision Support in an Imperfect World. *Proc. ACM/IEEE International Symposium on Empirical Software Engineering* 2: 33–35.

[Foss et al. 2003] Foss, T., E. Stensrud, B. Kitchenham, and I. Myrtveit. 2003. A Simulation Study of the Model Evaluation Criterion MMRE. *IEEE Transactions on Software Engineering* 29(11): 985–995.

[Green et al. 2009] Green, P., T. Menzies, S. Williams, and O. El-waras. 2009. Understanding the Value of Software Engineering Technologies. *Proceedings of the 2009 IEEE/ACM International Conference on Automated Software Engineering*: 52–61. Also available at *http://menzies.us/pdf/09value.pdf*.

[Hall et al. 2008] Hall, T., H. Sharp, S. Beecham, N. Baddoo, and H. Robinson. 2008. What Do We Know About Developer Motivation? *IEEE Software* 25(4): 92–94.

[Kitchenham 2004] Kitchenham, B. 2004. Procedures for undertaking systematic reviews. Technical Report TR/SE-0401, Department of Computer Science, Keele University, and National ICT, Australia Ltd.

[Kitchenham et al. 2007] Kitchenham, B., E. Mendes, and G. H. Travassos. 2007. Cross Versus Within-Company Cost Estimation Studies: A Systematic Review. *IEEE Trans. Software Eng.* 33(5): 316–329.

[Menzies 2008] Menzies, T. 2008. Editorial, special issue, repeatable experiments in software engineering. *Empirical Software Engineering* 13(5): 469–471.

[Menzies and Marcus 2008] Menzies, T., and A. Marcus. 2008. Automated Severity Assessment of Software Defect Reports. Paper presented at IEEE International Conference on Software Maintenance, September 28–October 4, in Beijing, China.

[Menzies et al. 2008] Menzies, T., M. Benson, K. Costello, C. Moats, M. Northey, and J. Richardson. 2008. Learning Better IV & V Practices. *Innovations in Systems and Software Engineering* 4(2): 169–183. Also available at *http://menzies.us/pdf/07ivv.pdf*.

[Menzies et al. 2009] Menzies, T., O. El-waras, J. Hihn, and B. Boehm. 2009. Can We Build Software Faster and Better and Cheaper? Paper presented at the International Conference on Predictor Models in Software Engineering (PROMISE09), May 18–19, in Vancouver, Canada. Available at *http://promisedata.org/pdf/2009/01_Menzies.pdf*.

[Neto et al. 2008] Neto, A., R. Subramanyan, M. Vieira, G.H. Travassos, and F. Shull. 2008. Improving Evidence About Software Technologies: A Look at Model-Based Testing. *IEEE Software* 25(3): 10–13.

[Rogers 1962] Rogers, E.M. 1962. *Diffusion of innovations*. New York: Free Press.

[Runeson et al. 2006] Runeson, P., C. Andersson, T. Thelin, A. Andrews, and T. Berling. 2006. What do we know about defect detection methods? *IEEE Software* 23(3): 82–90.

[Seaman 2007] Seaman, C. 2007. Qualitative Methods. In *Guide to Advanced Empirical Software Engineering*, ed. F. Shull, J. Singer, and D. I. K. Sjøberg, 35–62. London: Springer.

[Shull 2002] Shull, F., V.R. Basili, B. Boehm, A.W. Brown, P. Costa, M. Lindvall, D. Port, I. Rus, R. Tesoriero, and M.V. Zelkowitz. 2002. What We Have Learned About Fighting Defects. Proc. *IEEE International Symposium on Software Metrics (METRICS02)*: 249–258.

[Shull and Seaman 2008] Shull, F., and C. Seaman. 2008. Inspecting the History of Inspections: An Example of Evidence-Based Technology Diffusion. *IEEE Software* 24(7): 88–90.

[Shull et al. 2001] Shull, F., J. Carver, and G.H. Travassos. 2001. An Empirical Methodology for Introducing Software Processes. *Proc. Joint European Software Engineering Conference and ACM SIGSOFT Symposium on Foundations of Software Engineering (ESEC/FSE)*: 288–296.

[Tosun et al. 2009] Tosun, A., A. Bener, and B. Turhan. 2009. Practical Considerations of Deploying AI in Defect Prediction: A Case Study within the Turkish Telecommunication Industry. Paper presented at the International Conference on Predictor Models in Software Engineering (PROMISE09), May 18–19, in Vancouver, Canada. Available at *http://promisedata .org/pdf/2009/09_Tosun.pdf*.

[Turham et al. 2009] Turhan, B., T. Menzies, A.B. Bener, and J. Di Stefano. 2009. On the relative value of cross-company and within-company data for defect prediction. *Empirical Software Engineering* 14(5):540–557.

[Weyuker et al. 2008] Weyuker, E.J., T.J. Ostrand, and R.M. Bell. 2008. Do too many cooks spoil the broth? Using the number of developers to enhance defect prediction models. *Empirical Software Engineering* 13(5): 539–559.

[Zannier et al. 2006] Zannier, C., G. Melnik, and F. Maurer. 2006. On the Success of Empirical Studies in the International Conference on Software Engineering. *Proceedings of the 28th international conference on software engineering*: 341–350.

[Zimmerman 2009] Zimmermann, T., N. Nagappan, H. Gall, E. Giger, and B. Murphy. 2009. Cross-Project Defect Prediction. *Proceedings of the 7th joint meeting of the European Software Engineering Conference and the ACM SIGSOFT Symposium on the Foundations of Software Engineering (ESEC/FSE)*: 91–100.

## CHAPTER TWO

Credibility, or Why Should I Insist on Being Convinced?

Lutz Prechelt
Marian Petre

As software engineers, we all have our opinions about what works and what does not (or not so well), and we share stories of practice and experience that are eventually distilled into cultural knowledge and received wisdom. The trouble is that "what everyone knows" is often wrong, and although we are continually collecting information, we may not be assessing and integrating that information critically, or even giving ourselves the wherewithal to do so.

How Evidence Turns Up in Software Engineering

In crime dramas, the most interesting moments are often when a new piece of *evidence* appears: someone presents a fact that was not previously known, and the clever detective revises his theory of the crime. Sometimes the new evidence adds an important dimension to our world view ("Oh, so he had *intended* all these things to happen!"), sometimes it just adds a little more conviction to a belief we already had ("She's *really* not as careful as she claims"), and sometimes it overturns something we were sure was reliable ("Golly! And I always thought he had arrived there an hour *after* her!"). The drama hinges on the critical thinking ability of the detective. Superior fictional detectives take into account every single bit of evidence, they work until they can integrate it all into a coherent whole, and they continually test their theory of the crime and revise it in the light of new evidence, whereas weak detectives get snagged on confirmatory bias, holding fast to theories even when they can't account for "loose ends" of evidence.

Software development is similar: evidence emerges over time, and the quality of the engineering hinges on the critical faculties of the engineer. If we succumb to confirmatory bias, we pay most attention to evidence that confirms our views. If we're more critically vigilant, we sometimes find that new information suggests we have overlooked some aspect that has to be added to the picture, or we even find that some dearly held belief is contradicted by reality.

Where does such relevant new information come from? It comes from a variety of *sources*:

Experience
Software engineers use technology and methods, participate in projects, and learn things along the way.

Other people
Software engineers talk to people they know, and they listen to recommendations from people they respect.

Reflection
Effective software engineers think hard about what they do, about what works, what doesn't, and why.

Reading
Written materials, both informal (such as high-quality blog posts) or formal (such as scientific articles) transport insights from other parties.

Scientific (or quasi-scientific) exploration
Software engineers conduct software experiments, undertake user studies, and make systematic comparison of alternatives.

Not everyone is satisfied that software engineering has an adequate mastery of evidence. There have been a number of calls for *evidence-based software engineering* (e.g., [Finkelstein 2003], [Kitchenham et al. 2004]), that is, for providing skills, habits, and infrastructure for integrating empirical research results in order to support decision making in software engineering. The comparison is usually made to evidence-based medicine and its reliance on rigorous clinical evidence. The point is not so much that software engineers ignore evidence (although arguably opinion- and superstition-based software engineering exist as well), but that the discipline lacks an organizational, cultural, and technical infrastructure to support the accumulation and aggregation of knowledge from a number of sources. Barbara Kitchenham presents this movement in Chapter 3.

It's also clear that there are a number of fine introspective and reflective accounts of engineering that inform software engineering practice. Writers such as Fred Brooks and Walter Vincenti bring practice into focus by distilling experience and by using illustrations from practice and experience to consider the nature of engineering activity. We would hardly reject their accounts just because they based their essays on reflective experience rather than on scientific experiment, although we may think hard about their interpretations, whether we agree with them, whether they fit our own contexts, and whether they match our own experience—that is, whether they are consistent with other evidence with which we're familiar.

But regardless of whether we resort to scientific studies (on which we will focus in the rest of this chapter) or rely on reports of enlightened practitioners, we argue that, as software engineers, we need a sufficiently sophisticated understanding of evidence to inform our decisions and to assess our evidence needs in terms of the questions we want to answer. It's not that we need more metrics *per se*, or a widespread application of scientific method, or a rigidly defined methodology and signed-off lab books. Imposing processes or method does not by itself produce quality and certainly does not guarantee it. Rather, such proposals are usually an attempt to approximate the real goal: systematic, well-informed, evidence-based *critical thinking*.

The meat of this discussion is the business of "thinking hard" about evidence: how we evaluate evidence in terms of its credibility and fitness for purpose.

Credibility and Relevance

Our discussion revolves around two central concepts: credibility and relevance.

Credibility
> The degree to which you are (or should be) willing to believe the evidence offered and the claims made about it. Part of credibility is validity, the extent to which a study and the claims made from it accurately represent the phenomenon of interest. Validity has a number of facets, including:
>
> - Whether what you observed was what you wanted to observe and thought you were observing
>
> - Whether measures used actually measure what they are intended to measure
>
> - Whether the account of why something is happening is accurate
>
> - Whether we can generalize from what has been studied to other, conceptually comparable settings
>
> Credibility requires a study to embody not just high validity but also *good reporting* so readers know how and when to apply the study.

Relevance
> The degree to which you are (or ought to be) interested in the evidence and claims. In most cases, you won't even *look* at an irrelevant study. The typical exception is when the question is of interest to you but the environment in which the answer was found is very different from yours. Relevance in that case is the degree to which the result can be generalized to your environment—which unfortunately is usually a difficult question.

Some people consider relevance to be a facet of credibility, but we believe it is helpful to keep them apart because a low-credibility statement is hardly more than noise (given the gazillions of things you would like to learn about), whereas a high-credibility, low-relevance statement is respectable information you just do not currently consider very important for your purpose—but that might change.

Fitness for Purpose, or Why What Convinces You Might Not Convince Me

Evidence is not proof. In general, evidence is whatever empirical data is sufficient to cause us to conclude that one account is more probably true than not, or is probably more true than another. Different purposes require different *standards of evidence*. Some purposes need strong evidence. For example, deciding whether to switch *all* software development to an aspect-oriented design and implementation approach demands compelling evidence that the benefits would exceed the investment (both financial and cultural). Some purposes need only weak evidence. For instance, an example application of aspect-orientation for tracing might be sufficient evidence that aspect-oriented programming (AOP) *can* be worthwhile, leaving it up to further research to clarify how well its goals are accomplished (and in what environments). An evaluation study whose goal is to identify deficiencies in a design may require responses from only a handful of participants. We know of one prototype voice feedback system for manufacturing that was abandoned after the initial users pointed out that they wore ear plugs to block out factory noise. Some purposes need only counter-examples. For example, when one is trying to dispute an assumption or a universal claim, one needs only a single counter-example. An example is the work that put the "it's good because it's graphical" claims of visual programming proponents in perspective by showing in an experiment that a nested structure was comprehended more effectively using a textual representation [Green and Petre 1992].

So there's a relationship between the question you want to answer and the respective evidence required for your particular context. And there's a relationship between the evidence you need and the sorts of *methods* that can provide that evidence. For example, you can't ask informants about their tacit knowledge, indicating one of the limitations of surveys. Software is created and deployed in a *socio-technical context*, so claims and arguments about software need to draw on evidence that takes into account both the social and the technical aspects as well as their inter-relationship.

For instance, understanding the implications of aspect-oriented design on your project's communication structure requires observing that technology in its full context of use. Good application of methods means matching the method to the question—and to the evidence you need to answer that question for your purposes.

Quantitative Versus Qualitative Evidence: A False Dichotomy

Discussions of research often distinguish studies as quantitative or qualitative. Roughly speaking, the difference resides in the questions of interest. Quantitative studies revolve around measurement and usually ask *comparison* questions ("Is A faster than B?"), *if* questions ("If A changes, does B change?"), or *how much* questions ("How much of their time do developers spend debugging?"). In contrast, qualitative studies revolve around description and categorization and usually ask *why* questions ("Why is A easier to learn than B?") or *how* questions ("How—by what methods—do developers approach debugging?").

Like most models, this is a simplification. Some issues regarding this notional distinction lead to confusion and deserve a short discussion:

It is nonsense to say that quantitative evidence is generally better than qualitative evidence (or vice versa).
Rather, the two have different purposes and are hence not directly comparable. Qualitative evidence is required to identify phenomena of interest and to untangle phenomena that are known to be of interest but are convoluted. Quantitative evidence is for "nailing down" phenomena that are well-enough understood or simple enough to be isolated for study.

Hence, qualitative research has to precede quantitative research and will look at situations that are *more complicated*. When only few different factors are involved (such as in physics), one can proceed to quantitative investigation quickly; when many are involved (such as in human social interactions), the transition either takes a lot longer or will involve premature simplification. Many of the credibility problems of software engineering evidence stem from such premature simplification.

It's not a dichotomy, but a continuum.
Qualitative and quantitative studies are not as distinct as the simplification suggests. Qualitative studies may collect qualitative data (e.g., records of utterances or actions), then code that data systematically (e.g., putting it into categories), and eventually quantify the coded data (i.e., count the instances in a category) and analyze it statistically. Quantitative studies may, in turn, have qualitative elements. For example, when one compares the efficacy of two methods A and B, one may compare the products of the methods, assessing them as "good," "adequate," or "poor." The answers are qualitative; they lie on an ordinal scale. However, one may then use a statistical procedure (such as the Wilcoxon rank-sum test) to determine whether the outcome with A is significantly better than with B. The study's structure is experimental, and the analysis is quantitative, using the same techniques as if the measure were centimeters or seconds. (Even in studies that use performance metrics, the choice of metrics and the association of metric with quality may be based on a qualitative assessment.)

Some of the most powerful studies of software systems combine quantitative evidence (e.g., performance measures) with qualitative evidence (e.g., descriptions of process) to document a phenomenon, identify key factors, and offer a well-founded explanation of the relationship between factors and phenomenon.

Qualitative studies are not necessarily "soft," nor are quantitative ones "hard."

The results of good studies are not at all arbitrary. Good science seeks *reproducible* ("hard") results because reproducing results suggests that they are reliable, and the process of reproduction exposes the study method to critical scrutiny. Reproducing a result means repeating ("replicating") the respective study, either under conditions that are almost exactly the same (*close replication*) or in a different but like-minded manner (*loose replication*). Qualitative studies almost always involve unique human contexts and are therefore hard to replicate closely. However, that does not mean the *result* of the study cannot be reproduced; it often can. And from the point of view of relevance, a loose replication is even *more* valuable than a close one because it signals that the result is more generalizable. On the other hand, the results of quantitative studies sometimes *cannot* be reproduced. For example, John Daly's experiments on inheritance depth were replicated by three different research groups, all with conflicting results [Prechelt et al. 2003].

Summing up, the strength of quantitative studies is that they capture a situation in a few simple statements and thus can sometimes make things very clear. Their disadvantage is that they ignore so much information that it is often difficult to decide what the results actually mean and when they apply. The strength of qualitative studies is that they reflect and exhibit the complexity of the real world in their results. The disadvantage is that they are therefore much harder to evaluate. Any research results may be hard to apply in real life if it is not clear how the results map onto one's real-world context, either because an experiment is too narrow to generalize or because an observational setting is too different.

The "bottom line" is that the method must be appropriate for the question. Issues about social context, process, and the contrast between what people believe they do and what they actually do require different forms of inquiry than issues about algorithm performance.

Aggregating Evidence

One way to deal with the limitations of evidence is to combine different forms or sources: to aggregate results from different studies on the same question. The notion behind combing evidence is that if different forms of evidence or evidence from independent sources agree (or at least don't contradict each other), they gather a sort of "weight" and are more credible together.

Software engineering does not yet have a consolidated body of evidence. However, various efforts are being made at consolidation. Barbara Kitchenham and colleagues have been fuelling a movement for *systematic literature reviews*, which examine and aggregate published evidence about a specific topic using a framework of assessment against specified criteria. For instance, Jørgensen and Shepperd's work on cost modeling compiles and integrates the evidence comparing the performance of models and humans in estimation and suggests that they are *roughly* comparable [Jørgensen and Shepperd 2007]. Interestingly, doing systematic

reviews—and doing tertiary reviews of systematic reviews, as done by Kitchenham et al.—
exposes interesting weaknesses in the evidence base [Kitchenham et al. 2009]:

- Little credible evidence exists on a variety of topics in software engineering.
- Concerns about the quality of published evidence plague the endeavor.
- Concerns about the quality of the *reporting* of evidence (e.g., whether the method is described fully and accurately) limit its evaluation.

Systematic reviews are not the final say in validating research results, however. One of their weaknesses is that their way of aggregating studies makes it difficult for them to pay proper attention to context, whose importance in validating and applying studies has been well-established in human studies. As one consequence, systematic reviewers find it difficult to handle qualitative studies, and therefore often exclude them from their reviews, thereby also excluding the evidence they offer. Another consequence is a danger of over-generalization when results from relevantly different contexts (say, student practice and professional practice) are put together as if those contexts were equivalent.

Methodologies—agreed systems of inquiry that include standard applications of methods— offer the important advantage of allowing researchers to compare and contrast results, so that evidence can accumulate over time and consistent evidence can provide a strong basis for knowledge. Disciplines such as chemistry, and particularly subdisciplines that have well-specified concerns and standard forms of questions, have well-defined methodologies. They may also have standard reporting practices that reinforce the standard methodologies through standard formats of reporting.

Any methodology can become a sort of lens through which researchers view the world, but it's important to recognize that not everything will be within focal range. Blind adherence to methodology can lead to all sorts of embarrassing slips, especially when the researcher has failed to understand the conventions and assumptions that underpin that methodology. The availability of an accepted methodology does not absolve researchers from justifying the choice of technique in terms of the evidence required.

Benchmarking is one example of a method used in software engineering that produces results suitable for aggregation. It involves measuring performance according to a very precisely defined procedure, or benchmark. A good example is the SPEC CPU benchmark, which measures, despite its name, the combined performance of a CPU, memory subsystem, operating system, and compiler for CPU-heavy applications. It consists of a collection of batch-mode application program source codes, plus detailed instructions for how to compile them and instructions for how to run inputs and measure them.

If the benchmark is well specified and fairly applied, you know very precisely what benchmarking results mean, and can without further ado compare Sun's results to HP's to Intel's and so on. This reliability and comparability is exactly what benchmarks where invented for and makes them a hallmark of credibility.

So is benchmarking a free lunch? Of course not. The real concern with benchmarking evidence is relevance: whether the measures used are appropriate for and representative of the phenomenon of interest. A benchmark's content is always a matter of concern and is usually in dispute. SPEC CPU is a quite successful benchmark in this regard, but others, such as TPC-C for transaction loads on RDBMSes, attract a good share of skepticism.

Limitations and Bias

Even high-quality evidence is usually partial. We're often unable to assess a phenomenon directly, and so we study those consequences of it that we *can* study directly, or we look at only a part of a phenomenon, or we look at it from a particular perspective, or we look at something that we can measure in the hope that it maps onto what we're interested in. Measures are a shorthand, a compact expression or reflection of the phenomenon. But they're often not the phenomenon; the measure is typically a simplification. Good credibility requires justifying the choices made.

Worse than that, evidence can be biased. How many software engineers would be convinced by the sort of "blind tests" and consumer experiments presented in old-fashioned detergent ads ("Duz washes more dishes...")? Advertising regulations mean that such consumer experiments must conform to certain standards to make conditions comparable: same dirt, same water, same amount of detergent, and so on. But the advertisers are free to shape the conditions; they can optimize things like the kind of dirt and the water temperature for their product. "Hah!" we say, "the bias is built-in." And yet many of the published evaluations of software engineering methods and tools follow the same model: wittingly or not, the setting is designed to demonstrate the virtues of the method or tool being promoted, rather than to make a fair comparison to other methods or tools based on well-founded criteria that were determined independently.

Bias occurs when things creep in unnoticed to corrupt or compromise the evidence. It is the distortion of results due to factors that have not been taken into consideration, such as other influences, conflated variables, inappropriate measures, or selectivity in a sample that renders it unrepresentative. Bias threatens the validity of research, and we look for possible bias when we're assessing credibility.

We need to understand not just the value of specific evidence and its limitations, but also how different *forms* of evidence compare, and how they might fit together to compensate for the limitations of each form.

Types of Evidence and Their Strengths and Weaknesses

For the sake of illustration, let's consider an example. Imagine that we are assessing a new software engineering technology, AWE (A Wonderfulnew Excitement), which has been developed to replace BURP (Boring but Usually Respected Predecessor). What sort of evidence might we consider in deciding whether to adopt AWE? In the following sections, we describe common types of studies and evaluate each for the issues that typically arise for credibility and relevance.

Controlled Experiments and Quasi-Experiments

Controlled experiments are suitable if we want to perform a *direct comparison* of two or more conditions (such as using AWE versus using BURP) with respect to one or more *criteria that can be measured reliably*, such as the amount of time needed to complete a certain task. These experiments also often can be helpful if measurement is tricky, such as counting the number of defects in the work products produced with AWE or BURP. "Control" means keeping everything else (other than exchanging AWE for BURP) constant, which we can do straightforwardly with the work conditions and the task to be solved. For the gazillions of human variables involved, the only way to implement control is to use a group of subjects (rather than just one) and count on all the differences to average out across that group. This hope is justified (at least statistically) if we assign the subjects to the groups at random (a *randomized experiment*), which makes sense only if all subjects are equally competent with using AWE as they are with BURP. Randomized experiments are the only research method that can prove causation: if all we changed is AWE versus BURP, any change in the results (except for statistical fluctuations) must be caused by this difference.

Sometimes we can't assign developers at random, because all we have are preexisting groups. Consider, for instance, the comparison of C, C++, Java, Perl, Python, Rexx, and TCL, described in Chapter 14. How many programmers do you know who are *equally* versed in all seven languages? For a randomized experiment, you would need enough of them to fill seven groups! Training enough people to that level is infeasible. In such cases, we use the groups as they are (*quasi-experiment*) and must be concerned about whether, say, all brainy, bright, brilliant people only use languages whose names start with B or P, which would mean that our groups reflect different talent pools and hence distort the comparison (although we could then attribute this effect to the languages themselves).

Credibility

Given a clear, well-formed hypothesis, a clean design and execution, and sensible measures, the credibility of controlled experiments is usually quite high. The setup is notionally fair and the interpretation of the results is in principle quite clear. The typical credibility issues with experiments are these:

Subject bias

Were the subjects really equally competent with AWE and BURP? If not, the experiment may reflect participant characteristics more than technology characteristics. Subtle variants of this problem involve motivational issues: BURP is boring and AWE is exciting, but this will not remain true in the long run. The difference is pronounced if the experimenter happens to be the inventor of AWE and is correspondingly enthusiastic about it.

Task bias

The task chosen by such an experimenter is likely to emphasize the strengths of AWE more than the strengths of BURP.

Group assignment bias

Distortions due to inherent group differences are always a risk in quasi-experiments.

Relevance

This is the real weak spot of experiments. A good experiment design is precise, and the narrowness of the experimental setting may make the results hard to apply to the outside world. Experiments are prone to a "sand through the fingers" effect: one may grasp at a concept such as productivity, but by the time the concept has been mapped through many refinements to a particular measure in a setting that has sufficient controls, it may seem to slip away.

Surveys

Surveys—simply asking many people the same questions about an issue—is the method of choice for measuring *attitude*. What do I *think* is great about AWE? About BURP? How boring do I personally find BURP? Why? Sociology and psychology have worked out an elaborate (and costly) methodology to figure out appropriate questions for measuring attitude correctly for a particular topic. Unfortunately, this methodology is typically ignored in surveys in software engineering.

Surveys can also be used (if less reliably) to *collect experiences*: for instance, the top five things that often go wrong with AWE or BURP. Surveys scale well and are the cheapest method for involving a large set of subjects. If they contain open questions with free text answers, they can be a foundation for qualitative studies along with quantitative ones.

Credibility

Although surveys are cheap and convenient, it is quite difficult to obtain high credibility with them. The typical credibility issues are these:

Unreliable questions

Questions that are vague, misleading, or ambiguous will be interpreted differently by different respondents and lead to results that are not meaningful. These issues can be quite subtle.

Invalid questions or conclusions

This happens in particular when surveys are abused to gather information about complex factual issues: "How many defects does your typical AWE transphyxication diagram contain?" People just do not know such things well enough to give accurate answers. This is not much of a problem if we view the answers as what they are: that the answer reveals what respondents *think*, and as we stressed at the beginning of this section, it reflects their *attitude*. Most often, however, the answers are treated like true facts and the conclusions are correspondingly wrong. (In such cases, critics will often call the survey "too subjective," but subjectivity is supposed to be what surveys are all about! If subjectivity is a problem, the method has been abused.)

Subject bias

Sometimes respondents will not answer what they really think but rather suppress or exaggerate some issues for socio-political reasons.

Unclear target population

The results of a survey can be generalized to any target population of which the respondents are a representative sample. Such a population always exists, but the researchers can rarely characterize what it is.

To generalize credibly, two conditions must be met. First, the survey has to be sent out to a well-defined and comprehensible population. "All readers of web forums X, Y, and Z in date range D to E" is well defined, but not comprehensible; we have no clear idea who these people are. Second, a large fraction (preferably 50% or more) of this population must answer, or else the respondents may be a biased sample. Perhaps the 4% AWE-fans ("the only thing that keeps me awake at work") and the 5% BURP-haters ("so boring that I make twice as many mistakes") in the population felt most motivated to participate and now represent half of our sample?

Relevance

The questions that can be addressed with surveys are often not the questions of most interest. The limited forms of response are often unsatisfying, can be hard to interpret satisfactorily, and are often hard to apply more generally. Surveys can be effective, however, in providing information that supplements and provides context for other forms of evidence: e.g., providing background information about participants in an experiment or providing satisfaction and preference information to supplement performance data.

Experience Reports and Case Studies

Given the limitations of experiments and surveys, and given an interest in assessments based on real-world experience, perhaps looking carefully and in depth at one or two realistic examples of adoption would give us the kind of information we need to make our decision, or at least focus our attention on the questions we would need to answer first.

A case study (or its less formal cousin, the *experience report*) describes a specific instance of a phenomenon (typically a series of events and their results) that happened in a real software engineering setting. In principle, a case study is the result of applying a specific, fairly sophisticated methodology, but the term is most often used more loosely. Although the phenomenon is inherently unique, it is described in the hope that other situations will be similar enough for this one to be interesting.

Case studies draw on many different kinds of data, such as conversations, activities, documents, and data records, that researchers collect by many different potential methods, such as direct observation, interviews, document analysis, and special-purpose data analysis programs. Case studies address a broad set of questions, such as: What were the main issues in this AWE process? How did AWE influence the design activities? How did it influence the resulting design? How did it structure the testing process? And so on.

In our AWE versus BURP example, BURP can be addressed either in a separate case study or in the same case study as a second case where the researchers attempt to match the structure of investigation and discussion as best they can. If the description is sufficiently detailed, we potentially can "convert" the observations to our own setting.

Credibility

For experience reports and case studies, credibility issues abound because these studies are so specific to their context. Most of the issues have to do with:

- Selectivity in what is recorded
- Ambiguity

Therefore, precise description of setup and data and careful interpretation of findings are of utmost importance. The credibility of case studies hinges crucially on the quality of the reporting.

Relevance

Experience reports and case studies are usually published because researchers and publishers believe them to have some general relevance. Interpreting relevance may be challenging, because there are likely to be many important differences between one setting and another. But often the relevance of the *questions* raised by such reports can be recognized, even if the relevance of the *conclusions* may be hard to ascertain.

Other Methods

The previous sections aren't comprehensive. For instance, we might evaluate tools that support AWE and BURP for their scalability using benchmarking methods or for their learnability and error-proneness by user studies. Each of these (and other) methods and approaches has its own credibility and relevance issues.

Indications of Credibility (or Lack Thereof) in Reporting

When one takes into account the fundamental issues discussed in the previous sections, credibility largely boils down to a handful of aspects that have been done well or poorly. We now discuss what to look for in a study report with respect to each of these.

General characteristics

For a highly credible study:

- Its report will be detailed (rather than vague) and precise (rather than ambiguous).
- The style of discussion will be honest (rather than perform window-dressing), and the logic and argumentation will be correct (rather than inconsistent, false, or inconsequential).
- The setup of the study will maximize relevance (rather than being too simple or demonstrate over-specialization).
- The writing style in reports of very good studies is engaging (rather than dull), despite their dryness.

A clear research question

A clearly stated and unambiguous research question is the mother of all credibility, because if the authors do not explain what they were looking for, what can they turn up for you to believe? The research question need not be announced with a fanfare, but it must be clearly discernible from the abstract and introduction.

Often there is a clearly discernible research question, but it's vague. In such cases, the results will either be vague as well, or they will be somewhat accidental and random. Such a study may sometimes be of sufficient interest to read on, but it likely has modest credibility at best.

An informative description of the study setup

Understanding the setup of the study is at the heart of credibility and is the main difference between press releases and scientific reports. Even the most appealing result has little credibility if it was generated by staring into a crystal ball. It may be quite impressive to read that "an empirical study with almost 600 participants has shown that Java is superior to C++ in almost all respects: programming times are shorter by 11%, debugging times are shorter by 47%, and long-term design stability is better by 42%. Only the runtime performance of C++ programs is still superior to Java by 23%."

The same results are far less credible if you know that they were found by means of a survey. And they may become still less credible if you look at the questions more closely: How did they compare programming and debugging times when the programs are all different? Ah, they asked how often these tasks took longer than expected! And what is "long-term design stability"? Ah, they asked what fraction of methods never changed! The devil is in the details: the method, the sample, the data, the analysis.

As a coarse rule of thumb, you can safely ignore all studies whose setup is not described at all, and you should be skeptical of all studies whose setup description leaves open any of your inquisitive "W-questions": What type of study is it? What tasks have the subjects undertaken? In what kind of work context? Who were the subjects? How was the data collected? How was it validated? How, precisely, are the main measures defined? A good report on an empirical study will answer all of these questions satisfactorily.

A meaningful and graspable data presentation

Once you know how the study was constructed and how the data were collected, you need information about the data itself. There may not be space to publish the raw data, so even small studies summarize data by what statisticians call *descriptive statistics*.

Assume you have a study involving six different groups and five different measures of interest. Some authors will present their data as a table, with each line listing the group name, group size, and, for instance, the minimum, maximum, average, and standard deviation of one measure. The table has five blocks of six such lines each, making a 37-line table that consumes more than half a page. What do you do when confronted with such information? You could ignore the table (thus failing to scrutinize the data), or you could delve into the table trying to compare the groups for each measure. In the latter case, you will create a *mental image* of the overall situation by first making sense of the individual entries and then visualizing their relationships. In more colorful terms, you will reanimate the corpses from this data graveyard and then teach them to dance to your music.

Preferably, the authors keep their data alive by presenting it in ways that help the reader engage: by finding visual representations that relate to the key questions and relationships the authors wish to discuss, and that relate clearly and directly to the tabular or textual data presentation. Good data visualizations associate salient visual qualities (e.g, scale, color) with information of interest in a consistent way. Poor data visualizations use visual qualities that obscure or distract viewers from the data, for example, by connecting discrete data with lines that imply some sort of continuity, or by using different scales on related graphs or scales not starting at zero, or by adding extraneous elements that are more salient than the data. Edward R. Tufte wrote the seminal book on proper visualization [Tufte 1983].

A transparent statistical analysis (if any)

Statistical analysis (*inferential statistics*) is about separating the "noise" from the "signal": separating results that are likely to have arisen from chance or error from results that are reasonably likely to have arisen as a meaningful part of the phenomenon under study. Statistics are applied in order to *reduce your uncertainty* about how your results should be interpreted.

In contrast, many authors use statistical analysis for *intimidation*. They present all sorts of alpha levels, p values, degrees of freedom, residual sum of squares, parameters mu, sigma, theta, coefficients beta, rho, tau, and so on, all the way to Crete and back—all to tell you, "Dare not doubt my declamations or I'll hit you over the head with my significance tests." *Credible* studies use statistics to *explain* and *reassure*; *bad* ones use them to *obfuscate* (because the authors have weaknesses to hide) or *daunt* (because the authors are not so sure themselves what all this statistical hocus pocus really means).

In a good study, the authors *explain* in simple words each statistical inference they are using. They prefer inferences whose meaning is *easy to grasp* (such as confidence intervals) over inferences whose meaning is difficult to interpret (such as p-values and power, or effect sizes that are normalized by standard deviations). They will clearly *interpret* each result as saying one of the following: "There is probably some real difference here" (a positive result), "There is likely no effect here or only a very small one; we see mostly random noise" (a negative result), or "It remains unclear what this means" (a null result). Even the latter case is reassuring because it tells you that the uncertainty you felt about the meaning of the data when you looked at it was there for a reason and cannot be removed, even by statistical inference (at least not by this one; there may be a different analysis that could shed more light on the situation).

An honest discussion of limitations

Any solid report of an empirical study needs to have a section discussing the limitations of the study, often titled "threats to validity." This discussion offers information about what could not be achieved by the study, what interpretations involved are problematic (*construct validity*), what has gone wrong or may have gone wrong in the execution of the study (*internal validity*), and what limits the generalizability of the results (*external validity*). For a good study and report, you are often already aware of these points and this section does not offer much surprising information. Authors of credible studies accept that possible points of criticism remain. It is not a good sign when a report attempts to discuss them all away.

If done well, the most interesting part is usually the discussion of generalizability, because it is directly relevant (forgive the pun) to the results' relevance. Good reports will offer points *both in favor of and against* generalizability in several respects and for different generalization target domains.

Conclusions that are solid yet relevant

Critical readers of reports on empirical studies will form their own opinions based on their own assessment of the evidence presented, and will not rely just on the statements provided by the authors in the abstract or conclusions.

If the authors' conclusions *oversell* the results, generalizing them to areas not backed by solid argumentation or even drawing conclusions regarding phenomena only loosely connected to the phenomenon being studied, you should be doubly wary regarding the credibility of the rest of the report. In particular, you should take your widest red pen and strike out the abstract and conclusion so you will never rely on them when refreshing your memory with respect to this particular study. Be advised that few readers ever do this, and yet all people need to refresh their memories. As a consequence, many references to a study in other reports or in textbooks will wrongly refer to overstated conclusions as if they were true. (Nobody's perfect, and scientists are no exception.)

If, on the other hand, the conclusions appear thoughtful and visibly attempt to strike a good balance between reliability and relevance, their credibility is reinforced and their relevance is maximized. Such authors put both the results and the limitations of their study into one scale pan and all possible generalizations (viewed in light of other results elsewhere in the literature) into the other, and then tell you what they think are *likely correct* generalizations. Such information is valuable because the authors possess a lot of information about the study that is not explicit anywhere in the article but has been used for this judgment.

Society, Culture, Software Engineering, and You

By now you will probably agree that high credibility is far from easy to obtain. However, that does not mean there are no (or almost no) credible studies; it is just that the credible ones are almost always limited. They are far more specialized than we would like them to be and burdened with more ifs, whens, and presumablys than we would prefer. There is not much sense in complaining about this situation; it is simply an unavoidable result of the complexity of the world in which we live and (as far as technology is concerned) that we have created. And it would not even be much of a problem if we were patient enough to be happy with the things we *do* find out.

And here is what we believe to be the real problem: although engineers and scientists understand a lot about complexity, have respect for it and for the effort it often implies, and are still capable of awe in that regard, our society and culture as a whole do not. We are surrounded by so many spectacular things and events that we come to feel that small news is no news. A finding that requires an intricate 50-word clause to summarize it without distortion is unlikely to receive our attention.

The general media act accordingly. In order to capture attention, they ignore, inflate, or distort the findings of an empirical study, often beyond recognition. Scientists often are not helpful either and write so-called abstracts that merely announce results rather than summarizing them. In either case, the burden is on the critical reader to take a closer look. You will have to dig out a report about the study, digest it, decide its credibility, and take home what is both credible and relevant for you. Your qualifications as a software engineer mean you are able to do this, and progress in software engineering depends on many engineers actually exercising this capability on a regular basis. This book represents a wonderful opportunity to do just that.

One thing that observational studies have shown is that *expert* software engineers *do* gather evidence when it matters to them, at a level of credibility pitched for their purpose. That is, if they're designing digital filters for professional audio, they may well do controlled experiments on outputs to determine whether the software produces the desired sound qualities for human hearing. If they're in a battle with marketing over whether customers who currently use analog controls are ready to handle a virtual interface, they may well send a researcher into the field to discover what parameters the customers are controlling, how their existing systems function, and how the customers think about their tasks. If they're designing frontends for safety-critical systems, they may well do user studies to determine which of several design alternatives best fit the human context of use. If they're designing backends for safety-critical systems, they may well use formal methods to establish correct implementation of the specified requirements. If they're optimizing scheduling algorithms, they may well run benchmarks against industrial inputs.

So rather than dismissing evidence of various forms, we should embrace it, and think hard and critically about it.

Acknowledgments

The authors thank colleagues who tolerated their indecision in grappling with evidence about evidence, including David Budgen, Gordon Rugg, and Judith Segal.

References

[Brooks 1975] Brooks, F. 1975. *The Mythical Man-Month*. Boston: Addison-Wesley.

[Eisenstadt 1993] Eisenstadt, M. 1993. Tales of Debugging from the Front Lines. In *Empirical Studies of Programmers: Fifth Workshop*, ed. C.R. Cook, J.C. Scholtz, and J.C. Spohrer, 86–112. Norwood, NJ: Ablex Publishing.

[Finkelstein 2003] Finkelstein, A. 2003. A call for evidence-based software engineering. Keynote address to Psychology of Programming Interest Group Annual Workshop, Keele University, April 8–10, in Keele, UK.

[Green and Petre 1992] Green, T.R.G., and M. Petre. 1992. When visual programs are harder to read than textual programs. *Proceedings of the Sixth European Conference on Cognitive Ergonomics*: 167–180.

[Jørgensen and Shepperd 2007] Jørgensen, M., and M. Shepperd. 2007. A Systematic Review of Software Development Cost Estimation Studies. *IEEE Transactions on Software Engineering* 33(1): 33–53.

[Kitchenham et al. 2004] Kitchenham, B.A., T. Dybå, and M. Jørgensen. 2004. Evidence-based software engineering. *Proceedings of the 26th International Conference on Software Engineering (ICSE)*: 273–281.

[Kitchenham et al. 2009] Kitchenham, B., O.P. Brereton, D. Budgen, M. Turner, J. Bailey, and S. Linkman. 2009. Systematic literature reviews in software engineering—A systematic literature review. *Information and Software Technology* 51(1): 7–15.

[Prechelt et al. 2003] Prechelt, L., B. Unger, M. Philippsen, and W.F. Tichy. A Controlled Experiment on Inheritance Depth as a Cost Factor for Maintenance. *Journal of Systems and Software* 65(2): 115–126.

[Tufte 1983] Tufte, E.R. 1983. *The Visual Display of Quantitative Information*. Cheshire, CT: Graphics Press.

[Vincenti 1993] Vincenti, W.A. 1993. *What Engineers Know and How They Know it: Analytical Studies from Aeronautical History*. Baltimore: Johns Hopkins University Press.

## CHAPTER THREE

What We Can Learn from Systematic Reviews

Barbara Kitchenham

As a strong advocate of evidence-based software engineering ([Dybå et al. 2005], [Kitchenham et al. 2004]), I am also a strong advocate of *systematic reviews* (SRs) ([Kitchenham 2004], [Kitchenham and Charters 2007]). These are sometimes referred to as systematic literature reviews in software engineering to avoid confusions with inspection methods (i.e., methods for reading and reviewing software engineering documents or code). We cannot have evidence-based software engineering without a sound methodology for aggregating evidence from different empirical studies. SRs provide that methodology.

SRs have been in widespread use in other disciplines for decades. Each SR is launched by a researcher to investigate all available evidence that supports or refutes a particular "topic of interest," which in software engineering typically involves asking about the effect of a method or process. A researcher conducting an SR selects empirical studies that are relevant to the particular research question, assesses the validity of each one, and then determines the trend shown by those studies. Thus, SRs aim to find, assess, and aggregate all relevant evidence about some topic of interest in a fair, repeatable, and auditable manner.

This chapter introduces the value of SRs to readers with a general interest in empirical software engineering. I also aim to help novice researchers (such as PhD students)—who might be looking for robust methods to undertake state-of-the-art reviews—get started with SRs.

This chapter should also be of interest to more experienced empirical researchers who are not yet confident of the value of the SR methodology. Many European researchers are publishing SRs in software engineering, but relatively few researchers from the U.S. do so ([Kitchenham et al. 2009b], [Kitchenham et al. 2010a]).

I also hope that this chapter will alert empirical researchers to the possibility that their studies will contribute to subsequent SRs and that they consequently will report their results with future aggregation in mind. A recent SR found it impossible to undertake a full meta-analysis because the individual primary studies used very disparate practices for reporting their results ([Turner et al. 2008], [Turner et al. 2010]).

The aim of systematic reviews in the context of evidence-based software engineering is not just to provide a methodology for researchers; the aim is to influence practice. I hope, therefore, that managers and decision makers in industry also will find something in this chapter relevant to their needs. The main lesson for industry is that "common knowledge" and expert opinion should not be the sole basis for the decisions about the choice of software engineering methods. Furthermore, unfortunately, individual empirical studies cannot be trusted automatically. For important decisions concerning the adoption of new methods, decision makers need unbiased summaries of all relevant evidence, and SRs provide a means to deliver such summaries.

An Overview of Systematic Reviews

Believable research starts with *primary studies*: experiments with qualitative or quantitative results relevant to the question one is researching. An SR aggregates results from different independent experiments sometimes using statistical *meta-analysis*.

The classic example demonstrating the need for SRs comes from the medical domain. In 1990, Crowley et al. published an SR that included a meta-analysis of 12 primary studies on the effect of giving corticosteroids to pregnant women expected to give premature birth [Crowley et al. 1990]. Corticosteroids were believed to reduce lung problems affecting premature babies. Crowley at al.'s SR confirmed that the use of corticosteroids substantially decreased the risk of infant death. Corticosteroid administration was not the standard treatment for premature babies at the time, and the publication of the SR resulted in a change of medical practice.

However, this was *not* considered a major triumph for evidence-based medicine. Out of those 12 studies, 8 were published before 1982. If those 8 studies had been aggregated in 1982, eight years of incorrect treatment and associated infant deaths would have been avoided. This led to a reassessment of the importance of aggregating evidence in a timely manner and to the establishment of the Cochrane Collaboration, a nonprofit organization that undertakes SRs of medical and health care issues and maintains a database of SR reports.

You can find an update of Crowley et al.'s report on corticosteroids available without cost from the Cochrane Collaboration library [Roberts and Dalziel 2006]. This is not just of historic interest; for researchers new to SRs, it is a good example of a good quality review.

You may ask what is new about SRs. After all, software engineering researchers have been doing state-of-the-art reports for many years, and summarize related work when they report their latest research results. The answer comes from research in other disciplines that utilize SRs (e.g., psychology and sociology as well as medicine), which has identified numerous problems with conventional reviews that lack a formal methodology:

Experts can be wrong

> Antman et al. confirmed that expert opinion did not always reflect the state of current medical knowledge [Antman et al. 1992].

Researcher's choice of "related studies" can be biased

> Shadish surveyed authors of over 280 articles in psychological journals and found that studies were often cited because they supported the author's argument, not because they were high-quality studies [Shadish 1995].

Informal reviews can miss important studies

> For example, an informal review convinced the Nobel Laureate Linus Pauling that mega-doses of vitamin C would protect against the common cold. However, an SR contradicted this conclusion and found that Pauling had not cited 5 of the 15 methodologically sound studies [Knipschild 1994].

The major advantage of an SR is that it is based on a well-defined methodology. The most important processes associated with undertaking SRs are:

Formulating the research question

> This is the starting point of any SR. It involves refining a recognized information need into one or more questions that can be answered by the current research literature.

Finding the relevant research

> This involves a team of researchers searching the research literature, as thoroughly as possible, to find papers that address the research questions. Sometimes a single researcher, such as a PhD student, needs to do this activity alone, but that limitation raises the risk of missing relevant papers. Best practice advises that each paper identified by the search process be checked by at least two researchers who independently assess whether the paper should be included in the SR. Disagreements about individual papers must be discussed and resolved (if necessary, by bringing in a third member of the team).

> The validity of the SR depends on finding sufficient empirical research to address the research question and showing that the search process meets the level of completeness needed for the SR.

Evaluating the quality of individual studies

This involves identifying appropriate criteria to assess the methodological rigor of each study, which then identifies whether it is qualified to be included in the aggregation. We want our aggregation to be based on best quality evidence. Quality assessment is difficult, so most standards advise that at least two researchers evaluate the quality of each study and resolve any disagreement through discussion.

Extracting and aggregating data

This involves extracting data that address the research question from each study and aggregating the data appropriately. Sometimes a formal meta-analysis can aggregate the data, but more often in software engineering and other nonmedical disciplines, the results of each study are simply tabulated to identify any underlying trends. Like quality evaluation, data extraction is usually performed by two researchers who discuss and resolve any disagreements.

Although I have criticized reliance on expert opinion, the best SRs of software engineering topics I have seen were performed by teams that included domain experts. The knowledge of a domain expert can be put to good use in an SR for identifying specialist conferences and journals that need to be searched, and identifying an initial set of research papers and studies that can be used as a baseline to check the effectiveness of any automated search process.

For new researchers starting to learn the SR process, I recommend they consider *mapping studies*. These are SRs that seek to find and categorize the literature concerning a broad research topic rather than answer a specific research question [Kitchenham et al. 2010b]. The difference between the two types of study can be seen by comparing two papers by Magne Jørgensen. The first is a conventional SR that investigates whether cost estimation model estimates are more accurate than expert judgment estimates for predicting project effort [Jørgensen 2007], which is discussed in the section "The accuracy of cost estimation models" on page 44. The second is a high-quality mapping study that categorizes the cost estimation literature [Jørgensen and Shepperd 2007].

The later section "Systematic Reviews in Software Engineering" on page 44 discusses some SRs that have challenged "common knowledge" in software engineering, to demonstrate the need for methodologically sound methods of aggregating evidence. However, before discussing these examples, I present an overview of the systematic literature process.

A reader interested in the outcomes of SRs rather than the detailed SR process is free to skip directly to "Systematic Reviews in Software Engineering" on page 44. The introduction to this chapter should be sufficient for you to appreciate the rigor of the SR process without overburdening you with too much detail.

However, if you are reading this as a new or experienced researcher wanting to assess the value of SRs, you should read the next section. It discusses steps in the SR process in more detail and identifies some of the practical difficulties inherent in the methodology.

The Strengths and Weaknesses of Systematic Reviews

I have defined, over time, two standards for performing SRs suitable for software engineering researchers. The first standard was based on medical SRs [Kitchenham 2004], whereas the second revised the first standard to take into account new ideas arising from sociological research [Kitchenham and Charters 2007].*

This section provides a brief summary of the guidelines documented in these reports. However, I caution readers not to assume they can successfully undertake an SR based on this brief overview. You should read the full technical reports, consult other references (for example, [Fink 2005], [Higgins and Green 2009], [Khan et al. 2003], [Petticrew and Roberts 2006]) and read examples of SRs, including the software engineering examples discussed later in this chapter. If you look at some good examples of SRs, you will appreciate that they are not an easy form of research. They take a long time and require meticulous planning, execution, and reporting [Brereton et al. 2007].

The Systematic Review Process

An SR has three main phases: planning, conducting the review, and reporting the results.

Planning the review

The stages of this phase are:

Identifying the need for a review
> Identification of an information need helps to define the context for the review and may place constraints on the research questions or the criteria used to include and exclude primary studies. For example, if you need to determine the best way to introduce a new technology, you might restrict the inclusion criteria to industry field studies. In addition, you should check whether there are any existing literature reviews in the topic area, and if there are, justify the need for another review.

Commissioning a review
> Policy makers in medicine and social studies often commission SRs on topics of current interest. A funding body usually invites experts who know both the subject matter and how to do SRs to submit a proposal to undertake the review. I have not heard of this commissioning stage taking place in software engineering, however.

Specifying the research question or questions
> The choice of questions impacts the whole of the review process, so they need to be clearly written and understood by all members of the review team.

---

* These reports and other empirical software engineering resources can be found at *http://www.ebse.org.uk*.

Developing a review protocol

This identifies all the processes that will be used to conduct the review and report its results: the detailed search process, the primary study inclusion and exclusion criteria, and the extraction and aggregation processes. These need to be trialled to confirm that they are appropriate for the task. The review protocol is one of the mechanisms used to reduce researcher bias (since the search strategy is defined in advance and is not under the control of a single researcher) and to increase the auditability and repeatability of the review (since the planned process is fully reported). This is an extremely time-consuming activity.

Evaluating the review protocol

Most standards suggest inviting researchers outside the team to review the protocol. However, in practice it is difficult to find external researchers willing to perform this role, and it may only be possible to have an internal review.

Conducting the review

The stages of this phase are:

Finding the relevant research literature

This involves identifying literature sources to search for research papers, deciding how the search will be organized, and identifying relevant research papers. Major issues include which digital libraries, indexing systems, journals, and conference proceedings to search, whether the search process will be automated, manual, or mixed, and how the search process will be validated. Finding the research is another time-consuming activity and is discussed later in more detail.

Selecting primary studies

The selection process means applying inclusion and exclusion criteria to decide whether each study identified in the search process should be included in the review.

Assessing the quality of studies

Primary studies need to be assessed for quality so that you either include only methodologically sound studies or, when there are relatively few studies of any kind, provide a warning to the reader. Generally, you need a quality evaluation questionnaire that asks questions related to the rigor of the empirical study.

For example, in the case of experiments, standard questions include: "Were subjects randomly allocated to treatments?" and "Were researchers kept in ignorance of the actual allocation of subjects to treatment until after the completion of the experiment?" For SRs in software engineering where a variety of different research methods may be used, I recommend the checklist developed by Dybå and Dingsøyr [Dybå and Dingsøyr 2008a] as a starting point, although I would suggest using an ordinal scale rather than a binary choice for answering the questions. You should also consult Chapter 2.

Data extraction and synthesis

The data extracted from each paper must be aggregated to answer the research questions. When there are sufficient comparable quantitative data, meta-analytic techniques can be applied [Lipsey and Wilson 2001]. When there are not, results should be tabulated in a way that addresses the research questions.

Meta-analysis is the most common form of aggregation in medical SRs, but is less common in other disciplines. In practice, meta-analysis is possible only if the results of each primary study are presented in terms of an appropriate statistical analysis. However, even in the presence of statistical results, it is not always possible to perform a full meta-analysis [Turner et al. 2010].

Reporting the review

The stages of this phase are:

Specifying dissemination mechanisms

Some SRs are extremely long and it is necessary to consider whether any paper submitted to a journal needs to be backed by a more detailed technical report.

Formatting the main report

SRs follow the normal reporting standards for empirical papers. I recommend using a structured abstract (such as the one in [Roberts and Dalziel 2006]) because evidence suggests they are a useful way of summarizing research results [Budgen et al. 2008]. If you have adhered to a good protocol and have kept good records of your search and data extraction processes, this is a relatively straightforward task.

Evaluating the report

The standards recommend external reviewers, but regardless of whether the SR is evaluated internally or externally, reviewers need to confirm that the processes used in the conduct of the SR are fully reported and that there is a clear link from the research questions to the search process, the data extraction process, and the aggregation process.

One of the claims for SRs is that results are repeatable, in the sense that if another research team followed the same protocol, they would obtain the same results. Repeatability depends on lack of ambiguity in the research questions, full reporting of the search and aggregation processes, and the scope of the study. A recent study compared two independent SRs undertaken using the same research question [Macdonell et al. pending]. This study concluded that in the context of a relatively small number of primary studies and review teams composed of domain experts, software engineering SRs are reasonably repeatable. Another SR, based on a very large body of empirical literature [Turner et al. 2010], found major differences between different literature reviews but explained that differences were implicit in the differences between the research questions addressed in the different reviews.

Problems Associated with Conducting a Review

Theoretically, an SR is conducted strictly according to the predefined research protocol. However, this is not as easy as it appears. In spite of being tested, the protocol may not have identified all the variations in the designing and reporting of relevant primary studies, so you may come across situations not covered by the protocol. In such circumstances, the protocol will need to be revised. Depending on the nature of the revision, you may have to review and even redo a substantial amount of work to ensure it is consistent with the revised protocol [Turner et al. 2008].

To identify relevant research, critical issues are the selection of the digital libraries to be searched and whether the search is automated or manual. A manual search involves looking at the back issues of a set of journals (either paper or online) and deciding from the title and abstract which individual papers are candidates for inclusion in the review. An automated search uses strings, usually based on complex Boolean formulas, to turn up papers in online catalogs. Medical texts advise procedures for deriving search strings from the research questions.

For automated searches, Hannay et al. recommend restricting the digital sources searched to ACM Digital Library, IEEE Xplore, Compendex, and ISI Web of Science because these libraries ensure coverage of ACM, IEEE, Kluwer Online, Science Direct, SpringerLink, and Wiley [Hannay et al. 2009]. The authors also recommend hand-searches of important thematic conference proceedings. However, if you need to find all relevant literature, whether or not it has been published, you should also use Google Scholar or CiteSeer. In addition, the digital libraries differ in subtle ways in their implementations of searches, so you would be well advised to consult a librarian about your search process and search strings. Issues that arise are:

- Software engineering digital libraries have different interfaces and different tolerances for the complex Boolean formulas typically used by SR researchers to turn up relevant papers.

- Software engineering digital libraries also have different procedures for searching the body of the paper, or only the title, abstract, and keywords. In addition, of course, indexing systems only search titles, keywords, and abstracts.

- Automated searches from different sources may overlap (i.e., the same paper may be found in different digital libraries), and every search includes a large number of irrelevant papers ([Brereton et al. 2007], [Dieste and Padua 2007]).

For manual searches, you will need to select the journals and conference proceedings you intend to search. You will also need to justify your selection of sources. However, rather surprisingly, in one case study we found that a targeted manual search was much quicker than a broad automated search [Kitchenham et al. 2009a]. In practice, you will probably need a mixed strategy. If you do a manual search of some sources (including specialist conference proceedings), this should give you a baseline set of candidate primary studies against which you can validate the efficacy of your automated search strings. Alternatively, a domain expert can identify a baseline set of papers.

The medical standards mandate that two researchers make the initial inclusion/exclusion decision independently. However, my experience of automated software engineering searches is that many papers are clearly irrelevant from the title alone. Thus, in practice many software engineering researchers (myself included) allow a single researcher to do an initial screening for complete irrelevance, with the understanding that if there is any doubt, the paper remains a candidate. However, for the next phase of screening, it is more important to have two or more independent assessments of each candidate primary study. In this stage, the reviewers read each of the remaining candidate papers in full and apply the inclusion/exclusion criteria to them.

Including the same study more than once would bias the aggregation. Therefore, papers must be checked to identify whether they include multiple studies or whether their results need to be blended because they refer to the same study. However, it is not always easy to recognize duplicate reports of the same study. In a recent SR, my colleagues and I were obliged to look for replicated sample sizes together with the same list of authors in order to identify multiple reports of the same study [Turner et al. 2010]. In another SR, the problem was even subtler because different researchers used the same data sets to investigate the same data analysis methods, but did not always explicitly identify the data sets they used [Kitchenham et al. 2007].

The medical standards require an SR to be performed by a team of researchers. This is because much of the process relies on human judgment, in particular:

- Deciding whether or not a paper is a candidate for primary study, both during the initial search and when the inclusion/exclusion criteria are applied
- Answering quality assessment questions
- Extracting data from each primary study

Assigning the SR to multiple researchers is hoped to undercut bias in human judgment. Originally my colleagues and I suggested that an extractor and checker process might be more efficient than two independent extractions for data extraction and quality assessment [Brereton et al. 2007], but in the end, it proved to be a poor option [Turner et al. 2008]. However, it is sometimes necessary for SRs to be undertaken by a single researcher, such as when doing research for a postgraduate degree or when resources are limited. For example, I undertook a preliminary mapping study by myself [Kitchenham 2010] as a result of tight timescales and limited resources. In such cases, researchers should use techniques to assess the accuracy of subjective decisions, such as the test-retest procedure suggested by Fink [Fink 2005].

Finally, with respect to quality criteria, I have found that relatively few software engineering SRs actually assess the quality of individual studies ([Kitchenham et al. 2009b], [Kitchenham et al. 2010a]). However, such a quality judgment is an essential element of the SR process and is very important for appropriately aggregating primary study results and interpreting the results. An example of the impact of poor quality on results can be seen in a recent SR of the efficacy of homeopathy [Shang et al 2005]. If all studies are included, it appears that homeopathy is more effective than a placebo, whereas an SR excluding poor-quality studies clearly reveals that homeopathy is no more effective than a placebo. I will discuss a software engineering example of problems with poor-quality primary studies later.

Systematic Reviews in Software Engineering

In this section I present the results of some SRs that have challenged "common knowledge" and, in some cases, forced me to revise some of my ideas about software engineering.

Cost Estimation Studies

Cost estimation studies often report empirical studies of industry data sets, so research questions related to cost estimation would appear to be obvious candidates for SRs. Indeed, a review of SRs published between January 2004 and June 2007 found that cost estimation topics were the most common subject for SRs [Kitchenham et al. 2009b]. Two of these reviews are of particular interest because they overturn some of our preconceptions about software cost estimation.

The accuracy of cost estimation models

In two SRs, Magne Jørgensen addressed the issue of whether estimates from cost models (mathematical formulas usually generated from data collected on past projects) are more accurate than expert judgment estimates (estimates based on the subjective opinion of software developers or managers) [Jørgensen 2004], [Jørgensen 2007]. Since the publication of the books by Boehm [Boehm 1981] and DeMarco [DeMarco 1982] in the early 1980s, it has been an article of faith among cost estimation researchers that cost estimation models must be better than expert judgment, but Jørgensen's reviews were the first attempt to determine whether this belief was supported by empirical evidence.

In [Jørgensen 2004], Jørgensen found 15 primary studies that compared expert judgment models and cost estimation models. He categorized 5 to be in favor of expert judgment, 5 to find no difference, and 5 to be in favor of model-based estimation. In [Jørgensen 2007], he identified 16 primary studies that compared expert judgment estimates with formal cost models and found that the average accuracy of the expert-judgment models was better in 12.

The differences between the two SRs reflect differences in the included studies and the focus of the review. In the more recent SR, he omitted three of the primary studies included in the first SR and included four additional primary studies. The reason for including different studies was that the initial SR was aimed at justifying the need to improve procedures by which experts made their subjective estimates. The second SR was concerned with identifying the context within which an expert opinion estimate would more likely be accurate than the estimate from a formal model and vice versa. However, in spite of differences between the two SRs, the results are clearly not consistent with the view that cost model estimates are necessarily better than expert judgment estimates.

With respect to possible bias in "related research" sections in papers, I was the coauthor of one of the papers included in both of Jørgensen's reviews [Kitchenham et al 2002]. In our paper, my colleagues and I were able to identify only 2 of the 12 papers published before 2002 found by Jørgensen, and both of them found expert judgment better than model-based estimation, as we ourselves did.

The accuracy of cost estimates in industry

The 1994 CHAOS Report from the Standish Group [The Standish Group 2003] stated that project overruns in the software industry averaged 189% and that only 16% of projects were successful (i.e., within budget and schedule). Subsequent reports from the Standish Group have found lower levels of overruns, with 34% of projects being classified as successful, a change observers have hailed as demonstrating how much software engineering techniques are improving. However, when Moløkken-Østvold and Jørgensen undertook a literature review of software effort estimation surveys ([Moløkken-Østvold et al. 2004], [Moløkken-Østvold and Jørgensen 2003]), they found three industrial surveys undertaken before the CHAOS report that found average cost overruns of between 30% and 50%. This was so different from the CHAOS report results that they reviewed the CHAOS report carefully to understand why the overrun rates were so high, and as a result of their investigation, omitted the CHAOS report from their survey.

The details of their investigation of the CHAOS report are given in [Jørgensen and Moløkken-Østvold 2006]. They found that the methodology adopted by the Standish Group left much to be desired:

- The method of calculating the overruns was not specified. When Moløkken-Østvold and Jørgensen ran their own calculations, they found that the overruns should have been close to 89%, not 189%.
- The Standish Group appeared to have deliberately solicited failure stories.
- There was no category for under-budget projects.
- Cost overruns were not well-defined and could have included costs on canceled projects.

They concluded that although the CHAOS report is one of the most frequently cited papers on estimate overruns, its results cannot be trusted.

Agile Methods

Currently there is a great deal of interest in Agile methods, both in industry and academia. Agile methods aim to deliver applications that match user requirements as quickly as possible while ensuring high quality. Many different approaches fall under the Agile rubric, but they all emphasize the practices of minimizing unnecessary overheads (i.e., excessive planning and documentation) while concentrating on incremental delivery of client-specified functions. Some of the best-known approaches are:

Extreme programming (XP, XP2)
> The original XP method comprises 12 practices: the planning game, small releases, metaphor, simple design, test first, refactoring, pair programming, collective ownership, continuous integration, 40-hour week, on-site customers, and coding standards [Beck 2000]. The revised XP2 method consists of the following "primary practices": sit together, whole team, informative workspace, energized work, pair programming, stories, weekly cycle, quarterly cycle, slack, 10-minute build, continuous integration, test-first programming, and incremental design [Beck 2004].

Scrum [Schwaber and Beedle 2001]
> This method focuses on project management in situations where it is difficult to plan ahead by adopting mechanisms for "empirical process control" that focus on feedback loops. Software is developed by a self-organizing team in increments (called "sprints"), starting with planning and ending with a review. Features to be implemented in the system are registered in a backlog. Then, the product owner decides which backlog items should be developed in the following sprint. Team members coordinate their work in a daily stand-up meeting. One team member, the Scrum master, is in charge of solving problems that stop the team from working effectively.

Dynamic software development method (DSDM) [Stapleton 2003]
> This method divides projects into three phases: pre-project, project life cycle, and post-project. It is based on nine principles: user involvement, empowering the project team, frequent delivery, addressing current business needs, iterative and incremental development, allow for reversing changes, high-level scope being fixed before project starts, testing throughout the life cycle, and efficient and effective communication.

Lean software development [Poppendieck and Poppendieck 2003]
> This adapts principles from lean production, the Toyota production system in particular, to software development. It consists of seven principles: eliminate waste, amplify learning, decide as late as possible, deliver as fast as possible, empower the team, build integrity, and see the whole.

One of the possible limitations of SRs is that they may progress too slowly to be of value in a fast-moving domain such as software engineering. However, there have already been two recent SRs addressing Agile methods: [Dybå and Dingsøyr 2008a] and [Hannay et al. 2009].

Dybå and Dingsøyr

These researchers [Dybå and Dingsøyr 2008a] had three goals:

- To assess current knowledge of the benefits and limitations of Agile methods
- To assess the strength of evidence behind that knowledge
- To apply their results to industry and the research community

They concentrated on Agile development as a whole, and therefore excluded papers that investigated specific methods, such as pair-programming in isolation. They identified 33 relevant primary studies. Most (24) of the studies they included examined professional software engineers. Nine studies took place in a university setting.

With respect to the differences between SRs and informal reviews, Dybå and Dingsøyr report that they found five papers published in or before 2003 that were not reported by two informal reviews published in 2004. With respect to the need for good-quality evidence, they rejected all the papers reported in the two informal reviews because they were either lessons-learned papers or single-practice studies that did not compare the technique they focused on with any alternative.

Dybå and Dingsøyr found that although some studies reported problems with XP (in the context of large, complex projects), most papers discussing XP found that it was easy to introduce and that the approach worked well in a variety of different environments. With respect to the limitations of XP, they found primary studies that reported that the role of the on-site customer was unsustainable in the long term.

However, they found many limitations with the empirical studies of Agile methods. Most of the studies concerned XP, with Scrum and Lean software development discussed in only one paper each. Furthermore, only one research team (which carried out four of the primary studies included) had looked at Agile methods being used by mature teams.

In addition, Dybå and Dingsøyr assessed the quality of the existing evidence in terms of the rigor of the study design, the quality of the individual primary studies (within the constraint of the basic design), the extent to which results from different studies gave consistent results, and the extent to which the studies were representative of real software development. They found the overall quality of evidence very low, and concluded that more research is needed of Agile methods other than XP, particularly studies of mature teams, where the researchers adopt more rigorous methods.

Hannay, Dybå, Arisholm, and Sjøberg

These researchers [Hannay et al. 2009] investigated pair-programming and undertook a meta-analysis to aggregate their results. If you are interested in how to do a meta-analysis, this paper provides a sound introduction. Their SR identified 18 primary studies, all of which were experiments. Of the 18 studies, 4 of the experiments involved only professional subjects, 1 involved professionals and students, and the remaining 13 used students. Hannay et al.

investigated three different outcomes: quality, duration, and effort (although not every study addressed every outcome). Their initial analysis showed that the use of pair-programming had:

- A small positive impact on quality
- A medium positive effect on duration
- A medium negative effect on effort

These results would seem to support the standard view of the impact of pair-programming. However, the results also indicated that there was significant *heterogeneity* among the studies. Heterogeneity means that the individual studies arise from different populations, so study results cannot be properly understood unless the different populations can be identified.

Hannay et al. found more problems when they investigated the possibility of *publication bias*. This occurs when papers that fail to demonstrate a significant effect are less likely to be accepted for publication than papers that show a significant effect. Their analysis suggested the likelihood of publication bias and found that adjusting for possible bias eliminated the quality effect completely, reduced the duration effect from moderate to small, but slightly increased the effort effect (although this occurred for only one particular analysis model).

They pointed out that the heterogeneity and possible publication bias could have been caused by the presence of moderating variables (i.e., variables that account for differences among study results). To investigate the impact of possible moderating variables, they looked at one study in detail. It was by far the largest study, involving 295 subjects, and used professional software engineers with three levels of experience (senior, intermediate, and junior). They concluded that there is likely to be an interaction between task complexity and outcome such that very complex tasks may achieve high quality using pair-programming but at the cost of considerably greater effort, whereas low-complexity tasks can be performed quickly but at a cost of poor quality. They recommend that researchers focus on moderating variables in future primary studies.

Dybå and Dingsøyr's study suggests there are some benefits to be obtained from Agile methods [Dybå and Dingsøyr 2008a]. However, Hannay et al.'s meta-analysis suggests that the effects of pair-programming are not as strong as might have been hoped [Hannay et al. 2009]. Overall, the results of both studies suggest not only that the impact of Agile methods needs more research, but more generally, that we also need to improve the research methods we use for primary studies.

Inspection Methods

Inspection techniques are methods of reading code and documents with the aim of identifying defects. They are arguably one of the most researched topics in empirical software engineering. There were 103 human-centered experiments performed between 1993 and 2002 [Sjøberg et al. 2005]; 37 (36%) of them were inspection-related studies. The next largest category was object-oriented (OO) design methods, which were investigated in 8 (7.8%) of these 103 papers. It would seem, therefore, that inspections are a strong candidate for a SR.

Recently Ciolkowski performed a SR including a meta-analysis to test the claims made concerning perspective-based reading (PBR) [Ciolkowski 2009]. For example, many researchers had suggested that PBR was better than either "ad hoc" reading or checklist-based reading (CBR), and the experts involved in an electronic workshop rated the impact on the order of 35% [Boehm and Basili 2001], [Shull et al. 2002]. Other researchers were less enthusiastic. Wholin et al. undertook a study to investigate the feasibility of quantitative aggregation of inspection studies and concluded that CBR was the most effective technique [Wholin et al. 2003].

Ciolkowski's initial meta-analysis found *no* significant impact of PBR. This result showed small to moderate heterogeneity. A subset analysis suggested that PBR was better than ad hoc reading and that CBR was better than PBR for requirements documents but worse for design documents. He also noted that the results were affected by moderating variables such as the origin of the inspection materials and whether the studies were performed by independent research groups. Overall, studies that used the same materials and the same group of researchers were more favorable to PBR than independent studies, although the subgroup analysis was not very robust. Nonetheless, he concluded that claims that PBR increased performance by 35% were not confirmed.

Conclusion

In the previous section I discussed some SRs that offer new insights into software engineering. Many other SRs and mapping studies over the past few years have covered a variety of topics (see [Kitchenham et al. 2009b], [Kitchenham et al. 2010a], the *IST* virtual special issue,† and Chapter 12). I believe these studies should start to change the way we do research in software engineering. Anyone interested in a particular topic needs to check for SRs addressing the topic. If no SRs exist, it may be a good idea to do one. If there are existing reviews, they can act as the starting point for your own literature search or can point you to topic areas where new research is necessary.

However, SRs have obvious limitations. First, just because something claims to be an SR doesn't mean it was necessarily a high-quality review. You should read SRs as critically as you read any other research paper. You can use Greenhalgh's evaluation criteria [Greenhalgh 2000] or the five criteria used by the Centre for Reviews and Dissemination [Centre for Reviews and Dissemination 2007]:

- Are the review's inclusion and exclusion criteria described and appropriate?
- Is the literature search likely to have covered all relevant studies?

---

† *http://www.elsevier.com/wps/find/P05.cws_home/infsof_vsi_sysreviews*

- Were the studies synthesized?
- Did the reviewers assess the quality/validity of the included studies?
- Were the basic data/studies adequately described?

The second major problem is that SRs rely on the availability of high-quality primary studies. The studies discussed in the previous section suggest that there are a relatively large number of primary studies but cast doubts on their quality. For SRs, we need primary studies that:

- Conform to best quality guidelines for the type of study being undertaken
- Report their results in sufficient detail for meta-analysis to be performed
- Are independent of one another in terms of research groups and research materials (in contrast to Basili's et al.'s suggestion for families of experiments [Basili et al. 1999])
- Collect data concerning possible moderating variables, e.g., subject type and experience, task complexity, size, and duration

Furthermore, even if our primary studies of human-centric methods adopt these best practices, I remain to be convinced that meta-analysis-based aggregation can reliably assess the impact of a method/technique unless we are able to use professional subjects in realistic situations (i.e., doing tasks of realistic complexity and duration).

Nonetheless, even if there are problems with primary studies and the interpretation of the results of meta-analyses, it seems to me to be pointless to undertake empirical studies if we don't attempt to organize results into an empirical body of knowledge about our methods and techniques. Furthermore, we need to adopt the discipline of SRs to ensure that we aggregate our results as fairly and openly as possible.

References

[Antman et al. 1992] Antman, E.M., J. Lau, B. Kupelnick, F. Mosteller, and T.C. Chalmers. 1992. A comparison of results of meta-analysis of randomized controlled trials and recommendations of clinical experts. *Journal of the American Medical Association* 268(2): 240–248.

[Basili et al. 1999] Basili, V.R., F. Shull, and F. Lanubile. 1999. Building knowledge through families of experiments. *IEEE Transactions on Software Engineering*. 25(4): 456–473.

[Beck 2000] Beck, K. 2000. *Extreme Programming Explained: Embrace Change*. Boston: Addison-Wesley.

[Beck 2004] Beck, K. 2004. *Extreme Programming Explained: Embrace Change*, Second Edition. Boston: Addison-Wesley.

[Boehm 1981] Boehm, B.W. 1981. *Software engineering economics*. Upper Saddle River, NJ: Prentice-Hall.

[Boehm and Basili 2001] Boehm, B.W. and V.R. Basili. 2001. Software Defect Reduction Top 10 List. *Computer* 31(1): 135–137.

[Brereton 2007] Brereton, O.P., B.A. Kitchenham, D. Budgen, M. Turner, and M. Khalil. 2007. Lessons from applying the systematic literature process within the software engineering domain. *Journal of Systems and Software* 80(4): 571–583.

[Budgen et al. 2008] Budgen, D., B. Kitchenham, S. Charters, M. Turner, P. Brereton, and S. Linkman. 2008. Presenting Software Engineering Results Using Structured Abstracts: A Randomised Experiment. *Empirical Software Engineering* 13(4): 435–468.

[Centre for Reviews and Dissemination 2010] Centre for Reviews and Dissemination. 2007. "DARE" section in the online HELP section. Available at *http://www.york.ac.uk/inst/crd/darefaq .htm*.

[Ciolkowski 2009] Ciolkowski, M. 2009. What Do We Know About Perspective-Based Reading? An Approach for Quantitative Aggregation in Software Engineering. *Proceedings of the Third International Symposium on Empirical Software Engineering and Measurement*: 133–144.

[Crowley et al. 1990] Crowley, P., I. Chalmers, and M.J.N.C. Keirse. 1990. The effects of corticosteroid administration: an overview of the evidence from controlled trials. *British Journal of Obstetrics and Gynaecology* 97: 11–25.

[DeMarco 1982] DeMarco, T. 1982. *Controlling Software Projects: Management, measurement, and estimation*. Englewood Cliffs, NJ: Yourdon Press (Prentice-Hall).

[Dieste and Padua 2007] Dieste, O., and A.G. Padua. 2007. Developing Search Strategies for Detecting Relevant Experiments for Systematic Reviews. *Proceedings of the 1st International Symposium on Empirical Software Engineering and Measurement (ESEM'07)*: 215–224.

[Dybå and Dingsøyr 2008a] Dybå, T., and T. Dingsøyr. 2008. Empirical studies of agile software development: A systematic review. *Information and Software Technology* 50(9–10): 833–859.

[Dybå and Dingsøyr 2008b] Dybå, T., and T. Dingsøyr. 2008. Strength of Evidence in Systematic Reviews in Software Engineering. *Proceedings of the 2nd International Symposium on Empirical Software Engineering and Measurement (ESEM'08)*: 178–187.

[Dybå et al. 2005] Dybå, T., B.A. Kitchenham, and M. Jørgensen. 2005. Evidence-based Software Engineering for Practitioners. *IEEE Software* 22(1): 58–65.

[Fink 2005] Fink, A. 2005. *Conducting Research Literature Reviews: From the Internet to Paper*. Thousand Oaks, CA: Sage Publications, Inc.

[Greenhalgh 2000] Greenhalgh, Trisha. 2000. *How to Read a Paper: The Basics of Evidence-Based Medicine*. Hoboken, NJ: BMJ Books.

[Hannay et al. 2009] Hannay, J.E., T. Dybå, E. Arisholm, and D.I.K. Sjøberg. 2009. The effectiveness of pair-programming: A meta-analysis. *Information and Software Technology* 54(7): 1110–1122.

[Higgins and Green 2009] Higgins, J.P.T., and S. Green, ed. 2009. *Cochrane Handbook for Systematic Reviews of Interventions,* Version 5.0.2 [updated September 2009]. The Cochrane Collaboration. Available from *http://www.cochrane-handbook.org.*

[Jørgensen 2004] Jørgensen, M. 2004. A review of studies on expert estimation of software development effort. *Journal of Systems and Software* 70(1–2): 37–60.

[Jørgensen 2007] Jørgensen, M. 2007. Forecasting of software development work effort: Evidence on expert judgement and formal models. *International Journal of Forecasting* 23(3): 449–462.

[Jørgensen and Moløkken-Østvold 2006] Jørgensen, M., and K. Moløkken-Østvold. 2006. How large are software cost overruns? A review of the 1994 CHAOS report. *Information and Software Technology* 48: 297–301.

[Jørgensen and Shepperd 2007] Jørgensen, M., and M. Shepperd. 2007. A Systematic Review of Software Development Cost Estimation Studies. *IEEE Transactions on Software Engineering* 33(1): 33–53.

[Khan et al. 2003] Khan, K.S., R. Kunz, J. Kleijnen, and G. Antes. 2003. *Systematic Reviews to Support Evidence-Based Medicine: How to Review and Apply Findings of Healthcare Research.* London: The Royal Society of Medicine Press Ltd.

[Kitchenham 2004] Kitchenham, B. 2004. Procedures for Performing Systematic Reviews. Joint Technical Report, Keele University TR/SE-0401 and NICTA 0400011T.1, July.

[Kitchenham 2010] Kitchenham, B. What's up with software metrics—A preliminary mapping study. *Journal of Systems and Software* 83(1): 37–51.

[Kitchenham and Charters 2007] Kitchenham, B.A., and S.M. Charters. 2007. Guidelines for Performing Systematic Literature Reviews in Software Engineering, Version 2.3. EBSE Technical Report EBSE-2007-01, Keele University and Durham University, July.

[Kitchenham et al. 2002] Kitchenham, B., S.L. Pfleeger, B. McColl, and S. Eagan. 2002. An empirical study of maintenance and development accuracy. *Journal of Systems and Software* 64: 57–77.

[Kitchenham et al. 2004] Kitchenham, B.A., T. Dybå, and M. Jørgensen. 2004. Evidence-based Software Engineering. *Proceedings of the 26th International Conference on Software Engineering (ICSE'04)*: 273–281.

[Kitchenham et al. 2007] Kitchenham, B., E. Mendes, G.H. Travassos. 2007. A Systematic Review of Cross- vs. Within-Company Cost Estimation Studies. *IEEE Transactions on Software Engineering* 33(5): 316–329.

[Kitchenham et al. 2009a] Kitchenham, B., P. Brereton, M. Turner, M. Niazi, S. Linkman, R. Pretorius, and D. Budgen. 2009. The Impact of Limited Search Procedures for Systematic Literature Reviews—An Observer-Participant Case Study. *Proceedings of the 3rd International Symposium on Empirical Software Engineering and Measurement (ESEM'09)*: 336–345.

[Kitchenham et al. 2009b] Kitchenham, B., O.P. Brereton, D. Budgen, M. Turner, J. Bailey, and S. Linkman. 2009. Systematic literature reviews in software engineering—A systematic literature review. *Information and Software Technology* 51(1): 7–15.

[Kitchenham et al. 2010a] Kitchenham, B., R. Pretorius, D. Budgen, O.P. Brereton, M. Turner, M. Niazi, and S. Linkman. Systematic Literature Review in Software Engineering—A Tertiary Study. *Information and Software Technology* 52(8): 792–805.

[Kitchenham et al. 2010b] Kitchenham, B., O.P. Brereton, and D. Budgen. 2010. The Educational Value of Mapping Studies of the Software Engineering Literature. *Proceedings of the 32nd ACM/IEEE International Conference on Software Engineering* 1: 589–598.

[Knipschild 1994] Knipschild, P. 1994. Some examples of systematic reviews. *British Medical Journal* 309: 719–721.

[Lipsey and Wilson 2001] Lipsey, M.W., and D.B. Wilson. 2001. *Practical Meta-Analysis: Applied Social Research Methods Series*, Volume 49. Thousand Oaks, CA: Sage Publications, Inc.

[Macdonell et al. pending] Macdonell, S., M. Shepperd, B. Kitchenham, and E. Mendes. How Reliable Are Systematic Reviews in Empirical Software Engineering? Accepted for publication in *IEEE Transactions on Software Engineering*.

[Moløkken-Østvold and Jørgensen 2003] Moløkken-Østvold, K.J., and M. Jørgensen. 2003. A Review of Surveys on Software Effort Estimation. *Proceedings of the 2003 International Symposium on Empirical Software Engineering*: 223.

[Moløkken-Østvold et al. 2004] Moløkken-Østvold, K.J., M. Jørgensen, S.S. Tanilkan, H. Gallis, A.C. Lien, and S.E. Hove. 2004. A Survey on Software Estimation in the Norwegian Industry. *Proceedings of the 10th International Symposium on Software Metrics*: 208–219.

[Petticrew and Roberts 2006] Petticrew, M., and H. Roberts. 2006. *Systematic Reviews in the Social Sciences: A Practical Guide*. Malden, MA: Blackwell Publishing.

[Poppendieck and Poppendieck 2003] Poppendieck, M., and T. Poppendieck. 2003. *Lean Software Development: An Agile Toolkit*. Boston: Addison-Wesley.

[Roberts and Dalziel 2006] Roberts, D., and S. Dalziel. 2006. Antenatal corticosteroids for accelerating fetal lung maturation for women at risk of preterm birth. *Cochrane Database of Systematic Reviews* 2006, Issue 3. Art. No.: CD004454. Available at *http://www2.cochrane.org/reviews/CD004454.pdf*.

[Schwaber and Beedle 2001] Schwaber, K., and M. Beedle. 2001. *Agile Software Development with Scrum*. Upper Saddle River, NJ: Prentice Hall.

[Shadish 1995] Shadish, W. 1995. Author judgements about work they cite: Three studies from psychological journals. *Social Studies of Science* 25: 477–498.

[Shang et al. 2005] Shang, A., K. Huwiler-Müntener, L. Nartney, P. Jüni, S. Dörig, D. Pwesner, and M. Egger. 2005. Are the clinical effects of homeopathy placebo effects? Comparative study of placebo-controlled trials of homeopathy and allopathy. *Lancet* 366(9487): 726–732.

[Shull et al. 2002] Shull, F., V. Basili, B. Boehm, A. Brown, P. Costa, M. Lindvall, D. Port, I. Rus, R. Tesoriero, and M. Zelowitz. 2002. What We Have Learned About Fighting Defects. *Proc 8th IEEE Symposium on Software Metrics*: 249–258.

[Sjøberg et al. 2005] Sjøberg, D.I.K., J.E. Hannay, O. Hansen, V.B. Kampenes, A. Karahasanovic, N.K. Liborg, and A.C. Rekdal. 2005. A survey of controlled experiments in software engineering. *IEEE Transactions on Software Engineering* 31(9): 733–753.

[The Standish Group 2003] The Standish Group. 2003. Chaos Chronicles Version 3.0. Available at *http://www.standishgroup.com/chaos/intro1.php*.

[Stapleton 2003] Stapleton, J. 2003. *DSDM: Business Focused Development*, Second Edition. Upper Saddle River, NJ: Pearson Education.

[Turner et al. 2008] Turner, M., B. Kitchenham, D. Budgen, and P. Brereton. 2008. Lessons Learnt Undertaking a Large-scale Systematic Literature Review. *Proceedings of EASE 2008*, BCS-eWiC. Available at *http://www.bcs.org/upload/pdf/ewic_ea08_paper12.pdf*.

[Turner et al. 2010] Turner, M., B. Kitchenham, P. Brereton, S. Charters, and D. Budgen. 2009. Does the Technology Acceptance Model Predict Actual Use? A Systematic Literature Review. *Information and Systems Technology* 52(5): 463–476.

[Wholin et al. 2003] Wholin, C., H. Petersson, and A. Aurum. 2003. Combining data from reading experiments in software inspections: A feasibility study. In *Lecture Notes on Empirical Software Engineering*, ed. N. Juristo and A. Moreno, 85–132. Singapore: World Scientific Publishing.

## CHAPTER FOUR

Understanding Software Engineering Through Qualitative Methods

Andrew Ko

People trust numbers. They are the core of computation, the fundamentals of finance, and an essential part of human progress in the past century. And for the majority of modern societies, numbers are how we know things: we use them to study which drugs are safe, what policies work, and how our universe evolves. They are, perhaps, one of the most powerful and potent of human tools.

But like any tool, numbers aren't good for everything. There are some kinds of questions for which numbers answer little. For example, public health researchers in the 1980s wanted to explain epileptic patients' difficulties with taking their medication regularly. Researchers measured how many people failed to comply; they looked for statistical differences between those who complied and those who didn't; they even ran elaborate longitudinal controlled experiments to measure the consequences of noncompliance. But none of these approaches explained the lack of compliance; they just described it in rigorous but shallow ways.

Then, a groundbreaking study [Conrad 1985] took a different approach. Instead of trying to measure compliance quantitatively, the researchers performed 80 interviews of people with epilepsy, focusing on the situations in which their informants were expected to take their medications but did not. The researchers found that the lack of compliance was due not to irrational, erratic behavior, but to patients' deliberate choice. For example, some patients were aware of the potential of becoming chemically dependent on the drugs and carefully regulated their use of the drug to avoid tolerance. These qualitative findings, one of the first of their kind in public health research, became a critical part of redefining how epilepsy medication is delivered to society.

What does all of this have to do with software engineering? Like public health, software engineering is full of *why* and *how* questions for which numbers and statistics are of little help. For example, if you've managed a software team, you've probably asked yourself a number of questions. Why won't my developers write unit tests? Why do users keep filling out this form incorrectly? Why are some of my developers 10 times as productive as the others? These questions can't be answered with numbers, but they can with the careful application of *qualitative methods*.

But using qualitative methods isn't as simple as asking people a few questions, nor is reading reports of qualitative studies as simple as reading the abstract. This chapter explains what qualitative methods are, how to interpret the results of qualitative studies, and how you might use them in your own work to improve software process and quality.

What Are Qualitative Methods?

Put simply, qualitative methods entail the *systematic gathering and interpretation of nonnumerical data* (including words, pictures, etc.). Like quantitative methods, qualitative methods can be used to gather data to confirm or reject beliefs (deductive reasoning). However, qualitative methods can also be used to support inductive reasoning: gather data to arrive at new explanations. Because qualitative methods gather nonnumerical data, they also lend themselves to being used in more natural settings.

To illustrate, let's focus on a specific scenario and discuss how qualitative methods might be used to understand it. Imagine you've just started managing a software team. You're leading a new project and have just adopted a new bug tracking system with some great features your team has been dying to have. Over the next few months, you see your team patching a lot of code and making great progress, but every time you check the bug list in the new system, there are only a few reports from the same few testers and they never seem to change. Then, one morning you walk by your best developer's desk and see the old bug tracker up on his screen. Your team has been secretly using the old system for weeks! After all of that training, the careful transition, and the costly licensing, *why aren't they using the new tracker*?

One obvious thing to do is simply ask. For example, you could call a meeting and just ask the team to explain why they're avoiding the new system. You'd get some explanation, but it may not be entirely trustworthy, especially if the developers find themselves opposing your decision to adopt the new tracker. Moreover, the fact that they're in a social context will also make the less talkative members of your team less likely to speak, biasing the explanations you get to your most vocal employees. A biased, warped explanation won't be helpful to anyone.

To take yourself out of the equation, perhaps you could ask a trustworthy friend to ask around during coffee breaks, conducting brief, informal interviews. That would give each person a chance to state his opinion outside of a group context, perhaps freeing him to be more vocal and more honest. But you'll still be limited to the views of your friend's friends. Even worse, your friend might not be impartial; maybe he particularly dislikes the new tracker and unintentionally biases his report back to you.

The issue with the approaches I've just suggested is that they are secondhand or even thirdhand accounts. Ideally, you would be able to observe the moment of interest. For example, when people on the team decided to use the old tracker instead of the new one, what was going on in their heads? What were the other constraints on their time? Who were they collaborating with? What data were they entering? To get at these questions, you might sit next to developers for a day, watching what they do. This would allow you to directly observe the moments when they decide to use the old tracker instead of the new one.

Of course, directly observing people in these moments is often unfeasible. People don't like being watched, and often adapt their behavior to preserve their privacy or avoid embarrassment or anxiety. Moreover, since you'd be the sole observer, you're likely to bring biases to your observations.

It might also be possible to take people out of the picture altogether and just study the documents. Which bugs are getting reported in the old system, and which are reported in the new system? This might uncover differences in the type of reports that the team hasn't been filing in the new system. This might give you a hunch about the reasons for using the old tracker, but it still wouldn't tell you the actual reasons inside the minds of your team.

All of these approaches are qualitative methods and all of them have limitations. The solution to getting around these limitations is to *embrace* them: no one approach will reveal the whole unbiased truth. Instead, good qualitative research combines multiple methods, allowing one to triangulate evidence from multiple sources. For example, suppose you interviewed individual employees about the tracker but also studied which bugs were being filed in the new tracker. Each approach will give you a distinct story, more or less consistent with the stories from other approaches. By comparing and contrasting these stories, one can uncover the ground truth behind a question.

Aside from gaining understanding, qualitative methods are also good for gaining *empathy*. More often than not, the cause of communication breakdowns, broken processes, and user frustration is people's inability to see the world from another person's perspective. And this is precisely what qualitative methods are designed to correct. This perspective-taking is often precisely the goal of qualitative methods. For example, suppose you manage a team and have noticed that every Friday the build breaks, people spend the whole day trying to fix it, and everyone goes home frustrated. Using a qualitative approach to diagnose the cause of these broken builds might lead you to discover that Thursday nights are a big night for check-ins because you've decided Friday is meeting day. Knowledge like this can help you see the world from the developers' perspective and find solutions that make everyone happy.

Reading Qualitative Research

Having described what qualitative methods are, we now turn to a discussion of how to read qualitative studies like the ones that appear throughout this book. For example, what does a particular study teach? When can you trust a study's results? When can you generalize a study's results to the larger world? To discuss these issues, let's consider *The Errors of TeX*, published in 1989 by the Turing Award winner Donald Knuth [Knuth 1989].

In this classic article, Knuth analyzes more than 850 errors he logged while writing the TeX software. The study, as Knuth described it, was "to present a list of all the errors that were corrected in TeX while it was being developed, and to attempt to analyse those errors." Knuth describes the rationale for his approach as overcoming the limitations of quantitative methods:

> The concept of scale cannot easily be communicated by means of numerical data alone; I believe that a detailed list gives important insights that cannot be gained from statistical summaries.

What did Knuth discover in this study? He presents 15 categories of errors, gleaned from a much larger catalog, and then describes them with examples from his log. For example, Knuth describes the "blunder or blotch" category, which included program statements that were syntactically correct but semantically wrong. The root cause of these errors was variable names that were closely related conceptually but led to very different program semantics (e.g., reversing variables named *before* and *after*, or *next_line* and *new_line*). Knuth goes on to describe the other error categories, the history behind the TeX software project, his personal experiences in writing the software, and how he recorded errors in his log.

At the end of the article, he concludes:

> What have I really learned then? I think I have learned, primarily, to have a better sense of balance and proportion. I now understand the complexities of a medium-size software system, and the ways in which it can be expected to evolve. I now understand that there are so many kinds of errors, we cannot stamp them out by systematically eliminating everything that might be 'considered harmful.' I now understand enough about my propensity to err that I can accept it as an act of life; I can now be convinced more easily of my fallacy when I have made a mistake.

Now let us step back and reflect on the merits of this work: what did we learn, as readers? The first time I read this article in the mid-1990s, I learned a great deal: I had never written a medium-sized software system, and the rich details, both contextual and historical, helped me understand the experience of undertaking such a large system by one's self. I recognized many of the error categories that Knuth described in my own programming, but also learned to spot new ones, which helped me become better at thinking of possible explanations for why my code wasn't working. It also taught me, as a researcher, that the human factors behind software development—how we think, how our memory works, how we plan and reason—are powerful forces behind software quality. This was one of just a few articles that compelled me to a career in understanding these human factors and exploiting them to improve software quality through better languages, tools, and processes.

But few of these lessons came immediately after reading. I only started to notice Knuth's categories in my own work over a period of months, and the article was just one of many articles that inspired my interests in research. And this is a key point in how to read reports on qualitative research critically: not only do the implications of their results take time to set in, but you have to be open to reflecting on them. If you dismiss an article entirely because of some flaw you notice or a conclusion you disagree with, you'll miss out on all of the other insights you might gain through careful, sustained reflection on the study's results.

Of course, that's not to say you should trust Knuth's results in their entirety. But rather than just reacting to studies emotionally, it's important to read them in a more systematic way. I usually focus on three things about a study: its *inputs*, its *execution*, and its *outputs*. (Sounds like software testing, doesn't it?) Let's discuss these in the context of Knuth's study.

First, do you trust the inputs into Knuth's study? For example, do you think TeX is a representative program? Do you think Knuth is a representative programmer? Do you trust Knuth himself? All of these factors might affect whether you think Knuth's 15 categories are comprehensive and representative, and whether they still occur in practice, decades after his report. If you think that Knuth isn't a representative programmer, how might the results have changed if someone else did this? For example, let's imagine that Knuth, like many academics, was an absent-minded professor. Perhaps that would explain why so many of the categories have to do with forgetting or lack of foresight (such as the categories *a forgotten function, a mismatch between modules, a surprising scenario*, etc.). Maybe a more disciplined individual, or one working in a context where code was the sole focus, would not have had these issues. None of these potential confounding factors are damning to the study's results, but they ought to be considered carefully before generalizing from them.

Do you trust Knuth's *execution* of his study? In other words, did Knuth follow the method that he described, and when he did not, how might these deviations have affected the results? Knuth used a *diary study* methodology, which is often used today to understand people's experiences over long periods of time without the direct observation of a researcher. One key to a good diary study is that you don't tell the participants of the study what you expect to find, lest you bias what they write and how they write it. But Knuth was both the experimenter and the participant in his study. What kinds of expectations did he have about the results? Did he already have categories in mind before starting the log? Did he categorize the errors throughout the development of TeX, or retrospectively after TeX was done? He doesn't describe any of these details in his report, but the answers to these questions could significantly change how we interpret the results.

Diary studies also have inherent limitations. For example, they can invoke a Heisenberg-style problem, where the process of observing may compel the diary writer to reflect on the work being captured to such a degree that the nature of the work itself changes. In Knuth's study, this might have meant that by logging errors, Knuth was reflecting so much about the causes of errors that he subconsciously averted whole classes of errors, and thus never observed them. Diary studies can also be difficult for participants to work on consistently over time. For example, there was a period where Knuth halted his study temporarily, noting, "I did not keep any record of errors removed during the hectic period when TeX82 was being debugged...." What kinds of errors would Knuth have found had he logged during this period? Would they be different from those he found in less stressful, hectic periods?

Finally, do you trust the *outputs* of the study, its implications? It is standard practice in academic writing to separate the discussion of results and implications, to enable readers to decide whether they would draw the same conclusions from the evidence that the authors did. But Knuth combines these two throughout his article, providing both rich descriptions of the faults in TeX and the implications of his observations. For example, after a series of fascinating stories about errors in his *Surprises* category (which Knuth describes as global misunderstandings), he reflects:

> This experience suggests that all software systems be subjected to the meanest, nastiest torture tests imaginable; otherwise they will almost certainly continue to exhibit bugs for years after they have begun to produce satisfactory results in large applications.

When results and implications appear side-by-side, it can be easy to forget that they are two separate things, to be evaluated independently. I trust Knuth's memory of the stories that inspired the implication quoted here because he explained his process for recording these stories. However, I think Knuth over-interpreted his stories in forming his recommendation. Would Knuth have finished TeX if he spent so much time on torture tests? I trust his diary, but I'm skeptical about his resulting advice.

Of course, it's important to reiterate that *every* qualitative study has limitations, but most studies have valuable insights. To be an objective reader of qualitative research, one has to accept this fact and meticulously identify the two. A good report will do this for you, as do the chapters in this book.

Using Qualitative Methods in Practice

While qualitative methods are usually applied in research settings, they can be incredibly useful in practice. In fact, they are useful in any setting where you don't know the entire universe of possible answers to a question. And in software engineering, when is that *not* the case? Software testers might use qualitative methods to answer questions about inefficiencies in the human aspects of a testing procedure; project managers can use qualitative methods to understand how the social dimensions of their team might be impacting productivity. Designers, developers, and requirements engineers can use qualitative methods to get a deeper understanding of the users they serve, ensuring a closer fit between user needs and the feature list. Any time you need to analyze the dynamics between *who, what, when, where, how* and *why*, qualitative methods can help.

Using qualitative methods is a lot like being a good detective or journalist: the point is to uncover truth, and tell a story people can trust—but also realize that there are usually many truths and many perspectives. How you go about uncovering these perspectives depends a lot on the situation. In particular, you need an instinct for the social context of what you want to understand, so you know whom you can trust, what their biases are, and how their motives might affect your sleuthing. Only with this knowledge can you decide what combination of direct observation, shadowing, interviews, document analysis, diary studies, or other approaches you might take.

To illustrate, let's go back to our bug tracker example. One of the most important factors in choosing which methods to use is *you*, and so there are a number of things to consider:

- Do your employees like you?
- Do they respect you?
- Do they trust you?

If the answer to any of these questions is no, you're probably not the one to do the sleuthing. Instead, you might need to find a more impartial party. For example, a perfect role for sleuthing is an *ombudsperson*. Her job is to be a neutral party, a person who can see multiple perspectives to support effective communication and problem solving. If your organization has an ombudsperson, she would be a great candidate for a class on qualitative methods and could play an instrumental role in improving your workplace.

If your employees do like you, the next most important factor is your employees. Are they good communicators? Are they honest? Do they hide things? Are there rival factions on your team? Is there a culture of process improvement, or is the environment rigid and conservative? All of these social factors are going to determine the viability of applying any particular qualitative method. For example, direct observation is out of the question if your employees like to hide things, because they'll know they're being observed. Document analysis might work in this case, but what will your team think about their privacy? Interviews work quite well when the *interviewer* can establish rapport, but otherwise they're a garbage-in, garbage-out process. The goal of a good qualitative approach to answering a question is to find ways of probing that minimize bias and maximize objectivity.

Regardless of whether you or someone else is doing the sleuthing, another important consideration is how you explain to your team what you're sleuthing about. In all of the cases I can imagine, keeping the sleuthing a secret is a terrible idea. You're probably asking a question because you want to solve a problem, and you're managing a team of problem solvers: get them to help! It's important to point out to them, however, that your agenda is to understand, not to dictate. It's also important to say that there's probably not a single explanation and everybody's perspective will differ at least a little. Communicating these points creates an expectation that you'll be seeking your informants' perspectives and empathizing with them, which makes them more likely to reflect honestly.

Finally, qualitative methods can feel loose and arbitrary at times. How can you really trust the results of a process without structure? The trick is to realize that bias is all around you and embrace it. You as the researcher are biased, your informants are biased, and the different methods you use to understand a context are biased toward revealing certain phenomena. The more you can explicitly identify the bias around you and understand how it affects your interpretations of what you see, the more objective your findings.

Generalizing from Qualitative Results

Whether you find qualitative results in a research paper or you get them yourself, one issue that always comes up is how much you can generalize from it.

For example, qualitative methods are can identify *common* behavior, but they cannot identify *average* behavior. Averages and other aggregate statistics require some ability to count, and that's not what qualitative methods are about. Moreover, because the gathering of nonnumerical data can be more labor-intensive, qualitative methods often end up with smaller sample sizes, making it difficult to generalize to the broader population of situations under study.

Nevertheless, qualitative studies can and do generalize. For example, they can demonstrate that the cause and effect relationships present in one context are similar to those in another context. Suppose you were part of a user interface team for a web application, trying to understand why code reviews were always taking so long. Although your findings might not generalize to the team managing the database backend, they might generalize to other frontend teams for web applications in a similar domain. Knowing when the study generalizes is no less challenging than for quantitative studies; in both cases, it's a subjective matter of knowing which assumptions still apply in new contexts.

Qualitative Methods Are Systematic

Qualitative methods are increasingly important in research on software engineering, and they can be quite important in software engineering practice as well. But there's a significant difference between simply understanding problems and understanding problems *systematically*. Therefore, the next time you read the results of a qualitative study or set out to do your own, make sure you or the article are following a process like this:

Formulate the question
What knowledge is desired and why? How will the knowledge be used?

Consider viable sources of objective evidence
What data can be gathered *objectively*, with as little bias as possible? Can you gather from multiple sources to account for biases in individual sources?

Interpret patterns in the evidence

Are the sources of evidence consistent with one another or do they conflict? What new questions does the evidence data raise? Do they lead to a hypothesis that can be tested with further data?

Although this cycle of question formulation, evidence gathering, and interpretation can be a long process, each iteration can lead to more confidence in your understanding, which means better decisions and better outcomes. Moreover, when you combine qualitative methods with quantitative tools, you'll have a powerful toolbox with which to understand and improve software engineering practice.

References

[Conrad 1985] Conrad, P. 1985. The meaning of medications: Another look at compliance. *Social Science and Medicine* 20: 29–37.

[Knuth 1989] Knuth, D. 1989. The Errors of TeX. *Software Practice and Experience* 19(7): 607–685.

## CHAPTER FIVE

Learning Through Application: The Maturing of the QIP in the SEL

Victor R. Basili

Empirical studies—formal research that uses respected, validated methods for establishing the truth of an assertion—have started to make headway within software engineering. The good news is that these studies have finally become recognized as an important component of the discipline. One sees more and more empirical studies and experiments in the literature to confirm or reject the effectiveness of some method, technique, or tool.

The bad news is that these studies are not yet used for discovery. The experiment is an add-on, tried after the concept is considered complete. The scientific method, however, is classically based on applying a method, technique, or tool and learning from the results how to evolve the concept. This is how theories are tested and evolved over time. In the software engineering discipline, where the theories and models are still in the formative stages and processes are applied by humans as part of a creative process, observing the application or performing exploratory studies should be an important step in the evolution of the discipline.

What Makes Software Engineering Uniquely Hard to Research

Software engineering has several characteristics that that distinguish it from other disciplines. Software is *developed* in the creative, intellectual sense, rather than being *produced* in the manufacturing sense. Software processes are development processes, not production processes. In other words, they are not replicated over and over again. This unique aspect of the discipline is probably the most important one, and greatly affects how we learn. We always need to be on the lookout for the effect of context variables. Because software engineering is a human-based discipline, there will always be variation in study results and we will never be able to control or even identify all the context variables. The discipline creates a need for continual experimentation, as we explore how to modify and tailor processes for people.

The variation in context springs from more than just the people who create the software; each piece of software itself is different, as are software development environments. One consequence of this is that process is a variable, goals are variables, etc. That is, we need to select the right processes for the right goals for the environment we are analyzing. So, before we decide how to study a technique, we need to know something about the environment and the characteristics of what we are about to build.

A second distinguishing characteristic of the software engineering discipline is software's *intangibility*, or one might say the invisibility of its structure, components, and forms of development. This is compounded by a third characteristic, the field's *immaturity*, in the sense that we haven't developed sufficient models that allow us to reason about processes, products, and their relationships. These difficulties intensify the need to learn from the application of ideas in different situations and the requirement to abstract from what we see.

A final problem is that developing models of our experiences for future use (that is, reuse) requires additional resources in the form of money, organizational support, processes, people, etc. Building models, taking measurements, experimenting to find the most effective technologies, and feeding back information for corporate learning cost both time and money. These activities are not a byproduct of software development. If these activities are not explicitly supported, independent of the product development, they will not occur and we will not make quality improvements in the development process.

All this makes good experimentation difficult and expensive. Experiments can be confirmatory only in the small scale and are subject to problems in understanding scale-up, the integration of one process with another, the understanding of the effect of context variables, etc.

A Realistic Approach to Empirical Research

I believe we need to focus more attention on informal exploratory studies that provide insights into directions software development can take. We should couple these, when appropriate, with more formal empirical studies to test out pieces of the whole that can be added to the tapestry that helps make the discipline clear. I believe that the study of the software engineering discipline is exploratory and evolutionary. It follows the scientific method, but because of its nature, real experiments are not always possible or useful.

I like to say that the study of software engineering is a laboratory science, and it is a big science. So the laboratory is quite grand and we need methods that support the exploratory nature of this big science. The discipline cannot be understood only by analysis. We need to learn from applying the discipline whether relationships hold, how they vary, and what the limits of various technologies are, so we can know how to configure process to develop software better.

We need to take advantage of all opportunities we can find to explore various ideas in practice—e.g., test their feasibility, find out whether humans can apply them, understand what skills are required to apply them, and test their interactions with other concepts. Based upon that knowledge, we need to refine and tailor each idea to the application environment in which we are studying it so it can be transferred easily into practice. Even before we build models, we need to try out our ideas in practice and evolve them. We are, in short, an exploratory science: we are more dependent on empirical application of methods and techniques than many disciplines.

Variety is an important aspect of applying the scientific method to software engineering. We need many applications of a process, taking place in different environments, each application providing a better understanding of the concepts and their interaction. Over time, all context variables need to be considered. Many of them will not even pop up until we have seen applications of the approach in practice by different people at different sites.

The building of the tapestry is too grand for any one group to perform. This is big science and it requires the collaboration of many groups. Results need to be shared in an effective way, a repository of evolving models and lessons learned that can be added to and used by researchers.

The NASA Software Engineering Laboratory: A Vibrant Testbed for Empirical Research

To support the argument for informal learning I make in this chapter, I'll summarize our experiences in the NASA Software Engineering Laboratory (SEL) over a period of 25 years, where we learned a great deal not just through experiments, but also by trying to understand the problems, applying potential solutions, and learning where they fell short. We did run controlled experiments and performed case studies, but they were done in the context of the larger evolutionary learning process.

The SEL was established in 1976 with the goals of understanding ground-support software development for satellites, and where possible, improving the process and product quality in the Flight Dynamics Division at Goddard using observation, experimentation, learning, and model building [Basili and Zelkowitz 1977]. The laboratory had a team that was supportive of learning, consisting of developers from both NASA and Computer Sciences Corporation (CSC), along with a research group at the University of Maryland (UMD). The three groups formed a consortium. The organization made a decision to support our empirical research and integrate it into the overall activities of the organization. Support came from the project budget, rather than the research budget at NASA.

In 1976, very few empirical studies were being performed in software engineering. The idea of creating a laboratory environment to study software development was perhaps unprecedented. But it provided an excellent learning environment where potential solutions to problems were proposed, applied, examined for their effectiveness and lessons, and evolved into potentially better solutions. Characteristics that made this setup a good place for empirical research included the limited domain of the application, the use of professional developers, firm support from the local organization, the presence of a research team to interact closely with the practical developers, and a mix of developers and managers with different goals, personalities, and responsibilities. The balance created an ideal learning environment with lots of feedback and collaboration.

From 1976 to 2001, we learned a great deal while making a lot of mistakes. Examples of these mistakes include:

- Trying to make assessments before fully understanding the environment
- Being data-driven rather than goal- and model-driven
- Drawing on other people's models derived from other environments to explain our own environment

The learning process was more evolutionary than revolutionary. With each learning experience, we tried to package what we had learned into our models of the processes, products and organizational structure.

The SEL used the University researchers to test high-risk ideas. We built models and tested hypotheses. We developed technologies, methods, and theories as needed to solve a problem, learned what worked and didn't work, applied ideas that we read about or developed on our own when applicable, and all along kept the business going.

The most important thing we learned was how to apply the scientific method to the software domain—i.e., how to evolve the process of software development in a particular environment by learning from informal feedback from the application of the concepts, case studies, and controlled experiments. The informal feedback created the opportunity to understand where to focus our case studies and experiments. Informal feedback also, and perhaps surprisingly, provided the major insights.

What follows in this chapter is a retrospective look at our attempts to instantiate the scientific method and how our approach evolved over time based upon feedback concerning our application of the ideas.

The Quality Improvement Paradigm

I will begin with a distillation of our journey, a process for applying the scientific method to software engineering in an industrial environment. We called our version of the scientific method the Quality Improvement Paradigm (QIP) [Basili 1985], [Basili and Green 1994]. It consists of six basic steps:

1. *Characterize* the current project and its environment with respect to the appropriate models and metrics. (*What does our world look like?*)

2. *Set quantifiable goals* for successful project performance and improvement. (*What do we want to know about our world and what do we want to accomplish?*)

3. *Choose the process model* and supporting methods and tools for this project. (*What processes might work for these goals in this environment?*)

4. *Execute* the processes, construct the products, and collect, validate, and analyze the data to provide real-time feedback for corrective action. (*What happens during the application of the selected processes?*)

5. *Analyze* the data to evaluate the current practices, determine problems, record findings, and make recommendations for future project improvements. (*How well did the proposed solutions work, what was missing, and how should we fix it?*)

6. *Package* the experience in the form of updated and refined models and other forms of structured knowledge gained from this and prior projects, and save it in an experience base to be reused on future projects. (*How do we integrate what we learned into the organization?*)

The Quality Improvement Paradigm is a double-loop process, as shown by Figure 5-1. Research interacts with practice, represented by project learning and corporate learning based upon feedback from application of the ideas.

But that is not where we started. Each of *these* steps evolved over time as we learned from observation of the application of the ideas. In what follows, I will discuss that evolution and the insights it provided, with formal experiments playing only a support role for the main ideas.

The learning covered a period of 25 years, although here I concentrate on what we learned mostly in the first 20. The discussion is organized around the six steps of the QIP, although there is overlap in the role of many of the steps. In each case I say what we learned about applying the scientific method and what we learned about improving software development in the Flight Dynamics Division of NASA/GSFC.

We started in 1976 with the following activities, representing each step of the approach: characterize, set goals, select process, execute process, analyze, and package.

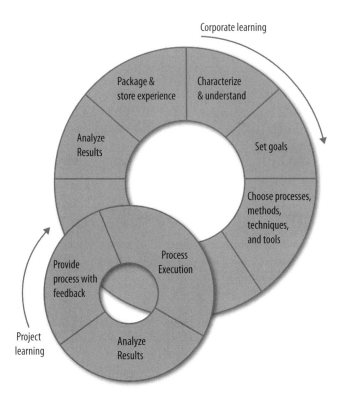

FIGURE 5-1. Quality Improvement Paradigm

Characterize

In the beginning, we looked at various models in the literature and tried to apply them to help us understand our environment (e.g., Raleigh curve or MTTF models). We found they were not necessarily appropriate. Either they were defined for larger systems than what we were building (on the order of 100KSLOC) or they were applied at different points in time than what we needed. This led to the insight that we needed to build our own environment-appropriate models using our own data. We needed to better understand and characterize our own environment, projects, processes, products, etc., because we could not use other people's models that were derived for different environments [Basili and Zelkowitz 1978], [Basili and Freburger 1981], [Basili and Beane 1981].

We needed to understand our own problem areas. So over time, we began to build baselines to help us understand the local environment; see Figure 5-2. Each box represents the ground support software for a particular satellite. We built baselines of cost, defects, percent reuse, classes of defects, effort distribution, source code growth in the library, etc. We used these baselines to help define goals, and as historical data to establish the basis for showing improvement.

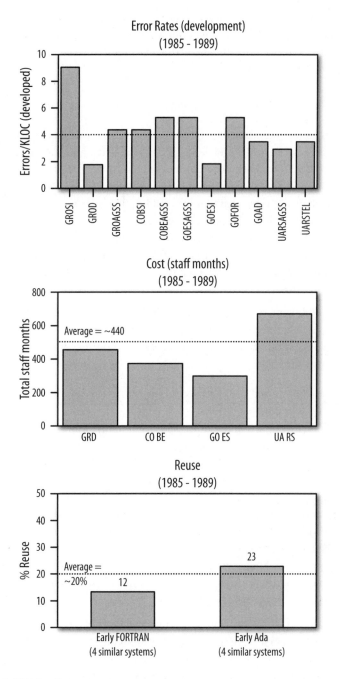

FIGURE 5-2. Example NASA baselines

As we progressed over time, we learned that we needed to better understand the factors that created similarities and differences among projects so we would know the appropriate model to apply and what variables were influencing the effectiveness of the processes. Context, even within the local environment, was important.

Set Goals

From the very beginning, we decided to use measurement as the abstraction process to provide visibility into what was occurring, and developed data collection forms and a measurement tool. We collected data from half a dozen projects in a simple database and tried to interpret that data, discovering that sometimes we did not have the right data or sufficient information to answer our questions. We realized that we couldn't just collect data and then figure out what to do with it; data collection needed to be goal-driven. This led to the development of the Goal Question Metric (GQM) approach to help us organize the data around a particular study [Basili and Weiss 1984]. You can also drown in too much data, especially if you don't have goals. We have continued to evolve the GQM, for example, by defining goal templates [Basili and Rombach 1988].

We also understood the important role that nominal and ordinal data played in capturing information that was hard to measure in other ways. We moved from a database to a model-based experience base as our models evolved, based upon our experiences with over 100 projects in that environment.

Select Process

We began by minimally impacting the processes, using heuristically defined combinations of existing processes. We began to run controlled experiments at the university, with students, to isolate the effects of small sets of variables at minimal cost [Basili and Reiter 1981]. When we understood the effects of those processes, we began to experiment with well-defined technologies and high-impact technology sets. Many of these technologies were studied first at the university in controlled experiments before being brought to the SEL for use on live projects, e.g., Code Reading by stepwise abstraction [Basili and Selby 1987], Cleanroom [Selby et al. 1987], and Ada and Object oriented design [Basili et al. 1997]. The university studies diminished the risks of applying these techniques in the SEL. Over time we began to understand how to combine controlled experiments and case studies to provide a more formal analysis of isolated activities [Basili 1997].

We began to experiment with new technologies to learn more about the relationships between the application of processes and the resulting product characteristics. But the motivation for choosing these techniques was based upon the insights we gained from observing the problems that arose in the SEL and were aimed at specific goals, e.g., minimizing defects. Based upon recognition of problems with requirements, for example, we developed a set of reading techniques for identifying defects in requirements documents [Basili et al. 1996].

We recognized the obvious fact that we needed to understand how to choose the right processes to create the desired product characteristics and that some form of evaluation and feedback were necessary for project control. Reusing experience in the form of processes, products, and other forms of knowledge is essential for improvement. We learned to tailor and evolve technologies based upon experience.

Execute Process

When we started, data collection was an add-on activity; we expected the developers to perform their normal development processes and fill out the data forms we provided. The process was loosely monitored to see that the data forms were being filled out and the developers understood how to fill out the forms. The lack of consistent terminal use and support tools forced the data collection to be manual. Sharing the intermediate results with the developers allowed them to provide feedback, identify misunderstandings, and suggest better ways to collect data. Over time, using GQM, we collected less data, and embedded data collection into the development processes so the data were more accurate, required less overhead, and allowed us to evaluate process conformance. We captured the details of developer experiences via interaction between developers and experimenters, providing effective feedback about local needs and goals. We combined controlled experiments and case studies with our general feedback process to provide more formal analysis of specific methods and techniques.

Analyze

We began by building and analyzing the baselines to characterize the environment. Baselines were built of many variables, including where effort was spent, what kinds of faults were made, and even source code growth over time. These provided insights into the environment, showed us where to focus process improvement, and offered a better understanding of the commonality and differences among projects. We began to view the study of software development as following an experimental paradigm—i.e., design of experiments, evaluation, and feedback are necessary for learning. Our evolution of analysis methods went from correlations among the variables [Basili et al. 1983] to building regression models [Bailey and Basili 1983] and more sophisticated quantitative analyses [Briand et al. 1992], to including all forms of qualitative analysis [Seaman and Basili 1998]. Qualitative analysis played a major role in our learning process, as it allowed us to gain insights into the causes of effects. Little by little, we recognized the importance of simple application of the ideas followed by observation and feedback to evolve our understanding, which we incorporated into our models and guided where and when to use the more formal analytic approaches.

We realized it was impossible to run valid experiments on a large scale that covered all context variables. The insights gained from pre-experimental designs and quasi-experiments became critical, and we combined them with what we learned from the controlled experiments and case studies.

Package

Our understanding of the importance, complexity, and subtlety of packaging evolved slowly. In the beginning we recorded our baselines and models. Then, we recognized the need for focused, tailored packages—e.g., generic code components and techniques that could be tailored to the specific project. What we learned had to become usable in the environment, and we needed to constantly change the environment based on what we learned. Technology transfer involved a new organizational structure, experimentation, and evolutionary culture change. We built what we called *experience models*—i.e., models of behavior based upon observation and feedback in a particular organization. We built focused, tailorable models of processes, products, defects, and quality, and packaged our experiences with them in a variety of ways (e.g., equations, histograms, and parameterized process definitions). The hard part was integrating these packaged experiences. All this culminated in the development of the Experience Factory Organization [Basili 1989]; see Figure 5-3.

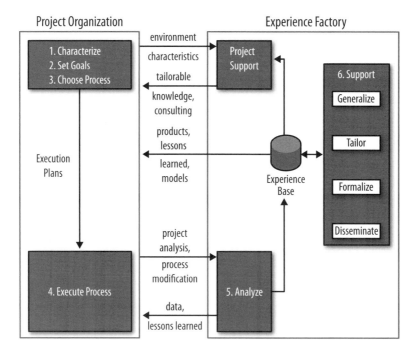

FIGURE 5-3. The Experience Factory Organization

The Experience Factory of processes, products, and other forms of knowledge is essential for improvement [Basili 1989]. It recognizes the need to separate the activities of the project development organization from the building of knowledge based upon experiences within the organization. Sample activities of the project organization are decomposing a problem into simpler ones, instantiation of the solution, design and implementation, validation, and verification. The goal is to deliver a product within cost and schedule. The activities of the Experience Factory are the unification of different solutions and redefinition of the problem, generalization, formalization, and integration of experiences. It does this by analyzing and synthesizing what it observes and experimenting to test out the ideas. Its goal is experience and delivering recommendations to the projects. It is responsible for the evaluation, tailoring, and packaging of experiences for reuse.

The Experience Factory cannot be built solely on the basis of small, validated experiments. It requires the use of insights and intelligent judgment based upon observation for the application of ideas, concepts, processes, etc.

Once we felt we understood how to learn from our observations and how to combine the results of case studies and controlled experiments (which was more publishable than our insights), we continued with our process of application, observation, and learning. We dealt with such topics as commercial off-the-shelf (COTS) development, reading techniques, etc.

Learning in an organization is time-consuming and sequential, so we need to provide projects with short-term results to keep the development team interested. We need to find ways to speed up the learning process and feed interim results back into the project faster. If we are successful in evolving, our baselines and the environment are always changing, so we must continue to reanalyze the environment. We need to be conscious of the trade-off between making improvements and the reuse of experience.

Conclusion

This tells the story of over 25 years of evolution and tailoring the goals and processes for a particular environment. The continuous improvement was measured by taking values of three data points: the development defect rates, the reduced cost for development, and the improvement of reuse of code at three points in time: 1987, 1991, and 1995. Each data point represents the average of the three years around it [Basili et al. 1995]; see Table 5-1.

TABLE 5-1. The results of the QIP approach in the SEL

Continuous improvement in the SEL	1987–1991	1991–1995
Development defect rates	75%	37%
Reduced cost	55%	42%
Improved reuse	300%	8%

During this period there was a continual increase in the functionality of the systems being built. An independent study estimated it to be a five-fold increase from 1976 to 1992.

The cost of this activity was about 10% of the development costs. However, the data shows an order of magnitude improvement for that 10% cost, which is a pretty good ROI.

But the data in Table 5-1 are not the results of a controlled experiment or even a well-defined case study. One can argue that these results might have occurred anyway, even if we did nothing. There is no control group. But the people involved believe differently. We believe the learning process worked and delivered these results. No controlled experiment could have been developed for this 25-year study, as we did not know when we started what we would do and how it would evolve.

During the 25 years of the SEL, we learned a great deal about software improvement. Our learning process was continuous and evolutionary, like the evolution of the software development process itself. We packaged what we learned into our process, product, and organizational structure. The evolution was supported by the symbiotic relationship between research and practice. This relationship requires patience and understanding on both sides, but when nurtured, really pays dividends.

The insights gained from learning by application, supplemented where appropriate by pre-experimental designs, quasi-experiments, controlled experiments, and case studies, provided a wealth of practical and theoretical results that could not have been gathered from formal experiments alone. It was the large-scale learning that allowed for the development of such things as the GQM approach, the QIP, and the Experience Factory, as well as the development and evaluation of various techniques and methods.

References

[Bailey and Basili 1983] Bailey, J. and V. Basili. 1983. A Meta-Model for Software Development Resource Expenditures. *Proceedings of the Fifth International Conference on Software Engineering*: 107–116.

[Basili 1985] Basili, V. 1985. Quantitative Evaluation of Software Methodology. Keynote Address, *Proceedings of the First Pan Pacific Computer Conference* 1: 379–398.

[Basili 1989] Basili, V. 1989. Software Development: A Paradigm for the Future. *Proceedings of COMPSAC '89*: 471–485.

[Basili 1997] Basili, V. 1997. Evolving and Packaging Reading Technologies. *Journal of Systems and Software* 38(1): 3–12.

[Basili and Beane 1981] Basili, V., and J. Beane. 1981. Can the Parr Curve Help with the Manpower Distribution and Resource Estimation Problems? *Journal of Systems and Software* 2(1): 59–69.

[Basili and Freburger 1981] Basili, V., and K. Freburger. 1981. Programming Measurement and Estimation in the Software Engineering Laboratory. *Journal of Systems and Software* 2(1): 47–57.

[Basili and Green 1994] Basili, V., and S. Green. 1994. Software Process Evolution at the SEL. *IEEE Software* 11(4): 58–66.

[Basili and Hutchens 1983] Basili, V., and D. Hutchens. 1983. An Empirical Study of a Syntactic Complexity Family. *IEEE Transactions on Software Engineering* 9(6): 664–672.

[Basili and Reiter 1981] Basili, V., and R. Reiter, Jr. 1981. A Controlled Experiment Quantitatively Comparing Software Development Approaches. *IEEE Transactions on Software Engineering* 7(3): 299–320 (IEEE Computer Society Outstanding Paper Award).

[Basili and Rombach 1988] Basili, V., and H.D. Rombach. 1988. The TAME Project: Towards Improvement-Oriented Software Environments. *IEEE Transactions on Software Engineering* 14(6): 758–773.

[Basili and Selby 1987] Basili, V., and R. Selby. 1987. Comparing the Effectiveness of Software Testing Strategies. *IEEE Transactions on Software Engineering* 13(12): 1278–1296.

[Basili and Weiss 1984] Basili, V., and D. Weiss. 1984. A Methodology for Collecting Valid Software Engineering Data. *IEEE Transactions on Software Engineering* 10(3): 728–738.

[Basili and Zelkowitz 1977] Basili, V., and M. Zelkowitz. 1977. The Software Engineering Laboratory: Objectives. *Proceedings of the Fifteenth Annual Conference on Computer Personnel Research*: 256–269.

[Basili and Zelkowitz 1978] Basili, V., and M. Zelkowitz. 1978. Analyzing Medium-Scale Software Development. *Proceedings of the Third International Conference on Software Engineering*: 116–123.

[Basili et al. 1983] Basili, V., R. Selby, and T. Phillips. 1983. Metric Analysis and Data Validation Across FORTRAN Projects. *IEEE Transactions on Software Engineering* 9(6): 652–663.

[Basili et al. 1995] Basili, V., M. Zelkowitz, F. McGarry, J. Page, S. Waligora, and R. Pajerski. 1995. Special Report: SEL's Software Process-Improvement Program. *IEEE Software* 12(6): 83–87.

[Basili et al. 1996] Basili, V., S. Green, O. Laitenberger, F. Shull, S. Sorumgaard, and M. Zelkowitz. 1986. The Empirical Investigation of Perspective-Based Reading. *Empirical Software Engineering: An International Journal* 1(2): 133–164.

[Basili et al. 1997] Basili, V., S. Condon, K. Emam, R. Hendrick, and W. Melo. 1997. Characterizing and Modeling the Cost of Rework in a Library of Reusable Software Components. *Proceedings of the Nineteenth International Conference on Software Engineering (ICSE)*: 282–291.

[Briand et al. 1992] Briand, L., V. Basili, and W. Thomas. 1992. A Pattern Recognition Approach for Software Engineering Data Analysis. *IEEE Transactions on Software Engineering* 18(11): 931–942.

[Seaman and Basili 1998] Seaman, C., and V. Basili. 1998. Communication and Organization: An Empirical Study of Discussion in Inspection Meetings. *IEEE Transactions on Software Engineering* 24(7): 559–572.

[Selby et al. 1987] Selby, R., V. Basili, and T. Baker. 1987. Cleanroom Software Development: An Empirical Evaluation. *IEEE Transactions on Software Engineering* 13(9): 1027–1037.

## CHAPTER SIX

Personality, Intelligence, and Expertise: Impacts on Software Development

Jo E. Hannay

The most important factor in software work is not the tools and techniques used by the programmers, but rather the quality of the programmers themselves.

—*Robert Glass (Fact 1 of Facts and Fallacies of Software Engineering [2002])*

Good programmers are up to 28 times better than mediocre programmers, according to "individual differences" research. Given that their pay is never commensurate, they are the biggest bargains in the software field.

—*Robert Glass (Fact 2 of Facts and Fallacies of Software Engineering [2002])*

Robert Glass's two postulates (of which he reminds us in "Frequently Forgotten Fundamental Facts about Software Engineering" on the IEEE Computer Society web pages) reflect several important issues. First off, they accommodate the focus on "people issues" in the otherwise technological domain of computer programming. Among other things, this focus has helped the research discipline of empirical software engineering to address the practice of software engineering from additional viewpoints (managerial, sociological, and psychological) to the purely technological one. A necessity, one would say, in order to make the practice of software engineering more evidence-based.

For the purpose of our discussion, let's assume that the two postulates from Robert Glass hold. Mind you, we've made it our business to constantly reevaluate and refine such assertions, even when the assertions may be based on empirical evidence. Knowledge is never static, so Glass's facts might, in fact, need some refinement. But let's postpone that. What we are interested in right now are three questions that these facts entail, and which stand on their own accord. They are more general because they consider software development as a whole, and not only programming:

- Can you actually define what it means to be a good software developer?
- If so, can you find ways to reliably and efficiently determine that one developer is better than another?
- If you can't, should you focus on tools and techniques instead?

A confirmatory answer to the first two questions would be nothing less than a small revolution, and people like Joel Spolsky would be delighted. He writes that hiring superstar (rather than average) programmers determines whether you produce a truly great product that will bring the world forward or whether you'll just produce mediocre code that will give the rest of your team a series of redesign, reconstruction, and debugging headaches [Spolsky 2007]. The truth, however, is that it is extremely hard to get hold of top-notch programmers. People long in the business of hiring software professionals have sensible ideas and useful advice as to what to look for (see Spolsky again), but the problem remains hard. In general, finding, keeping, and developing talent is very much in the front of HR managers' minds, but there is a lack of evidence-based methodology to follow through on this, according to the 2010 Global Assessment Trends Report [Fallaw and Solomonsen 2010].

The third question touches upon the distinction between a focus on capacities in the individual (e.g., skills and personality) and a focus on facilitating the environment (e.g., using tools and putting people together in pairs to program). It probably isn't sufficient to hire the best programmers, just as it isn't enough to hire the best pilots for an airline to minimize the risk of air disasters; you also need a lot of safety features in the environment, along with the ability to work with other people.

Striking the optimal balance between human expertise and tools is nontrivial. But if you can't even determine what an expert is, then you might not have the option to balance anything. Moreover, if you think you know what a good programmer is, and your intuitions are wrong, then your project might be in dire shape, unless it is facilitated by environmental measures designed to detect and adjust for unforeseen contingencies. The operability of Glass's insights therefore depends on reliably discerning clever people from the crowd. As we'll see, it's not at all obvious that you can do that. Software engineering consists of diverse tasks, and the nature of the task at hand influences the degree to which you can determine expertise.

Let's start by looking at programming.

How to Recognize Good Programmers

Determining whether one can define what it is to be a good programmer demands that we consider two deeper questions:

- What in a programmer gives good programming performance? Should you care about the amount of experience she has? Should you worry about her personality? Should you attempt to measure her IQ? And what about all this in the context of pair programming and team work?

- What is good programming performance? For example, should you hire the person who can produce the most lines of code per unit time or the person who produces the code of highest quality (whatever that means), no matter the amount of time spent producing it?

These questions touch on fundamental and difficult issues. In the work life where one has to make strategic decisions, such issues are explicitly or implicitly dealt with on the fly by following intuitions or applying more or less ill-founded personal profile and aptitude tests. In academic research, the deeper and more general meaning of these questions has led to huge research efforts across several disciplines in attempts to gain some insight into these issues.

Individual Differences: Fixed or Malleable

Characteristics that separate one individual from another—or *individual differences*, as researchers call them for short—can be classified along a continuum from *fixed* to *malleable*. Toward the fixed end, you find things such as personality and cognitive predispositions that are assumed to be relatively stable throughout a person's life time. Malleable characteristics, on the other hand, include task-related skills, knowledge, and motivation, all of which are assumed to be affected by shorter-term circumstance, training, and learning, and hence may be subject to deliberate manipulation, e.g., improvement.

It is relatively quick, inexpensive, and easy to distinguish people by fixed characteristics, whereas it is a comparatively lengthy process to assess and develop someone's skills. It is also perhaps human nature to discern people by stereotypes. No wonder, then, that the recruitment industry offers a range of tests to measure a person's fixed characteristics.

We can discuss at length different opinions on how you should view your fellow human beings. Is hiring someone based on their fixed characteristics bordering on discrimination? Is it unethical to submit your staff to intelligence or personality tests? In some countries (especially in Europe), it is indeed considered *non comme il faut* to do so, and it is well known that IQ tests are biased across ethnic groups (resulting in lawsuits in the U.S.). But industries and governments continue to deploy their tests in various guises. So what predicts job performance better: fixed characteristics such as personality and intelligence or malleable characteristics such as skill and expertise?

Personality

Personality has been a subject of interest in the context of programming and software engineering for some time. For example, Weinberg predicted in *The Psychology of Computer Programming* that "attention to the subject of personality should make substantial contributions to increased programmer performance" [Weinberg 1971], a position he reaffirms in the 1998 edition of the book [Weinberg 1998]. Shneiderman states in *Software Psychology* that, "Personality variables play a critical role in determining interaction among programmers and in the work style of individual programmers" [Shneiderman 1980]. However, both authors admit to a lack of empirical evidence on the impact of personality on performance: "Personality tests have not been used successfully for selecting programmers who will become good programmers" [Weinberg 1971], [Weinberg 1998], "Unfortunately too little is known about the impact of personality factors" [Shneiderman 1980].

Since then, empirical studies have been conducted on personality and software development. For example, Dick and Zarnett conclude that "[b]uilding a development team with the necessary personality traits that are beneficial to pair programming will result in greater success with extreme programming than a team built based on technical skills alone" [Dick and Zarnett 2002]. Beyond the specific task of programming, Devito Da Cunha and Greathead conclude that "if a company organizes its employees according to personality types and their potential abilities, productivity and quality may be improved" [Devito Da Cunha and Greathead 2007], and there are arguments that one should map personality types onto specific roles in software development [Capretz and Ahmed 2010], [Acuña et al. 2006].

So what is personality? Informally, we speak of people's personality all the time. "She has the perfect personality for being a lawyer," or "He really has personality problems." Indeed, important decisions are made every day based on such informal hunches. Maybe some of them turn out to be right, and maybe some turn out to be wrong. Adopting an evidence-based approach means to structure such decisions on knowledge that is obtained in a systematic (read, scientific) manner. I will say right now that this systematic approach has inherent limitations, but more on that later.

One must first ask whether it is possible to define and measure personality in the first place. That this should be possible is perhaps not obvious for technologists such as ourselves. We may soon be able to point to tangible (say, genetic or psychophysiological) mechanisms of a person's personality [Read et al. 2010]. However, the main development of personality theory over the past century has followed a different path. Scientists have inferred that there might be differences in something we might call "personality" based on how people act or on what they say. These lines of research have been able to come up with convincing models of personality based on said behavioral and linguistic inferences. The most acclaimed models are perhaps the

Big Five model and the related Five Factor Model (see "Factors of Personality" next). So yes, personality is definable and measurable. It makes scientific sense to speak of a person's personality, and there are tests that can reliably establish a person's personality. Scientists would say that we have *construct validity* for the concept of personality.

FACTORS OF PERSONALITY

A number of models of personality exist, and each model has its own battery of tests to measure a person's personality according to that model. Personality tests are in extensive commercial and governmental use by, among others, recruitment and career counseling agencies and the military. Although several of these tests may originally have had theoretical or empirical underpinnings in psychological research, many of them have been simplified or altered over time for specific purposes, with little or no scientific control. (See [Paul 2005] for critical anecdotes and the history of personality testing.)

At the same time, personality research in academia has developed well-researched models and tests. Two models that have dominated personality research in recent years [Barrick et al. 2001] consist of five factors and go under the names of the *Five Factor Model* (FFM) [Costa and McCrae 1985] and the *Big Five* [Goldberg 1990] ,[Goldberg 1993]. The FFM posits that traits are situated in a comprehensive model of genetic and environmental causes and contexts. The Big Five posits that the most important personality differences in people's lives will become encoded as terms in their natural language, the so-called *Lexical Hypothesis* [Goldberg 1990]. These two models are often seen as one, and their respective factors correlate quite well, e.g., [Goldberg et al. 2006]. However, the two models are conceptually different, and their theoretical bases imply different approaches to designing tests for the factors.

The five factors are (with descriptions from [Pervin and John 1997]):

1. Extraversion

   Assesses quantity and intensity of interpersonal interaction, activity level, need for stimulation, and capacity for joy.

2. Agreeableness

   Assesses the quality of one's interpersonal orientation along a continuum from compassion to antagonism in thoughts, feelings, and actions.

3. Conscientiousness

   Assesses the individual's degree of organization, persistence, and motivation in goal-directed behavior. Contrasts dependable, fastidious people with those who are lackadaisical and sloppy.

4. Emotional stability/Neuroticism

   Assesses adjustment versus emotional stability. Identifies individuals prone to psychological distress, unrealistic ideas, excessive cravings or urges, and maladaptive coping responses.

5. Openness to experience

   Assesses proactive seeking and appreciation of experience for its own sake, and toleration for and exploration of the unfamiliar.

Several commercially used models and tests have been criticized in the academic community for having poor conceptual foundations, low reliability, and low validity ([Furnham 1996], [Saggio et al. 2001], [Saggio and Kline 1996]). In particular, many personality tests have been associated with the "Forer Effect," * which applies to general and vague descriptions that are likely to evoke feelings of recognition in anyone, regardless of actual personality.

Definitions of personality have been used to categorize people in a number of ways. For example, relating to the Big Five Model, we found that programmers deviated from a reference group in that they are lower on Extraversion, lower on Emotional Stability, and higher on Openness to Experience [Hannay et al. 2010]. See also [Moore 1991], [Smith 1989], [Woodruff 1979], [Capretz 2003], and [Turley and Bieman 1995] for related results. Programmers are also more homogeneous than the population as a whole; that is, programmers vary less in personality than do people in general. This confirms the stereotype of programmers being neurotic, introverted, and intellectual—and, by the way, male (which I know for a fact some people consider tantamount to a personality trait!).

As I said earlier, the systematic scientific approach has inherent limitations, in part as a result of its strengths. The one limitation to point out here, is what scientists call *content validity*: how reasonable is it to claim that your definition of personality captures all there is to what might be reasonably understood as personality? For example, most people would be reluctant to claim that a person can be characterized by only five factors. Other models of personality attempt to capture more complex types and subtle, complicated combinations of personality factors, but these lack construct validity. Being systematic inherently restricts what one can be systematic about! We're running into a classic trade-off here. Simple models (such as the five factors) simplify reality and are amenable to validation and measurement. More complicated models pretend to capture reality better, but are hard to validate.

* B. T. Forer [Forer 1949] administered a personality test to his students. He then simply discarded their responses and gave all students the exact same personality analysis copied from an astrology book. The students were subsequently asked to rate the evaluation on a five-point low to high scale according to how accurately they felt that the evaluation described them. The mean was 4.26. Forer's study has been replicated numerous times, and averages remain around 4 [Dickson and Kelly 1985], [Hanson and Claiborn 2006]. The Forer effect is also referred to as the "Barnum Effect" [Meehl 1956].

The ultimate question for us, though, is the utility of measuring personality. How much of a difference in performance does a certain difference in personality yield? How viable is it to use someone's personality to predict other behavior, and programming performance in particular? There is a substantial body of research conducted on the link between personality and general job performance. This research has been summarized in large meta-analyses [Barrick et al. 2001], [Peeters et al. 2006], [Bell 2007]. According to Barrick et al., the general effects of personality on job performance are "somewhat disappointing" and "modest…even in the best of cases" [Barrick et al. 2001]. Thus, personality may have little direct effect on job performance in terms of efficiency.

Maybe, though, personality could have more substantial indirect effects on job performance via social factors that influence teamwork. In fact, the effects on teamwork are higher than on overall job performance for all of the Big Five factors [Barrick et al. 2001]. This suggests that it may be more relevant to study effects of personality in the context of collaborative performance rather than on individual performance. We investigated this prospect in the context of 198 professional programmers pair programming over one day [Hannay et al. 2010]. We found that personality was a weak predictor of pair programming performance. Even crude measures of expertise, task complexity, and even the country in which the programmers where employed had greater predictive power than personality. The study also included an analysis of personality on individual programming and whether the effect on performance of pairing up had anything to do with personality. Again, expertise and task complexity are stronger predictors than personality.

By the way, the extent to which a construct—here, personality—has predictive value on something else, is called *criterion validity*. For more on construct, content, and criterion validity, see "Three Great Challenges of Empirical Science" next.

THREE GREAT CHALLENGES OF EMPIRICAL SCIENCE

Say you want to install a new cupboard between two existing ones in your IKEA kitchen. You use a tape measure to measure the space where you want to put it. But you notice that the metal clamp at the end of the tape looks a bit haphazardly mounted. It's a really tight fit, so you need to be sure of the space available. So, just in case, you use a folding ruler as well (which you also notice has metal clamps inaccurately mounted at each end). Your two measurements deviate by about one millimeter (as far as you can see while bending your neck in the semi-darkness). Your neighbor shows up with a laser measurement device with a digital display, but it only guarantees accuracy up to half a millimeter. It seem you'll never be quite sure, but you decide to buy the cupboard, and if worse comes to worst, you figure it can be jammed in somehow.

Your problem in this scenario is your instruments of measurement; they simply aren't accurate enough. You address this problem by using several instruments to add confidence so you at least know that you won't be too far off the mark. Frustrating as this situation might be, the measurement of physical objects (at least macroscopic objects here on earth) is relatively unproblematic compared to the measurement of nonphysical concepts such as psychological traits and the quality of programmers. Unlike physical objects, nonphysical concepts are hard to define in the first place. (At a certain level this is true for physical objects, too. We don't really understand what makes up physical objects and the space between them, but our everyday understanding of "physical object" seems to work for many purposes.)

Thus the first great challenge of empirical science is *construct validity*: how do you know that your measurement instruments are measuring whatever you want to measure, and do you really know what you want to measure in the first place? The combination of a concept and its means of measurement (its indicators) is called a *construct*; see Figure 6-1(a). For example, each of the personality factors in the Big Five model are measured by 20 questionnaire items, so the construct for Extraversion would be illustrated by an oval labeled "Extraversion" with 20 indicator boxes connected to it.

Usually, construct validity is achieved by attacking the problem both top-down and bottom-up: one devises some measures that one thinks might represent the concept to be measured, and in so doing one gains a greater understanding of the concept, which then guides one in devising further measures, and so forth, in a bootstrapping manner. There are certain statistical standards that any such instrument should live up to, and the degree to which these standards are fulfilled also warrants for the quality and meaningfulness of the construct. Achieving high construct validity is hard, and it usually takes years of research to gain usable levels of it. Commercial actors often don't have time for this or don't care, and therefore, the world is filled with tests that measure, well, most likely, nothing at all!

The second great challenge is *content validity*. A construct represents the part of a concept of which we have scientific control. However, it's important to keep in mind that there may be more to a concept than what is represented by a construct. Content validity is the extent to which a construct reasonably captures our understanding of a concept; see Figure 6-1(b), where a construct is seen as covering only a part of a concept. Efforts should always be made to ascertain whether one should expand the region of control in a concept (the dashed oval in Figure 6-1(b)). One of the great arrogances of science is the claim that whatever we have control over is all there is, such as that IQ tests measure all there is to the human intellect.

The third great challenge is *criterion validity*. This pertains to how useful a construct is at predicting changes in a different construct. Can you use personality to predict programming performance? Can you use programming skill to predict how productive a person will be as a developer in the next large development project? And so on. See Figure 6-1(c), where variation in one construct (the predictor) predicts variation in a second construct (the criterion).

It's easy to make a blunder here and confound criterion validity with construct validity. For instance, if you want to define a construct of collaboration, and you know you want to use this construct to predict a construct of team performance, it is very tempting to simply define collaboration in terms of whatever gives good or bad performance, i.e., to say that good collaboration is whatever gives good performance. This automatically gives good criterion validity, but in actual fact, the collaboration construct will then not be a genuine construct in itself. Instead, it will merely be another aspect of team performance.

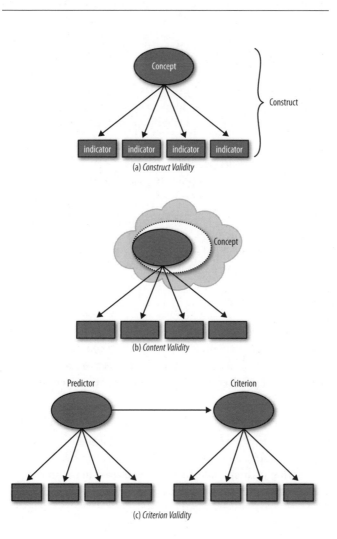

FIGURE 6-1. Types of validity

It may well be the case that effects of personality only manifest themselves after a while. In particular, pair programming over one day may not give sufficient time for the peers' personalities to bring about any serious effect. There is also debate around short tests that may be conducted almost automatically (such as personality and intelligence tests) versus more holistic assessment methods that require a specialist interpretation. Take the case for a personality trait called *Need for Achievement*. Meta-analyses suggest that a controversial procedure for measuring Need for Achievement called the Thematic Apperception Test (TAT) has better predictive validity on real-world performance than standard questionnaire-based tests, which are better for predicting performance in controlled environments [Spangler 1992].[†] The TAT continues to receive skepticism from the scientific community. However, Spangler states that "[a]n unintended consequence of the scientific method may be to minimize the expression of individual differences and the interaction of individual differences and environmental characteristics" [Spangler 1992]. There you have your content validity challenge again! Note also that measuring long-term real-world performance is much harder than measuring performance in controlled conditions in the laboratory.

In summary, personality does not seem to be a very strong predictor of performance. Let's briefly look at what effects there are. Conscientiousness is, in general, the most persistent of the personality factors when it comes to predicting both academic and job performance [Schmidt and Hunter 1998]. Guess what: this seems not to be the case for pair programming [Saleh et al. 2010]. In fact, in our data, we even found that conscientiousness had a negative effect (also for solo programmers). What seems to have a positive effect is openness to experience [Saleh et al. 2010] and difference in extraversion [Hannay et al. 2010]. Pairs whose peers have different levels of extraversion work quicker than those with more similar levels.

Intelligence

When given the prospect of trying out a scientifically validated test for measuring programming skill, an HR manager in a fairly large software development company stated that in her opinion, there is one, and one only, factor that predicts developer performance—namely, IQ. This view is interesting and illustrative: in a sense it is not wrong, but it is far enough off the mark to lead you down the wrong path.

General mental ability, or GMA for short, is a very general concept of intelligence or cognitive ability that one thinks resides in every human being. It is, roughly, what IQ tests purport to measure. See "Factors of Intelligence" on page 89 for more on intelligence. GMA is a pretty good predictor of learning [Schmidt and Hunter 1998]. In other words, a person with a lot of GMA will likely learn new tasks quicker than a person with not as much GMA. GMA is also a

---

[†] There are additional factors here: the TAT criterion validity is conditional on motivational incentives related to task activities, whereas the criterion validity of the questionnaires is conditional on motivational incentives related to social achievement. This illustrates that research findings are hardly ever as clean cut as you might wish them to be, but they are still worth considering.

pretty good predictor of future job performance for employees without previous experience [Schmidt and Hunter 1998]. So if our HR manager wants to hire inexperienced programmers who don't yet know how to work with large, complex systems, then she's not wrong; maybe she should indeed calculate their IQ.

The effect of GMA depends on the type of task at hand. A task is said to be *consistent* if, over time, the best performers develop similar strategies to solving the task. An inconsistent task, on the other hand, is a task for which substantially different strategies for solving the task emerge. When acquiring skills on consistent tasks, the effect of intelligence levels off or diminishes after a while, and job performance soon depends on other factors, such as experience and training ([Ackerman and Beier 2006], [Schmidt et al. 1988], [Schmidt et al. 1986]). This is especially the case for tasks that are highly dependent on domain knowledge, such as software development ([Bergersen and Gustafsson 2010], [Ackerman and Beier 2006]). Software development in general and programming in particular have both consistent and inconsistent task properties. This means that intelligence is important, but not all-important. For experienced job performers, GMA alone is not the ultimate predictor ([Ericsson 2006], [Schmidt and Hunter 1998], [Ackerman and Beier 2006]). So what is? The answer: intelligence *and* skill [Schmidt and Hunter 1998].

What these studies tell us is that relying solely on GMA isn't "intelligent" in the long run. The problem with general mental ability is that it is too general. It is conceptualized as a universal human trait, and its means of measurement are purposefully designed to be independent of any task domain. (The weakness of depending on GMA is compounded by the observation that it isn't really all that universal after all, but dependent on, for example, culture [Bond 1995].) This means that if you want to hire people who are good software developers, you need to assess them on something relevant to the job in addition to a general ability.

FACTORS OF INTELLIGENCE

Modern scientific views of intelligence encompass several aspects. A model of intelligence that is accepted by many researchers is that of Carroll [Carroll 1993], which consists of the following eight primary factors:

> Gf: Fluid reasoning
> Gc: Acculturation knowledge
> SAR: Short-term apprehension and retrieval from short-term working memory (STWM)
> TSR: Fluency of retrieval from long-term storage
> Gv: Visual processing
> Ga: Auditory processing
> Gs: Processing speed
> Gq: Quantitative knowledge

These factors (each of which has a number of subfactors) include aspects that are arguably dependent on culture (such as Gc, acculturation knowledge, the extent to which an individual has incorporated the knowledge and language of the dominant culture, which is why IQ tests for instance do not treat minorities fairly) and factors that are supposed to be independent of culture (such as Gf, fluid reasoning, which represents reasoning abilities in a short-term perspective).

Although several researchers have proposed one, there is little empirical evidence of an all-encompassing factor of general intelligence (GI) [Horn and Masunaga 2006]. Earlier, Spearman [Spearman 1923] argued that his concept of intelligence (called simply g) represented the essence of intelligence, but this notion is now recognized as corresponding to the one factor Gf. What we refer to in this chapter as "general mental ability" (GMA) is actually a coagulation of the factors Gf and Gc [Valentin Kvist and Gustafsson 2008]; see Figure 6-2. There are dependencies between these factors. For example, Gf aids in building Gc. There is also evidence that some of the factors deteriorate with age.

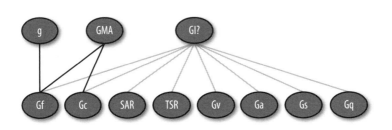

FIGURE 6-2. Factors of intelligence

The Task of Programming

Skills are often measured by means of work-sample tests. These are tests that consist of small, representative tasks. The definition presents two challenges: "small" and "representative." If you want to test potential or current employees' programming skill, you need this to take as little time as possible. So test tasks need to be much smaller than what might be encountered in a normal job situation. But then, how can you be sure that you are testing something relevant? That is where representativeness comes in.

In fact, here you have construct and content validity again: how do you know that your measurement instrument is measuring what you want to measure, and do you really know what you want to measure in the first place? We had this for personality, we have this for intelligence (although we didn't make a fuss about it), and here it shows up again in programming skill: define "programming skill" (this includes defining the task of programming), and then devise a rapid test that can assess it! In general, the construct validity of work-sample tests is problematic [Campbell et al. 1993].

At our research laboratory, we're developing a measurement instrument for assessing programming skill [Bergersen 2010]. It is based on work-sample tests. The work-sample tests are small-sized to medium-sized programming tasks that have been carefully selected, replaced, and modified according to a growing understanding of the concept of programming skill.

The instrument is heavily based on measurement theory and satisfies stringent statistical standards. It is also based on theories of skill and expertise, all in the effort of obtaining construct validity. The instrument is therefore double-tuned: it keeps track of task difficulty, and it keeps track of the skill of the person solving the tasks. Like intelligence and personality, a person will be assessed relatively to the rest of the population who have taken the test. Unlike intelligence and personality, programming skill is directly relevant for hiring and keeping good programmers.

Programming Performance

What, then, is good programming performance? Clearly, quality of code is one criterion. The meaning of "good quality" when it comes to code, of course, has been the subject of endless discussions. But for work-sample tests, there are some obvious as well as evidence-based quality measures, such as functional correctness, depth of inheritance, and so forth. Another criterion is the time spent producing it. You want good quality code in as little time as possible. You might expect that these two criteria are in conflict with each other, that you need more time to produce better quality code. This isn't necessarily true [Arisholm and Sjøberg 2004], [Bergersen 2010b]. For some programming tasks, a given programmer either "gets it" or doesn't, and if he does get it, he'll get it quickly. For other programming tasks, however, the solution gets better the more time is spent on the task. It is important to know what kind of programming task in this respect one is dealing with.

Expertise

Skill is something that can be improved. What's actually a skill and how to improve it has been extensively researched in the field of expertise and learning. Expertise in general, and skill in particular, is related to a specific task or set of tasks. This is very different from both personality and intelligence.

There are other aspects of expertise beside skill. Expert knowledge (in our case, programming knowledge) is an important ingredient in expertise. So is experience (in our case, programming experience); see "Factors of Expertise" on page 92. There are dependencies between these factors. For example, experience contributes to knowledge, which contributes to skill.

FACTORS OF EXPERTISE

Expertise is defined in several ways [Ericsson 2006]:

1. In terms of *extended experience*

2. In terms of *superior knowledge representation and organization*; more specifically [Horn and Masunaga 2006]:

   • Expert knowledge

   • Expert reasoning

   • Expert memory

3. In terms of *reliably superior performance on representative tasks* (so-called *expert performance*)

Expertise is usually understood as related to specific tasks within a given domain. Being an expert on one task does not necessarily relate to being an expert on a different task.

Great care must be taken when giving measures to the various aspects of expertise. For example, extended experience (Option 1) has quite often been measured simply by years on the job, but a more relevant measure might be a more task-specific count of experience [Sonnentag 1998], [Shaft and Vessey 1998]. Superior knowledge representation and organization (Option 2) is a more cognitive aspect of expertise. It is very common to measure this complex aspect in terms of years on the job too, since it is not obvious how to measure someone's cognitive structures. It is postulated that the superior mental representations develop over time as a result of task-relevant experience. This is often, but not necessarily, true. When specifically referring to skill, researchers usually relate to superior performance on representative tasks; i.e., work-samples (Option 3).

Two other aspects of expertise that are widely recognized include these:

• Expertise on consistent tasks is asymptotic. There is a limit to how good anyone can get. This is less so for inconsistent tasks.

• Expertise comes and goes with practice. If you stop practicing, your expertise will likely drop below your optimal level.

Intelligence aids in this process of acquiring skill, but it does not determine skill. According to Cattell's investment theory, the "investment" of Gf (so-called *fluid reasoning*, or the capacity to solve problems in a short-term perspective; see "Factors of Intelligence" on page 89) in learning situations that demand insights into complex relations, will benefit the acquisition of knowledge and skill. Recently, evidence was provided that suggests that this holds true for programming [Bergersen and Gustafsson 2010]; see Figure 6-3. Here, Working Memory Capacity (WMC) is used as a substitute for Gf. WMC has a substantial positive effect on programming knowledge, which in turn positively affects programming skill. However, the

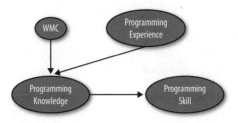

FIGURE 6-3. Investment Theory for Programming Skill [Bergersen and Gustafsson 2010]

direct effect of WMC on programming skill seems to be negligible! In other words, WMC does not make someone skillful just like that, as a direct cause. It does so via facilitating the attainment of knowledge. Similarly, programming experience has an indirect (rather than a direct) effect on programming skill, but not as strongly as WMC.

The upshot of all this is that intelligence is an asset when acquiring a skill. If you want good programmers, go ahead and test their intelligence, if you must, but be sure to test their programming skill first and foremost.

Success calls for both intelligence and skill. Combining intelligence and expertise in this manner draws attention to merit in a way that is more to the point of interest and perhaps less stigmatizing. In fact, efforts are being made to merge intelligence and expertise into a unified theory; see "Combining Intelligence and Expertise" next. The common ground here is cognitive structures in the brain. Some are stable, some deteriorate with age, and some are improved by deliberate practice.

COMBINING INTELLIGENCE AND EXPERTISE

Cognitive structures are building blocks in both intelligence and expertise. Efforts have been made to merge these two cognitive themes into a joint theory of expertise and intelligence [Horn and Masunaga 2006]. Interesting contrasts then emerge: whereas Gf (fluid intelligence) is inductive reasoning from first principles (e.g., the rules of chess), expert reasoning is deductive and inferential (e.g., from the battery of experienced and learned chess positions). Whereas SAR is retrieval from short-term working memory, which holds seven chunks of information, plus or minus two, experts seem to be able to use an expanded expert working memory in their domain of expertise that holds much more than SAR's short-term working memory. Whereas Gs is speed of recall on nonsense tasks, expert cognitive speed is speed of recall on domain-specific things. Thus, one may add three new aspects to the eight aspects of intelligence to get a combined theory:

> ExpDR: Expert deductive reasoning
> ExpSAR: Short-term apprehension and retrieval from expert working memory (ExpWM)
> ExpCS: Expert cognitive speed

Software Effort Estimation

So what about other software engineering tasks? Can they be learned, and can the resulting skill on those tasks be measured? Let's look at a notoriously hard task: software effort estimation, which is the task of estimating the effort of developing software.

The development of a software system is an inherently complex process. Estimating the effort needed to run a large software development project lifts this complexity to a higher order. Visible effects of the difficulty of this task are that effort estimates of software development are inaccurate and generally too low [Moløkken-Østvold and Jørgensen 2003], that software professionals tend to exhibit more confidence in their estimates than is warranted [Jørgensen et al. 2004], and that estimates are unreliable, in that the same person may judge the same project differently on separate occasions [Grimstad and Jørgensen (2007)]. There also seems to be no substantial improvement (learning from history) in estimation accuracy over the past decades, and learning from outcome feedback seems difficult [Gruschke and Jørgensen 2005].

As if complexity wasn't enough, we know that the human judgment processes involved in forecasting an estimate are subject to a range of unconscious processes [Kahneman and Frederick 2004], [LeBoeuf and Shafir 2004], [Jørgensen and Sjøberg 2001], [Jørgensen and Carelius 2004], [Jørgensen and Sjøberg 2004]. For example, it is easy to manipulate the estimates that people produce by simply feeding them various base estimates beforehand (the anchor effect). The human judgment processes are also sensitive to the nature and format of the information (e.g., requirement documents) available when producing the estimate [Jørgensen and Grimstad 2008], [Jørgensen and Grimstad 2010], [Jørgensen and Halkjelsvik 2010], [Jørgensen 2010]. For example, it makes a significant difference whether you ask someone how much time he needs to complete a given amount of work, or whether you ask how much work he can complete in a given amount of time. The latter is the *modus operandi* for agile development's time boxing. The result? Asking people to time box seems to increase underestimation. In addition, time boxing seems to reverse the tendency to overestimate the effort for completing small tasks while underestimating the effort for completing large tasks [Halkjelsvik et al. 2010].

Unlike for the task of programming, it seems that it is not enough simply to do more estimation of software development effort to become good at it. Evidence suggests that on-the-job feedback regarding the accuracy of estimation (either passive, in the form of historical data, or active, in the form of direct management assessment) doesn't improve the tendency to be overly optimistic, overly confident, or unreliable in one's estimations. According to classic learning theory, this in turn suggests that more refined feedback and active training of skills (so-called deliberate practice) is necessary. In other words, one needs to build estimation expertise in a conscious and deliberate manner.

The question is, however: is this possible? Targeted training, requires that one knows what the target is. In other words, one must know what expertise to induce. But when it comes to estimating the effort of software projects, the nature of expertise seems to elude us; it is not readily observable, because experienced project managers do not really stand out from inexperienced estimators, and further, the theoretical foundations of expertise do not give clear answers to what exactly the expertise of interest is. Moreover, software effort estimation is an instance of so-called *ill-defined* tasks. They transcend merely inconsistent tasks in that successful strategies seem to be difficult even to define. Neither the task of software effort estimation nor the expertise required to be good at this task are within our scientific grasp yet; in other words, we're struggling with construct validity on these two concepts.

Individual or Environment

We now turn to the third question with which we started this chapter, which we can now formulate a bit more precisely. If you know that it isn't trivial to determine software developer expertise, should you focus on tools and techniques instead? Imagine a policy maker in charge of reducing the number and severity of road traffic collisions, the leading cause of death among children worldwide 10–19 years old and the sixth leading preventable cause of death in the United States. Should she prioritize efforts on increasing driving skills and driver awareness, or should she spend more money on environmental measures, such as improving the road standard, lowering speed limits, and lobbying for more safety features in cars? Both, you might say, but then, within a limited budget, how much on each?

Research on road traffic collisions is, unfortunately, in a fortunate position: there is a tremendous amount of data worldwide available for analysis. It is therefore actually possible to make rational decisions on where to spend resources. Software engineering is not in a position to make such clear-cut decisions. We don't yet have enough data, and our tasks are extremely diverse.

Skill or Safety in Software Engineering

Programming skill is becoming measurable. This means we may get a better grasp on both the task of programming and what it means to be an expert programmer. We've made progress on construct validity (that is, our measures consistently reflect aspects of programming skill and task difficulty), and we're increasing our content and criterion validity (that is, we're working on expanding our scientific grasp on the concepts of programming skill and task difficulty, as well as validating the constructs with regards to real-life programming success). This makes it possible to develop and improve our training programs for programmers.

Not so with software effort estimation. Forecasting how much effort a team or a project will spend on developing some part of a system is in general not within our grasp of understanding, to the extent that we can reliably measure task difficulty or estimation skill—which also means that we don't yet know how to train people to become better at it.

We do know, though, that facilitating the environment seems to help. A few examples are: deleting irrelevant information from requirements documents, avoiding distortions of thinking by discouraging tentative base estimates, and asking people to estimate ideal effort prior to estimating most likely effort (see also [Jørgensen 2005]). These measures are intended to alter the environment in which the judgment (i.e., estimation) process occurs, and the purpose is to counter known psychological biases in those who perform the judgment. Other environmental measures are group estimation, which is on average more accurate than single estimates, and using the appropriate process model: estimates associated with iterative development are often better than those associated with relay-style development [Moløkken-Østvold and Jørgensen 2005]. It is possible to develop tools and techniques that support all these environmental measures.

Pair programming (examined in Chapter 17 by Laurie Williams, and to a lesser extent in Chapter 18 by Jason Cohen) is an example of an environmental measure taken to improve code production. Rather than improving the programmers themselves, one relies on social processes that are meant to enhance productivity of both the individual programmer and the team. It's important to know under which circumstances pairing people up is beneficial. For example, pairing up seems to be most beneficial for novices on complex programming tasks [Arisholm et al. 2007]; see also the meta-analysis in [Hannay et al. 2009] or [Dybå et al. 2007].

Collaboration

Teamwork and collaboration are in vogue now. For example, it is generally seen as beneficial to involve and collaborate with various stakeholders throughout the stages of the software development process. Thus, introducing more explicit collaboration is meant as a major environmental facilitator.

It should be worth looking into exactly what successful collaboration is. So instead of (or in addition to) looking at, say, personality, one should look at how people collaborate. There is extensive research into collaboration, team composition, and group processes. In fact, there is almost too much! I once tried to wrap my brain around relevant basic group processes for pair programming (see Figure 6-4), but it soon became apparent that unless you know what sort of collaboration that is actually going on, it is impossible to decide which theory to apply. Quite often researchers apply some theory or another as a *post hoc* explanation for their observations [Hannay et al. 2007]. And quite often, this is easy. There is always some theory that fits! For example, social facilitation might explain why a team performs well, while social inhibition might explain why a team doesn't perform well. So you can use either theory to explain whatever outcome you might observe. This is, of course, possible only if you don't really know what's going on, because if you did, you'd probably see that the underlying mechanisms of at least one of the theories do not fit with what's going on.

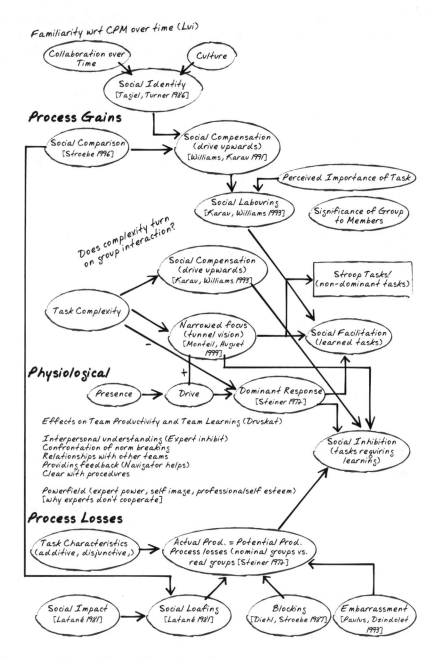

FIGURE 6-4. Too much theory! (If you don't know what's really going on.)

To find out what kind of collaboration goes on in pair programming, we listened to audio tapes of 43 professional pair programmers solving a pair programming task. We classified their mode of collaboration according to their verbal interaction [Walle and Hannay 2009]. The classification scheme we used was developed in a boot-strapping manner, both top-down from existing schemes and bottom-up from the specific collaboration that was apparent in the audio recordings. You can see the resulting scheme in Figure 6-5.

The scheme has two levels. The first level distinguishes according to the main focus of the discourse—for example, whether the pair is discussing the task description, or trying to comprehend the code, or writing code together, or talking about something else, like last night's soccer game. The second level analyzes so-called *interaction sequences* [Hogan et al. 2000]. The central element here is the *interaction patterns*. For example, verbal passages are classified as *Elaborative* if both peers contribute substantive statements to the discussion and the speakers make multiple contributions that build on or clarify another's prior statement.

One would think that the presence of elaborative verbal collaboration would be beneficial for performance. However, we didn't find evidence for this in our data. Tentative results are that spending more time discussing the task description leads to less time spent overall in solving the task. It is too early to reach a conclusion, though, so you should not take this as evidence, but rather as input to your reflective process as a practitioner. Efforts to understand the collaboration that goes on in software effort estimation are also ongoing [Børte and Nerland 2010], [Jørgensen 2004].

Personality Again

Personality inevitably enters the scene when it comes to collaboration. For example, in ethnographic studies focusing on personality issues and disruption in software engineering team collaboration, it was found that disruption is bad, but lack of debate (which is a mild form of disruption) is worse [Karn and Cowling 2006], [Karn and Cowling 2005]. It is argued that pairs or teams with personalities that are too alike will lead to lack of debate. This finds empirical confirmation in [Williams et al. 2006] and [Walle and Hannay 2009]. In particular, differences in Extraversion has the largest effect: pairs whose peers have different levels of Extraversion collaborate more intensely (that is, engage in more discussion) than those with more similar levels.

A Broader View of Intelligence

People who score high on IQ tests are not necessarily good at planning or at prioritizing when to plan and when to move forward and take action [Sternberg 2005]. Planning is important. Remember our tentative findings that the quickest pair programmers were those who spent relatively more time to understand the task description, which can be taken as spending more time planning. One might further argue that "classical" intelligence tests, with their emphasis

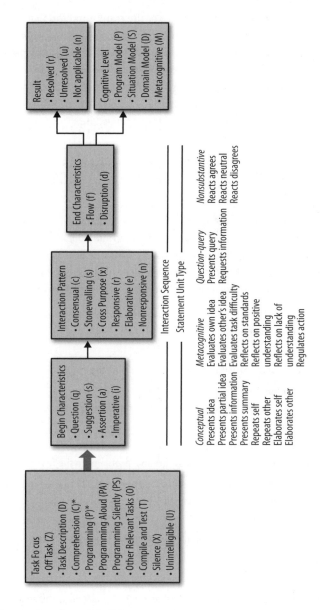

FIGURE 6-5. Classification scheme for verbal collaboration

on processing speed, show merely that high scorers are good at solving IQ test items, but fail to measure their ability to find the best solution for actual real-life needs [Schweizer 2005].

There has been concern that the content validity of the traditional intelligence constructs are not adequate. Based on input from cognitive psychologists specializing in intelligence, Robert Sternberg and his colleagues found that intelligence should include the capacity to learn from experience, to use metacognitive processes (i.e., to plan) to enhance learning, and the ability to adapt to the environment. Also, what is considered intelligent in one culture might be seen as silly in another culture [Sternberg 2005]. The "classic" constructs of intelligence, thus, may not be extensive enough. See "Other Aspects of Intelligence" next.

OTHER ASPECTS OF INTELLIGENCE

Sternberg's *Triarchic Theory of Intelligence* or *Theory of Successful Intelligence* [Sternberg 2003] presents three aspects of intelligence: Analytical, Creative, and Practical (Figure 6-6). The theory offers a description of intellectual competence according to an individual's own personal standards and sociocultural context. Success is achieved by using combinations of all three aspects, and by utilizing one's strengths and compensating for one's weaknesses in any of the three aspects. The theory subsumes the concepts of intelligence in "Factors of Intelligence" on page 89.

- Analytical intelligence: How intelligence relates to the internal world of information processing. This aspect has three components:

    Metacomponents
    Higher-order processes used in planning and monitoring the use of the other components

    Performance components
    Lower-order cognitive processes used to implement the decisions of the metacomponents. Akin to GMA

    Knowledge-Acquisition Components
    Cognitive processes used to learn how to solve problems in the first place

- Creative intelligence: How intelligence relates to experience. This aspect describes how prior and new experience interact with the analytical aspect, and includes:

    Dealing with novelty
    The ability to learn and think within new conceptual systems

    Automatizing information processing
    Familiarizing a task

- Practical intelligence: How intelligence relates to the external world. This includes:

    — Adapting to one's environment

    — Shaping one's environment

    — Selecting a different environment

There are many other models of intelligence; see [Sternberg 2005] for pointers.

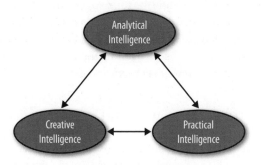

FIGURE 6-6. Triarchic Theory of Intelligence

According to Sternberg, intelligence manifests itself strongly in the ability to be street-wise and to exhibit adaptive behavior. Adaptive behavior consists of practical problem-solving ability, verbal ability, and social competence. The latter includes things such as accepting others for what they are, admitting mistakes, and displaying interest in the world at large. Invaluable stuff for collaboration!

Adaptive behavior is also the tenet of Gerd Gigerenzer and the Adaptive Behavior and Cognition research group. When faced with complex tasks, Western science and engineering disciplines usually teach us to analyze and get a full overview of all relevant factors and then to take appropriate action. However, many tasks, especially ill-defined ones such as software effort estimation, are beyond our capabilities of a thorough enough analysis for ever reaching an overview of all such relevant factors. By the sheer effort we put into it, we might think we're cataloging a lot of relevant factors, but we're probably missing out on more factors than we're including. Thus, the argument goes, such an analytical approach is bound to fall short of the target. Man has adapted to and survived complex situations not by thorough analysis, but by eliminating irrelevant factors and focusing on a few critical ones [Gigerenzer 2007], [Gigerenzer and Todd 1999]. Thus, adaptive behavior means to acknowledge your shortcomings and to choose your strategy accordingly. This bears relevance for software development and software effort estimation, because it is impossible to specify and analyze everything beforehand. Approaches to focus on the few most critical factors for software effort estimation include analogical reasoning and top-down estimation [Li et al. 2007], [Jørgensen 2004], [Hertwig et al. 1999].

Concluding Remarks

Readers of this book should have an affinity to the *reflective practitioner view* [Jarvis 1999], [Argyris and Schön 1996], where practitioners reflect on what they do in their daily work and develop better ways of performing work tasks. To get hold of the usually implicit understandings of practitioners should be a main focus of disciplines such as ours. I must mention that our HR manager from earlier also stated that her company didn't really want their programmers to spend time reflecting too much upon what they did. Rather, they should just implement what they were told to implement. I'm sure most of us, together with Joel Spolsky, would not find this view particularly appealing, but it is all too easy to revert to such strategies in pressed lead-time situations, i.e., getting trapped in the *urgent/important* quadrant at the expense of the *important/not urgent* planning and development quadrant [Covey et al. 1999].

With our insights, however, we can lay a logical trap for our already time-trapped HR manager: her previous remark on IQ entailed that (1) GMA predicts programming performance, but (2) since GMA predicts learning ability first and foremost, this must mean that she wants programmers who are fast at learning, and (3) learning is done through reflective practice, but (4) once she has her programmers, she doesn't want them to reflect, hence she doesn't want them to learn. I'll call this the unreflective time-trapped HR manager's paradox.

In fact, our HR manager isn't totally unreflective. She knows that intelligence matters. Maybe she has also read some of the literature on it cited in this chapter. But perhaps she didn't turn to the page where it says more specifically that intelligence is good for acquiring skill rather than good for predicting skill already acquired. Intelligence is also more than IQ (which is just a measure of one aspect of intelligence). It's easy to lose the details when reading scientific literature, and this wouldn't be the first time. An urban legend in software engineering tells us that this was the case for Royce's article [Royce 1970] where he argued against the waterfall model, but the industry failed to turn to the next page, where it said that the model on the previous page was not to be recommended. There are sure to be many more incidents of getting only half the picture; among practitioners and researchers alike. Remember to include the fuller picture when basing your decisions on evidence!

So how did we fare with our three questions posed at the start of this chapter? The first question concerned whether one can define what a good software developer is. The answer is that for certain tasks of software development (e.g., programming), it seems we might soon be able to. For other tasks (e.g., software effort estimation), it is much harder to define what a good performer is. Before you object that a good performer on the task of estimation is simply a person who estimates accurately and reliably with the correct level of confidence, remember that our discourse in this chapter filled this first question with a great deal more meaning than that. To define a good performer means to define the task and the expertise to go with it, to the degree that you can say what it takes for a novice to become an expert, and an expert to become an even better expert.

The answer to the second question follows suit. For certain tasks it seems that we'll be able to measure expertise and task difficulty, but for other tasks the road there seems much longer. Note that we're asking to determine a degree of expertise by efficient means: that is, without having to observe performance over a long period of time. This, therefore, includes predicting future performance.

The two protagonist tasks in this chapter—programming and software effort estimation—are quite different in nature; one relates to planning, and the other relates to doing. And our answers to our first two questions might seem to broaden this divide. But just because we have a beginning grasp on one task but not the other doesn't mean that the two tasks are unrelated. On the contrary, it is natural to ask whether performance on one coincides with performance on the other.

Tentatively, it seems that programming skill and estimation accuracy and reliability on one's own tasks are positively related, which goes against the common belief that even good programmers can't estimate their own effort. If the positive relationship turns out to be true, you could ask your best programmers to estimate and then calculate the correction to this estimate according to the skill levels of the programmers who will actually do the job. This would be a vast improvement on the skill-insensitive compensation factors that are currently in circulation. Using one concept vicariously for another concept in this manner is an interesting prospect. For example, can you improve estimation skill indirectly by improving programming skill?

The third question asked whether one should focus on tools if one can't reliably determine expertise. If one does understand the task and the expertise needed for it, then one should definitely focus more on expertise, since large bodies of research show the increased business value of just increasing the organization's expertise a few percent. But clearly, Glass's facts aren't useful unless you know how to recognize expertise in software developers. When you do not have a grasp on expertise and how to develop it, the alternative is to rely on the environment and to develop facilitating tools and techniques. The relevant skill then becomes once removed to that of mastering the tool or technique. Maybe this is the way to transform ill-defined tasks such as software effort estimation into at least an inconsistent task, if not a consistent task.

References

[Ackerman and Beier 2006] Ackerman, P.L., and Beier, M.E. 2006. Methods for studying the structure of expertise: Psychometric approaches. In *The Cambridge Handbook of Expertise and Expert Performance*, ed. K.A. Ericsson, N. Charness, P.J. Feltovich, and R.R. Hoffman, 147–166. New York: Cambridge University Press.

[Acuña et al. 2006] Acuña, S.T., N. Juristo, and M. Moreno. 2006. Emphasizing human capabilities in software development. *IEEE Software*, 23(2): 94–101.

[Argyris and Schön 1996] Argyris, C., and D.A. Schön. 1996. *Organizational Learning II. Theory, Method, and Practice*. Boston: Addison-Wesley.

[Arisholm and Sjøberg 2004] Arisholm, E., and D.I.K. Sjøberg. 2004. Evaluating the effect of a delegated versus centralized control style on the maintainability of object-oriented software. *IEEE Transactions on Software Engineering*. 30: 521–534.

[Arisholm et al. 2007] Arisholm, E., H. Gallis, T. Dybå, and D.I.K. Sjøberg. 2007. Evaluating pair programming with respect to system complexity and programmer expertise. *IEEE Transactions on Software Engineering*. 33: 65–86.

[Barrick et al. 2001] Barrick, M.B., M.K. Mount, and T.A. Judge. 2001. Personality and performance at the beginning of the new millennium: What do we know and where do we go next? *International Journal of Selection and Assessment* 9(1/2): 9–30.

[Bell 2007] Bell, S.T. 2007. Deep-level composition variables as predictors of team performance: A meta-analysis. *Journal of Applied Psychology* 92(3): 595–615.

[Bergersen 2010a] Bergersen, G.R. 2010. *Assessing Programming Skill*, to be submitted in 2010. PhD thesis, Simula Research Laboratory/University of Oslo.

[Bergersen 2010b] Bergersen, G.R. 2010. Combining time and correctness in the scoring of performance on items. Presentation at Rasch Conference 2010, Probabilistic models for measurement in education, psychology, social science and health, June 13–16, in Copenhagen, Denmark. *https://conference.cbs.dk/index.php/rasch/Rasch2010/paper/view/596*.

[Bergersen and Gustafsson 2010] Bergersen, G.R., and J.-E. Gustafsson. Programming skill, knowledge and working memory among software developers from an investment theory perspective. Forthcoming in *Journal of Individual Differences*.

[Bond 1995] Bond, L., 1995. Unintended consequences of performance assessment: Issues of bias and fairness. *Educational Measurement: Issues and Practice* 14(4): 21–24.

[Børte and Nerland 2010] Børte, K., and M. Nerland. Software effort estimation as collective accomplishment: An analysis of estimation practice in a multi-specialist team. To appear in *Scandinavian Journal of Information Systems*.

[Campbell et al. 1993] Campbell, J.P., R.A. McCloy, S.H. Oppler, and C.E. Sager. 1993. A theory of performance. In *Personnel Selection in Organizations*, ed. N. Scmitt and W.C. Borman, 35–70. San Francisco: Jossey-Bass.

[Capretz 2003] Capretz, L.F. 2003. Personality types in software engineering. *Journal of Human-Computer Studies* 58: 207–214.

[Capretz and Ahmed 2010] Capretz, L.F., and F. Ahmed. 2010. Making sense of software development and personality types. *IT Professional* 12(1): 6–13.

[Carroll 1993] Carroll, J.B. 1993. *Human Cognitive Abilities: A Survey of Factor-Analytic Studies*. New York: Cambridge University Press.

[Cegielski and Hall 2006] Cegielski, C.G., and D.J. Hall. 2006. What makes a good programmer? *Communications of the ACM* 49(10): 73–75.

[Chi 2006] Chi, M.T.H. 2006. "Two approaches to the study of experts' characteristics." In *The Cambridge Handbook of Expertise and Expert Performance*, ed. K.A. Ericsson, N. Charness, P.J. Feltovich, and R.R. Hoffman, 21–30. New York: Cambridge University Press.

[Costa and McCrae 1985] Costa, P.T., and R.R. McCrae. 1985. *The NEO Personality Inventory Manual*. Lutz, FL: Psychological Assessment Resources.

[Covey et al. 1999] Covey, S.R., A. Roger Merill, and R.R. Merill. 1999. *First Things First*. New York: Simon & Schuster.

[Devito Da Cunha and Greathead 2007] Devito Da Cunha, A., and D. Greathead. 2007. Does personality matter? An analysis of code-review ability. *Communications of the ACM* 50(5): 109–112.

[Dick and Zarnett 2002] Dick, A.J., and B. Zarnett. 2002. Paired programming and personality traits. *Proc. Third Int'l Conf. Extreme Programming and Agile Processes in Software Engineering (XP 2002)*: 82–85.

[Dickson and Kelly 1985] Dickson, D.H., and I.W. Kelly. 1985. The "Barnum Effect" in personality assessment: A review of the literature. *Psychological Reports* 57: 367–382.

[Dybå et al. 2007] Dybå, T., E. Arisholm, D.I.K. Sjøberg, J.E. Hannay, and F. Shull. 2007. Are two heads better than one? On the effectiveness of pair programming. *IEEE Software* 24(6): 12–15.

[Ericsson 2006] Ericsson, K.A. 2006. "An introduction to The Cambridge Handbook of Expertise and Expert Performance: Its development, organization, and content." In *The Cambridge Handbook of Expertise and Expert Performance*, ed. K.A. Ericsson, N. Charness, P.J. Feltovich, and R.R. Hoffman, 3–20. New York: Cambridge University Press.

[Fallaw and Solomonsen 2010] Fallaw, S.S., and A.L. Solomonsen. 2010. Global assessment trends report. Technical report, PreVisor Talent Measurement.

[Forer 1949] Forer, B.R. 1949. The fallacy of personal validation: A classroom demonstration of gullibility. *Journal of Abnormal and Social Psychology* 44: 118–123.

[Furnham 1996] Furnham, A. 1996. The big five versus the big four: The relationship between the Myers-Briggs Type Indicator (MBTI) and NEO-PI five factor model of personality. *Personality and Individual Differences* 21(2): 303–307.

[Gigerenzer 2007] Gigerenzer, G. 2007. *Gut Feelings: The Intelligence of the Unconscious*. New York: Viking.

[Gigerenzer and Todd 1999] Gigerenzer, G., and P.M. Todd, editors. 1999. *Simple Heuristics That Make Us Smart*. New York: Oxford University Press.

[Glass 2002] Glass, R.L. 2002. *Facts and Fallacies of Software Engineering*. Boston: Addison-Wesley Professional.

[Goldberg 1990] Goldberg, L.R. 1990. An alternative description of personality: The big-five factor structure. *Journal of Personality and Social Psychology* 59: 1216–1229.

[Goldberg 1993] Goldberg, L.R. 1993. The structure of phenotypic personality traits. *American Psychologist* 48: 26–34.

[Goldberg et al. 2006] Goldberg, L.R., J.A. Johnson, H.W. Eber, R. Hogan, M.C. Ashton, C.R. Cloninger, and H.C. Gough. 2006. The international personality item pool and the future of public-domain personality measures. *Journal of Research in Personality* 40: 84–96.

[Grimstad and Jørgensen 2007] Grimstad, S., and M. Jørgensen. 2007. Inconsistency in expert judgment-based estimates of software development effort. *Journal of Systems and Software* 80(11): 1770–1777.

[Gruschke and Jørgensen 2005] Gruschke, T.M., and M. Jørgensen. 2005. Assessing uncertainty of software development effort estimates: Learning from outcome feedback. *Proceedings of the 11th IEEE International Software Metrics Symposium*: 4.

[Hærem 2002] Hærem, T. 2002. *Task Complexity and Expertise as Determinants of Task Perceptions and Performance: Why Technology-Structure Research has been Unreliable and Inconclusive*. PhD thesis, Norwegian School of Management BI.

[Halkjelsvik et al. 2010] Halkjelsvik, T., M. Jørgensen, and K.H. Teigen. 2010. To read two pages, I need 5 minutes, but give me 5 minutes and I will read four: How to change productivity estimates by inverting the question. Forthcoming in *Applied Cognitive Psychology*.

[Hannay et al. 2007] Hannay, J.E., D.I.K. Sjøberg, and T. Dybå. 2007. A systematic review of theory use in software engineering experiments. *IEEE Transactions on Software Engineering*. 33: 87–107.

[Hannay et al. 2009] Hannay, J.E., T. Dybå, E. Arisholm, and D.I.K. Sjøberg. 2009. The effectiveness of pair programming: A meta-analysis. *Information & Software Technology* 55(7): 1110–1122.

[Hannay et al. 2010] Hannay, J.E., E. Arisholm, H. Engvik, and D.I.K. Sjøberg. 2010. Personality and pair programming. *IEEE Transactions on Software Engineering* 36(1): 61–80.

[Hanson and Claiborn 2006] Hanson, W.E., and C.D. Claiborn. 2006. Effects of test interpretation style and favorability in the counseling process. *Journal of Counseling and Development* 84(3): 349–358.

[Hertwig et al. 1999] Hertwig, R., U. Hoffrage, and L. Martignon. 1999. Quick estimation: Letting the environment do the work. In *Simple Heuristics That Make Us Smart*, ed. G. Gigerenzer and P.M. Todd, 75–95. New York: Oxford University Press.

[Hogan et al. 2000] Hogan, K., B.K. Nastasi, and M. Pressley. 2000. Discourse patterns and collaborative scientific reasoning in peer and teacher-guided discussions. *Cognition and Instruction*, 17(4): 379–432.

[Horn and Masunaga 2006] Horn, J., and H. Masunaga. 2006. A merging theory of expertise and intelligence. In *The Cambridge Handbook of Expertise and Expert Performance*, ed. K.A. Ericsson, N. Charness, P.J. Feltovich, and R.R. Hoffman, 587–612. New York: Cambridge University Press.

[Jarvis 1999] Jarvis, P. 1999. *The Practitioner-Researcher*. San Francisco: Jossey-Bass.

[Jørgensen 2004] Jørgensen, M. 2004. Top-down and bottom-up expert estimation of software development effort. *Information and Software Technology* 46(1): 3–16.

[Jørgensen 2005] Jørgensen, M. 2005. Practical guidelines for expert-judgment-based software effort estimation. *IEEE Software* 22(3): 57–63.

[Jørgensen 2010] Jørgensen, M. 2010. Selection of strategies in judgment-based effort estimation. *Journal of Systems and Software* 83(6): 1039–1050.

[Jørgensen and Carelius 2004] Jørgensen, M., and G.J. Carelius. 2004. An empirical study of software project bidding. *IEEE Transactions on Software Engineering* 30(12): 953–969.

[Jørgensen and Grimstad 2008]] Jørgensen, M., and S. Grimstad. 2008. Avoiding irrelevant and misleading information when estimating development effort. *IEEE Software* 25(3): 78–83.

[Jørgensen and Grimstad 2010] Jørgensen, M., and S. Grimstad. 2010. The impact of irrelevant and misleading information on software development effort estimates: A randomized controlled field experiment. *IEEE Transactions on Software Engineering* Preprint(99).

[Jørgensen and Halkjelsvik 2010] Jørgensen, M. and T. Halkjelsvik. 2010. The effects of request formats on judgment-based effort estimation. *Journal of Systems and Software* 83(1): 29–36.

[Jørgensen and Sjøberg 2001] Jørgensen, M., and D.I.K. Sjøberg. 2001. Impact of effort estimates on software project work. *Information and Software Technology* 43(15): 939–948.

[Jørgensen and Sjøberg 2004] Jørgensen, M., and D.I.K. Sjøberg. 2004. The impact of customer expectation on software development effort estimates. *Journal of Project Management* 22(4): 317–325.

[Jørgensen et al. 2004] Jørgensen, M., K.H. Teigen, and K.J. Moløkken-Østvold. 2004. Better sure than safe? Over-confidence in judgment based software development effort prediction intervals. *Journal of Systems and Software* 70(1-2): 79–93.

[Kahneman and Frederick 2004] Kahneman, D., and S. Frederick. 2004. "A Model of Heuristic Judgment" in *The Cambridge Handbook of Thinking and Reasoning*, eds. K.J. Holyoak and R.G. Morrison. Cambridge: Cambridge University Press, 267–294.

[Karn and Cowling 2005] Karn, J.S., and A.J. Cowling. 2005. A study of the effect of personality on the performance of software engineering teams. *Proc. Fourth International Symposium on Empirical Software Engineering* (ISESE'05): 417–427.

[Karn and Cowling 2006] Karn, J.S., and A.J. Cowling. 2006. A follow up study of the effect of personality on the performance of software engineering teams. *Proc. Fifth International Symposium on Empirical Software Engineering* (ISESE'06): 232–241.

[LeBoeuf and Shafir 2004] LeBoeuf, R.A., and E.B. Shafir. 2004. "Decision Making" in *The Cambridge Handbook of Thinking and Reasoning*, eds. K.J. Holyoak and R.G. Morrison. Cambridge: Cambridge University Press, 243–266.

[Li et al. 2007] Li, J., G. Ruhe, A. Al-Emran, and M.M. Richter. 2007. A flexible method for software effort estimation by analogy. *Empirical Software Engineering* 12(1): 1382–3256.

[Meehl 1956] Meehl, P.E. 1956. Wanted—A good cookbook. *American Psychologist* 11(3): 263–272.

[Moløkken-Østvold and Jørgensen 2003] Moløkken-Østvold, K.J., and M. Jørgensen. 2003. A review of surveys on software effort estimation. *Proc. Int'l Symp. Empirical Software Engineering* (ISESE 2003): 223–230.

[Moløken-Østvold and Jørgensen 2005] Moløkken-Østvold, K.J., and M. Jørgensen. 2005. A comparison of software project overruns—flexible vs. sequential development models. *IEEE Transactions on Software Engineering* 31(9): 754–766.

[Moore 1991] Moore, J.E. 1991. Personality characteristics of information systems professionals. *Proc. 1991 Special Interest Group on Computer Personnel Research (SIGCPR) Annual Conference*: 140–155.

[Paul 2005] Paul, A.M. 2005. *The Cult of Personality Testing: How Personality Tests Are Leading Us to Miseducate Our Children, Mismanage Our Companies, and Misunderstand Ourselves*. New York: Free Press.

[Peeters et al. 2006] Peeters, M.A.G., H.F.J.M. van Tuijl, C.G. Rutte, and I.M.M.J. Reymen. Personality and team performance: A meta-analysis. *European Journal of Personality* 20: 377–396.

[Pervin and John 1997] Pervin, L.A., and O.P. John. 1997. *Personality: Theory and Research*, Seventh Edition. Hoboken, NJ: John Wiley & Sons.

[Read et al. 2010] Read, J.S., B.M. Monroe, A.L. Brownstein, Y. Yang, G. Chopra, and L.C. Miller. 2010. A Neural Network Model of the Structure and Dynamics of Human Personality. *Psychological Review* 117(1): 61–92.

[Royce 1970] Royce, W.W. 1970. Managing the development of large software systems. *Proc. IEEE WESCON*: 1–9.

[Saggio and Kline 1996] Saggio, A., and P. Kline. 1996. The location of the Myers-Briggs Type Indicator in personality factor space. *Personality and Individual Differences* 21(4): 591–597.

[Saggio et al. 2001] Saggio, A., C. Cooper, and P. Kline. 2001. A confirmatory factor analysis of the Myers-Briggs Type Indicator. *Personality and Individual Differences* 30: 3–9.

[Saleh et al. 2010] Saleh, N., E. Mendes, J. Grundy, and G. St. J. Burch. 2010. An empirical study of the effects of conscientiousness in pair programming using the five-factor personality model. *Proc. of the 32nd ACM/IEEE Int'l Conf. Software Engineering* 1: 577–586.

[Schmidt and Hunter 1998] Schmidt, F.L., and J.E. Hunter. 1998. The validity and utility of selection methods in personnel psychology: Practical and theoretical implications of 85 years of research findings. *Psychological Bulletin* 124(2): 262–274.

[Schmidt et al. 1986] Schmidt, F.L., J.E. Hunter, and A.N. Outerbridge. 1986. Impact of job experience and ability on job knowledge, work sample performance, and supervisory ratings of job performance. *Journal of Applied Psychology* 71(3): 432–439.

[Schmidt et al. 1988] Schmidt, F.L., J.E. Hunter, A.N. Outerbridge, and S. Goff. 1988. Joint relation of experience and ability with job performance: Test of three hypotheses. *J. Applied Psychology* 73(1): 46–57.

[Schweizer 2005] Schweizer, K. 2005. An overview of research into the cognitive basis of intelligence. *Journal of Individual Differences* 26(1): 43–51.

[Shaft and Vessey 1998] Shaft, T.M., and I. Vessey. 1998. The relevance of application domain knowledge. *Journal of Management Information Systems* 15(1): 51–78.

[Shneiderman 1980] Shneiderman, B. 1980. *Software Psychology: Human Factors in Computer and Information Systems*. Cambridge, MA: Winthrop Publishers.

[Smith 1989] Smith, D.C. 1989. The personality of the systems analyst: An investigation. *SIGCPR Computer Personnel* 12(2): 12–14.

[Sonnentag 1998] Sonnentag, S. 1998. Expertise in professional software design. *Journal of Applied Psychology* 83(5): 703–715.

[Spangler 1992]] Spangler, W.D. 1992. Validity of questionnaire and TAT measures of need for achievement: Two meta-analyses. *Psychological Bulletin* 112(1): 140–154.

[Spearman 1923] Spearman, C. *The Nature of "Intelligence" and the Principles of Cognition*, Second Edition. New York: Macmillan.

[Spolsky 2007] Spolsky, J. 2007. *Smart and Gets Things Done*. New York: Apress.

[Sternberg 2003] Sternberg, R.J. 2003. A broad view of intelligence: The theory of successful intelligence. *Consulting Psychology Journal: Practice and Research* 55(3): 139–154.

[Sternberg 2005] Sternberg, R.J. 2005. Intelligence. In *The Cambridge Handbook of Thinking and Reasoning*, ed. K.J. Holyoak and R.G. Morrison, pp. 751-774. New York: Cambridge University Press.

[Turley and Bieman 1995] Turley, R.T., and J.M. Bieman. 1995. Competencies of exceptional and non-exceptional software engineers. *Journal of Systems and Software* 28(1): 19–38.

[Valentin Kvist and Gustafsson 2008] Valentin Kvist, A., and J.-E. Gustafsson. 2008. The relation between fluid intelligence and the general factor as a function of cultural background: A test of Cattell's investment theory. *Intelligence* 36: 422–436.

[Walle and Hannay 2009] Walle, T., and J.E. Hannay. Personality and the nature of collaboration in pair programming. *Proc. 3rd Int'l Symp. Empirical Software Engineering and Measurement* (ESEM): 203–213.

[Weinberg 1971] Weinberg, G.M. 1971. *The Psychology of Computer Programming*. New York: Van Nostrand Reinhold.

[Weinberg 1998] Weinberg, G.M. 1998. *The Psychology of Computer Programming*. New York: Dorset House Publishing.

[Williams et al. 2006] Williams, L., L. Layman, J. Osborne, and N. Katira. 2006. Examining the compatibility of student pair programmers. *Proc. AGILE 2006*: 411–420.

[Woodruff 1979] Woodruff, C.K. 1979. Personality profiles of male and female data processing personnel. *Proc. 17th Annual Southeast Regional Conference*: 124–128.

## CHAPTER SEVEN

Why Is It So Hard to Learn to Program?

Mark Guzdial

Most of the topics in this book—the best ways to develop software, the costs of developing software, what communications facilitate programming—revolve in some way around programmers. But it's hard even to become a programmer in the first place. Few people try to enter the field, and even fewer succeed. In this chapter, we ask why it's so hard to learn to program.

Whether we need to develop more programmers at this moment is a point of dispute. The United States Bureau of Labor Statistics recently predicted an enormous demand for computing professionals. According to the November 2008 report [Association 2008], the demand for "IT Professionals" from 2006–2016 will be twice the growth rate of the rest of the workforce. The updated estimate of November 2009 said: "'Computer and mathematical' occupations are the fastest growing occupational cluster within the fastest growing major occupational group" [Consortium 2010]. But what does "IT Professional" mean? A "computer and mathematical" occupation? The experience of many newly unemployed IT workers, especially during the current downturn, suggests that maybe there are *too many* programmers in the United States today [Rampell 2010].

Although it may not be clear whether we *need* more programmers, it is clear that many start down the path of programming and fail early. Rumors of high failure rates in introductory computing courses (typically referred to as "CS1" in reference to an early curriculum standards report) are common in the literature and in hallway discussions at conferences such as the ACM Special Interest Group in Computer Science Education (SIGCSE) Symposium. Jens Bennedsen and Michael Caspersen made the first reasonable attempt to find out what failure rates really look like [Bennedsen and Caspersen 2007]. They asked for data from faculty around the world via several computer science (CS) educator mailing lists. Sixty-three institutions provided their failure rates in introductory courses, which means that these data are self-selected and self-reported (e.g., schools with really embarrassing results may have chosen not to participate, or to lie, and the results can be skewed because the sampling was not random). Overall, 30% of students fail or withdraw from the first course, with higher rates in colleges than universities (40% versus 30%). Thus, we have indications that roughly one out of every three students who start a CS1 course, around the world in all kinds of institutions, fails or gives up. Why is that?

The Bennedsen and Caspersen results report success or failure in taking a class. A CS1 teacher's criteria aren't the only possible definition of success, however. There are many programmers who never took a course at all, yet are successful. So we first need to establish that students really do have a hard time learning programming, apart from the evidence of grades. If we can establish that, the next question is, "Why?" Is programming an unnatural activity? Could programming be made easier in a different form? Could programming be taught in a different way that makes learning easier? Or maybe we just have no idea how to actually measure what students know about programming.

Do Students Have Difficulty Learning to Program?

At Yale University in the 1980s, Elliot Soloway gave the same assignment regularly in his Pascal programming class [Soloway et al. 1983]:

> Write a program that repeatedly reads in positive integers, until it reads the integer 99999. After seeing 99999, it should print out the average.

Called "The Rainfall Problem," it became one of the most studied problems in the early years of computing education research. In the 1983 paper from which this formulation of the problem is taken (other formulations were explored in other papers), the Yale team was exploring whether having a *leave* statement (a *break* in C or Python) improved student performance on the problem. They gave the problem to three groups of students:

- First-semester CS1 students after learning and using WHILE, REPEAT, and FOR, 3/4 of the way through the term
- CS2 (second semester of computing coursework, typically a data structures course) students 3/4 of the way through the term
- Juniors and seniors in a systems programming course

In each class of students, half the students used traditional Pascal and the other half had the opportunity to use Pascal with an added *leave* statement. The results, summarized in Table 7-1, may shock those who have successfully entered a programming career. Only 14% of the introductory students could solve this problem in raw Pascal? And 30% of the *most advanced* students couldn't solve it either? This study was repeated in the literature several times (e.g., dissertations by both Jim Spohrer [Spohrer 1992] and Lewis Johnson [Johnson and Soloway 1987] studied students working on the Rainfall Problem), and has been repeated informally many times since—with surprisingly similar results every time.

TABLE 7-1. Performance of Yale students on the Rainfall Problem

Class group	% correct using raw Pascal	% correct using Pascal with *leave*
CS1	14%	24%
CS2	36%	61%
Systems course	69%	96%

The problem requires a relatively complex conditional controlling the loop. *If the input is negative, ignore it but continue to accept input. If the input is positive and not 99999, add it to the total and increment the count. If the input is 99999, ignore the input and leave the loop.* It's easy to get an error where negative input or 99999 gets added into the sum.

These results were at Yale University. Could it be that Yale was just really bad at teaching programming? Few students in those years might have learned programming before entering college, so whatever instruction they received came from the CS1 course. Researchers for many years wondered how to conduct a study of programming that would avoid the complicating factor of possibly bad instruction at a particular school.

The 2001 McCracken Working Group

In 2001, Mike McCracken [McCracken et al. 2001] organized a group of researchers to meet at the Innovation and Technology in Computer Science Education (ITICSE) conference held at the University of Canterbury at Kent. ITICSE is a European conference, and it draws participants from all over the world. Teachers in McCracken's group were to conduct the same study in each of their CS1 or CS2 classes: assign the same problem, and give students 90 minutes to complete the assignment on paper. All the student data were submitted and analyzed by the participants at the conference. Four institutions from three countries participated in this first *multi-institutional, multi-national* (MIMN) study of student performance in computing. By comparing students across institutional and country borders, the researchers hoped to get a clear picture of just what students *really* can do in their first courses.

The problem was to evaluate arithmetic expressions (prefix, infix, or postfix) with only numbers, binary operators (+, -, /, *), or unary negation (~ in order to avoid the complication of overloading the minus character). Overall, 216 students submitted answers. The average score on a language-independent grading rubric of 110 points was 22.89 (21%). Students did *horribly* on this problem. One teacher even "cheated" by explicitly lecturing on expression evaluation before the problem was assigned. That class performed no better.

The McCracken Working Group did several evaluations of their data. They found that performance varied dramatically between classes. They also saw evidence of the "two hump effect" that many computing teachers have noted and several papers have tried to explain. Some students just "get it" and perform very well. The larger hump of students performs much worse. Why is it that some students just "get" programming and others don't? Variables ranging from past computing experience to mathematical background have been explored [Bennedsen and Caspersen 2005], and there is still no convincing explanation for this effect.

The Lister Working Group

Some students may not respond to a particular teacher or teaching style, but why did so many students at different institutions do *so* badly? Are we teaching badly *everywhere*? Are we overestimating what the students should be able to do? Or are we not measuring the right things? Raymond Lister organized a second ITICSE Working Group in 2004 to explore some of these questions [Lister et al. 2004].

The Lister group's idea was that the McCracken group asked too much of students. Giving them a problem required a very high level of thinking to design and implement a solution. The Lister group decided to focus instead on the lower-level abilities to read and trace code. They created a multiple-choice questionnaire (MCQ) that asked students to perform tasks such as reading code and identifying outcomes, or identifying the correct code for the empty gaps in a program fragment. The questions focused on array manipulation. They asked their participants from around the world to try the same MCQ with their students, and to bring their results to ITICSE.

The Lister group results were better, but still disappointing. The 556 students had an average score of 60%. Although those results did suggest that the McCracken group overestimated what students could do, Lister and his group expected much better performance on their questions.

The McCracken and Lister efforts taught researchers that it is hard to underestimate how much students understand about programming in their first course. They are clearly learning far less than we realize. Now, *some* students are learning. But the majority are not. What's so hard about programming that most students can't easily pick it up?

What Do People Understand Naturally About Programming?

Linguists generally agree that humans are "wired" for language. Our brains have evolved to pick up language quickly and efficiently. We are wired specifically for *natural* language. Programming is the manipulation of an artificial language invented for a particular, relatively unnatural purpose—telling a nonhuman agent (a computer) *exactly* what to do. Maybe programming is not a natural activity for us, and only a few humans are able to do the complex mental gymnastics to succeed at this unnatural act.

How might we answer this question? We can try an approach similar to Lister's modification to McCracken's approach: choose a smaller part of the task and focus just on that. To program requires telling a machine what to do in an unnatural language. What if we asked study participants to tell another human being to accomplish some task, in natural language? How would participants define their "programs"? If we remove the artificial language, is programming now "natural" or "commonsense"?

L.A. Miller asked participants in his studies to create directions for someone else to perform [Miller 1981]. The participants were given descriptions of various files (such as employees, jobs, and salary information) and tasks like:

> Make one list of employees who meet either of the following criteria:
>
> (1) They have a job title of technician and they make 6 dollars/hr. or more.
>
> (2) They are unmarried and make less than 6 dollars/hr.
>
> List should be organized by employee name.

Miller learned a lot about what was hard and what was easy for his participants. First, his subjects completed their tasks. He doesn't say that 1/3 of all the subjects gave up or failed, as happens all the time in programming classes. The basic challenge of specifying a process for someone else doesn't seem to be the problem.

A key difference between the natural language solutions to Miller's problems and the programming problems studied by earlier researchers is the structure of the solution. Miller's subjects didn't define iterations, but set operations. For instance, they didn't say, "Take each folder and look at the last name. If it starts with 'G'...." Instead, they talked about doing things "for all the last names starting with 'G'...." Miller was surprised at this: no one ever specified the ending conditions for their loops. Some people talked about testable IF-like conditions, but none ever used an ELSE. These results alone point to the possibility of defining a programming language that is *naturally* easier for novices.

Miller ran a separate experiment where he gave other participants the instructions from the first experiment with the vague loops. Nobody had any problem with the instructions. It was obvious that you stopped when you were done with data. Subjects processed the set; they didn't increment an index.

John Pane took up this exploration again in the late 1990s and early 2000s [Pane et al. 2001]. Pane was explicitly interested in creating a programming language that would be closer to how people "naturally" described processes to one another. He replicated Miller's experiments, but with a different task and different input. He was worried that by providing "files" and asking for "lists," Miller may have been leading the witness, so to speak. Instead, Pane showed the subjects images and movies of videogames, then asked them how they would want to tell the computer to make *that* happen, e.g., "Write a statement that summarizes how I (as the computer) should move Pac-Man in relation to the presence or absence of other things."

Pane, like Miller, found that people weren't explicit about their looping. He went further to characterize the kinds of instructions they wrote in terms of programming paradigms. He found lots of use of constraints ("This one is always doing that"), event-driven programming ("When Pac-Man gets all the dots, he goes to the next level"), and imperative programming. Nobody ever talked about *objects* even once. They talked about characteristics and behaviors of entities in the video game, but no groupings of those entities (e.g., into classes). They never talked about the behaviors from the perspective of the entities themselves; everything was from the perspective of the player or the programmer.

Based on Miller and Pane's experiments, we might claim that people may be able to specify tasks to another agent, but that our current programming languages do not allow people to program the way that they think about the tasks. If the programming languages were made more natural, would the majority of student then be able to program? Could people solve complex problems involving significant algorithms in the more natural language? Would a more natural language be good for both novices' tasks and professionals' tasks? And if not, might students of CS still have to deal with learning the professionals' language at some point?

A group of researchers who call themselves the Commonsense Computing Group have been asking some of these questions. They ask pre-CS1 students to solve significant algorithmic tasks, such as sorting or parallelizing a process, in natural language and before they have learned any programming languages. They find their subjects to be surprisingly successful at these tasks.

In one study [Lewandowski et al. 2007], they asked students to create a process for a theater that decides to have two ticket sellers.

> Suppose we sell concert tickets over the telephone in the following way—when a customer calls in and asks for a number (n) of seats, the seller (1) finds the n best seats that are available, (2) marks those n seats as unavailable, and (3) deals with payment options for the customer (e.g., getting a credit or debit card number, or sending the tickets to the Will Call window for pickup).

> Suppose we have more than one seller working at the same time. What problems might we see, and how might we avoid those problems?

Some 66 participants across five institutions attempted to solve this problem—with surprising success! As seen in Table 7-2, almost all the students recognized what the real challenge of the problem was, and 71% came up with a solution that would work. Most of these solutions were inefficient—because they involved a centralized arbiter—so there is still much for these students to learn. However, the point that they could solve a parallel processing problem suggests that the problem of getting students to program may be in the tools. Students may be more capable of computational thinking than we give them credit for.

TABLE 7-2. Number of solutions and problems identified by students (n=66), from [Lewandowski et al. 2007]

Accomplishment	Percent of students
Problems identified:	
• Sell ticket more than once	97%
• Other	41%
Provided "reasonable" solutions to concurrency problems	71%

Making the Tools Better by Shifting to Visual Programming

How do we make the tools better? One obvious possible answer is by moving to a more visual notation. Since David Smith's icon-based programming language *Pygmalion* emerged [Smith 1975], the theory has been that maybe visual reasoning is easier for students. There certainly have been a lot of studies showing that visualizations in general helped students in computing [Naps et al. 2003], but relatively few careful studies.

Then, Thomas Green and Marian Petre did a head-to-head comparison between a dataflow-like programming language and a textual programming language [Green and Petre 1992]. They created programs in two visual languages that had been shown to work well in previous studies and in a textual language that had also tested well. Subjects were shown a visual program or a textual program for a short time, and then asked a question about it (e.g., shown input data or output results). *Understanding the graphical language always took more time.* It didn't matter how much experience the subject had with visual or textual languages, or what kind of visual language. Subjects comprehended visual languages more slowly than textual languages.

Green and Petre published several papers on variations of this study [Green et al. 1991]; [Green and Petre 1996], but the real test came when Tom Moher and his colleagues [Moher et al. 1993] stacked the deck in favor of visual languages. Tom and his graduate students were using a visual notation, Petri Nets, to teach programming to high school students. He got a copy of Green and Petre's materials and created a version where the only visual language used was Petri Nets. Then, Tom reran the study with *himself and his students as subjects*. The surprising result was that textual languages were more easily comprehended again, under every condition.

Are we wrong about our intuition about visual languages? Does visualization actually reduce one's understanding of software? What about those studies that Naps et al. were talking about [Naps et al. 2003]? Were they wrong?

There is a standard method for comparing multiple studies, called a *meta-study*. Barbara Kitchenham describes this procedure in Chapter 3 of this book. Chris Hundhausen, Sarah Douglas, and John Stasko did this type of analysis on studies of algorithm visualizations [Hundhausen et al. 2002]. They found that yes, there are a lot of studies showing significant benefits for algorithm visualizations for students. There are a lot of studies with nonsignificant results. Some studies had significant results but didn't make it obvious *how* algorithmic visualizations might be helping (Figure 7-1). Hundhausen and colleagues found that *how* the visualizations were used matters a *lot*. For example, using visualizations in lecture demonstration had little impact on student learning. But having students build their own visualizations had significant impact on those students' learning.

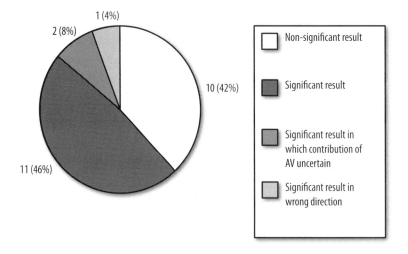

FIGURE 7-1. Summary of 24 studies in Hundhausen, Douglas, and Stasko paper [Hundhausen et al. 2002]

A few studies varied the use of visualization while holding all other variables constant (e.g., type of class, type of student, teacher, subject). Although Hundhausen and colleagues suspect the way visualization is used is important after their analysis of 24 studies, that result is not the same as *testing* the suspicion. One thing we have learned from studies in education is that it is actually quite difficult to predict the outcomes. Humans are not as predictable as a falling projectile or chemical cocktails. We actually have to test our suspicions and hypotheses, and sometimes test them repeatedly under different conditions, until we are convinced about some finding.

Contextualizing for Motivation

What we know thus far is that beginning computing students learn far less about design and programming than we might predict, and they fail their first course at a pretty high rate. We find that changing from textual to visual modalities does not consistently result in better results, which suggests that another variable may be at play. The previous section explored the possibility that differences in how visualizations are used may be one such variable. What other variables might we manipulate in order to improve student success and learning?

In 1999, Georgia Tech decided to require introductory computing of all undergraduate students. For the first few years of this requirement, only one course satisfied this requirement. Overall, the pass rate in this course was 78%, which is quite good by Bennedsen and Caspersen's analysis [Bennedsen and Caspersen 2007]. However, that number wasn't so good when we start disaggregating it. The pass rate for students from the Liberal Arts, Architecture, and Management colleges was less than 50% [Tew et al. 2005a]. Women failed at *nearly twice* the rate of men. A course aimed at *all* students, but at which mostly males in technical majors pass, highlights general problems in teaching computing.

In 2003, we started an experiment to teach students in those classes a different kind of introductory course, one *contextualized* around manipulating media [Forte and Guzdial 2004]. Students worked on essentially the same kinds of programming as in any other introductory computer science course. In fact, we worked hard to cover all the topics [Guzdial 2003] that were recommended by the then-current ACM and IEEE Computing Standards [IEEE-CS/ACM 2001]. However, all the textbook examples, sample code in lectures, and homework assignments had students manipulating digital media as the data in these programs. Students learned how to iterate through the elements of an array, for instance, by converting all the pixels in a picture to grayscale. Instead of concatenating strings, they concatenated sound buffers to do digital splicing. Iteration through a subrange of an array is introduced by removing red-eye from a picture without messing up any other red in the picture.

The response was positive and dramatic. Students found the new course more relevant and compelling, particularly women, whose pass rate rose above men's (but not with any statistical significance) [Rich et al. 2004]. The average pass rate over the next three years rose to 85%, and that applies even to those majors who were passing at less than 50% per semester before [Tew et al. 2005a].

Sounds like a big success, but what do these papers really say? Do we know that the new approach is the *only* thing that changed? Maybe those colleges suddenly started accepting much smarter students. Maybe Georgia Tech hired a new, charismatic instructor who charmed the students into caring about the content. Social science researchers refer to these factors that keep us from claiming what we might *want* to claim from a study *threats to validity.** We can state, in defense of the value of our change, that the [Tew et al. 2005a] paper included semesters with different instructors, and the results covered three years' worth of results, so it's unlikely that the students were suddenly much different.

Even if we felt confident concluding that Georgia Tech's success was the result of introducing Media Computation, and that all other factors with respect to students and teaching remained the same, we should wonder what we can claim. Georgia Tech is a pretty good school. Smart students go there. They hire and retain good teachers. Could *your* school get better success in introductory computing by introducing Media Computation?

---

* *http://www.creative-wisdom.com/teaching/WBI/threat.shtml*

The first trial of Media Computation at a different kind of school was by Charles Fowler at Gainesville State College in Georgia. Gainesville State College is a two-year (not undergraduate and post-graduate) public college. The results were reported in the same [Tew et al. 2005a] paper. Fowler also found dramatically improved success rates among his students. Fowler's students ranged from computer science to nursing students. However, both the Georgia Tech and Gainesville students were predominantly white. Would this approach work with minority students?

At the University of Illinois-Chicago (UIC), Pat Troy and Bob Sloan introduced Media Computation into their "CS 0.5" class [Sloan and Troy 2008]. Their class was for students who wanted to major in computer science but had no background in programming. A CS 0.5 class is meant to get them ready for the first ("CS1") course. Over multiple semesters, these students' pass rate also rose. UIC has a much more ethnically diverse student population, where a majority of their students belong to minority ethnic groups.

Are you now convinced that you should use Media Computation with your students? You might argue that these are still unusual cases. The studies at Georgia Tech and Gainesville were with nonmajors (as well as majors at Gainesville). Although Troy and Sloan are dealing with students who want to major in computer science, their class is not the normal introductory computer science course for undergraduate majors.

Beth Simon and her colleagues at the University of California at San Diego (UCSD) started using Media Computation two years ago as the main introductory course ("CS1") for CS majors [Simon et al. 2010]. More students pass with the new course. What's more, the Media Computation students are doing better in the *second* course, the one after Media Computation, than the students who had the traditional CS1.

Is that it? Is Media Computation a slam dunk? Should *everyone* use Media Computation? Although my publisher would like you to believe that [Guzdial and Ericson 2009a]; [Guzdial and Ericson 2009b], the research does not unambiguously bear it out.

First, I haven't claimed that students learn the same amount with Media Computation. If anyone tells you that students learn the same amount with their approach compared to another, be very skeptical, because we currently do not have reliable and valid measures of introductory computing learning to make that claim. Allison Tew (also in [Tew et al. 2005a]) first tried to answer the question of whether students learn the same in different CS1s in 2005 [Tew et al. 2005b]. She developed two multiple-choice question tests in each of the CS1 languages she wanted to compare. She meant them to be *isomorphic*: a problem meant to evaluate a particular concept (say, iteration over an array) would be essentially the same across both tests and all languages. She used these tests before and after a second CS course (CS2) in order to measure how much difference there was in student learning between the different CS1s. Tew found that students *did* learn different things in their CS1 class (as measured by the start-of-CS2 test), but that those differences disappeared by the end of CS2. That's a great finding, suggesting that the differences in CS1 weren't all that critical to future success. But in future trials, she never found the same result.

How could that be? One real possibility is that her tests *weren't* exactly the same. Students might interpret them differently. They might not measure exactly the kind of learning that she aimed to test. For instance, maybe the answer to some of the multiple-choice questions could be guessed because the distractors (wrong answers) were so far from being feasible that students could dismiss them without really knowing the right answer. A good test for measuring learning should be *reliable* and *valid*—in other words, it measures the right thing, and it's interpreted the same way by all students all the time.

As of this writing we have no measure of CS1 learning that is language-independent, reliable, and valid. Tew is testing one now. But until one exists, it is not possible to determine for sure that students are learning the same things in different approaches. It's great that students succeed more in Media Computation, and it's great that UCSD students do better even in the second course, but we really can't say for sure that students learn the same things.

Second, even if Georgia Tech, Gainesville, UIC, and UCSD were all able to show that students learned the same amount in the introductory course, what would all that prove? That the course will work for *everyone*? That it will be better than the "traditional" course, no matter how marvelous or successful the "traditional" course is? For every kind of student, no matter how ill-prepared or uninterested? No matter how bad the teacher is? That's ridiculous, of course. We can always imagine something that could go wrong.

In general, curricular approaches offer us *prescriptive* models, but not *predictive* theories. Media Computation studies show us evidence that, for a variety of students and teachers, the success rate for the introductory course *can* be improved, but not that it inevitably *will* improve. Being able to promise improvement would be a prescription. It is not a predictive theory in the sense that it can predict improvement, not without knowing many more variables that have not yet been tested with studies. It also can't be predictive because we can't say that *not* using Media Computation *guarantees* failure.

Conclusion: A Fledgling Field

Computing Education Research, as a field of study, is still a fledgling discipline [Fincher and Petre 2004]. We are just recently realizing the importance of computing education and the need to support the teaching of computing. The ACM organization that supports computing teachers, Computer Science Teachers Association (CSTA), was formed only in 2005. In contrast, the National Council of Teachers of Mathematics was formed in 1920.

Most of our studies point more toward how complex it is for humans to learn how to program a computer. We continue to marvel at the intelligence and creativity of humans, and that even students without training in computing can already think in algorithmic terms. However, developing that skill to the point that it can be used to give directions to a machine in the machine's language occurs more slowly than we might expect. We can get students through the process, but we still don't have effective measures of how much they're learning.

What we really need as a field are predictive theories, based on models of how people really come to develop their understanding of computing. On those theories, we can build curricula in which we can have confidence. ACM's International Computing Education Research workshop is only five years old this year, and the number of attendees has never topped 100. We have few workers, and they have only just started at a difficult task. We have taken only the first steps toward understanding why it is that students find it so hard to learn to program.

References

[Bennedsen and Caspersen 2005] Bennedsen, J., and M.E. Caspersen. 2005. An investigation of potential success factors for an introductory model-driven programming course. *Proceedings of the first international workshop on computing education research*: 155–163.

[Bennedsen and Caspersen 2007] Bennedsen, J., and M.E. Caspersen. 2007. Failure rates in introductory programming. *SIGCSE Bull.* 39(2): 32–36.

[Computing Community 2010] Computing Community Consortium. 2010. Where the jobs are.... *http://www.cccblog.org/2010/01/04/where-the-jobs-are/*.

[Computing Research 2008] Computing Research Association. 2008. BLS predicts strong job growth and high salaries for IT workforce. Retrieved May 2010 from *http://www.cra.org/resources/crn-archive-view-detail/bls_predicts_strong_job_growth_and_high_salaries_for_it_workforce_through_2/*.

[Fincher and Petre 2004] Fincher, S., and M. Petre. 2004. *Computer Science Education Research*. New York: RoutledgeFalmer.

[Forte and Guzdial 2004] Forte, A., and M. Guzdial. 2004. Computers for Communication, Not Calculation: Media As a Motivation and Context for Learning. *Proceedings of the 37th Annual Hawaii International Conference on System Sciences (HICSS'04)* 4: 40096.1.

[Green and Petre 1992] Green, T.R.G., and M. Petre. 1992. When visual programs are harder to read than textual programs. In *Human-Computer Interaction: Tasks and Organisation, Proceedings EECE-6 (6th European Conference on Cognitive Ergonomics)*, ed. G.C.v.d. Veer, M.J. Tauber, S. Bagnarola, and M. Antavolits, 167–180. Rome: CUD.

[Green and Petre 1996] Green, T.R.G., and M. Petre. 1996. Usability analysis of visual programming environments: A "cognitive dimensions" framework. *Journal of Visual Languages and Computing* 7(2): 131–174.

[Green et al. 1991] Green, T.R.G., M. Petre, et al. 1991. Comprehensibility of visual and textual programs: A test of "superlativism" against the "match-mismatch" conjecture. In *Empirical Studies of Programmers: Fourth Workshop*, ed. J. Koenemann-Belliveau, T. Moher, and S. Robertson, 121–146. Norwood, NJ, Ablex.

[Guzdial 2003] Guzdial, M. 2003. A media computation course for non-majors. *ACM SIGCSE Bulletin* 35(3): 104–108.

[Guzdial and Ericson 2009a] Guzdial, M., and B. Ericson. 2009. *Introduction to Computing and Programming in Python: A Multimedia Approach*, Second Edition. Upper Saddle River, NJ: Pearson Prentice Hall.

[Guzdial and Ericson 2009b] Guzdial, M., and B. Ericson. 2009. *Problem Solving with Data Structures Using Java: A Multimedia Approach*. Upper Saddle River, NJ: Pearson Prentice Hall

[Hundhausen et al. 2002] Hundhausen, C.D., S.H. Douglas, et al. 2002. A meta-study of algorithm visualization effectiveness. *Journal of Visual Languages and Computing* 13: 259–290.

[IEEE-CS/ACM 2001] IEEE Computer Society and Association for Computing Machinery, The Joint Task Force on Computing Curricula. 2001. Computing curricula 2001. *Journal of Educational Resources in Computing.* 1(3): 1.

[Johnson and Soloway 1987] Johnson, W.L., and E. Soloway. 1987. PROUST: An automatic debugger for Pascal programs. In *Artificial intelligence and instruction: Applications and methods*, ed. G. Kearsley, 49–67. Boston: Addison-Wesley Longman Publishing Co., Inc.

[Lewandowski et al. 2007] Lewandowski, G., D.J. Bouvier, et al. 2007. Commonsense computing (episode 3): Concurrency and concert tickets. *Proceedings of the third international workshop on computing education research*: 133–144.

[Lister et al. 2004] Lister, R., E.S. Adams, et al. 2004. A multi-national study of reading and tracing skills in novice programmers. *Working group reports from ITiCSE on Innovation and technology in computer science education*: 119–150.

[McCracken et al. 2001] McCracken, M., V. Almstrum, et al. 2001. A multi-national, multi-institutional study of assessment of programming skills of first-year CS students. *SIGCSE Bulletin.* 33(4): 125–180.

[Miller 1981] Miller, L.A. 1981. Natural language programming: Styles, strategies, and contrasts. *IBM Systems Journal* 29(2): 184–215.

[Moher et al. 1993] Moher, T.G., D.C. Mak, et al. 1993. Comparing the comprehensibility of textual and graphical programs: the case of Petri nets. In *Empirical Studies of Programmers: Fifth Workshop*, ed. C.R. Cook, J.C. Scholtz, and J.C. Spohrer, 137–161. Norwood, NJ, Ablex.

[Naps et al. 2003] Naps, T., S. Cooper, et al. 2003. Evaluating the educational impact of visualization. *Working group reports from ITiCSE on innovation and technology in computer science education*: 124–136.

[Pane et al. 2001] Pane, J.F., B.A. Myers, et al. 2001. Studying the language and structure in non-programmers' solutions to programming problems. *International Journal of Human-Computer Studies.* 54(2): 237–264.

[Rampell 2010] Rampell, Catherine. "Once a Dynamo, the Tech Sector Is Slow to Hire." *The New York Times*, Sept. 7, 2010.

[Rich et al. 2004] Rich, L., H. Perry, et al. 2004. A CS1 course designed to address interests of women. *Proceedings of the 35th SIGCSE technical symposium on computer science education*: 190–194.

[Simon et al. 2010] Simon, B., P. Kinnunen, et al. 2010. Experience Report: CS1 for Majors with Media Computation. Paper presented at ACM Innovation and Technology in Computer Science Education Conference, June 26–30, in Ankara, Turkey.

[Sloan and Troy 2008] Sloan, R.H., and P. Troy. 2008. CS 0.5: A better approach to introductory computer science for majors. *Proceedings of the 39th SIGCSE technical symposium on computer science education*: 271–275.

[Smith 1975] Smith, D.C. 1975. PYGMALION: A creative programming environment. Computer Science PhD diss., Stanford University.

[Soloway et al. 1983] Soloway, E., J. Bonar, et al. 1983. Cognitive strategies and looping constructs: An empirical study. *Communications of the ACM* 26(11): 853–860.

[Spohrer 1992] Spohrer, J.C. 1992. *Marcel: Simulating the novice programmer*. Norwood, NJ: Ablex.

[Tew et al. 2005a] Tew, A.E., C. Fowler, et al. 2005. Tracking an innovation in introductory CS education from a research university to a two-year college. *Proceedings of the 36th SIGCSE technical symposium on computer science education*: 416–420.

[Tew et al. 2005b] Tew, A.E., W.M. McCracken, et al. 2005. Impact of alternative introductory courses on programming concept understanding. *Proceedings of the first international workshop on computing education research*: 25–35.

## CHAPTER EIGHT

Beyond Lines of Code: Do We Need More Complexity Metrics?

Israel Herraiz
Ahmed E. Hassan

Complexity is everywhere in the software life cycle: requirements, analysis, design, and of course, implementation. Complexity is usually an undesired property of software because complexity makes software harder to read and understand, and therefore harder to change; also, it is believed to be one cause of the presence of defects. Of all the artifacts produced in a software project, source code is the easiest option to measure complexity. However, several decades of software research have failed to produce a consensus about what metrics best reflect the complexity of a given piece of code. It's hard even to compare two pieces of code written in different programming languages and say which code is more complex. Because of this lack of resolution, a myriad of possible metrics are currently offered to measure the complexity of a program. What does the research say are the best metrics for each particular case? Are all these metrics any better than very simple source code metrics, such as lines of code?

In this chapter, we take advantage of the huge amount of open source software available to study the relationships between different size and complexity metrics. To avoid suffocating in the myriads of attributes and metrics, we focus only on one programming language: C, a "classic" in software development that remains one of the most popular programming languages. We measure a grab-bag of metrics ranging from the simplest and most commonly cited (lines of code) to some rather sophisticated syntactic metrics for a set of about 300,000 files. From this we have found out which metrics are independent from a statistical point of view—that is to say, whether traditional complexity metrics actually provided more information than the simple lines-of-code approach.

Surveying Software

The first step in this study was to select a representative sample of software, just like surveys in the social sciences. From a known population, statistical methods allow us to obtain the minimum sample size that lets us extract conclusions with a given uncertainty. For instance, the U.S. population is about 300 million people at the moment of writing this text; exit polls can accurately predict the results of elections if the size of the polled sample is large enough, say, 30,000 people.

The problem with this approach when carried over to software engineering is that we do not know the size of the world's software. So we cannot determine a minimum sample that can answer our questions with a given uncertainty, and the classic "survey approach" to the whole population of software becomes unfeasible.

However, even though the whole population of software is indeterminable, a portion of that population is open, accessible for research, and willing to share its source code with the world: open source software. Of course, restricting our population to this kind of software should theoretically bind the answer to our initial question to this kind of software. But when all is said and done, the only difference between open source and closed source software is the license. Although open source software is usually developed using particular practices (projects that are community-driven, source code available, etc.), the open source software population is very heterogeneous, ranging from projects that are completely community-driven to projects that remain under the close control of companies. The only feature held in common by open source software is the set of licenses under which it is released, making its source code publicly available. Therefore, we can assume that the best complexity metrics for source code obtained from open source projects are also the best complexity metrics for any other source code, whether open source or not.

Open source software also presents some other interesting properties for research. Open source software repositories are usually completely available to researchers. Software repositories contain all the artifacts produced by the software project—source code releases, control version systems, issue tracking systems, mailing lists archives, etc.—and often all the previous versions of those artifacts. All that information is available for anyone interested in studying it. Thus, open source not only offers a huge amount of code, allowing us to study samples as large as we might want, but also makes possible repeatable and verifiable studies, which are fundamental and minimal requirements to ensure that the conclusions of empirical studies can be trusted.

There are some perils and pitfalls when using open source software, though. It is hard to obtain data for a large sample of open source software projects because of the heterogeneity in the data sources. Not all projects use the same tools for the different repositories, or even the same kind of repositories, and often those repositories are dispersed across different sites. Some efforts, such as the FLOSSMetrics (*http://flossmetrics.org*) and FLOSSMole (*http://flossmole.org*) projects, deliver databases containing metrics and facts about open source projects, which alleviate the heterogeneity of data when mining open source software repositories. And this problem is partially solved by the open source software community itself in the form of software distributions, such as the well-known Ubuntu and Debian distributions. Distributions gather source code from open source projects, adapt it to the rest of the distribution, and make it available as compiled binary and source code packages. These packages are tagged with meta-information that helps classify them and retrieve the different dependencies needed to install them. Some of these distributions are huge, encompassing thousands of packages and million of lines of source code. So they are ideal for any study that needs to gather a large amount of source code, like the one in this chapter.

Measuring the Source Code

We have selected for our case study the ArchLinux software distribution (*http://archlinux.org*), which contains thousands of packages, all open source. ArchLinux is a lightweight GNU/Linux distribution whose maintainers refuse to modify the source code packaged for the distribution, in order to meet the goal of drastically reducing the time that elapses between the official release of a package and its integration into the distribution. There are two ways to install a package in ArchLinux: using the official precompiled packages, or installing from source code using the Arch Build System (ABS).

ABS makes it possible to retrieve the original, pristine source code of all the packages. This is different from other distributions, which make copies of the source code of the packages and often patch it to adapt it to the rest of the distribution. With ABS, we can gather source code from its original location, at the upstream projects' websites and repositories, in an automatic fashion. This ensures that the source code has not been modified, and therefore that the case studies in our sample are independent. As we will show later in the results section, this property of independence is crucial for the validity of the results.

Because of the size of ArchLinux, using it as a case study gives us access to the original source code of thousands of open source projects, through the build scripts used by ABS (see Example 8-1).

EXAMPLE 8-1. Header of a sample build script in ArchLinux

```
pkgname=ppl
pkgver=0.10.2 ❶
pkgrel=2 ❷
pkgdesc="A modern library for convex polyhedra and other numerical abstractions."
arch=('i686' 'x86_64')
url="http://www.cs.unipr.it/ppl"
license=('GPL3')
depends=('gmp>=4.1.3')
options=('!docs' '!libtool')
source=(http://www.cs.unipr.it/ppl/Download/ftp/releases/$pkgver/ppl-$pkgver.tar.gz) ❸
md5sums=('e7dd265afdeaea81f7e87a72b182d875') ❹
```

❶ Version of the package. Used to build the download URL.

❷ Minor release version number. Also used to build the download URL.

❸ Source code download URL.

❹ Checksum of the source tarball.

Example 8-1 shows the header of sample build script in ABS. The header contains meta-information that is used to gather the sources, retrieve other dependencies from the package archives, and classify the package in the archives once it is built. We have used the fields highlighted in Example 8-1 to retrieve the source code of all the packages in the ArchLinux archives.

For all the source code gathered, we determined the programming language of every file using the *SlocCount* tool (*http://www.dwheeler.com/sloccount*). Using only C language code for our sample, we measured several size and complexity metrics using the Libresoft tools' *cmetrics* package (*http://tools.libresoft.es/cmetrics*).

A Sample Measurement

Table 8-1 contains a summary of all the metrics used in this study, and the symbols denoting these metrics in the rest of the tables and figures.

TABLE 8-1. Selected metrics for the study

Variable	Metric (symbol)
Size	Source Lines of Code (SLOC), Lines of Code (LOC)
	Number of C functions (FUNC)
Complexity	McCabe's cyclomatic complexity—maximum of all functions (MCYCLO)
	McCabe's cyclomatic complexity—average (ACYCLO)
	Halstead's length (HLENG), volume (HVOLUM), level (HLEVE), and mental discriminations (HMD)

The elements of code that provide input to all these metrics are illustrated in the sample source code file shown in Example 8-2. This file was extracted from the package urlgfe, a cross-platform download manager. (urlgfe has recently changed its name to uget, so it is no longer found in the ArchLinux repositories with its original name.) The file contains preprocessor directives (such as ❶), comments (such as ❸), and only one function (starting at line ❹) containing a while loop.

EXAMPLE 8-2. A sample C source code file

```
#ifdef HAVE_CONFIG_H ❶
# include <config.h>
#endif
❷
/* Specification.  */ ❸
#include "hash-string.h"


/* Defines the so called `hashpjw' function by P.J. Weinberger
   [see Aho/Sethi/Ullman, COMPILERS: Principles, Techniques and Tools,
   1986, 1987 Bell Telephone Laboratories, Inc.]  */
unsigned long int ❹
_hash_string (const char *str_param)
{
  unsigned long int hval, g;
  const char *str = str_param;

  /* Compute the hash value for the given string.  */
  hval = 0;
  while (*str != '\0')
    {
      hval <<= 4;
      hval += (unsigned char) *str++;
      g = hval & ((unsigned long int) 0xf << (HASHWORDBITS - 4));
      if (g != 0)
        {
          hval ^= g >> (HASHWORDBITS - 8);
      hval ^= g;
        }
    }
  return hval;
}
```

❶ Preprocessor directives, counted both for LOC and SLOC.

❷ Blank lines. Counted for LOC but not for SLOC.

❸ Comment lines. Counted for LOC but not for SLOC.

❹ Code, counted both for LOC and SLOC.

The simplest complexity metrics that we can measure are the ones related to lines of code (total lines of code and source lines of code). The number of functions also can be extracted easily from the source code. The rest of the complexity metrics that we measured are slightly more sophisticated: McCabe's cyclomatic complexity and the set of Halstead's Software Science metrics.

Except for McCabe's cyclomatic complexity, all the metrics are defined at the file level. So we measured all of them for all the C files (as identified by *SlocCount*), ignoring header files, which we identified by filename (all files ending in *.h*).

Because of the definition of McCabe's cyclomatic complexity, it must be measured over complete functions or programs because it is defined for entities that have one starting point and one or more exit points. We decided to run the formula over each function and to summarize the cyclomatic complexity of a whole file using two values: the maximum of all the functions included in the file and the average value over all the functions in the file.

Additionally, we also calculated the MD5 hash for every file, so we could discard repeated files from the statistical analysis, as including the same file more than once would introduce a bias in the results.

Source Lines of Code (SLOC)

For this classic measure, we use the definition given by Conte [Conte 1986]:

> A line of code is any line of program text that is not a comment or blank line, regardless of the number of statements or fragments of statements on the line. This specifically includes all lines containing program headers, declarations, and executable and non-executable statements.

In the case of our sample file in Example 8-2, when we ignore blanks and comments but include preprocessor directives and all the rest of the lines, the file contains 23 SLOC.

Lines of Code (LOC)

For this we measured the total number of lines in each source code file, including comments, blank lines, etc., using the Unix *wc* utility.

This is straightforward to measure because it counts blanks, comments, etc. Example 8-2 contains 32 LOC (plus 18 LOC of the license comment text, which was removed for clarity purposes).

Number of C Functions

We counted the number of functions inside each file using the *exuberant-ctags* tool combined with *wc*.

This metric is even easier to measure. Example 8-2 contains only one function, so CFUNC is 1 for this file.

McCabe's Cyclomatic Complexity

We use the definition given in the original paper by McCabe [McCabe 1976], which indicates the number of regions in a graph representing a source code file. Any program can be represented as a graph. The simplest element is a *flat* series of statements with no conditions, loops, or branches, which is represented by graph (a) in Figure 8-1. An if statement is a bifurcation, as shown in graph (b) in Figure 8-1. A loop would be shown through an edge that returns back to an earlier node.

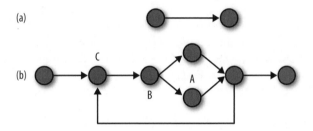

FIGURE 8-1. Two sample graphs. Graph (a) has a CYCLO of 1, and graph (b) has a CYCLO of 3.

For a graph G with n vertices, e edges, and p exit points (e.g., function returns in the case of C), the complexity v is defined as follows:

$$v(G) = e - n + 2p$$

The minimum value for the cyclomatic complexity metric (CYCLO) is 1, corresponding to the flat series of statements with no bifurcations or loops. Every additional region in the control flow graph increases the CYCLO by one unit. For instance, a program that contains an if statement (with no else) has a CYCLO of 2, because it creates a new region in the control flow graph, in addition to the surrounding region.

The program shown in Example 8-2, whose control flow graph is shown in the (b) graph of Figure 8-1, has a CYCLO of 3. The if bifurcation creates one new region (A in Figure 8-1), and the while loop creates another (B in Figure 8-1). Finally, C is the surrounding region, which always counts as 1 in the cyclomatic complexity.

Halstead's Software Science Metrics

For this we use the definition given by Kan [Kan 2003]. We measured four metrics: length, volume, level, and mental discriminations. These metrics are based on the redundancy of *operands* and *operators* in a program.

In the C language, operands are string constants and variable names. Operators are symbols (such as +, -, ++, and --), the * indirection operator, the sizeof operator, preprocessor constants, control flow statements (such as if and while), storage class specifiers (such as static and extern), type specifiers (such as int and char), and structure specifiers (struct and union).

The metrics are obtained by counting the number of distinct operators n_1, the number of distinct operands n_2, along with the total number of operators N_1, and the total number of operands N_2. The length L of a program is the total number of operators and operands:

$$L = N_1 + N_2$$

The volume V of a program is its physical size, defined as:

$$V = N \cdot log_2(n_1 + n_2)$$

The level lv of a program is a parameter with an upper limit of 1; the closer it is to 1, the less complex is the program. The level is defined as the ratio between the volume of the program and its potential volume (the least redundant implementation of the algorithm):

$$lv = \frac{2}{n_1} \frac{n_2}{N_2}$$

The inverse of this metric is sometimes called the code's *difficulty*. The minimum *difficulty* is 1, and it increases without an upper bound.

The effort E that a programmer needs to invest to comprehend a program is defined as:

$$E = \frac{V}{lv}$$

This metric is sometimes called the *number of mental discriminations* that a developer must do to understand a program.

Halstead obtained all these formulas by making an analogy between programming and natural languages. The main idea is that the implementation of an algorithm is an expression written in a language, and this expression will be easier to understand if it is shorter or contains more redundancy of operators and operands because the number of different concepts that a programmer must retain in memory at once will be smaller. For instance, Halstead's level is related to the redundancy of operands. If the redundancy is very high, with lots of repeated operands, the Halstead value will be lower, indicating a less complex program. This approach makes intuitive sense, because redundancy should help one learn and understand a program more quickly.

Halstead's Software Science metrics are similar to McCabe's cyclomatic complexity, being defined over whole, non-modular programs, without imports. But contrary to McCabe's metric, Halstead's metrics do not rely on the structure of the code to measure complexity. This is to say, Halstead's metrics are defined purely for the textual elements making up a program, not for any kind of semantic unit such as functions, and so we apply Halstead's metrics to whole files.

The sample file shown in Example 8-2 has a Halstead's length of 97, which represents the total number of operators (string constants and variable names) and operands (symbols, statements, etc.). The Halstead's volume is 526, and the Halstead's level is 0.036. The number of mental discriminations is 14,490, the quotient between the volume and level. All those metrics indicate a greater complexity for higher values, except in the case of Halstead's level, where a lower value indicates a more complex program.

Statistical Analysis

The ArchLinux repositories contained 4,069 packages (as of April 2010), with some of the packages being different versions of the same upstream project. After removing different versions, we obtained a sample of 4,015 packages, containing 1,272,748 source code files. Among all those files, 576,511 were written in C. However, there were repeated files. In the overall sample, only 776,573 were unique files; in the C subsample, only 338,831 were unique files. From these unique C files, 212,167 were nonheader files and 126,664 were header files.

The same measurements shown in the previous section for the file included in Example 8-2 were repeated in our study for all the files written in C. Thus, we ended up with a set of more than 300,000 measurements. Each element of the set contained a tuple for each file containing the metrics (nine values in each tuple).

Overall Analysis

The basic analysis on the sample correlated each of the nine metrics defined at the file level with the rest of the metrics. The goal is to extract a set of orthogonal metrics that can characterize software size and complexity. Our goal was to discover, from all the metrics we gathered, which ones do not provide any further information and therefore can be discarded.

For the analysis, we considered each file of the sample as an independent point, which is a fair assumption because we discarded all the repeated files, and because all files came from projects that can be considered independent. For the correlation, we decided to use the logarithm of the value of the metrics. The logarithm was chosen after calculating the ideal Box-Cox power transformation of the data. With the logarithms of all the metrics, we performed a linear regression and calculated the Pearson correlation coefficient. Pearson coefficients close to 1 correspond to highly correlated variables; if they are closer to 0, they indicate independent variables.[*]

---

[*] Wikipedia contains detailed information about correlation analysis and the Box-Cox power transformation: see *http://en.wikipedia.org/wiki/Correlation_coefficient* and *http://en.wikipedia.org/wiki/Box -Cox_transformation* (consulted as of April 3, 2010).

Table 8-2 shows the Pearson correlation coefficient among the logarithms of all the metrics. This matrix is symmetrical; that is to say, values above and below the diagonal are the same, because the correlation coefficient between two variables is the same, regardless of which variable depends on the other one. So we have removed half of the values from Table 8-2 for clarity's sake. For most of the metrics, the coefficients are very high, indicating a strong correlation between the pair of metrics. We have highlighted the higher correlation coefficients of LOC and SLOC with the rest of metrics; those values show that most of the complexity metrics are correlated with these two simple size metrics. A high correlation means that either of the metrics provides as much information about complexity as the other metric. For instance, Halstead's length and SLOC are correlated with a coefficient of 0.97, so it doesn't matter which one we use to determine a file's complexity.

TABLE 8-2. Correlation coefficients among all the metrics

	SLOC	LOC	NFUNC	MCYCLO	ACYCLO	HLENG	HVOLU	HLEVE	HMD
SLOC	1.00	**0.97**	0.68	**0.77**	0.63	**0.97**	**0.97**	0.88	**0.96**
LOC		1.00	0.67	**0.75**	0.60	**0.94**	**0.94**	0.84	**0.92**
NFUNC			1.00	0.63	0.32	0.64	0.63	0.67	0.66
MCYCLO				1.00	0.91	0.76	0.75	0.82	0.80
ACYCLO					1.00	0.63	0.62	0.72	0.68
HLENG						1.00	0.99	0.90	0.99
HVOLU							1.00	0.90	0.98
HLEVE								1.00	0.96
HMD									1.00

Some of the complexity metrics are not very well correlated. For instance, both the maximum McCabe's complexity (MCYCLO in Table 8-2) and the average McCabe's complexity (ACYCLO) are poorly correlated with SLOC and LOC. Can we find a reason for this?

MCYCLO and ACYCLO are related to the structure of the code: the more bifurcations and loops, the higher their values will be. This produces a possible source of inconsistencies between McCabe's metrics and lines of code: the difference between header and nonheader files.

Our analysis studied both sets of files. In C, header files include mostly specifications about the different functions and entities. But they may also contain conditional preprocessor directives, which are resolved at compilation time, not at runtime. Although conditional preprocessor directives are bifurcations of a sort, our tools do not consider them to be new regions in the control flow graph of the program. Therefore, header files will probably be quite flat in terms of McCabe's cyclomatic complexity, regardless of their size in lines of code. Consequently, to find out whether there is indeed a correlation between size and cyclomatic complexity, we should remove header files from the sample.

Differences Between Header and Nonheader Files

If we divide the sample into two subsamples, one corresponding to header files and the other one to nonheader files, the values of the correlation coefficients change.

We include here only a subset of the metrics. The rest of the metrics presented very high correlation coefficients both in the original overall analysis and in the two subsamples. So, for more clarity, we have removed those metrics from the results tables.

Table 8-3 shows the results for header files. We have highlighted two correlation coefficients, showing the low dependence between cyclomatic complexity and SLOC for header files. The other complexity metric, Halstead's level (HLEVE in the table), is highly correlated with SLOC. This result is expected because header files are flat, regardless of their size. Therefore, the cyclomatic complexity of these files will always be low, and the correlation with size will be poor. For instance, for the maximum cyclomatic complexity (MCYCLO), the mean value over all the files is 2, and the median is 1, indicating that most of the files have a MCYCLO of 2 or less. However, the independence between size and cyclomatic complexity does not indicate that we can use the cyclomatic complexity of a header file to measure its complexity. Moreover, interestingly, all other complexity metrics are highly correlated with size.

TABLE 8-3. Correlation coefficients for header files

	SLOC	MCYCLO	ACYCLO	HLEVE
SLOC	1.00	**0.37**	**0.34**	0.72
MCYCLO		1.00	0.97	0.49
ACYCLO			1.00	0.46
HLEVE				1.00

The results for nonheader files are shown in Table 8-4. In this case, all correlation coefficients are high. The only metric that is not so highly correlated with size is ACYCLO, the average cyclomatic complexity. However, it is highly correlated with the maximum cyclomatic complexity, MCYCLO, which is highly correlated with size itself. Halstead's level (HLEVE) is also highly correlated with size for nonheader files.

TABLE 8-4. Correlation coefficients for nonheader files

	SLOC	MCYCLO	ACYCLO	HLEVE
SLOC	1.00	0.83	0.60	0.91
MCYCLO		1.00	0.86	0.82
ACYCLO			1.00	0.65
HLEVE				1.00

What results, then, can we draw from the high correlations between metrics in our study? Are lines of code just as good as the fancy metrics defined by McCabe and Halstead? Let's look at some of the literature on software metrics before jumping to conclusions.

The Confounding Effect: Influence of File Size in the Intensity of Correlation

The empirical validation of metrics with samples of source code is a popular topic in the research community. Most of these studies are similar to the one presented in this chapter. El Emam et al. [El Emam et al. 2001] includes a detailed review of many of these validation works, and raises a concern about the validity of this kind of statistical study. In particular, the authors show how class size threatens the validity of object-oriented metrics for fault prediction; when repeating the same validation studies and controlling for size, some of the conclusions do not hold.

Although the methodology cannot be directly applied to this case, because we are dealing with files and not classes, and the rationale behind the metrics is also different, we should consider the risk that our metrics are affected by file size. To test for this confounding effect, we broke down all the results shown here by file size, to test how the correlation was affected by the size of files, and find out whether some of the conclusions could not be validated for all the size ranges.

Effects of size on correlations for header files

One of the results previously shown is that McCabe's cyclomatic complexity is very poorly correlated with size, and we suggested that this metric should not be used with header files, because of their ambiguous relationship to bifurcation. Figure 8-2 shows the variation of the value of the correlation coefficient of cyclomatic complexity (vertical axis) versus SLOC (horizontal axis) when file size changes. It was obtained by dividing the files into 20 intervals, each one containing the same amount of files, and calculating the correlation coefficient using only those files. The horizontal axis is in logarithmic scale because of the wide range of file sizes. There are two curves, one corresponding to the maximum cyclomatic complexity of the file (MCYCLO) and the other to the average cyclomatic complexity (ACYCLO).

At first glance, there is no correlation at all for very small files (a correlation coefficient close to zero), and the correlation coefficient grows until it stabilizes at approximately 500 SLOC. The coefficient does not change much for very large files.

We can extract two conclusions from Figure 8-2. First of all, there are huge files that should probably be removed from the sample. However, those files affect the value of the correlation coefficient only slightly, as evidenced by the small increase in that part of the plot. The second conclusion is that there is indeed an influence of file size on the value of the correlation. That influence does not affect our results for header files, because the correlation coefficient remains very low regardless of file size. But how will the rest of correlations be affected by this issue?

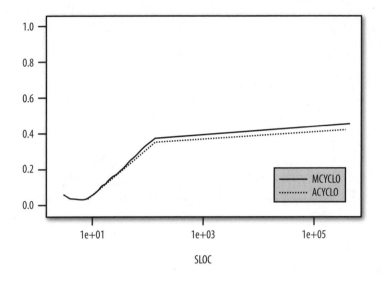

FIGURE 8-2. *Effect of file size on the correlation between cyclomatic complexity and SLOC in header files*

Effects of size on correlations for nonheader files

Figure 8-3 shows the influence of file size on the correlation coefficient between cyclomatic complexity and SLOC for the case of nonheader files. The vertical axis shows the value of the correlation coefficient, and the horizontal axis, in logarithmic scale, shows the value of the file size in SLOC. There are two curves: the maximum cyclomatic complexity (MCYCLO) and the average cyclomatic complexity (ACYCLO).

Again, we can observe that file size does influence the value of the correlation coefficient. However, the values stabilize beyond a certain file size (around 1,000 SLOC for MCYCLO and 500 SLOC for ACYCLO). For very small files, low correlation coefficients are reasonable, because the variability of files at that end is very high. For medium file sizes, the values of the correlation coefficients are similar to those shown in previous sections.

Effect on the Halstead's Software Science metrics

Figure 8-4 shows the influence of file size on the correlation coefficient of Halstead's metrics versus SLOC. Again, the vertical axis shows the correlation coefficient, the horizontal axis shows file size in logarithmic scale, and there is a curve for each one of the metrics (four in total).

The pattern is similar to the previous cases, albeit even more uniform across all the metrics. Even though file size influences the value of the correlation coefficient, all the coefficients remain high, regardless of file size.

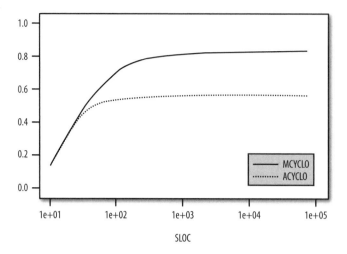

FIGURE 8-3. Effect of file size on the correlation between cyclomatic complexity and SLOC in nonheader files

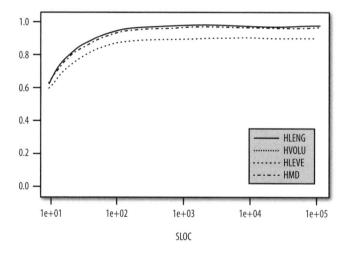

FIGURE 8-4. Effect of file size on the correlation between Halstead's Software Science metrics and SLOC in nonheader files

Summary of the confounding effect of file size

Although file size certainly influences the values of correlations, this influence does not substantially change the conclusions extracted from those correlations in any case. And indeed, the argument about the confounding effect of class size on the correlation of object-oriented metrics has faced some criticism [Evanco 2003].

In the case of our sample, we should probably remove very large files from the analysis because those probably introduce bias in the results. We randomly inspected some of these files. Some seem to have an automatic origin, and therefore should not be taken into account for an analysis of the complexity of source code. That is, no programmer has to read and edit those files, because they are automatically derived from the source files written by programmers. In any case, this bias is not significant, as shown in the previous figures.

As some practical advice, when applying the methodology shown in this chapter to other projects, we recommend that researchers break down the analysis by file size, to test whether the correlation coefficient changes with the size of files.

Some Comments on the Statistical Methodology

Statistical analyses are subject to threats to the validity of the conclusions extracted from the data. Returning to the exit poll example given in the introduction to this chapter, the socioeconomic profile of the interviewees might bias the results of the exit poll. A robust exit poll requires a random sample to be selected; otherwise, the poll will not accurately predict the actual results of the elections. Along the same lines, the results shown in this chapter might be biased because of some threats to validity, and the conclusions might not hold for other software projects. For the sake of the completeness of our analysis, we discuss the threats to validity:

- The first problem you might have spotted is regarding the level of significance of the correlations shown in the previous sections. Because of the statistical properties and the size of the samples (in the range of hundred of thousands), this level of significance will always be very high (in the order of 99.99%).

- From a software development point of view, this study should be extended to other programming languages. The conclusions shown here for C might not hold for other languages. Although C is currently the most popular language in the open source community (in terms of available code), other languages are also very popular, growing much faster than C, and have vast amounts of code available.

- Finally, all the source code used for this study was released as open source. Although we believe there are no technical differences between open source and other forms of software releases, the selection of the sample might affect the validity of the conclusions. In particular, the conclusions might not hold for software developed under different conditions. To solve this threat to validity, this study should be repeated with code obtained from other domains (e.g., industry, scientific software).

So Do We Need More Complexity Metrics?

The results shown in this chapter suggest that for non-header files written in C language, all the complexity metrics are highly correlated with lines of code, and therefore the more complex metrics provide no further information that could not be measured simply with lines of code.

However, these results must be accepted with some caution. Header files show poor correlation between cyclomatic complexity and the rest of metrics. We argue that this is because of the nature of this kind of file. In other words, header files do not contain implementations, only specifications. We are trying to measure the complexity of source code in terms of program comprehension. Programmers must of course read and comprehend header files, which means that header files can contribute to complexity to a certain extent. However, even though cyclomatic complexity is poorly correlated with lines of code in this case, that does not mean that it is a good complexity metric for header files. On the contrary, the poor correlation is due only to the lack of control structures in header files. These files do not contain loops, bifurcations, etc., so their cyclomatic complexity will always be minimal, regardless of their size.

For nonheader files, all the metrics show a high degree of correlation with lines of code. We accounted for the confounding effect of size, showing that the high correlation coefficients remain for different size ranges.

In our opinion, there is a clear lesson from this study: syntactic complexity metrics cannot capture the whole picture of software complexity. Complexity metrics that are exclusively based on the structure of the program or the properties of the text (for example, redundancy, as Halstead's metrics do), do not provide information on the amount of effort that is needed to comprehend a piece of code—or, at least, no more information than lines of code do. This has implications for how these metrics are used. In particular, defect prediction, development and maintenance effort models, and statistical models in general cannot benefit from these metrics, and lines of code should be considered always as the first and only metric for these models.

The problem of code complexity versus comprehension complexity has been faced in the research community before. In particular, a *semantic entropy* metric has been proposed, based on how obscure the identifiers used in a program are (for instance, names of variables). Interestingly, those kind of measurements are good defect predictors [Etzkorn et al. 2002].

This does not mean there are no useful lessons to take from traditional complexity metrics. First, cyclomatic complexity is a great indicator for the amount of paths that need to be tested in a program. Halstead's Software Science metrics also provide an interesting lesson: there are always several ways of doing the same thing in a program. So if you choose one way and use it in many parts of the program, you'll make your code more redundant, in turn making it more readable and less complex—in spite of what other statistics might say.

References

[Conte 1986] Conte, S.D. 1986. *Software Engineering Metrics and Models*. San Francisco: Benjamin Cummings.

[El Emam et al. 2001] El Emam, K., S. Benlarbi, N. Goel, and S. Rai. 2001. The confounding effect of class size on the validity of object-oriented metrics. *IEEE Transactions on Software Engineering* 27(7): 630–650.

[Etzkorn et al. 2002] Etzkorn, L.H., S. Gholston, and W.E. Hughes, Jr. 2002. A semantic entropy metric. *Journal of Software Maintenance and Evolution: Research and Practice* 14(4): 293–310.

[Evanco 2003] Evanco, W. 2003. Comments on "The confounding effect of class size on the validity of object-oriented metrics." *IEEE Transactions on Software Engineering* 29(7): 670–672.

[Kan 2003] Kan, S.H. 2003. *Metrics and Models in Software Quality Engineering* (2nd Edition). Boston: Addison-Wesley Professional.

[McCabe 1976] McCabe, T.J. 1976. A complexity measure. *IEEE Transactions on Software Engineering* SE-2(4): 308–320.

## PART II

Specific Topics in Software Engineering

This part of *Making Software* applies the ideas in the previous part to several pressing topics in the field of programming and software development. Most of these topics are widely debated, with ardent proponents on several sides. The beliefs programmers hold on these issues influence their day-to-day behavior and control hiring and budgetary decisions. You'll learn in this part of the book how much we can trust current beliefs.

## CHAPTER NINE

An Automated Fault Prediction System

Elaine J. Weyuker
Thomas J. Ostrand

Everyone wants their software to be perfect and contain no *faults* (or *defects* or *bugs*). Typically, developers use software testing techniques to identify these problems so that they can be removed, but when the software system is large, thorough testing can require a huge amount of resources.

Accurate prediction of the parts of a system that are most likely to have faults can provide developers, testers, and managers with a large head start on finding problems, increase the efficiency of testing, and help make the most of resources that are usually in short supply. Over the past several years, we have built models that predict the expected number of defects in each file of a software system in its next release. The files can then be arranged in decreasing order of predicted numbers of faults, so the files most likely to have defects are easily identified.

We have now used one of these prediction models to build an automated tool that can help a project manager prioritize effort for the files predicted to be most defect-prone. For example, the project manager might schedule more test time for these files, assign the team's best developers to make changes to them, or do code inspections for the files predicted to be most problematic. This should lead to faster identification of defects and therefore to reduced testing costs. It might also free up resources, allowing additional testing for the entire system, and lead to higher levels of reliability.

Fault Distribution

Large enterprise systems typically have a long lifespan, are built by many programmers, and are developed and released to the field at regular intervals. Anecdotal reports have stated that after a large system has gone through a few early releases, bugs in later versions tend to be concentrated in relatively small sections of the code. The bug distribution is frequently described as a *Pareto distribution*, with 80% of the bugs being located in just 20% of the code entities such as files or methods. This situation can be very helpful for system testers and debuggers if they can identify just which files fall into the 20% that contain problems because it would allow them to focus their Quality Assurance efforts such as testing, inspections, and debugging most effectively.

Working at AT&T, we have access to quite a few large systems with extended lifetimes, so we started a project to:

- Identify the parts of the code most likely to have bugs prior to the system testing phase
- Design and implement a programming environment tool that identifies the most bug-prone parts of the system and presents the information to developers and testers

The concept of the "most bug-prone parts of the system" is meaningful only if faults really are highly concentrated in certain parts of the system, so in order for these to be feasible goals, we first need to provide evidence that bugs are indeed distributed throughout the code with a highly skewed Pareto-like distribution.

We have examined six large systems that are used continuously in various parts of AT&T's operations, shown in Table 9-1. Their purposes include inventory control, provisioning, maintenance support, and automated voice response processing. These are real industrial systems, with bugs that actually occurred and were identified primarily during in-house testing, but sometimes by customers in the field.

Three of the systems have been developed and maintained by internal software development organizations, and the other three by an outside company. Their sizes range from 300,000 to over a half million lines of source code, and their lifetimes range from 2 years to almost 10 years. Each system includes code in a variety of different programming languages, sometimes as few as 4, but at least one system has code written in over 50 languages. With one exception (described later), the life history of these systems follows a disciplined pattern of regularly spaced versions, which are usually released to users approximately every three months.

The evidence collected from these systems overwhelmingly supports the Pareto hypothesis about bug distribution. A preliminary study on the first system we examined showed its bugs to be concentrated in fewer than 20% of the system's files for releases 2–9, and fewer than 10% for every release past the ninth.

TABLE 9-1. *Overview of systems*

System	Total releases	Years in the field	Avg files per release	Avg KLOC per release	Avg bugs per release	Avg % buggy files	% LOC in buggy files
Inventory	17	4	1318	363	301	10.4	28.7
Provisioning	9	2	2178	416	34	1.3	5.7
Voice Response	9	2.25	1341	228	165	10.1	16.9
Maintenance Support A	35	9	550	333	44	4.8	17.4
Maintenance Support B	35	9	1237	300	36	1.9	13.7
Maintenance Support C	27	7	437	219	42	4.8	14.3

This convinced us that it made sense to proceed with developing a fault prediction model. Each system we've studied subsequently has provided additional evidence that this Pareto distribution occurs, with faults concentrated in surprisingly small portions of the code. For two of the systems, the average percent of buggy files over all releases was less than 10.5%. For two other systems, faults were found in fewer than 5% of the files. And for the two remaining systems, fewer than 2% of the files contained any faults. Stated another way, for the six systems studied, roughly 90% or more of the files had no bugs detected either during pre-release system tests or in the field. Although the buggy files tended to be larger than non-buggy files, for five of the six systems they nevertheless contained less than 18% of the total lines of code in the system.

Table 9-1 has the system-specific values for bug concentration, as well as other key figures about each system. The second and third columns indicate the system's age in terms of the number of releases and the number of years in the field. The remaining columns are all averages calculated over all the releases for each system. They show the size of the system in terms of the number of files and the number of thousands of lines of code (KLOC), the average number of bugs, the percent of the system's files that have one or more bugs, and the percent of the system's code that is included in these buggy files.

Usually, as a system's lifetime increases, the number of files typically increases as new functionality is added. Therefore, the average number of files and the average number of lines of code shown in Table 9-1 are typically smaller than those values for releases late in the system's life. Table 9-2 shows the size of the latest release that we studied for each system, measured in terms of the number of files and the number of lines of code, along with our prediction findings for each of the six systems.

When systems are developed by large organizations with many programmers and testers, it's crucial to have systematic defect reporting, change management, and version control. The systems that we've studied use a single tool that fulfills all those functions. Changes that are recorded by the tool are documented in a *modification request*, or *MR*, which starts out as a description of a desired change and is updated with a description of the actual change that is eventually made. An MR can request a change to any aspect of the system, including to the system requirements, to a design document, to the code, or to user documentation.

TABLE 9-2. Percentage of faults in top 20% of files for previously studied systems

System	Final release files	Final release KLOC	% faults in top 20% files
Inventory	1950	538	83%
Provisioning	2308	438	83%
Voice Response	1888	329	75%
Maintenance Support A	668	442	81%
Maintenance Support B	1413	384	93%
Maintenance Support C	584	329	76%

The submitter of an MR could be, for example, a system designer who wants to change the way some function performs, a programmer who has discovered a more efficient algorithm for part of his code, or a tester who has discovered a flaw in the program's behavior. The actual change to the system might take place immediately and be performed by the MR submitter (in the case of the programmer), or it might be done hours or days later by a second person who is responsible for the code but did not submit the original MR. This is the typical scenario when an MR was initiated by a tester. The MR documents all aspects of the change, including the dates and phases of the development process when it is submitted and when it is implemented, the identity of the submitter and the implementor, attribute tags that characterize the MR, and any written description of the change that is provided by the submitter or the implementor.

The change itself is also recorded as part of the MR, and provides the information used by the version control component of the tool to create a build of the system at any point in its lifetime. The MR information is stored in a database that gives our fault prediction tool all the information we need to analyze past releases and predict future faults.

Although all our systems use the same underlying tool to record MRs, they may use it in different ways. The most significant difference is the stage of the development process when a project starts requiring changes to be made formally with MRs. One common practice is for MRs to be required only after the system has reached the stage of system testing, so that the MR database contains no information about changes made or defects found in any phases prior to system test. This practice was followed by four of the six systems we studied. For those systems, our models predict faults that are expected to be detected in system testing or field operation, as the models are based on past faults from those phases.

The Inventory System recorded defects found and corrected for all development phases starting with unit testing, going through system testing and release. Roughly 80% of its identified faults were reported during unit and integration testing, preceding the system test phase, and inflating the average fault count relative to the other systems. This explains why the Inventory System has substantially more faults, on average, than any of the other systems. It is *not* necessarily an indication that it is more problematic than the others.

The Voice Response system was a special case that will be discussed in the next section.

Characteristics of Faulty Files

Once we had evidence of bug concentration, we were able to start looking for characteristics of the buggy code that would allow us to identify it. The software in an ongoing project provides two classes of properties that potentially can be used to characterize particular code units. The first class consists of *static structural code properties* that can be extracted directly from the source code. They include things such as programming language, the number of lines of code in a file, the number of method calls, and various software complexity metrics.

The second class consists of *process properties*, which relate to the history of the system's development and testing. They include information such as the number of changes and faults that were detected in previous releases, and the length of time that a particular code unit has been part of the system.

The goal of our early research was to find properties of the files from both of these classes that had a strong correlation with the occurrence of faults in the files. The first two systems that we studied provided enough evidence for us to build preliminary models that did a creditable job of predicting which files would be the most likely to have the largest number of faults in future releases of those systems.

The third system we examined, the Voice Response system, was similar to the first two systems in size, duration of time in the field, and multideveloper team, but it used a development process that was different from the usual sequence of phases and did not release versions at regular release intervals. Its defects could not be associated with any particular development phase.

This Voice Response system was released continuously, with new builds being created and released whenever bugs were fixed or new functionality was introduced. Without the discipline of regular releases and their associated substantial system test phase, it wasn't obvious that the models developed for the first two systems would be applicable to this system, but we were pleasantly surprised to discover that with some variation, these models performed very well. The "releases" shown in Tables 9-1 and 9-2 for Voice Response are simply consecutive three-month periods of time in the system's life, and the bugs reported for each release are just those bugs that were first reported during that three-month time period. This different development paradigm might explain why this system had a larger number of faults per release than most of the others. Many of its MRs reported changes made by developers relatively early in a module's life, corresponding to a traditional project's usual phase of unit testing.

Based on our experiments with the first three systems, we settled on a standard prediction model that we applied to the three Maintenance Support systems, with excellent results.

Overview of the Prediction Model

Fault prediction for a given release N of a system is based on a model built by analyzing the code properties, process properties, and fault counts from earlier releases. The fundamental assumption is that properties associated with faulty files in earlier releases will also be associated with faulty files in the next release. A model consists of an equation whose variables are the code and process properties for a file of release N, and whose value is a predicted number of faults for the file. Creation of the model requires data from at least two prior releases, but can make use of data from as many prior releases as are available. The data used to construct a model are referred to as *training data*.

Because we have fault data available for the entire history of these systems, we can generate predictions for release N using information from releases 1 through $N - 1$, and then check the prediction quality by looking at the actual numbers of faults that occur in files of release N. Our fundamental way of evaluating the quality of the predictions for release N is to measure how many of the faults actually detected in N occurred in the files that appear in the first 20% of the prediction list. Table 9-2 shows that the top 20% always includes at least 75% of the faults, and usually more than 80%. The table provides compelling evidence that the prediction method will be applicable to other large systems.

You might be wondering why we have chosen to use the admittedly arbitrary cutoff value of 20% to assess our predictions. There are two basic reasons. First, the evidence that we and others have collected tells us that the top 20% of the files usually contains the majority of the defects, which encourages us to feel that if our predictions really do help us identify the files containing around 80% of the faults, we are doing an excellent job of pinpointing the right files.

Second, 20% of the files often represents a small enough number of files to make it practical to target them for special attention. We are certainly not advocating that other files should not be tested or carefully scrutinized, only that the first 20% are likely to warrant increased attention.

The prediction models we use are based on *negative binomial regression* (NBR) [McCullagh and Nelder 1989], which we have found to be the most effective statistical approach for our purpose. We have developed a single form of the NBR model and have applied it successfully to many different systems. Negative binomial regression is a well-known statistical modeling method that is an extension of linear regression. It is especially suitable to model situations where the outcomes of trials are nonnegative integers, such as the number of faults expected in each file of a system. With NBR, the logarithm of the outcome (expected number of faults) is modeled as a linear combination of the independent variables. In other words, the expected number of faults is assumed to be a multiplicative function of the independent variables.

The following variables make up what we call the *standard model* for our predictions. They are input to the model's equation for each file, and produce a predicted fault count for the file in release N:

- The size of the file in number of lines of code (LOC)
- Whether the file was part of the system in the previous release or was new to this release (a binary variable)
- The number of changes made to the file in release $N - 1$
- The number of changes made to the file in release $N - 2$
- The number of faults detected in the file in release $N - 1$, either during testing or during operation in the field
- The programming language in which the file was written

A detailed technical description of our standard NBR model can be found in [Weyuker et al. 2009].

In our empirical studies, we evaluate a model's success by adding up the faults that actually were detected in the files predicted to be among the top 20%, and then dividing that number by the total number of faults that were identified in all of the files in that release. Thus, if the files predicted to be in the top 20% contain 80 faults and collectively there is a total of 100 faults in all the files of release N, then we would say that the model correctly identifies 80% of the faults in the top 20% of the files for release N. Of course, when the models are used in practice in an ongoing development environment, the developers don't know exactly which files in release N will turn out to be faulty or not faulty.

Replication and Variations of the Prediction Model

It is really important to provide evidence that methods work by replicating studies. Using the same statistical model with the same releases of a given subject system generally will not provide new information, because the algorithms used to make the predictions are deterministic. Therefore, replication in this arena usually means either applying the same model to different releases of the same system or applying the model to different systems.

We have demonstrated both types of replication. In Table 9-1, we indicated the number of different releases included in the study for each of six different systems. In this section, we discuss another form of replication involving model variations.

Although the prediction accuracies achieved by the negative binomial models described in the previous section have generally been very good, we have continued to investigate ways to further improve our predictions.

This has led us to experiment with the use of different predictor variables for the NBR model, as well as comparing the NBR model against other statistical models. These trials have shown that it's very difficult to improve on the standard NBR model. The best we've achieved with additional predictor variables is accuracy improvements of roughly 1%, and none of the other statistical models produced better results than those achieved by the NBR model.

In addition to being a search for improved prediction methods, these studies are another form of evidence that our approach to fault prediction is fundamentally sound.

The Role of Developers

Many software engineering professionals are convinced that an important issue related to software quality, and therefore to fault prediction, is who or how many people wrote or changed the code recently. A common belief is that the more different programmers who work on a given piece of code, the more bugs that code is likely to have. When we present our prediction work and the standard NBR model, one of the most commonly asked questions is whether information about the programmers who wrote and modified the code might provide more accurate predictions of the most faulty files. For this reason, we decided to augment the standard model by adding developer information and then compare the results from augmented models to those achieved with the standard model.

Each change to a given file in a given release that is recorded in the MR database includes a coded ID of the developer who modified the file. This lets us track all the developers who changed the file over its lifetime. Unfortunately, the database does not identify the developer responsible for the initial version of the file. However, the IDs let us calculate the following three additional numbers for each file in release N, which we used as variables for the prediction models:

Cumulative developers
    The number of different people who modified the file in all previous releases 1 through $N-1$

Recent developers
    The number of people who modified the file in the most recent previous release $N-1$

New developers
    The number of people who modified the file in release $N-1$, and who never modified the file in any earlier release

Although each of the three developer variables generally improved the prediction results slightly when added alone, the cumulative developers variable always yielded the best improvement. For this reason, we present results for only that variable, comparing it to the original standard NBR model.

Figures 9-1, 9-2, and 9-3 show information about Maintenance Systems A, B, and C, respectively. These figures originally appeared in [Weyuker et al. 2008]. Each figure is divided into two parts, with the upper and lower parts aligned by release number. The upper portion is a bar graph showing a count of the total number of faults identified during each release. In each case, bugs were always concentrated in a small proportion of the files.

The lower portion of the figures contains two graphs, to compare the performances of the standard model and the model augmented with the cumulative number of developers. Each graph shows the percentages of the actual faults for each release in the 20% of files predicted to have the largest numbers of faults.

We see very little difference between the results with and without developer information included in the model. For System A, the improvement in predictions over all releases is only 0.2%, and for System C there is no improvement. Even for System B, which shows the greatest improvement, there is just a 1% improvement in the percentage of identified faults by augmenting the model with the cumulative number of developers changing the file. It is also interesting to notice that for each of the three systems, there is at least one release for which adding the developer information actually makes the predictions less accurate.

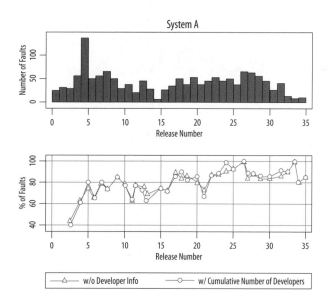

FIGURE 9-1. Prediction models with and without cumulative developer counts: number of faults and percentage of faults in top 20% of files, by release number for System A

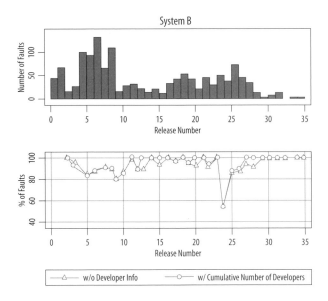

FIGURE 9-2. Prediction models with and without cumulative developer counts: number of faults and percentage of faults in top 20% of files, by release number for System B

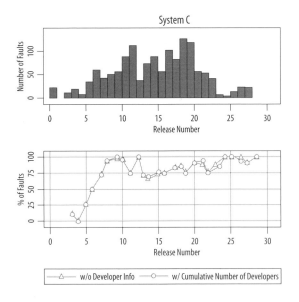

FIGURE 9-3. Prediction models with and without cumulative developer counts: number of faults and percentage of faults in top 20% of files, by release number for System C

Additional details about our findings can be found in [Weyuker et al. 2008].

Predicting Faults with Other Types of Models

Although we have generally found that the negative binomial regression models were able to identify a large majority of the defects by selecting a small percentage of the files, we wanted to compare the performance of NBR against results that could be achieved with different prediction methods. We created prediction models for three of the systems in Table 9-1, using the following three alternate model-building methods: *recursive partitioning, random forests*, and *Bayesian additive regression trees* (BART). Random forests and BART are extensions of recursive partitioning and were designed to deal with some of this method's limitations.

Recursive partitioning attempts to construct a binary decision tree based on the training data, such that each leaf node represents a set of similar input values, whose outputs (the predicted number of faults) are reasonably close to each other. To understand how the tree works, remember that the goal is to assign a predicted number of faults to each file in the new release. A file is an input to the prediction process, and the output is the file's predicted fault count.

Each file has a number of attributes that characterize it, including its length, its past history of faults and changes, its programming language, etc. These attributes are the independent variables, or predictor variables, of the process. For each file, the decision tree defines a path from the root to a leaf node, using the attribute values of the file. Each internal node of the tree splits the inputs into two sets, based on the value of a single predictor variable. An input follows either the left or right branch from an internal node, based on the input's value of the predictor variable associated with the node. When the input reaches a leaf node, its predicted number of faults is given as the average value of the fault count for all the training data inputs at that node.

The tree is constructed from the top down, starting by splitting all the training data into two sets, based on the single variable that minimizes the total squared error of all the data in each set. The error for each file in the training data is the difference between that file's fault count and the average of all the fault counts at the node. Each resulting node is again split on the single variable that yields the smallest squared error. This process of *recursive partitioning* is repeated for all subsequent nodes until a stopping condition is met.

Since the idea for recursive partitioning is completely different from the idea behind regression, it produces models that are very different from the negative binomial models.

One drawback to recursive partitioning is that the decision tree is very dependent on the first few splits that are made. Once a set of training values is assigned to one side of the tree, none of those values can ever be associated with values on the other side of the tree, which may have very similar fault counts. The random forests method attempts to overcome this problem by constructing a large set of decision trees and using the average prediction over all the trees as the predicted output for any given input. Our implementation of this method constructed 500 trees for each fault-predicting forest. Naturally the running time for random forests is considerably longer than for either negative binomial regression or recursive partitioning.

The final method we tried is called Bayesian additive regression trees (BART). It attempts to overcome the recursive partitioning problem by splitting the prediction into many small pieces and modeling the predicted fault count as the sum of predictions by many trees. For this method, we used 100 trees for each model.

More details about our use of all these methods appear in [Weyuker et al. 2009], as well as some of the limitations we observed when using them. To construct the models and make our predictions, we used implementations of all three methods in the R [R Project Statistical Computing] library: the rpart package [rpart Package] for the recursive partitioning model, the randomForest package [randomForest Package] to make predictions using random forests, and the BayesTrees package [BayesTree Package] for fitting BART models to our data.

The subjects of this model-comparing empirical study were Maintenance Support Systems A, B, and C, described in Tables 9-1 and 9-2. Figure 9-4, which originally appeared in [Weyuker et al. 2009], shows the percent of faults detected in the top 20% of files identified by each of the prediction models. The bars for each system are the average over all of the system's releases for which we made predictions. The chart shows that the NBR and random forests models performed significantly better than BART or recursive partitioning for each of the three systems. However, although there was no statistically significant difference between the prediction results for NBR and random forests, NBR required far lower execution times than random forests. We therefore concluded that using NBR was the best choice, at least for these systems.

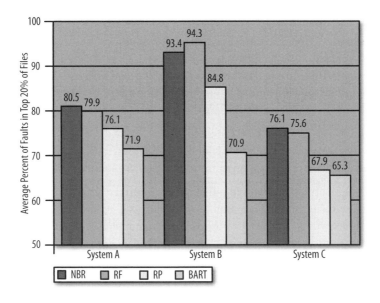

FIGURE 9-4. Prediction results for four different models, Systems A, B, C

Building a Tool

The successful predictive ability of our standard negative binomial regression model, and the interest among practitioners to be able to use our technology, led us to build an automated programming environment tool that gives users the ability to generate fault predictions for the files in a release that is about to enter the system testing phase.

A prototype of this tool is now operational, and requires minimal user expertise and input. The user identifies the particular release of the system under development for which predictions are wanted and the specific file types that should be included in the predictions. In addition, the user tells the tool how to identify entries in the MR database that represent past changes that were made to correct defects. Defects are typically identified either by the development stage at which the MR was written, such as system testing, or by the role of the person who initiated the MR, such as a system tester.

The tool returns its results as a sorted list of files, in decreasing order of the predicted number of faults. Users can indicate the percentage of the files for which they are interested in seeing results, and can optionally restrict the output to only certain file types. Thus a user might ask to see the worst 10% of the Java files or the predicted most faulty 20% of files written in C, C++, Java, or SQL. The results are generally produced very quickly.

The tool *does not* require the user to have any knowledge of data mining algorithms or statistics, the parameters used in the model, or any understanding of the internal workings of the tool.

Several of our development and testing managers have seen the prototype in action and plan to use this technology to make predictions for their software systems to guide requirements and design reviews, as well as to guide testing.

The Warning Label

In the process of developing our fault prediction technology and tool, we did a large series of empirical studies. Because it is fairly unusual to see repeated large industrial empirical studies that follow multiple systems for multiple years, it would perhaps be interesting for readers to hear which parts of the work are most challenging and why, so they can understand why this sort of evidence is so critical even though it is difficult to provide.

Where will I get systems to study?

Many people seem to feel that since we work for a large company that has hundreds of millions or perhaps billions of lines of code that run continuously, obtaining systems to study would be trivial. Nothing could be further from the truth, especially at early stages of the research. It's sort of a chicken and egg syndrome. System owners are reluctant to allow you access to their systems for a number of reasons, most of which are perfectly sensible from their points of view.

The first thing they worry about is that you will take time, and they typically have very tight deadlines. If they spend time answering your questions, they will see no direct benefit and will have less chance of deploying their system on schedule. Therefore they are unwilling to get involved with what they perceive to be high-risk research projects. Most research projects are in fact high-risk because they never get to a stage that can be used by practitioners.

System owners may also fear that you will modify the system or their data in some way that will have a negative impact on their project. Although you may promise to look and not touch, they fear you will deliberately or inadvertently impact their system.

A third issue is similar to a problem common to studies in other fields of research. For example, in medical treatment or drug trials, it is rare that the people who are the study subjects will actually benefit from the study, and it is critical to make sure that subjects understand that and know the risks of participation.

In fact, the projects that served as our earliest study subjects derived no benefit, because we were only identifying the characteristics most closely associated with faulty files and just beginning to develop the prediction models.

Even after we had a prediction model that seemed to work, the next couple of systems were used to validate the model. Only after that was done did we begin to build an automated tool. Until the tool was complete, doing the predictions required an understanding of data mining and statistics, and familiarity with a statistics tool such as R. This knowledge is outside the normal set of skills held by software developers or testers.

Once you have a number of successes with the technology under your belt, it will be much easier to find projects eager to try it, but of course, there first need to be projects willing to act as guinea pigs. This usually requires previous relationships developed by working with project personnel that convince them you understand their time constraints and the importance of not impacting the project while studying it.

Preliminary studies are difficult and time-consuming

As explained earlier, before we could begin to do any actual work on fault prediction, we had to first assure ourselves that faults were not uniformly distributed and determine which characteristics were most closely correlated with faulty files by doing preliminary empirical studies to collect evidence. Of course, there was a fair amount of anecdotal evidence, especially about the Pareto distribution, and there had been earlier studies that considered which properties were associated with fault-proneness, but anecdotal evidence is not the same as a careful study done on a large industrial system. We needed to verify that we would observe this behavior in our environment. Finally, some of the earlier studies had conflicting results about the importance of different file characteristics or did not consider both code-based and history-based characteristics.

We spent roughly two years doing these preliminary studies and getting to the point at which we were ready to consider building a statistical prediction model for the first system.

Data acquisition and analysis is difficult and time-consuming

Once we had determined the most important code and history metrics to use to build the statistical model, we had to understand the change management and version control system that the projects use and determine exactly how to extract the necessary data. In the course of looking at the second system we studied, we learned that different projects used certain fields of the underlying database in different or non-obvious ways. This helped us determine which data was usable and which was not. Following that, we needed to write scripts to actually do the data extraction, and build the initial prediction model.

This took us roughly one additional year until we were able to make the preliminary predictions for the first system using a custom-built prediction model.

Measuring success is difficult

Our model associates a predicted number of faults in the next release with every file. We considered a number of different ways of measuring how well the predictions were doing.

One way might be to compare how close the predicted numbers of faults came to the actual numbers of faults in each file. For the first system we studied, we observed that typically, the numbers of faults did not match closely. However, the files with the largest numbers of actual faults tended to be among those files with the largest numbers of predicted faults. Discussing this with practitioners, we decided that the most useful information and best way to assess our success was using the 20% metric described earlier in this chapter.

We have considered other metrics proposed in the literature and found many other metrics inappropriate for this work because they were designed for predicting binary decisions, such as whether or not a file will contain faults, rather than ranking the files as our model does. We have continued to assess and propose alternative metrics to make sure that the assessment used is most appropriate for our needs.

Getting "customers" is difficult

Even after completing several large empirical studies that showed consistently good results, and having developed a fully automated tool, it is still difficult to convince project leaders that they should change their development methodology and incorporate our prediction models and tool into their process. We have recently identified a project whose management believes this will be very useful and we are negotiating the transfer of our technology. It remains to be seen whether the use of the prediction tool will impact the types and numbers of faults identified by the users.

So what is the bottom line here? We have spent eight years working on this research. Was all that time necessary? It is our hope that some of the factors outlined earlier will convince you that this was indeed time well spent. If you want to be able to collect evidence on the scope that we did, it is often very time-consuming, especially in the early stages while the technology is still being developed and matured, during which most stages need to be done manually. But having provided a considerable amount of evidence that our prediction model works well in many different settings and circumstances, and having built a fully automated tool, we believe we are now ready for prime time!

References

[BayesTree Package] The BayesTree Package. *http://cran.rproject.org/web/packages/BayesTree*

[McCullagh and Nelder 1989] McCullagh, P., and J.A. Nelder. 1989. *Generalized Linear Models*, Second Edition. London: Chapman and Hall.

[Ostrand and Weyuker 2002] Ostrand, T.J., and E.J. Weyuker. 2002. The Distribution of Faults in a Large Industrial Software System. *Proc. ACM/International Symposium on Software Testing and Analysis (ISSTA2002)*: 55–64.

[Ostrand et al. 2005a] Ostrand, T.J., E.J. Weyuker, and R.M. Bell. 2005. Predicting the Location and Number of Faults in Large Software Systems. *IEEE Transactions on Software Engineering* 31(4): 340–355.

[Ostrand et al. 2005b] Ostrand, T.J., E.J. Weyuker, and R.M. Bell. 2005. A Different View of Fault Prediction. *Proc. 29th IEEE Annual International Computer Software and Applications Conference (COMPSAC 2005)* 2: 3–4.

[R Project Statistical Computing] The R Project for Statistical Computing. *http://www.r-project .org/*

[randomForest Package] The randomForest Package. *http://cran.rproject.org/web/packages/ randomForest*

[rpart Package] The rpart Package. *http://cran.rproject.org/web/packages/rpart*

[Weyuker et al. 2008] Weyuker, E.J., T.J. Ostrand, and R.M. Bell. 2008. Do Too Many Cooks Spoil the Broth? Using the Number of Developers to Enhance Defect Prediction Models. *Empirical Software Engineering Journal* 13(5): 539–559.

[Weyuker et al. 2010] Weyuker, E.J., T.J. Ostrand, and R.M. Bell. 2010. Comparing the Effectiveness of Several Modeling Methods for Fault Prediction. *Empirical Software Engineering Journal* 15(3): 277–295.

## CHAPTER TEN

Architecting: How Much and When?

Barry Boehm

This chapter presents research that can help projects and organizations determine whether and when to use Agile methods versus architecting approaches to software development. Even when the managers of software or software-intensive projects appreciate the importance of architecting, they all have limited resources to spend and frequently ask, "How much architecting is enough?" (See "How Much Architecting Is Enough?" on page 162.)

To provide practical guidelines for this inquiry, this chapter summarizes and ties together two sources of evidence that I and other researchers have accumulated across 40 years of software practice, and discusses some insights for software that have been drawn from these inquiries. The questions we've researched can be framed as follows:

- By how much should you expect the cost of making changes or fixing defects to increase as a function of project time or product size?

- How much should you invest in early architecting and evidence-based project reviews before proceeding into product development?

In this context, "architecting" does not refer to producing the equivalent of blueprints for the software, but to the overall set of concurrent frontend activities (site surveys, operations analysis, needs and opportunities analysis, economic analysis, requirements and architecture definition, planning and scheduling, verifying and validating feasibility evidence) that are key to creating and sustaining a successful building or software product, as elaborated in the book *Systems Architecting* [Rechtin 1991].

Does the Cost of Fixing Software Increase over the Project Life Cycle?

The significance of the first question has been expressed well by Agile methods pioneer Kent Beck in his book *Extreme Programming Explained* [Beck 1999]:

> Figure 10-1 is "the technical premise for XP" (eXtreme Programming). If the cost of making a software change "rose slowly over time...you would make decisions as late in the process as possible...and...only implement what you need to."
>
> However, "if a flattened cost curve makes XP possible, a steep change cost curve makes XP impossible."

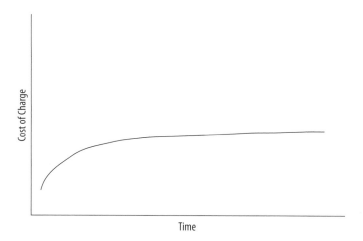

FIGURE 10-1. The cost of change may not rise dramatically over time

We can therefore ask whether XP or other Agile methods can ensure a flattened cost-of-change curve. We can also ask what other strategies can flatten the curve—so that late fixes do not threaten a project's costs and delivery dates—as well as how to reduce fixes for projects that have a steep cost-to-fix curve. This chapter will provide some answers to these questions.

How Much Architecting Is Enough?

If a steep change-of-cost curve makes Agile methods such as XP impossible, how much should you invest in making preparations for a development project? Some decision makers draw on analogies such as, "We pay an architect 10% of the cost of a building, so that's what we'll pay for software architecting." But what percentage is really appropriate for software? Perhaps 10% is way too little or way too much. Many cost-cutting decision makers see that software architecting doesn't directly produce the product, and as a result try to minimize its cost. But this often leads to an increased amount of late rework and embarrassing overruns in time and costs. Here again, any relevant evidence on "how much architecting is enough?" would be highly valuable for enterprise or project decision makers.

Cost-to-Fix Growth Evidence

Evidence on how the costs of making changes or fixes vary phase by phase for large software projects was reported by several organizations in the 1970s, including IBM [Fagan 1976], GTE [Daly 1977], TRW [Boehm 1976], and Bell Labs' Safeguard project [Stephenson 1976]. These studies found rather consistently that a post-delivery software change was about 100 times as expensive as a requirements-phase software change. Figure 10-2, taken from the 1981 book *Software Engineering Economics* [Boehm 1981], summarizes the results of these studies and a few others. It shows that, although the 100:1 ratio was generally true for large systems, a 5:1 ratio was more characteristic of smaller systems (2,000–5,000 source lines of code) [Boehm 1980].

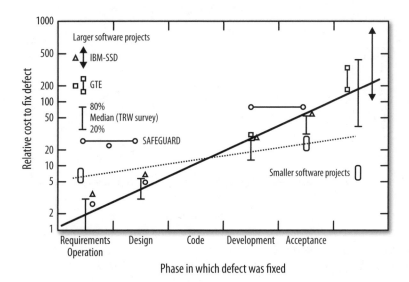

FIGURE 10-2. Relative cost to fix defects by phase (1970s)

Considerable uncertainty has arisen over whether these escalation factors remain representative in today's software development environment. To explore this and related questions, the National Science Foundation–sponsored Center for Empirically-Based Software Engineering (CeBASE), formed by the University of Maryland and the University of Southern California, performed a literature search and held three e-workshops involving people with relevant experience and data [Shull et al. 2002]. The results tended to confirm the 100:1 ratio for large projects, with factors of 117:1 and 137:1 recorded, and a 1996 survey showing a range of 70–125:1 [McGibbon 1996]. However, related e-workshop discussions indicated that investments in early requirements and design verification and validation by large projects could reduce the slope of the cost-to-fix curve from 100:1 down to as low as 20:1. A major success story that did even better in this regard—and the only project to my knowledge with experience data to match the flat curve in Figure 10-1—is the million-line CCPDS-R project described in the next section [Royce 1998].

Although Beck and others have provided anecdotal data on Agile change experiences fitting Figure 10-1, empirical data on small Agile projects fails to bear out the claims. For example, a recent summary of two small commercial Java projects mostly following some XP practices (pair programming, test first, on-site customer) and compliant with the remaining practices, does provide empirical data on Agile cost-of-change, as shown in Figures 10-3 and 10-4 [Li and Alshayeb 2002].

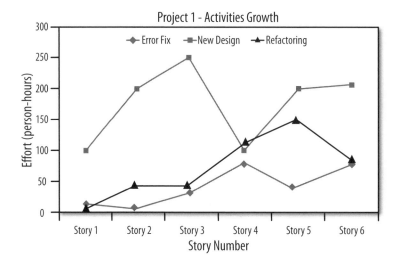

FIGURE 10-3. Project 1: Cost-of-change growth

No data was available in these studies on the number of changes and the effort per change, but the percentage of total story development effort for Project 1 shows an average increase from one story to the next of roughly 6% per story for refactoring (from 0% of total effort to roughly 35% of total effort across six new stories), and about 4% per story for error fixes (from 0% of total effort to roughly 25% of total effort across six new stories). The corresponding figures for Project 2 are roughly 5% and 3%. These are nontrivial rates of increase, and although clearly not as good as the anecdotal experiences of Agile experts, more likely to represent mainstream XP experience. The small decrease in rates from Project 1 to Project 2 indicates a small, but not dominant, learning curve effect for the XP process.

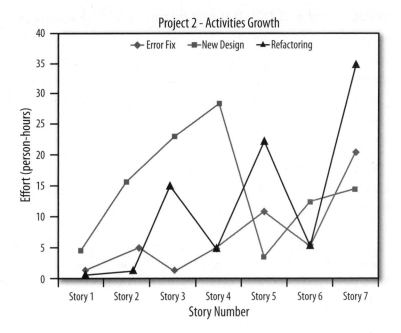

FIGURE 10-4. Project 2: Cost-of-change growth

[Reifer 2002] cites some proprietary empirical data with similar characteristics. Another corroborative data point is the XP ThoughtWorks lease management project experience report in [Elssamadisy and Schalliol 2002]. Once the project size reached over 50 people, 1,000 stories, and 500,000 lines of code, they noted that "[e]veryone says that all the story cards were finished at the proper times [in 30 days], but it still takes 12 weeks of full-time development effort to deliver a quality application to the customer."

Using What We Can Learn from Cost-to-Fix Data About the Value of Architecting

It is useful first of all to isolate architecting as a set of early concurrent system and project definition activities and determine the effect of its use to reduce later rework and consequent project costs. We show how to tie architecting to costs in this section, and then proceed in later parts of the chapter to come up with some figures about when to do architecting and how much to do on various types of projects.

The Foundations of the COCOMO II Architecture and Risk Resolution (RESL) Factor

This chapter is based on decades of research that my colleagues and I invested in two generations of developing a Constructive Cost Model (COCOMO) for estimating software costs and project duration. By incorporating estimations of risk into this model, we succeeded in showing the value of architecting and (as will be shown later in this chapter) how much is enough.

Economies and diseconomies of scale

Our original COCOMO [Boehm 1981] did not include a factor measuring thoroughness of architecting. We did not consider whether projects have any control over the diseconomies of scale that many projects and teams suffer from.

What are diseconomies (and economies, for that matter) of scale? These are economic terms that relate the number of units of something produced to their cost per unit. An economy of scale is achieved when producing more units leads to a lower cost per unit. A diseconomy of scale is the opposite: when producing more units leads to a higher cost per unit.

One reason that these quantities are important is that software products are getting larger and larger, and you would like to minimize any diseconomies of scale. Another is that they often cause a clash of mental models between hardware people and software people. Hardware people think of units produced as things like cars or cell phones: the more you produce, the cheaper they are per unit. In other words, hardware tends to experience economies of scale. For software, the cost of making more copies is essentially zero, and the cost-related unit of production is the source lines of code (SLOC). For this unit of production, the larger the number of new SLOC, the higher the cost per unit, leading to a diseconomy of scale for software.

To see why, consider the cost of producing two software components having 10,000 new SLOC. If the development cost is \$20/SLOC, the cost of each will be 10,000 * \$20 = \$200,000.

But suppose that these two components need to be combined into a single product. In addition to the \$200,000 it costs to develop each component, the project will incur additional design costs to make them interoperate, integration costs in order to deliver them, testing costs on the integrated system, and rework costs to fix any integration defects.

The total number of delivered SLOC is still 20,000, but the cost will be greater than 2 * \$200,000 = \$400,000, and the cost per SLOC will be higher, producing a diseconomy of scale. This is often difficult for software developers to explain to hardware-oriented project managers, who expect larger numbers of units to be cheaper per unit.

Reducing software rework via architecture and risk resolution

In the original COCOMO model, the closest factor to architecting thoroughness was called Modern Programming Practices, which included such practices as top-down development, structured programming, and design and code inspections. These were assumed to affect small and large projects equally. But diseconomies of scale were assumed to be built into a project's development mode. For instance:

- A low-criticality Organic-mode project had an exponent of 1.05 relating software project size to project development effort. This meant that doubling the product size increased effort by a factor of 2.07.

- A mission-critical Embedded-mode project had an exponent of 1.20, which meant that doubling product size increased effort by a factor of 2.30.

The exponent values were determined by fitting curves to each mode's size and effort data in the 63-project COCOMO database.

Subsequent experience and analyses at TRW during the 1980s indicated that some sources of software development diseconomies of scale, such as rework, could be reduced by improved practices, and that architecting thoroughness was one of the most significant improvements. For example, some large TRW software projects that did insufficient software architecture and risk resolution had very high rework costs [Boehm 2000], while similar smaller projects had smaller rework costs.

Analysis of project defect tracking cost-to-fix data (a major source of rework costs) showed that 20% of the defects accounted for 80% of the rework costs, and that these 20% were primarily due to inadequate architecture definition and risk resolution.

For example, in TRW Project A in Figure 10-5, most of the rework was the result of using a nominal-case architecture for the network operating system. The systems engineering of the architecture neglected to address the risk that the operating system architecture would not support the project requirements of successful system fail-over if one or more of the processors in the network failed to function. Once this was discovered during system test, it turned out to be an "architecture-breaker," causing several sources of expensive rework to software that was already developed. A similar "architecture-breaker," the late discovery of the importance of handling extra-long messages (over 1 million characters), was the cause of most of the rework in Project B, whose original nominal-case architecture assumed that almost all messages would be short and easy to handle with a fully packet-switched network architecture. (This assumption was partly due to a vague requirements statement of the form: "The system shall satisfactorily deliver all messages submitted to it.")

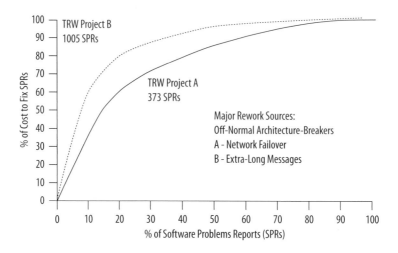

FIGURE 10-5. Steeper cost-to-fix for high-risk elements

These results caused TRW to develop policies requiring thorough risk analyses of all requirements by the project's Preliminary Design Review (PDR). With TRW's adoption of the Ada programming language and associated ability to verify the consistency of Ada module specifications, the risk policy was extended into an Ada Process Model for software, also requiring that the software architecture pass an Ada compiler module consistency check prior to its PDR [Royce 1998]. This enabled subsequent projects to perform much of the systems integration before providing the module specifications to programmers for coding and unit test.

A successful example: CCPDS-R

By assimilating the lessons described in the previous section and eliminating architecture risks prior to PDR, subsequent projects were able to significantly reduce late architecture-breaker rework and the steep slope of the cost-to-fix curve. A good example was the Command Center Processing and Display System-Replacement (CCPDS-R) project described in [Royce 1998], whose flattened cost-to-fix curve is shown in Figure 10-6. It delivered over a million lines of Ada code within its original budget and schedule.

CCPDS-R was able to reinterpret its waterfall-model contract process by deferring its milestone dates to enable early risk-driven spiral-model cycles. For example, its PDR was held in month 14 of a 35-month initial-delivery schedule and covered about 25% of the initial-delivery budget, including development and validation of its working high-risk software, such as its network operating system and the key portions of its user interface software.

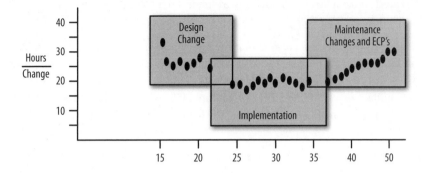

FIGURE 10-6. Reducing software cost-to-fix: CCPDS-R [Royce 1998]

The Architecture and Risk Resolution Factor in Ada COCOMO and COCOMO II

The flattened cost-to-fix curve for large projects exemplified in Figure 10-6 confirmed that increased emphasis on architecture and risk resolution reduced the rework and diseconomies of scale on large projects. From 1987 to 1989, TRW developed a version of COCOMO for large mission-critical projects using the Ada Process Model, called Ada COCOMO [Boehm and Royce 1989]. It reduced the 1.20 exponent relating product size to project effort in proportion to the project's adherence to the Ada Process Model. It consequently also reduced software project diseconomies of scale through architecting and risk resolution, reduced software cost estimates, and helped managers in government and industry move from relatively rigid, pipelined, documentation-driven processes toward more risk-driven concurrently engineered processes.

How the Ada Process Model promoted risk-driven concurrent engineering software processes

The Ada Process Model and the CCPDS-R project showed that it was possible to reformulate the sequential waterfall process model as a more modern form of risk-driven concurrent engineering of requirements, architecture, and plans. The model applied review criteria that focused on the compatibility and feasibility of these artifacts.

Subsequently, the researchers elaborated these practices into general processes for software engineering and systems engineering for software-intensive systems. The models emphasized risk-driven concurrent engineering and associated milestone review pass-fail criteria [Boehm 1996]. The models included:

- The Rational Unified Process (RUP) [Royce 1998]; [Jacobson et al. 1999]; [Kruchten 1999]
- The USC Model-Based (System) Architecting and Software Engineering (MBASE) model [Boehm and Port 1999]; [Boehm and Port 2001]. This in turn integrated:
  — The risk-driven concurrent engineering WinWin spiral model [Boehm et al. 1998]

— The Rechtin concurrent engineering Systems Architecting approach [Rechtin 1991]; [Rechtin and Maier 1997]

Both RUP and MBASE used a set of anchor point milestones, including the Life Cycle Objectives (LCO) and Life Cycle Architecture (LCA), as their model phase gates. The milestones were chosen in a series of workshops involving the USC Center for Software Engineering and its 30 government and industry affiliates, including Rational, Inc., as phase boundaries for COCOMO II cost and schedule estimates [Boehm 1996]. The pass/fail criteria for the LCO and LCA anchor point milestones are:

- Evidence provided by developer and validated by independent experts that if the system is built to the specified architecture, it will:
  — Satisfy the requirements: capability, interfaces, levels of service, and evolution
  — Support the operational concept
  — Be buildable within the budgets and schedules in the plan
  — Generate a viable return on investment
  — Generate satisfactory outcomes for all of the success-critical stakeholders
- All major risks resolved or covered by risk management plans

More recently, the MBASE approach has been extended into an Incremental Commitment Model (ICM) for overall systems and software engineering. It uses the anchor point milestones and feasibility rationales to synchronize and stabilize the concurrent engineering of the hardware, software, and human factors in a system's architecture, requirements, operational concept, plans, and business case [Pew and Mavor 2007]; [Boehm and Lane 2007]; [Boehm and Lane 2009]. A strong feasibility rationale includes evidence of feasibility resulting from architecture trade-off and feasibility analyses such as those discussed in [Clements et al. 2002] and [Maranzano et al. 2005].

Shortfalls in feasibility evidence are reflected as uncertainties or probabilities of project loss, which when multiplied by the associated size of the project loss equals Risk Exposure. Key stakeholders can use a project's level of Risk Exposure to determine whether to proceed into the next phase (acceptable risk), skip the next phase (negligible risk), extend the current phase (high but workable risk), or terminate or rescope the project (unacceptable risk). To ensure that this risk information is available, feasibility evidence needs to become a first-class project deliverable rather than an optional appendix that is dropped when budgets and schedules approach overruns.

Architecture and risk resolution (RESL) factor in COCOMO II

To persuade project managers to invest in feasibility evidence, we need to provide empirical evidence that the time spent on feasibility evidence offers a robust return on investment (ROI). The conditions under which feasibility evidence are worthwhile were established in the calibration of the COCOMO II cost estimation model to 161 representative projects.

The definition of the COCOMO II software cost estimation model [Boehm et al. 2000] evolved during 1995–1997 in workshops involving USC and its 30 industry and government affiliates. Its diseconomy-of-scale factor is a function of the Architecture and Risk Resolution (RESL) factor and four other scale factors: Capability Maturity Model maturity level, Developer-customer-user team cohesion, Precedentedness, and Development Flexibility.

The definition of the RESL rating scale was elaborated into the seven contributing factors shown in Table 10-1. As indicated in the section "How the Ada Process Model promoted risk-driven concurrent engineering software processes" on page 169, architecture and risk resolution include the concurrent engineering of the system's operational concept, requirements, plans, business case, and feasibility rationale, as well as its architecture, thus covering most of the key elements that are part of the software systems engineering function.

TABLE 10-1. RESL rating scale

Characteristic	Very Low	Low	Nominal	High	Very High	Extra High
Risk Management Plan identifies all critical risk items and establishes milestones for resolving them by PDR or LCA.	None	Little	Some	Generally	Mostly	Fully
Schedule, budget, and internal milestones through PDR or LCA compatible with Risk Management Plan.	None	Little	Some	Generally	Mostly	Fully
Percent of development schedule devoted to establishing architecture, given general product objectives.	5	10	17	25	33	40
Percent of required top software architects available to project.	20	40	60	80	100	120

Characteristic	Very Low	Low	Nominal	High	Very High	Extra High
Tool support available for resolving risk items, and developing and verifying architectural specs.	None	Little	Some	Good	Strong	Full
Level of uncertainty in key architecture drivers: mission, user interface, COTS, hardware, technology, and performance.	Extreme	Significant	Considerable	Some	Little	Very little
Number and criticality of risk items.	> 10 critical	5–10 critical	2–4 critical	1 critical	> 5 noncritical	< 5 noncritical

Each project contributing data to the COCOMO II database used Table 10-1 as a guide for rating its RESL factor. For each project, the data contributors and COCOMO II researchers decided during the data collection sessions how to relatively weight the ratings for each row. The RESL factor ratings of the 161 projects in the COCOMO II database fall roughly along a normal distribution, as shown in Figure 10-7.

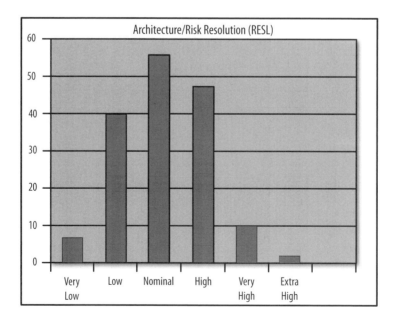

FIGURE 10-7. RESL ratings for the 161 projects in the COCOMO II database

The contribution of a project's RESL rating to its diseconomy-of-scale factor was determined by a Bayesian combination of expert judgment and a multiple regression analysis of the size, effort, and cost driver ratings of 161 representative software development projects in the COCOMO II database. These include commercial information technology applications, electronic services, telecommunications, middleware, engineering and science, command and control, and real-time process control software projects. Project sizes range from 2.6 thousand equivalent software lines of code (KSLOC) to 1,300 KSLOC, with 13 projects below 10 KSLOC and 5 projects above 1,000 KSLOC. The measure of equivalent lines of code accounts for the software's degrees of reuse and requirements volatility.

The expert-judgment means and standard deviations of the COCOMO II cost driver parameters were treated as *a priori* knowledge in the Bayesian calibration, and the corresponding means and standard deviations resulting from the multiple regression analysis of the historical data were treated as an *a posteriori* update of the parameter values. The Bayesian approach produces a weighted average of the expert and historical data values, which gives higher weights to parameter values with smaller standard deviations. The detailed approach and formulas are provided in Chapter 4 of the COCOMO II text [Boehm et al. 2000].

Improvement shown by incorporating architecture and risk resolution

Our calibration of the RESL scale factor tested our hypothesis that proceeding into software development with inadequate architecture and risk resolution results (i.e., inadequate systems engineering results) would cause project effort to increase because significant software rework would be necessary to overcome the architecture deficiencies and resolve the risks late in the development cycle. We also hypothesized, in accordance with our beliefs about diseconomies of scale in software, that the percentage of rework cost would be larger for larger projects.

The regression analysis to calibrate the RESL factor and the other 22 COCOMO II cost drivers confirmed these hypotheses with a statistically significant result. The calibration results determined that for this sample of 161 projects, the difference between a Very Low RESL rating and an Extra High rating added an extra 0.0707 to the exponent that related project effort to product size. This translates to an extra 18% effort for a small 10 KSLOC project, and an extra 92% effort for an extra-large 10,000 KSLOC project.

Figure 10-8 summarizes the results of the analysis. It shows that at least for this sample of 161 software projects, larger projects will see correspondingly larger upward scaling in overall project effort and cost, independent of the effects of the other 22 COCOMO II cost drivers. We demonstrated this independence through a regression analysis that accounted for the other 22 factors. The level of statistical significance of the RESL parameter was 2.084, which is above the significance value of 1.96 for the analysis of 23 variables and 161 data points, as shown in Table 10-2. Moreover, the pair-wise correlation analysis shows that no variable was correlated more than 0.4 with RESL.

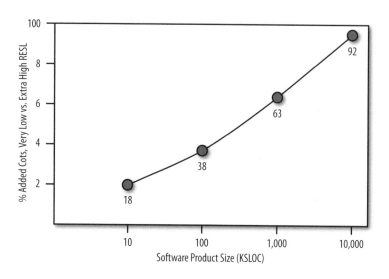

FIGURE 10-8. Added cost of minimal software systems engineering

TABLE 10-2. COCOMO II regression run

Data set = COCOMO II.2000			
Response = log[PM]			
Coefficient Estimates			
Label	**Estimate**	**Std. error**	**t-value**
Constant_A	0.961552	0.103346	9.304
log[SIZE]	0.921827	0.0460578	20.015
PMAT*log[SIZE]	0.684836	0.481078	1.424
PREC*log[SIZE]	1.10203	0.373961	2.947
TEAM*log[SIZE]	0.323318	0.497475	0.650
FLEX*log[SIZE]	0.354658	0.686944	0.516
RESL*log[SIZE]	1.32890	0.637678	2.084
log[PCAP]	1.20332	0.307956	3.907
log[RELY]	0.641228	0.246435	2.602
log[CPLX]	1.03515	0.232735	4.448
log[TIME]	1.58101	0.385646	4.100
log[STOR]	0.784218	0.352459	2.225

Data set = COCOMO II.2000			
Response = log[PM]			
Coefficient Estimates			
Label	Estimate	Std. error	t-value
log[ACAP]	0.926205	0.272413	3.400
log[PLEX]	0.755345	0.356509	2.119
log[LTEX]	0.171569	0.416269	0.412
log[DATA]	0.783232	0.218376	3.587
log[RUSE]	-0.339964	0.286225	-1.188
log[DOCU]	2.05772	0.622163	3.31
log[PVOL]	0.867162	0.227311	3.815
log[APEX]	0.137859	0.330482	0.417
log[PCON]	0.488392	0.322021	1.517
log[TOOL]	0.551063	0.221514	2.488
log[SITE]	0.674702	0.498431	1.354

ROI for Software Systems Engineering Improvement Investments

The previous sections showed that software engineering should focus effort on the risk-driven concurrent engineering of software system requirements, architecture, plans, budgets, and schedules. Investment is also needed to assure the consistency and feasibility of requirements via prototyping, modeling, and analysis. Stakeholder review at each phase of the project, and a commitment to support the next phase, are also critical to success, as discussed earlier in this chapter.

The results of the COCOMO II calibration of the RESL factor shown in Figure 10-8 enable us to determine the ROI for such investments, in terms of the added effort required for architecture and risk resolution, and the resulting savings for various sizes of software systems measured in KSLOC. Table 10-3 summarizes these results for a range of software system sizes from 10 to 10,000 KSLOC. Following the table is an explanation of how the values were calculated.

TABLE 10-3. Software systems engineering/RESL ROI

COCOMO II RESL rating	Very Low	Low	Nominal	High	Very High	Extra High
RESL time invested %	5	10	17	25	33	>40 (50)
Level of effort	0.3	0.4	0.5	0.6	0.7	0.75
RESL investment cost %	1.5	4	8.5	15	23	37.5
Incremental investment cost		2.5	4.5	6.5	8	14.5
Scale factor exponent for rework effort	1.0707	1.0565	1.0424	1.0283	1.0141	1.0
10 KSLOC project						
Added effort %	17.7	13.9	10.3	6.7	3.3	0
Incremental benefit, cost		3.8, 2.5	3.6, 4.5	3.6, 6.5	3.4, 8	3.3, 14.5
Incremental ROI		0.52	-0.20	-0.45	-0.58	-0.77
100 KSLOC project						
Added effort %	38.4	29.7	21.6	13.9	6.7	0
Incremental benefit, cost		8.7, 2.5	8.1, 4.5	7.7, 6.5	7.2, 8	6.7, 14.5
Incremental ROI		2.48	0.80	0.18	-0.10	-0.54
1,000 KSLOC project						
Added effort %	63	47.7	34.0	21.6	10.2	0
Incremental benefit, cost		15.3, 2.5	13.7, 4.5	12.4, 6.5	11.4, 8	10.2, 14.5
Incremental ROI		5.12	2.04	0.91	0.42	-0.30
10,000 KSLOC project						
Added effort %	91.8	68.3	47.8	29.8	13.9	0
Incremental benefit, cost		23.5, 2.5	20.5, 4.5	18.0, 6.5	15.9, 8	13.9, 14.5

The first rows in Table 10-3 show combined statistics for all projects measured:

RESL time invested %

> This is the key scale against which all other values are measured. It is the percentage of time invested in architecting for each RESL rating level.

Level of effort

> The fraction of the average project staff level on the job doing systems engineering at this rating level. The result looks roughly like the Rayleigh curve observed in the early phases of software projects [Boehm 1981].

RESL investment cost %

The percent of proposed budget allocated to architecture and risk resolution. This is calculated by multiplying the RESL percentage calendar time invested by the fraction of the average level of project staffing incurred for each rating level. For example, the RESL investment cost for the Very Low case is calculated as 5 * 0.3 = 1.5.

Incremental investment

The difference between the RESL investment cost % of rating level *n* minus rating level *n*-1. For instance, the incremental investment for the Low case is calculated as 4 − 1.5 = 2.5%.

Scale factor exponent for rework effort

The exponential effect of the RESL driver on software project effort, as calibrated from 161 projects.

The rest of the table shows four different system sizes (10 through 10,000 KSLOC) and how the ROI was calculated for the five different rating scale levels. The sequence of calculations is:

Added effort

Calculated by applying the scale factor exponent for rework (e.g., 1.0707) to the size of the system (e.g., 10 KSLOC) and calculating the added effort introduced. For instance, on the 10 KSLOC project, the added effort for the Very Low case is calculated as follows:

$$ROI = \frac{(B - C)}{C}$$

Incremental benefit

The difference between the added effort for rating level *n* minus rating level *n*-1. Thus, the incremental benefit for the Low case is 17.7 - 13.9 = 3.8.

Incremental cost

Same as the value for incremental investment, explained earlier.

Incremental ROI

The difference between the benefit and the cost divided by the cost:

$$= \frac{10^{1.0707} - 10}{10} *100$$
$$= 17.7$$

For instance, in the 10 KSLOC project, the incremental ROI for the Low case is calculated as follows:

$$= \frac{(3.8 - 2.5)}{2.5}$$
$$= 0.52$$

The calculations make it evident that architecting has a decreasing amount of incremental ROI as a function of RESL effort invested. Larger projects enjoy higher levels of ROI and longer spans of positive ROI because they start from higher levels of rework to improve upon. These results are presented graphically in Figure 10-9.

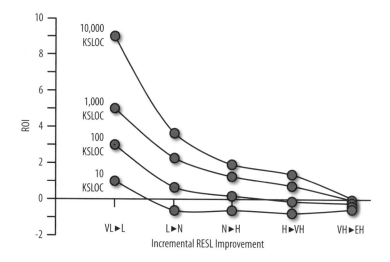

FIGURE 10-9. Incremental software systems engineering ROI

So How Much Architecting Is Enough?

We can now use the calculations in the previous sections to provide a rough answer to this central question in project planning.

The project that motivated this analysis was a very large software project (over 10,000 KSLOC) that wanted to get the suppliers on the job quickly, at the risk of spending an inadequate amount of time in system architecture and risk resolution before putting supplier plans and specifications into their Requests for Proposals (RFPs). The project needed to determine its "sweet spot" between the risk of having the suppliers deliver incompatible components, thus incurring schedule overruns due to rework, and the risk of spending too much time on system architecting and risk resolution, which might not leave enough time for the suppliers to develop their system components. This section shows how the COCOMO II RESL factor results were used to determine an adequate architecting "sweet spot" for this project and other sizes of projects.

The full set of effects for each of the RESL rating levels and corresponding architecting investment percentages are shown in Table 10-4 for projects of size 10, 100, and 10,000 KSLOC. Also shown are the corresponding percentages of total delays in delivery, obtained by adding the architecting investment time to the rework time, assuming constant team size during rework in order to translate added effort into added schedule. The bottom two rows of Table 10-4 show that the added investments in architecture definition and risk resolution are more than repaid by savings in rework time for a 10,000 KSLOC project up to an investment of 33% in architecting, after which the total delay percentage increases. In short, the minimum-delay architecting investment "sweet spot" for the 10,000 KSLOC project is 33%.

TABLE 10-4. Effect of architecting investment level on total project delay

COCOMO II RESL rating	Very Low	Low	Nominal	High	Very High	Extra High
% architecting investment	5	10	17	25	33	>40 (50)
Scale factor exponent for rework effort	1.0707	1.0565	1.0424	1.0283	1.0141	1.0
10 KSLOC project						
Added effort %	17.7	13.9	10.3	6.7	3.3	0
Project delay %	23	24	27	32	36	50
100 KSLOC project						
Added effort %	38.4	29.7	21.6	13.9	6.7	0
Project delay %	43	40	38	39	40	50
10,000 KSLOC project						
Added effort %	91.8	68.3	47.8	29.8	13.9	0
Project delay %	96	78	65	55	47	50

The top graph in Figure 10-10 shows the results of Table 10-4 graphically. It indicates that for a 10,000 KSLOC project, the sweet spot was actually a flat region around a 37% architecting investment (as a result of this analysis, the project added another 18 months to its architecting schedule). For a 100 KSLOC project, the sweet spot is a flat region around 20%. For a 10 KSLOC project, the sweet spot is around 5%. Thus, the results in the graph and Table 10-4 confirm that investments in architecting are less valuable for small projects but increasingly necessary as the project size increases.

Recent further analyses of the COCOMO II database on the effects of requirements volatility and system criticality are shown in the bottom graph of Figure 10-10. Here, the solid black lines represent the average-case cost of rework, architecting, and total cost for a 100-KSLOC project, as shown at the left. The dotted red lines show the effect on the cost of architecting and total cost if rapid change adds 50% to the cost of architecture and risk resolution. Quantitatively, this moves the sweet spot from roughly 20% to 10% of effective architecture investment (but actually 15%, due to the 50% cost penalty). Thus, high investments in architecture, feasibility analysis, and other documentation do not have a positive return on investment for very high volatility projects, due to the high costs of analysis and documentation rework for rapid-change adaptation.

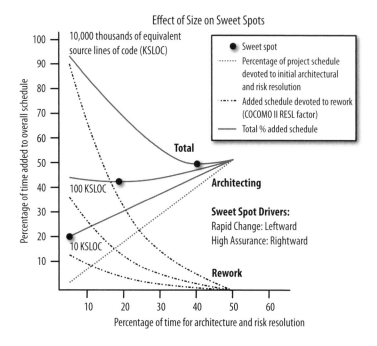

Effect of Size on Sweet Spots

10,000 thousands of equivalent source lines of code (KSLOC)

Legend:
- ● Sweet spot
- .... Percentage of project schedule devoted to initial architectural and risk resolution
- ·—·—· Added schedule devoted to rework (COCOMO II RESL factor)
- ——— Total % added schedule

Total

100 KSLOC

Architecting

Sweet Spot Drivers:
Rapid Change: Leftward
High Assurance: Rightward

10 KSLOC

Rework

Percentage of time added to overall schedule (y-axis)

Percentage of time for architecture and risk resolution (x-axis)

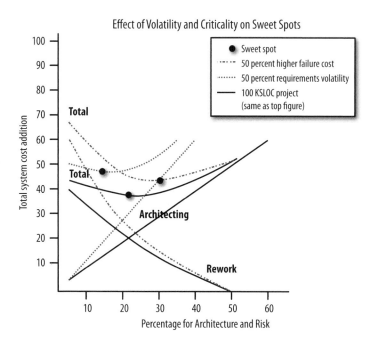

Effect of Volatility and Criticality on Sweet Spots

Legend:
- ● Sweet spot
- ·—·—· 50 percent higher failure cost
- .... 50 percent requirements volatility
- ——— 100 KSLOC project (same as top figure)

Total

Total

Architecting

Rework

Total system cost addition (y-axis)

Percentage for Architecture and Risk (x-axis)

FIGURE 10-10. *Penalties for architecture evidence shortfalls and resulting architecting investment sweet spots*

The dashed lines in the bottom graph of Figure 10-10 represent a conservative analysis of the external cost effects of system failure due to unidentified architecting shortfalls. These estimates of the costs of architecting shortfalls include not only added development project rework, but also losses to the organization's operational effectiveness and productivity. These are conservatively assumed to add 50% to the project-rework cost of architecture shortfalls. In most cases, for high-assurance systems, the added cost would be considerably higher.

Quantitatively, this moves the sweet spot from roughly 20% to over 30% as the most cost-effective investment in architecting and development of feasibility evidence for a 100 KSLOC project. As mentioned earlier, all the "sweet spots" are actually relatively flat "sweet regions" extending 5–10% to the left and right of the "sweet spots." However, moving to the edges of a sweet region increases the risk of significant losses if some project assumptions turn out to be optimistic.

To summarize the lessons from Figure 10-10, the greater the project's size, criticality, and stability, the greater the need for validated architecture feasibility evidence. However, for very small low-criticality projects with high volatility, the architecting efforts make little difference and don't need to be redone continuously, which would produce a negative return on investment. In such cases, Agile methods such as XP will be more effective. Overall, evidence-based specifications and plans will not guarantee a successful project, but in general will eliminate many of the software delivery overruns and shortfalls experienced on current software projects.

As one final caveat, the sweet spot investment numbers in Figure 10-10 are not one-size-fits-all architecting investment numbers for projects to put into their budgets, but instead early indicators of the right planning range for the architecting investments. Once the project reaches the detailed planning and budgeting stage, other cost drivers—such as personnel capability and experience, application complexity, legacy migration complexity, technology risk, process maturity, and tool support—can also influence the appropriate level of architecting investment. A more recent Constructive Systems Engineering Model (COSYSMO) has been developed and calibrated to support a project's more detailed determination of its needed amount of architecting investment [Valerdi 2005]; [Valerdi and Boehm 2010].

Does the Architecting Need to Be Done Up Front?

Many Agile projects succeed by doing a lot of architecting, but by spreading it out across the life cycle through refactoring. This is an effective process as long as the project stays small and noncritical, but can run into "easiest-first" difficulties otherwise.

One example is when a small project grows large and finds that tacit interpersonal knowledge and local refactoring do not scale up very well, as in the lease management project described in [Elssamadisy and Schalliol 2002]. Another class of difficulties arises from choosing commercial off-the-shelf (COTS) products to get a quick start and early customer satisfaction, but finding that the COTS products do not scale up to handle increased workloads and that their source code is unavailable for refactoring. A related problem is when a project delays a pervasive concern such as security—scheduling it for the sixth quarter, for instance—only to find that security is a pervasive quality attribute that cannot be bolted on or refactored into the project's previous architectural commitments. Thus, such evolution requirements need to be anticipated and architected-for in advance.

Conclusions

The evidence provided across 40 years of data on the degree of increase in software cost-to-fix versus delay-of-fix is that for large projects, the increase from fixing requirements changes and defects during requirements definition to fixing them once the product is fielded continues to be around 100:1. However, this ratio can be significantly reduced by higher investments in early requirements and architecture verification and validation. As shown by the CCPDS-R project data in Figure 10-6, the ratio can approach 1:1 if the high-risk fixes are addressed early.

The evidence for small projects continues to show ratios around 5:1, but these can also be flattened by the use of outstanding personnel and by Agile methods, such as pair programming and continuous integration, that shorten the delay-of-fix time. Small, noncritical projects can also spread their architecting activity across the life cycle via refactoring, but need to watch out for making easiest-first architectural commitments that cannot be easily undone by refactoring, such as committing to unscalable COTS products or security-incompatible data and control structures.

The evidence provided more recently on the payoff of architecting and risk resolution efforts, such as those on CCPDS-R, is that the location of the highest-payoff "how much architecting is enough" sweet spot is a function of project size and criticality (larger, more critical projects require more architecting investment), but also a function of requirements volatility (more volatile projects would be slowed down by the need to revise extensive documentation). For detailed project planning and budgeting, the sweet-spot numbers need to be adjusted to reflect additional project, personnel, and product-related cost drivers. A recent COSYSMO model is now available to support such adjustments.

Very large projects are likely to have elements that are high in criticality and stability (e.g., safety and security-critical elements), as well as elements that are high in requirements volatility (e.g., user interfaces, external-system interfaces, device drivers, database schemas). In such cases, a hybrid approach using Agile methods for the rapidly changing parts and plan-driven methods for the more stable and high-criticality parts will work, as long as the overall system is based on an architecture using the [Parnas 1979] information-hiding approach of encapsulating sources of change within modules.

Thus, there are no one-size-fits-all solutions for the increasingly rapid change that projects will experience in the future. Large projects or enterprises with a mix of critical and volatile elements are best served by risk-driven process generators, such as the Incremental Commitment Model and risk-driven versions of the Rational Unified Process. These model generators use the degree of developer-supplied evidence of project feasibility to determine project risk. Such evidence is critical to the success of many future projects facing the prospect of having to cope with increasing size, criticality, volatility, and complexity. In addition, the use of such evidence-based models will have the double benefit of reducing risk and adding to the knowledge base of evidence that can be analyzed for further sources of project and enterprise improvement.

References

[Beck 1999] Beck, K. 1999. *Extreme Programming Explained*. Boston: Addison-Wesley.

[Boehm 1976] Boehm, B. 1976. Software engineering. *IEEE Transactions on Computers* 25(12): 1226–1241.

[Boehm 1980] Boehm, B. 1980. Developing small-scale software application products: Some experimental results. *Proceedings of the IFIP Congress 1980*: 321–326.

[Boehm 1981] Boehm, B. 1981. *Software Engineering Economics*. Upper Saddle River, NJ: Prentice-Hall.

[Boehm 1996] Boehm, B. 1996. Anchoring the software process. *Software* 13(4): 73–82.

[Boehm 2000] Boehm, B. 2000. Unifying software engineering and systems engineering. *Computer* 33(3): 114–116.

[Boehm and Lane 2007] Boehm, B., and J. Lane. 2007. Using the incremental commitment model to integrate system acquisition, systems engineering, and software engineering. *CrossTalk* (Oct. 2007): 4–9.

[Boehm and Lane 2009] Boehm, B., J. Lane. 2009. Guide for Using the Incremental Commitment Model (ICM) for Systems Engineering of DoD Projects, Version 0.5. USC-CSSE-2009-500. Available at *http://csse.usc.edu/csse/TECHRPTS/2009/usc-csse-2009-500/usc-csse-2009-500.pdf*.

[Boehm and Port 1999] Boehm, B., and D. Port. 1999. Escaping the software tar pit: Model clashes and how to avoid them. *ACM Software Engineering Notes* 24(1): 36–48.

[Boehm and Port 2001] Boehm, B., and D. Port. 2001. Balancing discipline and flexibility with the spiral model and MBASE. *CrossTalk* (Dec. 2001): 23–28.

[Boehm and Royce 1989] Boehm, B., and W. Royce. 1989. Ada COCOMO and the Ada process model. Paper presented at the 5th COCOMO Users' Group, October 17–19, in Pittsburgh, PA. Available at *http://csse.usc.edu/csse/TECHRPTS/1989/usccse89-503/usccse89-503.pdf*.

[Boehm et al. 1998] Boehm, B.A., Egyed, J. Kwan, D. Port, A. Shah, and R. Madachy. 1998. Using the WinWin spiral model: a case study. *IEEE Computer* 31(7): 33–44.

[Boehm et al. 2000] Boehm, B., C. Abts, A.W. Brown, S. Chulani, B. Clark, E. Horowitz, R. Madachy, D. Reifer, and B. Steece. 2000. *Software Cost Estimation with COCOMO II*. Upper Saddle River, NJ: Prentice-Hall.

[Boehm et al. 2010] Boehm, B., J. Lane, S. Koolmanojwong, and R. Turner. 2010. Architected Agile Solutions for Software-Reliant Systems. In *Agile Software Development: Current Research and Future Directions*, ed. T. Dingsøtr, T. Dybå, and N.B. Moe, 165–184. Berlin: Springer-Verlag.

[Clements et al. 2002] Clements, P., R. Kazman, and M. Klein. 2002. *Evaluating Software Architectures*. Boston: Addison-Wesley.

[Daly 1977] Daly, E. 1977. Management of software engineering. *IEEE Transactions on Software Engineering*. 3(3): 229–242.

[Elssamadisy and Schalliol 2002] Elssamadisy, A., and G. Schalliol. 2002. Recognizing and Responding to "Bad Smells" in Extreme Programming. *Proceedings of the 24th International Conference on Software Engineering*: 617–622.

[Fagan 1976] Fagan, M. 1976. Design and code inspections to reduce errors in program development. *IBM Systems Journal* 15(3): 182–211.

[Jacobson et al. 1999] Jacobson, I., G. Booch, and J. Rumbaugh. 1999. *The Unified Software Development Process*. Reading, MA: Addison-Wesley.

[Kruchten 1999] Kruchten, P. 1999. *The Rational Unified Process: An Introduction*. Reading, MA: Addison-Wesley.

[Li and Alshayeb 2002] Li, W., and M. Alshayeb. 2002. An Empirical Study of XP Effort. Paper presented at the 17th International Forum on COCOMO and Software Cost Modeling, October 22–25, in Los Angeles, CA.

[Maranzano et al. 2005] Maranzano, J., S.A. Rozsypal, G.H. Zimmerman, G.W. Warnken, P.E. Wirth, and D.M. Weiss. 2005. Architecture reviews: Practice and experience. *Software* 22(2): 34–43.

[McGibbon 1996] McGibbon, T. 1996. Software reliability data summary. Data & Analysis Center for Software Technical Report.

[Parnas 1979] Parnas, D. 1979. Designing software for ease of extension and contraction, *IEEE Transactions on Software Engineering* 5(2): 128–138.

[Pew and Mavor 2007] Pew, R., and A. Mavor, ed. 2007. *Human-System Integration in the System Development Process*. Washington, D.C.: National Academies Press.

[Rechtin 1991] Rechtin, E. 1991. *Systems Architecting*. Englewood Cliffs, NJ: Prentice-Hall.

[Rechtin and Maier 1997] Rechtin, E., and M. Maier. 1997. *The Art of Systems Architecting*. Boca Raton, FL: CRC Press.

[Reifer 2002] Reifer, D. 2002. How to get the most out of extreme programming/agile methods. *Proceedings of the Second XP Universe and First Agile Universe Conference on Extreme Programming and Agile Methods*: 185–196.

[Royce 1998] Royce, W. 1998. *Software Project Management: A Unified Framework*. Reading, MA: Addison-Wesley.

[Shull et al. 2002] Shull, F., V. Basili, B. Boehm, A.W. Brown, P. Costa, M. Lindvall, D. Port, I. Rus, R. Tesoreiro, and M. Zelkowitz. 2002. What we have learned about fighting defects. *Proceedings of the 8th International Symposium on Software Metrics*: 249–258.

[Stephenson 1976] Stephenson, W. 1976. An analysis of the resources used in the SAFEGUARD software system development. *Proceedings of the 2nd international conference on software engineering*: 312–321.

[Valerdi 2005] Valerdi, R. 2005. The constructive systems engineering cost model (COSYSMO). PhD diss., University of Southern California.

[Valerdi and Boehm 2010] Valerdi, R., and B. Boehm. 2010. COSYSMO: A systems engineering cost model. *Génie Logiciel* 92: 2–6.

NOTE

Pre-publication versions of most USC papers are available at *http://csse.usc.edu/csse/ TECHRPTS/.*

## CHAPTER ELEVEN

Conway's Corollary

Christian Bird

**Design and programming are human activities; forget that and
all is lost.**

—Bjarne Stroustrop

Conway's Law

In 1967, Melvin Conway, an early computer scientist, computer programmer, and hacker,
submitted a paper entitled "How Do Committees Invent?" to the *Harvard Business Review* (HBR),
which summarily rejected it on the grounds that Conway "had not proved [the] thesis."

Fortunately for the world of software design, the same paper was later accepted by
Datamation, a major IT magazine of the time, and published in April 1968 [Conway 1968].
Later, in Fred Brooks' seminal work "The Mythical Man-Month" [Brooks 1974], he referred
to one of Conway's assertions as "Conway's Law," and the name stuck. While there was little
in the way of empirical evidence to support Conway's assertions at the time, this "law" has
received no small amount of attention in recent years. This chapter contains evidence that
would no doubt have been helpful to Conway in 1967 to gather support for this assertion. This
evidence is valuable today to help establish the "law" as a touchstone for modern software
developers.

At the heart of Conway's paper is the thesis:

> Any organization that designs a system (defined broadly) will produce a design whose structure is a copy of the organization's communication structure.

As anecdotal evidence, Conway cites the following: A contract research organization had eight people who were to produce a COBOL and an ALGOL compiler. After some initial estimates of difficulty and time, five people were assigned to the COBOL job and three to the ALGOL job. The resulting COBOL compiler ran in five phases, and the ALGOL compiler ran in three.

Though simple and inconclusive, this real-world example provides a striking demonstration of the possible effect that the organizational structure of a development team has on artifact design and architecture.

Conway stated that *HBR*'s basis for rejecting the paper "says more about differences in notions of 'proof' than it does about the paper."

Empirical software engineering has come a long way since 1967 and this chapter presents some important studies that evaluate the validity of Conway's Law. Many empirical studies have major flaws and none are perfect, but these studies were conducted according to established empirical guidelines, and we have reason to cite them as strong evidence of not only the tendency but also the *need* for organizational structure to mirror architectural structure.

Any system of consequence is fashioned from smaller *subsystems* that are interconnected in some fashion. These subsystems in turn can be viewed as systems made up of even smaller modules. The design of a system is made up of the modules, each of which accomplishes some part of the whole, and of the interconnections between the modules. In software development, as in many other disciplines, the term *interface* describes the mechanism by which one module is connected to another (or exposes services that it provides). Thus a system can be described by a graph made up of nodes (module/subsystems) and edges (interconnections by means of interfaces).

Conway provides a "proof," based on design origins of a system, for the assertion that artifact structure mirrors organizational structure. For any module x in the system, we can identify the set of people in the design organization that designed x; call this set X. Thus, for every module in the system, there is a corresponding set of people that we call a design group. Note that there may not be a one-to-one correspondence, however, as the same design group may design multiple modules. For any two modules or subsystems, x and y, designed by design groups X and Y, a connection either exists or is absent. If there is a connection, then X and Y must have negotiated and agreed upon an interface specification to permit communication between the two corresponding modules. If there is no connection, then there was nothing for the two design groups to negotiate and thus no need for communication between X and Y.

Thus, at least at the outset, there is a close relationship between the structure of a system and the structure that created it. However, both the software artifact and the organization that develops and maintains it are dynamic. Requirements change, people transfer to different teams, and designs drift.

While Conway's claims focus on the initial design stages of software development, many observers have found that this intuition holds during later phases as well. Thus a possible corollary of Conway's Law is:

> A software system whose structure closely matches its organization's communication structure works "better" (defined broadly) than a subsystem whose structure differs from its organization's communication structure.

The term "better" may take on different definitions depending on the project's context. Most software development organizations express two high-level goals: to sustain high levels of productivity while maintaining software quality. This chapter presents one study that examined the relationship of Conway's Law to the ability of developers to complete tasks quickly (productivity) and another study that investigated the effects of Conway's Law on post-release failures (quality). Both cases support this corollary to Conway's assertions. We also present one study that examined the structure of five prominent open source software (OSS) projects to derive evidence that when left to their own devices, the communication structure of a successful project (at least in the area of OSS) tends to become modular in a fashion that mirrors software structure.

For each study, we present the context, the methods used, the results, and the implications. In addition, we describe the practical changes we should make to software projects in view of the findings. In particular, we suggest that we should not let the system's structure evolve haphazardly from the breakdown of tasks among programmers, but instead should anticipate the structure of the software we want and make sure to structure our organization accordingly.

We take the positivist view that it is difficult to prove a theory, but that we can increase our confidence in the theory each time we fail to refute it. To this end, it is hoped that the following sections increase a reader's confidence in Conway's Law, as well as the corollary.

Coordination, Congruence, and Productivity

In 2006, Marcelo Cataldo et al. [Cataldo et al. 2006] asked the question, *"How much does coordination affect productivity in a large real-world software project?"* The implications of the answer are clear: if coordination plays a large role in productivity, organizations have a vested interest in doing whatever they can to ease coordination. If coordination does not have much of an effect, time and money should be focused on other aspects of a project (e.g., more manpower, better equipment, or siting facilities in economically better locations).

To answer this question, they examined work dependencies, coordination needs, and the time that it took to complete software development tasks for an important project in a large company. The project represented a unit of work as a modification request (MR). An MR is any requested change to the system, whether it be adding a feature, fixing a problem, or performing maintenance to improve the code base. Team members working to complete MRs often need to coordinate their changes for two key reasons:

- Some MRs have dependencies on other MRs. For instance, a request to add a spellchecker to a word processor cannot be completed until the request to add a dictionary to the project has been completed.

- A software project is almost always made up of a number of interdependent modules. Thus, changes made to the system are rarely made in isolation and often affect "nearby" modules.

For these reasons, Cataldo and company posit that when there is "fit" between the task dependencies that developers have and the coordination activities performed by these developers, it will be easier to complete tasks (MRs). They call this fit *congruence* and use data from a large software project to evaluate their hypothesis. This seems relatively simple until we think about how to measure coordination activities within a software team, something that is not straightforward at all. Half the difficulty of any empirical study is finding ways to measure what is desired with the data that is actually available. Cataldo et al. devised four measures for examining the congruence of the coordination of software developers with the modification requests that they needed to complete. These measures capture both direct observations of communication and team characteristics that facilitate communication. The direct observations came from comments made on particular MRs and content within Internet Relay Chat (IRC) messages. The likelihood of communication was judged by team members' geographic proximity and their positions within the organization. The four measures of congruence are:

Structural congruence
> Measures the ease of coordination among developers in the same team. There are many reasons to believe that communication between team members is easier than between members of different teams. Team members communicate by way of team meetings and other work-related activities. They often know each other and have communicated previously. Further, management puts developers into teams because they expect that their assigned work will require them to work together.

Geographical congruence
> Measures the physical distance between developers as a proxy for difficulty in communication. When two developers work in the same building, it is much easier for one to contact the other, by arriving unannounced, planning an impromptu meeting, or some other means. Time zone issues are not a problem when working at the same site. In addition, because communication can take place in person, the communication itself can be richer. Developers can use social cues such as facial expressions. They can sketch out ideas and plans on a whiteboard or look at code on a screen together in a way that is much more difficult over a greater distance.

Task congruence

> Measures communication via comments associated with a particular task (MR). In the software project that Cataldo studied, the online MR tracking system allowed developers to record comments on MRs for other people to see. This allowed the developers who had an interest in a particular MR to communicate with each other. When multiple developers made comments to an MR, this indicated some level of coordination, and a flow of technical information regarding the MR.

IRC communication congruence

> Measures coordination between developers that occurs on IRC, a form of instant messaging. Although not as rich as face-to-face communication, IRC can be used for synchronous communication between developers to ask questions or plan coordinated changes. In order to relate IRC conversations to specific modification requests, Cataldo enlisted the help of two additional raters to read the IRC logs and manually associate them with the MRs that the developers were discussing. To assess consistency, 10% of the MRs were associated by all three raters, and there was 97.5% agreement between them, indicating high confidence that the IRC chat to MR association was fairly accurate.

The software project comprised the activity of 114 developers grouped into eight development teams distributed across three locations. The period during which data was collected encompassed three years and four releases of the product. The crux of the idea was to look at the *task assignments* for each developer and the *task dependencies* for each task. If Alice is working on some task, *t1*, that has a dependency on a different task, *t2*, which is assigned to Bob, there may be need for Alice and Bob to coordinate their changes. Cataldo et al. measured task assignment by looking at which MRs were completed by each developer and which files were changed to complete each MR. Therefore, the task associated with each developer was a set of files. Often, completing an MR required making changes to multiple files. Then, counting the number of times over the life of the system that two files were changed together to complete a single MR represents the interdependence of the files. Concretely, if two files *f1* and *f2* have been changed together in the past many times to complete MRs, and if Alice needs to change *f1* to complete an MR while Bob needs to change *f2* to complete his MR, then it would probably be a good idea for them to communicate.

These patterns were used to determine the developer coordination that we *expect* to see when MRs are being completed. Cataldo measured the *actual* coordination patterns of developers via the four measures of coordination introduced. When the expected coordination closely matched what actually happened, this indicated high congruence, and when the expected coordination did not occur, congruence was said to be low. Using this approach, they calculated the congruence level for each MR for each of the four forms of congruence. They then examined the relationship of each type of congruence with the time that it took to complete the MR.

The four forms of coordination indicate the communication structure of the entire development organization. At a high level, Cataldo et al. are asking the question, "Is a task completed more quickly when the communication structure mirrors the artifact structure?" If the answer is yes, this is strong evidence that teams are more productive when Conway's Law is adhered to, and Conway's Corollary is true with respect to the time required to complete tasks.

In their analysis, the authors were careful to control for factors that were already known to have an effect on the time required to complete an MR. For instance, MRs that have many dependencies will take longer, and those that are in a higher-priority category will be completed more quickly. In all, they controlled for dependencies, priority, task reassignment, the number of files that were changed to complete an MR, whether the MR was internal or requested by a customer, the experience of the developer that the MR was assigned to (in terms of time spent programming in general, time with the company, and time working on the component associated with the MR), the particular release that the MR occurred in, and the load on the developer in terms of number of other MRs he or she was assigned. This approach avoids a situation in which the time required for an MR that has low priority and is worked on by a new developer during an initial release is compared to that required for a different MR that is high priority during a maintenance release and assigned to a seasoned project veteran. Without controlling for such factors, one might falsely conclude that lack of coordination caused an MR to take longer to complete, when in fact, the real reason was lack of experience or the phase of the project. Such rigor and attention to detail is one of the reasons that the results of this study represent real evidence rather than "deception by statistics."

After a careful quantitative analysis (I'll leave out the gory details of lognormal distributions and multiple regression models, but for extra fun, take a look at the original paper), the authors found that when an MR had a high level of congruence, or "coordination fit," it was completed in less time than a similar MR with a low level of congruence.

Interestingly, *structural congruence*, the measure that takes team makeup into account, reduced the time required by MRs the most, followed by *geographical congruence*, a measure of distance between developers working on related tasks.

The other important finding was that the effect of *IRC congruence* was stronger in later releases than in earlier ones. Figure 11-1 indicates that there was likely architectural drift over time, as the *structural congruence* (congruence along team makeup) appears to drop, meaning that more MRs required work from people in multiple teams. IRC communication would make up for the difficulty in cross-team coordination. It is also likely that developers became more adept at using IRC to coordinate changes with others who were on different teams or at different sites.

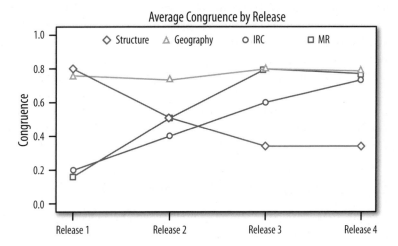

FIGURE 11-1. Average congruence by release

Implications

This is all well and good, but what does it mean for *your* project? As with any case study, we have to think about whether we can generalize from the results. Findings from a study are likely to hold for a software project, to the degree that the project is similar to the project in the study. Fortunately, the project studied by Cataldo et al. was large, made up of over 100 developers and thousands of files and work tasks (MRs). The project was made up of multiple teams that were geographically distributed, and the results held across both an initial release and subsequent releases. Thus, we have some confidence in the applicability of the study to many situations in software development.

Although you can't anticipate all of the bugs that your team will need to fix or all the features they will need to implement, it may well be reasonable to have an idea of where most strong dependencies will be during the design phase of a software project. These dependencies between components indicate parts of the system that are likely to feel more repercussions when changes are made without coordination. When possible, the allocation of tasks and components to developers and teams should be made to facilitate communication between parties working on interdependent components. This implies that it would be better to delay finalizing team structure until *after* the design phase, or at least to allow flexibility in the makeup of teams. Cataldo et al. noted that structural congruence decreased over time, indicating that the mapping of teams to dependencies within the code changed. Reorganizing teams of developers between releases may mitigate this problem, leading to higher structural congruence and decreased time for MR completion. Similarly, the allocation of tasks and components to developers should take geography into account. When possible, components that have high levels of interdependence should be given to teams and developers that work at the same site to allow richer forms of coordination.

MR and IRC coordination are much more dynamic and can change during the course of a project. Clearly, MRs take less time to complete when more of the developers working on related tasks are coordinating via MR comments. This behavior should be recognized and encouraged. Current research is investigating the use of tools to help developers and managers identify tasks that lack such coordination and determine who *should* be coordinating. Further, development organizations should embrace any communication medium that enhances coordination across both geographical and organizational distance. An investment in such technology and infrastructure up front may well pay for itself in the form of fewer tasks blocked by coordination needs and thus in increased productivity.

Organizational Complexity Within Microsoft

We've explored the relationship of Conway's Corollary with developer productivity by examining how "congruence," Cataldo's term for conforming to Conway's Corollary, yields faster task completion. The other important outcome in any software development project is software quality. It is well known that a defect identified later in the development cycle has a much higher cost to correct. Defects that are not identified until after release are the most costly and therefore the most important to minimize. The cost associated with such defects have more than just monetary effects; perceived quality and company reputation drops when users encounter bugs in software, which can have lasting effects in the marketplace.

In light of Conway's claims and the cost associated with defects, Nachi Nagappan, Brendan Murphy, and Vic Basili studied organizational structure and post-release defects in Windows Vista [Nagappan et al. 2008] and found a surprisingly strong relationship between the two. In fact, they found that measures of organizational structure *were better indicators of software quality than any attributes of the software itself.* Put more simply, in the case of Vista, if you want to know whether a piece of software has bugs, you'll know better by looking at how the people who wrote it were organized than by looking at the code!

At the heart of their study is the premise that software development is a group effort and organizational complexity makes coordinating that effort difficult. As with any empirical study, they had to map their phenomenon down to something that is actually measurable. Measuring software quality is fairly easy. Windows Vista shipped with thousands of "binaries," which are any piece of compiled code that exists in one file. So this includes all executables (*.exe*), shared libraries (*.dll*), and drivers (*.sys*). Whenever a component fails, the failure can be isolated to the binary that caused it, and reports of failures that are sent to Microsoft (remember that fun dialog you see whenever something crashes?) are recorded and used in decision making about how to prioritize bug fixing efforts. This information, along with other bug reports and their associated fixes, indicate how prone to failure each individual binary is. To evaluate Conway's Corollary, Nagappan classified each binary in Vista as either failure-prone or not failure-prone based on how many distinct failures were associated with the binary. Note that if thousands of users send reports of crashes due to one defect, this is still only counted as *one* defect. Thus, failure-proneness is a measure of the number of defects known to be in a binary.

Measuring organizational complexity is a bit more difficult. Nagappan, Murphy, and Basili proposed eight metrics for organizational complexity, examined the individual correlation of each metric with failure-proneness, and built a regression model to examine the effect of each metric when controlling for the effects of each of the others. They used data from the version control system to determine which software engineers made changes to source files. Build information indicated which source files are used to build each binary. For simplicity, we say that an engineer contributed to, or touched, a binary if he or she made changes to any of the source files that were compiled into that binary.

Nagappan, Murphy, and Basili also gathered data from the company's organizational chart to see how engineers were related organizationally. Each of their metrics uses information from at least one of these sources (and no other additional information was used). The eight organizational structure metrics are presented here:

Number of engineers
> The number of engineers simply indicates how many individual software engineers contributed to a particular binary and are still employed by the company. We expect that higher values will result in more failure-prone binaries. The intuition behind this expectation is based on Brooks' assertion [Brooks 1974] that if there are n engineers working on one component, there are $n(n-1)/2$ possible communication paths. The communication overhead grows *more than linearly* when a software team grows. The more communication paths that can break down, the more likely there will be a coordination problem, leading to design mismatches, one engineer breaking another's code, misunderstandings about design rationale, etc. Therefore, we expect to see more failures when more engineers work on a binary.

Number of ex-engineers
> The number of ex-engineers is a measure of the engineers who worked on a binary and left the company prior to the release date. We expect that a higher value will lead to more defects. This is a measure of required knowledge transfer. When an engineer working on a binary leaves, another engineer who is less experienced with the code may step in to perform required work. This new engineer likely is not as familiar with the component's design, the reasoning behind bug fixes, or who all of the stakeholders in the code are. This therefore increases the probability of mistakes being made and defects being introduced into the binary.

Edit frequency
> The edit frequency is the total number of times that a binary was changed, independent of the number of lines in each change. A change is simply a unique commit in the version control system. Higher values of this metric are considered bad for code quality. If a binary has too many changes, this could indicate a lack of stability or control in the code, even if a small group of engineers are responsible for the changes. When taken together with the

number of engineers and number of ex-engineers, this metric provides a comprehensive view of the distribution of changes. For instance, did a single engineer make the majority of the changes, or were they widely distributed across a large group? Correlating engineers with edits avoids a situation in which a few engineers making all of the changes can inflate this metric and lead to incorrect conclusions.

Depth of master ownership (DMO)

This measures how widely the work on a binary is distributed within an organization. For a particular binary, each person in the organization is labeled with the number of changes made to the binary by that person and all the people below him or her in the organizational hierarchy. In other words, the changes by individual contributors are summed and assigned to their manager along with his or her personal changes. The depth of master ownership is simply the lowest organizational level of the person labeled with at least 75% of the changes (the master owner). The higher this metric, the lower the master owner in the organization. We expect that a higher metric will be associated with less failures. If the majority of the changes to a binary come from a group of organizationally close engineers with a common manager, this low-level manager has ownership and the depth of master ownership is high. This indicates that the engineers working on a binary are in close contact and that coordination doesn't require communication at high levels of the hierarchy. If we need to move up to a high-level manager to find someone responsible for 75% of the commits, there is no clear owner and changes are coming from many different parts of the organization. This may lead to problems regarding decision making due to many interested parties with different goals. Because a high-level manager has more people beneath him or her and is further removed from most of the actual work, communication is more likely to be delayed, lost, or misunderstood.

Percentage of organization contributing to development

This measures the proportion of the people in an organization that report to the level of the DMO, the previous metric. If the organization that owns a binary has 100 people in it and 25 of those people report to the master owner, for instance, this metric has a value of 0.25. We expect that lower values will indicate less failure-prone binaries. This metric aids the DMO metric when considering organizations that are unbalanced, for instance, if an organization has two managers but one manager deals with 50 people and the other only 10. A lower value indicates that ownership is more concentrated and that there is less coordination overhead across the organization.

Level of organizational code ownership

This is the percent of changes from the owning organization, or, when there is no defined owning organization, the largest contributing organization. Higher values are better. Different organizations within the same company will often have differing goals, work practices, and culture. Coordination between parties across organizational boundaries will need to deal with these differences, increasing the likelihood of broken builds, synchronization problems, and defects in the code. If there is an owner from a binary, then it is better for the majority of the changes to come from the same organization as the owner. If there is no clear owner, we still expect better outcomes if one organization makes the vast majority of the changes.

Overall organizational ownership

This measure is the ratio of the number of engineers who made changes to a binary and report to the master owner to the total number of engineers who made changes to the binary. We expect higher values to be associated with less failures. If the majority of the people making changes to a binary are managed by the owning manager, there is less required coordination outside the scope of that manager and therefore a lower chance of a coordination breakdown. This metric complements the DMO metric in that a low depth of master ownership (considered bad) may be offset by a high overall organizational ownership level (considered good).

Organization intersection factor

This measures the number of organizations that make at least 10% of the changes to a binary. Higher values indicate more organizationally distributed binaries, which we expect to lead to more failures. When more organizations make changes to a binary, this indicates no clear owner. There also may be competing goals within organizations touching the binary. The interest that multiple organizations show in the binary may also indicate that it represents an important "join-point" within the system architecture.

Each of these metrics measures some form of organizational complexity per binary. More organizational complexity indicates that the structure of the organization is poorly aligned with the structure of the software system itself. If our corollary to Conway's Law is correct, we will observe better outcomes when there is less organizational complexity and more "fit" between the social and technical structures.

So how did these organizational measures hold up when compared to post-release defects in Windows Vista? To answer this question, Nagappan, Murphy, and Basili used a form of quantitative analysis known as *logistic regression*. Logistic regression takes as input a series of independent variables and produces a classification as output. In this case, each of the organizational metrics is measured for each binary and is used as the independent variables. Nagappan, Murphy, and Basili used post-release defect data to classify the binaries into failure-prone and not failure-prone. They then used logistic regression to determine whether there was a relationship between an independent variable (an organizational metric) and a classification (failure-prone or not). What's more, this form of analysis can determine whether one organizational metric is related to failure-proneness *when controlling for the effects of the other organizational metrics.*

This is a little like studying the effect of a person's age and height on his weight. If we examine the relationship of age with weight, a strong relationship will emerge, and likewise with height and weight. However, if you control for the height of a person, there is little to no relationship between age and weight (on average, someone in the U.S. who is six feet tall weighs about 210 lbs., regardless of whether he is 30 or 60). Logistic regression can also be used to make predictions. One can "train" a logistic regression model using a sample of people whose age, height, and weight are known, and then predict the weight of a new person by examining only his age and height.

The results of the study by Nagappan, Murphy, and Basili showed that each of the eight organizational metrics studied had a statistically significant effect on failure, even when controlling for the effects of the other seven metrics. That is, the higher the number of ex-engineers that worked on a binary, the more failures in that binary, even when removing the effects of the total number of engineers, depth of master ownership, etc. This indicates not only that organizational complexity is related to post-release defects, but also that each of the organizational metrics is measuring something at least slightly different from the others.

Next, Nagappan, Murphy, and Basili attempted to *predict* the failure-prone binaries based on the organizational metrics. Prediction is more difficult than simply finding a relationship because there are many factors that can affect an outcome. One might determine that age is strongly related to weight, but that doesn't mean that one can accurately *predict* the weight of someone given only her age. The researchers found, however, that these organizational complexity metrics actually could predict failure-proneness with surprising accuracy. In fact, the organizational metrics were far better predictors than characteristics of the source code itself that have been shown to be highly indicative of failures (e.g., lines of code, cyclomatic complexity, dependencies, code coverage by testing).

The standard way to compare different prediction techniques is to examine precision and recall, two complementary measures of a predictor's accuracy:

- *Precision*, in this case, indicates how many of the binaries that a predictor classifies as failure-prone actually are failure-prone. A low value indicates many false positives, i.e., binaries that were predicted to be failure-prone but actually are not.

- *Recall* indicates how many of the binaries that actually are failure-prone binaries are predicted to be failure-prone. A low value indicates that there are many failure-prone binaries that the predictor is incorrectly classifying as not failure-prone.

If possible, we would like to maximize both prediction and recall. An ideal predictor would predict all the actually failure-prone binaries as such and not predict any others as failure-prone. Table 11-1 shows the recall and precision for the organizational structure regression model compared to other methods of predicting failure-prone binaries in the past that have used aspects of the source code.

TABLE 11-1. Prediction accuracy

Model	Precision	Recall
Organizational structure	86.2%	84.0%
Code churn	78.6%	79.9%
Code complexity	79.3%	66.0%
Dependencies	74.4%	69.9%
Code coverage	83.8%	54.4%
Pre-release bugs	73.8%	62.9%

Implications

What do these results actually mean? First, within the context of Windows Vista development, it is clear that organizational complexity has a strong relationship with post-release defects. These results confirm our corollary that (at least in within the context of Windows Vista) when communication and coordination mirrors the technical artifact itself, the software is "better." When developers from different organizations are working on a common binary, that binary is much more likely to be failure-prone. There are many possible explanations for this. In the case of engineers leaving the company, binary-specific domain knowledge is lost, and low depth of master ownership means that communication between engineers working on the same binary must flow through upper levels of management and deal with the accompanying overhead, delay, and information loss.

Nagappan, Murphy, and Basili didn't identify exactly which factors were *causing* the post-release defects. Such an endeavor would be quite difficult and most likely economically infeasible given the scale of Windows Vista. It would require something akin to a controlled "clinical trial" in which one group of engineers writes an operating system in a setting where organizational structure is minimized while another "placebo" group does the same thing in a more traditional structure as it exists at present.

Despite the lack of a detailed causality analysis, we can still benefit a great deal from these results. If practitioners believe that there is a causal relationship between organizational complexity and post-release defects, they may use such knowledge to minimize this complexity. Instead of allowing engineers throughout the organization to make changes to a binary, a clear owning team may be appointed to act as a gatekeeper or change reviewer. Due to interdependencies within any non-trivial software project, it is unlikely that organizationally complex components can be avoided entirely, but they may be identified up front. Stabilizing the interfaces of such components early in the development cycle may mitigate the negative effects of organizational complexity later on. An analysis of which binaries suffer from the most organizational complexity can be used late in the development cycle to direct testing resources to the components most likely to exhibit problems after release.

How much can we trust these results? To answer this question we have to understand the context of the study. It compared software components (binaries) that had different characteristics but were part of the same project. This approach avoids a number of confounding factors because it is more of an apples-to-apples comparison than comparing components from two different projects. Attempting to isolate the effects of a particular factor by examining different projects is prone to problems because each project is inherently different in many regards. A difference in outcomes may be due to the factor under study or to some external, unobserved factor, such as team experience, software domain, or tools used. Within the Windows organization inside of Microsoft, there is a consistent process, the same tools are used throughout, and decisions are made in similar ways. There is even a strong effort to make the process consistent and integrated across development sites in different countries. The consistency of the Windows development effort mitigates threats to the internal validity of this study and provides confidence that the relationships Nagappan, Murphy, and Basili observed between organizational complexity and post-release defects are not the result of some other form of bias due to differences in the binaries.

This study was also large-scale, comprising thousands of developers and binaries and tens of millions of lines of code. Given Brooks' observations about the super-linear growth of coordination and communication requirements, it would seem that the effects of coordination mismatches would be magnified in larger projects. Windows Vista is clearly one of the largest pieces of software in use today, both in terms of developer teams and code size. It is therefore reasonable to expect that smaller projects (at least in terms of number of engineers) would not suffer as much from organizational complexity. The authors replicated their study on a reduced data set to determine the level at which the organizational metrics were good indicators of failure-proneness and found that the effects could be observed on a team size of 30 engineers and three levels of depth in the management hierarchy.

A reading of the original study shows careful attention to detail, a clear knowledge of the issues involved in a quantitative study (e.g., the authors used principal component analysis to mitigate the threat of multicolinearity in organizational metrics), and a fairly comprehensive examination of the results. The hypotheses are supported by both prior theory (Conway's Law, Brooks' Law, etc.) *and* empirical evidence. Further, discussions with those who have management experience in software projects indicate that these results match their intuition and experiences. As scientists, our confidence in theories increases as experiments and studies fail to refute them. Replications of this study on additional projects and in other contexts are beneficial because they can indicate whether the findings are fairly universal, specific to Vista, or more generally true under certain constraints. Ultimately, practitioners must examine both the context and results of empirical studies to make informed judgments about how well the results may generalize to their own particular scenarios.

Chapels in the Bazaar of Open Source Software

The previous two studies have looked at commercial software. The past two decades have seen a new style of development termed *free* or *open source* software that occurs primarily over the Internet between parties who have never met and who do not (often) share a financial interest. It differs from "traditional" development in a number of ways. Although OSS contributors may be paid by their own employers to work on the projects, the OSS project itself rarely pays contributors directly. Thus, most people can come and go as they please. Since no one company "runs" the project, there is no mandated organizational structure.

Eric Raymond, who emerged as a spokesperson for this movement by writing a series of essays, has posited that this form of development can be characterized as an ad-hoc *bazaar* in which contributors meander around the code base, talk to others somewhat at random, and work on whatever they please. In contrast, he characterizes a controlled and planned development process in an industrial setting as a *cathedral* model where workers are directed to work on clearly delineated tasks and everything is planned up front. Of course, the dichotomy involves a bit of hyperbole. Even characterizing open source development and industrial development as two distinct styles is quite a generalization.

We've seen that studies of industrial projects tend to follow Conway's Corollary, but what about open source software? One of the reasons that Brooks' law holds is due to the communication overhead involved in large teams. If OSS is really a bazaar that lacks structure, then how does it overcome the quadratic increase in possible communication paths as the project grows? We decided to investigate the social structure of a number of prominent OSS projects to see whether they really do resemble a bazaar, and additionally to look at the relationship between the organizational structure and the architecture of the system [Bird et al. 2008].

Unlike commercial entities, OSS projects lack a mandated and clearly defined organizational structure. In order to recover the social structure of each OSS project, we gathered the historical archives of the developer mailing lists. These lists comprise discussions regarding decisions, fixes, policies, and nearly all communication required to run an OSS project. Some OSS projects also use IRC, but those that we selected require discussions of import to be conducted on the mailing lists. The participants on these lists are the project developers (i.e., those with write access to the source code repository), contributors who submit patches, and others who simply want to participate in discussions regarding features, bugs, and everything else. Many of the active participants in these projects use multiple email addresses, and we want to be able to attribute each email that a particular person uses to that one person rather than a number of entities. To address this issue, we resolved email aliases using heuristics and manual inspection. We also matched email addresses to source code repository accounts for the developers. We were able to reconstruct the social organization by examining interactions on these mailing lists to create social networks. If Alice posted a message to the developer mailing list and Bob read it and posted a response, there is evidence of information flow and possible collaboration between Alice and Bob. We therefore create an organizational network of all project mailing list participants based on these interactions. The network edges are weighted based on the number of interactions between each pair of participants.

We examined the Perl and Python projects, the Apache webserver, the PostgreSQL database system, and the Ant Java build system. The number of mailing list participants ranged from 1,329 for Python to 3,621 for Perl and the number of actual project developers ranged from 25 for Perl to 92 for Python. Table 11-2 shows statistics for the projects that we studied.

TABLE 11-2. Open source project statistics

Project	Apache	Ant	Python	Perl	PostgreSQL
Begin date	1995-02-27	2000-01-12	1999-04-21	1999-03-01	1998-01-03
End date	2005-07-13	2006-08-31	2006-07-27	2007-06-20	2007-03-01
Messages	101,250	73,157	66,541	112,514	132,698
List participants	2,017	1,960	1,329	3,621	3,607
Developers	57	40	92	25	29

We drew on the social network along with the commit activity of developers to answer two important questions:

- Do teams of participants form spontaneously and organically in the social network revealed by communication in the OSS projects?
- What is the relationship between the technical structure of the software and the teams of participants?

To answer the first question, we turn to the area of network analysis in complex physics. One active research topic in this community is the detection of *community structure*, the existence of strongly connected subnetworks within a network. Community structure detection techniques attempt to partition a network into groups of nodes such that the connections *within* groups are dense and the connections *between* groups are sparse. The level of community structure is quantified by a measure called *modularity*. Modularity can range from 0, which represents a completely random network, to 1, which represents a network of a number of disconnected cliques. Prior research has found that naturally occurring networks with clear clusters (e.g., networks that are modular) have values of modularity ranging from 0.3 to 0.7.

Figure 11-2 shows the boxplots of the modularity for three-month snapshots in each of these projects. The vast majority of modularity values shown are well above the 0.3 threshold, indicating strong community structure. Put more concretely, although the networks are too large and complex to easily visualize, the communication network is modular, with well-defined groups of developers who interact with each other much more than with other developers in other modules. This is evidence that these projects are not disorganized, chaotic groups of developers with everyone talking to everyone else in a haphazard manner. When left to their own devices, it appears that (at least for these projects) OSS projects actually *are* characterized by organized teams of developers. The key difference between industrial teams and these teams is that the OSS teams are formed organically rather than having their structure imposed by management. Further, we observed that the makeup of the teams was more dynamic than industrial software teams, with teams rarely lasting more than six months before disbanding and reforming in different ways.

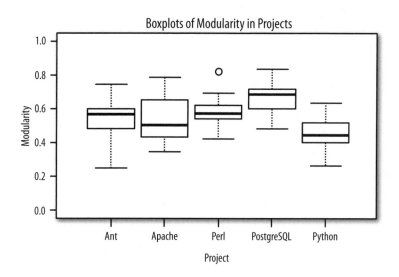

FIGURE 11-2. *Average congruence by release*

The mere existence of tightly connected subgraphs within the communication network for these projects is not in and of itself a validation of Conway's Law or our corollary. We are also interested in the relationship between these groups of participants who are talking to one another and the technical tasks that they are working on. Is the social structure tied to the software structure? To answer this question, we looked at the development activity, characterized by the files, function, and classes of the developers involved in each team. Based on our examination of the development behavior, we present two observations.

First, those who talk together work on related parts of the system. If two developers were found to be in the same software team by community structure detection algorithms, they were *much* more likely to be working on the same files and functions. Further, these same functions and files were often mentioned in the bodies of the email communication between members of the same team. Thus, the communication patterns are reflective of collaborative development behavior.

Second, we looked closely at the actual development to see what was really happening. We present a few examples here and refer the reader to our paper for a more in-depth analysis.

In the Apache webserver project, from May to July of 2003, one team consisted of Rowe and Thorpe (developers) as well as Deaves, Adkins, and Chandran. They discussed a number of bug fixes to mod_ssl, the Apache interface to the Secure Sockets Layer (SSL). Topics in the discussion included issues with incorrect input/output code; module loading, unloading, and initialization; and integration of mod_ssl with the server. Nearly all the discussion was about the SSL code, and virtually all of the files modified by people in this group during this time period are in the *modules/ssl* directory, as shown here:

> *modules/arch/win32/mod_isapi.h*
> *modules/ssl/mod_ssl.c*
> *modules/ssl/mod_ssl.h*
> *modules/ssl/ssl_engine_config.c*
> *modules/ssl/ssl_engine_init.c*
> *modules/ssl/ssl_engine_io.c*
> *modules/ssl/ssl_engine_kernel.c*
> *modules/ssl/ssl_engine_pphrase.c*
> *modules/ssl/ssl_toolkit_compat.h*
> *modules/ssl/ssl_util.c*
> *modules/ssl/ssl_util_ssl.c*
> *modules/ssl/ssl_util_ssl.h*
> *support/ab.c*

In another example, from October to December of 2002 in PostgreSQL, one team worked solely on embedded SQL in C, while another focused on updating the SGML documentation source. In the following time period, a group emerged whose activity and discussion concerned the development and testing of the PostgreSQL JDBC driver (with source code and test code changes spanning the code base within the JDBC subtree), and another much smaller group worked on Unicode support.

We found many more examples of teams of project participants forming around tasks that were directly related to portions of the code base. The discussion of approaches, delegation of work, and decision making in the communication was reflective of the actual development work (and in some cases, contributed patches) that was going on. Clearly, Conway's Corollary is at work in these projects.

So why do these findings matter? First, this shows that the strong ties between software structure and social structure appear to transcend different development processes and that even open source software projects seem to work well when these relationships are followed. Second, we've learned that OSS solves the problem of scalability and delegation of work in ways that are similar to more traditional development styles. Teams made up of a few individuals (we saw team sizes range from three to seven participants on average) work together to accomplish tasks within limited portions of the software. The common claim (though still open to debate) that successful OSS projects are self-adapting and self-optimizing communities is supported by their conformance to Conway's Corollary, as shown by our study. Also, although it might have been thought that OSS is able to somehow avoid the effects of Brooks' Law and Conway's Law, it appears that they adhere to both.

Conclusions

In the aggregate, what do these studies tell us and how can they help the state of practice in developing software?

They all provide evidence that when the organization of people in a software effort is similar to the organization of the software, the project does better than when they differ. Software projects should take both types of organization into account when making decisions, especially in the initial design and planning stages. When possible and economically feasible, projects should be organized (or, after a period of time, perhaps even reorganized) to ensure a strong relationship between social and software structure.

Conway's Corollary can have a negative or a positive effect on a development endeavor and can empower stakeholders in the projects if they take advantage of it. Now that evidence exists to support it, one ignores it at one's own peril. Clearly, you need to preserve independent judgment. If a software project consists of only five developers, the effects of violating Conway's Corollary are most likely minimal. In the age of global software development, it is probably unrealistic to relocate engineers simply to leverage the corollary. Nonetheless, we believe that, all things being equal, a software effort that pays attention to and actively aligns social structure with technical structure will fare better than one that does not.

As software teams continue to grow in size, they can derive more and more value from understanding the dynamics of collaboration and coordination. We encourage software projects that observe the negative or positive effects of Conway's Corollary (or that look for the effect and don't find it) to share their stories to increase our knowledge of the interaction of social and technical project structure. Only by sharing our evidence or the lack thereof can we hope to continue to understand and improve our craft.

References

[Bird et al. 2008] Bird, C., D. Pattison, R. D'Souza, V. Filkov, and P. Devanbu. 2008. Latent Social Structure in Open Source Projects. *SIGSOFT '08/FSE-16: Proceedings of the 16th ACM SIGSOFT Symposium on Foundations of Software Engineering*: 24–35.

[Brooks 1974] Brooks, F.P. 1974. The Mythical Man-Month. *Datamation* 20(12): 44–52.

[Cataldo et al. 2006] Cataldo, M., P.A. Wagstrom, J.D. Herbsleb, and K.M. Carley. 2006. Identification of Coordination Requirements: Implications for the Design of Collaboration and Awareness Tools. *Proceedings of the 20th Conference on Computer Supported Cooperative Work*: 353–362.

[Conway 1968] Conway, M.E. 1968. How do committees invent? *Datamation* 14(4): 28–31.

[Nagappan et al. 2008] Nagappan, N., B. Murphy, and V. Basili. 2008. The influence of organizational structure on software quality: An empirical case study. *Proceedings of the 30th International Conference on Software Engineering*: 521–530.

## CHAPTER TWELVE

How Effective Is Test-Driven Development?

Burak Turhan
Lucas Layman
Madeline Diep
Hakan Erdogmus
Forrest Shull

Test-Driven Development (TDD) [Beck 2002] is one of the most referenced, yet least used agile practices in industry. Its neglect is due mostly to our lack of understanding of its effects on people, processes, and products. Although most people agree that writing a test case before code promotes more robust implementation and a better design, the unknown costs associated with TDD's effects and the inversion of the ubiquitous programmer "code-then-test" paradigm has impeded TDD's adoption.

To provide an overview of current evidence on the effects of TDD, we conducted a systematic review of TDD research in online databases and scientific publications. Systematic review is a research method popularized in the medical community for aggregating and analyzing the results of clinical trials. A systematic review seeks to answer the general question, "*What does the published evidence say about the effects of using technique X?*" In medicine, systematic reviews play a critical role in evaluating the effectiveness of pharmaceutical drugs and alternative treatments for illnesses. Empirical software engineering researchers have adopted this approach for summarizing and analyzing evidence about the effects of software development practices. It is covered in Chapter 3, *What We Can Learn from Systematic Reviews*, by Barbara Kitchenham, and in [Kitchenham 2004] and [Dybå et al. 2005].

In this chapter, we treat TDD as an imaginary medical pill and describe its effects with a narrative from a pharmacological point of view, instead of providing a formal systematic review report. We invite the reader to imagine that the rest of this chapter is a medical fact sheet for the TDD "pill" and to continue reading with the following question in mind:

> "If TDD were a pill, would you take it to improve your health?"

The TDD Pill—What Is It?

The ingredients of the TDD pill are as follows and should be prepared following the given order *exactly*:

1. Choose a small task.
2. Write a test for that task.
3. Run all the tests to verify that the new test fails.
4. Write minimal production code to complete the task.
5. Run all tests (including the new one) to verify that they pass.
6. Refactor the code as necessary.
7. Repeat from step 1.

The active ingredient in the TDD pill is the authoring of test cases before production code. Authoring test cases before code requires the patient to consider the design of the solution, how information will flow, the possible outputs of the code, and exceptional scenarios that might occur. Running the newly written test case before writing production code helps to verify that the test is written correctly (a passing test case at this point is not testing the intended effects) and that the system compiles. The TDD pill also involves writing just enough production code to pass the test case, which encourages an uncluttered, modular design. Furthermore, TDD users create a growing library of automated test cases that can be executed at any time to verify the correctness of the existing system whenever changes are made.

Like many drugs, the TDD pill has some official variants, including ATDD (Acceptance-Test-Driven Development), BDD (Behavior-Driven Development) and STDD (Story-Test-Driven Development). ATDD replaces the "small task" step with "functional level business logic tasks," whereas BDD uses "behavioral specifications" instead. The ordering of tasks in TDD differentiates it from other treatments, but official varieties of TDD pills may also contain sets of other ingredients, such as breaking work down into simple tasks, refactoring, keeping the test-code cycles short, and relentless regression testing.

Summary of Clinical TDD Trials

The focus of our review was to gather *quantitative* evidence on the effects of the TDD pill on internal code quality (see "Measuring Code Quality" below), external quality, productivity, and test quality. The evaluation of the TDD pill is based on data gathered from 32 clinical trials. In the first quarter of 2009, the authors gathered 325 TDD research reports from online comprehensive indices, major scientific publishers (ACM, IEEE, Elsevier), and "gray literature" (technical reports, theses). The initial set of 325 reports was narrowed down to 22 reports through a two-level screening process. Four researchers filtered out studies conducted prior to 2000, qualitative studies, surveys, and wholly subjective analyses of the TDD pill. Some of these reports contained multiple or overlapping trials (i.e., the same trial was reported in multiple papers); in such cases, the trial was counted only once. A team of five researchers then extracted key information from the reports regarding study design, study context, participants, treatments and controls, and study results. In total, the research team analyzed 22 reports containing 32 unique trials.

MEASURING CODE QUALITY

The *internal quality* of a system is related to its design quality, usually with the interpretation that good designs are simple, modular, and easy to maintain and understand. Though TDD is primarily interpreted as a development practice, it is considered as a design practice as well. An incremental and simple design is expected to emerge when using the TDD pill. The simple design is driven by the modularity needed to make code testable, by writing minimal production code to complete simple tasks, and by constant refactoring. To assess the internal quality of a system, the TDD trials use one or more of the following measures:

- Object-oriented metrics. These involve weighted methods on a per-class basis (WMC, depth of inheritance tree), DIT, etc. [Chidamber et al. 1994]
- Cyclomatic complexity
- Code density (e.g., lines of code per method)
- Code size per feature

The *external quality* of a system is usually measured by the number of pre-release or post-release defects. TDD is associated with the important claim that it increases external quality because it encourages writing lots of test cases, developers work on simple tasks that are easy to comprehend, the system is under frequent regression testing, and errors due to changes can be easily detected by the fine-grained tests. In TDD trials, external quality is reported by one or more of the following:

- Test cases passed
- Number of defects
- Defect density
- Defects per test
- Effort required to fix defects
- Change density
- Percentage of preventative changes

The 32 trials were conducted in academic or industrial settings in the form of controlled experiments, pilot studies, or commercial projects. Controlled experiments were conducted in academic laboratories or controlled industry environments with a defined research protocol, pilot studies were carried out using less-structured experimental tasks, and commercial projects described industry teams using TDD as part of their everyday work. Participants in these trials had different experience levels, ranging from undergraduate students to graduate students to professionals. The number of participants per trial ranged from a single individual to 132 persons. The effort spent on the trials spans a wide interval, ranging from a few person-hours to 21,600 person-hours. Each trial compares the effects of the TDD pill with respect to another treatment—usually traditional test-last development. The subjects in the treatment groups were comprised of various units, such as individuals, pairs, teams, and projects.

We have classified the 32 trials into four levels based on the experience of participants, the detail of the experimental construct, and the scale of the trial. The experience of participants is determined by whether they were undergraduate students, graduate students, or professionals.

The descriptions of the dynamics of TDD and the control treatment were used to evaluate the construct of the trial as either good, adequate, poor, or unknown. A *good* construct enforced all prescribed TDD ingredients from the prior section, an *adequate* construct prescribed writing tests first but not all of the TDD ingredients, a *poor* construct did not enforce the TDD steps, and an *unknown* construct did not specify whether the TDD steps were enforced or not.

Finally, the scale of a trial is recorded as small, medium or large, depending on the reported effort or estimated effort based on duration and number of participants. Small projects involved less than 170 person-hours of total effort across all subjects, whereas large projects ranged from 3,000 to 21,600 person-hours. A simple clustering algorithm was used to categorize the scale of the projects, while the experience of participants and the details of the construct were based on descriptive data found in the trial reports.

Our confidence that the results of using the TDD pill will generalize to "real-life" cases increases as the level of the trial increases. The lowest level, L0, contains all small-scale trials. These trials report less than 170 person-hours of effort or less than 11 participants. The next level, L1, consists of medium- or large-scale trials with unknown or poor constructs. The L2 level consists of medium- or large-scale trials with adequate or good constructs and undergraduate student participants. Finally, the highest level, L3, contains medium- or large-scale trials with adequate or good constructs and graduate student or professional participants.

Table 12-1 summarizes the attributes we used to classify trials into levels, and Table 12-2 shows how many trials we examined at each level.

TABLE 12-1. Levels of clinical TDD trials

	L0	L1	L2	L3
Experience	Any	Any	Undergraduate student	Graduate student or professional
Construct	Any	Poor or unknown	Adequate or good	Adequate or good
Scale	Small	Medium or large	Medium or large	Medium or large

TABLE 12-2. Types of clinical TDD trials

Type	L0	L1	L2	L3	Total
Controlled experiment	2	0	2	4	8
Pilot study	2	0	5	7	14
Industrial use	1	7	0	2	10
Total	5	7	7	13	32

The Effectiveness of TDD

We analyzed the TDD trials that reported quantitative results of the TDD pill's effects on productivity, internal and external quality, and test quality. Direct comparison of the quantitative results across trials was impossible, since the trials measured TDD's effectiveness in different ways. Instead, we assign each trial a summary value of "better," "worse," "mixed," or "inconclusive/no-difference." The summary value is determined by the quantitative results reported for the TDD pill compared with a control. The summary value also incorporates the report author's interpretation of the trial results. In trials with a summary value of "better," a majority of quantitative measures favor the TDD pill in comparison to the control treatment. In trials with a summary value of "worse," a majority of measures favor the control treatment. Trials with a summary value of "inconclusive/no-difference" were inconclusive or report no observed differences. Finally, in trials with a summary value of "mixed," some measures favor TDD while others don't. In all cases, the summary assignation was guided by the report author's interpretation of the study findings because, in many cases, the reports omitted details of the trial that would have enabled an objective external evaluation.

In the following sections we do our best to draw some conclusions about the value of TDD from the trials.

Internal Quality

Available evidence from the trials suggests that TDD does not have a consistent effect on internal quality. Although TDD appears to yield better results over the control group for certain types of metrics (complexity and reuse), other metrics (coupling and cohesion) are often worse in the TDD treatment. Another observation from the trial data is that TDD yields production code that is less complex at the method/class level, but more complex at the package/project level. This inconsistent effect is more visible in more rigorous trials (i.e., L2 and L3 trials). The differences in internal quality may be due to other factors, such as motivation, skill, experience, and learning effects. Table 12-3 classifies the trials according to internal quality metrics.

> NOTE
>
> **In the following tables, the first number in each cell reports all trials, whereas the number in parentheses reports only L2 and L3 trials.**

TABLE 12-3. Effects on internal quality

Type	BETTER	WORSE	MIXED	INC | NO-DIFF	Total
Controlled experiment	1 (0)	0 (0)	0 (0)	2 (2)	3 (2)
Pilot study	1 (1)	1 (1)	3 (1)	2 (2)	7 (5)
Industrial use	3 (1)	1 (1)	0 (0)	0 (0)	4 (2)
Total	5 (2)	2 (2)	3 (1)	4 (4)	14 (9)

External Quality

There is some evidence to suggest that TDD improves external quality. Although the outcomes of controlled experiments are mostly inconclusive, industrial use and pilot studies strongly favor TDD. However, the supporting evidence from industrial use and controlled experiments disappears after filtering out the less rigorous studies (i.e., L0 and L1 trials). Furthermore, the evidence from pilot studies and controlled experiments is contradictory once L0 and L1 trials are filtered out. If all studies are counted equally, however, the evidence suggests that the TDD pill can improve external quality. Table 12-4 classifies the trials according to external quality metrics.

TABLE 12-4. Effects on external quality

Type	BETTER	WORSE	MIXED	INC | NO-DIFF	Total
Controlled experiment	1 (0)	2 (2)	0 (0)	3 (3)	6 (5)
Pilot study	6 (5)	1 (1)	0 (0)	2 (2)	9 (8)
Industrial use	6 (0)	0 (0)	0 (0)	1 (1)	7 (1)
Total	13 (5)	3 (3)	0 (0)	6 (6)	22 (14)

Productivity

The productivity dimension engenders the most controversial discussion of TDD. Although many admit that adopting TDD may require a steep learning curve that may decrease the productivity initially, there is no consensus on the long-term effects. One line of argument expects productivity to increase with TDD; reasons include easy context switching from one simple task to another, improved external quality (i.e., there are few errors and errors can be detected quickly), improved internal quality (i.e., fixing errors is easier due to simpler design), and improved test quality (i.e., chances of introducing new errors is low due to automated tests). The opposite line argues that TDD incurs too much overhead and will negatively impact productivity because too much time and focus may be spent on authoring tests as opposed to adding new functionality. The different measures used in TDD trials for evaluating productivity included development and maintenance effort, the amount of code or features produced over time, and the amount of code or features produced per unit of development effort.

The available evidence from the trials suggests that TDD does not have a consistent effect on productivity. The evidence from controlled experiments suggests an improvement in productivity when TDD is used. However, the pilot studies provide mixed evidence, some in favor of and others against TDD. In the industrial studies, the evidence suggests that TDD yields worse productivity. Even when considering only the more rigorous studies (L2 and L3), the evidence is equally split for and against a positive effect on productivity. Table 12-5 classifies the trials according to effects on productivity.

TABLE 12-5. Effects on productivity

Type	BETTER	WORSE	MIXED	INC | NO-DIFF	Total
Controlled experiment	3 (1)	0 (0)	0 (0)	1 (1)	4 (2)
Pilot study	6 (5)	4 (4)	0 (0)	4 (3)	14 (12)
Industrial use	1 (0)	5 (1)	0 (0)	1 (0)	7 (1)
Total	10 (6)	9 (5)	0 (0)	6 (4)	25 (15)

Test Quality

Because test cases precede all development activities with TDD, testing the correctness of an evolving system is expected to be made easier by a growing library of automated tests. Further, the testing process is expected to be of high quality due to the fine granularity of the tests produced. In the trials, test quality is captured by test density, test coverage, test productivity, or test effort.

There is some evidence to suggest that TDD improves test quality. Most of the evidence comes from pilot studies and is in favor of TDD, even after filtering out less rigorous studies. Controlled experiments suggest that TDD fares at least as well as the control treatments. There is insufficient evidence from industrial use to reach a conclusion.

Therefore, the test quality associated with TDD seems at least not worse and often better than alternative approaches. Here we would have expected stronger results: since encouraging test case development is one of the primary active ingredients of TDD, the overall evidence should have favored TDD in promoting the test quality measures reported in these studies.

Table 12-6 classifies the trials according to test quality.

TABLE 12-6. Effects on test quality

Type	BETTER	WORSE	MIXED	INC | NO-DIFF	Total
Controlled experiment	2 (1)	0 (0)	0 (0)	3 (3)	5 (4)
Pilot study	7 (5)	1 (1)	0 (0)	1 (1)	9 (7)
Industrial use	1 (0)	1 (1)	0 (0)	1 (0)	3 (1)
Total	10 (6)	2 (2)	0 (0)	5 (4)	17 (12)

Enforcing Correct TDD Dosage in Trials

Although most of the trials did not measure or control the amount of the TDD pill taken (which in software parlance translates into a lack of attention to process conformance), we believe that the dosage ended up being variable across trials and subjects. Trials with poor or unknown constructs may not have strictly enforced TDD usage, and we believe it is highly likely that the trial participants customized the pill with a selection of ingredients rather than following the strict textbook definition of TDD. This issue poses a serious threat to drawing generalized conclusions. In the medical context, not enforcing or measuring TDD usage is analogous to failing to ensure that the patients took a pill for some treatment or not knowing which dosage the patient took. Thus, the observed effects of the TDD pill may be due to process conformance or other factors that are not adequately described or controlled. In future trials, conformance to the treatment and the control should be carefully monitored.

Regardless of the reporting quality of the TDD trials, a related question is raised: "Should the textbook definition of TDD be followed in all real-life cases?" Sometimes patients get better even with a half-sized or quarter-sized pill modified for their specific work context and personal style. Micro-level logging tools for development activity are available and can be used to investigate these issues. Such logging tools can be helpful both for controlling the conformance to TDD processes and for understanding real-life, practical implementations of TDD.

Cautions and Side Effects

In this section we pose several questions about the TDD pill that may temper TDD's effectiveness in different contexts.

Is it reactive to the environment?

> There is no recommended best context for the use of TDD. We do not know whether it is applicable to all domains, to all kinds of tasks within a domain, or to projects of all sizes and complexities. For example, the trials do not make it clear whether TDD is an applicable practice for developing embedded systems or for developing highly decentralized systems where incremental testing may not be feasible. Furthermore, it is often considered a challenge to use TDD for legacy systems that may require considerable refactoring of existing code to become testable.

Is it for everyone?

> One basic fact on which almost everyone agrees is that TDD is difficult to learn. It involves a steep learning curve that requires skill, maturity, and time, particularly when developers are entrenched in the code-then-test paradigm. Better tool support for test-case generation and early exposure in the classroom to a test-then-code mentality may encourage TDD adoption.

Could it be addictive?

> Personal communications with TDD developers suggest that it is an addictive practice. It changes the way people think and their approach to coding in a way that is difficult to roll back. Therefore, leaving TDD practices may be as difficult as adopting them.

Does it interact with other medications?

> No studies focus specifically on whether TDD performs better or worse when used with other medications. In one trial, it is suggested that, when coupled with up-front design, TDD results in a 40% improvement in external quality [Williams et al. 2003]. Another trial compares solo and pair developers who practice TDD and incremental test-last development [Madeyski 2005]. That trial reports no difference in the external quality of software produced by solo or pair programmers using TDD. It is not known which practices go well or poorly with TDD. Although there may be practices that stimulate its desired effects, there also may be some that inhibit them. The examples just mentioned are probably case-specific, but they point out the need to investigate further TDD's interaction with other medications.

Conclusions

The effects of TDD still involve many unknowns. Indeed, the evidence is not undisputedly consistent regarding TDD's effects on any of the measures we applied: internal and external quality, productivity, or test quality. Much of the inconsistency likely can be attributed to internal factors not fully described in the TDD trials. Thus, TDD is bound to remain a controversial topic of debate and research.

For practitioners looking for some actionable advice, our expert panel recommends taking the TDD pill, carefully monitoring its interactions and side effects, and increasing or decreasing the dosage accordingly. So we end with some specific prescriptions from individual members of our team, after reviewing the data:

> We've been able to compile the evidence, but each reader has to make up his or her own mind. First, decide which qualities matter most to you. For example, do you care more about productivity or external quality? Can you justify spending more effort to create higher-quality tests? The evidence in this chapter is useful only for making decisions based on each reader's specific goals.

> I have taken the TDD pill and become hooked. My personal experience has been that TDD improves productivity, although evidence from our study is lacking in this regard. Perhaps mine was simply a perception. Based on these results, especially based on the evidence regarding its conservatively positive impact on external quality, if I weren't already using TDD, I'd start having my team take it in small doses and see whether they find a long-term productivity improvement of their own. If there are no adverse reactions, I'd increase the dosage gradually and keep observing.

> Although TDD is promising, its adoption can be impeded by uncertainties about its effectiveness and by high up-front adoption cost. Still, its ingredients seem to encourage good programming and development habits to flourish, yielding better-quality programmers and tests in the long run.

> TDD seems promising, but let's face it, it tastes bad when you first start. A lot of people like the old stuff better. After all, it's hard to feel productive when you spend a large amount of your time writing test cases that fail. On the other hand, I've never written cleaner code in my life, and it feels great to make a change to that old code, hit the "Run Tests" button, and be confident that I didn't break anything.

> The evidence packed into this chapter shows that TDD might be a cure for you, yet you should not try to use it as a panacea. Your TDD adventure is likely to vary with certain factors, including your experience and the context you are working in. As a practitioner, developing an insight about when to expect improvements from TDD would be a valuable asset.

Acknowledgments

Dr. Janice Singer was one of the researchers who participated in the screening of the studies in the initial stages of the systematic review. We gratefully acknowledge her contributions to this work.

General References

[Beck 2002] Beck, Kent. 2002. *Test-Driven Development: By Example*. Boston: Addison-Wesley.

[Chidamber et al. 1994] Chidamber, S.R., and C.F. Kemerer. 1994. A Metrics Suite for Object Oriented Design. *IEEE Transactions on Software Engineering* 20(6): 476–493.

[Dybå et al. 2005] Dybå, Tore, Barbara Kitchenham, and Magne Jørgensen. 2005. Evidence-Based Software Engineering for Practitioners. *IEEE Software* 22(1): 58-65.

[Kitchenham 2004] Kitchenham, Barbara. 2004. Procedures for Performing Systematic Reviews. Keele University Technical Report TR/SE0401.

Clinical TDD Trial References

[Canfora et al. 2006] Canfora, Gerardo, Aniello Cimitile, Felix Garcia, Mario Piattini, and Corrado Aaron Visaggio. 2006. Evaluating advantages of test-driven development: A controlled experiment with professionals. *Proceedings of the ACM/IEEE international symposium on empirical software engineering*: 364–371.

[Erdogmus et al. 2005] Erdogmus, Hakan, Maurizio Morisio, and Marco Torchiano. 2005. On the Effectiveness of the Test-First Approach to Programming. *IEEE Transactions on Software Engineering* 31(3): 226–237.

[Flohr et al. 2006] Flohr, Thomas, and Thorsten Schneider. 2006. Lessons Learned from an XP Experiment with Students: Test-First Needs More Teachings. In *Product-Focused Software Process Improvement: 7th International Conference, PROFES 2006, Proceedings*, ed. J. Münch and M. Vierimaa, 305–318. Berlin: Springer-Verlag.

[George 2002] George, Boby. 2002. *Analysis and Quantification of Test-Driven Development Approach*. MS thesis, North Carolina State University.

[Geras 2004] Geras, Adam. 2004. *The effectiveness of test-driven development*. MSc thesis, University of Calgary.

[Geras et al. 2004] Geras, A., M. Smith, and J. Miller. 2004. A Prototype Empirical Evaluation of Test-Driven Development. *Proceedings of the 10th International Symposium on Software Metrics*: 405–416.

[Gupta et al. 2007] Gupta, Atul, and Pankaj Jaloye. 2007. An Experimental Evaluation of the Effectiveness and Efficiency of the Test-Driven Development. *Proceedings of the First International Symposium on Empirical Software Engineering and Measurement*: 285–294.

[Huang et al. 2009] Huang, Liang, and Mike Holcombe. 2009. Empirical investigation towards the effectiveness of Test First programming. *Information & Software Technology* 51(1): 182–194.

[Janzen 2006] Janzen, David Scott. 2006. *An Empirical Evaluation of the Impact of Test-Driven Development on Software Quality*. PhD thesis, University of Kansas.

[Kaufmann et al. 2003] Kaufmann, Reid, and David Janzen. 2003. Implications of test-driven development: A pilot study. *Companion of the 18th annual ACM SIGPLAN conference on object-oriented programming, systems, languages, and applications*: 298–299.

[Madeyski 2005] Madeyski, Lech. 2005. Preliminary Analysis of the Effects of Pair Programming and Test-Driven Development on the External Code Quality. *Proceedings of the 2005 Conference on Software Engineering: Evolution and Emerging Technologies*: 113-123.

[Madeyski 2006] Madeyski, Lech. 2006. The Impact of Pair Programming and Test-Driven Development on Package Dependencies in Object-Oriented Design—An Experiment. In *Product-Focused Software Process Improvement: 7th International Conference, PROFES 2006, Proceedings*, ed. J. Münch and M. Vierimaa, 278-289. Berlin: Springer-Verlag.

[Madeyski et al. 2007] Madeyski, Lech, and Lukasz Szala. 2007. The Impact of Test-Driven Development on Software Development Productivity — An Empirical Study. *Software Process Improvement, 4th European Conference, EuroSPI 2007, Proceedings*, ed. P. Abrahamsson, N. Baddoo, T. Margaria, and R. Massnarz, 200-211. Berlin: Springer-Verlag.

[Muller et al. 2002] Muller, M.M., and O. Hagner. 2002. Experiment about test-first programming. *Software, IEEE Proceedings* 149(5): 131–136.

[Nagappan et al. 2008] Nagappan, Nachiappan, E. Michael Maximilien, Thirumalesh Bhat, and Laurie Williams. 2008. Realizing quality improvement through test-driven development: results and experiences of four industrial teams. *Empirical Software Engineering* 13(3): 289-302.

[Pancur et al. 2003] Pancur, M., M. Ciglaric, M. Trampus, and T. Vidmar. 2003. Towards empirical evaluation of test-driven development in a university environment. *The IEEE Region 8 EUROCON Computer as a Tool* (2): 83–86.

[Siniaalto et al. 2008] Siniaalto, Maria, and Pekka Abrahamsson. 2008. Does Test-Driven Development Improve the Program Code? Alarming Results from a Comparative Case Study. In *Balancing Agility and Formalism in Software Engineering*, ed. B. Meyer, J. Nawrocki, and B. Walter, 143–156. Berlin: Springer-Verlag.

[Slyngstad et al. 2008] Slyngstad, Odd Petter N., Jingyue Li, Reidar Conradi, Harald Ronneberg, Einar Landre, and Harald Wesenberg. 2008. The Impact of Test Driven Development on the Evolution of a Reusable Framework of Components—An Industrial Case Study. *Proceedings of the Third International Conference on Software Engineering Advances*: 214–223.

[Vu et al. 2009] Vu, John, Niklas Frojd, Clay Shenkel-Therolf, and David Janzen. 2009. Evaluating Test-Driven Development in an Industry-Sponsored Capstone Project. *Proceedings of the 2009 Sixth International Conference on Information Technology: New Generations*: 229–234.

[Williams et al. 2003] Williams, Laurie, E. Michael Maximilien, and Mladen Vouk. 2003. Test-Driven Development As a Defect-Reduction Practice. *Proceedings of the 14th International Symposium on Software Reliability Engineering*: 34.

[Yenduri et al. 2006] Yenduri, Sumanth, and Louise A. Perkins. 2006. Impact of Using Test-Driven Development: A Case Study. *Proceedings of the International Conference on Software Engineering Research and Practice & Conference on Programming Languages and Compilers, SERP 2006*: 126–129.

[Zhang et al. 2006] Zhang, Lei, Shunsuke Akifuji, Katsumi Kawai, and Tsuyoshi Morioka. 2006. Comparison Between Test-Driven Development and Waterfall Development in a Small-Scale Project. *Extreme Programming and Agile Processes in Software Engineering, 7th International Conference, XP 2006, Proceedings*, ed. P. Abrahamsson, M. Marchesi, and G. Succi, 211–212. Berlin: Springer-Verlag.

## CHAPTER THIRTEEN

Why Aren't More Women in Computer Science?

Michele A. Whitecraft
Wendy M. Williams

> **"You cannot solve a problem from the frame of mind that created the problem in the first place."**
>
> —*Albert Einstein*

Consider the following statistics.

Girls receive higher grades than do boys, from kindergarten through college, including grades in mathematics. In the latest year for which we have data, girls comprised 48% of all college math majors, took 56% of all Advanced Placement exams, and took 51% of AP calculus exams [College Board 2008]. Yet, only 17% of AP computer science test-takers in that year were female [College Board 2008].

Likewise, although 57% of all 2008 undergraduate degree recipients were female, women comprised only 18% of computer science (CS) and information (IT) degree recipients [National Center for Education Statistics 2008].

Curiously, 23 years earlier (in 1985), 37% of computer science bachelor's degrees were awarded to women [National Center for Education Statistics 2008]. Between 2001 and 2008 alone, there was a 79% decline in the number of incoming undergraduate women interested in majoring in computer science [Higher Education Research Institute 2008].

Why are so few women in computer science? Should we care? And, if we should, can anything be done to reverse these trends? Debates over these issues fall into three major categories.

Some argue that women are less likely than men to possess cognitive abilities at the extreme right tail of the distribution, which are necessary to compete in computer science (see [Ceci and Williams 2007], [Ceci and Williams 2010], and [Halpernet al. 2007]).

Others say that women are not as interested in computer science and simply prefer to study other subjects [Ferriman et al. 2009]; [Durndell and Lightbody 1993]; [Seymour and Hewitt 1994], and still others argue that women are directed out of the field by stereotypes, biases, and "male culture" [American Association of University Women 2000]; [Margolis et al. 2000].

This chapter reviews the research pertaining to each of these three positions and follows each argument through to its logical implications.

Why So Few Women?

First, we'll review the common explanations given for this situation and the formal research that investigates them.

Ability Deficits, Preferences, and Cultural Biases

Much research has been done on innate ability differences, preferences, and cultural biases as reasons for the underrepresentation of women in science, technology, engineering, and mathematics (STEM) fields. Ceci, Williams, and Barnett developed a framework to understand how these all interact [Ceci et al. 2009]. Next, we address the research on each factor and then work it through Ceci et al.'s more integrative framework. The picture that emerges (see Figure 13-1) gives the reader a feel for the complexity of the interactions between the contributing factors. Although there are certainly biologically rooted gender differences at work, the research suggests that there also may be some detrimental gender biases involved, which raises further questions.

Evidence for deficits in female mathematical-spatial abilities

Innate ability differences between males and females (as well as environmentally mediated differences traceable to experiences during childhood) have been explored as one possible reason for the declining number of women in computer-related fields. Substantial evidence supports the argument that women are not as capable at highly math-intensive pursuits as are men. This sex asymmetry is found at the very upper end of the ability distribution. For example, the top 1% of scores on the mathematics SAT shows a 2-to-1 ratio of males to females, and the top .01% shows a ratio of 4-to-1 [Hyde and Lynn 2008]; [Lubinski et al. 2001]. Males also earn most of the very low scores, meaning that males' performance is simply more variable overall.

Ceci, Williams, and Barnett [Ceci et al. 2009] divide the evidence on cognitive sex differences into mean differences (at the midpoint of the distribution) and right-tail differences in proportions in the top 10%, 5%, and 1%, the latter being a better representation of those in the science, technology, engineering, and math (STEM) professions. Based on a national probability sampling of adolescents between 1960 and 1992, Hedges and Nowell found that the distribution of test scores for male and female test-takers differed substantially at the top and bottom 1%, 5%, and 10% [Hedges and Nowell 1995]. Males excelled in science, mathematics, spatial reasoning, social studies, and mechanical skills. Females excelled in verbal abilities, associative memory performance, and perceptual speed. These findings raise the possibility that biology accounts for some of the observed gender patterns of participation in related fields of STEM, CS, and IT.

Research on relative brain size, brain organization, and hormonal differences is also relevant. Ceci and Williams review the recent biological work on cognitive sex differences, investigating brain size, brain organization, and hormonal differences [Ceci and Williams 2010]. Discussing Deary et al.'s finding of a modest correlation (.33–.37) between intelligence and brain volume [Deary et al. 2007], in which men on average have slightly bigger brains, Ceci and Williams note that "in most of the research on biological correlates of sex differences, the focus is on means, whereas the focus on sex differences in the STEM fields is on the extreme right tail (the top 1% or even the top .1% or the top 0.01%)." In other words, many studies of average brain differences are not pertinent to our question, because strong evidence of mathematical and spatial ability differences between men and women appear only at the very top (or bottom) of the range of ability scores.

Other research cited in Ceci and Williams' review suggests that males and females use different parts of their brains to complete the same tasks [Haier et al. 2005]. Ceci and Williams conclude that "with additional independent replications and representative sampling, it can be concluded that men and women achieve the same general cognitive capability using somewhat different brain architectures."

Additionally, Ceci and Williams cite research that investigates the role of pre- and postnatal hormones in understanding cognitive sex differences. In one study, male rats were superior at figuring their way around a maze, compared with female rats. Once the male rats were castrated, their superiority disappeared. Ceci and Williams also review research in which biological females, given estrogen-suppressing drugs coupled with large doses of male hormones during sex-change operations, developed enhanced spatial abilities. The large body of research in this area suggests that hormonal factors might affect professional choices of women. However, it is unclear how much. Ceci and Williams conclude that the evidence is "not strong and consistent enough to justify claiming that hormones are the primary cause of sex differences in STEM careers."

Before we leave the subject of hormonal differences, however, we should consider the possibility that they underlie some behavioral differences that predispose women not to be as attracted as men to working in computer science.

Statistics show that women are committed to the professional work force. They hold 57% of all professional occupations in the U.S. in 2008 [Ashcraft and Blithe 2009]; [National Center for Education Statistics 2008], and they are also successful in math (as measured by grades), a closely related academic discipline. Thus, it seems important to go beyond the explanation of ability deficits and to ask about women's choices. The statistics call for a gender-sensitive analysis of the factors influencing women's decisions to participate in the field of Computer Science—or not—and we also need to address the possibility that women find themselves disenfranchised by the male culture of CS. If, in fact, significant reasons for a gender imbalance lie here, then here, too, may exist an opportunity to reverse a portion of this trend.

The role of preferences and lifestyle choices

Accordingly, some researchers have addressed preferences and cultural forces. Some claim that culturally inscribed career and lifestyle choices are the major reason for the small number of women in computer science, and others claim more strongly that discouraging cultural forces are the most instrumental causes. Next, we review evidence for each of these positions.

With respect to career choice, gender shifts within professions have occurred throughout history, notably within teaching, secretarial work, and medicine [Ceci and Williams 2010]. These shifts are easily explained by changes over time in these careers' prestige levels and financial remuneration, rather than by hormones or genes. Repeatedly, men have taken over whatever kind of work is considered more economically valuable, suggesting that gender workforce patterns are driven more by cultural and political forces rather than simple biological differences. In a recent longitudinal study of women's choices to work in health-related careers, we can find an interesting parallel case in which cultural values drive career choices. Jacqueline Eccles and colleagues at the University of Michigan found that even when mathematical ability was taken into consideration, young women were more attracted to health-related careers because they placed a higher value on a people/society-oriented job than did their male peers [Eccles et al. 1999].

Margolis, Fisher, and Miller [Margolis et al. 2000] provide further evidence of a "female" inclination—or values choice—to serve people and society in their 2000 study involving 51 male and 46 female computer science majors at Carnegie Mellon University (comprising a total of 210 interviews). A representative quote from a female computer science interviewee resonates with Eccles's research:

> The idea is that you can save lives, and that's not detaching yourself from society. That's actually being a part of it. That's actually helping. Because I have this thing in me that wants to help. I felt the only problem I had in computer science was that I would be detaching myself from society a lot, that I wouldn't be helping; that there would be people in third-world countries that I couldn't do anything about...I would like to find a way that I could help—that's where I would like to go with computer science.

Margolis, Fisher, and Miller found that women's quest for people-oriented purposes for computers was in concordance with other research in the field of computer science [Honey 1994]; [Martin 1992]; [Schofield 1995]. They report that 44% of the female students in their study (as compared to 9% of the male students) emphasized the importance of integrating computing with people through projects with a more human appeal. Overall, women preferred computing for medical purposes (e.g., pacemakers, renal dialysis machines, and figuring out diseases), communication, and solving community problems over computing for the sake of computing, developing better computers, or programming for games.

Tagging some similar values issues, Ferriman, Lubinski, and Benbow point to gender differences in lifestyle preferences and orientation toward life as the main reason for women's underrepresentation in high-intensity STEM careers [Ferriman et al. 2009]. Their research is unique in that they were able to hold ability constant and narrow the population down to only those who excel in STEM careers. By following mathematically precocious youth over 20 years, they found that "following the completion of their terminal graduate degrees, men seem to be more career-focused and agentic, whereas women appear to be more holistic and communal in their orientation toward life and more attendant to family, friends, and the social well-being of themselves and others more generally." By this argument, then, there are few women in CS simply because women are more interested in and prefer other disciplines and areas.

Biases, Stereotypes, and the Role of Male Computer-Science Culture

Some researchers reject the notion that any inherently female quality (whether ability or interest) causes women's underrepresentation in CS and IT careers. They argue instead that the culture of CS and IT discourages women. In "The Anatomy of Interest: Women in Undergraduate Computer Science," Margolis, Fisher, and Miller focus on how women students who enter CS with high enthusiasm and interest in computing quickly lose their ability and interest in the subject [Margolis et al. 2000]. They looked at factors beyond intellectual preference that influenced interest in an abstract body of knowledge. For example, they explored how gender-biased norms eroded confidence, and also how a masculinized standard for success shaded women's interest and ability in computing. The authors suggest that there may be some "pernicious ways in which male behavior and interest become the standards for 'the right fit' and success," and this, in turn, contributes to women's waning enthusiasm in the subject. In other words, as their interviews showed, women who refused to conform to the image of the myopically focused "computer geek" who "hacks for hacking's sake" might feel out of place.

For those who perceive the culture of computing as one in which the "boy wonder" icon is up all night programming feverishly in isolation, Margolis, Fisher, and Miller offer this insight from a female computer science teacher:

My point is that staying up all night doing something is a sign of single-mindedness and possibly immaturity as well as love for the subject. The girls may show their love for computers and computer science very differently. If you are looking for this type of obsessive behavior, then you are looking for a typically young, male behavior. While some girls will exhibit it, most won't. But it doesn't mean that they don't love computer science!

Shortcomings of the Margolis, Fisher, and Miller case study include the fact that it examines just one small subset of the general population of students pursuing computer science, and thus, we should be wary of extrapolating these personal accounts to the broader population. We should not make broad assumptions based on this small sample. Furthermore, even though their interview questions were designed to elicit students' own experiences rather than their abstract thoughts, the authors admit that this interviewing technique was not conducive to assigning relative weight to different detachment factors, as "factors frequently shifted and appeared enmeshed with one another" [Margolis et al. 2000].

At the same time, these findings resonate with other studies of computer culture, such as one by the Educational Foundation of the American Association of University Women (AAUW), which combines input from its 14 commissioners (researchers, educators, journalists, and entrepreneurs) in cyberculture and education. Their report covers the Foundation's online survey of 900 teachers, qualitative focus research on more than 70 girls, and reviews of existing research, in order to provide insight into perspectives on computer culture, teacher perspectives and classroom dynamics, educational software and games, computer science classrooms, and home community and work [AAUW 2000]. Like Margolis, Fisher, and Miller, the AAUW found cultural deterrents to female participation in computer science. They found that girls are concerned about the passivity of their interactions with the computer as a "tool." Additionally, they found that girls rejected the violence, redundancy, and tedium of computer games and expressed dislike for narrowly and technically focused programming classes. Furthermore, the AAUW contends that these concerns are dismissed as symptoms of anxiety or incompetence that will diminish once girls "catch up" with the technology.

Finally, in a comprehensive compilation of research in IT, CS, and CE, McGrath Cohoon and Aspray integrated research from over 34 key researchers in the field [McGrath Cohoon and Aspray 2006]. Their potential explanations for the underrepresentation of women include experience, barriers to entry, role models, mentoring, student-faculty interaction, peer support, curricula, and pedagogy, as well as student characteristics such as academic fitness, values, confidence, and response to competition, plus the culture of computing.

In light of these culturally based concerns, we might ask what, exactly, high-ability women who opt out of disciplines such as CS *do* choose to do with their intellectual lives? Ceci, Williams, and Barnett remind us that women with high math competence are disproportionately more likely than men to also have high verbal competence, allowing them greater choice of professions [Ceci et al. 2009]. Hence, issues of culture and choice likely dovetail, directing capable women out of the computer field, thus revealing that more than biology, and factors other than raw ability, are at play. Figure 13-1 depicts the interplay of all these factors, both biological and cultural.

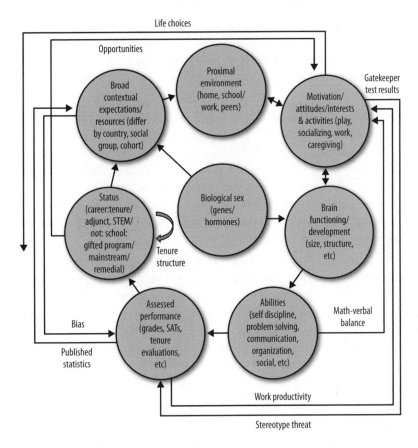

FIGURE 13-1. General causal model for gender disparity in science, technology, engineering, and mathematics. Figure copyright 2009 by Stephen J. Ceci, Wendy M. Williams, and Susan M. Barnett; used with permission.

With so many confounding factors, it is no surprise that we have no clear solution to the barriers that some women may face in CS and related fields. On the other hand, we do have an emerging picture of multiple and interacting forces potentially acting against women's full participation, which raises implications to which we now turn.

Should We Care?

To the extent that women do not choose CS because of troubling aspects of culture that could be changed, we must ask ourselves whether we ought to push for more women in CS, for instance, through educational policy. Since CS is a desirable professional field, women might benefit by enhanced opportunities to take part. Furthermore, insofar as CS is a key area for global competition, it may be beneficial for CS to become more gender-inclusive. Diversity may improve the products of computer and software teams.

Ultimately, however, the issue might go beyond any immediately measurable benefit. The inadequacies of the research at hand might actually suggest that we need to think within a different frame of mind: one that recognizes possible biological differences *and* a broad range of culturally determined qualities as key elements of a complex equation.

First, let us address the potential benefits to women of participating in CS. First, IT jobs pay considerably more than most female-dominated occupations [Bureau of Labor Statistics 2004]; [National Center for Education Statistics 2008]. According to the National Association of Colleges and Employers, starting salary offers for graduates with a bachelor's degree in computer science averaged $61,407 in July 2009 [Bureau of Labor Statistics 2010]. For computer systems software engineers, the median annual wages in the industries employing the largest numbers in May 2008 were: scientific research and development services, $102,090; computer and peripheral equipment manufacturing, $101,270; software publishers, $93,5790; and computer systems design and related services, $91,610.

The Bureau of Labor Statistics classifies computer software engineers' prospects of landing a job as *excellent*. Projecting ahead from 2008 to 2018, the percentage change projections as indicated on the Bureau of Labor Statistics website are: computer software engineers and computer programmers show an increase of 283,000 jobs, representing a 21% increase; computer software engineers show an increase in 295,000 jobs, representing a 32% increase; and computer software engineers show an increase of 34%. The only decline in projected jobs occurs in computer programming, at 3%. Thus, CS is a burgeoning field, with good pay and good job prospects.

Compared to other STEM occupations, the computer industry will see the greatest percentage of growth and demand, projected to 2016 (Figure 13-2).

Technology job opportunities are predicted to grow at a faster rate than jobs in all other professional sectors, up to 25% over the next decade [Ashcraft and Blithe 2009]. Considering the huge demand and projected employment to 2018, it might not be optimal that a possibly male-focused work culture may prevent some women from reaping the benefits of a career in CS.

The financial benefits to women of greater participation in CS are clear, but beyond these are the benefits that might accrue across the board when women are enabled to participate in all professional fields, including CS. The United States needs competent people to fill computer-related jobs and do them well. The United States Department of Labor estimates that by 2016 there will be more than 1.5 million computer-related jobs available [Bureau of Labor Statistics 2004].

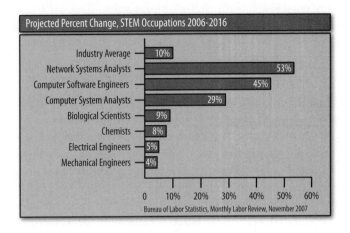

FIGURE 13-2. Projected percent change, STEM occupations 2006–2016

Despite the technology industry being one of the fastest growing industries in the U.S., if current trends continue, by 2016 the technology industry will be able to fill only half of its available jobs with candidates holding computer science bachelor's degrees from U.S. universities [Bureau of Labor Statistics, 2004]. In other words, we will benefit from participation by all people who show promise and capability, of both sexes.

Beyond this, gender balance might provide some benefits that some people have attributed to diversity. Indeed, some scholars have advanced the notion that diversity—including gender diversity—improves team performance, though not all scholars agree with this assertion, which frequently is made more on sociopolitical grounds than on scholarly ones. Research oriented around self-categorization/social identity and similarity-attraction tends to result in a pessimistic view of diversity, whereas the information-processing approach tends to give rise to more optimistic outcomes. As Mannix and Neale explain [Mannix and Neale 2005]:

> The self-categorization/social-identity and similarity-attraction approaches both tend to lead to the pessimistic view of diversity in teams. In these paradigms, individuals will be more attracted to similar others and will experience more cohesion and social integration in homogeneous groups. The information-processing approach, by contrast, offers a more optimistic view: that diversity creates an atmosphere for enhancing group performance. The information-processing approach argues that individuals in diverse groups have access to other individuals with different backgrounds, networks, information, and skills. This added information should improve the group outcome even though it might create coordination problems for the group.

Page, an advocate of diversity, says that under the right conditions, teams comprising diverse members consistently outperform teams comprising "highest-ability" members [Page 2007]. From his extensive work in complex systems, economics, and political science, Page asserts that progress depends as much on our collective differences as it does our individual IQ scores.

The research on the benefits of diversity in the IT workplace suggests that teams with equal numbers of women and men are more likely (than teams of any other composition) to experiment, be creative, share knowledge, and fulfill tasks [London Business School 2007], and that teams comprising women and men produce IT patents that are cited 26–42% more often than the norm for similar types of patents [Ashcraft and Breitzman 2007].

Research on this topic often credits diversity with a myriad of positive outcomes for team performance, yet it must be acknowledged that 50 years of research by social scientists has shown that performance advantages are not so clear-cut. As Mannix and Neale [2005] on page 237 point out, whereas tenure diversity (diversity in employee length of service) has particularly negative effects on performance, diversity based on social-category variables such as age, sex, and race seems to produce mixed effects, and the effect particularly depends on proportions (ratios of minority to majority members). In a large-scale, four-study project in which the authors measured the effects of racial and gender diversity on team process and performance, Kochan and colleagues found that gender diversity had either no effect or positive effects on team process, whereas racial diversity tended to have negative effects [Kochan et al. 2003]. Although Kochan and colleagues reported few direct effects for either type of diversity on team performance, they did indicate that contextual conditions (such as high competition among teams) exacerbated racial diversity's negative effects on performance.

Interestingly, Sackett and colleagues pose the question of how, exactly, performance is being assessed throughout the literature evaluating the benefits of diversity [Sackett et al. 1991]. That is, the authors note that performance ratings are tricky. After controlling for differences in male-female cognitive ability, psychomotor ability, education, and experience, when the proportion of women was small, women received lower performance ratings. Sackett and colleagues found that when women formed less than 20% of a group, they received lower performance ratings than did men, but when their proportion was greater than 50%, they were rated higher than the men. The authors did not find any parallel effects of proportion of representation on the performance ratings of men. Because the sex of the rater was not recorded, other potentially plausible explanations, including fear of class-action lawsuits or claims of discrimination, are difficult to evaluate.

In other words, researchers may lack credible measures for valuing gender diversity, at least with respect to performance. Does proportion truly enhance performance, or is there some other underlying factor giving the perception of enhanced performance? How can overt diversity (male/female, black/white) be studied while also appropriately assessing values and attitudes for similarities and differences? Would a gender- or ethnically-diverse work group whose members share similar attitudes and values be considered homogeneous or heterogeneous? Clearly, parameters need to be defined, and creating valid measures is part of the difficulty for research in this area.

Amidst these confusions, the fact that potential benefits of a diverse workforce may also include financial rewards is worth noting. A 2006 Catalyst study found higher average financial performance for companies with a higher representation of female board members. The study claims that for return on equity, sales, and invested capital, companies with the highest percentages of women board members outperformed those with the least by 53, 42, and 66%, respectively [Joy and Carter 2007]. Previously, a 2004 Catalyst study indicated that companies with the highest percentage of women leaders experienced a 35.1% higher return on equity and a 34% higher total return to shareholders. However, it could be argued that these results stem from progressive attitudes, not gender per se. Furthermore, Adams and Ferreira found that the average effect of gender diversity on both market valuation and operating performance was negative [Adams and Ferreira 2008]. This negative effect, they explain, may be driven by companies with greater shareholder rights. In firms with weaker shareholder rights, gender diversity has positive effects. Therefore, given the Catalyst researchers' inability to control for variables such as business attitudes and shareholder involvement, we need to question their "face-value" conclusions.

Of additional concern should be politically forced and mandated measures creating gender diversity on boards. In 2003, the Norwegian Parliament passed a law requiring all public limited firms to have at least 40% women on their boards. Since then, researchers from the University of Michigan have investigated the consequences of this law. Ahern and Dittmar found negative impacts on firm value; however, they are quick to point out that the value loss was not caused by the sex of the new board members, but rather by their younger age and lack of high-level work experience [Ahern and Dittmar 2009]. Forcing gender diversity on boards for the sake of social equity produces inexperienced boards that can be detrimental to the value of individual companies, at least for the short run. What remains to be seen are the long-term consequences of such mandates.

Finally, some have argued that a diverse workforce fosters innovation. Overall patenting in all IT subcategories grew substantially between 1980 and 2005, but U.S. female patenting grew even more dramatically. All U.S. IT patenting for both genders combined grew from 32,000-plus patents in the period from 1980–1985 to 176,000-plus patents—a five-fold increase [Ashcraft and Blithe 2009]. For the same period, U.S. female IT patenting grew from 707 patents to more than 10,000—a 14-fold increase. This is particularly noteworthy because the percentage of women employed in IT remained relatively flat [Ashcraft and Blithe 2009]. Also, because women influence 80% of consumer spending decisions, and yet 90% of technology products and services are designed by men, there is a potential untapped market representing women's product needs [Harris and Raskino 2007]. Including women in the technological design process may mean more competitive products in the marketplace.

W. A. Wulf, the president of the National Academy of Engineering, notes one perspective on diversity: "Without diversity, we limit the set of life experiences that are applied, and as a result, we pay an opportunity cost—a cost in products not built, in designs not considered, in constraints not understood, and in processes not invented." On the other hand, concerning the research on diversity, Thomas A. Kochan, MIT Professor of Management and Engineering Systems, has said: "The diversity industry is built on sand. The business case rhetoric for diversity is simply naïve and overdone. There are no strong positive or negative effects of gender or racial diversity on business performance." Kochan does, however, acknowledge, "there is a strong social case for why we should be promoting diversity in all our organizations and over time as the labor market becomes more diverse, organizations will absolutely need to build these capabilities to stay effective" [Kochan 2010]. The most parsimonious current summary is that there may be some benefits of gender diversity, but that there may be costs as well.

What Can Society Do to Reverse the Trend?

The research on the causes of the gender imbalance in CS professions has created many passionate debates that suggest a need for change. Some argue that women are choosing what they wish to do—and it is medicine (where women are 50% of new MDs), veterinary medicine (where women are 76% of new DVMs), and fields such as biology (where women are also at parity with men; see [Ceci and Williams 2010]). But if our society were to wish to explore options for encouraging more women to enter CS, what might we do? Can the trend toward an overwhelmingly male CS field be reversed? Fortunately, research has looked beyond why so few women are in CS; studies have also examined potential interventions dealing with culture, curriculum, confidence, and policy.

Research and initiatives at Carnegie Mellon serve as an excellent paradigm for evidence-based intervention in CS instruction at the post-secondary level. Some of these approaches include interdisciplinary courses that bring students of diverse backgrounds together to work on multifaceted problems, an undergraduate concentration on human-computer interaction, and a course that engages students with nonprofit groups in the local community, applying their skills to community issues [Margolis et al. 2000]. Additionally, Carnegie Mellon has found that directly recruiting women has a strong effect on increasing women's participation in computer science. Through their recruitment program and the programs previously outlined, they raised their proportion of women undergraduate CS majors from 7% in 1995 to 40% in 2000. Despite an overall decrease in enrollments in computer science across the country, in 2007, Carnegie Mellon represents a positive outlier, with 23% female enrollment.

Implications of Cross-National Data

In 2004, Charles and Bradley analyzed data from the Organization for Economic Cooperation and Development (OECD), focusing on higher-education degrees awarded in 21 industrialized countries. As expected, women predominated in traditionally female-typed fields such as health and education, and lagged behind in stereotypically masculine fields [Charles and Bradley 2006]. In all 21 countries, women were underrepresented in computer science (Table 13-1). What was surprising, however, were the results as far as egalitarian versus nonegalitarian countries are concerned. One might expect the underrepresentation of females (or the overrepresentation of males) to be greatest in nonegalitarian countries. However, Turkey and Korea, countries not known for equality of the sexes, have *smaller* male overrepresentation factors (see Table 13-1). This could, in part, be due to policy issues mandating both genders' participation in computer science experiences. Note that the overrepresentation values show the factor by which men are overrepresented in computer science programs in each respective country (see [Charles and Bradley 2006] for a complete discussion on how these values were calculated).

TABLE 13-1. Male "overrepresentation factor" in computer science programs, 2001[a]

Country	Factor of overrepresentation
Australia	2.86
Austria	5.37
Belgium	5.58
Czech Republic	6.42
Denmark	5.47
Finland	2.29
France	4.57
Germany	5.58
Hungary	4.66
Ireland	1.84
Korea, Republic	1.92
Netherlands	4.39
New Zealand	2.92
Norway	2.75
Slovak Republic	6.36
Spain	3.67
Sweden	1.95
Switzerland	4.66
Turkey	1.79
United Kingdom	3.10
United States	2.10

[a] Values give the factor by which men are overrepresented in computer science programs in the respective country. They are calculated by taking inverse values of the "computer science" parameters from previous calculations (see McGrath Cahoon and Aspray, 2006 in Chapter 6 and [Charles and Bradley 2006]) and converting the resultant positive values into exponential form.

Charles and Bradley's research does not support standard arguments of social evolution theory, since the most economically developed countries are not producing greater numbers of women in computer science. Likewise, the authors show that there is not a strong correlation between the number of women in the workforce or in high-status jobs and the number going into computer science. These findings again suggest that the reasons for women's underrepresentation in computer professions are more likely found in the realm of culture than biology, a realm in which change is possible. But it is critically important to note that this research also provides little evidence that women's representation in computer science programs is stronger in the most economically developed countries, or that it is stronger in countries in which women participate at higher rates in the labor market, higher education, or high-status professional occupations [Charles and Bradley 2006]. Thus, the role of women's preferences emerges as the most likely explanation for where women end up, as opposed to explanations implicating biases as preventing women from entering CS.

The underrepresentation of women in computer science in all 21 countries studied indicates that there is a deep, shared belief in a given culture that women and men are better suited for different jobs. What makes the work of Charles and Bradley so interesting is that, with so much cross-national variability, there is a lot of room for social and cultural influences to play out. In the United States, we emphasize free choice and self-realization as societal goals that education seeks to nurture; yet the prevailing stereotypes may secretly stifle students' "free" choice as they pursue fields that are in line with the conventional identity of being male or female in our culture. Charles and Bradley observed that the governments exerting strong controls over curricular trajectories, such as Korea and Ireland, had less female underrepresentation in computer science. This suggests that we may want to defer adolescents' career choices to a time when gender stereotypes do not have such a stronghold on them, and implement policies in which students explore math and science, including computer science, from kindergarten to 12th grade and beyond.

Conclusion

In this chapter we have provided recent evidence to help the reader navigate and explore the question of why so few women pursue CS careers, why we should care, and what, if anything, should be done about it. We have looked at areas of biological differences between males and females that are coupled with cognitive-ability differences, especially in gifted individuals; differences in career and lifestyle preferences; and the culture of the computer science milieu. Despite clear gaps in understanding about the relationship between gender and participation in CS/IT, it is worth debating the costs of acting versus not acting to encourage more women to participate in CS, within the context of the empirical literature on women in science.

In short, some in industry and business argue that the paucity of women in CS/IT-related fields is a detriment to the economic advancement of women and the economic development of our nation—and some have argued the opposite. Although some transnational comparisons of women's underrepresentation in CS [Charles and Bradley 2006] call into question the value of interventions, on the whole it does seem wiser for policy-makers to work toward broadening both genders' exposure to computers at an early age, when students are not so entrenched in gender identity roles. Given potential benefits to women and society, it seems advisable to consider steps that may encourage women to enter the fields of Information Technology, Computer Science, and Computer Engineering. Cultural, curricular, and confidence-oriented interventions have been suggested by various authors [Margolis et al. 2000]; [AAUW 2000]; [McGrath Cohoon and Aspray 2006], and should continually be assessed regarding whether they are effective in the first place, whether they advance or hinder female participation in the field of computer science, and whether these changes in fact enhance the field. The ultimate goal should be the quality, effectiveness, and advancement of the CS profession, regardless of whether this means that the futuristic view of CS is largely male, largely female, or somewhat more gender balanced.

References

[Adams and Ferreira 2009] Adams, R., and D. Ferreira. 2009. Women in the boardroom and their impact on governance and performance. *Journal of Financial Economics* 94(2): 291–309.

[Ahern and Dittmar 2009] Ahern, K., and K. Dittmar. 2009. The changing of the boards: The value effect of a massive exogenous shock. Under review.

[AAUW 2000] American Association of University Women. 2000. *Tech-Savvy: Educating Girls in the New Computer Age*. Washington, DC: American Association of University Women Educational Foundation. Retrieved from *http://www.aauw.org/research/upload/TechSavvy.pdf*.

[Ashcraft and Blithe 2009] Ashcraft, C., and S. Blithe. 2009. *Women in IT: The Facts*. Boulder, CO: National Center for Women & Information Technology.

[Ashcraft and Breitzman 2007] Ashcraft, C., and A. Breitzman. 2007. Who invents IT? An analysis of women's participation in information technology patenting. National Center for Women & Information Technology. Retrieved from *http://www.ncwit.org/pdf/PatentExecSumm .pdf*.

[Bureau of Labor Statistics 2004] Bureau of Labor Statistics. 2004. *Occupational Outlook Handbook*, 2004–05 Edition. Washington, DC: Labor Department, Labor Statistics Bureau. Retrieved from *http://www.bls.gov/oco/ocos267.htm*.

[Bureau of Labor Statistics 2010] Bureau of Labor Statistics. 2010. *Occupational Outlook Handbook*, 2010–11 Edition. Washington, DC: Labor Department, Labor Statistics Bureau. Available at *http://www.umsl.edu/services/govdocs/ooh20042005/www.bls.gov/OCO/index.html*.

[Ceci and Williams 2010] Ceci, S.J., and W.M. Williams. 2010. *The mathematics of sex: How biology and society conspire to limit talented women and girls*. New York, NY: Oxford University Press.

[Ceci and Williams 2007] Ceci, S.J., and W.M. Williams, ed. 2007. *Why aren't more women in science? Top researchers debate the evidence.* Washington, DC: American Psychological Association Books.

[Ceci et al. 2009] Ceci, S.J., W.M. Williams, and S.M. Barnett. 2009. Women's underrepresentation in science: Sociocultural and biological considerations. *Psychological Bulletin* 135(2): 218–261.

[Charles and Bradley 2006] Charles, M., and K. Bradley. 2006. A matter of degrees—Female underrepresentation in computer science programs cross-nationally. In *Women and Information Technology: Research on Underrepresentation*, ed. J. McGrath Cohoon and W. Aspray, 183–204. Cambridge, MA: MIT Press.

[College Board 2008] College Board. 2008. *AP summary report (calculus AB, computer science A and AB).* Princeton, N.J.: College Board. Retrieved from *http://professionals.collegeboard.com/data -reports-research/ap/archived/2008.*

[Deary et al. 2007] Deary, I., K. Ferguson, M. Bastin, G. Barrow, L. Reid, J. Seckl, J. Wardlaw, and A. MacLullich. 2007. Skull size and intelligence and King Robert Bruce's IQ. *Intelligence* 31: 519–525.

[Durndell and Lightbody 1993] Durndell, A., and P. Lightbody 1993. Gender and computing: Change over time? *Computers and Education* 21(4): 331–336.

[Eccles et al. 1999] Eccles, J., B. Barber, and D. Jozfowicz. 1999. Linking gender to educational, occupational and recreational choices: Applying the Eccles et al. related model of achievement related choices. In *Sexism and stereotypes in modern society: The gender science of Janet Taylor Spence*, ed. W. Swan, J. Langlois, and L. Gilbert, 153–192. Washington, DC: American Psychological Association Books.

[Ferriman et al. 2009] Ferriman, K., D. Lubinski, and C. Benbow. 2009. Work preferences, life values, and personal views of top math/science graduate students and the profoundly gifted: Developmental changes and gender differences during emerging adulthood and parenthood. *Journal of Personality and Social Psychology* 97(3): 517–532.

[Haier et al. 2005] Haier, R., R. Jung, R. Yeo, and M. Alkire. 2005. The neuroanatomy of general intelligence: Sex matters. *Neuroimage* 25(1): 320–327.

[Halpern et al. 2007] Halpern, D., C. Benbow, D.C. Geary, R. Gur, J. Hyde, and M.A. Gernsbacher. 2007. The science of sex differences in science and mathematics. *Psychological Science in the Public Interest*, 8(1): 1–52.

[Harris and Raskino 2007] Harris, K., and M. Raskino. 2007. *Women and men in IT: Breaking sexual stereotypes.* Stamford, CT: Gartner.

[Hedges and Nowell 1995] Hedges, L., and A. Nowell. 1995. Sex differences in mental test scores: variability and numbers of high-scoring individuals. *Science* 269: 41–45.

[Higher Education Research Institute 2008] Higher Education Research Institute. 2008. *Freshman: Forty year trends, 1966–2006.* Los Angeles, CA: Higher Education Research Institute.

[Honey 1994] Honey, M. 1994. The maternal voice in the technological universe. In *Representations of Motherhood,* ed. D. Bassin, M. Honey, and M.M. Kaplan, 220–239. New Haven: Yale University Press.

[Hyde and Lynn 2008] Hyde, J., and M. Lynn. 2008. Gender similarities in mathematics and science. *Science* 321: 599–600.

[Joy and Carter 2007] Joy, L., and N. Carter. 2007. The bottom line: Corporate performance and women's representation on boards. *Catalyst Research Reports.* Retrieved January 29, 2009, from *http://www.catalyst.org/publication/200/the-bottom-line-corporate-performance-and-womens-representation-on-boards.*

[Kochan 2010] Kochan, T. 2010. Personal communication, March 16.

[Kochan et al. 2003] Kochan, T., K. Bezrukova, R. Ely, S. Jackson, A. Joshi, K. Jehn, J. Leonard, D. Levine, and D. Thomas. 2003. The effects of diversity on business performance: Report of the diversity research network. *Human Resource Management* 42:3–21.

[London Business School 2007] London Business School. 2007. Innovative potential: Men and women in teams. Available at *http://www.london.edu/newsandevents/news/2007/11/Women_in_Business_Conference_725.html.*

[Lubinski et al. 2001] Lubinski, D., C. Benbow, D. Shea, H. Eftekhari-Sanjani, and B. Halvorson. 2001. Men and women at promise for scientific excellence: Similarity not dissimilarity. *Psychological Science* 12: 309–317.

[Mannix and Neale 2005] Mannix, E., and M. Neale. 2005. What differences make a difference? The promise and reality of diverse teams in organizations. *Psychological Science in the Public Interest* 6(4): 31–55.

[Margolis et al. 2000] Margolis, J., A. Fisher, and F. Miller. 2000. The anatomy of interest. *Women's Studies Quarterly* 28(1/2): 104.

[Martin 1992] Martin, C., ed. 1992. *In search of gender-free paradigms for computer science education.* Eugene, OR: International Society for Technology in Education.

[McGrath Cohoon and Aspray 2006] McGrath Cohoon, J., and W. Aspray, ed. 2006. *Women and Information Technology: Research on Underrepresentation.* Cambridge, MA: MIT Press.

[National Center for Education Statistics 2008] National Center for Education Statistics. 2008. *Classification of Instructional Program 11.* Washington, DC: U.S. Department of Education Institute of Education Sciences.

[Page 2007] Page, S. 2007. *The Difference: How the power of diversity helps create better groups, firms, schools, and societies.* Princeton, NJ: Princeton University Press.

[Sackett et al. 1991] Sackett, P., C. Dubois, and A. Noe. 1991. Tokenism in performance evaluation: The effects of work group representation on male-female and White-Black differences in performance ratings. *Journal of Applied Psychology* 76(2): 263–267.

[Schofield 1995] Schofield, J. 1995. *Computers and classroom culture.* New York: Cambridge University Press.

[Seymour and Hewitt 1994] Seymour, E., and N. Hewitt. 1994. *Talking About Leaving: Factors Contributing to High Attrition Rates Among Science, Mathematics, and Engineering Undergraduate Majors.* Boulder, CO: University of Colorado, Bureau of Sociological Research.

## CHAPTER FOURTEEN

Two Comparisons of Programming Languages

Lutz Prechelt

At parties, stereotypical programmers tend to be the quiet kind. There is one topic, however, that is sure to produce not only their rapt attention, but also plenty of verbal contribution: programming languages! Everyone has lots of factual knowledge of several languages, accompanied by plenty of opinion regarding which one is best and why. Any evidence, too? Yes, seasoned programmers will also have a number of war stories to tell where something went particularly well or not well because of the language used: "I estimated this to be a ten- or fifteen-hour job, but then I decided to use language X instead and had it all up and running after just three hours—and mighty readable, too!"

The problem with such evidence is that it usually doesn't involve any direct comparison of languages, and if it does, you are lucky if that comparison is apples-to-oranges; more likely it is apples-to-orangutans.

One would think that scientists would have jumped at this opportunity to make an immensely popular and hugely relevant contribution to the field of computer programming and would have produced a long series of wonderful, clean studies comparing the pros and cons of various programming languages. Candidate topics for research projects abound: such topics as execution speed, memory consumption, defect rates, defect types, reliability, robustness, readability, modifiability, programming productivity, and many more.

But for reasons that so far I have been unable to determine, this has never happened. The scientific evidence available in this regard is scarce. And though serious studies tend to be much less entertaining than the war stories told at parties, the latter often do *not* offer more credibility [Hudak and Jones 1994].

In my career, I have encountered two opportunities to perform reasonably convincing language comparisons and grabbed them. This chapter tells the story of these two studies.

A Language Shoot-Out over a Peculiar Search Algorithm

The first opportunity arose after I had collected a number of implementations of the same program for a different study. That study [Prechelt and Unger 2001] measured the effects of receiving a training in Watts Humphrey's Personal Software Process (PSP, [Humphrey 1995]). The PSP claims big improvements in estimation accuracy, defect density, and productivity, yet our study found the effect to be a lot smaller than expected.

Half of the graduate student subjects in that study had received PSP training, and the others had received other programming-related training. In the study, they all solved exactly the same task (described in the next section), but could choose their programming language freely. I ended up with 40 implementations (24 in Java, 11 in C++, and 5 in C), and it occurred to me that it would be quite interesting to compare not just the PSP-trained programmers against the non-PSP-trained programmers, but to treat the programs as three sets stemming from different languages. It would be even more interesting to have further implementations in several scripting languages to compare.

I posted a public "call for implementations" in several Usenet newsgroups (this was in 1999), and within four weeks received another 40 implementations from volunteers: 13 in Perl, 13 in Python, 4 in Rexx, and 10 in TCL.

At this point, your skeptical brain ought to yell, "Wait! How can he know these people are of comparable competence?" A very good question, indeed; we will come back to it in the credibility discussion at the end.

The Programming Task: Phonecode

The programmers were told to implement the following program.

The program first loads a dictionary into memory (a flat text file containing one word per line; the full test file contained 73,113 words and was 938 KB in size). Then, it reads "telephone numbers" from another file (in fact long, nonsensical strings of up to 50 arbitrary digits, dashes, and slashes), converts them one by one into word sequences, and prints the results. The conversion is defined by a fixed mapping of characters to digits (designed to balance digit frequencies) as follows:

```
e jnq rwx dsy ft am civ bku lop ghz
0 111 222 333 44 55 666 777 888 999
```

The program's task is to find a sequence of words such that the sequence of characters in these words exactly corresponds to the sequence of digits in the phone number. All possible solutions must be found and printed. The solutions are created word-by-word, and if no word from the dictionary can be inserted at some point during that process, a single digit from the phone number can appear in the result at that position. Many phone numbers have no solution at all.

Here is an example of the program output for the phone number 3586-75. Among the words in the dictionary were Dali, um, Sao, da, and Pik.

```
3586-75: Dali um
3586-75: Sao 6 um
3586-75: da Pik 5
```

A list of partial solutions needs to be maintained by the program while processing each number. This requires the program to read the dictionary into an efficiency-supporting data structure, as it was explicitly prohibited to scan the whole dictionary for each digit to be encoded.

The programmers were asked to make sure their implementation was 100% reliable. They were given a small dictionary for testing purposes and one set of example telephone numbers for input plus the corresponding output—all correct encodings of these numbers with respect to the given dictionary.

Comparing Execution Speed

Figure 14-1 shows a run-time comparison across the seven languages. (Refer to "How to read the boxplot diagrams" on page 242 to interpret the figure's boxplot format.)

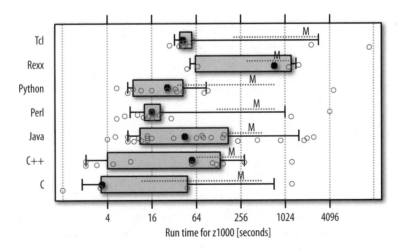

FIGURE 14-1. *Program runtime for 1,000 inputs in different languages. The bad/good ratios range from 1.5 for Tcl up to 27 for C++. Note the logarithmic axis; for instance, the Java runtimes differ by up to a factor of 500!*

HOW TO READ THE BOXPLOT DIAGRAMS

Boxplots are a good tool for visually comparing the location and spread of multiple samples of data quickly. In our particular style of boxplots, each of the small circles represents one datapoint.

The box marks the "middle half" of these data: its left edge is the 25-percentile, meaning 25% of the datapoints are less than or equal to this point (interpolated if necessary); its right edge is the 75-percentile.

The fat dot is the 50-percentile (median), not to be confused with the arithmetic mean, which is marked by the letter M. The dotted line around the M is plus/minus one standard error of the mean, which indicates how accurately the present sample allows one to estimate the mean of the respective population with 68% confidence.

The whiskers on the left and right of the box indicate the 10-percentile and 90-percentile, which are better representatives of extreme values than minimum and maximum. Wide boxes or long dashed lines indicate data with high variability, which implies high uncertainty, which in turn, for software development, implies high risk. We use the ratio of the right versus left box edge as a measure of variability and call it the *good/bad* or *bad/good ratio*. The left edge is the median of the bottom half of the data, and if the data shown is the consumption of something, the bottom half is the "good" part of the data because lower consumption is better. Likewise for the top half.

When comparing languages visually, we may choose to compare the location of the fat dots, the Ms (means), or the whole boxes. The latter makes us most conscious of the uncertainty involved and makes hasty conclusions less likely.

More reliable than a visual comparison (but less clear) is a numerical comparison based on appropriate statistical techniques—in the present case, confidence intervals computed via bootstrapping. Note that sometimes the variability is so large that the plots need to use a logarithmic scale, which reliably baffles your imagination. Think!

Also, treat the plots for Rexx and for C as somewhat unreliable, as they represent only four and five programs, respectively.

Remember that you are looking at data on a logarithmic scale. This means the within-language variabilities shown are actually *huge*! So huge that not a single one of the 21 pairwise differences of mean runtimes per language is statistically significant. This can be seen by the high degree of overlap among the dashed lines for essentially all languages in the figure. It means there is some non-negligible chance (clearly more than 5%, the commonly used threshold for statistical significance) that the observed differences are there *only* due to random fluctuations and are hence not "real."

As a different way to put this, we could say the differences between programmers outweigh the differences between languages. There are a few significant differences for *median* runtimes (both Perl and Python are faster than both Rexx and Tcl), but medians are far less relevant because their use would imply that you only care *whether* one program is faster than another and not *how much* faster it is.

To squeeze more information out of the data, we have to aggregate the languages into just three groups: Java forms one, C and C++ form the second, and all four scripting languages form the third. In this aggregation, statistical analysis reveals that with 80% confidence, a script program will run at least 1.29 times as long as a C/C++ program, and a Java program will run at least 1.22 times as long as a C/C++ program. No big deal. "I don't believe this!" I hear you say. "C and C++ are a *hell* of a lot faster than scripts. Where have these differences gone?"

There are two answers to this question. The first is revealed when we split up each runtime into two pieces. The execution of the phonecode program has two phases: first, load the dictionary and create the corresponding data structure, and second, perform the actual search for each input phone number. For the search phase, the within-language differences are quite large for the script languages, very large for Java, and enormous for C/C++. This within-language variability is so large that it renders the between-language differences statistically insignificant. For the dictionary load phase, the C/C++ programs *are* indeed the fastest. The Java programs need at least 1.3 times as long to complete this phase, and the script programs need at least 5.5 times as long, on average (again with 80% confidence).

The second answer has to do with the within-language variability, which is mind-boggling, particularly for C and C++. This blurs language differences a lot. Remember the good/bad ratio mentioned earlier: the median run time of the slower half of the C++ programs is 27 times as large as for the faster half. Are these slower-half programmers complete cretins? No, they are not. The upcoming discussion of program structure will reveal where these differences come from.

Comparing Memory Consumption

For the same program runs we considered in the previous sections, see the corresponding plots for the memory consumption in Figure 14-2.

From these results we can derive the following observations:

- Nothing beats the low memory consumption of the smaller C/C++ programs.
- The C++ and Java groups are clearly partitioned into two subgroups (look at the small circles!) that have small versus large memory consumption.
- Scripting languages tend to be worse than C/C++.

- Java is, on average, clearly worse than everything else.
- But you can shoot yourself in the memory footprint with any language.
- Java shows the largest variability and hence the largest planning risk.

We'll find the reason for the partitioning of programs in our upcoming analysis.

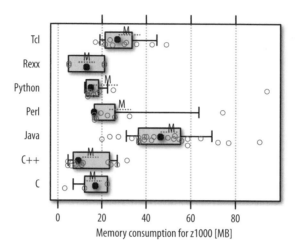

FIGURE 14-2. Memory consumption for 1,000 inputs, including the runtime system, program code, and data. The bad/good ratios range from 1.2 for Python up to 4.9 for C++.

Comparing Productivity and Program Length

In a time of multigigabyte memories and multigigahertz, multicore processors, often both runtime and memory consumption are not critical. Saving programmer effort, however, will never go out of fashion. Figure 14-3 shows how long the programmers took to write each implementation, probably the most spectacular result of this study.

We see that the average work times are roughly in the range of 3 to 5 hours for the scripting languages, but 9 to 16 hours for the nonscript languages. Nonscripts take about three times as long! I can almost see all you nonscripting programmers shift uneasily in your seat now. Should we be willing to believe these data? Or have many of the scripting programmers cheated about their work time? Figure 14-4 offers evidence that their reports can be trusted, because the scripts are also hardly more than one-third as long as the nonscripts. However, please see "Should I Believe This?" on page 247 for a caveat when interpreting these data.

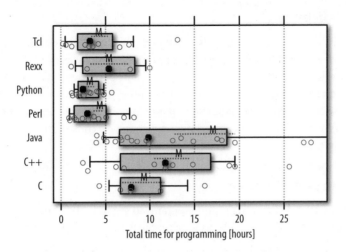

FIGURE 14-3. Total programmer work time. Script groups show times as measured and reported by the programmers; nonscript groups show times as measured by the experimenter. The bad/good ratios range from 1.5 for C up to 3.2 for Perl. Three Java work times at 40, 49, and 63 hours are not shown.

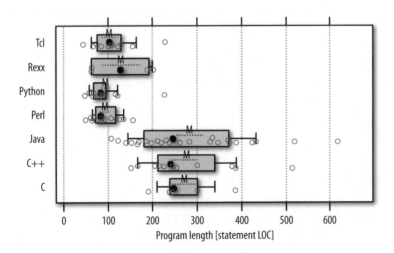

FIGURE 14-4. Program length in number of noncomment source lines of code. The bad/good ratios range from 1.3 for C up to 2.1 for Java and 3.7 for Rexx. Comment densities (not shown) are higher for scripts than for nonscripts.

Comparing Reliability

In a mass reliability testing of all programs, we found that most implementations worked perfectly. Those few that failed were spread about evenly over all languages—at least when one considers the somewhat different working conditions of the script versus the nonscript programmers, described in [Prechelt 2000a]. Furthermore, the failures also tended to occur for the same inputs across all languages: devious "phone numbers" that contained no digit at all, only dashes and slashes. In short, the experiment did not reveal consistent reliability differences between the languages.

Comparing Program Structure

When we looked at the source code of the programs to see how they are designed, we found the second really spectacular result of this experiment.

Programs used one of three basic data structures to represent the dictionary content so as to speed up the search:

- A simple partitioning of the dictionary into 10 subsets based on the digit corresponding to the first character. This is a simple but also very inefficient solution.

- An associative array (hash table) indexed by phone numbers and mapping to a set of all corresponding words from the dictionary. This is hardly more difficult to program, but is very efficient.

- A 10-ary tree where any path corresponds to a digit sequence and dictionary words are attached to all leaf nodes and some inner nodes. This requires the most program code, but is blazingly fast in the search phase.

And here is the fascinating observation: First, all C, C++, and Java programs used either solution 1 or solution 3. The difference between these two solutions explains the huge within-language runtime variability in these three groups seen in Figure 14-1. Second, all script programs used solution 2.

Solution 2 can be considered the best solution, in that it provides high efficiency at rather low coding effort. But, of course, although suitable hash map implementations were available to at least the C++ and Java programmers, apparently none of them thought of using them. For the script programmers, in contrast, using associative arrays for many things appears to be second nature, so they all came up with the corresponding straightforward and compact search routine.

The language used really shaped the programmers' thinking here—even though many of them also knew a language of the other type. The observation also explains some part of the between-languages difference in program length: the loop using the associative array needs fewer statements.

I do not believe that this effect is about "better" or "worse" languages. I think that particular languages incline programmers toward particular solution styles. Which of these styles is better depends on the particular problem at hand.

Should I Believe This?

Remember, we still have a nagging question open:

> How do we know that the programmers in different languages being compared are of similar competence?

We can find an answer through the same technique we already used in the section on productivity: compare the productivity across languages measured in lines of code per reported work hour. It has long been known that the effort per line of code depends on the program requirements and various constraints, but hardly on the programming language ([Boehm 1981], p. 477), so higher language expressiveness is a most promising source of productivity improvements. Thus, if the range found for lines of code per hour is similar for each language, we can be reasonably confident that the programmer group for each language is comparable to the others (and also that at most, a few of the script programmers reported too-low work times).

The results, as shown in Figure 14-5, show that there are at most four abnormally high productivity values (three for TCL and one for Perl); all others are in the range established by the carefully supervised Java, C, and C++ programmers from the PSP study, and all averages are reasonably similar. This means it is fair to assume that the groups are indeed comparable and the times reported for scripting are at least approximately correct.

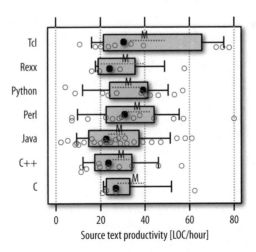

FIGURE 14-5. Source code productivity in noncomment lines of code per work hour. Work hours are measured for C, C++, and Java and are self-reported for the script groups.

OK, so if we are willing to accept the results at face value, what limitations should we keep in mind when interpreting them? There are basically three:

- The measurements are old (1999). The efficiency results might be different today because of differently sized improvements in the language implementations; in particular, Java (version 1.2 at that time) and Python (version 1.5 at that time) have likely improved a lot in the meantime. Also, Java was so new at the time of the data collection that the Java programmers were naive about their language. For instance, some of them simply used `Strings` where `StringBuffers` were called for, which explains part of the worse results reported for them in the memory usage and runtime categories.

- The task solved in this study is small and hence rather specific. Its nature is also quite idiosyncratic. Different tasks might bring forth different results, but we cannot know for sure.

- The working conditions for the scripting groups were rather different from conditions for the Java/C/C++ groups. The latter worked under laboratory conditions, and the former under field conditions. In particular, some of the scripting participants reported they had not started implementation right after they had read the task description, which puts them at an advantage because the background thinking they performed in the meantime does not show up in the time measurements. Fortunately, the difference in work times is huge enough that a meaningful amount remains even if one applies a hefty rebate to the nonscript work times.

A number of other considerations may also hedge the results of this study. If you want to learn about them, have a look at the original source for this study [Prechelt 2000a]. A much shorter report, but still more detailed than the description here, can be found in [Prechelt 2000b].

Plat_Forms: Web Development Technologies and Cultures

The second opportunity for a language comparison arose after a software manager named Gaylord Aulke called me in 2005 and said, "I own a service company that builds web applications. I have read your Phonecode report and use it to explain to my customers why they need not be afraid of scripting languages. But I would like to have something more specific. Couldn't you do something like that for PHP?"

It was a fascinating thought, but it took me only two seconds to decide that no, I could not. I explained the reasons to him: to be credible, comparing web development platforms would need to involve a much bigger task (at least several days long, to make interesting aspects of web applications visible), platform groups of *teams* (at least three people each, to make interesting aspects of web development processes visible) rather than language groups of individuals, and high-quality professionals rather than arbitrary folks or students (because of the greater depth of knowledge required for a realistic use of web platforms). Also, the evaluation would be much more complicated. I simply could not imagine how anybody would pay for a study of this size.

His reaction was "Hmm, I see. I will talk to someone. Maybe we can do something about it." Months later, the person he had talked to put me in contact with Richard Seibt and Eduard Heilmayr, who eventually were able to attract teams to participate in the experiment, which I had been able to scale down a great deal and which was now called Plat_Forms. The mission of the experiment was to look for any and all characteristics of the solutions or development processes that were consistent within a platform, yet different between platforms. These characteristics could then be considered emergent properties of the platforms—that is, effects on development that probably weren't designed into the platforms or motivations for adopting them, but that nevertheless had a consistent impact.

The data collection, announced as a contest, went smoothly, except that we could not find enough teams for .NET, Python, and Ruby, and so had teams for only Java, Perl, and PHP. The evaluation was indeed quite difficult, but eventually we found some intriguing results.

The Development Task: People-by-Temperament

In the morning of January 25, 2007, nine competent professional teams (three using Java, three Perl, and three PHP) were handed a 20-page document (spelling out 127 fine-grained functional, 19 nonfunctional, and 5 organizational requirements) and two data files on a CD. The next afternoon, they handed in a DVD containing the source code, version archive, and turnkey-runnable VMware virtual machine of their solution. In the meantime, they worked in whatever style suited them (even including field tests via a public prototype server and blog comments), using all the available software and tools they wanted.

The functional requirements came in use-case format, were prioritized as MUST, SHOULD, or MAY, and described a community portal called "People by Temperament" (PbT). They asked for:

- A user registration, including uncommon attributes such as GPS coordinates.
- The "Trivial Temperament Test" (TTT), a questionnaire of 40 binary questions (provided as a structured text file on the CD) leading to a four-dimensional classification of personality type.
- Search for users, based on 17 different search criteria (all combinable), some of them complicated, such as selecting a subset of the 16 personality types or coarsely classifying distance based on the GPS coordinates.
- A user list, used for representing search results, users "in contact" with myself, etc., including a graphical summary of the list as a 2D Cartesian coordinate plot visualizing the users as symbols based on two selectable criteria.

- User status page, displaying details about a user (with some attributes visible only under certain conditions) and implementing a protocol by which users can reveal their email address to each other ("get in contact") by sending and answering "requests for contact details" (RCDs).

- An additional SOAP-based web-service interface conforming to a WSDL file provided on the CD.

The nonfunctional requirements talked about scalability, persistence, programming style, and some user interface characteristics, among other things.

The participants could ask clarification questions, but each group did so less than twice per hour overall. The task turned out to be suitable and interesting for the comparison, but also somewhat too large for the given time frame.

Lay Your Bets

Being the scientist that I am, I was completely blank with respect to what the experiment would find and had no prejudices whatsoever regarding the characteristics of the three platforms. Do you believe that? Laughable! I was indeed neutral (in the sense of nonpartisan), but of course I *had* some expectations, and it was both entertaining and instructive to see that many of them crumbled. To get the most fun as well as knowledge out of this chapter, I encourage you to formulate your own expectations as well. Now. I mean it.

Here is an approximate summary of my assumptions:

Productivity
    Higher for PHP and Perl

Length of source code
    Lowest for Perl, low for PHP, high for Java

Execution speed
    Fastest for Java

Security
    Best for Java, worst for PHP

Architecture style
    "Clean" for Java, "pragmatic" for Perl and PHP (whatever that would mean; I wasn't sure myself)

Development style
    Less incremental for Java and with more up-front design

Some of these expectations were more or less fulfilled, but others held a big surprise.

Comparing Productivity

Since all teams had the same amount of time (two days) and worked towards the same set of fine-grained requirements, and no team finished early, we measured productivity by counting how many of the requirements were implemented and working. The result is shown in Figure 14-6.

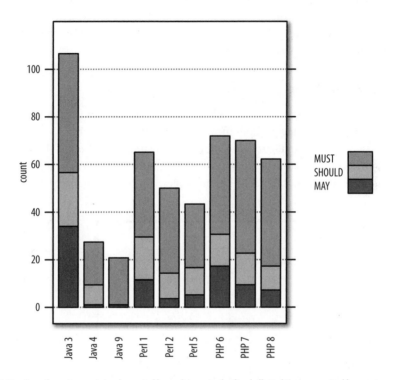

FIGURE 14-6. Number of requirements implemented by each team in the fixed allotted time, separated by requirement priority (essential, important, optional)

Please note that team 9 should be ignored for this evaluation. They used an immature framework in pre-alpha stage whose limitations kept them from achieving much. They had been very reluctant to participate, but we had urged them because we had no other third Java team. Team 4 also should be interpreted with care: they lost a lot of time on problems with their VMware setup that had nothing to do with Java. That said, the data holds the following interesting insights:

- The most productive team was actually from the least expected platform: Java. We can only speculate why this is so. Some participants (not from Team 3) pointed out that Team 3 was the only one who used a commercial framework. It is possible that this difference indeed allowed for higher productivity or that Team 3 was most versed in the use of its respective framework, perhaps because of a well-refined "company style."

- The highest average productivity was found for PHP.
- PHP also had the most even productivity. If this is a systematic effect, it would mean that PHP projects (at least with teams as competent as these) are least risky.

That last finding is something for which I had formulated no expectations at all, but it clearly calls for further research, as risk is a very important project characteristic [Hearty et al. 2008]. In hindsight, I would expect such smooth productivity more in a "high-ceremony" (statically typed) language than in a dynamic language.

Comparing Artifact Size

Although the projects varied widely in the number of requirements they implemented, this was nothing compared to the size differences we found when we opened the hood and looked at the solutions' source code. Figure 14-7 provides an overview of the size (in lines of code) of each team's deliverable, when one takes into account only programming language and templating files (not data files, binary files, build files, or documentation).

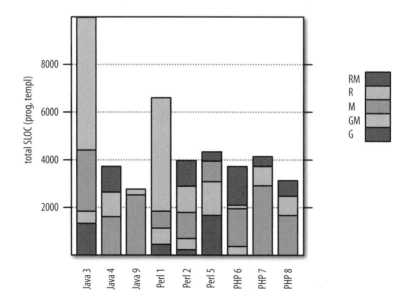

FIGURE 14-7. Total artifact size in source lines of code (SLOC) for each team, separated by origin of the respective file: reused-then-modified (RM), reused (R), manually written (M), generated-automatically-then-modified (GM), and generated automatically (G). Note that the Java 3 bar extends all the way up to 80,000 (with almost no RM), dwarfing all others by a factor of 10 to 20.

Again, we can make a number of interesting observations:

- Some teams modify reused or generated files and others do not, but no platform-dependent pattern is visible.

- Generating files appears to be most common for Perl.

- The fraction of reused code differs wildly, again without a clear platform-dependent pattern.

- Team 3's commercial framework is particularly heavyweight.

Although these are interesting academically, they are hardly of much practical interest. The curiosity of a pragmatic person would be much better satisfied by the representation shown in Figure 14-8, which considers manually written files only and relates their size to the number of requirements implemented.

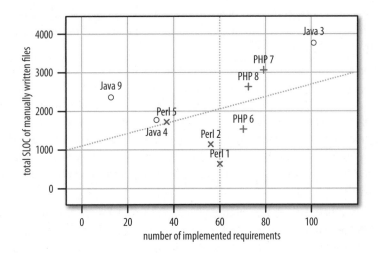

FIGURE 14-8. Total length of manually written files (as shown in Figure 14-7) depending on the number of requirements implemented (as shown in Figure 14-6)

This data shows that at least one of my initial expectations is right on target: the Java solutions are larger than average (above the trend line), and the Perl solutions are smaller than average (below the trend line).

Comparing Modifiability

There are normally two reasons why we are interested in artifact size. First, it can be used as a proxy for effort: larger artifacts tend to take longer to produce. The productivity data listed earlier has already shown us that this rule has to be taken with a grain of salt. Second, artifact size can be used as a proxy for modifiability: larger artifacts tend to require more effort for a given change. How about this in our case?

Modifiability is governed by two other *-ities*: understandability (how long do I need to find out where the change needs to be done and how?) and modularity (are the change spots widely spread or confined to a narrow region of the product?). Since the 1970s, researchers have been looking for ways to quantify these properties, but so far all metrics suggested [Fenton and Pfleeger 2000] have proven unsatisfactory. We have therefore investigated modifiability through two simple modification requests we made:

- Add another text field in the registration dialog for representing the user's middle initial, and handle this data throughout the user data model. What changes are required to the GUI form, program logic, user data structure, or database?

- Add another question to the TTT questionnaire and its evaluation.

In each scenario, we listed for each solution what changes were needed in which files.

With respect to scenario 1, Perl is the clear winner with the smallest number of change spots throughout. Java and PHP needed to make more changes, and some of the changes were also much less obvious.

With respect to scenario 2, the solutions of teams Perl 1, Perl 5, PHP 7, and PHP 8 implemented an interpreter for the original structured text file containing the TTT questionnaire, so the change amounted to just adding the new question to that text file and you were done. Neat! Team Java 9 had also started in that direction, but had not implemented the actual evaluation. The other teams all used approaches that were much less straightforward, involving separate property files (Java 3 and Java 4), a hard-coded array in the source code (PHP 6), or database tables (Perl 2). All of these are much more difficult to change and require modifications in more than one place.

The message from these experiments in modification is mixed, but we interpret them to mean that the users of dynamic languages tend more strongly toward ad-hoc (as opposed to standardized) solution approaches. With the right design idea (as teams 1, 5, 7, 8 had), this can be better for modifiability.

Internationalization, by the way, was explicitly not a requirement, but could be done easily, even with the interpreter approach. Before implementing the property file approach, teams Java 3 and Java 4 (as well as Perl 1) had queried the "customer" whether they should allow for dynamic modification of the questionnaire at run time and had received a "no" answer.

Regarding the expectation of a "clean" architectural style for Java and a "pragmatic" one for Perl and PHP, my personal conclusion is that our study does not indicate, at least for the system we asked teams to implement, any particular cleanness (or other advantage) for Java. But a pragmatic style is visible for Perl and fares quite well!

Comparing Robustness and Security

The last area with fairly spectacular results (at least in my opinion) concerns the related questions of input validation, error checking, and security. It is very difficult to perform a fair security evaluation for nine systems that are so different both externally (the amount and representation of implemented functionality) and internally (the structure and technology used). We eventually settled for a fixed set of scenarios, as in the modifiability test, that did not attempt actual penetration, but just collected symptoms of potential vulnerabilities. We used a purely black-box approach restricted to unfriendly inputs at the user interface level: inputs involving HTML tags, SQL quotes, Chinese characters, very many characters, and so on. Figure 14-9 summarizes the results. The items on the X axis are:

</...>
> HTML tags

Long
> Very long inputs

Int'l
> Nonwestern 8-bit ISO characters and non-8-bit Unicode characters

Email
> Invalid email addresses

SQL
> Quotes in text and number fields

Cookie
> Operation with cookies turned off

The reaction of the system in each case was classified as correct (**OK**), acceptable (**(OK)**), broken (**!**), or security risk (**!!!**).

To summarize our findings:

HTML-based cross-site scripting (CSS)
> Two PHP solutions and one Perl solution appear susceptible. The Java 4 solution lacked the output functionality for this test, but the other two Java solutions came out clean.

SQL injection
> All three Perl solutions and one Java solution can be provoked to produce SQL exceptions by malign user input, which may or may not represent an actual vulnerability. All three PHP solutions came out clean here.

Long inputs
> Perl 2 fails in an uncontrolled way, but all other solutions behave acceptably.

International characters
> Perl 2 and Java 3 reject even short Chinese inputs as too long, whereas all PHP solutions work correctly.

Email address checking

    Two Java and two Perl solutions performed no email address validity checking; all PHP solutions did.

Operation with cookies turned off

    These made Java 9 fail silently and Perl 5 fail incomprehensibly. For the other (including all PHP) solutions, the operation was either possible or was rejected with a clean error message.

Summing this up, we have two findings that may be surprising for many people. First, the only solution that is correct or acceptable in each respect tested is a PHP solution, PHP 6. Second, with the exception of the CSS test, every other test had at least one broken Java solution and one broken Perl solution—but zero broken PHP solutions. It appears that, at least in the hands of capable teams, PHP is more robust than is often thought.

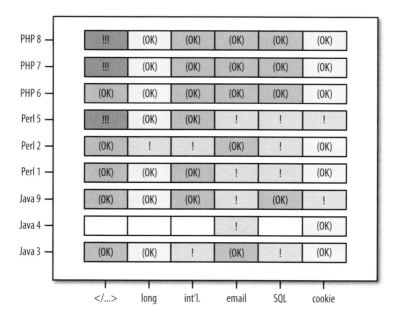

FIGURE 14-9. *Results of black-box robustness and security testing. We evaluated the handling of six scenarios of potentially difficult dialog inputs. We report vulnerable-looking behavior only; we have not attempted to actually break in. The Java 4 solution lacks some functionality required for the tests.*

Hey, What About <Insert-Your-Favorite-Topic>?

We attempted to evaluate a number of other aspects in our Plat_Forms study, but some turned out to be too difficult to investigate and others returned no interesting differences between the platforms.

For instance, we had expected that teams on different platforms would exhibit different development styles in their processes. We attempted to capture these differences using a simple classification of who-is-doing-what in 15-minute intervals based on human observation (a single person going around to all nine teams). We also analyzed the time/person/file patterns of check-in activity in each team's version repository. But neither data source indicated identifiable platform differences.

Of course, we also intended to investigate performance and scalability. Unfortunately, the intersection of the functionalities implemented in the nine solutions was too small for a meaningful comparison.

Again, many relevant details have been glossed over in this chapter. The original, very detailed source for this study is [Prechelt 2007]. A shorter but still fairly precise article is [Prechelt 2010].

So What?

Hmm, so what is the overall take-home message from these two quite different studies? The amount of evidence available is far too small to draw strong, generalizable conclusions, but one can combine the results with one's personal understanding of the world of software development and come out with at least better-founded prejudices than one had before. When I do this, the result reads somewhat like this:

- With respect to programming languages, at least for small programs that perform some kind of text handling (or some such general activity), it appears safe to say that scripting languages are more productive than conventional, statically typed languages.

- With respect to the efficiency of such programs, it is usually much more important to avoid the wrong programmer than to avoid the wrong language. There are many ways (and languages to use) to get it right.

- If very high performance or very low memory usage are needed, C and C++ are still superior if (but perhaps only if) the programmers are sufficiently capable.

- There appear to be language-specific cultures that can sometimes lead programmers using different languages to take different approaches to design.

- Regarding web development platforms in particular, for straightforward web-based systems in the hands of capable teams, it appears that the language is the particular framework used and the level of mastery the team has with that framework are much more important than the language.

- In particular, when capable professionals are using it, PHP is a lot better than its reputation.

- There appear to be cultures particular to web platforms that can sometimes lead teams working on different platforms in different directions.

Your own view may vary, and your mileage will vary as well. A lot more studies like these are needed before we really understand where the individual strengths of individual languages and platforms lie or what typical characteristics emerge from their use. Furthermore, both of these questions are moving targets.

References

[Boehm 1981] Boehm, B.W. 1981. *Software Engineering Economics*. Englewood Cliffs, NJ: Prentice Hall.

[Fenton and Pfleeger 2000] Fenton, N.E., and S.L. Pfleeger. 2000. *Software Metrics: A Rigorous and Practical Approach*. Boston: Thomson.

[Hearty et al. 2008] Hearty, P., N. Fenton, D. Marquez, and M. Neil. 2008. Predicting project velocity in XP using a learning dynamic Bayesian network model. *IEEE Transactions on Software Engineering* 35: 124–137. *http://doi.ieeecomputersociety.org/10.1109/TSE.2008.76*.

[Hudak and Jones 1994] Hudak, P., and M.P. Jones. 1994. Haskell vs. Ada vs. C++ vs. awk vs....: An experiment in software prototyping productivity. Yale University, Dept. of CS, New Haven, CT. *http://www.haskell.org/papers/NSWC/jfp.ps*.

[Humphrey 1995] Humphrey, W.S. 1995. A Discipline for Software Engineering. Reading, MA: Addison-Wesley.

[Prechelt 2000a] Prechelt, L. 2000. An empirical comparison of C, C++, Java, Perl, Python, Rexx, and Tcl for a search/string-processing program. Fakultät für Informatik, Universität Karlsruhe, Germany. *http://page.inf.fu-berlin.de/prechelt/Biblio/jccpprtTR.pdf*.

[Prechelt 2000b] Prechelt, L. 2000. An empirical comparison of seven programming languages. *IEEE Computer* 33(10): 23–29.

[Prechelt 2007] Prechelt, L. 2007. Plat_Forms 2007: The web development platform comparison—Evaluation and results. Freie Universität Berlin, Institut für Informatik, Germany. *http://www.plat-forms.org/sites/default/files/platformsTR.pdf*.

[Prechelt 2010] Prechelt, L. 2010. Plat_forms: A web development platform comparison by an exploratory experiment searching for emergent platform properties. Preprint. Forthcoming in *IEEE Transactions on Software Engineering*. *http://doi.ieeecomputersociety.org/10.1109/TSE.2010 .22*.

[Prechelt and Unger 2001] Prechelt, L., and B. Unger 2001. An experiment measuring the effects of Personal Software Process (PSP) training. *IEEE Transactions on Software Engineering* 27(5): 465–472.

## CHAPTER FIFTEEN

Quality Wars: Open Source Versus Proprietary Software

Diomidis Spinellis

Talk is cheap. Show me the code.

—Linus Torvalds

When developers compare open source with proprietary software, what should be a civilized debate often degenerates into a flame war. This need not be so, because there is plenty of room for a cool-headed, objective comparison.

Researchers examine the efficacy of open source development processes through various complementary approaches:

- One method involves looking at the quality of the code, its *internal quality attributes*, such as the density of comments or the use of global variables [Stamelos et al. 2002].

- Another approach involves examining the software's *external quality attributes*, which reflect how the software appears to its end users [Kuan 2003].

- Then, instead of the product, one can look at the *process* and examine measures related to the code's construction and maintenance, such as the how much code is being added each week or how swiftly bugs are closed [Paulson et al. 2004].

- Another approach involves discussing specific scenarios. For instance, Hoepman and Jacobs [Hoepman and Jacobs 2007] examine the security of open source software by looking at how leaked source code from Windows NT and Diebold voting machines led to attacks and how open source practices lead to cleaner code and allow the use of security-verification tools.

- Finally, a number of arguments are based on plain hand waving. More than a decade ago, Bob Glass [Glass 1999] identified this trend in the hype associated with the emergence of Linux in the IT industry.

Although many researchers over the years have examined open source artifacts and processes [Fitzgerald and Feller 2002], [Spinellis and Szyperski 2004], [Feller 2005], [Feller et al. 2005], [von Krogh and von Hippel 2006], [Capiluppi and Robles 2007], [Sowe et al. 2007], [Stol et al. 2009], the direct comparison of open source systems with corresponding proprietary products has remained an elusive goal. The reason for this is that it used to be difficult to find a proprietary product comparable to an open source equivalent, and then convince the proprietary product's owner to provide its source code for an objective comparison. However, the open-sourcing of Sun's Solaris kernel (now part of Oracle's portfolio) and the distribution of large parts of the Windows kernel source code to research institutions provided me with a window of opportunity to perform a comparative evaluation between the open source code and the code of systems developed as proprietary software.

Here I report on code quality metrics (measures) I collected from four large industrial-scale operating systems: FreeBSD, Linux, OpenSolaris, and the Windows Research Kernel (WRK). This chapter is not a crime mystery, so I'm revealing my main finding right up front: there are no significant across-the-board code quality differences between these four systems. Now that you know the ending, let me suggest that you keep on reading, because in the following sections you'll find not only how I arrived at this finding, but also numerous code quality metrics for objectively evaluating software written in C, which you can also apply to your code. Although some of these metrics have not been empirically validated, they are based on generally accepted coding guidelines, and therefore represent the rough consensus of developers concerning desirable code attributes. I first reported these findings at the 2008 International Conference of Software Engineering [Spinellis 2008]; this chapter contains many additional details.

Past Skirmishes

> The very ink with which all history is written is merely
> fluid prejudice.
>
> —Mark Twain

Researchers have been studying the quality attributes of operating system code for more than two decades [Henry and Kafura 1981], [Yu et al. 2004]. Particularly close to the work you're reading here are comparative studies of open source operating systems [Yu et al. 2006], [Izurieta and Bieman 2006], and studies comparing open and closed source systems [Stamelos et al. 2002], [Paulson et al. 2004], [Samoladas et al. 2004].

A comparison of maintainability attributes between the Linux and various Berkeley Software Distribution (BSD) operating systems found that Linux contained more instances of module communication through global variables (known as *common coupling*) than the BSD variants. The results I report here corroborate this finding for file-scoped identifiers, but not for global identifiers (see Figure 15-11). Furthermore, an evaluation of growth dynamics of the FreeBSD and Linux operating systems found that both grow at a linear rate, and that claims of open source systems growing at a faster rate than commercial systems are unfounded [Izurieta and Bieman 2006].

A study by Paulson and his colleagues [Paulson et al. 2004] compares evolutionary patterns between three open source projects (Linux, GCC, and Apache) and three non-disclosed commercial ones. They found a faster rate of bug fixing and feature addition in the open source projects, which is something we would expect for very popular projects like those they examine. In another study focusing on the quality of the code (its internal quality attributes) [Stamelos et al. 2002] the authors used a commercial tool to evaluate 100 open source applications using metrics similar to those reported here, but measured on a scale ranging from *accept* to *rewrite*. They then compared the results against benchmarks supplied by the tool's vendor for commercial projects. The authors found that only half of the modules they examined would be considered acceptable by software organizations applying programming standards based on software metrics. A related study by the same group [Samoladas et al. 2004] examined the evolution of a measure called *maintainability index* [Coleman et al. 1994] between an open source application and its (semi)proprietary forks. They concluded that all projects suffered from a similar deterioration of the maintainability index over time.

The Battlefield

> You cannot choose your battlefield, God does that for you; but
> you can plant a standard where a standard never flew.
>
> —*Nathalia Crane*

Figure 15-1 shows the history and genealogy of the systems I examine.[*] All four systems started their independent life in 1991–1993. At that time affordable microprocessor-based computers that supported a 32-bit address space and memory management led to the Cambrian explosion for modern operating systems. Two of the systems, FreeBSD and OpenSolaris, share common ancestry that goes back to the 1978 1BSD version of Unix. FreeBSD is based on BSD/Net2, a

---

[*] If you think that the arrows point the wrong way round, you're in good company. Nevertheless, take some time to look them up in your favorite UML reference.

distribution of the Berkeley Unix source code that was purged from proprietary AT&T code. Consequently, whereas both FreeBSD and OpenSolaris contain code written at Berkeley, only OpenSolaris contains AT&T code. Specifically, the code behind OpenSolaris traces its origins back to the 1973 version of Unix, which was the first written in C [Salus 1994] (page 54 in the reference). In 2005, Sun released most of the Solaris source code under an open source license.

Linux was developed from scratch in an effort to build a more feature-rich version of Tanenbaum's teaching-oriented, POSIX-compatible Minix operating system [Tanenbaum 1987]. Thus, though Linux borrowed ideas from both Minix and Unix, it did not derive from their code [Torvalds and Diamond 2001].

The intellectual roots of Windows NT go back to DEC's VMS through the common involvement of the lead engineer David Cutler in both projects. Windows NT was developed as Microsoft's answer to Unix, initially as an alternative of IBM's OS/2 and later as a replacement of the 16-bit Windows code base. The Windows Research Kernel (WRK) whose code I examine in this chapter includes major portions of the 64-bit Windows kernel, which Microsoft distributes for research use [Polze and Probert 2006]. The kernel is written in C with some small extensions. Excluded from the kernel code are the device drivers, and the plug-and-play, power management, and virtual DOS subsystems. The missing parts explain the large size difference between the WRK and the other three kernels.

Although all four systems I examine are available in source code form, their development methodologies are markedly different. Microsoft and Sun engineers built Windows NT and Solaris within their companies as proprietary systems with minimal, if any, involvement of outsiders in the development process. (OpenSolaris had a very short life as an open source project, and therefore only minimal code could have been contributed by developers outside Sun in the snapshot I examined.) Furthermore, Solaris has been developed with emphasis on a formal process [Dickinson 1996], whereas the development of Windows NT employed more lightweight methods [Cusumano and Selby 1995] (pages 223, 263, and 273-74 in reference). FreeBSD and Linux are both developed using open source development methods [Feller and Fitzgerald 2001], but their development processes are also dissimilar. FreeBSD is mainly developed by a non-hierarchical group of about 220 committers who have access to a shared software repository that was initially based on CVS and currently on Subversion [Jørgensen 2001]. In contrast, Linux's developers are organized in a four-tier pyramid. At the bottom two levels, thousands of developers contribute patches to about 560 subsystem maintainers. At the top of the pyramid, Linus Torvalds, assisted by a group of trusted lieutenants, is the sole person responsible for adding the patches to the Linux tree [Rigby and German 2006]. Nowadays, Linux developers coordinate their code changes through git, a purpose-built distributed version control system.

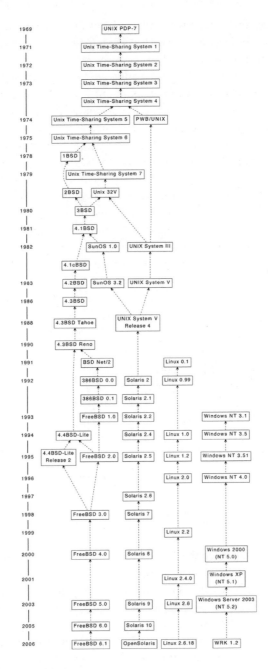

FIGURE 15-1. History and genealogy of the four systems

I calculated most of the metrics reported here by issuing SQL queries on a relational database containing the code elements comprising each system: modules, identifiers, tokens, functions, files, comments, and their relationships. The database's schema appears in Figure 15-2.[†] I constructed the database for each system by running the CScout refactoring browser for C code ([Spinellis 2003], [Spinellis 2010]) on a number of processor-specific configurations of each operating system. (A processor-specific configuration comprises some unique macro definitions and files, and will therefore process code in a different way.) To process the source code of a complete system, CScout must be given a configuration file that will specify the precise environment used for processing each compilation unit (C file). For the FreeBSD and the Linux kernels, I constructed this configuration file by instrumenting proxies for the GNU C compiler, the linker, and some shell commands. These recorded their arguments (mainly the include file path and macro definitions) in a format that could then be used to construct a CScout configuration file. For OpenSolaris and the WRK, I simply performed a full build for the configurations I investigated, recorded the commands that were executed in a log file, and then processed the compilation and linking commands appearing in the build's log.

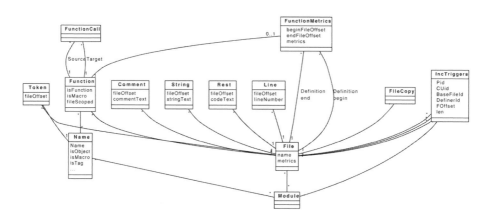

FIGURE 15-2. Schema of the database containing the code's analysis

In order to limit bias introduced in the selection of metrics, I chose and defined the metrics I would collect before setting up the mechanisms to measure them. This helped me avoid the biased selection of metrics based on results I obtained along the way. However, this *ex ante* selection also resulted in many metrics—such as the number of characters per line—that did not supply any interesting information, failing to provide a clear winner or loser. On the other hand, my selection of metrics was not completely blind, because at the time I designed the experiment I was already familiar with the source code of the FreeBSD kernel and had seen source code from Linux, the 9th Research Edition Unix, and some Windows device drivers.

† The databases (141 million records) and all the corresponding queries are available online at *http://www .spinellis.gr/sw/4kernel/*.

Other methodological limitations of this study are the small number of (admittedly large and important) systems studied, the language specificity of the employed metrics, and the coverage of only maintainability and portability from the space of all software quality attributes. This last limitation means that the study fails to take into account the large and important set of quality attributes that are typically determined at runtime: functionality, reliability, usability, and efficiency. However, these missing attributes often depend on factors that are beyond the control of the system's developers: configuration, tuning, and workload selection. Studying them would introduce additional subjective biases, such as configurations that were unsuitable for some workloads or operating environments. The controversy surrounding studies comparing competing operating systems in areas such as security or performance demonstrates the difficulty of such approaches.

The large size difference between the WRK source code and the other systems is not as problematic as it may initially appear. An earlier study on the distribution of the maintainability index [Coleman et al. 1994] across various FreeBSD modules showed that their maintainability was evenly distributed, with few outliers at each end [Spinellis 2006](in Figure 7-3). This means that we can form an opinion about a large software system by looking at a small sample of it. Therefore, the WRK code I examine can be treated as a representative subset of the complete Windows operating system kernel.

Into the Battle

No battle plan survives contact with the enemy.

—Helmuth von Moltke the Elder

The key properties of the systems I examine appear in Table 15-1. The quality metrics I collected can be roughly categorized into the areas of file organization, code structure, code style, preprocessing, and data organization. When it is easy to represent a metric with a single number, I list its values for each of the four systems in a table, and on the left I indicate whether ideally that number should be high ($\uparrow$), low ($\downarrow$), or near a particular value (e.g., $\cong 1$). In other cases we must look at the distribution of the various values, and for this I use so-called candlestick figures, as in Figure 15-3. Each element in such a figure depicts five values:

- The minimum, at the bottom of the line
- The lower (25%) quartile, at the bottom of the box
- The median (the numeric value separating the higher half of the values from the lower half), as a horizontal line within the box
- The upper (75%) quartile, at the top of the box
- The maximum value, at the top of the line
- The arithmetic mean, as a diamond

Minima and maxima lying outside the graph's range are indicated with a dashed line, along with a figure of their actual value.

TABLE 15-1. Key metrics of the four systems

Metric	FreeBSD	Linux	Solaris	WRK
Version	HEAD 2006-09-18	2.6.18.8-0.5	2007-08-28	1.2
Configuration	i386 AMD64 SPARC64	AMD64	Sun4v Sun4u SPARC	i386 AMD64
Lines (thousands)	2,599	4,150	3,000	829
Comments (thousands)	232	377	299	190
Statements (thousands)	948	1,772	1,042	192
Source files	4,479	8,372	3,851	653
Linked modules	1,224	1,563	561	3
C functions	38,371	86,245	39,966	4,820
Macro definitions	727,410	703,940	136,953	31,908

File Organization

In the C programming language, source code files play a significant role in structuring a system. A file forms a scope boundary, while the directory in which it is located may determine the search path for included header files [Harbison and Steele Jr. 1991]. Thus, the appropriate organization of definitions and declarations into files and files into directories is a measure of the system's modularity [Parnas 1972].

Figure 15-3 shows the length of C and header files. Most files are less than 2,000 lines long. Overly long files (such as the C files in OpenSolaris and the WRK) are often problematic because they can be difficult to manage, they may create many dependencies, and they may violate modularity. Indeed the longest header file (WRK's *winerror.h*) at 27,000 lines lumps together error messages from 30 different areas, most of which are not related to the Windows kernel.

A related measure examines the contents of files not in terms of lines, but in terms of defined entities. In C source files, I count global functions. In header files an important entity is a structure, the closest abstraction to a class that is available in C. Figure 15-4 shows the number of global functions that are declared in each C file and the number of aggregates (structures or unions) that are defined in each header file. Ideally, both numbers should be small, indicating an appropriate separation of concerns. The C files of OpenSolaris and WRK come out worse than the other systems, while a significant number of WRK's header files look bad, because they define more than 10 structures each.

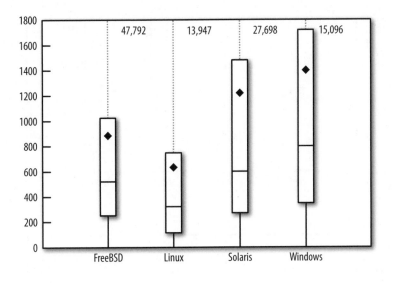

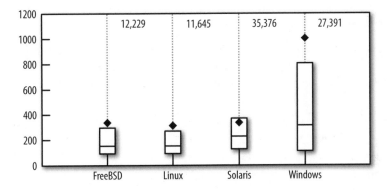

FIGURE 15-3. File length in lines of C files (top) and headers (bottom)

The four systems I've examined have interesting directory structures. As you can see in Figures 15-5 through 15-8, three of the four systems have similarly wide structures. The small size and complexity of the WRK reflects the fact that Microsoft has excluded from it many large parts of the Windows kernel. We see that the directories in Linux are relatively evenly distributed across the whole source code tree, whereas in FreeBSD and OpenSolaris, some directories lump together in clusters. This can be the result of organic growth over a longer period of time, because both systems have 20 more years of history on their backs (Figure 15-1). The more even distribution of Linux's directories may also reflect the decentralized nature of its development.

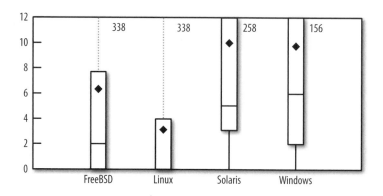

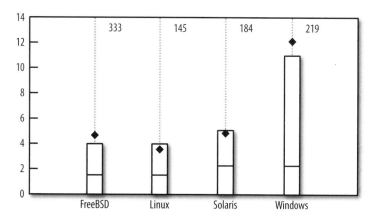

FIGURE 15-4. Defined global functions (top) and structures (bottom)

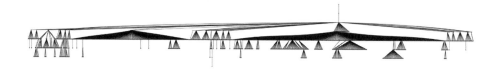

FIGURE 15-5. The directory structure of FreeBSD

FIGURE 15-6. The directory structure of Linux

FIGURE 15-7. The directory structure of OpenSolaris

FIGURE 15-8. The directory structure of the Windows Research Kernel

At a higher level of granularity, I examine the number of files located in a single directory. Again, putting many files in a directory is like having many elements in a module. A large number of files can confuse developers, who often search through these files as a group with tools such as *grep*, and lead to accidental identifier collisions through shared header files. The numbers I found in the examined systems can be seen in Table 15-2, and show Linux lagging the other systems.

TABLE 15-2. File organization metrics

Metric	Ideal	FreeBSD	Linux	Solaris	WRK
Files per directory	↓	6.8	20.4	8.9	15.9
Header files per C source file	≅ 1	1.05	1.96	1.09	1.92
Average structure complexity in files	↓	2.2×10^{14}	1.3×10^{13}	5.4×10^{12}	2.6×10^{13}

The next line in the table describes the ratio between header files and C files. I used the following SQL query to calculate these numbers:

```
select (select count(*) from FILES where name like '%.c') /
  (select count(*) from FILES where name like '%.h')
```

A common style guideline for C code involves putting each module's interface in a separate header file and its implementation in a corresponding C file. Thus a ratio of header to C files around 1 is the optimum; numbers significantly diverging from 1 may indicate an unclear distinction between interface and implementation. This can be acceptable for a small system (the ratio in the implementation of the *awk* programming language is 3/11), but will be a problem in a system consisting of thousands of files. All the systems score acceptably in this metric.

Finally, the last line in Table 15-2 provides a metric related to the complexity of file relationships. I study this by looking at files as nodes in a directed graph. I define a file's *fan-out* as the number of efferent (outgoing) references it makes to elements declared or defined in other files. For instance, a C file that uses the symbols FILE, putc, and malloc (defined outside the C file in the *stdio.h* and *stdlib.h* header files) has a fan-out of 3. Correspondingly, I define a file's *fan-in* as the number of afferent (incoming) references made by other files. Thus, in the previous example, the fan-in of *stdio.h* would be 2. I used Henry and Kafura's information flow metric [Henry and Kafura 1981] to look at the corresponding relationships between files.

The value I report is:

$$(fanIn \times fanOut)^2$$

I calculated the value based on the contents of the CScout database table INCTRIGGERS, which stores data about symbols in each file that are linked with other files.

```
select avg(pow(fanout.c * fanin.c, 2)) from
  (select basefileid fid, count(definerid) c from
    (select distinct BASEFILEID, DEFINERID, FOFFSET from INCTRIGGERS) i2
    group by basefileid) fanout
  inner join
  (select definerid fid, count(basefileid) c from
    (select distinct BASEFILEID, DEFINERID, FOFFSET from INCTRIGGERS) i2
    group by definerid) fanin
  on fanout.fid = fanin.fid
```

The calculation works as follows. The innermost select statements derive, for all the external definitions or references associated with each file, a set of unique identifiers, and the files where these are defined or referenced. Then, the middle select statements count the number of identifiers per file, and the outermost select statement joins each file's definitions with its references and calculates the corresponding information flow metric. A large value for this metric has been associated with a high occurrence of changes and structural flaws.

Code Structure

The code structure of the four systems illustrates how similar problems can be tackled through diverse control structures and separation of concerns. It also allows us to peer into the design of each system.

Figure 15-9 shows the distribution across functions of the extended cyclomatic complexity metric [McCabe 1976]. This is a measure of the number of independent paths contained in each function. The number shown takes into account Boolean and conditional evaluation operators (because these introduce additional paths), but not multi-way switch statements, because these would disproportionally affect the result for code that is typically cookie-cutter similar. The metric was designed to measure a program's testability, understandability, and maintainability [Gill and Kemerer 1991]. In this regard Linux scores better than the other systems and the WRK worse. The same figure also shows the number of C statements per function. Ideally, this should be a small number (e.g., around 20), allowing the function's complete code to fit on the developer's screen. Linux again scores better than the other systems.

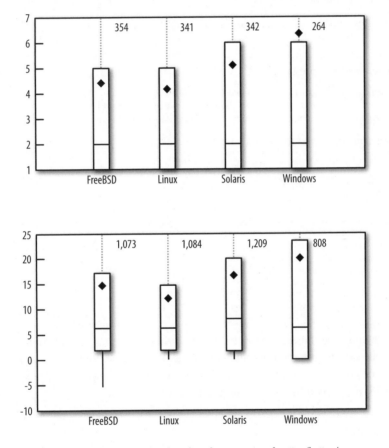

FIGURE 15-9. Extended cyclomatic complexity (top) and number of statements per function (bottom)

In Figure 15-10 we can see the distribution of the Halstead volume complexity [Halstead 1977]. For a given piece of code this is based on four numbers:

n1

Number of distinct operators

n2

Number of distinct operands

N1

Total number of operators

N2

Total number of operands

Given these four numbers, we calculate the program's so-called volume as:

$$(N1 + N2) \times \log_2(n1 + n2)$$

For instance, for the expression:

```
op = &(!x ? (!y ? upleft : (y == bottom ? lowleft : left)) :
(x == last ? (!y ? upright : (y == bottom ? lowright : right)) :
(!y ? upper : (y == bottom ? lower : normal))))[w->orientation];
```

the four variables have the following values:

n1

= & () ! ?: == [] -> (8)

n2

bottom last left lower lowleft lowright normal op orientation right upleft upper upright w x y (16)

N1

27

N2

24

The theory behind the Halstead volume complexity number states that it should be low, reflecting code that doesn't require a lot of mental effort to comprehend. This metric, however, has often been criticized. As was the case with the cyclomatic complexity, Linux scores better and the WRK worse than the other systems.

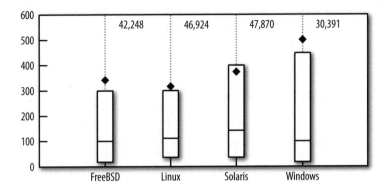

FreeBSD 42,248   Linux 46,924   Solaris 47,870   Windows 30,391

FIGURE 15-10. Halstead complexity per function

Taking a step back to look at interactions between functions, Figure 15-11 depicts common coupling in functions by showing the percentage of the unique identifiers appearing in a function's body that come either from the scope of the compilation unit (file-scoped identifiers declared as static) or from the project scope (global objects). Both forms of coupling are undesirable, with the global identifiers considered worse than the file-scoped ones. Linux scores better than the other systems in the case of common coupling at the global scope, but (probably because of this) scores worse than the other systems when looking at the file scope. All other systems are more evenly balanced.

Other metrics associated with code structure appear in Table 15-3. The percentage of global functions indicates the functions visible throughout the system. The number of such functions in the WRK (nearly 100%, also verified by hand) is shockingly high. It may however reflect Microsoft's use of different techniques—such as linking into shared libraries (DLLs) with explicitly exported symbols—for avoiding identifier clashes.

TABLE 15-3. Code structure metrics

Metric	Ideal	FreeBSD	Linux	Solaris	WRK
% global functions	↓	36.7	21.2	45.9	99.8
% strictly structured functions	↑	27.1	68.4	65.8	72.1
% labeled statements	↓	0.64	0.93	0.44	0.28
Average number of parameters to functions	↓	2.08	1.97	2.20	2.13
Average depth of maximum nesting	↓	0.86	0.88	1.06	1.16
Tokens per statement	↓	9.14	9.07	9.19	8.44
% of tokens in replicated code	↓	4.68	4.60	3.00	3.81
Average structure complexity in functions	↓	7.1×10^4	1.3×10^8	3.0×10^6	6.6×10^5

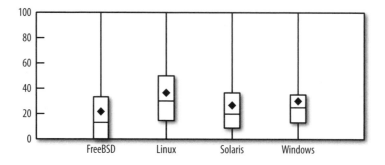

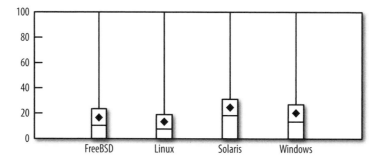

FIGURE 15-11. Common coupling at file (top) and global (bottom) scope

Strictly structured functions are those following the rules of structured programming: a single point of exit and no goto statements. The simplicity of such functions makes it easier to reason about them. Their percentage is calculated by looking at the number of keywords within each function through the following SQL query.

```
select 100 -
(select count(*) from FUNCTIONMETRICS where nreturn > 1 or ngoto > 0) /
(select count(*) from FUNCTIONMETRICS) * 100
```

Along the same lines, the percentage of labeled statements indicates goto targets: a severe violation of structured programming principles. I measured labeled statements rather than goto statements, because many branch targets are a lot more confusing than many branch sources. Often multiple goto statements to a single label are used to exit from a function while performing some cleanup—the equivalent of an exception's `finally` clause.

The number of arguments to a function is an indicator of the interface's quality; when many arguments must be passed, packaging them into a single structure reduces clutter and opens up opportunities for optimization in style and performance.

Two metrics tracking the code's understandability are the average depth of maximum nesting and the number of tokens per statement. These metrics are based on the theories that both deeply nested structures and long statements are difficult to comprehend [Cant et al. 1995].

Replicated code has been associated with bugs [Li et al. 2006] and maintainability problems [Spinellis 2006](pages 413–416 in the reference). The corresponding metric (% of tokens in replicated code) shows the percentage of the code's tokens that participate in at least one clone set. To obtain this metric, I used the *CCFinderX*‡ tool to locate the duplicated code lines and a Perl script (Example 15-1) to measure the ratio of such lines.

EXAMPLE 15-1. Determining the percentage of code duplication from the CCFinderX report

```
# Process CCFinderX results
open(IN, "ccfx.exe P $ARGV[0].ccfxd|") || die;
while (<IN>) {
    chop;
    if (/^source_files/ .. /^\}/) {
        # Process file definition lines like the following:
        # 611     /src/sys/amd64/pci/pci_bus.c         1041
        ($id, $name, $tok) = split;
        $file[$id][$tok - 1] = 0 if ($tok > 0);
        $nfile++;
    } elseif (/^clone_pairs/ .. /^\}/) {
        # Process pair identification lines like the following for files 14 and 363:
        # 1908    14.1753-1832    363.1909-1988
        ($id, $c1, $c2) = split;
        mapfile($c1);
        mapfile($c2);
    }
}

# Add up and report tokens and cloned tokens
for ($fid = 0; $fid <= $#file; $fid++) {
    for ($tokid = 0; $tokid <= $#{$file[$fid]}; $tokid++) {
        $ntok++;
        $nclone += $file[$fid][$tokid];
    }
}
print "$ARGV[0] nfiles=$nfile ntok=$ntok nclone=$nclone ", $nclone / $ntok * 100, "\n";

# Set the file's cloned lines to 1
sub mapfile
{
    my($clone) = @_;
    my ($fid, $start, $end) = ($clone =~ m/^(\d+)\.(\d+)\-(\d+)$/);
    for ($i = $start; $i <= $end; $i++) {
        $file[$id][$i] = 1;
    }
}
```

‡ *http://www.ccfinder.net/*

Finally, the average structure complexity in functions again uses Henry and Kafura's information flow metric [Henry and Kafura 1981] to look at the relationships between functions. Ideally we would want this number to be low, indicating an appropriate separation between suppliers and consumers of functionality.

Code Style

Various choices of indentation, spacing, identifier names, representations for constants, and naming conventions can affect the presentation of code without altering its functionality. [Kernighan and Plauger 1978], [The FreeBSD Project 1995], [Cannon et al.], [Stallman et al. 2005]. In most sane cases, consistency is more important than the specific code style convention that was chosen.

For this study, I measured each system's consistency of style by applying the formatting program indent§ on the complete source code of each system and counting the lines that indent modified. The result appears on the first line of Table 15-4. The behavior of indent can be modified using various options in order to match a formatting style's guidelines. For instance, one can specify the amount of indentation and the placement of braces. In order to determine each system's formatting style and use the appropriate formatting options, I first run indent on each system with various values of the 15 numerical flags, and turned on or off each one of the 55 Boolean flags (see the shell script in Examples 15-2 and 15-3). I then chose the set of flags that produced the largest number of conforming lines. For example, on the OpenSolaris source code, indent with its default flags would reformat 74% of the lines. This number shrank to 16% once the appropriate flags were determined (-i8 -bli0 -cbi0 -ci4 -ip0 -bad -bbb -br -brs -ce -nbbo -ncs -nlp -npcs).

TABLE 15-4. Code style metrics

Metric	Ideal	FreeBSD	Linux	Solaris	WRK
% style conforming lines	↑	77.27	77.96	84.32	33.30
% style conforming typedef identifiers	↑	57.1	59.2	86.9	100.0
% style conforming aggregate tags	↑	0.0	0.0	20.7	98.2
Characters per line	↓	30.8	29.4	27.2	28.6
% of numeric constants in operands	↓	10.6	13.3	7.7	7.7
% unsafe function-like macros	↓	3.99	4.44	9.79	4.04
% misspelled comment words	↓	33.0	31.5	46.4	10.1
% unique misspelled comment words	↓	6.33	6.16	5.76	3.23

§ *http://www.gnu.org/software/indent/*

EXAMPLE 15-2. Determining a system's indent formatting options

```
DIR=$1
NFILES=0
RNFILES=0

# Determine the files that are OK for indent
for f in `find $DIR -name '*.c'`
do
    # The error code is not always correct, so we have to grep for errors
    if indent -st $f 2>&1 >/dev/null | grep -q Error:
    then
        REJECTED="$REJECTED $f"
        RNFILES=`expr $RNFILES + 1`
        echo -n "Rejecting $f - number of lines: "
        wc -l <$f
    else
        FILES="$FILES $f"
        NFILES=`expr $NFILES + 1`
    fi
done

LINES=`echo $FILES | xargs cat | wc -l`
RLINES=`echo $REJECTED | xargs cat | wc -l`

# Format the files with the specified options
# Return the number of mismatched lines
try()
{
    for f in $FILES
    do
        indent -st $IOPT $1 $f |
        diff $f -
    done |
    grep '^<' |
    wc -l
}

# Report the results in a format suitable for further processing
status()
{
    echo "$IOPT: $VIOLATIONS violations in $LINES lines of $NFILES files \
($RLINES of $RNFILES files not processed)"
}

# Determine base case
VIOLATIONS=`try`
status
```

```
# Try various numerical options with values 0-8
for try_opt in i ts bli c cbi cd ci cli cp d di ip l lc pi
do
    BEST=$VIOLATIONS
    for n in 0 1 2 3 4 5 6 7 8
    do
        NEW=`try -$try_opt$n`
        if [ $NEW -lt $BEST ]
        then
            BNUM=$n
            BEST=$NEW
        fi
    done
    if [ $BEST -lt $VIOLATIONS ]
    then
        IOPT="$IOPT -$try_opt$BNUM"
        VIOLATIONS=$BEST
        status
    fi
done

# Try the various Boolean options
for try_opt in bad bap bbb bbo bc bl bls br brs bs cdb cdw ce cs bfda \
    bfde fc1 fca hnl lp lps nbad nbap nbbo nbc nbfda ncdb ncdw nce \
    ncs nfc1 nfca nhnl nip nlp npcs nprs npsl nsaf nsai nsaw nsc nsob \
    nss nut pcs prs psl saf sai saw sc sob ss ut
do
    NEW=`try -$try_opt`
    if [ $NEW -lt $VIOLATIONS ]
    then
        IOPT="$IOPT -$try_opt"
        VIOLATIONS=$NEW
    fi
    status
done
```

Figure 15-12 depicts the length distribution of two important classes of C identifiers: those of globally visible objects (variables and functions) and the tags used for identifying aggregates (structures and unions). Because each class typically uses a single name space, it is important to choose distinct and recognizable names (see Chapter 31 in [McConnell 2004]). For these classes of identifiers, longer names are preferable, and the WRK excels in both cases, as anyone who has programmed using the Windows API could easily guess.

Some other metrics related to code style appear in Table 15-4. To measure consistency, I also determined through code inspection the convention used for naming typedefs and aggregate tags, and then counted the identifiers of those classes that did not match the convention. Here are the two SQL queries I ran, one on the Unix-like systems and the other on the WRK:

```
select 100 * (select count(*) from IDS where typedef and name like '%_t') /
  (select count(*) from IDS where typedef)

select 100 * (select count(*) from IDS where typedef and name regexp '^[A-Z0-9_]*$') /
  (select count(*) from IDS where typedef)
```

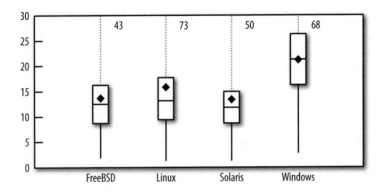

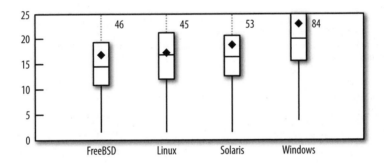

FIGURE 15-12. Length of global (top) and aggregate (bottom) identifiers

The following are three other metrics aimed at identifying programming practices that style guidelines typically discourage:

- Overly long lines of code (characters per line metric)
- The direct use of "magic" numbers in the code (% of numeric constants in operands),
- The definition of function-like macros that can misbehave when placed after an if statement (% unsafe function-like macros)[||]

The following SQL query roughly calculates the percentage of unsafe function-like macros by looking for bodies of such macros that contain more than one statement but no do keywords.

[||] Function-like macros containing more than one statement should have their body enclosed in a dummy do ... while(0) block in order to make them behave like a call to a real function.

The result represents a lower bound because the query can miss other unsafe macros, such as those consisting of an if statement.

```
select 100.0 * (select count(*) from FUNCTIONMETRICS left join
    FUNCTIONS on functionid = id where defined and ismacro and ndo = 0 and nstmt > 1) /
(select count(*) from FUNCTIONS where defined and ismacro)
```

Another important element of style involves commenting. It is difficult to objectively judge the quality of code comments. Comments can be superfluous or even wrong. We can't programmatically judge quality on that level, but we can easily measure the comment density. So Figure 15-13 shows the the comment density in C files as the ratio of comment characters to statements. In header files, I measured it as the ratio of defined elements that typically require an explanatory comment (enumerations, aggregates and their members, variable declarations, and function-like macros) to the number of comments. In both cases I excluded files with trivially little content. With remarkable consistency, the WRK scores better than the other systems in this regard and Linux worse. Interestingly, the mean value of comment density is a lot higher than the median, indicating that some files require substantially more commenting than others.

```
select nccomment / nstatement from FILES where name like '%.c' and nstatement > 0

select (nlcomment + nbcomment) / (naggregate + namember + nppfmacro + nppomacro +
    nenum + npfunction + nffunction + npvar + nfvar) from FILES
    where name like '%.h' and naggregate + namember + nppfmacro + nppomacro > 0
        and nuline / nline < .2
```

I also measured the number of spelling errors in the comments as a proxy for their quality. For this I ran the text of the comments through the *aspell* spell checker with a custom dictionary consisting of all the system's identifiers and file names (see the shell script in Example 15-4). The low number of errors in the WRK reflects the explicit spellchecking that, according to accompanying documentation, was performed before the code was released.

EXAMPLE 15-4. Counting comment words and misspellings in a CScout database

```
# Create personal dictionary of correct words
# from identifier names appearing in the code
PERS=$1.en.pws
(
echo personal_ws-1.1 en 0
    (
    mysql -e 'select name from IDS union select name from FUNCTIONS union
        select name from FILES' $1 |
    tr /._ \\n |
    sed 's/\([a-z]\)\([A-Z]\)/\1\
\2/g'
    mysql -e 'select name from IDS union select name from FUNCTIONS union
        select name from FILES' $1 |
    tr /. \\n
    ) |
sort -u
) >$PERS
```

```
# Get comments from source code files and spell check them
mysql -e 'select comment from COMMENTS left join FILES
    on COMMENTS.FID = FILES.FID where not name like "%.cs"' $1 |
sed 's/\\[ntrb]//g' |
tee $1.comments |
aspell --lang=en --personal=$PERS -C --ignore=3 --ignore-case=true  \
    --run-together-limit=10 list >$1.err
wc -w $1.comments    # Number of words
wc -l $1.err         # Number of errors
```

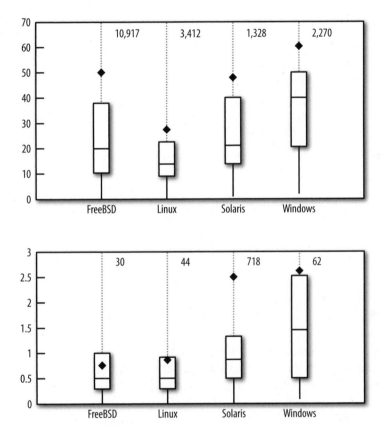

FIGURE 15-13. Comment density in C (top) and header (bottom) files

Although I did not measure portability objectively, the work involved in processing the source code with CScout allowed me to get a feeling of the portability of each system's source code between different compilers. The code of Linux and WRK appears to be the one most tightly bound to a specific compiler. Linux uses numerous language extensions provided by the GNU C compiler, sometimes including assembly code thinly disguised in what passes as C syntax in *gcc* (see Example 15-5). The WRK uses considerably fewer language extensions, but relies significantly on the try catch extension to C that the Microsoft compiler supports. The FreeBSD kernel uses only a few *gcc* extensions, and these are often isolated inside wrapping macros. The OpenSolaris kernel was a welcome surprise: it was the only body of source code that did not require any extensions to CScout in order to compile.

EXAMPLE 15-5. The definition of memmove in the Linux kernel

```
void *memmove(void *dest, const void *src, size_t n)
{
        int d0, d1, d2;

        if (dest < src) {
                memcpy(dest,src,n);
        } else {
                __asm__ __volatile__(
                        "std\n\t"
                        "rep\n\t"
                        "movsb\n\t"
                        "cld"
                        : "=&c" (d0), "=&S" (d1), "=&D" (d2)
                        :"0" (n),
                         "1" (n-1+(const char *)src),
                         "2" (n-1+(char *)dest)
                        :"memory");
        }
        return dest;
}
```

Preprocessing

The relationship between the C language proper and its (integral) preprocessor can at best be described as uneasy. Although C and real-life programs rely significantly on the preprocessor, its features often create portability, maintainability, and reliability problems. The preprocessor, as a powerful but blunt instrument, wreaks havoc with identifier scopes, the ability to parse and refactor unpreprocessed code, and the way code is compiled on different platforms. Thus most C programming guidelines recommend moderation in the use of preprocessor constructs. Also for this reason, modern languages based on C have tried to replace features provided by the C preprocessor with more disciplined alternatives. For instance, C++ provides constants and powerful templates as alternatives to the C macros, and C# provides preprocessor-like functionality only to aid conditional compilation and code generators.

The use of preprocessor features can be measured by the amount of expansion or contraction that occurs when the preprocessor runs over the code. Figure 15-14 contains two such measures: one for the body of functions (representing expansion of code), and one for elements outside the body of functions (representing data definitions and declarations). The two measurements were made by calculating the ratio of tokens arriving into the preprocessor to those coming out of it. Here is the SQL query I used for calculating the expansion of code inside functions:

```
select nctoken / npptoken from FUNCTIONS
inner join FUNCTIONMETRICS on id = functionid
where defined and not ismacro and npptoken > 0
```

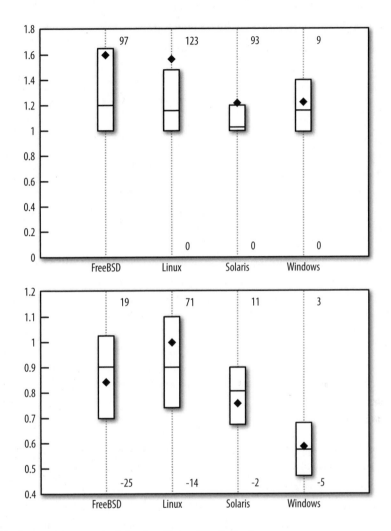

FIGURE 15-14. Preprocessing expansion in functions (top) and files (bottom)

Both expansion and contraction are worrisome. Expansion signifies the occurrence of complex macros, and contraction is a sign of conditional compilation, which is also considered harmful [Spencer and Collyer 1992]. Therefore, the values of these metrics should hover around 1. In the case of functions, OpenSolaris scores better than the other systems and FreeBSD worse, whereas in the case of files, the WRK scores substantially worse than all other systems.

Four further metrics listed in Table 15-5 measure increasingly unsafe uses of the preprocessor:

- Directives in header files (often required)
- Non-#include directives in C files (rarely needed)
- Preprocessor directives in functions (of dubious value)
- Preprocessor conditionals in functions (a portability risk)

TABLE 15-5. Preprocessing metrics

Metric	Ideal	FreeBSD	Linux	Solaris	WRK
% of preprocessor directives in header files	↓	22.4	21.9	21.6	10.8
% of non-#include directives in C files	↓	2.2	1.9	1.2	1.7
% of preprocessor directives in functions	↓	1.56	0.85	0.75	1.07
% of preprocessor conditionals in functions	↓	0.68	0.38	0.34	0.48
% of function-like macros in defined functions	↓	26	20	25	64
% of macros in unique identifiers	↓	66	50	24	25
% of macros in identifiers	↓	32.5	26.7	22.0	27.1

Preprocessor macros are typically used instead of variables (where we call these macros *object-like macros*) and functions (where we call them *function-like macros*). In modern C, object-like macros often can be replaced through enumeration members and function-like macros through inline functions. Both alternatives adhere to the scoping rules of C blocks and are therefore considerably safer than macros, whose scope typically spans a whole compilation unit. The last three metrics of preprocessor use in Table 15-5 measure the occurrence of function-like and object-like macros. Given the availability of viable alternatives and the dangers associated with macros, all should ideally have low values.

Data Organization

The final set of measurements concerns the organization of each kernel's (in-memory) data. A measure of the quality of this organization in C code can be determined by the scoping of identifiers and the use of structures.

In contrast to many modern languages, C provides few mechanisms for controlling namespace pollution. Functions can be defined in only two possible scopes (file and global), macros are visible throughout the compilation unit in which they are defined, and aggregate tags typically live all together in the global namespace. For the sake of maintainability, it's important for large-scale systems such as the four examined in this chapter to judiciously use the few mechanisms available to control the large number of identifiers that can clash.

Figure 15-15 shows the level of namespace pollution in C files by averaging the number of identifiers and macros that are visible at the start of each function. With roughly 10,000 identifiers visible on average at any given point across the systems I examine, it is obvious that namespace pollution is a problem in C code. Nevertheless, FreeBSD fares better than the other systems and the WRK worse.

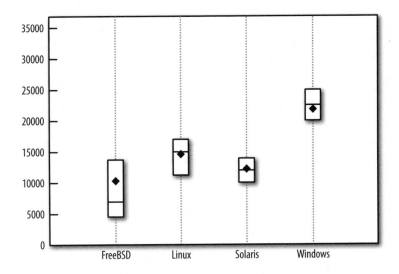

FIGURE 15-15. Average level of namespace pollution in C files

The first three measures in Table 15-6 examine how each system deals with its scarcest naming resource, global variable identifiers. One would like to minimize the number of variable declarations that take place at the global scope in order to minimize namespace pollution. Furthermore, minimizing the percentage of operands that refer to global variables reduces coupling and lessens the cognitive load on the reader of the code (global identifiers can be declared anywhere in the millions of lines comprising the system). The last metric concerning global objects counts identifiers that are declared as global, but could have been declared with a static scope, because they are accessed only within a single file. The corresponding SQL query calculates the percentage of identifiers with global (linkage unit) scope that exist only in a single file:

```
select 100.0 * (select count(*) from
  (select  TOKENS.eid from TOKENS
    left join IDS on TOKENS.eid = IDS.eid
    where ordinary and lscope group by eid having min(fid) = max(fid) ) static) /
  (select count(*) from IDS)
```

The next two metrics look at variable declarations and operands with file scope. These are more benign than global variables, but still worse than variables scoped at a block level.

TABLE 15-6. Data organization metrics

Metric	Ideal	FreeBSD	Linux	Solaris	WRK
% of variable declarations with global scope	↓	0.36	0.19	1.02	1.86
% of variable operands with global scope	↓	3.3	0.5	1.3	2.3
% of identifiers with wrongly global scope	↓	0.28	0.17	1.51	3.53
% of variable declarations with file scope	↓	2.4	4.0	4.5	6.4
% of variable operands with file scope	↓	10.0	6.1	12.7	16.7
Variables per typedef or aggregate	↓	15.13	25.90	15.49	7.70
Data elements per aggregate or enumeration	↓	8.5	10.0	8.6	7.3

The last two metrics concerning the organization of data provide a crude measure of the abstraction mechanisms used in the code. Type and aggregate definitions are the two main data abstraction mechanisms available to C programs. Therefore, counting the number of variable declarations that correspond to each type or aggregate definition provides an indication of how much these abstraction mechanisms have been employed.

```
select ((select count(*) from IDS where ordinary and not fun) /
    (select count(*) from IDS where suetag or typedef))
```

```
select ((select count(*) from IDS where sumember or enum)  /
    (select count(*) from IDS where suetag))
```

These statements measure the number of data elements per aggregate or enumeration in relation to data elements as a whole. This is similar to the relation that Chidamber and Kemerer's object-oriented weighted methods per class (WMC) metric [Chidamber and Kemerer 1994] has to code. A high value could indicate that a structure tries to store too many disparate elements.

Outcome and Aftermath

> **There are two kinds of statistics, the kind you look up and the kind you make up.**
>
> —Archie Goodwin

Table 15-7 summarizes my results. I have marked cells where an operating system excels with a + and corresponding laggards with a –. For a number of reasons it would be a mistake to read too much from this table. First of all, the weights of the table's metrics are not calibrated according to their importance. In addition, it is far from clear that the metrics I used are functionally independent, or that they provide a complete or even representative picture of the quality of C code. Finally, I entered the +/– markings subjectively, trying to identify clear cases of differentiation in particular metrics.

TABLE 15-7. Result summary

Metric	FreeBSD	Linux	Solaris	WRK
File organization				
Length of C files			−	−
Length of header files		+		−
Defined global functions in C files			−	−
Defined structures in header files				−
Directory organization		+		
Files per directory		−		
Header files per C source file				
Average structure complexity in files	−		+	
Code structure				
Extended cyclomatic complexity		+		−
Statements per function		+		
Halstead complexity		+		−
Common coupling at file scope		−		
Common coupling at global scope		+		
% global functions		+		−
% strictly structured functions	−			+
% labeled statements		−		+
Average number of parameters to functions				
Average depth of maximum nesting			−	−
Tokens per statement				
% of tokens in replicated code	−	−	+	
Average structure complexity in functions	+	−		
Code style				
Length of global identifiers				+
Length of aggregate identifiers				+
% style conforming lines			+	−
% style conforming typedef identifiers	−	−		+
% style conforming aggregate tags	−	−	−	+
Characters per line				
% of numeric constants in operands		−	+	+
% unsafe function–like macros			−	
Comment density in C files		−		+
Comment density in header files		−		+
% misspelled comment words				+
% unique misspelled comment words				+

Metric	FreeBSD	Linux	Solaris	WRK
Preprocessing				
Preprocessing expansion in functions	–		+	
Preprocessing expansion in files				–
% of preprocessor directives in header files		–	–	+
% of non–#include directives in C files	–		+	
% of preprocessor directives in functions	–		+	
% of preprocessor conditionals in functions	–	+	+	
% of function–like macros in defined functions		+		–
% of macros in unique identifiers	–		+	+
% of macros in identifiers	–		+	
Data organization				
Average level of namespace pollution in C files	+			–
% of variable declarations with global scope		+		–
% of variable operands with global scope	–	+		
% of identifiers with wrongly global scope		+		–
% of variable declarations with file scope	+			–
% of variable operands with file scope		+		–
Variables per typedef or aggregate		–		+
Data elements per aggregate or enumeration		–		+

Nevertheless, by looking at the distribution and clustering of markings, we can arrive at some important and plausible conclusions. The most interesting finding, which I drew from both the detailed results listed in the previous sections and the summary in Table 15-7, is the similarity of the values among the systems. Across various areas and many different metrics, four systems developed using wildly different processes score comparably. At the very least, the results indicate that the structure and internal quality attributes of a large and complex working software artifact, will represent first and foremost the formidable engineering requirements of its construction, with the influence of process being marginal, if any. If you're building a real-world operating system, a car's electronic control units, an air traffic control system, or the software for landing a probe on Mars, it doesn't matter whether you're managing a proprietary software development team or running an open source project: you can't skimp on quality. This does not mean that process is irrelevant, but it does mean that processes compatible with the artifact's requirements lead to roughly similar results. In the field of architecture this phenomenon has been popularized under the motto "form follows function" [Small 1947].

One can also draw interesting conclusions from the clustering of marks in particular areas. Linux excels in various code structure metrics, but lags in code style. This could be attributed to the work of brilliant, motivated programmers who aren't, however, effectively managed to pay attention to the details of style. In contrast, the high marks of WRK in code style and low marks in code structure could be attributed to the opposite effect: programmers who are effectively micro-managed to care about the details of style, but are not given sufficient creative freedom to develop techniques, design patterns, and tools that would allow them to conquer large-scale complexity.

The high marks of OpenSolaris in preprocessing could also be attributed to programming discipline. The problems from the use of the preprocessor are well-known, but its allure is seductive. It is often tempting to use the preprocessor to create elaborate domain-specific programming constructs. It is also often easy to fix a portability problem by means of conditional compilation directives. However, both approaches can be problematic in the long run, and we can hypothesize that in an organization such as Sun, programmers were discouraged from relying on the preprocessor.

A final interesting cluster appears in the low marks for preprocessor use in the FreeBSD kernel. This could be attributed to the age of the code base in conjunction with a gung-ho programming attitude that assumes code will be read by developers at least as smart as the one who wrote it. However, a particularly low level of namespace pollution across the FreeBSD source code could be a result of using the preprocessor to set up and access conservatively scoped data structures.

Despite various claims regarding the efficacy of particular open or closed source development methods, we can see from the results that there is no clear winner (or loser). One system with a commercial pedigree (OpenSolaris) has the highest balance between positive and negative marks. On the other hand, WRK has the largest number of negative marks, and OpenSolaris has the second-lowest number of positive marks. Looking at the open source systems, although FreeBSD has the highest number of negative marks and the lowest number of positive marks, Linux has the second-highest number of positive marks. Therefore, the most we can read from the overall balance of marks is that open source development approaches do not produce software of markedly higher quality than proprietary software development.

Acknowledgments and Disclosure of Interest

I wish to thank Microsoft, Sun, and the members of the FreeBSD and Linux communities for making their source code available in a form that allows analysis and experimentation. I also thank Fotis Draganidis, Robert L. Glass, Markos Gogoulos, Georgios Gousios, Panos Louridas, and Konstantinos Stroggylos for their help, comments, and advice on earlier drafts of this work. This work was partially funded by the European Community's Sixth Framework Programme under the contract IST-2005-033331 "Software Quality Observatory for Open Source Software (SQO-OSS)."

I've been a source code committer in the FreeBSD project since 2003, I have participated as an invited guest in three Microsoft-sponsored academic initiatives, and I've been using all four systems for more than a decade.

References

[Cannon et al.] Cannon, L.W., and others. Recommended C style and coding standards. Archived by WebCite® at *http://www.webcitation.org/5svpriKD3*.

[Cant et al. 1995] Cant, S.N., D.R. Jeffery, and B.L. Henderson-Sellers. 1995. A conceptual model of cognitive complexity of elements of the programming process. *Information and Software Technology* 37(7): 351–362.

[Capiluppi and Robles 2007] Capiluppi, A., and G. Robles, ed. 2007. *FLOSS '07: Proceedings of the First International Workshop on Emerging Trends in FLOSS Research and Development*. IEEE Computer Society.

[Chidamber and Kemerer 1994] Chidamber, S.R., and C.F. Kemerer. 1994. A metrics suite for object oriented design. *IEEE Transactions on Software Engineering* 20(6): 476–493.

[Coleman et al. 1994] Coleman, D., D. Ash, B. Lowther, and P.W. Oman. 1994. Using metrics to evaluate software system maintainability. *Computer* 27(8): 44–49.

[Cusumano and Selby 1995] Cusumano, M.A., and R.W. Selby. 1995. *Microsoft Secrets*. New York: The Free Press.

[Dickinson 1996] K. Dickinson. 1996. Software process framework at Sun. *StandardView* 4(3): 161–165.

[Feller 2005] FellerJ., ed. 2005. *5-WOSSE: Proceedings of the Fifth Workshop on Open Source Software Engineering*. ACM Press.

[Feller and Fitzgerald 2001] Feller, J., and B. Fitzgerald. 2001. *Understanding Open Source Software Development*. Reading, MA: Addison-Wesley.

[Feller et al. 2005] Feller, J., B. Fitzgerald, S. Hissam, and K. Lakhani, ed. 2005. *Perspectives on Free and Open Source Software*. Cambridge, MA: MIT Press.

[Fitzgerald and Feller 2002] Fitzgerald, B., and J. Feller. 2002. A further investigation of open source software: Community, co-ordination, code quality and security issues. *Information Systems Journal* 12(1): 3–5.

[The FreeBSD Project 1995] The FreeBSD Project. 1995. Style—Kernel Source File Style Guide. The FreeBSD Project. FreeBSD Kernel Developer's Manual: style(9). Archived by WebCite® at *http://www.webcitation.org/5svq73uER*.

[Gill and Kemerer 1991] Gill, G.K., and C.F. Kemerer. 1991. Cyclomatic complexity density and software maintenance productivity. *IEEE Transactions on Software Engineering* 17(12): 1284–1288.

[Glass 1999] R.L. Glass. 1999. Of open source, Linux...and hype. *IEEE Software* 16(1): 126–128.

[Halstead 1977] M.H. Halstead. 1977. *Elements of Software Science*. New York: Elsevier New Holland.

[Harbison and Steele Jr. 1991] Harbison, S.P., and G.L. Steele Jr. 1991. *C: A Reference Manual*, Third Edition. Englewood Cliffs, NJ: Prentice Hall.

[Henry and Kafura 1981] Henry, S.M., and D. Kafura. 1981. Software structure metrics based on information flow. *IEEE Transactions on Software Engineering* SE-7(5), 510–518.

[Hoepman and Jacobs 2007] Hoepman, J.H., and B. Jacobs. 2007. Increased security through open source. *Communications of the ACM* 50(1), 79–83.

[Izurieta and Bieman 2006] Izurieta, C., and J. Bieman. 2006. The evolution of FreeBSD and Linux. *Proceedings of the 2006 ACM/IEEE International Symposium on Empirical Software Engineering*, 204–211.

[Jørgensen 2001] N. Jørgensen. 2001. Putting it all in the trunk: Incremental software development in the FreeBSD open source project. *Information Systems Journal* 11(4): 321–336.

[Kernighan and Plauger 1978] Kernighan, B.W., and P.J. Plauger. 1978. *The Elements of Programming Style*, Second Edition. New York: McGraw-Hill.

[Kuan 2003] J. Kuan. 2003. Open source software as lead user's make or buy decision: A study of open and closed source quality. Paper presented at the second conference on the Economics of the Software and Internet Industries, January 17-18, in Toulouse, France. Archived by WebCite® at *http://www.webcitation.org/5svpriKD3*.

[Li et al. 2006] Li, Z., S. Lu, S. Myagmar, and Y. Zhou. 2006. CP-miner: Finding copy-paste and related bugs in large-scale software code. *IEEE Transactions on Software Engineering* 32(3): 176–192.

[McCabe 1976] T.J. McCabe. 1976. A complexity measure. *IEEE Transactions on Software Engineering* 2(4): 308–320.

[McConnell 2004] , S.C. McConnell. 2004. *Code Complete: A Practical Handbook of Software Construction*, Second Edition. Redmond, WA: Microsoft Press.

[Parnas 1972] D.L. Parnas. 1972. On the criteria to be used for decomposing systems into modules. *Communications of the ACM* 15(12): 1053–1058.

[Paulson et al. 2004] Paulson, J.W., G. Succi, and A. Eberlein. 2004. An empirical study of open-source and closed-source software products. *IEEE Transactions on Software Engineering* 30(4): 246–256.

[Polze and Probert 2006] Polze, A., and D. Probert. 2006. Teaching operating systems: The Windows case. *Proceedings of the 37th SIGCSE Technical Symposium on Computer Science Education*: 298–302.

[Rigby and German 2006] Rigby, P.C., and D.M. German. 2006. A preliminary examination of code review processes in open source projects. Technical Report DCS-305-IR, University of Victoria. Archived by WebCite® at *http://www.webcitation.org/5svoPB5t5*.

[Salus 1994] P.H. Salus. 1994. *A Quarter Century of UNIX*. Boston, MA: Addison-Wesley.

[Samoladas et al. 2004] Samoladas, I., I. Stamelos, L. Angelis, and A. Oikonomou. 2004. Open source software development should strive for even greater code maintainability. *Communications of the ACM* 47(10): 83–87.

[Small 1947] Small,H.A., ed. 1947. *Form and Function: Remarks on Art by Horatio Greenough*. Berkeley and Los Angeles: University of California Press.

[Sowe et al. 2007] Sowe, S.K., I.G. Stamelos, and I. Samoladas, ed. 2007. *Emerging Free and Open Source Software Practices*. Hershey, PA: IGI Publishing.

[Spencer and Collyer 1992] Spencer, H., and G. Collyer. 1992. #ifdef considered harmful or portability experience with C news. *Proceedings of the Summer 1992 USENIX Conference*: 185–198.

[Spinellis 2003] D. Spinellis. 2003. Global analysis and transformations in preprocessed languages. *IEEE Transactions on Software Engineering* 29(11): 1019–1030.

[Spinellis 2006] D. Spinellis. 2006. *Code Quality: The Open Source Perspective*. Boston, MA: Addison-Wesley.

[Spinellis 2008] D. Spinellis. 2008. A tale of four kernels. *ICSE '08: Proceedings of the 30th International Conference on Software Engineering*: 381-390.

[Spinellis 2010] D. Spinellis. 2010. CScout: A refactoring browser for C. *Science of Computer Programming* 75(4): 216–231.

[Spinellis and Szyperski 2004] Spinellis, D., and C. Szyperski. 2004. How is open source affecting software development? *IEEE Software* 21(1): 28–33.

[Stallman et al. 2005] Stallman, R., and others. 2005. GNU coding standards. Archived by WebCite® at *http://www.webcitation.org/5svos1oZq*.

[Stamelos et al. 2002] Stamelos, I., L. Angelis, A. Oikonomou, and G.L. Bleris. 2002. Code quality analysis in open source software development. *Information Systems Journal* 12(1): 43–60.

[Stol et al. 2009] Stol, K.J., M.A. Babar, B. Russo, and B. Fitzgerald. 2009. The use of empirical methods in open source software research: Facts, trends and future directions. *Proceedings of the 2009 ICSE Workshop on Emerging Trends in Free/Libre/Open Source Software Research and Development*: 19-24.

[Tanenbaum 1987] A.S. Tanenbaum. 1987. *Operating Systems: Design and Implementation*. Englewood Cliffs, NJ: Prentice Hall.

[Torvalds and Diamond 2001] Torvalds, L., and D. Diamond. 2001. *Just for Fun: The Story of an Accidental Revolutionary*. New York: HarperInformation.

[von Krogh and von Hippel 2006] von Krogh, G., and E. von Hippel. 2006. The promise of research on open source software. *Management Science* 52(7): 975–983.

[Yu et al. 2004] Yu, L., S.R. Schach, K. Chen, and J. Offutt. 2004. Categorization of common coupling and its application to the maintainability of the Linux kernel. *IEEE Transactions on Software Engineering* 30(10): 694–706.

[Yu et al. 2006] Yu, L., S.R. Schach, K. Chen, G.Z. Heller, and J. Offutt. 2006. Maintainability of the kernels of open source operating systems: A comparison of Linux with FreeBSD, NetBSD and OpenBSD. *Journal of Systems and Software* 79(6): 807–815.

## CHAPTER SIXTEEN

Code Talkers

Robert DeLine

The way programmers are portrayed in pop culture, you would think that they're all cubicle-dwelling nerds with no social graces, like Dilbert and Wally in *Dilbert* or Roy and Moss on *The IT Crowd*. According to the stereotype, the only time these geeks *do* talk to each other, it's to debate the merits of Kirk versus Picard.

The truth, though, is that many programmers spend large fractions of their day away from their desks, talking to each other. In this chapter, we look at several studies of how programmers spend their time at work and see that communication is a huge part of the job. These conversations aren't idle distractions around the water cooler: they help programmers stay aware of project status, coordinate activities, and spread knowledge around the team. Instead of seeing these conversations as disruptive hiccups in the machinery of a development team, we should see them as the lubricant that keeps the machinery running smoothly.

A Day in the Life of a Programmer

So, how does a typical programmer spend his or her time at work, and how do we know?

There's a long tradition of studying workers to account for their time and to look for possible productivity improvements. Starting in the early 20th century, pioneers such as Frank and Lillian Gilbreth, immortalized in the book *Cheaper by the Dozen*, did *time and motion studies* to reduce the time and effort needed for factory workers and office clerks to perform repeated tasks. In such studies, a researcher, equipped with a stopwatch, clipboard, and camera, observes a worker performing his or her normal work activities. The researcher then measures the time each body movement takes and looks for new possibilities that are quicker, more accurate, or less fatiguing. As one example, the Gilbreths observed surgeons fumbling to pick up instruments during surgeries and invented the now familiar protocol by which a surgeon asks an assisting nurse for each instrument as it is needed. This innovation both reduces the time surgeries take and avoids mistakes.

Of course, software development isn't factory work or surgery. Time and motion studies focus on physical movement, whereas software development is mostly brain work. Nonetheless, the same study techniques can be useful.

In the early 1990s, Perry, Staudenmayer, and Votta ran a study, in the spirit of a time and motion study, with a group of programmers working on real-time switching systems [Perry et al. 1994]. Because there was no established methodology for studying programmer work practice, they tried two different methods: a diary study and an observational study.

Diary Study

First, the researchers asked some of the participating programmers to fill out daily *diaries* of their work activities, for the period of a full year. Their custom diary form had a box for each hour of the work day, in which the participant summarized what he did during that hour. In each box, he would write down what aspect of his assigned task he worked on (planning, requirements, design, coding, testing, etc.) or, if he did not work on their assigned task, the reason why (higher-priority task, blocked waiting on resources, or personal choice to work on something else). Amazingly, 13 programmers from four teams were willing to do this.

Based on this data, their biggest result was that the participants spent only 40% of their time working on their assigned tasks. The rest of the time they were either blocked or doing other work. The researchers noticed that, because of the frequent blocking, programmers would often keep two assigned tasks close at hand. That way, if they were blocked on one task, they could always switch to the other to keep from being idle.

Of course, given that the participants were recording their own time usage, it's possible that their diaries were not very accurate. Even if every participant acted diligently about filling out the diary every hour on the hour, a one-hour time period is very coarse-grained—a lot happens in an hour! So, both to double-check the accuracy of the diary data and to get more detailed data, the researchers ran a second study where they shadowed programmers to see how they spent their time.

Observational Study

In their second study, Perry, Staudenmayer, and Votta directly observed five participants during their work days. They shadowed these developers for their entire work days, typically eight to ten hours long, for five work days for each participant, totaling an impressive 300 hours of data. During an observed work day, the researcher would ask to be treated like a student trying to learn the job and would prompt participants with questions such as, "What are you working on now?" when the answer wasn't obvious just from watching [Perry et al. 1996]. These observations provided much a finer level of detail about what the programmers were doing than the diary study, down to intervals of three minutes.

From the observation data, they saw that programmers spent an average of 75 minutes of each work day in informal communication, which took the form of email, phone calls, voice mail, and face-to-face visits. This 75 minutes was *in addition to* their scheduled meetings for design reviews, code reviews, organizational updates, etc., which clearly also involve a lot of communication. Aside from incoming emails with broadcast announcements, the most frequent type of communication was face-to-face visits, which occurred about two to three times as often as other media. Programmers spoke with an average of seven different people throughout the day. The maximum seen in this study was 17 unique visitors in one day. Most of these interactions were short—68% under five minutes—but it was not uncommon for some observed phone calls to last a half hour and some in-person visits to last up to an hour. Clearly, this is a lot of talk!

Were the Programmers on Their Best Behavior?

If we naively think that programmers are productive when they are pounding out code at the keyboard, these results might seem alarming. After all, the studies claim that programmers spend the majority of their time away from their assigned tasks, a lot of that time just talking with other programmers. We might then wonder whether there was something wrong with the studies.

One concern is that the diary study relies on self-reported data. To reduce this risk, the researchers chose to overlap some participants in both the diary and observational studies. On many days, therefore, the researchers had both the participant's self-reported diaries and the researcher's observed data. As you might expect, programmers differed in the accuracy with which they estimated the time spent on tasks, sometimes over-reporting and sometimes under-reporting. However, the programmers often were not off by much: the average amount of over-reporting was 2.8% [Perry et al. 1996]. In many cases, the under-reporting resulted from ignoring the time lost to interruptions and blockages.

Of course, we might also be suspicious of the observed data itself. Intuitively, we would assume that the participating programmers were acting "on their best behavior" during the observations, or maybe even showing off. In fact, this phenomenon is so familiar in experimental psychology that it has a name: the *Hawthorne Effect*.

In the late 1920s, researchers at the Hawthorne Works electronics factory in Chicago ran experiments to see whether improving the lighting on the factory floor would make the workers more productive. They tried many different lighting levels over the course of many weeks. The funny thing was that, no matter how minute a lighting change they tried, the workers were always more productive! But, as soon as the study was over, productivity would slump back to its normal levels. The one common factor across all these experiments was that the workers knew they were the subjects of experiments. Today, we use the term Hawthorne Effect to refer to the tendency people have to improve their work behavior when they know that researchers are observing them.

So, were the participants in Perry, Staudenmayer, and Votta's study influenced by the Hawthorne Effect? Since the effect is unavoidable, the answer is undoubtedly "yes" to some extent. So a better question is: how much inaccuracy did the Hawthorne Effect cause in their observational data? Because the researchers knew about the effect, they designed their study to mitigate it. First, they had several participants in the diary study who were not in the observational study, which allowed them to see how programmers being observed compared with those not being observed. Second, they made sure that several of the observed work days were not scheduled in advance. Because the researchers just showed up at random, the programmers could not arrange their work days to be as "interesting" as possible for the observer. In the end, these random days were not particularly different from the scheduled days. Finally, in both studies, all of the data was kept completely anonymous, which reduced the motivation for the programmers to make themselves "look good" for their coworkers, managers, or anyone else.

What Is All This Talk About?

Given that programmers spend a large fraction of their work days in conversation, you might wonder what they're talking about. A pair of recent studies that my colleagues and I conducted at Microsoft Corporation provides some insight into this question. Through surveys, interviews, and direct observation, we learned that a lot of the conversations are for *information seeking*—that is, looking for answers to questions that come up during programming tasks. These studies taught us a lot about why programmers often prefer face-to-face meetings and exactly what questions come up the most.

Getting Answers to Questions

In the first study, from 2006, we conducted a survey of 157 randomly chosen programmers and follow-up interviews with 11 of them. We asked them about their daily work activities, and in particular what they found difficult [LaToza et al. 2006]. Their responses about the time they spent on various work activities were consistent with the findings of Perry et al. The average percentage of time spent on communication was higher than for any other activity. The survey also asked respondents to estimate the percentage of time they spent using various communication media and to rate how effective they thought each medium was. The results are shown in Figure 16-1. These results are also in line with Perry et al., in that respondents spent the most of their time in unplanned face-to-face meetings. They also rated this as the most effective type of communication.

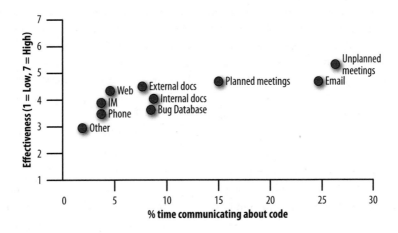

FIGURE 16-1. *Ratings of usage and effectiveness of various forms of communication*

In the interviews, we asked for examples of the difficulties they encountered in their daily work. One common thread was that the interviewed programmers would often get stuck in their tasks because they were missing some necessary information. They typically felt that walking down the hall and talking to a colleague was not only an effective way to get the information, but was sometimes the only way.

The following story, taken from one of our interviews (and reported in [LaToza et al. 2006]), illustrates how communication is an integral part of programming activities, in this case debugging:

> After being assigned a new bug through a bug tracking tool, the developer first reproduced the bug by navigating to a web page and ensuring that *error 500 – internal error* was received as reported in the bug. Next, the developer attached the Visual Studio debugger to the web server, set it to break on exceptions, reproduced the error again, and was presented with a null reference exception in Visual Studio. From an inspection of the call stack window, the developer considered the functions that might be responsible for producing the erroneous value. The developer switched to Emacs to read the methods and used *ctags.exe* to browse callers of methods. The developer then switched back to the Visual Studio debugger to change values at runtime and see what the effects were. The developer made a change, recompiled, and found that the same exception was still being produced. Finally, the developer browsed further up the call stack, tracing the erroneous value to one object, then to another object, and finally to a third object protected with mutexes.
>
> By this time, the developer had wandered into code that he did not understand and did not "own" or have primary responsibility for maintaining. But a second developer was working on a high-profile feature that touched this code, and the respondent knew that this second developer would understand this code. He went to the second developer's office, interrupted the second developer, and engaged him in a discussion about the rationale behind the code.

He walked back to his office and made a change based on this information, but determined that the change wouldn't work, leaving him with a new problem in this unowned code. He walked back to the second developer's office, who then told him that the functionality causing the problem was actually related to code that a third developer was working on. They both went to visit the third developer's office, only to find the third developer was at lunch. The first developer, now blocked, switched to another task. After lunch, both developers returned to the third developer's office, had a design discussion about how the functionality should behave, and finally passed the first developer's bug to the third developer to make the fix.

This story exemplifies points that we heard repeatedly in the interviews. When a programmer gets stuck on an issue he doesn't understand, he does his "due diligence" before turning to a colleague for help. That is, he spends time learning about the code and its execution in order to ask educated questions. After the interviews, we conducted a follow-up survey of 187 programmers to get more details about what we learned from the interviews [LaToza et al. 2006]. From this, we learned that during this "due diligence" phase, on average, respondents spent 42% of their time examining the source code, 20% using the debugger, 16% examining check-in comments or version diffs, 9% examining the results, 8% using debug or trace statements, and 5% using other means.

The Search for Rationale

Often, examining the code and its behavior is not enough to reach a full understanding. In the story I cited in the previous section, the interviewed programmer turned to colleagues to learn the *rationale* behind the code—a kind of information that is not typically recorded, but exists only in the team's collective memory. As one interviewed programmer put it, "Lots of design information is kept in people's heads." In fact, in our initial survey, "understanding the rationale behind a code" was the highest-ranked problem, with 66% agreeing that they have difficulty with this.

What do we mean by the term *rationale*? In the follow-up survey, we asked what aspect of rationale is the most difficult. Out of the 187 respondents, 82% agreed that it takes a lot of effort to understand "why the code is implemented the way it is," 73% "whether the code was written as a temporary workaround," 69% "how the code works," and 62% "what the code is trying to accomplish." In short, rationale is the "back story" behind decisions—sometimes about decisions that were made, and sometimes about alternatives that were rejected.

Interruptions and Multitasking

Returning to the interview story, when this programmer had a rationale question, he walked down the hall for a face-to-face visit, first with one colleague and then another. This choice to visit colleagues is consistent with both the communication preferences in Figure 16-1 and the observed programmer behavior in Perry et al. Unfortunately, every unscheduled face-to-face visit represents an interruption for at least one person. An interruption, in turn, often requires a task switch. The interrupted person might stop writing code, for instance, and start browsing around for the answer to the question the visitor is asking. In our survey, the second-highest-rated problem was "having to switch tasks often because of requests from my teammates or manager," with 62% of respondents agreeing that this is difficult.

We also see in this story that the interviewed programmer's first attempt to get an answer was blocked because his colleague was away. As a result, the interviewed programmer switched tasks to keep from being idle. Later, when the colleague came back, together they were able to make progress on the task—namely, they made some decisions about how the program should behave and who should be responsible for implementing it. Perry et al. observed this same tasking-switching behavior. So for the interrupted person, the conversation might feel like a productivity drain, but for the interrupting person, the conversation can convey information that is vital for staying productive.

In summary, when programmers work on their assigned tasks, questions often come up. When the answers cannot be found through "due diligence" of poking around the code, programmers often walk the halls, interrupting their colleagues to look for answers. The most difficult kind of question that they face has to do with rationale. For this kind of question, often the only place to look for answers is "inside people's heads." But is rationale the only problem? What other types of questions come up as programmers try to get their work done?

What Questions Do Programmers Ask?

To understand the questions that programmers have as they do their daily work, we ran a second study at Microsoft [Ko et al. 2007]. We used an observational protocol very similar to the one that Perry et al. used in their study. We observed 17 programmers in their offices as they did their typical work, for roughly 90 minutes apiece. Like Perry et al., we asked the programmers to treat us like students trying to learn the job and would ask them questions when we couldn't tell what they were doing.

We also used what psychologists and social scientists call a *think-aloud* protocol. That is, we asked the programmers to chatter continually at us, telling us every thought that occurred to them and narrating every action they were taking. Here's a made-up example to illustrate what this sounds like:

> So, I'm looking for the code that opens the database, so I hit Ctrl-F to bring up the search box. I'm typing in "open". Damn, it didn't find anything. Let me try "database" instead. OK, here's the code I was looking for. It was called "access database", not "open"—that's why I didn't find anything before.

Although this kind of chatter may seem awkward or even annoying, participants get used to it very quickly. Without the think-aloud protocol, it would be impossible to understand the programmer's mental state. In particular, we would never have known most of the questions that our participants were wondering about, if they didn't say them aloud.

As our participants chattered away, we used a small digital clock and notepad to create a minute-by-minute transcript of everything they said and did. Whenever they got up to ask a colleague a question, we followed them and transcribed the conversations. After we recorded this data, we analyzed the transcripts and created a catalogue of all the information needs we witnessed, shown in Table 16-1.

TABLE 16-1. Programmers' observed information needs, sorted by frequency

Information type	Duration		Frequency and outcome of searches
	Avg	Max	Acquired ■ Deferred □ Gave up ⊠ Beyond obs. −
What have my coworkers been doing?	1	11	■■□□□□□□
What code caused this program state?	2	21	■■■■■■■■■■■□□□□□□□□□□□□□□□□□□□⊠ −
In what situations does this failure occur?	2	49	■■■■■■■■■■■■■■□□□□□□□□□□⊠ −
What is the program *supposed* to do?	1	21	■■■■■■■■■■■■■■■■■■■■■□□□□
How have resources I depend on changed?	1	9	■■■■■■■■■■■■■■■■■□□□□□□⊠
What code *could* have caused this behavior?	2	17	■■■■■■■■■■■■■■□□□□□□□⊠⊠ −
How do I use this data structure or function?	1	14	■■■■■■■■■■■■■■■■■■■□⊠
Why was this code implemented this way?	2	21	■■■■■□□□□□□□□□⊠ − − − − −
Is this problem worth fixing?	2	6	■■■■■■■■■■■■■■■□
What are the implications of this change?	2	9	■■■■■■■■■■■■■■■
What is the purpose of this code?	1	5	■■■■■■■■■□⊠⊠
What's statically related to this code?	1	7	■■■■■■■■■■□
Is this a legitimate problem?	1	2	■■■■■■■■
Did I follow my team's conventions?	7	25	■■□□□□
What does the failure look like?	0	2	■■■■■
Which changes are part of this submission?	2	3	■■■■□
How can I coordinate this with other code?	1	4	■■⊠ −
How difficult will this problem be to fix?	2	4	■■■
What can be used to implement this behavior?	2	2	■■
What information was relevant to my task?	1	1	■■

The information needs in the table are generalized forms of the particular questions we heard the participants ask. Alongside each information need, we show two pieces of information. First, the "duration" column shows the average and maximum number of minutes we saw programmers searching for answers to that information need. Second, the "frequency and outcomes" column has a symbol for every instance of the information need that we saw: a black box for successfully finding the answer; a white box for deferring the search to some later time; a box with an X for giving up on the search; and a dash for unknown outcomes because the observation session ended before the question was answered.

Where did programmers look for answers? Table 16-2 shows the sources of information consulted by the programmers we observed. Consistent with the previous studies, coworkers are consulted more often than any other source of information. The other sources, in order from most consulted to least consulted, were:

1. Various team-specific or company-specific *tools*
2. The programmer's own intuition, logical inferences, or memory (*brain*)
3. The bug database (*bugs*)
4. The debugger (*dbug*)
5. The source code, its comments, or its history (*code*)
6. Documents other than specifications (*docs*)
7. *Email*
8. Specification documents (*specs*)
9. The *log*files from program executions
10. Instant messages (*im*)

In addition to looking at the frequency of questions, we can also look at the most frustrating information needs—namely, those that had the longest search times and that were unsatisfied (deferred or given up) the most often. Based on these criteria, here are the seven most frustrating information needs:

1. What code caused this program state? (61% unsatisfied, max 21 minutes)
2. Why was the code implemented this way? (44%, 21 minutes)
3. In what situations does this failure occur? (41%, 49 minutes)
4. What code *could* have caused this behavior? (36%, 17 minutes)
5. How have the resources I depend on changed? (24%, 9 minutes)
6. What is the program supposed to do? (15%, 21 minutes)
7. What have my coworkers been doing? (14%, 11 minutes)

For all seven, the observed programmers turned to colleagues for answers, but also turned to other sources as well, often as part of their "due diligence."

So in addition to knowing that developers frequently talk to each other to ask each other questions, we also know which questions come up the most often and which ones are the most difficult to answer.

TABLE 16-2. Frequency of sources that programmers consulted for information needs

	coworker	tools	brain	bugs	dbug	code	docs	email	specs	log	im	TOTAL
What have my coworkers been doing?	20	8						13			2	43
What code caused this program state?	1	3	3	3	16	2				3		31
What is the program supposed to do?	9						5	1	13			28
In what situations does this failure occur?	8	3	5	8	2	1						27
How have resources I depend on changed?	6	12		2		1		4				25
What code could have caused this behavior?	5		4	4	2	1			1	4	1	22
How do I use this data structure or function?	4					5	11		1			21
Why was this code implemented this way?	2	2	4	1	2	8						19
Is this problem worth fixing?	12		1	1				2				16
What are the implications of this change?	13									1		14

	coworker	tools	brain	bugs	dbug	code	docs	email	specs	log	im	TOTAL
What is the purpose of this code?		2	5		2	2	1		1			13
What's statically related to this code?		8	2					1				11
Is this a legitimate problem?	1			5						1		7
Did I follow my team's conventions?		2	1				2					5
What does the failure look like?				5								5
Which changes are part of this submission?		2	2									4
How can I coordinate this with other code?	1					1	2					4
How difficult will this problem be to fix?	1			1		1						3
What can be used to implement this behavior?			1				1					2
What information was relevant to my task?			2									2
TOTAL	83	42	30	30	24	22	22	21	16	9	3	

Are Agile Methods Better for Communication?

The behavior described earlier comes from two specific studies, one at a telephony company in the mid-1990s and the other at Microsoft in the mid-2000s. The companies differ in the products they produce, the development tools they use, and because of the decade between them, the communication tools used (the earlier study did not mention cell phones or instant messaging, for example). However, both companies use a variation on the traditional waterfall approach to development—that is, fairly lengthy development cycles with separate phases for planning, writing specs, coding, testing, and shipping. Would the communication behavior be different for a team that follows Agile practices?

In 2006, Chong and Siino studied the differences between Agile and non-Agile teams in two Bay Area start up companies [Chong and Siino 2006]. They observed one team, which they call Team Solo, using traditional methods in a workplace where programmers work alone in cubicles. The other team, which they call Team Pair, used pair programming in an open "bullpen" environment. Overall, the communication behavior they observed was largely the same as in the telephony and Microsoft studies. On both teams, programmers would communicate regularly to ask for help or information, to coordinate actions, or to share status. However, the exact nature of that communication varied because of differences in their development approach and work environment.

Some of the differences in communication were due to the physical setup of the office environment. Both teams worked in large spaces, but Team Pair organized their space as an open "bullpen," whereas Team Solo split up the space with cubicles. Because of Team Pair's open environment, programmers could overhear each other's conversations, picking up relevant information just by eavesdropping and jumping into the conversation when they had something to add. Because of this, Team Pair tended to keep their bullpen conversations on work topics. Team Solo, in contrast, tried to keep their environment quiet because noise easily carried over the cubicle walls. Despite this effort, some members of Team Solo worked from home to avoid disruption. (This need for a quiet workplace was a major topic of DeMarco and Lister's widely read manifesto *Peopleware* [DeMarco and Lister 1987].) Team Solo also relied heavily on a chat system to allow them to exchange information nonverbally and to communicate with people working from home.

Chong and Siino were particularly interested in differences in the use of interruption. Interruptions were consistently shorter in length for Team Pair than for Team Solo (on average, 1 minute 55 seconds versus 2 minutes 45 seconds). The use of pair programming also affected the findings. When questions arose in Team Pair, often one member of the pair would engage in discussion to answer the question, leaving the other member of the pair to carry on with the task. Also, on Team Pair, an interrupted programmer would walk over to the interrupting programmer's desk to have the discussion. This meant that the interrupted programmer could control when the interruption would end by returning to his or her own desk. In contrast, interruptions on Team Solo were similar to those described in the two earlier studies, where a programmer with a question would visit other people's cubicles and interrupt their work to get an answer. This left the interrupting programmer in control of when the interruption would end.

In short, this study indicates that some aspects of Agile methods do offer some unique advantages for communication. In particular, the use of a bullpen setting tended to spread knowledge and awareness by allowing eavesdropping and encouraged programmers to keep conversations (at least those in the bullpen) short and on business topics. The use of pair programming allowed one member of the pair to handle interrupting questions while the other carried on. These advantages, though, may come with a downside. Team Solo used email and their chat system for a lot of communication. This use of written media, unlike conversations, leaves behind a record that can be consulted later. Whether the heavy use of conversations hurts Agile teams in the long run has yet to be studied.

A Model for Thinking About Communication

By way of summary, here's a metaphor for thinking about the communication behavior that these studies document. We can think of a programmer as a thread scheduler in an operating system. The "algorithm" of a programmer's work practice is sketched in Example 16-1.

To flesh out the metaphor, here's a quick and dirty overview of how an operating system schedules threads. The scheduler keeps a queue of threads that are ready to run. It picks one and runs it until that thread gets blocked on input.* The blocked threads then get put on the pending queue until the input is available. Input arrives asynchronously in the form of an interrupt (for example, a network packet arriving or a disk block getting copied to memory). When input arrives, the scheduler finds the thread that was blocked waiting for that input and moves that thread from the pending queue back to the active queue. After handling the interrupt, the scheduler goes back to running a thread from the active queue.

EXAMPLE 16-1. A developer's day is like thread scheduling

```
void beProductiveProgrammer()
{
    while (!quittingTime)
        try {
            var task = readyTasks.pickOne();
            while (!task.isDone && !task.isBlocked)
                task.makeProgress();
            if (task.isBlocked)
                blockedTasks.add(task);
            readyTasks.remove(task);
        }
```

---

* A scheduler will also stop a thread if it runs for too long without blocking, but this aspect isn't especially relevant for the metaphor. We could use it to model programmer boredom!

```
        catch (Interruption interruption) {
            var info = interruption.informationContent;
            for (var task in blockedTasks)
                if (task.blockedOn(info)) {
                    blockedTasks.remove(task);
                    readyTasks.add(task);
                }
        }
    }
}
```

This thread scheduling behavior is strikingly similar to the work practices observed in the studies in this chapter. A programmer carries out a programming task (the thread) until she can't make further progress without getting some information (the thread is blocked on input). She then puts this task away and picks another one to work on to keep from being idle. When an interruption happens (an in-office visit, a phone call, an incoming email), this interruption often carries relevant information, such as the answer to a question that was posed. When this information arrives, the programmer can then resume the task that was blocked waiting for that information.

Naively, we could think of the inner loop as being a programmer's only "productive time." However, as the studies discussed earlier show, this view isn't realistic. Programmers stay in the inner loop only when they have no questions or can immediately find the answers without having to communicate with others. But these studies show that many times a day, programmers *do* have questions that require communication. A major source of such questions is the need for rationale information, which often is recorded only in the team's collective memory.

Could we ever hope to eliminate such questions, say, through good documentation? Economically, we wouldn't want to do this. A development team collectively makes thousands of choices each day, ranging in scope from tiny decisions about local variable names up to decisions about requirements or architecture that affect the entire product and team. As a project matures, some of these decisions will be revisited over and over again, while others are made once and remain stable. So documentation amounts to speculative investment (or, put more crudely, gambling). It's worthwhile documenting a decision only when these conditions are met:

- Some future programmer will care about it.
- The impacts of the decision last long enough for a future programmer to encounter one of them.
- The documentation is sufficient to answer future programmers' questions.
- The cost of writing the documentation is less than the cost of answering future questions directly through communication.

All of these conditions are speculative and uncertain. Looked at this way, we can see that many teams do their best to invest wisely in documentation in the face of uncertainty. They write documentation about the decisions with the biggest scope, most stability, and widest audience. The rest they handle on-demand through communication.

References

[Chong and Siino 2006] Chong, Jan, and Rosanne Siino.2006. Interruptions on Software Teams: A Comparison of Paired and Solo Programmers. *Proceedings of the ACM 2006 Conference on Computer Supported Cooperative Work.*

[DeMarco and Lister 1987] DeMarco, Tom, and Timothy Lister. 1987. *Peopleware: Productive Products and Teams.* New York: Dorset House Publishing Company, Inc.

[Ko et al. 2007] Ko, Andrew J., Robert DeLine, and Gina Venolia.2007. Information Needs in Collocated Software Development Teams.*Proceedings of the International Conference on Software Engineering.*

[LaToza et al. 2006] LaToza, Thomas D., Gina Venolia, and Robert DeLine.2006. Maintaining mental models: a study of developer work habits. *Proceedings of the International Conference on Software Engineering.*

[Perry et al. 1994] Perry, Dewayne, Nancy A. Staudenmayer, and Lawrence G. Votta. 1994.People, organizations, and process improvement. *IEEE Software* 11(4): 36-45.

[Perry et al. 1996] Perry, Dewayne, Nancy A. Staudenmayer, and Lawrence G. Votta. 1996.Understanding and Improving Time Usage in Software Development. In*Process-Centered Environments,* eds. Fuggetta and Wolf.Hoboken, NJ: John Wiley and Sons.

## CHAPTER SEVENTEEN

Pair Programming

Laurie Williams

Pair programming is a style of programming in which *two* programmers work side-by-side at *one* computer, continuously collaborating on the same design, algorithm, code, or test. Pair programming has been practiced sporadically for decades [Williams and Kessler 2003]. However, the emergence of Agile methodologies and Extreme Programming (XP) [Beck 2005] in the late 1990s brought the pair programming practice to more recent prominence.

With pair programming, one of the pair, called the *driver*, types at the computer or writes down a design. The other partner, called the *navigator*, has many jobs. One of these is to observe the work of the driver—looking for tactical and strategic defects in the driver's work. Some tactical defects might be syntax errors, typos, and calling the wrong method. Strategic defects occur when the driver's implementation or design ultimately will fail to accomplish its goals. The navigator is the strategic, long-range thinker of the programming pair. Because the navigator is not as deeply involved with the design, algorithm, code, or test, he or she can have a more objective point of view and can better think strategically about the direction of the work. Both in the pair are constant brainstorming and chatting partners [Wray 2010]. An effective pair will be constantly discussing alternative approaches and solutions to the problem [Vanhanen and Korpi 2007], [Williams and Kessler 2003]. A sign of a dysfunctional pair is a quiet navigator. Periodically, the driver and the navigator should switch roles. On a software development team, team members should pair program with a variety of other team members to leverage a variety of expertise.

The name of the technique, pair *programming*, can lead people to incorrectly assume that software engineers and others on a software development team pair only during code development. However, pairing can occur during all phases of the development process—in pair design, pair debugging, pair testing, and so on. Programmers could pair up at any time during development, in particular when they are working on a complex or unfamiliar problem. Additionally, a product manager may pair with a user interface designer to collaboratively develop the user experience. A tester and a developer may pair during the creation of automated tests. In short, the side-by-side collaboration style of pair programming can be done by many in the team, at all phases of development.

This chapter starts with a brief history of the use of pair programming. Then, I provide information on the use of pair programming in industry and in academia, respectively. Following that, I discuss distributed pair programming, which is the use of pair programming when the programmers are not co-located. Finally, I present the challenges in transitioning to pair programming.

A History of Pair Programming

People have advocated and practiced pair programming for decades, long before it was ever called pair programming. Fred Brooks, author of *The Mythical Man-Month* [Brooks 1975], has communicated: "Fellow graduate student Bill Wright and I first tried pair programming when I was a grad student (1953–1956). We produced 1,500 lines of defect-free code; it ran correctly first try" [Williams and Kessler 2003].

In the early 1980s, Larry Constantine, author of more than 150 technical articles and 16 books, reported observing "Dynamic Duos" at Whitesmiths, Ltd., producing code faster and more bug-free than ever before [Constantine 1995]. He commented that the code benefited from the thinking of two bright minds and the steady dialog between two trusted programmers. He concluded that two programmers in tandem was not redundancy, but rather it was a direct route to greater efficiency and better quality.

Based upon research findings of the Pasteur project (a large sociological/anthropological study of 50 highly effective software development organizations) at Bell Labs Research, James Coplien published the "Developing in Pairs" Organizational Pattern [Coplien 1995], [Coplien and Harrison 2005] in 1995. Coplien identified the forces of this pattern as "people sometimes feel they can solve a problem only if they have help. Some problems are bigger than any one individual." The proposed solution of the organizational pattern is to "pair compatible designers to work together; together they can produce more than the sum of the two individually." The result of applying the pattern is "a more effective implementation process. A pair of people is less likely to be blindsided than an individual developer."

In 1998, Temple University professor John Nosek was the first to run an empirical study on the efficacy of pair programmers [Nosek 1998]. Nosek reported the results of 15 full-time, experienced programmers working for a maximum of 45 minutes on a challenging problem important to their organization. In their own environments and with their own equipment, 5 worked individually and 10 worked collaboratively in 5 pairs. The conditions and materials were the same for both the experimental (team) and control (individual) groups. A two-sided t-test showed that the study provided statistically significant results. The pairs spent a total of 60% more total minutes on the task. However, because they worked in tandem, they completed the task 20% faster than the control groups. Nosek also reports that the pairs produced better algorithms and code.

As I mentioned earlier, the emergence of the XP software development methodology in the late 1990s/early 2000s brought the pair programming practice to the forefront. As XP emerged, many people were doubtful about pair programming because they believed that the amount of effort spent on a programming task would double if two programmers worked together.

This incredulousness motivated an extensive empirical study that was run at the University of Utah in 1999 ([Williams et al. 2000], [Williams 2000]), [Williams and Kessler 2000] to isolate and study the costs and benefits of pair programming. Forty-one third- and fourth-year undergraduate students in a software engineering class participated in a structured experiment for the duration of a 15-week semester. On the first day of class, the students were asked whether they preferred to work in pairs or individually, with whom they wanted to work, and with whom they did not want to work. The students were also classified as "High" (top 25%), "Average," or "Low" (bottom 25%) academic performers based on the grade point average (GPA) in their academic records. Twenty-eight students were assigned to the paired group and thirteen to the solo group. The GPA was used to ensure the groups were academically equivalent. Of the 14 pairs, 13 pairs were mutually chosen, in that each student had asked to work with her partner. The last pair was assigned because the students did not express a partner preference.

All students received instruction in effective pair-programming and were given a paper [Williams and Kessler 2000] on strategies for successful collaboration to help prepare them. Specific measures were taken to ensure that the pairs worked together consistently each week. One class period each week was allotted for the students to work on their projects. Additionally, the students were required to attend two hours of office hours with their partners each week, where they also worked on their projects. During these regular meeting times, the pairs gelled or bonded and were much more likely to establish additional meeting times to complete their work.

The pairs passed significantly more of the automated post-development test cases run by an impartial teaching assistant (see Table 17-1). On average, students who worked in pairs passed 15% more of the instructor's test cases. This quality difference was statistically significant at p < .01.

TABLE 17-1. University of Utah pair programming comparison

	Test cases passed by solo students	Test cases passed by paired students
Program 1	73.4%	86.4%
Program 2	78.1%	88.6%
Program 3	70.4%	87.1%
Program 4	78.1%	94.4%

The results also indicated that on average the pairs spent 15% more programmer-hours than the individuals to complete their projects. For example, if one individual spent 10 hours on an assignment, each partner in the pair would spend approximately 5 hours and 45 minutes, on average. The median time spent was essentially equal for the two groups, and the average difference was not statistically significant. Even with a 15% increase in programmer time, the improved quality makes pair programming an economically-viable software development practice [Erdogmus and Williams 2003]. The University of Utah study was conducted over a 16-week semester with advanced undergraduates with industry experience. However, these empirical results may be applicable only in an academic setting.

Between the use of the practice in XP and the results of the University of Utah study that indicated the benefits of pair programming without doubling resources, pair programming began to be used more prevalently in industry and education. The next two sections outline the use of pair programming in each of these environments.

Pair Programming in an Industrial Setting

This section outlines some of the pair programming practices that have been demonstrated in industrial organizations and the results cited for these practices.

Industry Practices in Pair Programming

Industrial teams have reported their experiences with sustained use of pair programming. Developers often require several days (approximately 8–12 hours) to become familiar and comfortable with the dynamics and practices of pair programming when transitioning from solo programming [Vanhanen and Korpi 2007]. In the University of Utah study referenced in the previous section, the students were acclimated to pair programming after the first program, which took approximately 8–10 hours to complete. Often programmers do not work in pairs for the full work day; a suitable length of time for pairs to work together is between 1.5 and 4 hours [Vanhanen and Lassenius 2007]. Extended pair programming sessions can be difficult for developers because pairing can be mentally exhausting [Vanhanen and Lassenius 2007], [Williams and Kessler 2003], due to the rapid pace a pair can work at and the constant focus on the task at hand.

In industry teams, pair rotation is a common practice to keep the pairs dynamic, rather than having assigned pairing partners for days or weeks at a time. Many teams rotate pairs several times per day [Belshee 2005] or once per day [Frever and Ingalls 2006]. Frequent pair rotation is beneficial for knowledge transfer among the team [Vanhanen and Korpi 2007]. Additionally, pair rotations aid in indoctrinating and training new team members, as empirically demonstrated at Menlo Innovations, Microsoft, Motorola, Silver Platter Software, and a large Italian manufacturer* [Belshee 2005], [Fronza et al. 2009], [Lacey 2006], [Williams et al. 2004b]. Deciding whom to pair with is usually done casually and without difficulty [Chong and Hurlbutt 2007], [Vanhanen and Korpi 2007], often during a short daily meeting, such as a "stand up meeting" or Daily Scrum meeting (Scrum is an Agile software development methodology) [Schwaber and Beedle 2002], in which daily activities and current challenges are discussed.

Rotating the roles of driver and navigator is considered important for keeping both software engineers engaged [Vanhanen and Korpi 2007], [Williams and Kessler 2003]. However, in a four-month ethnographic study, Chong and Hurlbutt did not observe driver/navigator roles in the pairs on two professional software development teams practicing pair programming [Chong and Hurlbutt 2007]. Rather, when the programmers had equivalent expertise, they engaged jointly in discussion and brainstorming. In this case, the driver mainly served the role of typist. When the programmers had different levels of expertise, the software engineer with more expertise dominated the interaction.

Chong and Hurlbutt also noted that possession of the keyboard had a subtle but consistent effect on decision making, with the driver often being the final decision maker. They noted that the keyboard is often passed back and forth pervasively, and that engineers were most effective when they jointly took on the roles of driver and navigator. Engineers seemed more engaged when they were in possession of the keyboard or perceived keyboard control was imminent. As a result, they advocate the use of dual keyboards and mice. Analyses performed by Höfer [Höfer 2008] and Freudenberg et al. [Freudenberg et al. 2007] support the findings of Chong and Hurlbutt.

Development teams at IBM and Guidant were given the choice of using pair programming or having their code inspected. When given this choice, some teams increased the use of pair programming from 5% to 50% of the time [Williams et al. 2004a] at IBM to essentially all the time [Pandey et al. 2003] at Guidant.

Often software engineers feel pair programming should be saved for specification, design, and more complex programming tasks [Dybå et al. 2007], [Hulkko and Abrahamsson 2005], [Luck 2004], [Vanhanen and Korpi 2007], [Vanhanen and Lassenius 2007], [Vanhanen et al. 2007]. One large experiment of 295 consultants demonstrated a quality improvement with pairs on complex tasks but no quality improvement on simpler tasks [Arisholm et al. 2007].

* The manufacturer wishes to remain anonymous.

Teams have been more successful when having a structured, organized approach to pair programming, such as proclaimed pair programming hours or having pairs assigned daily in a meeting, rather than voluntary and unstructured use. In one organization [Vanhanen et al. 2007], a survey indicated positive feelings toward pair programming and a desire to do more pair programming. However, these engineers cited the reasons for not pair programming more as difficulties in organization, such as in finding common time, lack of encouragement from team leaders, and not considering pair programming in project planning.

Professional pair programmers have been shown to have more communication-intensive collaboration when they have different personality types based upon the Big Five Personality Index [Walle and Hannay 2009], though these differences do not seem to impact the performance of the pairs [Hannay et al. 2010]. (For more information on the Big Five Personality Index, see Chapter 6.) Microsoft software engineers, however, perceive that personality clashes can disrupt productivity among pairs [Begel and Nagappan 2008]. These same Microsoft software engineers felt pair programming works best when each in the pair has complementary skills.

Finally, pair programmers have found it beneficial to have larger desks, larger screens, wireless mice and keyboards, and whiteboards on the walls. Noise from a pair can disturb others who work alone. A room or area set aside for pair programming can help mitigate this problem [Vanhanen et al. 2007].

Results of Using Pair Programming in Industry

The teams who have reported sustained use of pair programming have provided insight into the results of the use of the practice. Many teams report improved product quality [Begel and Nagappan 2008], [Dybå et al. 2007], [Jensen 2003], [Luck 2004], [Vanhanen and Korpi 2007] when using pair programming. Specifically, one large telecommunications company in Finland whose software engineers almost exclusively worked in pairs had only five field failures in one and a half years of production [Vanhanen and Korpi 2007], though no baseline comparison data was available. A different controlled case study in Finland [Hulkko and Abrahamsson 2005] demonstrated equal defect density for paired/solo developers for one project and a six-fold reduction for paired developers on another project.

Teams can be motivated to institute pair programming because of the positive effect of improved knowledge sharing [Begel and Nagappan 2008], [Luck 2004], including that of the development environment [Begel and Nagappan 2008], [Vanhanen and Korpi 2007], [Vanhanen and Lassenius 2007]. If only one person understands an area of code, the team can suffer if this person leaves the team or is unavailable due to sickness or vacation. When more than one person is at least casually familiar with each area of the code, risk is reduced for the team.

Teams find code written by a pair to be more understandable [Vanhanen and Korpi 2007], [Vanhanen and Lassenius 2007]. Code is written by a driver to be understandable by the navigator, motivating the driver to be clearer. Alternatively, if the driver does not understand the code, the navigator will stop the driver to ask for clarification, which may prompt the driver to rewrite the code more simply.

An initial decline in productivity is sometimes observed when engineers start to pair program [Arisholm et al. 2007], [Nosek 1998]. With sustained use of pair programming on one development team, pair programming was considered to have a positive effect on productivity when the software engineers worked on complex tasks [Vanhanen and Korpi 2007]. They surmise that other studies that showed a productivity decline [Nawrocki and Wojciechowski 2001], [Nosek 1998], [Williams 2000] were because these studies examined individual tasks or small projects. Another team perceived they had a small decline in productivity [Vanhanen and Lassenius 2007], as has been observed by earlier studies [Nawrocki and Wojciechowski 2001], [Nosek 1998], [Williams 2000]. A controlled case study of four teams in Finland [Hulkko and Abrahamsson 2005] did not demonstrate any patterns of higher or lower productivity by solo or pair programmers. In general, these studies used a "lines of code per person month" measure of productivity, which is often acknowledged to be an imprecise measure.

Teams report the use of pair programming contributed to their team morale. They also report that the use of pair programming increases discipline in the use of other prescribed practices, such as test-driven development, the use of coding standards, and frequent integration [Vanhanen and Korpi 2007], [Vanhanen and Lassenius 2007].

A structured experiment of eight professional software developers in Thailand was conducted to compare the use of Fagan inspections with pair programming [Fagan 1986]. Product development took 4% more time for the pairs, but the pairs produced a product with 39% fewer defects in user acceptance testing [Phongpaibul and Boehm 2006].

Pair Programming in an Educational Setting

For the most part, students do pair programming in much the same way as do practitioners. In this section, we discuss some pair programming practices specifically used with students and cite results of using pair programming in educational literature.

Practices Specific to Education

The teaching staff may allow the students to choose their partners [Cicirello 2009], [Jacobson and Schaefer 2008], or the teaching staff may proactively form student pairs that are most likely to work well together. Those that select pairs may use heuristics to guide them in forming pairs most likely to be effective. One study indicates that heterogeneous pairs formed of a male and a female had high quality and more creative solutions [Mujeeb-u-Rehman et al. 2005]. A study of 58 undergraduates indicates pairs work best if they rate themselves similarly when asked about their open-mindedness and level of responsibility [Chao and Atli 2006]. Another study of 54 undergraduates demonstrated a positive correlation between conscientiousness and assignment scores and between "openness to experience" and test performance based upon the Five Factor Model [Salleh et al. 2009].

A large empirical study of more than 1,350 students was conducted to examine factors the teaching staff can use to proactively form pairs that are most likely to be compatible [Williams et al. 2006]. The study indicated that most often (93% of pairs) students report being compatible with their partners. The results also indicated that the teaching staff can use one or more of the following criteria to form pairs that are more likely to be compatible:

- Pair students together who have a similar skill level, as measured by computer science and/or total grade point average (qualitative results by Toll et al. [Van Toll et al. 2007]; Grant Braught et al. [Grant Braught and Wahls 2010]; and Sennett and Sherriff also support having students of similar skill level [Sennett and Sherriff 2010]).
- Pair a Myers-Briggs sensor with a Myers-Briggs intuitor.
- Pair students together who have a similar work ethic, determined by asking students to provide a number from 1 to 9, where a 1 indicates the student works hard enough to just barely get by and a 9 indicates he works hard enough to get the best possible grade.

Pair rotation is done less frequently in an educational setting than in industry. Most often pairs stay together for the duration of an assignment (generally one to three weeks) [Srikanth et al. 2004]. Some educators prefer pairs to remain consistent for a whole semester [McDowell et al. 2002].

Results of Using Pair Programming in Education

Studies have shown that pair programming creates an environment conducive to more advanced active learning and social interaction, leading to students being less frustrated, more confident [Salleh et al. 2009], and more interested in IT [Berenson et al. 2005], [Layman 2006], [Layman et al. 2005], [Nagappan et al. 2003], [Slaten et al. 2005]. The benefits to pair programming contrast with the negative aspects of traditional solo programming pedagogies, which can leave students feeling isolated, frustrated, and unsure of their abilities. Pair programming encourages students to interact with peers in their classes and laboratories, thereby creating a more communal and supportive environment. Students of the current Millennial generation place particular value on collaborative environments [Oblinger 2003]. Furthermore, the collaboration inherent in pair programming exposes and reinforces students to the collaboration, teamwork, and communication skills required in industry. These benefits appear to help increase retention in computer science, particularly among women [Carver et al. 2007], [McDowell et al. 2003], [McDowell et al. 2006], [Williams et al. 2003]. In general, pair programming provides a way to mirror the "laboratory model" that is common practice in natural science fields such as chemistry or physics [Williams and Layman 2007].

Students who work in pairs tend to produce projects of higher quality and have higher course passing rates [Braught et al. 2008], [McDowell et al. 2006], [Mendes et al. 2006], [Williams et al. 2003], [Xu and Rajlich 2005], even when students pair program in a distributed manner (see the next section, "Distributed Pair Programming") [Hanks 2005]. Paired teams in the introductory class are successful in future classes that require solo programming [Jacobson and Schaefer 2008], [Williams et al. 2003]. A study of undergraduate students at Pace University found a positive correlation between out-of-class collaboration and student achievement based on student projects and examination grades [Joseph and Payne 2003]. In an experiment involving undergraduates at Dickinson College, a liberal arts college, students with lower SAT scores were able to achieve higher lab scores when using pair programming [Braught et al. 2008].

Pair programming also benefits the teaching staff. Less grading is required due to half the number of assignment submissions. A pair of students can oftentimes figure out the low-level technical or procedural questions that typically burden the teaching assistants in the laboratory [Hanks 2007], [Williams et al. 2002] and the instructor's office hours and email inbox. Finally, there are fewer "problem students" to deal with because the peer pressure involved in pair programming encourages all students to be active participants in the class. Students become concerned about jeopardizing their partner's grade and work harder on assignments, often getting started earlier than if they worked alone (though not all students report starting earlier [Simon and Hanks 2007]).

Alas, there are some costs to implementing pair programming. For students, there are two major costs that persist without apparent recourse. A small segment of students (approximately 5%) will always desire to work alone [Williams et al. 2006]. Most often, these are the top students who do not want to be "slowed down" by another student and who do not see the benefit in teaching others. Another problem for students is the need to coordinate schedules when pair programming is required outside of a classroom or laboratory setting.

Distributed Pair Programming

Distributed software development is becoming common practice in industry. In education, students may also prefer to work from their dorm rooms or homes, rather than going to the lab to work with their partners. Furthermore, students enrolled in distance education courses may never be able to meet each other face-to-face. These distributed workers can practice pair programming through the Internet using a variety of tools. In the simplest of cases, programmers can use VNC[†] or Windows Meeting Space[‡] (previously Net Meeting) to share desktops. These tools broadcast the display of the output of any application from a member to all the others, requiring sufficient bandwidth, trust, and security between the parties. Other

---

† *http://www.realvnc.com/*

‡ *http://www.microsoft.com/windows/products/windowsvista/features/details/meetingspace.mspx*

tools, such as Sangam [Ho et al. 2004], xpairtise§, COPPER [Natsu et al. 2003], or Facetop [Navoraphan et al. 2006] have been designed to transmit only those messages that are important for pair programming, such as the latest change made by the driver.

Distributed cognition expert Nick Flor stresses the importance of distributed pair programming systems to support cross-workspace visual, manual, and audio channels [Flor 2006]. These channels allow pairs to collaborate and provide subtle yet significant catalysts for ongoing knowledge-sharing and helping activities. For example, subtle gestures such as a shake of the head or a mumble can be the catalyst for an exchange between the pair. Transparent images of the partner shown in the screen by Facetop [Navoraphan et al. 2006] can aid in the transmission of these channels. Additionally, Chong and Hurlbutt [Chong and Hurlbutt 2007] discourage tools that have defined driver/navigator roles, such as Sangam [Devide et al. 2008], [Ho et al. 2004], because they inhibit the behaviors of more effective pair programmers who share the driver/navigator role throughout the session.

Some studies of distributed pair programming have been done with students at both North Carolina State University and the University of North Carolina at Chapel Hill [Baheti et al. 2002a], [Baheti et al. 2002b]. These studies indicated that pairing over the Internet shows a great deal of potential when compared with distributed nonpaired teams in which programmers work alone and code is integrated later. In these studies, the students used desktop-sharing software, NetMeeting, and Yahoo! Messenger/headsets/microphones to communicate. A survey was conducted of undergraduate informatics students in introductory computer science classes at Indiana University Bloomington who used the Adobe Connect Now web conferencing software for distributed pair programming [Edwards et al. 2010]. The results indicated that students viewed pair programming positively in general, but viewed distributed pair programming significantly less favorably.

Challenges

The results discussed previously indicate that teams benefit in a range of ways when using the pair programming practice. However, several challenges prevent widespread adoption of pair programming. Four of these challenges are now presented. In this section, we also suggest how these challenges can be overcome.

Bias/habit

Software engineers can be conditioned to work alone, particularly those who were not educated using the pair programming practice. As a result, many can be concerned that they will not be able to concentrate when working with others, that they may be "wasting their time" with slower programmers, that they will feel inadequate compared to their peers, and other concerns. However, of those who try the practice, more than 90% prefer pair programming over solo programming [Succi et al. 2002], [Williams et al. 2000].

§ *http://xpairtise.sourceforge.net/*

Because most engineers eventually learn to like the practice, a strategy for overcoming this challenge is to institute pair programming as a nonthreatening pilot with a small number of engineers. These engineers are likely to find the practice beneficial and will be more likely to ask a colleague for a spontaneous pair programming session when facing a challenging programming task.

Economics

Despite research results to the contrary, software organizations can be concerned that pair programming will double software development cost, as two programmers are working on one task [Begel and Nagappan 2008]. A manager at Microsoft was quoted as saying, "[I]f I have a choice, I can employ one star programmer instead of two programmers who need to code in a pair" [Begel and Nagappan 2008]. The management should be enlightened with the research and experiential results of the use of pair programming. The practice can be started on a small scale, which would cause only a minimal economic risk. The management can gain firsthand understanding that the practice does not cause an increase in product life cycle costs, particularly when the benefits of improved quality are considered.

Coordination

When engineers on a team practice pair programming, the team must decide who works with whom each day and must coordinate schedules [Begel and Nagappan 2008]. Additionally, the team may need to choose which hours of the day are considered pair programming hours, during which no meetings would take place. An ideal time to determine the composition of the pairs is during a daily 10–15 minute Scrum [Schwaber and Beedle 2002] meeting. During the Scrum meeting, engineers talk about their obstacles and the tasks that they will do each day. During this meeting, pairs can be dynamically assigned based upon the tasks of the day and their current challenges.

Distributed teams

Some teams may feel they cannot pair program because their team members are not all physically co-located. As discussed in the previous section, distributed pair programming has been shown to be a viable and beneficial practice.

Lessons Learned

Industrial teams that have used pair programming have realized the many benefits from the practice, including higher product quality, improved cycle time, enhanced learning, reduced product risk due to improved knowledge management, and enhanced team spirit. Despite these benefits, overall adoption of pair programming in industry is relatively slow, primarily for the reasons discussed in the previous section, "Challenges." A small percentage of industrial organizations are professed pair programming shops whereby programmers who interview for employment at these organizations know about the use of the practice. In many other organizations, pair programming is often done spontaneously when a team member faces a challenge and/or complex task or as part of training a new employee.

Students realize the same benefits as industrial teams, but research results have shown additional benefits in academic settings: retention in an information technology field of study; reduced frustration in completing course work; and increased satisfaction with getting to know their classmates. Many instructors around the world have realized these pedagogical benefits as well as an easing of their own workloads due to reduced grading and the reduced burden of answering all of the students' technical questions. As a result, pair programming will likely become more and more common in education. Students will graduate with pair programming as a more natural practice. Consequently, the use of pair programming is likely to increase in industry in the coming years.

Acknowledgments

Some of this material is based upon the work supported by the National Science Foundation under Grants ITWF 00305917 and BPC 0540523. Any opinions, findings, and conclusions or recommendations expressed in this material are those of the authors and do not necessarily reflect the views of the National Science Foundation.

References

[Arisholm et al. 2007] Arisholm, E., H. Gallis, T. Dybå, and D. Sjøberg. 2007. Evaluating Pair Programming with Respect to System Complexity and Programmer Expertise. *IEEE Transactions in Software Engineering* 33(2): 65–86.

[Baheti et al. 2002a] Baheti, P., E. Gehringer, and D. Stotts. 2002. Exploring the Efficacy of Distributed Pair Programming. In *Lecture Notes in Computer Science, volume 2418: Extreme Programming and Agile Methods – XP/Agile Universe 2002*, ed. D. Wells and L. Williams, 208–220. Berlin: Springer-Verlag.

[Baheti et al. 2002b] Baheti, P., L. Williams, E. Gehringer, and D. Stotts. 2002. Exploring Pair Programming in Distributed Object-Oriented Team Projects. Paper presented at the 11th OOPSLA Educators' Symposium, November 4–8, in Seattle, WA.

[Beck 2005] Beck, K. 2005. *Extreme Programming Explained: Embrace Change*, Second Edition. Reading, MA: Addison-Wesley.

[Begel and Nagappan 2008] Begel, A., and N. Nagappan. 2008. Pair programming: What's in it for me? *Proceedings of the ACM-IEEE international symposium on empirical software engineering and measurement*: 120–128.

[Belshee 2005] Belshee, A. 2005. Promiscuous pairing and beginner's mind: embrace inexperience. *Proceedings of the Agile Development Conference*: 125–131.

[Berenson et al. 2005] Berenson, S.B., L. Williams, and K.M. Slaten. 2005. Using Pair Programming and Agile Development Methods in a University Software Engineering Course to Develop a Model of Social Interactions. Paper presented at Crossing Cultures, Changing Lives Conference, July 31–August 3, in Oxford, UK.

[Braught et al. 2008] Braught, G., L.M. Eby, and T. Wahls. 2008. The effects of pair-programming on individual programming skill. *Proceedings of the 39th SIGCSE technical symposium on computer science education*: 200–204.

[Brooks 1975] Brooks, F.P. 1975. *Mythical Man-Month: Essays on Software Engineering*. Reading, MA: Addison-Wesley.

[Carver et al. 2007] Carver, J., L. Henderson, L. He, J. Hodges, and D. Reese. 2007. Increased Retention of Early Computer Science and Software Engineering Students Using Pair Programming. *Proceedings of the 20th Conference on Software Engineering Education and Training*: 115–122.

[Chao and Atli 2006] Chao, J., and G. Atli. 2006. Critical personality traits in successful pair programming. *Proceedings of the conference on AGILE 2006*: 89–93.

[Chong and Hurlbutt 2007] Chong, J and T. Hurlbutt. 2007. The Social Dynamics of Pair Programming. *Proceedings of the 29th International Conference on Software Engineering*: 354–363.

[Cicirello 2009] Cicirello, V.A. 2009. On self-selected pairing in CS1: who pairs with whom? *Journal of Computing Sciences in Colleges* 24(6): 43–49.

[Constantine 1995] Constantine, L.L. 1995. *Constantine on Peopleware*. Englewood Cliffs, NJ: Yourdon Press.

[Coplien 1995] Coplien, J.O. 1995. A Development Process Generative Pattern Language. In *Pattern Languages of Program Design*, ed. James O. Coplien and Douglas C. Schmidt, 183–237. Reading, MA: Addison-Wesley.

[Coplien and Harrison 2005] Coplien, J.O., and N.B. Harrison. 2005. *Organizational Patterns of Agile Software Development*. Upper Saddle River, NJ: Pearson Prentice-Hall.

[Devide et al. 2008] Devide, J.V.S., A. Meneely, C.-W. Ho, L. Williams, and M. Devetsikiotis. 2008. Jazz Sangam: A Real-Time Tool for Distributed Pair Programming on a Team Development Platform. Paper presented at the First International Workshop on Infrastructure for Research in Collaborative Software Engineering, November 9, in Atlanta, GA.

[Dybå et al. 2007] Dybå, T., E. Arisholm, D. Sjøberg, J. Hannay, and F. Shull. 2007. Are Two Heads Better Than One? On the Effectiveness of Pair Programming. *IEEE Software* 24(6): 12–15.

[Edwards et al. 2010] Edwards, R.L., J.K. Stewart, and M. Ferati. 2010. Assessing the effectiveness of distributed pair programming for an online informatics curriculum. *Inroads* 1(1): 48–54.

[Erdogmus and Williams 2003] Erdogmus, H., and L. Williams. 2003. The Economics of Software Development by Pair Programmers. *The Engineering Economist* 48(4): 283–319.

[Fagan 1986] Fagan, M.E. 1986. Advances in Software Inspection. *IEEE Transactions on Software Engineering* 12(7): 744–751.

[Flor 2006] Flor, N. 2006. Globally Distributed Software Development and Pair Programming. *Communications of the ACM* 49(10): 57–58.

[Freudenberg et al. 2007] Freudenberg, S., P. Romero, and B. du Boulay. 2007. "Talking the talk": Is intermediate-level conversation the key to the pair programming success story? *Proceedings of AGILE 2007*: 84–91.

[Frever and Ingalls 2006] Frever, T., and P. Ingalls. 2006. The pairing session as the atomic unit of work. *Proceedings of the Conference on AGILE 2006*: 165–169.

[Fronza et al. 2009] Fronza, I., A. Sillitti, and G. Succi. 2009. An interpretation of the results of the analysis of pair programming during novices integration in a team. *Proceedings of the 3rd International Symposium on Empirical Software Engineering and Measurement*: 225–235.

[Grant Braught and Wahls 2010] Grant Braught, J.M. and Tim Wahls. 2010. The benefits of pairing by ability. *Proceedings of the 41st ACM technical symposium on computer science education*: 249–253.

[Hanks 2005] Hanks, B. 2005. Student Performance in CS1 with Distributed Pair Programming. *Proceedings of the 10th Annual SIGCSE Conference on Innovation and Technology in Computer Science Education*: 316–320.

[Hanks 2007] Hanks, B. 2007. Problems Encountered by Novice Pair Programmers. *Proceedings of the Third International Workshop on Computing Education Research*: 159–164.

[Hannay et al. 2010] Hannay, J.E., E. Arisholm, H. Engvik, and D.I.K. Sjøberg. 2010. Effects of Personality on Pair Programming. *IEEE Transactions on Software Engineering* 36(1): 61–80.

[Ho et al. 2004] Ho, C-w., S. Raha, E. Gehringer, and L. Williams. 2004. Sangam: A Distributed Pair Programming Plug-in for Eclipse. *Proceedings of the 2004 OOPSLA workshop on Eclipse technology eXchange*: 73–77.

[Höfer 2008] Höfer, A. 2008. Video Analysis of Pair Programming. *Proceedings of the 2008 International Workshop on Scrutinizing Agile Practices*:37–41.

[Hulkko and Abrahamsson 2005] Hulkko, H., and P. Abrahamsson. 2005. A Multiple Case Study on the Impact of Pair Programming on Product Quality. *Proceedings of the 27th International Conference on Software Engineering*: 495–504.

[Jacobson and Schaefer 2008] Jacobson, N., and S.K. Schaefer. 2008. Pair programming in CS1: overcoming objections to its adoption. *SIGCSE Bulletin* 40(2): 93–96.

[Jensen 2003] Jensen, R. 2003. A Pair Programming Experience. *CrossTalk* 16(3): 22–24.

[Joseph and Payne 2003] Joseph, A., and M. Payne. 2003. Group Dynamics and Collaborative Group Performance. *Proceedings of the 34th SIGCSE Technical Symposium on Computer Science Education*: 368–371.

[Lacey 2006] Lacey, M. 2006. Adventures in Promiscuous Pairing: Seeking Beginner's Mind. *Proceedings of the conference on AGILE 2006*: 263–269.

[Layman 2006] Layman, L. 2006. Changing Students' Perceptions: An Analysis of the Supplementary Benefits of Collaborative Software Development. *Proceedings of the 19th Conference on Software Engineering Education and Training*: 156–166.

[Layman et al. 2005] Layman, L., L. Williams, J. Osborne, S. Berenson, K. Slaten, and M. Vouk. 2005. How and Why Collaborative Software Development Impacts the Software Engineering Course. *Proceedings of the 35th Annual Conference on Frontiers in Education*: T4C 9–14.

[Luck 2004] Luck, G. 2004. Subclassing XP: Breaking its rules the right way. *Proceedings of the Agile Development Conference 2004*: 114–119.

[McDowell et al. 2002] McDowell, C., L. Werner, H. Bullock, and J. Fernald. 2002. The Effects of Pair Programming on Performance in an Introductory Programming Course. *Proceedings of the 33rd SIGCSE technical symposium on computer science education*: 38–42.

[McDowell et al. 2003] McDowell, C., L. Werner, H. Bullock, and J. Fernald. 2003. The Impact of Pair Programming on Student Performance, Perception, and Persistence. *Proceedings of the 25th International Conference on Software Engineering*: 602–607.

[McDowell et al. 2006] McDowell, C., L. Werner, H. Bullock, and J. Fernald. 2006. Pair Programming Improves Student Retention, Confidence, and Program Quality. *Communications of the ACM* 49(8): 90–95.

[Mendes et al. 2006] Mendes, E., L. Al-Fakhri, and A. Luxton-Reilly. 2006. A Replicated Experiment of Pair Programming in a 2nd Year Software Development and Design Computer Science Course. *Proceedings of the 11th Annual SIGCSE Conference on Innovation and Technology in Computer Science Education*: 108–112.

[Mujeeb-u-Rehman et al. 2005] Mujeeb-u-Rehman, M., X. Yang, J. Dong, and M. Abdul Ghafoor. 2005. Heterogeneous and homogenous pairs in pair programming: an empirical analysis. *Proceedings of the Canadian Conference on Electrical and Computer Engineering 2005*: 1116–1119.

[Nagappan et al. 2003] Nagappan, N., L. Williams, M. Ferzli, K. Yang, E. Wiebe, C. Miller, and S. Balik. 2003. Improving the CS1 Experience with Pair Programming. *Proceedings of the 34th SIGCSE technical symposium on computer science education*: 359–362.

[Natsu et al. 2003] Natsu, H., J. Favela, A. Morán, D. Decouchant, and A. Martinez-Enriquez. 2003. Distributed Pair Programming on the Web. *Proceedings of the 4th Mexican International Conference on Computer Science*: 81–88.

[Navoraphan et al. 2006] Navoraphan, K., E. F. Gehringer, J. Culp, K. Gyllstrom, and D. Stotts. 2006. Next-generation DPP with Sangam and Facetop. Proceedings of the 2006 *OOPSLA workshop on Eclipse technology eXchange*: 6–10.

[Nawrocki and Wojciechowski 2001] Nawrocki, J., and A. Wojciechowski. 2001. Experimental Evaluation of Pair Programming. *Proceedings of the 12th European Software Control and Metrics Conference*: 269–276.

[Nosek 1998] Nosek, J.T. 1998. The Case for Collaborative Programming. *Communications of the ACM* 41(3): 105–108.

[Oblinger 2003] Oblinger, D. 2003. Boomers, Gen-Xers, and Millennials: Understanding the New Students. *Educause Review* 38(4): 37–47.

[Pandey et al. 2003] Pandey, A., C. Miklos, M. Paul, N. Kameli, F. Boudigou, V. Vijay, A. Eapen, I. Sutedjo, and W. Mcdermott. 2003. Application of tightly coupled engineering team for development of test automation software—a real world experience. *Proceedings of the 27th Annual International Computer Software and Applications Conference*: 56–63.

[Phongpaibul and Boehm 2006] Phongpaibul, M., and B. Boehm. 2006. An Empirical Comparison Between Pair Development and Software Inspection in Thailand. *Proceedings of the 2006 ACM/IEEE International Symposium on Empirical Software Engineering*: 85–94.

[Salleh et al. 2009] Salleh, N., E. Mendes, J. Grundy, and G.S.J. Burch. 2009. An empirical study of the effects of personality in pair programming using the five-factor model. *Proceedings of the 2009 3rd International Symposium on Empirical Software Engineering and Measurement*: 214–225.

[Schwaber and Beedle 2002] Schwaber, K., and M. Beedle. 2002. *Agile Software Development with SCRUM*. Upper Saddle River, NJ: Prentice-Hall.

[Sennett and Sherriff 2010] Sennett, J., and M. Sherriff. 2010. Compatibility of Partnered Students in Computer Science Education. *41st ACM Technical Symposium on Computer Science Education (SIGCSE)*: 244-248.

[Simon and Hanks 2007] Simon, B., and B. Hanks. 2007. First Year Students' Impressions of Pair Programming in CS1. *Proceedings of the Third International Workshop on Computing Education Research*: 73–86.

[Slaten et al. 2005] Slaten, K.M., M. Droujkova, S. Berenson, L. Williams, and L. Layman. 2005. Undergraduate Student Perceptions of Pair Programming and Agile Software Methodologies: Verifying a Model of Social Interaction. *Proceedings of the Agile Conference 2005*: 323–330.

[Srikanth et al. 2004] Srikanth, H., L. Williams, E. Wiebe, C. Miller, and S. Balik. 2004. On Pair Rotation in the Computer Science Course. *Proceedings of the 17th Conference on Software Engineering Education and Training*: 144–149.

[Succi et al. 2002] Succi, G., M. Marchesi, W. Pedrycz, and L. Williams. 2002. Preliminary analysis of the effects of pair programming on job satisfaction. *Proceedings of the Fourth International Conference on eXtreme Programming and Agile Processes in Software*: 212–215.

[Van Toll et al. 2007] Van Toll, T., III, T., R. Lee, and T. Ahlswede. 2007. Evaluating the Usefulness of Pair Programming in a Classroom Setting. *Proceedings of the 6th IEEE/ACIS International Conference on Computer and Information Science (ICIS) 2007*: 302–308.

[Vanhanen and Korpi 2007] Vanhanen, J., and H. Korpi. 2007. Experiences of Using Pair Programming in an Agile Project. *Proceedings of the 40th Annual Hawaii International Conference on System Sciences (HICSS) 2007*: 274b.

[Vanhanen and Lassenius 2007] Vanhanen, J., and C. Lassenius. 2007. Perceived Effects of Pair Programming in an Industrial Context. *Proceedings of the 33rd EUROMICRO Conference on Software Engineering and Advanced Applications*: 211–218.

[Vanhanen et al. 2007] Vanhanen, J., C. Lassenius, and M. Mäntylä. 2007. Issues and Tactics when Adopting Pair Programming: A Longitudinal Case Study. *Proceedings of the International Conference on Software Engineering Advances (ICSEA) 2007*: 70.

[Walle and Hannay 2009] Walle, T., and J.E. Hannay. 2009. Personality and the nature of collaboration in pair programming. *Proceedings of the 2009 3rd International Symposium on Empirical Software Engineering and Measurement*: 203–213.

[Williams 2000] Williams, L. A. 2000. The Collaborative Software Process. PhD diss., University of Utah.

[Williams and Kessler 2000] Williams, L. A. and R. R. Kessler. 2000. All I Ever Needed to Know About Pair Programming I Learned in Kindergarten. *Communications of the ACM*. 43(5): 108–114.

[Williams and Kessler 2003] Williams, L., and R. Kessler. 2003. *Pair Programming Illuminated*. Reading, MA: Addison-Wesley.

[Williams and Layman 2007] Williams, L,. and L. Layman. 2007. Lab Partners: If They're Good Enough for the Natural Sciences, Why Aren't They Good Enough for Us? *Proceedings of the 20th Conference on Software Engineering Education and Training*: 72–82.

[Williams et al. 2000] Williams, L., R. Kessler, W. Cunningham, and R. Jeffries. 2000. Strengthening the Case for Pair-Programming. *IEEE Software* 17(4):19–25.

[Williams et al. 2002] Williams, L., E. Wiebe, K. Yang, M. Ferzli, and C. Miller. 2002. In Support of Pair Programming in the Introductory Computer Science Course. *Computer Science Education* 12(3):197–212.

[Williams et al. 2003] Williams, L., C. McDowell, N. Nagappan, J. Fernald, and L. Werner. 2003. Building Pair Programming Knowledge Through a Family of Experiments. *Proceedings of the 2003 International Symposium on Empirical Software Engineering*: 143–152.

[Williams et al. 2004a] Williams, L., W. Krebs, L. Layman, A. Antón, and P. Abrahamsson. 2004. Toward a Framework for Evaluating Extreme Programming. *Proceedings of Empirical Assessment in Software Eng. (EASE) 2004*: 11–20.

[Williams et al. 2004b] Williams, L., A. Shukla, and A. Antón. 2004. An Initial Exploration of the Relationship Between Pair Programming and Brooks' Law. *Proceedings of the Agile Development Conference 2004*: 11–20.

[Williams et al. 2006] Williams, L., L. Layman, J. Osborne, and N. Katira. 2006. Examining the Compatibility of Student Pair Programmers. *Proceedings of the Conference on Agile 2006*: 411–420.

[Wray 2010] Wray, S. 2010. How Pair Programming Really Works. *IEEE Software* 27(1): 50–55.

[Xu and Rajlich 2005] Xu, S., and V. Rajlich. 2005. Pair Programming in Graduate Software Engineering Course Projects. *Proceedings of the 35th Annual Frontiers in Education Conference*: F1G7–F1G12.

## CHAPTER EIGHTEEN

Modern Code Review

Jason Cohen

Common Sense

Every page in this book has been checked over by an editor. Why?

Because even if you're the smartest, most capable, most experienced writer, you can't proofread your own work. You're too close to the concepts, and you've rolled the words around your head for so long you can't put yourself in the shoes of someone who is hearing them for the first time.

Writing code is no different. In fact, if it's impossible to write prose without independent scrutiny, surely it's also impossible to write code in isolation; code has to be correct to the minutest detail, *plus* it includes prose for humans as well! (You *do* write comments, don't you?)

It's common sense that two heads are better than one, especially when the second head is a domain expert or when the author is a junior developer who hasn't been around the block.

But it's not all rosy; it's also true that code review occupies expensive developer time. After all, four people in a meeting for 90 minutes is six on-task hours—an entire on-task person-day. That's a significant time investment, so we also have to ask whether the benefits outweigh the costs.

Fortunately, there's data. In the past 10 years we've made significant leaps in our knowledge of how to perform code reviews efficiently. Executed properly, code reviews find bugs faster than testing or other known debugging techniques—but when done inefficiently they can quickly become unproductive.

This survey will start by presenting findings that apply in any type of code review, from formal inspections to a single developer double-checking his own work. After establishing these fundamental best practices, we'll look at data from group reviews.

A Developer Does a Little Code Review

There are a million ways to do a code review, but there's one component that's common to all—a single developer critically examining code. So it makes sense to ask what the data tells us about developers diving into code by themselves, without distraction and without discussion.

What are the best practices during quiet contemplation?

Focus Fatigue

How much time should you spend on a code review in one sitting?

Figure 18-1 maps how efficient we are at finding defects over time [Dunsmore 2000]. The horizontal axis plots time passing; the vertical is the average number of defects a person found at this time index.

Looking early on in the code review, there's a clear linear relationship between time and defects: every 10 minutes another defect is found (on average). This is encouraging—the more time spent in the review, the more defects are found.

That's really efficient if you stop and think about it. What other software development processes do you know in which a new bug is found (and often fixed) every 10 minutes? Certainly not in the usual development/QA loop by the time you count the effort by both the tester and the developer.

But around the 60-minute mark, there's a sudden drop-off. Now another 10 minutes doesn't necessarily turn up another defect. The efficiency of finding defects drops sharply.

The usual theory explaining this effect is that around one hour we get mentally fatigued; it's just a long time to be concentrating on a technical task. But whatever the cause, it's clear that we shouldn't review code for more than an hour at a time.

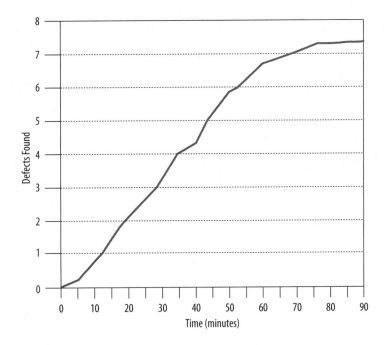

FIGURE 18-1. After 60–90 minutes, our ability to find defects drops off precipitously

Speed Kills

It's logical that the more time you spend on a piece of code, the deeper and more nuanced your analysis will be and the more bugs you'll find. It's similarly logical that if you race through a review, you'll find only the shallowest errors.

Where is the balance between spending enough time to root out important problems but not wasting time dwelling on decent code?

Figure 18-2 shows the effect of speed on ability to find defects in a study of 2,500 reviews [Cohen 2006].

On the horizontal axis we have the speed of the review measured in lines of code (LOC) per hour. The vertical axis shows defect density, which is the number of defects found per 1000 LOC (or kLOC). "Density" is used rather than "number of defects" because reviews with more lines of code will naturally have more defects, so this normalizes the results across reviews of different sizes.

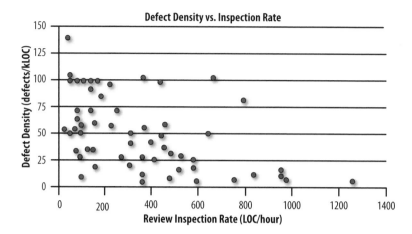

FIGURE 18-2. Defect detection drops at 400–500 lines of code per hour

Between zero and about 400 LOC/hour, you can see the defect density is evenly distributed between zero and 100 defects/kLOC. *This distribution is expected.* To see why, consider a review consisting of adding documentation to an interface. Three hundred lines of code might contain few or no defects—a low defect density. Now consider a review of brain-twisting, multithreaded, high-performance code in a core module that the entire application depends on. Perhaps just four lines of code were changed, but because of the complexity of the problem and the necessity of getting it right, several reviewers criticized the code and nitpicked the smallest of problems, and two defects were found—a high defect density.

In short, reviews will naturally have a range defect densities, so that spread is normal.

The problem comes with reviews faster than 400-500 LOC/hour. Suddenly we rarely see a review with a high defect density. Of course that's not because there are no defects, but because the reviewer is going too fast to find those defects.

Size Kills

Let's put the previous two results together. If we should spent at most one hour in review, and if we can review at most 400 LOC/hour, then we conclude that we shouldn't review more than 400 LOC at one time.

A sensible theory; let's put it to the test.

In Figure 18-3, we see how defect density is affected by the amount of code under review [Cohen 2006]. As in the last section, we expect to see a defect density spread between zero and 100 defects/kLOC, and we do see that with the smaller reviews. But as the review size increases, defect density drops off. As predicted, at around 300-500 LOC, it's clear that the reviews aren't being effective.

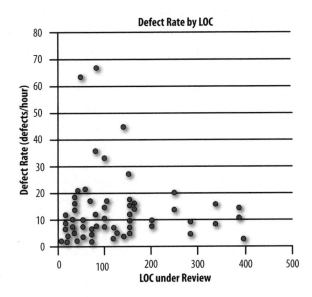

Defect Rate by LOC

FIGURE 18-3. As the size of the code under review increases, our ability to find all the defects decreases. Don't review more than 400 lines of code at a time.

The fact that this data matches the expected result so well lends credibility to all three results.

The Importance of Context

The typical version control "diff" utility displays modifications with only a few lines of surrounding context. Even more sophisticated tools typically display one file at a time.

Tools that limit your view result in similarly myopic code reviews. After all, you review what's put in front of you!

Upon reflection, this seems like a bad practice. Consider what happens when you're looking at a bug fix inside a single function. You inspect the change and see that it does fix the problem, but that's not the end of the story! The next question is: what other code depends on this function, and might depend on the original behavior? If there are side effects, what other code is affected by that? Are there accompanying unit tests? Did unit tests for completely different functions have to change because of this modification, and is that acceptable?

So how important is it to perform code reviews with additional files, classes, documentation, and other context, as opposed to just looking at the immediate changes? In an experiment, reviewers were given various amounts of "context"—files related to the change at hand [Dunsmore 2000]. With a simple, automated method for generating the list of "related files" based on methods called or called by the code in question, 15% more defects were found. When the automated process was replaced by a human being making a judgment call about what the right associated files were, a full 30% more defects were found.

This suggests that you shouldn't review snippets of code in isolation. At the very least you need to be in front of your IDE with the entire codebase at your fingertips. To the extent that the author of the code can highlight related code, that's probably a good use of time as well.

Group Dynamics

So far we've been considering a lone developer reviewing code in isolation, but that's almost never the entire process.

In fact, code review is one of the few activities developers do *together*. That in itself is an interesting argument for code review; everyone agrees that some level of interaction and collaboration is required to spread institutional knowledge, teach each other tricks, and solve particularly tricky problems.

Still, if wasting a single person's time is expensive, it's absolutely devastating to waste several people's time. So let's look at what the data tell us about how to ensure we're not flushing entire person-days down the toilet.

Are Meetings Required?

When you think of a "code review," you probably picture geeks huddled around a projector in a conference room criticizing a hapless developer as she walks through her code.

Besides putting the author in an unenviable position, this practice is also a potentially tremendous waste of time! Consider the traditional Formal Inspection, popularized by Michael Fagan [Fagan 1976], in which the focal point of the process is a two-hour meeting where four participants discuss the code.

Four people meeting for two hours is eight person-hours—an entire person-day of time! And that's not counting the overhead for scheduling a conference room and waiting for stragglers to show. There'd better be a large benefit in future time saved to justify such a process. Or ice cream.

In Fagan's theory the meeting is more than a convenience—it's an absolute requirement. His rationale is that when you have four people working together you can create "synergy" (his word), where the whole is more than the sum of the parts. It's almost as if there's a fifth person in the room, finding bugs that no one could find alone, a virtual person Fagan calls the "phantom inspector."

It's a colorful notion, but is it true? Unfortunately, Fagan didn't publish experiments testing this part of the theory; that would happen 17 years later [Votta 1993]. In 1993 Lawrence Votta measured the number of defects found *before* the meeting—when people went over the code themselves—and also the number of defects found *during* the meeting. His results are shown in Figure 18-4.

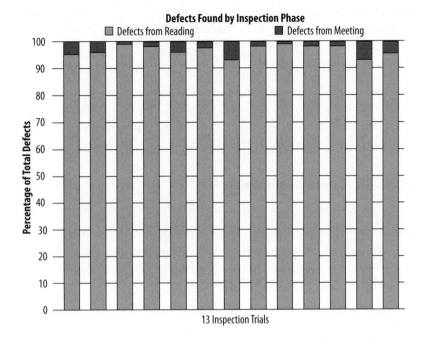

Defects Found by Inspection Phase

FIGURE 18-4. Votta demonstrated that inspection meetings contribute only an additional 4% to the number of defects already found by private code-readings

Of the defects found, 96% were identified just by looking at the code, not in the meeting. In retrospect this makes sense; the way you find subtle bugs is by spending alone-time with the code, not through a group walk-through where all your effort is spent just keeping up with the author as he explains each line.

To Fagan's credit, the defects found in meetings were generally more subtle, which means they would have taken significant effort to find and fix later on. Still, the massive time requirement implies that in-person meetings aren't worthwhile, except for the most vital source code.

False-Positives

Although meetings in general don't uncover enough new bugs to warrant the time, they do serve another useful purpose: they identify false positives where a reviewer thought there was a bug but there really wasn't. False-positives are an important drain on efficiency because they require developer time to fix and might create a true bug in the process.

In Votta's study [Votta 1993], 25% of the so-called defects identified before the meeting turned out not to be defects at all, but rather a misunderstanding by the reviewer. And it's not just Votta; other studies have shown false-positive rates between 15% and 30% [Conradi 2003] [Jazayeri 1997][Kelly et al. 2003].

The question is: What is the penalty for "fixing" these false-positives? And then, is this penalty greater than the time penalty incurred by the meeting?

Generally if one person was confused, someone else is likely to be confused as well. Therefore, even if the "fix" is just adding a comment, that's probably still a worthwhile use of time.

Finally, meeting together in the same room isn't the only way to identify false-positives! So long as the author and reviewers can communicate at all—through email, chat, or a tool—they can discuss questionable defects, and most false-positives can be dispensed with. The point is that the physicality and immediacy of the meeting room isn't necessary.

Are External Reviewers Required At All?

We've been assuming that two heads are better than one, but is that necessarily so?

Back to the analogy of editing your own writing, it's true that you can't see the errors on the screen, but if you print it out and view your text in a different medium, often the problems jump out. Or if you wait a week and come back to it, you can see a new problem. Could this apply to code reviews too?

This is a vital question because a self-check takes at most half the time of a code review involving another person.

A Cisco® study compared the results of 300 reviews where people reviewed their own work versus another 300 reviews where the author got a review without a self-check [Cohen 2006]. As demonstrated in Figure 18-5, self-check reviews had half the defect density of nonchecked reviews, indicating that people who double-check their work found half of the problems by themselves.

Whether a simple "self-check" *alone* is sufficient for your own process is a matter of opinion. After all, plenty of defects were still found by other reviewers. But one thing is clear: it's certainly an efficient use of time to self-check—and far better than nothing—since half the defects were found without any effort by external reviewers.

Conclusion

As with all processes in software development, the question isn't "is code review good or bad?" but rather: "When is code review useful, and when it is, what are the best practices?"

The studies given here address best-practices—preventing you from systematically and senselessly wasting time.

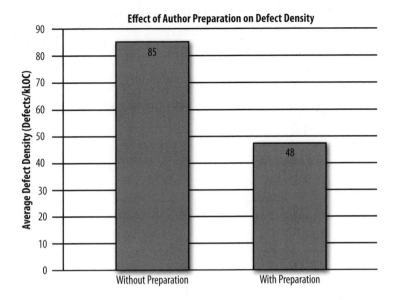

FIGURE 18-5. When authors proofed their own work, they found half of the defects that another reviewer would have found

References

[Cohen 2006] Cohen, Jason. 2006. *Best Kept Secrets of Peer Code Review.* Beverly, MA: SmartBear Software.

[Conradi 2003] Conradi, R., P. Mohagheghi, T. Arif, L. Hegde, G. Bunde, and A. Pedersen. 2003. Object-Oriented Reading Techniques for Inspection of UML Models—An Industrial Experiment. *European Conference on Object-Oriented Programming ECOOP'03*: 403–501.

[Dunsmore 2000] Dunsmore, A., M. Roper, and M. Wood. 2000. Object-Oriented Inspection in the Face of Delocalisation. *Proceedings of the 22nd International Conference on Software Engineering (ICSE) 2000*: 467–476.

[Fagan 1976] Fagan, M. 1976. Design and code inspections to reduce errors in program development. *IBM Systems Journal* 15(3): 182–211.

[Jazayeri 1997] Jazayeri, P., and H. Schauer. 1997. Validating the defect detection performance advantage of group designs for software reviews: report of a laboratory experiment using program code. *Proceedings of the 6th European Conference Held Jointly with the 5th ACM SIGSOFT International Symposium on Foundations of Software Engineering* (Zurich, Switzerland, September 22-25, 1997): 294–309.

[Kelly et al. 2003] Kelly, D., and T. Shepard. 2003. An experiment to investigate interacting versus nominal groups in software inspection. *Proceedings of the 2003 Conference of the Centre for Advanced Studies on Collaborative Research, IBM Centre for Advanced Studies Conference*: 122–134.

[Votta 1993] Votta, L. 1993. Does every inspection need a meeting? *Proceedings of the 1st ACM SIGSOFT Symposium on Foundations of Software Engineering, December 8-10*: 107–114.

## CHAPTER NINETEEN

A Communal Workshop or Doors That Close?

Jorge Aranda

This chapter deals with an apparently simple question: *what is the most convenient office space layout for collocated software teams?* Intuitively, we know that space and the distance and accessibility between members of a software team are factors that set the tone for their projects. Cubicle farms, telecommuting, shared rooms—these and other arrangements encourage some kinds of interactions and disable others, and in the extreme case, remotely distributed teams restrict team interaction almost exclusively down to electronic communication. But we know that even when team members live in the same city and work in the same building, their office layout has an effect on their performance. So, how important is office space layout, really? And what does our current evidence tell us about the best ways to design our working space?

Doors That Close

Let us begin with a straw man argument: money spent enhancing the workplace of software developers is money down the drain. Developers who insist on having individual offices with doors that close and phones that can be turned off are pampered *prima donnas* who can't ever be appeased. If you give each of them a nice office (and where will the space or the money for these offices even come from?), they'll start to complain about the kitchenette, or the lack of indoor bike parking, or the glare from the windows in their monitors. Inevitably they'll demand gourmet catering of organic, locally grown food, on-site massages, and ball pits, like those

Google folks. And even if developers don't go that far, individual offices are *expensive*, far more expensive than cubicles. Why should an organization choose to spend its money on perks with only marginal and dubious productivity gains—especially when most of its competitors aren't doing it?

As you may already know, there is a very important reason to do it. Anybody who has developed software knows how cognitively complex and demanding this work can be. Developers face problems so intricate and immaterial, and they struggle with so many implications and ramifications to their actions, that they often need to concentrate completely in their tasks, to the point where everything else becomes a blur, time drifts away, and their craft is all that matters. Csikszentmihalyi called that optimal state of deep concentration *flow*, an experience of full immersion, of harmony between one's actions, skills, and goals [Csikszentmihalyi 1990]. If you've heard about it, you've probably also heard that it takes time and effort to get into flow, that it is a relatively fragile state, and that it is extremely important for successful creative activities.

But if developers are constantly being distracted (by the conversation of the guys at the next cubicle, or a phone ringing, or the slurps and crunches and smells of someone having lunch nearby), they'll never get anything done—and they'll notice their failure, so they will not only achieve nothing, but they'll also come out frustrated and demoralized by their failure, leading to further failures down the road.

Unfortunately, flow is elusive for software developers in typical settings. We know this because many studies have reported that developers are routinely bombarded with interruptions. One of my favorite studies on this topic was executed by Andrew Ko, Rob DeLine, and Gina Venolia.* They observed developers over periods of up to 90 minutes, paying particular attention to circumstances where they had to stop what they were doing, either because they were interrupted by their colleagues or because they were blocked by a missing piece of information—and perhaps decided to interrupt their colleagues to get it [Ko et al. 2007].

The researchers found that, for these developers, work was extremely fragmented. They were constantly being interrupted, and they constantly interrupted others to find the piece of information that was blocking them. They were distracted by email, instant messaging, and people visiting their offices. The findings are even more troubling when we consider that these observations come from Microsoft, a company that prides itself on providing each of its developers with private, quiet space. An average software organization with cubicle farms or team rooms is likely to fare even worse in this sense.

---

* Disclosure: For one summer I was a research intern at Microsoft Research, working on Rob DeLine's Human Interactions of Programming group with Gina Venolia.

These considerations lead us to design an office space layout that maximizes the ability of developers to isolate themselves if needed, under the reasoning that isolation leads to less interruptions and more and deeper concentration, which in turn should lead to greater efficiency and product quality. What are the characteristics of such an office space? First, every developer should be guaranteed a private office, even if it is relatively small, with a door that closes. Of course, they should be able to mute their phones, and they should not be expected to be online and available constantly throughout working hours; they'll deal with their interruptions on their terms when they emerge from the flow. When team interaction is necessary, developers should be able to use shared spaces, such as meeting rooms, and they should also have access to recreational space to socialize and recharge for their next bouts of concentration. This maximizes the ability to concentrate deeply through isolation, bringing benefits such as greater productivity, better product quality, and higher team morale.

The theory makes sense, but is there any evidence that verifies it? As it happens, there is: such evidence is one of the central aspects of one of the most famous and celebrated books about software development, *Peopleware*, by Tom DeMarco and Tim Lister.

In their book, DeMarco and Lister explain that for several years they had been running a competition among software developers, implementing "a series of benchmark coding and testing tasks in minimal time and with minimal defects." They called these competitions Coding War Games. Participants record their time spent on a time log, and after they declare they are finished, their products are subjected to a standard acceptance test. Developers work "in their own work areas during normal work hours using the same languages, tools, terminals, and computers that they use for any other project."

DeMarco and Lister discovered that there was "a huge difference between competing individuals," and they found three rules of thumb that "seem to apply whenever you measure variations in performance" [DeMarco and Lister 1999]. They are:

- Count on the best people outperforming the worst by about 10:1.
- Count on the best performer being about 2.5 times better than the median performer.
- Count on the half who are better-than-median performers outdoing the other half by more than 2:1.

More importantly, DeMarco and Lister found that the best performers could not be predicted based on programming language, years of experience, salary, or number of defects submitted. The one strong predicting factor was where you worked: high-performance competitors often came from the same companies, and their companies had better environmental factors than those of low-performance competitors. They summarized these results in a table, reprinted here as Table 19-1.

TABLE 19-1. Environments of the best and worst performers in the Coding War Games

Environmental factor	Those who performed in the 1st quartile	Those who performed in the 4th quartile
How much dedicated workspace do you have?	78 sq. ft.	46 sq. ft.
Is it acceptably quiet?	57% yes	29% yes
Is it acceptably private?	62% yes	19% yes
Can you silence your phone?	52% yes	10% yes
Can you divert your calls?	76% yes	19% yes
Do people often interrupt you needlessly?	38% yes	76% yes

De Marco and Lister accept that these amazing results are only evidence of correlation, not of causation. As they put it: "The data presented [here] does not exactly prove that a better workplace will help people to perform better. It may only indicate that people who perform better tend to gravitate toward organizations that provide a better workplace. Does that really matter to you?"

The evidence for having private offices with doors that close and an environment as free of interruptions as possible is very compelling, and the extra cost in space is more than compensated by the resulting productivity gains. But the story is not over yet; there is a twist that leads us in an entirely different direction.

A Communal Workshop

Here is the problem with our previous discussion: in the DeMarco and Lister study, people work on a task *individually*. They code and test individually, and they will be ranked individually. All that matters is how much they can concentrate, *on their own*, on solving their problem in the best way possible.

But in most cases software isn't developed like that. People are not fighting a lone problem on their own: they are part of a team. The product of their individual work has to interact with that of many others. They get help, they provide help, they're in it together. Therefore, everyone on the team needs to coordinate and communicate with their peers, constantly, throughout the project.

These coordination and communication demands can be quite intense. As Brooks pointed out in that other classic text on software development, *The Mythical Man-Month* [Brooks 1975], they can be so intense that adding people to a late project can delay it further due to the resulting coordination overhead.

Thinking about coordination forces us to consider an alternative to our "doors that close" prescription. Perhaps what matters is to have an environment where people can coordinate and communicate constantly and swiftly. Perhaps an emphasis on coordination beats an emphasis on concentration.

It turns out that there are many theoretical reasons to emphasize coordination. First, we should remember that nowhere in Csikszentmihalyi's theory of flow does he say that flow happens exclusively in isolation. In fact, harmonious teamwork is one of the most accessible mechanisms to get into flow. Emphasizing coordination also brings other benefits. For instance, social psychologists have discovered that people in close relationships form a kind of partnership called a *transactive memory system* [Wegner et al. 1991]. You have probably experienced them with your partner or your family: someone (most likely you) becomes the "computer expert," someone is in charge of keeping track of birthdays, someone does the bills, and so on. In a transactive memory system, the people involved determine, often implicitly, what are everyone's areas of expertise. It's an efficient arrangement, as long as the areas of expertise are balanced. Nobody needs to keep track of everything; they just need to know who to ask. When left to their own devices, people in close relationships consistently score better at memory tests than pairs of strangers, and the effect occurs in both personal and professional relationships [Hollingshead 2000]. Therefore, if the members of a team frequently sit close to each other and are constantly available to answer their teammates' questions, they are more likely to develop efficient transactive memory systems—without even thinking about it.

There's more to this than developing a "team memory." Once we start thinking about efficient coordination and communication, other factors come into play. One has to do with the richness of the communication channels that we use. According to Olson and Olson, despite all our current technology for remote collaboration, distance still matters, and nothing beats collaborating face to face. Olson and Olson go further, in fact, and predict that distance will continue to matter *decades* from now, even if all of the reasonably feasible long-distance collaboration technologies materialize. Sharing our context with our interlocutors immediately transmits more information than we can consciously articulate, and this information often has an impact on our productivity and the quality of our work [Olson and Olson 2000].

Herbsleb and Grinter report on a case where a lack of immediacy became problematic. They observed the challenges of integrating the code built in a geographically distributed project, and reported that integration was the most difficult part of the project because of coordination problems caused by the breakdown of informal communication channels [Herbsleb and Grinter 1999]. There is nothing in their study to suggest that this was an extraordinary experience.

Their report is relevant for projects distributed across long distances, but it is fair to wonder whether informal communication channels would really break down that much when people work on different offices *in the same site*? Would individual offices really hamper informal communication significantly?

They would, although not as much as remote locations. One of the problems is that if people are located beyond a short walk from your desk (about 30 meters), they may as well be in a different city: your chances of visiting them for an informal chat decrease dramatically [Allen 1977]. Olson and Olson list many other reasons for the loss of communication when the team is not completely collocated: they lose access to rapid feedback, to multiple channels of communication, to nuanced information, and to implicit cues, to name a few. When people do not share the same room constantly, their communication efforts are simply less effective. They are also less cohesive, and my colleagues and I have hypothesized that cohesion may be a key success factor in software organizations [Aranda et al. 2007].

People in the Agile community stress these points. They call for constant, intense interaction, and most Agile proposals, if not all, focus on the importance of team collocation. Beck's Extreme Programming approach, in particular, explicitly recommends practices such as having the team *Sit Together* throughout the project, in an *Informative Workspace* room [Beck 2004]. Instinctively, or through trial and error, some Agile proponents have concluded that collocation, though perhaps distracting, is better than isolation. But what direct evidence is there to back up this strategy?

The most convincing evidence I've found comes from a study by Teasley et al. They studied a Fortune 100 automobile company that decided to try out *war rooms*[†] for their software development projects, first as a pilot program, and later for most of their development. The war rooms had a workstation for every project member, most of whom were sitting around a large desk, with whiteboards on the walls. There were also some private cubicles available nearby, outfitted with phones and computers, so team members could choose to go there if they needed silence and privacy. The researchers tracked several productivity metrics and the degree of team member satisfaction with the war rooms [Teasley et al. 2002].

The results were strongly in favor of the pilot teams: they outperformed their company baseline by a factor of two in terms of productivity, and though a few team members were uncomfortable with the arrangement, most of them liked the war rooms, grew comfortable with their more intense interaction, and preferred them over their old cubicles. Once the program had been institutionalized, subsequent teams had an *even better* performance, improving upon the pilot teams in all productivity metrics significantly while keeping the same degree of user and team satisfaction. Radical collocation was a success in this case, as it has been in others reported in the scientific literature.

You might wonder at this point what happened to that idea that developers need to concentrate so much. Aren't communal workshops completely disruptive? Chong and Siino addressed this question: they studied interruptions of paired (and radically collocated) programmers versus solo programmers [Chong and Siino 2006]. They found that the nature of our interruptions is different in collocated settings. People working in pair programming sessions are interrupted for shorter times and for more work-related questions than people working solo. The communal workshop environment of the pair programmers was more distracting than the

---

† The term "war room" has an aggressive connotation, and I prefer "communal workshop" myself, but both are meant to represent the same thing.

cubicles of the solo programmers, but pair programmers "were accustomed to their work environment, and conversations of others only became problematic when they were held at particularly high volume." Chong and Siino also found that for solo programmers, when an interruptor took the trouble of walking to the cubicle of the person he wanted to talk to, he would interrupt his target no matter what the target was doing. In comparison, the communal workshop environment of the pair programmers would offer hints to potential interruptors for when it would be a good time to interrupt their targets and when they were busy collaborating.

Based on this evidence, it seems to be advantageous to have a kind of *communal workshop*, a fully collocated team sitting in the same room, around one or two large desks without partitions, with ample wall space for whiteboards and a few private rooms nearby for those times when someone truly needs isolation. This layout, it seems, would maximize their coordination and awareness abilities.

Work Patterns

So what is going on? Paradoxically, we went through evidence in favor of isolation and individual offices, based on the principle that developers should be able to concentrate as much as possible, and then we switched to evidence in favor of collocation and shared spaces, based on the contrasting principle that developers should be able to coordinate as much as possible. Is one piece of evidence wrong?

Thinking in terms of *work patterns* might give us a clue to this puzzle. According to Tesluk et al., team workflow can be categorized in several levels, depending on the kinds of interaction that the team's members need to engage in [Tesluk et al. 1997]. They offer the following classification:

Pooled workflow
> Involves tasks that aggregate individual performances to the group level. No interactions or exchanges between group members are required in this pattern.

Sequential workflow
> Describes tasks that move from one member of the team to another but not in a back-and-forth manner.

Reciprocal workflow
> Similar to sequential workflow in that work flows only from one member to another, but the flow is now bidirectional.

Intensive workflow
> Work has the opportunity to flow between all members of the group, and the entire group must collaborate to accomplish the task.

Of course, this taxonomy is just an abstraction; it is unlikely that teams will fall strictly on only one category. Generally speaking, however, software projects tend to fall in the last two levels, although the exact slot for any one team depends on the specific processes and practices that it uses. There are very few software projects for which the *pooled workflow* or the *sequential workflow* patterns are feasible. (Pure waterfalls, which do not allow backtracking to the previous stages of the project, would be an example of sequential workflow.) But the *reciprocal workflow* pattern adjusts closely to real-life waterfall and spiral project life cycles, whereas the *intensive workflow* pattern matches Agile strategies much better.

This is important because, to the best of our knowledge, the need to coordinate on the spot is particularly present in teams with more intensive workflow patterns. In a comprehensive literature review, Beal et al. conclude that group cohesion and performance are strongly correlated *for teams with complex workflow dynamics*, but not necessarily for teams with a straightforward and simple workflow [Beal 2003].

Think about your last software project. Did the team members have a clear idea of the requirements and of what they needed to do individually? Did they know exactly who to go to in order to extract the information they needed? Did they have a clear picture of how their pieces matched with those of their teammates? Was there a repository of information that they could access to answer their questions, and was it useful? If so, workflow was more sequential, and there were fewer coordination demands in the team. If not, workflow was more intensive, and there were more coordination demands.

Here is an alternative way to look at this. Imagine you are part of a hypothetical project that does not have any clear requirements, just a broad idea of what the system should do. There is no clear end point either, just a commitment to keep delivering functionality to the clients as often as possible. Furthermore, you and your teammates don't know each other very well; you have not worked together for an extended period before, and you are not familiar with everybody's strengths and weaknesses. Now imagine the team members locking themselves away in their own private offices, in an environment that discourages all but the most essential interruptions. How could you get anything done in this setting?

Picture now the opposite case: the team has a pretty clear idea of what it needs to do, there is a comprehensive, beautifully crafted specification, everyone's responsibilities are precisely delimited, and, thanks to careful planning, integration will probably not be a headache. If only you and your teammates could concentrate individually on your own tasks for a few hours a day, the project would proceed perfectly, but you are sitting in a large communal space where you're interrupted and distracted all the time. How could you get anything done in *this* setting?

Unfortunately, research still has not provided a clear guideline to making a choice in the particular case of software development teams. The most we can get from the evidence so far is that both the Doors that Close and the Communal Workshop layouts can be beneficial if they are in agreement with the practices and the workstyle of the team. If you are committed to an intensive workflow (or if your context demands it), you should allow for intensive coordination, and if you prefer sequential or reciprocal workflows, you should enable developers to concentrate and depend on each other only through the necessary interfaces.

One More Thing...

The answer to the question, "A communal workshop or doors that close?" is *yes*. That is, both configurations, even though they are at opposite ends of the spectrum, bring a significant improvement over the now-typical cubicle farm layout.

The problem with cubicles is that they provide most of the drawbacks of the two extreme configurations we discussed without providing any of their benefits. First, cubicles do not isolate workers like private offices would, so they are often interrupted and distracted by nearby conversations. But cubicles are not truly shared spaces either, and therefore they do not allow for the continuous coordination and awareness that a communal workshop provides. To my knowledge there is absolutely no evidence in the literature that shows that cubicle layouts are better than any of their alternatives for software development work; they should be avoided if at all possible. Choose the ability to concentrate or the ability to coordinate. It's rather foolish to choose neither.

References

[Allen 1977] Allen, T.J.1977. *Managing the Flow of Technology*. Cambridge, MA: MIT Press.

[Aranda et al. 2007] Aranda, Jorge, Steve Easterbrook, and Greg Wilson. 2007. Requirements in the Wild: How Small Companies Do It. *Proceedings of the 15th IEEE International Requirements Engineering Conference (RE'07)*.

[Beal 2003] Beal, Daniel J., Robin R. Cohen, Michael J. Burke, and Christy L. McLendon. 2003. Cohesion and Performance in Groups: A Meta-Analytic Clarification of Construct Relations. *Journal of Applied Psychology*: 88(6).

[Beck 2004] Beck, Kent. 2004. *Extreme Programming Explained: Embrace Change*. Boston: Addison-Wesley.

[Brooks 1975] Brooks, Fred. 1975. *The Mythical Man-Month*. Boston: Addison-Wesley.

[Chong and Siino 2006] Chong, Jan, and Rosanne Siino. 2006. Interruptions on Software Teams: A Comparison of Paired and Solo Programmers. *Proceedings of the ACM 2006 Conference on Computer Supported Cooperative Work*.

[Csikszentmihalyi 1990] Csikszentmihalyi, Mihaly. 1990. *Flow: The Psychology of Optimal Experience*. New York: Harper.

[DeMarco and Lister 1999] DeMarco, Tom, and Tim Lister. 1999. *Peopleware*. New York: Dorset House.

[Herbsleb and Grinter 1999] Herbsleb, James D., and Rebecca E. Grinter. 1999. Splitting the Organization and Integrating the Code: Conway's Law Revisited. *Proceedings of the 21st International Conference on Software Engineering*.

[Hollingshead 2000] Hollingshead, Andrea B.2000. Perceptions of Expertise and Transactive Memory in Work Relationships.*Group Processes and Intergroup Relations* 3: 257-267.

[Ko et al. 2007] Ko, Andrew J., Robert DeLine, and Gina Venolia. 2007. Information Needs in Collocated Software Development Teams. *Proceedings of the International Conference on Software Engineering.*

[Olson and Olson 2000] Olson, Gary M., and Judith S. Olson. 2000. Distance Matters. *Human-Computer Interaction* 15: 139-178.

[Teasley et al. 2002] Teasley, Stephanie D., Lisa A. Covi, M.S. Krishnan, and Judith S. Olson. 2002. Rapid Software Development Through Team Collocation. *IEEE Transactions on Software Engineering* 28: 671-683.

[Tesluk et al. 1997] Tesluk, P.E., J.E. Mathieu, S.J. Zaccaro, and M.A. Marks. 1997.Task and aggregation issues in the analysis and assessment of team performance. In *Team performance and measurement: Theory, methods, and applications*, ed.Brannick, M.T., E. Salas, and C. Prince. Mahwah, NJ: Lawrence Erlbaum Associates.

[Wegner et al. 1991] Wegner, Daniel M., Paula Raymond, and Ralph Erber. 1991. Transactive Memory in Close Relationships. *Journal of Personality and Social Psychology* 61: 923-929.

## CHAPTER TWENTY

Identifying and Managing Dependencies in Global Software Development

Marcelo Cataldo

Global software development (GSD) is becoming commonplace. The promise of lower costs, access to talent, and the opening of new markets has led large corporations as well as smaller ones to embark on GSD efforts. However, pulling together the work of tens or hundreds of geographically distributed project members towards a successful outcome is easier said than done. Coordinating design and development work in a GSD setting is quite challenging. For instance, there are numerous examples where new products never see the light of day or where it takes double the amount of time to develop a system. Fortunately, over the past two decades we have learned a lot about making GSD work better.

This chapter has two goals. First, we draw from a wide range of empirical studies to show that effectively coordinating development work in GSD settings involves combining an understanding of the technical and socio-organizational dimensions of software development projects. Then, we discuss how the empirical evidence can be put into action through a collection of pragmatic approaches applicable to various roles and phases of GSD projects.

The content of the chapter is woven together by the idea of socio-technical congruence (STC). So before we proceed, we briefly introduce the concept. STC refers to the relationships between the coordination needs that emerge from the technical context of a development project and the coordination capabilities provided by the socio-organizational structure of the project. When a project's coordination needs match its coordination capabilities, STC argues that it will lead to better outcomes, such as higher levels of quality or improved productivity.

Finally, STC also suggests measurements for coordination needs, coordination capabilities, and their relationships. Throughout this chapter, we will discuss those various elements in a practical context.

Why Is Coordination a Challenge in GSD?

Large multisite or multiorganization projects have existed for many decades. One of the first problems tackled by organizational researchers starting back in the 1950s was how best to organize work. Researchers such as Galbraith, March, Simon, and Thompson argued that interdependencies among tasks in a project or in an organization should be minimized. In those cases where coordination needs are unavoidable, they showed that if we know *a priori* (a) all the steps involved in a task and (b) the different interdependencies among tasks in a project, we can use mechanisms such as standard operating procedures to manage the interdependencies and efficiently coordinate work. However, when exceptions to the rules occur or uncertainty surrounds a task, we need more flexible coordination mechanisms, such as direct interaction among project members or meetings.

More recently, Malone and Crowston [1994] suggested additional coordination approaches using traditional software problems such as shared resources or producer/consumer relationships as analogies for ways to manage work dependencies.

In the technical domain, work on modular system designs has suggested very similar ideas. For instance, Parnas was one of the first to argue that systems should be decomposed into units (e.g., modules) and that dependencies among them should be minimized [Parnas 1972]. In this context, dependencies are represented by the interfaces exposed by each unit or module. As long as those interfaces are clearly defined at the beginning of the project and they remain stable, development of each unit can move forward in parallel. If changes are required, coordination can be managed by mechanisms such as meetings, where the relevant parties discuss and agree upon the modifications to the interfaces.

The approaches to coordination discussed in the previous paragraphs are commonplace mechanisms that we see today in any type of organization, including software development projects. However, software development presents unique and very difficult challenges in terms of coordination, stemming primarily from a complex interrelationship between the technical and social dimensions of software development projects.

We all know that knowledge and understanding of project requirements typically grow and change over the life of a project. As requirements change, the structure of a system under development changes and evolves. The uncertainty and complexity that stems from changes and evolution represent quite a challenge to understanding the dependencies among the various project members and how to manage them.

For instance, de Souza et al. [de Souza et al. 2004] and Grinter et al. [Grinter et al. 1999] studied several development projects and found that developers had major difficulties identifying how changes they were making could affect other parts of the system and the corresponding development tasks. Those coordination failures usually resulted in problems, sometime quite significant ones, during integration and testing.

The impact of coordination challenges in software development is severely augmented in global projects [Herbsleb and Mockus 2003] for several reasons:

- Physical separation prevents project members from easily walking down the hallway and interacting with other project members to discuss problems or find out about changes.

- The exchange of information and effective coordination are also hampered by time zone differences.

- The lack of opportunities for synchronous interaction (e.g., conference calls) forces project members to exchange information in an asynchronous way (e.g., email) which increases the chance for mistakes and misinterpretations.

- The more departments or locations are in involved in a project, the higher the chances are for organizational barriers (e.g., different management styles, incentive mechanisms, and goals) to interfere in a project member's ability to efficiently and effectively communicate and coordinate.

In sum, understanding with whom and when to coordinate in software development projects is not a trivial issue. Furthermore, the inherent characteristics of GSD settings magnify the problem.

Dependencies and Their Socio-Technical Duality

The design and implementation of complex software systems involve a wide range of dependencies among the various constituent parts of a system. Developers, managers, and other relevant stakeholders often can't recognize and manage all those dependencies. Such failures typically translate into lower productivity because, among other things, they require more rework and more time spent on integration and testing [Cataldo et al. 2006], Cataldo et al. 2008] [Herbsleb and Mockus 2003]. We also tend to see an impact on software quality, where unrecognized dependencies result in a higher number of defects [Cataldo 2010] [Herbsleb et al. 2006].

A major challenge we all face in software development is identifying dependencies. This is not easy, and two interrelated dimensions are at play: a technical component and a socio-organizational component. For example, in certain cases, the technical nature of a dependency makes it hard to recognize it. A classic example would be asynchronous remote procedure calls among a pair of components that can create timing, locking, and resource consumption dependencies that might become visible only when developers are faced with a particular defect that exposes such dependencies.

In other cases, dependencies fall into a socio-organizational category, stemming from the way work is organized and carried out in the development organization. For instance, it is quite common to allocate work based on the availability of development resources. Such an approach could create work dependencies, such as information sharing needs, between individuals located in different parts of the world, sometimes with minimal work time overlap (e.g., time zone difference larger than 7–8 hours, as one finds between the USA and India). Under such circumstances, it is highly likely that those dependencies would not be addressed during the work.

In order to illustrate some of the challenges involved in identifying the relevant dependencies in software projects, consider the following example described by Bass et al. which is representative of many large development projects [Bass et al. 2007]. System 1 was a software platform designed to support a family of real-time embedded products. Given the products' wide range of technical requirements (the features supported, memory requirements, timing requirements, etc.), new functionality was expected to be added regularly over the lifetime of the platform.

The architecture team designed System 1 utilizing several approaches that had proved successful in past projects. It was developed as a component-based solution using a component integration framework, where the coupling among components was minimal and based on well-defined interfaces, allowing for development by independent teams. The development teams were to ensure that they developed their particular modules against the interface specification.

The architecture team addressed the performance and resource utilization requirements by building on past experience and applying the principle of separation of concerns. For example, the RAM was divided into several logical partitions, each assigned to a particular part of the system, and a priority-based scheduler was used to satisfy the performance requirements. In other words, the overall design followed well-established principles and practices.

On the organizational side, the project involved a total of four development sites, two in Germany and two in France. There was a central architecture team made up of the most qualified representatives from each site, and each site had responsibility for the design and development of one or more subsystems. The project was managed from one of the development sites in Germany, and the project manager travelled quite frequently to all the development sites. Each site had about the same number of engineers.

Nevertheless, Bass et al. described several serious problems encountered by the project. I will focus on two problems that provide good examples of how challenging it is to identify technical and work dependencies in large distributed projects.

First, after the initial implementation, the system had serious performance problems, particularly during system startup. Based on the experience from past projects, the architecture team assumed that the prioritization rules implemented in the scheduler were adequate to allow the teams to work independently. However, they failed to recognize that a significant amount of tweaking of the prioritization rules from previous systems was required. Resolving the performance conflicts resulted in a significant coordination overhead.

Second, the organizational structure inhibited coordination around the performance issues. The architecture team deferred many of the design decisions required for each component or subsystem to the corresponding site. The impact of the local decisions was not recognized until late in the development life cycle. Once a dependency was recognized, it was difficult to coordinate effectively because the teams were distributed and were only vaguely familiar with the activities of the other sites.

This example shows that the technical and organizational dimensions of a project do not operate in isolation of each other. Quite the contrary: each dimension influences the other. In the following section, I discuss the various types of technical dependencies, how they can impact productivity and quality when they are not recognized and coordinated appropriately, and the traditional approaches used to discover such dependencies. I then present an overview of traditional types of work dependencies along similar lines. Following that, I explore the socio-technical duality of dependencies and its implications for productivity and software quality in the context of GSD.

The Technical Dimension

Technical dependencies are relationships among the various software entities that constitute a software system. During architectural or detail design, such entities can be components, modules, or classes. On the other hand, during implementation, the entities of interest are source code files.

Software engineers commonly think of technical dependencies as *syntactic* relationships; that is, they manifest themselves in terms of programming language constructs such as data structures or function and method calls. A different way of thinking about technical dependencies focuses on a *logical* or semantic relationship between software entities. For instance, two components that implement part of a requirement are logically related.

Publisher/subscriber systems represent another example of semantic or logical dependencies, where the relationship between software entities is not explicitly articulated by a call, for instance, from one module to the other. Our discussion focuses primarily on the distinction between syntactic and logical dependencies, because this distinction points directly to the issue of the ease with which the dependency can be identified.

The idea of syntactic dependencies has its origins in compiler optimizations, where the main goal was to understand control and dataflow relationships across statements. Most approaches in this line of work extract relational information, typically from source code or some sort of intermediate representation of the code, such as bytecodes or abstract syntax trees. Then, they analyze units such as statements, functions, or methods to identify relationships that can reveal data-related dependencies (e.g., a particular data structure modified by a function and used in another function) or functional dependencies (e.g., method A calls method B).

Syntactic dependency analyses are used in a wide variety of applications, ranging from static analysis to detect defects to tools that assist developers in understanding and debugging code. Unfortunately, this type of relational information has some problems. In certain cases, it tends not to be accurate. For instance, in programming languages such as C and C++, function pointers and conditional compilation directives tend to create a lot of difficulties for syntactic analyzers based on source code. In the case of object-oriented languages, polymorphism makes the identification of a relationship between two classes almost impossible prior to runtime. In other cases, syntactic dependency information is overwhelming, uncovering tens of hundreds of relationships between source code files and making the process of identifying the relevant relationships quite challenging.

An alternative mechanism for identifying technical dependencies consists of examining the set of source code files that are modified together as part of some unit of development work, such as the development of a new feature or fixing a defect. Gall et al. suggested that files that changed together—for instance, in a version control commit transaction—share some sort of dependency, which they called *logical* [Gall et al. 1998]. Certainly, logical dependencies are not completely different from syntactic dependencies. In fact, they can range from syntactic relationships (e.g., the commit was due to a change in the number of parameters to a function that is implemented in file A and called from file B) to more complex semantic dependencies where the computations done in one file affects the behavior of another file.

One attractive characteristic of this way of thinking about technical dependencies is that it provides a better estimate for semantic dependencies relative to call graphs or data graphs, because it does not rely on language constructs to establish the dependency relationship between source code files. For instance, in the case of remote procedure calls (RPCs), a syntactic dependency approach would provide the necessary information to relate a pair of modules. However, such information would be embedded in a long path of connections from the RPC caller through the RPC stubs and all the way to the RPC server module. Alternatively, when the module invoking the RPC and the module implementing the RPC server are changed together, a logical dependency is created, showing a direct dependency between the affected source code files.

The logical dependency approach is even more valuable in cases such as publisher/subscriber or event-based systems. Here, the call-graph approach would fail to relate the interdependent modules because no syntactically visible dependency would exist between, for instance, a module that generates an event and a module that registers to receive such an event. Therefore, the logical dependency approach has the potential to identify important dependencies not visible in syntactic code analyses.

Moreover, logical dependencies can filter syntactic dependencies that may be relevant in terms of the information needs of developers. For example, the syntactic dependency approach highlights relationships among basic libraries (e.g., memory management, printing functionality, etc.) because they contain highly coupled files. Yet they tend to be very stable and unlikely to fail, despite this high level of coupling.

However, the logical view of technical dependencies also has its problems. The main challenge is that the dependency information is extracted from historical data such as that provided by version control systems. Without such a resource, there is no efficient way to determine the logical dependencies among source code files.

Despite the limitations of the two ways of characterizing technical dependencies, both the syntactic and the logical approaches provide useful and complementary information that can support, in multiple ways, the identification and management of dependencies in software development projects. The following sections discuss the implications of both types of dependencies for productivity and quality in software development projects.

Syntactic dependencies and their impact on productivity and quality

Syntactic dependencies are a simple vehicle to understand how traditional software engineering concepts such as coupling and cohesion affect the ability of an organization to efficiently develop high-quality software. Unfortunately, there is a lot more evidence about the effect of syntactic-based coupling and cohesion on software quality than on development productivity.

Banker et al. found that the more syntactic dependencies a software component had, the higher the maintenance effort associated with the component [Banker et al.1998]. The increase in maintenance effort stems, primarily, from the challenge of understanding the higher levels of complexity associated with higher numbers of syntactic dependencies.

Ever since the ideas of coupling and cohesion were introduced in the mid-1970s, researchers focused a lot of attention on the relationship between these concepts and software quality. This line of work has contributed a large collection of metrics, ranging for simple quantification of the syntactic dependencies of a software entity (e.g., the number of data type references or number of function calls made in a source code file) to more complex measures that attempt to capture the structural characteristics of coupling (e.g., the depth of the inheritance tree). Some of these measures are explored in Chapter 8, *Beyond Lines of Code: Do We Need More Complexity Metrics?*, by Israel Herraiz and Ahmed E. Hassan in this book.

The simplest way to summarize the extensive body of research is to say, "the higher the number of syntactic dependencies a software entity (e.g., a file, module or component) has, the more defects it will have." However, the relationship between syntactic dependencies and software quality is not that simple. Recent research [Cataldo et al. 2009] has shown that data-related syntactic dependencies (e.g., data type references) are more likely to lead to defects than functional dependencies (e.g., function A calls function B). One possible reason for such a difference is that data-related dependencies tend to require more abstract thinking than functional relationships in order to understand how their content changes as a program executes.

The structure of the syntactic dependencies also matter. For instance, Zimmermann and Nagappan applied graph theoretic lenses to calculate network measures on the syntactic dependencies extracted from Windows binaries, and found that such measures, when combined with more traditional metrics (e.g., churn metrics), were useful for predicting post-release defects [Zimmermann and Nagappan 2008].

Logical dependencies and their impact on productivity and quality

Thinking of technical dependencies as logical relationships is a more recent idea than syntactic dependencies, which means, unfortunately, that we know a lot less about how logical dependencies affect software quality and development productivity. Earlier research results suggested that logical dependencies affected quality in ways similar to syntactic dependencies. However, recent findings suggest more interesting implications.

My colleagues and I [Cataldo et al. 2009] studied two large-scale systems from two distinct firms and found that the number of logical dependencies was a much better predictor of failures than syntactic dependencies. In fact, the impact of syntactic dependencies vanished when logical dependencies are considered. These results have important implications for developers because they suggest that the effort to identify and understand dependencies should focus on those less-explicit relationships rather than on the obvious and explicit syntactic dependencies.

A second useful finding is that the structure of the logical dependencies also affect quality. For instance, my colleagues and I, studying two large-scale systems [Cataldo et al. 2009], found that the likelihood of failures associated with a source code file, e.g., file A, decreases as the density of the logical dependencies among the files dependent on file A increases. Such results suggest that developers should become more cognizant of logical dependencies, how tight those relationships are among a set of files, and where to look to make sure that changes to one part of the system do not introduce problems elsewhere. More importantly, we know that the structure of logical dependencies matters more than the structure of syntactic dependencies. For instance, Nambiar and I studied a large-scale multinational development organization and found that the density of logical dependencies among architectural components was one of the more important factors affecting the quality outcomes of GSD projects, whereas no evidence of such effects was found for syntactic dependencies [Cataldo and Nambiar 2010].

The Socio-Organizational Dimension

The social side of dependencies in software development have to do with the communication, information sharing, and coordination needs that emerge from the set of tasks that need to be performed in a particular software development project. We refer to these dependencies as *work dependencies*. It will be relatively obvious to those who have been involved in development projects, in particular large-scale ones, that numerous factors—such as experience, organizational structure, geographic distribution, and schedule pressure—introduce barriers that constrain project members' ability to efficiently and effectively identify and manage all the relevant work dependencies.

For instance, when developers have limited experience of a system, they tend not to understand all the potential implications of the changes they make to the system as part of their tasks (e.g., satisfying pre-invocation and post-invocation assumptions of a method or function call). Those knowledge gaps, typically, result in lower productivity in the form of rework or in poorer quality.

However, experience can be important beyond the categories of technical or system know-how. Familiarity in working together with other team members could result in important improvements in productivity and quality because knowing the people you work with facilitates information sharing and coordination. For instance, engineers tend to develop implicit ways of coordinating with each other, learning for instance how and when to interrupt a colleague to ask for or share information.

An important and sometimes overlooked factor related to the identification and management of work dependencies is the structure of projects and the development organization. Such structures encompass several elements, such as the set of organizational units (e.g., teams, departments) involved, their geographical location, their formal reporting paths, their administrative and development processes, and even their incentive mechanisms. All those elements together play an important role in shaping the way project members interact, coordinate, and collaborate.

Geographically distributed software development organizations are at a disadvantage in terms of information sharing and integration. For instance, we know that developers share a lot of technical information related to their current activities through short, informal conversations that might take place in a hallway or around the coffee machine. When developers are physically separated, they no longer can have such impromptu communication. In turn, project members have a lot more difficulty staying aware of other people's activities, decisions, and difficulties. The end result is an increase in coordination breakdowns, integration problems, and, ultimately, decreases in productivity and quality [de Souza et al. 2004], [Grinter et al. 1999].

However, being geographically distributed has other drawbacks besides the elimination of impromptu conversation. Significant time zone difference (more than six hours) significantly reduce possibilities for real-time problem solving activities that require synchronous interaction, such as phone conversations or video conferencing. Typically, project members tend to opt for an asynchronous means of communication, such as email. Unfortunately, as Espinosa et al. has demonstrated, asynchronous communication tends to create a lot of misunderstanding and mistakes stemming from the complexity associated with adequate management of the flow of information in this type of communication [Espinosa et al. 2007].

Another problem with geographically distributed projects is that members are less likely to know each other. We tend to share more information with collocated colleagues for whom we have a certain level of rapport than with colleagues located in other offices or locations. In such cases, and when coworkers don't know each other, information requests are not likely to be addressed in a timely fashion and may even be completely ignored. The end result is that project members are likely to fail to identify relevant work dependencies, particularly when unanticipated changes take place.

Finally, the schedule pressure of a software project can have serious implications for the ability of project members to identify and manage work dependencies. An increase in schedule pressure is typically manifested as an increase in the number of concurrent, and potentially interdependent, development tasks. Imagine a particular functionality B that was planned to follow the development of functionality A, on which it depends. Due to time pressures, both functionalities may have to be developed concurrently. To make that possible, developers face a new and more complex set of coordination needs.

For instance, interfaces between the two functionalities might evolve as the work progresses, creating the need for constant coordination to avoid integration problems and hard-to-find defects. In addition, there might be a need for special "glue code" to incrementally test the code under development. In other words, successful completion of these tasks depends on a collection of appropriate coordination mechanisms that allow developers to identify the relevant dependencies and deal with them appropriately.

The following section discusses the various types of work dependencies and their impacts on development productivity and quality.

Different types of work dependencies and their impacts on productivity and quality

The most common way to think about work dependencies is to model the temporal relationships between tasks. These dependencies focus on the temporal precedence of tasks (e.g., task A needs to be completed before task B). Projects focused on this way of thinking use numerous approaches, ranging from analytical and graphical methods such as Gantt and PERT diagrams to tool support such as workflow-based tools, to identify and managed the dependencies.

We would all agree that if we fail to recognize these dependencies and manage accordingly, we end up with longer development times. However, more interesting analyses are also possible with this type of information. My colleagues and I [Cataldo et al. 2009] considered all the temporal dependencies among the development tasks in one release and applied a social network type of analysis to a workflow dependency graph, where the nodes were members of the development organization and the edges represented the handover of a particular development task from one individual to another. Such people-to-people relationships were examined through the lenses of social network analysis. We found that a high number of relationships require a significant effort by the individuals involved to maintain the relationships.

This point is particularly important in the context of workflow dependencies because it suggests that centrally located project members are more likely to be overloaded because of the extra effort associated with managing the work dependencies, increasing the likelihood for communication breakdowns and risking diminished quality in the software produced. In fact, our results supported this argument, showing that source code files were more likely to have failures when highly interdependent individuals modified them.

A variant of temporal or workflow types of dependencies relates to temporal work relationships, where the dependency is centered on information needs rather than completion or handover of the task. For instance, if we have two interdependent tasks—develop module A and develop module B, where module B invokes functionality in module A—the temporal dependency resides in the information related to how to materialize the call from module B to module A. Given this information, developers working on module A can define an interface and provide the information to the developers working on module B. Then, the tasks can proceed in parallel.

Concurrent engineering, a line of research focused on ways to manage interdependent and concurrent development tasks, proposes that appropriate coordination mechanisms can be put in place to deal with the information-related dependencies among overlapping development tasks when we *a priori* can determine those information needs. Unfortunately, the reality of a typical software development project is not that simple. Tens or hundreds of tasks tend to overlap over the life of a project. In many cases, the temporal precedence of those tasks as well as the information-related dependencies among the tasks is not completely understood or known *a priori*. In fact, as requirements become known and better understood, the dependencies among those tasks might change.

One of my recent studies [Cataldo 2010] examined 209 distributed projects in a large multi-national development organization and found that higher levels of overlap among development tasks, as represented in a task-tracking system, were associated with lower levels of software quality. More importantly, the impact of task overlap was consistent along the life cycle of the project. That is, the impact on quality was not conditional on being close, for instance, to a project milestone, where we typically see a surge in the amount of concurrent development work. These results are useful because they show the importance of keeping track of the type of dependencies, so managers or other stakeholders can act to address their negative impact on a particular project.

A third type of work dependencies has its roots in the role of the organizational structure in establishing useful communication and coordination paths to address information-sharing needs. Nagappan et al. constructed a collection of metrics based on the information available in a traditional organizational chart and studied their relationships to failures in Windows components and programs [Nagappan et al. 2008]. Although their measures do not specifically capture work dependencies, they represent good proxies for numerous organizational phenomena, including issues of work dependencies. Their analyses showed some interesting results.

For instance, the higher the number of departmental units involved in the development of a component or a binary, the lower the quality of the component or binary. In addition, the distance in the organizational hierarchy among the individuals who developed or modified a component also had negative effects on software quality. These results highlight the difficulties associated with communication and coordination across organizational boundaries (e.g., teams, departments, divisions, locations, etc.) and the negative consequences those barriers can have on software quality.

The development of a software system consists of a collection of design decisions, either at the architectural level or at the implementation level. Those design decisions introduce constraints that might establish new dependencies among the various parts of the system, modify existing ones, or even eliminate dependencies. The changes in dependencies can generate new coordination needs that are typically quite difficult to identify *a priori*.

Imagine, for instance, a task that requires the modification of the memory allocation policies of RPCs in one component in order to improve its performance. Such a change could affect the timing of RPC exchanges with other components, which in turn might break certain assumptions made by users of those RPCs. In order to better understand how to capture such dynamic dependencies, my colleagues and I [Cataldo et al. 2006] [Cataldo et al. 2008] proposed a socio-technical framework for examining the relationship between the logical software dependencies and the structure of the development work used to construct such systems.

Coordination requirements, one of the elements of that framework, is a measure of the extent to which the work of each project member depends on the work of other project members, given a set of development tasks and the technical dependencies among the parts of the system that those tasks affect. One important finding from this line of work is that the higher the number of coordination needs a developer is faced with, the lower the quality of the source code files modified by the developer. In other words, you are more likely to introduce bugs in the system the more that coordination needs emerge from the logical dependencies of the system as development work progresses.

The Socio-Technical Dimension

Software development, and product development in general, involves technical and socio-organizational elements. So far we have discussed dependencies in the context of each individual dimension. However, the technical and the socio-organizational dimensions are intertwined, and considering them in isolation of each other does not allow us to consider the whole picture.

The general idea behind the socio-technical perspective of dependencies in software development is quite simple. Development productivity and software quality improve when the coordination needs established by the dependencies among development tasks are matched by the actual coordination activities carried out by the engineers. However, the important contribution of the socio-technical perspective is identifying and tracking the dynamic relationship between social and technical dependencies, focusing on a fine-grained level of analysis of different types of technical dependencies (e.g., syntactic or logical software dependencies) and examining the coordination needs that such technical dependencies create over the life cycle of a development project.

For instance, my colleagues and I [Cataldo et al. 2006] [Cataldo et al. 2008] [Cataldo and Herbsleb 2010] used data from multiple software repositories (version control systems, defect tracking systems, etc.) from two large-scale projects to show that when engineers identified and managed the relevant coordination needs, development productivity and software quality improved. A key insight of this work is that the relevant work-related coordination needs, in fact, tend to stem from logical dependencies instead of from syntactic dependencies. Logical dependencies tend to capture relationships that are more semantic and tacit, unlike syntactic relationships, which are explicit in nature (engineers can easily identify these relationships by looking at a piece of software code).

For example, logical dependencies could represent publisher/subscriber relationship or a particular timing relationship between two different components of a software system. In such cases, syntactic language constructs tend not to provide all the necessary information to identify such dependencies.

A related finding is that a misalignment between dependencies and coordination activity is a key factor affecting development productivity and software quality, when we examine the right set of software dependencies that determine the relevant work dependencies.

Considering the technical and the socio-organizational dimensions together also allows us to understand better how we can improve large-scale development that involves multiple organizational boundaries. For instance, architectural dependencies that cross the boundaries of projects tend to be associated with lower levels of software quality, as reported in my past study of 209 projects in a large development organization [Cataldo 2010]. Such a result suggests the importance of coordination and awareness beyond the traditional small organizational entity, such as the team, and the importance of providing support at a larger scale within the development organization.

In addition, Nambiar and I explored how technical coupling affects quality in geographically distributed software development projects [Cataldo and Nambiar 2010]. Our main finding was that the higher the number of technical dependencies that are external to a project (e.g., a component A interfaces with component B, but component B was not changed in the project), the lower the software quality. In particular, logical dependencies that crossed the boundaries of projects increased the predicted number of defects in a project by 50%, an impact similar in size to traditional factors such as the amount of code produced or the level of Capability Maturity Model (CMM) process maturity.

From Research to Practice

The previous sections discussed what we have learned in the past decade or so in terms of managing dependencies in GSD. We now turn our attention to the practical implications of such research results.

Leveraging the Data in Software Repositories

A large portion of the research studies that have examined how technical and work dependencies can lead to coordination breakdowns, and consequently reduce productivity and quality, used data collected from software repositories. Examples of such repositories are version control systems, defect and task tracking systems, wikis, and obviously the source code itself. Certainly, such lines of research highlight the potentially enormous value of building and maintaining software repositories to assess a wide range of factors that affect software development projects. Since such repositories are quite pervasive in today's software development organizations, why not use the rich data stored in those repositories to improve software development practice? This section discusses several examples of how to go about this.

Possibly one of the simplest but most beneficial steps that a software development organization can take is to connect the data between the version control system and the defect or task tracking systems. The end result is a clear link between a development task or a defect representation and the set of changes in the source code (or other artifacts) committed to a version control system. Two chapters in this book—Chapter 9, *An Automated Fault Prediction System*, by Elaine J. Weyuker and Thomas J. Ostrand, and Chapter 25, *Where Do Most Software Flaws Come From?*, by Dewayne Perry—describe research in this area.

Obviously, such a connection between repositories provides some fundamental, traceable linkages in the development process. But most importantly, it opens the door for a range of analytics and tool support that can significantly improve the development organization's ability to coordinate efficiently and effectively, particularly in a globally distributed setting. For example, my colleagues and I [Cataldo et al. 2006] [Cataldo et al. 2008] [Cataldo and Herbsleb 2010] developed a framework that uses data from software repositories to compute a number of measures (e.g., technical dependency, churn metrics, and workload metrics) as well as coordination patterns (e.g., from the comments in a defect report). The studies not only showed that we can assess the impact of coordination failures on the resolution time of development tasks and on software failures, but also showed that reliable analyses (which could easily be automated) can be done using only the rich data available in most software development projects. Wagstrom replicated the same type of analyses in the context of open source projects, providing further support for the viability and usefulness of the analyses [Wagstrom 2009].

Software repositories have also become a central element in a wide range of awareness and collaborative tools that focus on supporting the software development effort, particularly in geographically distributed settings. These tools leverage the traditional infrastructure type of tools such as ClearQuest, ClearCase, Subversion, Bugzilla, or oMantis to enhance the communication and coordination capabilities of software development projects. These collaborative tools come in many varieties, including:

- Workspace awareness technologies (e.g., [Biehl et al. 2007])
- Expertise recommenders (e.g., [Minto and Murphy. 2007])
- Artifact recommendation systems (e.g., [Cubranic et al. 2005])
- Interruption management systems (e.g., [Fogarty et al. 2005])
- Project dashboards and status visualizations (e.g., [Ripley et al. 2007])

A more recent set of tools, such as Tesserac [Sarma et al. 2009] have taken a socio-technical perspective, combining technical and work dependency information with visualizations and analytics in order to facilitate the identification and management of dependencies. Although many of these tools emerge from research projects, many of their features and ideas are finding their way into commercially available products such as IBM's Rational Team Concert and Microsoft's Visual Studio, as well as into open source projects, particularly as plug-ins for the Eclipse platform.

Software repositories can also be leveraged to examine the way a system is modularized and to make decisions to reorganize or refactor the code. For instance, once developers, software architects, or other relevant stakeholders become aware of particular patterns of technical dependencies, they can utilize specific techniques to reduce those dependencies, in particular logical relationships. For instance, refactoring the system to reduce logical dependencies can have a positive impact on software quality.

Other code reorganization techniques, such as chunking (proposed by [Mockus and Weiss 2001]), could utilize the various types of technical dependencies in order to make the structure of the systems more suitable for geographically distributed software development organizations. Chunking provides a way to select tightly clustered groups of source code files (in terms of logical or syntactic dependencies) that exhibit few logical dependencies with the rest of the system. Equivalent approaches could be applied to work dependencies.

The Role of Team Leads and Managers in Supporting the Management of Dependencies

Research on the socio-organizational dimension and the socio-technical perspective of dependencies suggests that team leads and managers can play a significant role in two important aspects of GSD projects: organizational barriers and work allocation. Organizational barriers (e.g., departmental units, locations, projects) tend to create a wide range of challenges that hinder software development organizations or projects in effectively and efficiently identifying and managing the relevant dependencies.

A traditional approach to dealing with organizational barriers is the establishment of processes that provide a set of basic mechanisms for managing dependencies across interdependent teams or locations. However, as the number of boundaries (e.g., more locations), complexity, and uncertainty about requirements or features increase, software processes tend to become more of a roadblock than an enabling mechanism. In fact, Nambiar and I showed that the quality improvement benefits of software processes diminish as the degree of distribution increases [Cataldo and Nambiar 2009b]. Such a reduction in benefits tends to stem from processes being optimized for the local context (e.g., a development site or a division), leading to inconsistencies among processes across locations.

Team leads and managers can be instrumental in overcoming organizational barriers. First, they must recognize the tendency of leaders to think solely within their realm of their responsibility. Second, leaders need to facilitate the harmonization of processes across locations (or other relevant organizational entities) by identifying the key stakeholders and the key pieces and flows of information that interdependent locations should be aware of. Finally, leaders need to take an active and open attitude toward facilitating the exchange of information across the various locations.

For instance, Suzanne Weisband has studied for decades the role of managers in distributed work [Weisband 2008]. Her key finding is that when managers are active in collecting information from the various locations involved in a project and sharing it with the rest of the locations, project performance increases dramatically.

Work allocation is another important factor related to the management of dependencies. There are two relevant dimensions: where the work will be done and when it should be completed.

Managers typically consider competence and costs as the two main drivers for distributing work packages across locations. However, other socio-organizational factors should be considered that could affect productivity and quality to the extent of potentially offsetting the possible cost savings from competence-based or cost-based allocation. For example, in my recent research [Cataldo and Nambiar 2009a] [Cataldo 2010], I found that projects with significant imbalances in the distribution of developers (e.g., one location with a few developers and a second location with an order of magnitude more developers) tended to have 40 to 50% higher levels of defects than projects with a similar number of engineers across locations.

In addition, the higher the number of development tasks that run concurrently, the poorer is the quality of the system produced in the project. In fact, projects with relatively stable workloads over their life cycles tended to have half as many defects as equivalent projects that had high levels of task concurrency at one or more points in time. In contrast, technical and domain experience accounted only for 20% of the difference in quality among comparable projects.

Combined, those results point to two additional important factors: the balance of people and the temporal execution of tasks, that managers should consider when making work allocation decisions.

In summation, team leads and managers can make a big difference in the identification and management of dependencies, particularly on distributed projects.

Developers, Work Items, and Distributed Development

Software developers are constantly navigating a complex web of technical and work dependencies. For instance, developers spend significant amounts of time trying to understand how particular parts of the code interact or relate to each other or how a particular change might affect other parts of the code. Despite such efforts, more often than not, many technical and work dependencies go unrecognized.

The work on technical and work dependencies discussed earlier in this chapter suggests various strategies that developers can utilize to better identify and manage dependencies. First, logical dependencies provide valuable information complementing the information about syntactic dependencies. Next, developers can grasp a better understanding of the technical relationship between different source code files or modules, as well as the potential impact of a particular change. Certainly, tools that collect logical dependency information and display them to the developer in the appropriate context would be useful. However, it is also possible to use traditional infrastructure tools such as the version control system to inquire what other files have changed whenever a particular file or artifact of interest changed.

A second strategy consists of maintaining awareness of overlapping tasks on related components or modules. The design or implementation decisions or changes in those related software entities could have a significant impact in the area of developer responsibility. Developers often focus their attention (for good reasons) on the development tasks attached to their immediate area of responsibility, whether it is a component, a part of a component, a module, or a set of source code files. An approach commonly used to help them maintain some sort of awareness of other development activities is to subscribe to the tasks of a particular team or component in the task or defect tracking systems. However, such an approach becomes ineffective pretty fast, particularly in large projects. Developers tend to become overwhelmed by notification emails and after a while no longer pay attention to them. The use of information about specific dependencies, such as logical or particular work-related dependencies, helps manage the volume of information by filtering it, letting developers stay aware of those development tasks that are relevant.

Finally, building social ties with interdependent teams, particularly in a geographically distributed setting, is a valuable and effective way of gathering and sharing relevant dependency information. One consistent result from decades of research in communication, distributed teams, and social networks is that two individuals who have developed a rapport tend to share more work-related information, in a more timely fashion. Some of the techniques that research has found useful in developing valuable social ties are face-to-face interaction in a nonwork setting, the use of social networking tools, and demonstrations of competence and cooperative behavior.

Future Directions

This section touches on three areas of work that can potentially have a profound impact on the identification and management of dependencies in software development projects.

Software Architectures Suitable for Global Software Development

The socio-technical perspective of dependencies highlights the benefits of identifying relevant dependencies as early as possible in the development cycle, so that the project can institute appropriate coordination capabilities. As software architectures become an integral part of the development process, they represent a key source of technical and organizational information for identifying dependencies. However, software architectures represent a higher level of abstraction that could potentially hinder the identification of relevant technical dependencies and, consequently, important coordination requirements.

The growing usage of standardized design and modeling languages, such as UML, might represent a way of overcoming these challenges by using information extraction and graph-theoretic analytics similar to those used to mine software repositories, as discussed earlier in this chapter. We could then envision a "coordination view" of software architectures that combines the product's technical dependencies with relationships among the organizational units responsible for carrying out the development work.

A potentially even more promising future direction is to develop a better understanding of how software architects make design decisions, particularly pertaining to technical and work dependencies. Software architects rarely make design decisions under ideal conditions. In fact, software architects constantly face a collection of nontechnical as well as technical constraints. Therefore, making trade-offs is an integral part of the decision-making process of software architects.

Examples of the forces software architects have to consider when making decisions include:

- Legacy code and its implications when restructuring the system
- Legacy organization and its implications when reorganizing work
- The cost of resources allocated to changes unrelated to customer requirements (e.g., customers are not interested in absorbing the cost of refactoring the platform software to improve its modifiability attributes)
- Managing variations across projects and customers

Software architects tend to develop their own heuristics and evaluation approaches. To date, only a limited set of guidelines exist, derived from research work at Siemens [Sangwan et al. 2006], Philips [Kommeren and Parviainen 2007], and Motorola [Battin et al. 2001]. However, there is a growing interest among researchers and practitioners in developing a systematic way of evaluating software architectures and changes to them, a way that considers technical and organizational constraints, particularly in the context of large-scale distributed development projects.

Collaborative Software Engineering Tools

As discussed earlier, researchers have paid a great deal of attention to communication, awareness, and coordination tools for software development. Recent empirical studies have demonstrated the value of such tools in small work teams [Sarma et al. 2008]. Despite these positive results, the empirical evaluations of awareness tools have been performed only in small teams.

Current collaborative tools do not provide satisfactory support for larger teams or large-scale projects. In such settings, the complex web of technical and work dependencies creates awareness mechanisms that provide overwhelming amounts of information, diminishing the potential benefits of coordination. The issues of scalability and information overload highlight an important limitation of current collaborative environments. Traditionally, the central premise of awareness tools is to capture coordination information of a distributed team or project. However, presenting all the available coordination-related information is not the appropriate approach, especially if the information is not actionable.

There are two important dimensions of actionable information: *relevance* and *timeliness*. Evidence suggests that developers create informal practices that tend to "follow the dependencies" to self-coordinate based on their knowledge of dependencies in the code, in order to minimize the impact of their efforts on others and vice versa. For example, developers have been known to email specific developers in a team before a check-in to warn them of impending changes and potential conflicts.

However, we know that automating email notifications for every check tends to result in information overload, and at that point developers start to ignore the notifications. Awareness information is far more useful when it is directed only to users who will be affected by a particular change. Moreover, information needs are dynamic, so in addition to identifying the right people, coordination information should be delivered at the right time. Information needs change as the context of the developer's task changes.

In the future, we expect to see a new generation of tools that manage scale and information overload by combining new analytical and visualization techniques in a more social context, mimicking current social computing environments. Then we could expect to see new tools that apply social networking approaches to the many collaborative tools proposed by researchers and to commercial products, such as IBM Rational Team Concert, to identify particular organizational boundaries (e.g., departmental units or projects) and provide special support for such coordination barriers.

Balancing Standarization and Flexibility

Research on software processes shares several commonalities with research on socio-technical congruence, since an important aspect of software processes is the examination and management of relationships among the development organization's members, tools, and the product. Ongoing research efforts in the process community are focused on developing a better understanding of the issues of cross-enterprise collaboration and coordination, suggesting a move towards a socio-technical perspective.

Frameworks such as socio-technical congruence [Cataldo et al. 2006] [Cataldo et al. 2008] could be very useful in evaluating the coordination capabilities that a particular set of software processes offer for a development organization that has multiple actors or roles (e.g., a change management process) across multiple organizational units under varying levels of uncertainty. Such a novel approach would complement the traditional process modeling approaches used to design, simulate, and evaluate software processes.

Some of the open research questions to be addressed include the development of mechanisms for utilizing socio-technical measures to improve software design and development by combining novel processes and tools, as well as understanding how processes, personal interaction, and collaborative tools complement each other to improve coordination.

References

[Banker et al. 1998] Banker, R., et al. Software Development Practices, Software Complexity, and Software Maintenance Performance: A Field Study. *Management Science* 40(4): 433–450.

[Bass et al. 2007] Bass, M., L. Bass, J.D. Herbsleb, and M. Cataldo. 2007. Architectural Misalignment: An Experience Report. *Proceedings of the Sixth Working IEEE/IFIP Conference on Software Architecture*: 17.

[Battin et al. 2001] Battin, R.D., et al. Leveraging Resources in Global Software Development. *IEEE Software* 18: 70–77.

[Biehl et al. 2007] Biehl, J., et al. FASTDash: A Visual Dashboard for Fostering Awareness in Software Teams. *Proceedings of the SIGCHI conference on human factors in computing systems*: 1313–1322.

[Cataldo 2010] Cataldo, M. 2010. Sources of Errors in Distributed Development Projects: Implications for Collaborative Tools. *Proceedings of the 2010 ACM conference on computer supported cooperative work*: 281–290.

[Cataldo and Herbsleb 2008] Cataldo, M., and J. Herbsleb. 2008. Communication Networks in Geographically Distributed Software Development. *Proceedings of the 2008 ACM conference on computer supported cooperative work*: 579–588.

[Cataldo and Herbsleb 2010] Cataldo, M., and J.D. Herbsleb. 2010. Coordination Failures: Their Impact on Development Productivity and Software Failures. Technical Report CMU-ISR-2010-100, School of Computer Science, Carnegie Mellon University. *http://reports-archive .adm.cs.cmu.edu/anon/isr2010/CMU-ISR-10-104.pdf*.

[Cataldo and Nambiar 2009a] Cataldo, M., and S. Nambiar. 2009. Quality in Global Software Development Projects: A Closer Look at the Role of Distribution. *Proceedings of the 2009 Fourth IEEE International Conference on Global Software Engineering*: 163–172.

[Cataldo and Nambiar 2009b] Cataldo, M., and S. Nambiar. 2009. On the Relationship Between Process Maturity and Geographic Distribution: An Empirical Analysis of their Impact on Software Quality. *Proceedings of the 7th joint meeting of the European software engineering conference and the ACM SIGSOFT symposium on the foundations of software engineering*: 101–110.

[Cataldo and Nambiar 2010] Cataldo, M., and S. Nambiar. 2010. The Impact of Geographic Distribution and the Nature of Technical Coupling on the Quality of Global Software Development Projects. Forthcoming in *Journal of Software Maintenance and Evolution: Research and Practice*.

[Cataldo et al. 2006] Cataldo, M., P. Wagstrom, J. Herbsleb, and K. Carley. 2006. Identification of Coordination Requirements: Implications for the Design of Collaboration and Awareness Tools. *Proceedings of the 2006 20th anniversary conference on Computer supported cooperative work*: 353–362.

[Cataldo et al. 2007] Cataldo, M., et al. On Coordination Mechanisms in Global Software Development. *Proceedings of the International Conference on Global Software Engineering*: 71–80.

[Cataldo et al. 2008] Cataldo, M., et al. 2008. Socio-Technical Congruence: A Framework for Assessing the Impact of Technical and Work Dependencies on Software Development Productivity. *Proceedings of the Second ACM/IEEE International Symposium on Empirical Software Engineering and Measurement*: 2–11.

[Cataldo et al. 2009] Cataldo, M., et al. Software Dependencies, Work Dependencies and their Impact on Failures. *IEEE Transactions on Software Engineering* 35(6): 864–878.

[Cubranic et al. 2005] Cubranic, D., G.C. Murphy, J. Singer, and K.S. Booth. 2005. Hipikat: A Project Memory for Software Development. *IEEE Transactions on Software Engineering* 31(6): 446–465.

[de Souza et al. 2004] de Souza, C.R.B., et al. 2004. How a Good Software Practice Thwarts Collaboration: The Multiple Roles of APIs in Software Development. *Proceedings of the 12th International Symposium on Foundations of Software Engineering*: 221–230.

[Espinosa et al. 2007] Espinosa, J.A., et al. 2007. Do Gradations of Time Zone Separation Make a Difference in Performance? A First Laboratory Study. *Proceedings of the Int'l Conference on Global Software Engineering*: 12–22.

[Fogarty et al. 2005] Fogarty, J., A.J. Ko, H.H. Aung, E. Golden, K.P. Tang, and S.E. Hudson. 2005. Examining Task Engagement in Sensor-based Statistical Models of Human Interruptibility. *Proceedings of the SIGCHI Conference on Human factors in computing systems*: 331–340.

[Gall et al. 1998] Gall, H., K. Hajek, and M. Jazayeri. 1998. Detection of Logical Coupling Based on Product Release History. *Proceedings of the International Conference on Software Maintenance*: 190.

[Grinter et al. 1999] Grinter, R.E., et al. 1999. The Geography of Coordination Dealing with Distance in R&D Work. *Proceedings of the International ACM SIGGROUP Conference on Supporting Group Work*: 306–215.

[Herbsleb and Mockus 2003] Herbsleb, J.D., and A. Mockus. 2003. An Empirical Study of Speed and Communication in Globally Distributed Software Development. *IEEE Transactions on Software Engineering* 29(6): 481–494.

[Herbsleb et al. 2006] Herbsleb, J.D., A. Mockus, and J.A Roberts. 2006. Collaboration in Software Engineering Projects: A Theory of Coordination. *Proceedings of the International Conference on Information Systems*.

[Kommeren and Parviainen 2007] Kommeren, R., and P. Parviainen. 2007. Philips Experience in Global Distributed Software Development. *Empirical Software Engineering* 12(6): 647–660.

[Malone and Crowston 1994] Malone, T.W., and K. Crowston. 1994. The interdisciplinary study of coordination. *Comp. Surveys* 26(1): 87–119.

[Minto and Murphy 2007] Minto, S., and G.C. Murphy. 2007. Recommending Emergent Teams. *Proceedings of the Fourth International Workshop on Mining Software Repositories*: 5.

[Mockus and Weiss 2001] Mockus, A., and D. Weiss. 2001. Globalization by chunking: a quantitative approach. *IEEE Software* 18: 30–37.

[Nagappan and Ball 2007] Nagappan, N., and T. Ball. 2007. Using Software Dependencies and Churn Metrics to Predict Field Failures: An Empirical Case Study. *Proceedings of the 1st International Symposium on Empirical Software Engineering and Measurement*: 363–373.

[Nagappan et al. 2008] Nagappan, N., B. Murphy, and V.R. Basili. 2008. The Influence of Organizational Structure on Software Quality: An Empirical Case Study. *Proceedings of the International Conference on Software Engineering*: 521–530.

[Parnas 1972] Parnas, D.L. 1972. On the criteria to be used in decomposing systems into modules. *Communications of the ACM* 15(12): 1053–1058.

[Pieper et al. 2009] Pieper, J.H., et al. 2009. Team Analytics: Understanding Team in the Global Workplace. *Proceedings of the 27th International Conference on Human Factors in Computing Systems*: 83–86.

[Ripley et al. 2007] Ripley, R., et al. 2007. A Visualization for Software Project Awareness and Evolution. *Proceedings of the 4th IEEE International Workshop on Visualizing Software for Understanding and Analysis*: 137–144.

[Sangwan et al. 2006] Sangwan, R., et al. 2006. *Global Software Development Handbook*. Pennsauken, NJ: Auerbach Publications.

[Sarma et al. 2008] Sarma, A., D. Redmiles, and A. van der Hoek. 2008. Empirical Evidence of the Benefits of Workspace Awareness in Software Configuration Management. *Proceedings of the 16th International Symposium on Foundations of Software Engineering*: 113–123.

[Sarma et al. 2009] Sarma, A., L. Maccherone, P. Wagstrom, and J.D. Herbsleb. 2009. Tesseract: Interactive Visual Exploration of Socio-Technical Relationships in Software Development. *Proceedings of the 31st International Conference on Software Engineering*: 23–33.

[Wagstrom 2009] Wagstrom, P.A. 2009. *Vertical Interaction in Open Software Engineering Communities*. Unpublished PhD dissertation, School of Computer Science, Carnegie Mellon University.

[Weisband 2008] Weisband, S., ed. 2008. *Leadership at a Distance: Research in Technologically-Supported Work*. New York: Lawrence Erlbaum Associates.

[Zimmermann and Nagappan 2008] Zimmermann, T., and N. Nagappan. 2008. Predicting Defects Using Network Analysis on Dependency Graphs. *Proceedings of the 30th International Conference on Software Engineering*: 531–540.

## CHAPTER TWENTY-ONE

How Effective Is Modularization?

Neil Thomas
Gail Murphy

For more than 30 years, the concept of modularity has been seen as a key enabler for the development of large software systems. Modules help manage the complexity of development by breaking a system into units of software that individuals or teams can build [Dijkstra 1968], [Parnas 1972]. Modules enable the hiding of decisions behind an interface, allowing the individual or team responsible for a module to make progress independent of the decisions made by individuals and teams responsible for other modules [Parnas 1972]. Modules enable the enforcement of boundaries between parts of the software system, enabling the interchange of one part for another [Dijkstra 1968], minimizing the impact of changes made to a specific part of the system [Parnas 1972] and reducing the time to build the system when changes are made (separate compilation) [Liskov et al. 1977].

To help programmers maximize these benefits and more, most programming languages provide explicit support for expressing modules. For instance, many object-oriented programming languages, such as Java [Gosling et al. 1996], support a fine-grained notion of modularity through the definition and implementation of abstract data types. Support for coarser-grained modularity can sometimes be found in companion technologies. For instance, OSGi, a companion technology to Java, enables classes to be divided into bundles that are then restricted to communicating through well-defined interfaces [OSGi 2007]. Developers also often use informal means to express modularity, such as using a hierarchical file structure to distinguish modules.

Ideally, each module a developer expresses would capture one coherent concern. For example, in a software system that controls a train, a developer may define a module that interacts with the train's brake so as to ensure coherent reasoning about the operations of the brake. In reality, concerns cannot always be separated so cleanly. Returning to the train example, a developer might define a different module to interact with the signalling system of the track on which the train runs. In some cases, the brake and the signalling system functionality may have to interact so closely that there is a need to implement signalling system functionality in the brake module; for instance, emergency signals may require immediate application of the brake. These tight interactions can lead to the need for multiple modularizations of a system. This need has been well-articulated as the motivation for aspect-oriented software development [Kiczales et al. 1997], [Tarr et al. 1999] and emerging aspect-oriented programming languages, such as AspectJ [Kiczales et al. 2001], improve a developer's ability to modularize the system by enabling the modular expression of crosscutting concerns.

Modules are thus an entrenched organizational approach to constructing software. But is modularization providing the promised benefits? In this chapter, we investigate whether the promised benefits are being seen by analyzing the archives of three open source software systems to determine answers to the following questions:

- Are most changes made to the code of a system during a single bug fix or enhancement constrained to a single module?

- When a software developer makes a change to the code of a system, must the developer consult code in other modules?

- Do the patterns in the actual changes and modules consulted suggest a different modular breakdown for a system?

We begin our account of this investigation by describing the systems we chose to include in our analyses. Because answering these questions across different software developments requires a definition for what constitutes a comparable change to these systems and a definition for what constitutes a module across the systems, we then describe how we defined a "change" and a "module." These definitions provide a basis for our analyses, which we then describe in detail before summarizing our results.

The Systems

Software development projects vary in many dimensions: the domain of the project, the expertise of the developers, the size of the project, and the programming languages used to express the source code comprising the system, to name just a few. We want the projects we analyze for the purpose of investigating the questions of interest to vary across at least some of these dimensions. We also want projects that have archival information about the software development available. Many projects meet these criteria. We chose to include in our analyses the following three projects:

- Evolution (*http://projects.gnome.org/evolution*), an integrated email, address book, and calendar application included in the GNOME desktop (*http://gnome.org*)
- Mozilla Firefox (*http://www.mozilla.com/firefox*), a popular cross-platform web browser
- Mylyn (*http://www.eclipse.org/mylyn*), a task-focused interface for Eclipse (*http://www.eclipse.org*) that is included in the standard Eclipse distribution

Table 21-1 demonstrates the variability in these projects by providing an overview of these projects in terms of the length of the development, the primary language used to express the source code, the number of modules (see "What Is a Module?" on page 381), lines of code, and changes (see "What Is a Change?" on page 376). Only changes that were analyzed in our study are included in these counts.

TABLE 21-1. An overview of the three systems we analyzed

Project	First release	Primary language	Modules	Approximate SLOC[a]	Changes
Evolution	December 2001	C	43	300,000	1,939
Firefox	November 2004	C++	45	4,000,000	11,710
Mylyn	November 2006	Java	18	675,000	3,055

[a] Source lines of code were measured using *cloc* (*http://cloc.sourceforge.net*).

Aggregate statistics are a useful starting point for understanding the systems being analyzed, but they really tell only part of the story. In particular, these statistics treat the archives of these systems as static, hiding the dynamics of how developers make changes to the system over time. To better understand how the system developments compare, we also examine the rate at which the system changes.

We can characterize the rate of change within each system by looking at the number of lines of code modified per day. Figure 21-1 shows the activity on each project over time. Each dot in these graphs corresponds to a single day of data recorded in the project's code repository; the height of each dot on the vertical axis represents the number of lines of code that were committed to the repository on that day. We see that Evolution is characterized by a period of slow change initially, followed by a long period of sustained activity. Firefox changes less frequently and shows almost no activity after a certain point, as developers completed work on the 3.5 release branch and moved on to the next version of the project. Mylyn appears to grow in periodic bursts over time.

We can reach similar conclusions about the rates of change of these systems by looking at the cumulative sum of this data. Figure 21-2 is such a plot for Evolution, clearly showing the initial period of slow change and later sustained activity. Plots for the other systems look similar.

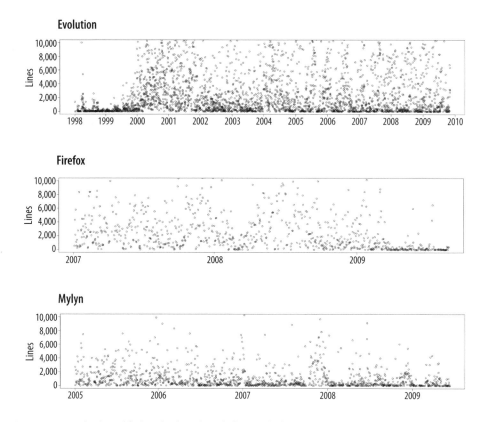

FIGURE 21-1. Lines of code modified per day throughout the history of Eclipse, Firefox, and Mylyn

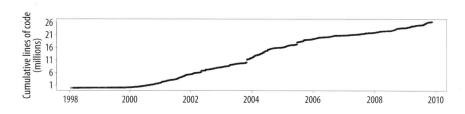

FIGURE 21-2. Cumulative sum of lines of code modified for Evolution

What Is a Change?

Before we can analyze the relationship between the modularity of a system and the changes developers make to that system, we first need a consistent definition of a change.

All of the projects we studied use Bugzilla (*http://www.bugzilla.org*) as a central bug-tracking system. Bug reports, despite their name, are not limited to just tracking defects; indeed, bug reports are also used to track feature requests (referred to as "enhancements" in Bugzilla). Thus, each report captures the notion of a single logical change to the system, which could be made either to fix a defect or to add new functionality to the system.

Table 21-2 shows the ratio of these two types of reports for the changes that we studied. For all three projects, the majority of the changes are fixes for defects in the system, although more than a quarter of the Mylyn changes are actually enhancements.

TABLE 21-2. Ratio of change types for each system

Project	Total changes	Defects (%)	Enhancements (%)
Evolution	1,939	1,792 (92.4%)	147 (7.6%)
Firefox	11,710	11,198 (95.6%)	512 (4.4%)
Mylyn	3,055	2,247 (73.6%)	808 (26.4%)

Each of these three projects uses a source control system that organizes and tracks changes using a notion of atomic commit operations. Each commit may modify multiple files and includes various metadata, including an identifier for the committer (typically a username or email address), the date and time at which the commit occurred, and a free-text description of the changes that were made.

A single change may correspond to more than one commit in the source control system. Developers may subdivide the work of one logical change into several smaller subtasks, completing and committing the code changes for each subtask before moving on to the next one. In some cases, multiple developers may contribute code to a new feature, each submitting their own part of the work as a separate commit. These commits are all part of the same logical change to the system, even though they happen to be committed to the source code repository separately.

We therefore define our unit of change as the aggregation of all commits associated with one bug report. Commits are grouped together by extracting bug IDs from the description field using the case-insensitive regular expression /bug #?(\d+)/, then taking the union of the code changes from all commits with the same bug ID. For example, these are the description fields of three commits from the Firefox project that combine to form a single logical change:

> Bug 385423. Refactor textrun cache so that all textrun clients use a single global word-based cache. Responsibility for stripping out problematic characters (e.g. newlines) is given to the word cache. r=vlad,smontagu

> Bug 385423. Force ZWSP, PSEP and LSEP to be treated as zero-width invisible and not passed into platform textrun creation. Avoids potential bugs and forces consistent handling. r=vlad

> [OS/2] Fix build break in gfxOS2Fonts.cpp (mimic gfxPangoFonts change that supposedly came from Bug 385423)

Commits with descriptions that did not match the specified regular expression were excluded from our analysis. For both Firefox and Mylyn, we were able to match approximately three-quarters of all commits (74.7% and 75.8%, respectively). For Evolution, only 19.5% of commits were matched, because most commits for this project did not explicitly reference a bug ID and therefore could not be analyzed.

Since our analysis will explore the scope of these changes (in particular, the number of modules consulted and modified by a developer as part of each change), it is useful to have a sense of the size of each change. Figure 21-3 shows the partial distribution of the number of lines of code modified in each change for Firefox; the distributions for the other two projects have a similar shape. Changes affecting over 1,000 lines are not shown in the histogram in order to save space, but are still counted in the summary statistics given in Table 21-3.

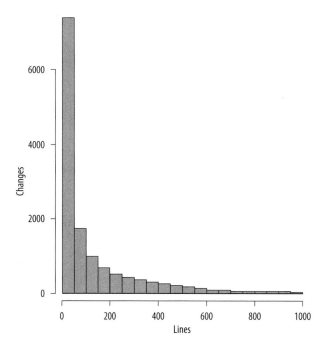

FIGURE 21-3. Distribution of the number of lines of code modified in each change to Firefox

TABLE 21-3. Lines of code modified in each change

Project	Median	Mean	% changes affecting over 100 lines
Evolution	24	157.2	2.0%
Firefox	26	383.3	3.6%
Mylyn	62	248.5	8.6%

We observe that most changes to all three systems are very small, with a few very large changes (e.g., refactoring a large component or moving code from one directory to another) in the right tail.

For the Mylyn project, additional information about each change is available via "task context" files that are attached to most of the project's bug reports. As we briefly mentioned earlier, Mylyn is a task-focused interface for the Eclipse IDE (*http://www.eclipse.org*). Among other features, Mylyn includes support for tracking all of the software artifacts a developer interacts with as he is working on a task. For each task, Mylyn maintains a set of "interesting" code elements (e.g., fields and methods) that includes not only those elements that have been modified but also those that have been navigated to in the editor [Kersten et al. 2006]. Many of the views within Eclipse can then be filtered to show only these interesting elements, allowing the developer to focus on only the subset of the larger system that is relevant to the task at hand.

As a matter of policy, whenever a developer is working to resolve a bug on the Mylyn project, she begins by opening a new task inside Mylyn that is linked directly to the bug report. When the developer has finished working on the bug, she publishes the task context information collected by Mylyn to the bug report. This posting allows other developers to import the task context into their own Mylyn instances if they wish to examine the system from the filtered perspective of the developer who worked on the bug.

Figure 21-4 shows a sample task context. Items in the context that are bold are so interesting to the developer as part of the task that they have become landmarks. The slider on the top left of the screenshot can be used to show elements only with interest greater than a threshold specified by the position of the slider. Developers do not typically work with the view shown in the screenshot, relying instead on filtering in other views in the IDE to show only the program elements related to the task context. The view in Figure 21-4 is used primarily to investigate the context prior to attaching to a bug.

Each task context stores timestamps that we can use to approximate the total amount of time the developer spent working on a change. Timestamps are recorded for many different types of "interaction events," including selection events (when the developer clicks on a source code element), edit events (when the developer modifies text in the editor), and command events (as the developer invokes commands in the IDE). We expect these events to be generated frequently while a developer is actively working. We can therefore compute an estimate for

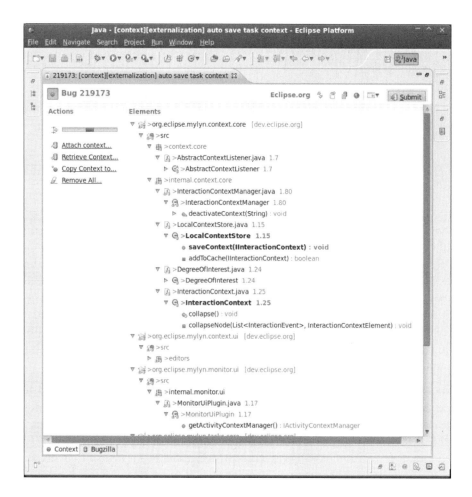

FIGURE 21-4. A task context attached to a change as viewed from within Mylyn

the time spent working on a change by simply sorting the interaction events chronologically, taking the difference between each pair of consecutive events and summing all of these differences. In order to account for breaks in a developer's work, we do not count the time that elapses between any pair of consecutive events that occur more than five minutes apart.

Thus when we analyze a change to Mylyn, we have two related sources of information: the commit logs from the source control system, which show the modifications a developer made to the code; and the task context files attached to the bug report, which show the path the developer took through the code in order to make those modifications. Using timestamps stored in the task context, we can also approximate how much time the developer spent working on the bug. This allows us, for at least one system, to answer questions about how a developer interacts with the system's modules in a much richer way than just looking at the changes that are ultimately made.

What Is a Module?

To be able to discuss how developers work with the modules in a software system, we need a consistent definition of what a module is and how the code in one module is separated from other modules in the system.

Although it would be convenient to define modules by reference to explicit declarations in the source code, this approach presents two difficulties for our analysis. First, the projects we selected for our study are implemented in a variety of programming languages, each of which treats modularity differently. Evolution is implemented in C, which provides minimal support for defining modules within source code. Firefox primarily uses C++, a language that supports modules at the language level through namespace declarations, but Firefox itself does not make consistent use of this language feature. Further, Firefox also includes code written in many other languages, such as JavaScript and XUL (the XML User Interface Language), which have completely different modularity constructs. Mylyn, a Java application, is the only one of the three systems that has clearly defined modules within source code, which it accomplishes using Java packages.

Second, the systems we chose to study are sufficiently large and long-lived that analysis at the fine-grained level of the programming language could be overwhelmed by development issues, such as changing members of the development team and refactorings of the code. To reduce the likelihood that such issues would impact our analysis, we chose to focus on a coarser granularity of modules that are more representative of architectural modules. It would be interesting to focus subsequent analysis on a finer-grained definition of module.

Rather than trying to define a module in terms of these programming-language-specific features, we instead turn to the directory structure used by each system to store its code. As we will see, all three of the projects we analyzed organize their filesystems in such a way that a consistent definition of a module can be applied to each. Further, this representation of modules as directories makes it trivial to identify the boundaries that separate each module from other modules in the system.

Both Evolution and Firefox use a simple directory structure that matches the way other data is typically stored on a computer: each top-level directory represents a major system component, with subdirectories dividing each component into several smaller subcomponents. Here's how that looks for one small part of the Firefox repository:

```
layout          netwerk         parser
   /base           /base           /expat
   /generic        /cache          /htmlparser
   /inspector      /cookie         /xml
   ...             ...
```

Each subdirectory may contain additional subdirectories dividing source code from test files and documentation.

Two possible definitions for a module emerge from this structure. At a high level, each top-level directory (e.g., *layout*) could be considered a module; at a lower level, each subdirectory of these top-level directories (e.g., *layout/base*) could be considered a separate module.

For Evolution, the smallest of the three projects in our study, we define a module as a top-level directory. For Firefox, which is an order of magnitude larger, we define a module as a subdirectory of a top-level directory. Applying the former definition to Firefox (i.e., using only top-level directories) results in extremely large modules that mask many of the interesting interactions within the system. Conversely, if we were to break Evolution down into subdirectory-level modules, there would be too much noise in the resulting data to perform a meaningful analysis.

Mylyn has a very different directory structure. Java source files are arranged in a nested directory structure that matches their package declarations, resulting in a much deeper folder hierarchy than we find with the C/C++ systems. These Java packages are in turn grouped together to form Eclipse projects (the top level of organization within the Eclipse IDE), which themselves are grouped by naming conventions. Part of the Mylyn repository looks like this:

```
org.eclipse.mylyn.bugzilla.core
  /src/org/eclipse/mylyn/internal/bugzilla/core
    /history
    /service
org.eclipse.mylyn.bugzilla.ui
  /src/org/eclipse/mylyn/internal/bugzilla/ui
    /action
    /editor
    /search
    ...
org.eclipse.mylyn.context.core
  /src/org/eclipse/mylyn/context
    /core
    /internal/core
```

As with the other systems, a couple of definitions for a module are readily apparent from this structure. The top-level directories, representing Eclipse projects, correspond roughly to the subdirectories in Evolution and Firefox. At an even higher level, we can group these directories together by the first component after *mylyn* in their names. For example, both *org.eclipse.mylyn.bugzilla.core* and *org.eclipse.mylyn.bugzilla* can be seen as part of a larger *bugzilla* component. Indeed, if we look at the Java package structure, both of these directories contain only code belonging to subpackages of *org.eclipse.mylyn.bugzilla*, so this choice of grouping matches the language semantics.

It is the latter top-tier model that we use here, rather than the Firefox second-tier model: we define a module in Mylyn as all the top-level directories that correspond to the same immediate subpackage of *org.eclipse.mylyn*. This choice allows the core logic and UI widgets, which typically reside in separate directories in this structure, to be viewed as a single module in the system.

The Results

Now that we have concrete definitions of changes and modules in each of our three systems, we can finally begin to investigate how developers work with these modules.

Change Locality

We begin our exploration with a simple question: are most changes to the code constrained to a single module? Figure 21-5 shows a histogram of the number of modules modified per change for each system, and Table 21-4 presents some summary statistics.

TABLE 21-4. Number of modules affected by each change

Project	% changes affecting only one module	Mean modules affected
Evolution	86.6%	1.243
Firefox	73.7%	1.577
Mylyn	69.7%	1.634

Examined Modules

When making these code changes, how many modules does a developer consult? We can answer this question quantitatively for Mylyn given the availability of task context data, but not for the other two systems.

Figure 21-6 shows the number of modules that were examined by a developer for each change. The mean number of examined modules is 2.365, with a median of 2. The mean of examined modules is higher than the mean number of modules that are actually modified (1.634), which suggests that developers occasionally consult modules that they do not end up actually changing.

If we take a closer look at the modules that are examined but not modified in each change, we find two of Mylyn's modules stand out. In 13% of changes, a developer examined the Tasks module without changing it, and in 8% of changes the same holds for the Bugzilla module. We might infer from this that the Tasks and Bugzilla modules are less cohesive than the other modules or are coupled to many other modules in the system. We will revisit this hypothesis later, when we look at how modules emerge from a developer's interaction with the system.

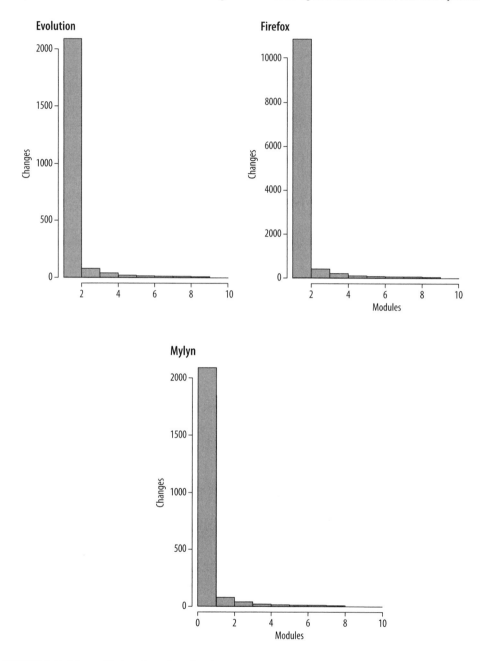

FIGURE 21-5. Modules modified per change in each system

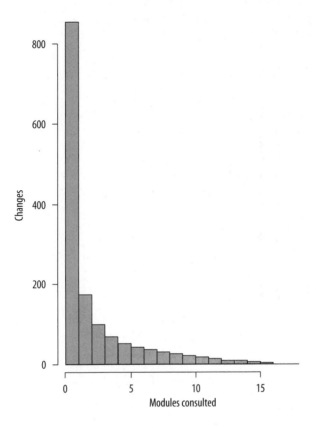

FIGURE 21-6. Number of modules examined per change to Mylyn

How does the number of modules examined affect the time required to complete a task? We hypothesize that when developers examine more modules, the time required for task completion increases. This hypothesis is indeed supported by our data, which show a weak correlation between the number of modules examined in a task context and the amount of time spent working on that task (Pearson's r=0.20, $p < 10^{-15}$).

Does the number of extra modules examined vary between developers? In particular, do more experienced developers need to consult fewer modules when making changes to the system? We can use the number of closed bug reports assigned to each developer as a heuristic for the developer's experience with the system. If we plot this against the number of modules examined but not modified in each change, we get the plot shown in Figure 21-7.

We observe that there seems to be little differentiation on the left side of the graph, with both new and experienced developers frequently consulting only a few extra modules when making changes. However, the story is quite different on the right side of the graph, where we see that most of the developers who consulted many extra modules had little experience.

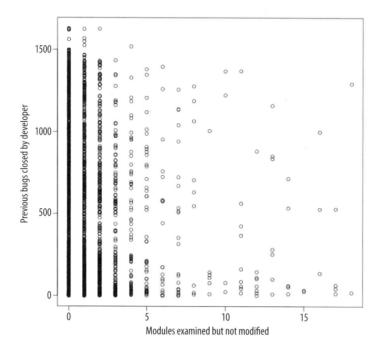

FIGURE 21-7. Developer experience versus number of modules examined but not modified in each change. Experience is measured by the number of bugs closed by the developer prior to making the change.

Emergent Modularity

All of our analysis so far has started from the assumption that the separation of each system into modules based on the filesystem structure is reasonable. We now approach these systems from a different perspective: can we infer modularity from the developers' interaction patterns? Do modules emerge as a developer works with the system that differ from those explicitly set out in the design? We have already shown that changes to Evolution almost always touch only a single module (86.6% of changes), so we focus on Firefox and Mylyn for this part of our analysis.

We begin with a simple count of the number of times each pair of modules is changed together. For Firefox, the pairs that occur in at least 1% of commits are:

```
browser/base, browser/themes
browser/places, toolkit/places
layout/base, layout/generic
browser/themes, toolkit/themes
toolkit/locales, toolkit/mozapps
browser/base, browser/locales
toolkit/content, toolkit/themes
```

There are a few observations we can make from this list. First, the "base" module inside each top-level directory seems to be tightly coupled to the other modules within the same top-level directory. This seems reasonable from a design perspective. Second, modules with the same name in different top-level directories change together: for example, *browser/places* and *toolkit/places* often change together, as do *browser/themes* and *toolkit/themes*. Here, the naming suggests that the system architects realized there were multiple ways in which the system could be sliced-and-diced, indicating possible crosscutting concerns, and that choosing one separation into modules would cause other cohesive parts of the system to be split up across multiple modules. In particular, choosing to divide the *browser* and *toolkit* components of Firefox has caused the *places* and *themes* components to become split.

The most interesting interactions are those that do not match either of these two explanations. From the previous list, we see that *toolkit/locales* and *toolkit/mozapps* seem to be related, as are *toolkit/content* and *toolkit/themes*. Further investigation into the details of the changes that modified each of these pairs of modules may reveal system functionality that could be extracted into a more cohesive module.

If we apply the same approach to Mylyn, we find the following pairs:

```
tasks, bugzilla
tasks, context
tasks, jira
tasks, help
tasks, commons
tasks, trac
```

A quick glance at this list reveals an obvious pattern: changes to the *tasks* module often involve changes to other modules in the system as well. Recall from our earlier analysis that in 13% of changes, more than for any other module, a developer examined the *tasks* module without ultimately changing it. Combined with this new data, there is evidence that the Mylyn *tasks* module is coupled to much of the rest of the system.

To explore the relationship between the *tasks* module and the rest of the system, we used association rule mining, specifically frequent pattern mining [Agrawal et al. 1993] on the Mylyn task context data to discover rules about how developers examine the system modules when working on a change.[*] In this context, association rule mining yields rules of the form "if a developer examines module X, he is likely to also examine module Y as part of the same change." Each rule has an associated confidence value that measures the percentage of the dataset over which the rule holds. Our data mining produced the following rules for the task context data:

```
doc -> tasks (100%)
help -> tasks (100%)
trac -> tasks (84%)
team -> tasks (82%)
bugzilla -> tasks (81%)
jira -> tasks (81%)
```

---

[*] Association rules were generated using the Apriori algorithm as implemented in *ARtool* (*http://www.cs.umb.edu/~laur/ARtool*).

These were the only rules found with a confidence level of at least 80%. We see that from the perspective of a developer working on the system, any consultation of the six modules listed as antecedents in the preceding rules (*doc, help*, etc.) is very likely to also include consultation of the *tasks* module as part of working on the same change.

Having established that "all roads lead to *tasks*" within Mylyn, we can dive deeper to see whether any relationships emerge at the class level as developers interact with the system. First, we consider the perspective of a developer examining the system by once again mining the task context data, which yields these rules at a confidence level of at least 60%:

```
NewBugzillaTaskEditor -> AbstractRepositoryTaskEditor (88%)
BugzillaTaskEditor -> AbstractRepositoryTaskEditor (85%)
NewBugzillaTaskEditor -> BugzillaTaskEditor (79%)
IBugzillaConstants -> BugzillaClient (71%)
JiraRepositoryConnector -> AbstractRepositoryConnector (63%)
BugzillaRepositorySettingsPage -> AbstractRepositorySettingsPage (62%)
SynchronizeTaskJob -> RepositorySynchronizationManager (61%)
```

The most common type of rule identified by this analysis relates a concrete implementation to its corresponding abstract base class. It seems reasonable that developers would navigate between an abstract class and its concrete subclasses while exploring the system, so these relationships are not unexpected.

If we instead mine the change data, looking only at classes that were actually modified rather than those that were consulted by the developer, we get a very different set of rules (with a minimum confidence of 70%):

```
ITaskListExternalizer -> BugzillaTaskExternalizer (87%)
NewAttachmentWizard -> AbstractRepositoryTaskEditor (81%)
AbstractJavaRelationshipProvider -> XmlReferencesProvider (80%)
ActiveHierarchyView -> ActiveSearchView (76%)
PdeStructureBridge -> AntStructureBridge (75%)
RepositoryTaskAttribute -> AbstractRepositoryTaskEditor (74%)
ContextRetrieveAction -> ContextAttachAction (74%)
TaskCategory -> TaskListView (71%)
ContextAttachAction -> ContextRetrieveAction (71%)
```

These rules present a different view of the system. For example, we observe there is a close relationship between the ActiveHierarchyView and ActiveSearchView, and similarly between the ContextRetrieveAction and ContextAttachAction. These views and actions, respectively, may contain common functionality that could be extracted to another class. Some of the relationships are unexpected. For example, it is unclear why PdeStructureBridge and AntStructureBridge are so closely related, as they are very different implementations of a common superclass.

This data shows that the modules of Mylyn from the perspective of a developer making changes to the project may be quite different from the modules built into the design through the separation of code into different classes and Java packages. Where these two views of modularity differ, developers may need to consider and reason about more of the system than desired, even when making only small logical changes.

Threats to Validity

The primary construct in our study is the use of bug reports as the logical unit of change to the analyzed systems. The first threat to the validity of this construct comes from the simple pattern-matching technique we use to associate commits with bug reports based on their description field. This technique does not guarantee that all of the links between bug reports and commits are found; some commit descriptions may report the associated bug ID in a nonstandard format that is missed by our regular expression, whereas other commits may describe the bug they address without explicitly mentioning the bug ID. In particular, we were only able to match approximately 20% of the commits for Evolution, which restricted our analysis to a small subset of the system's full history.

A second threat to the construct validity is due to noise in the Bugzilla repositories. We assumed that each bug report corresponds to a single logical change to the system, but this does not hold for all bug reports. For example, some reports describe routine software maintenance (e.g., upgrading a third-party library that is used by the system to the latest version) that could have very different characteristics than the defect reports and enhancement requests that we intended to study.

The internal validity of our study concerns the relationship between our data and the conclusions reached. Many of the conclusions are subjective interpretations of the data we present, and other inferences are certainly possible. There are two areas where we can quantify the validity of our results. First, for the analysis of how the number of modules examined correlates with the time spent working on a change, the Pearson correlation coefficient is significant at the 99% level. Second, for the association rules mined from the Mylyn task contexts and change data, the confidence level of each rule is reported and we restrict our analysis only to those rules above a certain confidence threshold.

It is possible that the results of our study do not generalize to systems that differ significantly from the ones that we studied. We can identify two threats to external validity. First, we examined only three systems. Although we tried to choose systems that varied in several characteristics (e.g., programming language, size, years of development), this is still a very small set of systems from which to generalize. For the analysis of how many modules a developer examines when making changes, we were only able to consider data from a single system (namely, Mylyn). Second, all of the systems we analyzed are open source, which may have different change patterns than industrial systems.

Summary

We studied archives from three open source systems of varying size to explore how developers interact with the modules expressed in these systems. Several patterns emerge from this analysis that transcend the size of the project, the problem domain, and the programming language used. First, as desired, we observed that most changes are isolated to a single module. However, we also saw that a large number of changes still require the modification of code in several different modules, causing developers to consult larger portions of the system and to spend more time making the changes. Second, looking at a system through the eyes of the developers making changes by mining data about which classes or files often change or are consulted together reveals that the modules designed into a system are not necessarily the same as those with which a developer works.

These results show that while current modularization techniques seem to be supporting developers in their work, there is room for improvement. Tools that help guide developers to look at modules that their colleagues have previously consulted to complete similar changes might help reduce the time needed to make a change. Analysis of developer work patterns with modules may help suggest remodularizations of the system or help suggest additional language features to better enable developers to express multiple perspectives of modularization for a single system.

References

[Agrawal et al. 1993] Agrawal, R., T. Imielinski, and A.N. Swami. 1993. Mining association rules between sets of items in large databases. *Proceedings of the 1993 ACM SIGMOD international conference on management of data*: 207–216.

[Dijkstra 1968] Dijkstra, Edsger W. 1968. The structure of "THE"—Multiprogramming System. *Communications of the ACM* 11(3): 341–346.

[Gosling et al. 1996] Gosling, James, Bill Joy, and Guy Steele. 1996. *The Java language specification*. Boston: Addison-Wesley.

[Kersten et al. 2006] Kersten, Mik, and Gail C. Murphy. 2006. Using task context to improve programmer productivity. *Proceedings of the 14th ACM SIGSOFT international symposium on foundations of software engineering*: 1–11.

[Kiczales et al. 1997] Kiczales, Gregor, John Irwin, John Lamping, Jean-Marc Loingtier, Christina Videira Lopes, Chris Maeda, and Anurag Mendhekar. 1997. Aspect-oriented programming. In *Lecture Notes in Computer Science, vol. 1241, Proceedings of ECOOP'97*, ed. M. Aksit and S. Matsuoka, 220–242. Berlin: Springer-Verlag.

[Kiczales et al. 2001] Kiczales, Gregor, Erik Hilsdale, Jim Hugunin, Mik Kersten, Jeffrey Palm, and William G. Griswold. 2001. An overview of AspectJ. In *Lecture Notes in Computer Science, vol. 2072, Proceedings of ECOOP 2001*, ed. J.L. Knudsen, 327–353. Berlin: Springer-Verlag.

[Liskov et al. 1977] Liskov, Barbara, Alan Snyder, Russel Atkinson, and Craig Schaffert. 1977. Abstraction mechanisms in CLU. *Communications of the ACM* 20(8): 565–576.

[OSGi 2007] OSGi Alliance. 2007. About the OSGi service platform: Technical Whitepaper. Available at *http://www.osgi.org/wiki/uploads/Links/OSGiTechnicalWhitePaper.pdf*.

[Parnas 1972] Parnas, David L. 1972. On the criteria to be used in decomposing systems into modules. *Communications of the ACM* 15(12): 1053–1058.

[Tarr et al. 1999] Tarr, Peri L., Harold Ossher, William H. Harrison, and Stanley M. Sutton, Jr. N degrees of separation: Multi-dimensional separation of concerns. *Proceedings of the International Conference on Software Engineering*: 107–119.

## CHAPTER TWENTY-TWO

The Evidence for Design Patterns

Walter Tichy

Design patterns are reusable solutions for design problems. They became popular in 1995 with a famous book by Erich Gamma et al. [Gamma et al. 1995]. Before design patterns were introduced, programmers had only a few general design principles to guide them when structuring software. These principles included the information hiding principle, which says to equip software modules with change-invariant interfaces. This principle assures that the insides of a module can be changed while keeping the interface the same, and therefore none of the software using the module needs to be updated. The principle was formulated by Parnas [Parnas 1972] in response to the observation that software changes frequently.

Design patterns go further than general principles: they suggest solutions for concrete design problems. In that sense, design patterns are to design what algorithms are to programming. Both algorithms and design patterns provide solutions for concrete problems. For instance, Quicksort provides a solution for sorting, whereas the Observer pattern is a solution for sending updates to interested software components. Textbook algorithms usually are not executable, because they are formulated in pseudo-language. The programmer must map them into the target programming language and make other adjustments. Similarly, design patterns are not finished designs. Instead, they describe a general software structure or interaction between software components that still must be adapted to circumstances.

Proponents claim the following advantages for design patterns:

- Higher software quality
- Greater programmer productivity

- Better team communication
- Improved design skills for inexperienced programmers

In the early years of design patterns, nobody knew whether these claims were true. At the time, experienced programmers had already lived through many programming fads and were unwilling to spend time and energy on another one. The zoo of design techniques was already crowded; it included structured design, functional design, data abstraction, modular design, object-oriented design, multi-paradigm design, architectural styles, refactoring, and others. Why would anyone waste time on something new and unproven called design patterns? But what if they were actually a good idea? How could we resolve this question? Should we rely on the authors of pattern books, personal experience, or the wisdom of consultants? All these were subjective or self-interested in some way. To objectively test whether the claims were true, there was only one way: objectively observing programmers in their work, or more precisely, conducting a scientific experiment. The experiment would measure the difference between using design patterns and not using them. If design patterns were such strong productivity and quality enhancers as claimed, then some difference should be measurable. Given the broad claims about patterns, a single experiment was not going to test all of them. So my students and I decided in 1996 to embark on a series of experiments. In the process, we not only learned a lot about design patterns, but also a lot about experimental methods in software research. But before reviewing them, a brief look at patterns will help grasp the ideas behind them.

Design Pattern Examples

The experiments discussed in this chapter involve a total of seven design patterns, sometimes in combination: Abstract Factory, Bridge, Compositum, Decorator, Observer, Template Method, and Visitor. Observer is a nice one to discuss in some detail; the rest will be characterized briefly. Exact specifications appear in [Gamma et al. 1995].

The Observer pattern solves the following design problem. Suppose an application contains an important data structure that is updated repeatedly. This data structure is called the *subject*. Suppose furthermore that there are a number of other components that need to be informed whenever the subject changes. These are called *observers*, because they watch the changes to the subject. An important aspect is that it is unknown how many observers there will be: observers should be independent and be able to come and go. This aspect precludes bundling the subject with the observers into a single class or module. Instead, there must be a dynamic link between subject and observers. The solution to this design problem is as follows: Both subject and observers are independent objects, and observers interested in a subject must register at the subject. When the subject changes, it sends a message, or an alert, to all registered observers. An example of the Observer pattern is a blog that readers might be interested in. Rather than monitoring the blog continuously, readers register at the blog and receive an alert—for example, an email message or notice in a message window—when a new blog entry has been added. Readers can then decide when to fetch and read the new entry.

Figure 22-1 shows the class diagram for the Observer pattern. Both the subject and observer classes have concrete subclasses, indicating that the pattern must be adapted to given circumstances. The observer class provides three important methods. The methods attach and detach are meant to register and deregister observers. The method notify goes through the list of observers and calls the function update on every registered observer. Each concrete observer class implements its own version of update. Each update method simply fetches relevant data from the concrete subject and updates its own variables. The important property of this pattern is that observers are independent of each other (no observer needs to pass data to another), but whenever the subject changes, all registered observers are updated automatically.

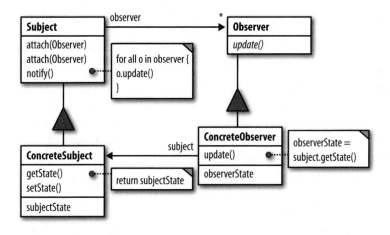

FIGURE 22-1. Observer design pattern (adapted from [Gamma et al. 1995])

Abstract Factory, also known as Kit, provides a mechanism for creating sets of matched objects. For example, consider the elements of a user interface toolkit, such as windows, buttons, scroll bars, icons, etc. When a user interface is initialized, it is necessary to select implementations of the graphical elements that are matched to the platform. To do so, one uses a factory object that delivers the right graphical elements for a given platform. If the platform changes, one chooses a different factory. All factories have the same interface specified in an abstract class, hence the name of the pattern. The advantage is that the program setting up a user interface needs to select the appropriate factory once, while the rest of the program is written independently of the actual choice by always going through the factory.

Bridge is also a pattern for handling different platforms. Suppose again that developers plan to build a user interface toolkit that runs on several platforms. Suppose furthermore that they decide to build all user interface elements from scratch, without using the native elements of the platform. To draw these elements, several primitive drawing operations are needed, such as drawing lines, drawing text, or setting colors. The Bridge pattern says to collect these primitive operations into an interface, and then to implement this interface on several platforms. When initializing the toolkit, select the implementation appropriate for the platform and store a pointer to it in every interface element. When it becomes necessary to draw a button or window, all calls to the primitive drawing operations will go through this pointer to the implementation chosen for the given platform. This pointer is the "bridge" that connects the interface elements with the platform-specific primitives.

Composite is used to construct parts hierarchies. The filesystem of a computer is a parts hierarchy: a root directory contains files and directories, the contained directories in turn list files and other directories, and so on. A parts hierarchy may cascade to arbitrary depth. The Composite pattern provides a standardized way to arrange such hierarchies. It distinguishes container nodes (in our example, the containers would be the directories) and leaf nodes (files in our examples). Leaf nodes are atomic, meaning they cannot contain other nodes. The interfaces of containers and leaves offer operations that are common to both. In our example, some of the common operations are renaming, moving a file or directory to another directory, or opening a file or directory.

Decorator is useful for adding information or functionality to an existing class, without modifying the class. A Decorator is a proxy that is used instead of the original. Whenever a decorator object receives a message, it executes its own function and then delegates to the original. For instance, a test decorator adds code that is executed before and after a test case is run, recording the identity of the test and its results.

Template Method is used to build extensible software. A template method is a larger function that calls helper methods, so-called hooks. Hooks are abstract, i.e., not implemented in the class defining the template. Subclasses of the class with the template method must provide these plug-ins. An Internet browser is a good example. It provides a method for playing media files, but this method must be extensible so that additional, unknown formats supplied by other manufacturers can be handled. The template method in the browser loads the media file, but provides hooks for playing, stopping, or rewinding. These hooks are then added later in the form of a subclass for each media type. The template method handles all organizational aspects of media files, but when it comes to playing the media, it delegates to the play method of the appropriate plug-in.

Visitor provides a bundle of methods that are used to walk a recursive data structure. Typically, Visitor is used together with Composite. For instance, a visitor for a file system might walk the directory tree to compute the space used by files and directories. Another visitor might extract keywords from files and enter them into an index that is used to find files that contain certain keywords. The interesting part of the Visitor pattern is that the visit-functions are not built into the Composite, as one would expect. Instead, a visitor can be built independently and "thrown at" a recursive data structure to traverse it.

Why Might Design Patterns Work?

Before embarking on an experiment, it is useful to develop an explanation, or theory, of why the hypothesized phenomena might occur. If one just compares method A with method B without an idea of why they might differ, it becomes difficult to build a convincing experiment. If, on the other hand, one has a notion of what the underlying cause might be, one can design an experiment that hinges on this underlying cause. Otherwise, one is just fishing in the dark. Also, generalization suffers: one can only claim that the observed differences hold in situations that are close to the conditions under which the experiment was conducted. For learning more about the interdependence of theory and experiment, we highly recommend Chalmers' book *What Is This Thing Called Science?* [Chalmers 1999].

Why might design patterns actually improve programmer productivity, software quality, and team communication? Chunking theory provides a possible explanation. This theory was first formulated in 1956, in George A. Miller's famous paper "The Magical Number Seven, Plus or Minus Two: Some Limits on our Capacity for Processing Information" [Miller 1956]. His theory assumes that human memory consists of short-term and long-term memory. Short-term memory is fast and accurate, but its capacity is limited to about seven, plus or minus two, "chunks." A chunk is a unit of information. Interestingly, the amount of information contained *within* a chunk is largely irrelevant. Long-term memory, on the other hand, has enormous capacity, but its recall is comparatively slow and occasionally inaccurate. In order to store information in long-term memory, humans must rehearse it, i.e., make repeated efforts to memorize it. Short-term memory requires no rehearsing; it seems to store information effortlessly, but forgets easily. When thinking, humans rely mostly on short-term memory, but when its capacity is exhausted, they also use long-term memory, which slows thinking down. For instance, when working with a large piece of software, programmers often go back and reread or recheck aspects they had already covered. A question such as, "How was this again?" is an indication of short-term memory overflow and the need to rehearse. Short-term memory acts somewhat like a cache in a microprocessor: if new information does not fit, older information is expelled. However, the expelled information is not automatically stored in long-term memory, unless it is rehearsed.

The limitation of short-term memory to about seven chunks is where design patterns might help: the patterns form units that group several design elements together. Without an understanding of the Observer pattern, for instance, a programmer needs to store four individual classes in short-term memory, plus the protocols for registration and update, using up several slots. If the programmer recognizes the Observer pattern, however, only a single chunk is needed, freeing up other slots for working on the rest of a design. Software designs typically consists of many classes, so this type of chunking could be useful. To help identify the chunks, a program's documentation could simply point the reader to the patterns and the classes that belong to them. For instance, if the documentation points out the Observer pattern, the programmer would get a quick overview of the classes involved and might even skip studying the code for registration and update. In essence, design patterns help keep more of a design in short-term memory and thus enable faster, more comprehensive, and more accurate thought processes, which should manifest themselves in increased programmer productivity and software quality. Team communication would also improve. For example, rather than launching into a long-winded explanation of how some objects register and receive updates, a programmer would merely mention to a partner that certain classes constitute the Observer pattern, and that would be all that would need to be said. Specialized terminology does have its advantages!

Though plausible, nobody knew whether design patterns would really exhibit the hypothesized phenomena, but chunking theory helped with developing suitable experiments. The experiments would need to test programmer performance when working with sets of classes or other software elements occurring in design patterns. The tasks would have to be large enough to tax short-term memory, but not huge. Differences could come from two sources: a more accurate grasp of the software by using patterns, or by having more short-term capacity left over to do other things. As the actual load on short-term memory is difficult to establish, the experiments here deal with the former approach.

The First Experiment: Testing Pattern Documentation

The first question we asked was whether merely documenting design patterns would improve programmer performance. The idea was to give two sets of subjects the same program to modify, but one group would get slightly extended program documentation pointing out the patterns present; the other group would get normal documentation, but no pattern information. This experiment would thus test only the presence or absence of pattern documentation, not the effect of patterns. We chose this approach partly because when designing the experiment in 1996, we hadn't figured out how to construct two versions of a program that were equivalent, but with only one containing patterns. In a later experiment we were able to overcome this hurdle. But testing pattern documentation alone still proved useful because it gave us a first indication of whether patterns could be effective. If documenting patterns alone would increase performance, even bigger effects could be expected when comparing programs with patterns against those without.

Design of the Experiment

The experiment question was this: does it help the software maintainer if the design patterns in the program code are documented explicitly (using source code comments), compared to a program without explicit reference to design patterns? The experiment question was refined into the following two hypotheses:

Hypothesis 1

Documentation of design patterns speeds up pattern relevant maintenance tasks

Hypothesis 2

Documentation of design patterns reduces errors in pattern relevant maintenance tasks

The experiment measures work time and errors when programmers perform maintenance tasks that involve design patterns. We actually conducted two experiments. The first experiment was performed in January 1997 at the University of Karlsruhe (UKA), and the second in May 1997 at Washington University St. Louis (WUSTL). In Karlsruhe, 64 graduate and 10 undergraduate students participated; in St. Louis, 22 undergraduate students participated. All students had been trained in Java (UKA) or C++ (WUSTL) and had written programs with design patterns prior to the experiment; a pretest made sure participants knew about the relevant patterns. Details are available in [Prechelt et al. 2002].

An oft-repeated complaint is that one should use professionals rather than students, but at that early time in design pattern history, professionals with pattern experience were extremely difficult to find. Even with students, the experiment would be useful, though. If patterns made no difference for students, then there was scant hope professionals would show a benefit from patterns. The reasons for this are several: professionals have experience in dealing with large systems, so they might need less help from design patterns, which reduces the effect size, i.e., the difference between pattern and no-pattern measurements. Second, professionals have more diverse backgrounds: many of them do not have formal training in computer science, and their programming experiences vary from several years to several decades. In contrast, students from a university computer science program have all seen the same material for the same time and have less diverse programming experience. So one needs to expect a lot more noise in experiments with professionals. More noise combined with a reduced effect size makes an insignificant difference all but disappear. In that case, one can save the expense of running an experiment with professionals—the result would be inconclusive. The student experiment can be seen as a preliminary test that tells the experimenter whether to pursue a hypothesis with professionals.

Although the two experiments were similar, there were some variations that turned out to complement the experiments rather nicely. In Karlsruhe, students wrote their solutions on paper using Java, whereas the WUSTL subjects produced running programs in C++. Working on paper avoids many problems that are unrelated to the experiment question, such as difficulties with the programming environment or programming language. Producing running programs, however, provides firmer evidence that programmers actually understood the design patterns. Using both scenarios and comparing the results allowed us to conclude that working on paper alone was good enough for later experiments. Also, using two different object-oriented languages supports the claim that results do not depend on the choice of object-oriented language.

Each of the experiments was performed in lieu of a final exam. Participants needed between two and four hours, but a number of WUSTL students gave up because of time constraints (they wanted to catch transportation home after the final). Experiments are conducted in the real world, and the real world tends to intrude in unplanned ways. We learned this lesson the hard way.

Since we knew that we had only a few participants, we planned to let each participant work once with design pattern documentation and once without. This way, we would get two data points from each participant. Obviously, it would not be appropriate to let participants solve the same maintenance problem twice. Hence, we needed two different programs, similar in size and complexity. Since we were going to combine the responses from both programs, they did not need to be identical in complexity, but they couldn't be vastly different, because in that case differences in response could be due to size and complexity rather than design pattern documentation. The first sample program is called Phonebook. It manages an address database and displays first and last names plus phone numbers in several different formats. It consists of 11 classes and 565 lines, 197 lines of which were comments. Phonebook contains the patterns Observer and Template Method. The second sample program implements an And-Or-Tree, a recursive data structure. With 7 classes and 362 lines (133 of which were comments), it is shorter, but somewhat more difficult to understand. It uses the patterns Composite and Visitor. When documenting the patterns, we added 14 lines to Phonebook and 18 lines to And-Or-Tree. (The line counts shown are for the Java versions; the counts for C++ are slightly different.) Here are two examples of the extra documentation:

```
*** DESIGN PATTERN: ***
the two TupleDisplays are registered as observers at the Tupleset.

*** DESIGN PATTERN: ***
newTuple together with its auxiliary method mergeIn() forms a
*** Template Method***. The hooks are the methods select(), format(), and compare().
```

Note that the programs were well documented, even without the design pattern information. Maintenance tasks were entirely manageable without this extra information. Thus, the experiment was designed extremely conservatively, almost against showing any effect. If any reduction in error count or work time in response to pattern documentation would show up, this reduction would probably be more pronounced in real programs, because of the often scant documentation of "professional" programs.

For Phonebook, the solution involved declaring and instantiating two new observers, one with and one without a template method. For And-Or-Tree, participants needed to declare and instantiate a new visitor. The description of the maintenance tasks did not mention patterns.

Because of two different sample programs, a potential threat to validity needed to be addressed. Suppose participants who are given pattern information in the first round start to look for patterns in the second round? Then the data points for the second round would be useless, because by hunting for patterns, participants would behave as if they had pattern information available. Similarly, suppose by starting with Phonebook, participants learn something they can use on the other program? Again, the effect of pattern documentation would then be confounded with something else. This threat to validity is called a sequence or learning effect. The answer to this threat is a counter-balanced experiment design. In this design, we divide participants into four groups that differ in the order in which they receive the programs and the order in which they receive the treatment (with or without design pattern documentation).

Figure 22-2 shows the counterbalanced experiment design. Group 1, for instance, works first on Phonebook with pattern documentation, and then on And-Or-Tree without pattern documentation. By comparing the results cross-wise, one can check whether providing pattern documentation initially makes a difference. For instance, Group 1 and Group 4 both work on Phonebook with pattern documentation, but in a different order; Group 2 and Group 3 do the same for And-Or-Tree. The experimenter checks whether the pooled results of the left circles differ noticeably from the pooled results of the right circles. If so, a learning effect is present. By comparing the results for the diamonds in a similar way, one checks for a learning effect (in the absence of pattern documentation). In our experiments, these checks showed no learning effects. (To be safe, we also asked in a post-questionnaire whether participants were looking for design patterns on their own, and none of them did.) Since there were no noticeable learning effects, it is permissible to compare the results from the circles with the results from the diamonds directly, without correction for learning.

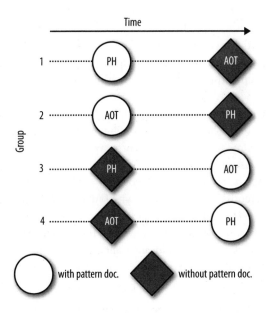

FIGURE 22-2. Counter-balanced design of the pattern documentation experiment (PH is Phonebook, AOT is And-Or-Tree)

Results

Solutions handed in by participants were graded on a point scale, and time was measured in minutes between assigning and handing in a task. Furthermore, we counted solutions that were completely correct. It turned out that the point scale did not show any significant differences. We therefore compare only time and completely correct solutions. The following table shows the results for And-Or-Tree.

Variable	With pattern documentation	Without pattern documentation	Significance (p-value)
UKA, And-Or-Tree			
correct solutions	15 of 38	7 of 36	0.077
time (min), mean	58.0	52.2	0.094
time (min) of 7 best	38.6	45.4	0.13
WUSTL, And-Or-Tree			
correct solutions	4 of 8	3 of 8	
time (min), mean	52.1	67.5	0.046

There are several things to note about this table. First, with design pattern documentation, UKA participants produced over double the number of completely correct solutions (15 versus 7 out of 36), a sizeable effect. The WUSTL students showed a smaller difference. Surprisingly, the average completion time with pattern documentation is longer for UKA (58 versus 52 minutes). However, this observation is misleading, because the number of correct solutions is much lower for the group without pattern information. Recall that UKA handed in solutions on paper. In a real maintenance environment, incorrect solutions would be detected and corrected, taking additional time not observed in this experiment. The work on paper made it difficult for participants to check their solutions; obviously, the time spent on incorrect work cannot be sensibly compared to time spent on correct work. We therefore reduced the sample: since the group without pattern documentation had only seven correct solutions, we compared these against the seven best solutions from the other group and found that the time spent with pattern documentation tends to be less, though with low statistical significance. Time difference is significant for the WUSTL group at the 0.05 level, presumably because this group not only designed, but also tested and corrected solutions, and thus produced more homogeneous quality. By comparing work time and solution quality, we also found out that without pattern documentation, the slower (less capable) subjects produced solutions of much lower quality, whereas with pattern documentation, quality is independent of the time required.

The discussion of time versus correctness reveals a flaw in the experimental design: quality and productivity are confounded, i.e., they depend on each other. Obviously, good quality takes time, so taking longer does not necessarily mean that patterns are worthless. The implication is that comparing time makes sense only if solution quality is the same. We corrected for this problem by comparing only totally correct solutions, but that cost us half of the data points and statistical significance. In retrospect, we could have avoided this problem entirely with an acceptance test that everyone had to pass. There will be more about this technique in the conclusions.

Overall, identifying patterns in And-Or-Tree saves maintenance time and produces better solutions, and even less capable programmers produce good solutions. For Phonebook, results (not shown) also suggest that pattern documentation saves time; results for quality are not available due to lack of data (students quitting).

We conclude that if maintenance tasks are performed on design patterns, including pattern documentation may reduce the time for implementing a program change or may help improve the quality of the change. We therefore recommend to always document design patterns in source code. As stated before, this experiment does not test the presence or absence of patterns, only the presence or absence of pattern documentation. Encouraged by the results, however, we started planning the second experiment. This time, we were going to check the more fundamental question and use professionals from the start.

The Second Experiment: Comparing Pattern Solutions to Simpler Ones

The second experiment came about in an unexpected way. The company sd&m held a technical conference near Frankfurt, Germany some time in 1997. A number of speakers were invited, and I was among them. I talked about design patterns, our early results with pattern documentation, and how important it was to see whether design patterns really worked. I ended by saying that I was looking for subjects in a pattern experiment, and as a benefit for participating, I would offer an intensive pattern course, discussing all the major patterns known at the time. The president and founder of the company, Ernst Denert, sat in the front row. When I had finished he stood up, walked to the stage, and asked for my microphone. What was going to happen next? Taking away the speaker's microphone is not exactly how the question-and-answer period after a talk works. He then turned to his employees (there were perhaps 150 in the room, most of them developers) and said: "You heard what Professor Tichy said. I don't have anything to add to that. Who is going to participate?" After a few seconds of silence, a lot of hands went up! I've never had more effective encouragement for participation in any experiment, ever. After preparation and with the various scheduling conflicts, we actually ended up with 29 professional developers from sd&m participating. The experiment was conducted at sd&m's Munich office in November 1997.

The experiment sought empirical evidence about whether using design patterns is beneficial, and whether some patterns are more difficult to use than others. In particular, we had noticed that developers sometimes went overboard in their pattern enthusiasm and used them in situations where simpler solutions would have been good enough. Was this overkill a problem? Chunking theory would suggest that it was not, because the size of a chunk does not matter.

But the answers could be discovered only by observing programmers modifying programs with patterns and equivalent ones without patterns.

As previously, the experiment investigated software maintenance scenarios that employ various design patterns. This time we worked with professionals. The structure of the experiment was similar to the previous one, except that it employed a pre- and a post-test, and in took two full days. In the morning of day 1, the pre-test assessed the performance of programmers who had no knowledge of design patterns. In the afternoon and the morning of day 2, participants took an intensive pattern course, followed by a post-test in the second afternoon. The participants were 29 professional software engineers with an average of 4.1 years of experience. Participants worked on paper and had unlimited time; they all handed in their solutions within three hours. There were four programs on which maintenance tasks were performed. Each program existed in two versions: a pattern version containing one or two design patterns and an alternative version that was functionally equivalent but used a simpler structure instead of the pattern. Maintenance tasks were performed on programs with patterns and alternate versions, both in pre- and in post-test. The pre- and post-test allowed us to check whether pattern knowledge improved performance and whether there were any patterns that were easy to grasp without prior familiarity.

Figure 22-3 summarizes the experimental design. In order to control learning and fatigue effects, the order of programs is varied (counterbalancing), and data are collected from each subject on both pattern (Pat) and alternative (Alt) programs. ST, GR, CO, and BO are the programs. The familiarization phase (letter F) introduces participants to the experiment process.

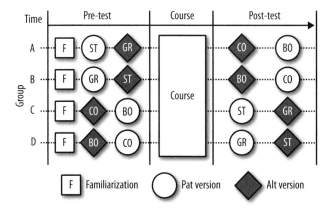

FIGURE 22-3. Experimental design: Circles denote pattern program versions, and shaded diamonds alternate versions. The two-letter codes are the program name abbreviations. Time runs from left to right.

The results varied by pattern. Figure 22-4 shows the time participants took to complete maintenance tasks on the Observer pattern in program ST. The diagram contains four boxplots showing how modification times are distributed. Inside the hourglasses are the inner 50% of the data points; the median value is in the middle of the hourglass. The left side shows the pre-test. The pattern solution took longer to modify than the alternative ("modular") solution. Apparently, an unknown pattern introduces additional complexity that costs extra time. After the pattern course, however, the situation changes. The alternative version still takes about the same time, but now the pattern solution is completed more quickly, even though it is more complex. This situation is exactly what chunking theory predicts.

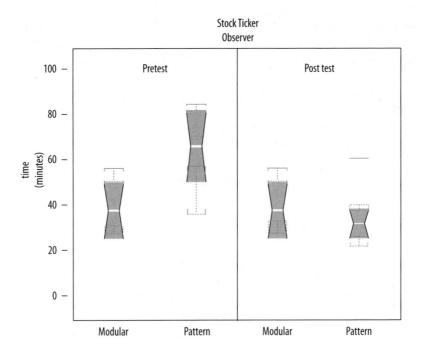

FIGURE 22-4. Results for Observer

Figure 22-5 shows the time taken for Decorator. Apparently, working with the pattern rather than the alternative saves quite a bit of time. However, there is a surprise: there is no difference between pre- and post-test! Apparently, Decorator is easy to grasp and modify, even if not known to the programmers. Participants need no prior exposure to the Decorator chunk.

Not all results are this clear, though. For instance, Composite and Abstract Factory together showed no difference between the two versions in either pre- or post-test. Visitor caused great confusion. In the pre-test, the alternative solution took longer than the Visitor solution, whereas in the post-test the relation was reversed. Apparently, Visitor is difficult to understand in the relatively short time it was covered in the course. Altogether, there were nine maintenance tasks. In most, we found positive effects from using design patterns: either their inherent extra flexibility required no more maintenance time, or maintenance time was reduced compared to the simpler alternative. In a few cases, we found negative effects: the alternative solution was less error-prone or required less maintenance time. In other words, not all design patterns are equally beneficial. More details, broken down by individual maintenance task, can be found in [Prechelt et al. 2001].

The original experiment was replicated at the Simula Lab in Norway in 2002, with major extensions. We used the same sample programs and maintenance tasks, and I even gave the same course with identical slides. However, realism was increased by using a real programming environment instead of pen and paper. A total of 44 paid professionals from multiple major consultancy companies participated. Elapsed time and correctness were analyzed using regression models. Together with online logging of participants' work, a better understanding of the results was possible. The data indicate quite strongly that some patterns are much easier to use than others. The patterns Observer and Decorator were grasped and used intuitively, even by subjects with little or no knowledge of patterns. Visitor caused difficulties. This confirmation of the earlier observations was important, because it applied to actual programming, not just exercises on paper. Also, participants varied greatly in professional experience (from less than a year to 20 years or more), so the results generalize much better.

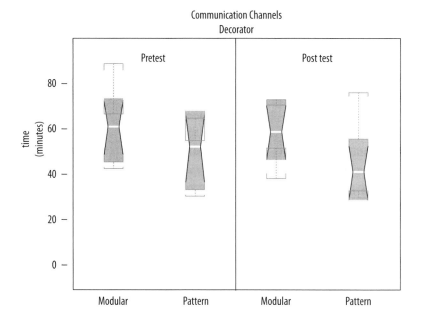

FIGURE 22-5. Results for Decorator

The implication is that design patterns are not universally good or bad, but must be used in a way that matches the problem and the programmers' knowledge. When approaching a program with documented design patterns, even short training can improve speed and quality of maintenance activities. When choosing between patterns and simpler, less flexible alternatives, it is probably wise to choose the patterns because unexpected new requirements often appear and the extra flexibility will be useful.

The Third Experiment: Patterns in Team Communication

Better team communication is the third major hypothesis about design patterns. The third experiment tests the hypothesis that if team members have common pattern knowledge, they can communicate more effectively than without. Obviously, there is no way around observing teams communicating when testing this hypothesis. The difficulty is how to elicit communication and how to evaluate it. Thinking-aloud or talking to an observer seemed unnatural for teamwork, so we decided to pair subjects and record their interactions (on audio and video) during design maintenance tasks, and then analyze the recordings.

The experimental setup was as follows. Pairs of subjects were given a design maintenance tasks. For eliciting an explanation phase, one subject of each pair was given extra time in advance. During this time, the subject studied requirements and design documents of the program. This member will be referred to as the *expert*. There was no time limit for preparation, but all subjects took about an hour. After preparation, the second team member joined as *novice*. The expert explained the program design to the novice. Subsequently, both team members collaborated on two maintenance tasks. This strategy provided a chance to observe two interesting communication phases: (1) the phase of explanation by expert to novice and (2) the teamwork phase between two maintainers.

The independent variable is design pattern knowledge. First, teams were given a pre-test, then they participated in a three-month lab course on design patterns, and finally they received a post-test. The whole experiment ran from April to August 1999. The lab course provided practical exercises for all patterns relevant for the tests (as well as other patterns). The experiment employed two different applications, one for pre-test and the other for post-test. For balancing differences in application complexity, the teams were divided into two groups that worked on the applications in alternate order. For balancing individual capability, the roles of expert and novice were also switched from pre- to post-test. Participants were 15 computer science graduate students in their eighth semester who had no prior experience with the design patterns used in the experiment.

The next question was how to analyze the recordings. One of the experimenters transcribed the audio and video tapes into written protocols and then coded them with a simple coding scheme. (This was a lot of work. Coding a single recording took four weeks or more, and there were 12 protocols to do.) The coding scheme identifies the speaker and the type of utterance, such as question, atomic assertion, answer, and feedback. Especially important are atomic assertions about the designs because they carry crucial design information. For analyzing the coded protocols, each assertion by the expert is counted as +1, and each assertion by the novice as −1. A moving average of 70 data points is computed and scaled to a range of −10~ ..~ +10. The plot of the moving average is called a *communication line*. Figure 22-6 shows what we hypothesize as the ideal communication line. During the explanation phase, when the expert explains the program, the communication line should be at +10. After the first task is distributed, the line should drop to 0 if both novice and expert contribute equally to the discussion. The time when the two tasks are distributed are indicated by solid vertical lines; the dashed lines indicate the range of the 70-point moving average around the solid lines. The drop from 10 to 0 is a slanted rather than vertical line because of the smoothing. When ideal and actual communication lines are superimposed, deviations from the ideal can indicate, for instance, dominance of a team member. Comparing the deviations for pre- and post-test of a team can show, both qualitatively and quantitatively, how effectively the expert explains the program and how balanced the communication is during the teamwork phase.

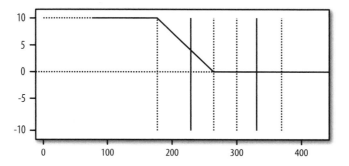

FIGURE 22-6. The ideal communication line

The results show that in the pre-test, all communication lines are heavily unbalanced, whereas most of the communication lines in the post-test exhibit a "hump" of explanation at the beginning and then become balanced around 0. Figure 22-7 shows the pre-test of Team T1. Here we have a case of *novice dominance*: the expert begins with explanations, but almost immediately the novice (who first knows nothing about the software) takes over and dominates the discussion, as seen by the communication line being drawn below the center. Compare the communication line in Figure 22-8, when T1 has passed the patterns course. Now the other team member is the expert. Recall that this is the dominant person in Figure 22-7 (roles have been switched). But now, when they start discussing the maintenance task, the formerly weaker team member pretty much balances the communication.

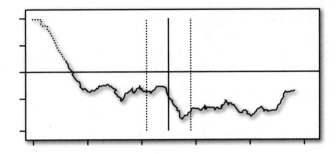

FIGURE 22-7. Communication line for team T1, pre-test

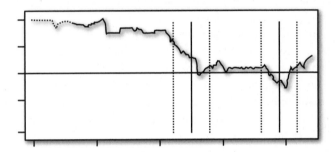

FIGURE 22-8. Communication line for team T1, post-test

A case of expert dominance can be seen in Figures 22-9 and 22-10. In the pre-test, the expert dominates the conversation throughout, but in the post-test, the conversation becomes balanced.

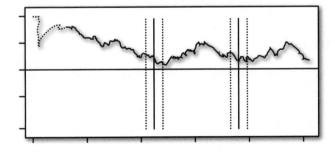

FIGURE 22-9. Communication line for team T4, pre-test

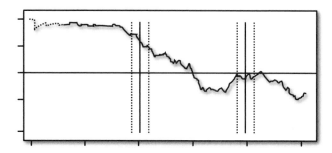

FIGURE 22-10. Communication line for team T4, post-test

For a quantitative analysis, we computed the difference between the ideal communication line and actual communication lines for all teams, pre- and post-test. First, we superimpose the ideal communication line over an actual communication line by lining up the points where the first task is distributed to the team members. Next, we sample the differences between the actual and ideal communication line 1,000 times in both the explanation and teamwork phases and compute the Euclidean distance. There is a pronounced difference between pre- and post-test in all cases; the Wilcoxon test[*] showed the difference as statistically significant at the 0.05 level. A qualitative analysis of the conversations showed that subjects talk about patterns in both pre- and post-test, but there is a more even flow of pattern information in the post-test. In the pre-test, pattern terminology is often used with little understanding.

The results show clear evidence that the communication lines of the design teams changed from pre- to post-test. Without shared pattern knowledge, the explanation phase is small or non existent, and the subsequent communication tends to be dominated by a single team member. After a three-month design pattern course, a clearly identifiable explanation phase is followed by a work phase with balanced communication. Even weaker team members can contribute equally to design discussions. These observations support the hypothesis that team members can communicate more effectively with design pattern knowledge. Apparently, using chunks that capture useful design abstractions improves communication.

Lessons Learned

This series of experiments was a tremendous learning experience. The experiments were difficult to construct. Adding pattern documentation was easy enough once we thought of it, but constructing "fair" comparisons for pattern programs was hard, because the alternative solutions always looked very much like the pattern solutions. The experimenters were already locked into thinking in patterns! We made progress only after we accepted that the alternative

---

[*] The Wilcoxon test evaluates whether two samples were drawn from the same population, without assuming normal distribution. For an explanation, look up the Mann-Whitney test in [Howell 1999].

solutions could be simpler and less flexible and that that was exactly what should be tested. Finding ways to capture communication stymied us for a long time. After a lot of reading about experimental design, we decided to use protocol analysis. But what to do with the protocols? The concept of the ideal communication line and comparing it with actual ones was a stroke of genius by Barbara Unger (see the Acknowledgments section). Preparing, running, and analyzing the experiments was unexpectedly time-consuming (three PhD dissertations' worth), but we did it at the right time, when the topic was fresh and subjects easy to find. In the end, we were thrilled with the results.

The book by Christensen [Christensen 2007] about experimental design was a godsend. It is in its 10th edition and covers all the major topics of experimental methodology.

I recommend to always use a counterbalanced design if subjects do more than one task. Counterbalancing does not cost anything except a bit of organization, and the ability to check for sequence effects provides peace of mind. Also, counterbalancing reduces the chance for copying, if one arranges for people sitting next to each other to be in different groups. (Copying can cost valuable data points and ruin an experiment.) For analyzing results, the free statistics package R was wonderful. It is available at *www.r-project.org*.

The following we would do differently. In statistical tests there is the concept of power. Power is the probability of finding a difference among treatments if there is one. One wants to keep this probability high (say, at 80%) because otherwise one might have an inconclusive result (the experiment does not show anything, because the chances for finding it are too low). Power analysis helps here. The process is briefly as follows: determine the approximate effect size with a few subjects in a pre-test. With this information, one can estimate the number of subjects needed for a given power and significance level. We were lucky that effect sizes in our experiments were large enough so we could get by with the number of subjects we had. For small effect sizes, the number of subjects can easily go to 80 or 120, and getting this many subjects is a major undertaking. Power analysis is described in statistics books, for instance, in Chapter 15 of [Howell 1999]. Statistics packages such as R provide packaged solutions for power analysis. Be sure to have enough participants before starting because otherwise you get into a never-ending search for additional subjects!

Another problem we did not recognize at first is that correctness of solutions and the time subjects take cannot be analyzed independently. Clearly, producing poor solutions takes hardly any time, whereas good solutions take a while. It seems obvious in hindsight, but blindly comparing work times is not acceptable; instead, one must compare work times on the basis of similar quality. For instance, one could devise three levels of quality, and then compare work times for each of those levels. The problem with that is the number of subjects needed. Each of the three correctness levels requires enough subjects to satisfy significance and power levels by itself, which in this case would triple the number of subjects. An alternative is to normalize quality by providing an acceptance tests. Every participant continues working until the solution handed in passes a pre-defined acceptance test. Thus, all participants provide a minimum of quality. The acceptance test can be an automatically executing test suit, and it can be run by the participants themselves or by the experimenters. It is also possible, but less objective, that the experimenters check solutions by hand (during the experiment!) and hand them back if unacceptable errors are present. Once the acceptance test is passed, one can measure time or other aspects. After the acceptance test, one can also apply a much larger test suite to differentiate quality in more detail. For one of the first experiments where an acceptance tests is used, see [Müller 2004].

Conclusions

A single experiment in a complex situation such as programming says little, except perhaps for rejecting a hypothesis. But for confirming hypotheses, more testing needs to be done. Three experiments, two of which were replicated, gathered evidence about the effectiveness of software design patterns. The first pair of experiments showed that merely documenting design patterns can already lead to an increase in programmer productivity and reduce errors during maintenance tasks. Another pair of experiments, conducted with professional programmers, compared design pattern solutions with simpler, ad hoc solutions. In these experiments, introducing design patterns caused a certain overhead, but in most cases this overhead was justified because it simplified maintenance. The final experiment showed improvements in communication when team members shared design pattern knowledge. In the first and third experiments, there was also some evidence that weaker designers catch up with more experienced ones when using patterns.

Taken together, strong empirical evidence emerges that software design patterns are an effective approach to improving software quality and productivity in a maintenance context. The trust in design patterns was not misplaced!

Whether patterns have a positive effect during initial development is still an open question. A first experiment in that direction examined Abstract Factory from an API usability point of view [Ellis et al. 2007]. It found that programmers require significantly more time to construct an object with a factory than with a constructor. However, the experiment did not use Abstract Factory in the way it was intended: it tested the creation of a single object rather than managing sets of matched objects. In the experiment, the pattern simply couldn't bring its (presumed) strength to bear. This example shows how difficult it is to design meaningful experiments. Nevertheless, more experiments that test patterns in initial development are desirable, and the API usability approach would certainly be helpful.

None of the experiments discussed in this chapter say anything about the potential cost savings when using patterns. These questions will perhaps be answered by future experiments.

Acknowledgments

Lots of people helped make these experiments possible. First and foremost, my thanks goes to the anonymous participants. They willingly put up with strange programs and strange problems to solve. My former PhD students, Lutz Prechelt, Michael Philippsen, and Barbara Unger, deserve the credit for making up and testing the programs and maintenance tasks, and collecting and analyzing the data. Thanks also go to Ernst Denert and Peter Brössler for encouraging sd&m engineers to participate. Lawrence Votta helped with experimental design. Marek Vokac, Dag Sjoberg, Erik Arisholm, and Magne Aldrin of Simula Labs provided the programming environment for monitoring participants. Marek Vokac did most of the analysis work at Simula. Dag Sjoberg had the (at the time radical) idea of paying consultants for participating in experiments; he also acquired the funding to do so.

References

[Chalmers 1999] Chalmers, Alan F. 1999. *What Is This Thing Called Science?*, Third Edition. Indianapolis, IN: Hackett Publishing Co.

[Christensen 2007] Christensen, Larry B. 2007. *Experimental Methodology*. Boston: Allyn and Bacon.

[Ellis et al. 2007] Ellis, Brian, Jeffrey Stylos, and Brad Myers. 2007. The Factory Pattern in API Design: A Usability Evaluation. *Proceedings of the 29th International Conference on Software Engineering*: 302–311.

[Gamma et al. 1995] Gamma, Erich, Richard Helm, Ralph Johnson, and John M. Vlissides. 1995. *Design Patterns: Elements of Reusable Object-Oriented Software*. Reading, MA: Addison-Wesley.

[Howell 1999] Howell, David C. 1999. *Fundamental Statistics for the Behavioral Sciences*. Pacific Grove, CA: Brooks/Cole Publishing Company.

[Miller 1956] Miller, George A. 1956. The Magical Number Seven, Plus or Minus Two: Some Limits on Our Capacity for Processing Information. *Psychological Review* 63: 81–97.

[Müller 2004] Müller, Matthias. 2004. Are Reviews an Alternative to Pair Programming? *Empirical Software Engineering* 9(4): 335–351.

[Parnas 1972] Parnas, David L. 1972. On the Criteria to be Used in Decomposing Systems into Modules. *Comm. of the ACM* 15(12): 1053–1058.

[Prechelt et al. 2001] Prechelt, Lutz, Barbara Unger, Walter F. Tichy, Peter Brössler, and Lawrence G. Votta. 2001. A Controlled Experiment in Maintenance Comparing Design Patterns to Simpler Solutions. *IEEE Transactions on Software Engineering* 27(12): 1134–1144.

[Prechelt et al. 2002] Prechelt, Lutz, Barbara Unger-Lamprecht, Michael Philippsen, and Walter F. Tichy. Two Controlled Experiments Assessing the Usefulness of Design Pattern Documentation in Program Maintenance. *IEEE Trans. on Software Engineering* 28(6): 595–606.

[Unger et al. 2000] Unger, Barbara, Walter F. Tichy. 2000. Do Design Patterns Improve Communication? An Experiment with Pair Design. Workshop on Empirical Studies of Software Maintenance. *http://www.ipd.uni-karlsruhe.de/Tichy/publications.php?id=149*.

[Vokac et al. 2004] Vokac, Marek, Walter Tichy, Dag Sjoberg, Erik Arisholm, Magne Aldrin. 2004. A Controlled Experiment Comparing the Maintainability of Programs Designed with and without Design Patterns—A Replication in a Real Programming Environment. *Empirical Software Engineering* 9: 149–195.

CHAPTER TWENTY-THREE

Evidence-Based Failure Prediction

Nachiappan Nagappan
Thomas Ball

Empirical software engineering (SE) studies collect and analyze data from software artifacts and the associated processes and variables to quantify, characterize, and explore the relationship between different variables to deliver high-quality, secure software on time and within budget. In this chapter we discuss empirical studies related to failure prediction on the Windows operating system family. Windows is a large commercial software system implemented predominantly in C/C++/C# and currently used by several hundreds of millions of users across the world. It contains 40+ million lines of code and is worked on by several hundreds of engineers.

Failure prediction forms a crucial part of empirical SE, as it can be used to understand the maintenance effort required for testing and resource allocation. For example:

Resource allocation
> Software quality assurance consumes a considerable effort in any large-scale software development. To raise the effectiveness of this effort, it is necessary to plan in advance for fixing issues in the components that are more likely to fail and thereby need quality assurance most.

Decision making
> Predictions on the number of failures can support other decisions, such as choosing the correct requirements or design, the ability to select the best possible fix for a problem, etc. The associated risk of a change (or likelihood to fail) can help in making decisions about

the risk introduced by the change. Failure predictions also help in assessing the overall stability of the system and help make decisions about the ability to release on time.

We explore the step-by-step progression of applying various metrics to predict failures. For each set for metrics we discuss the rationale behind metric selection, a description of the metric, and the results of applying the metrics for actual failure prediction in a large commercial software system.

Introduction

Software organizations can benefit greatly from an early estimation regarding the quality of their product. Because product quality information is available late in the process, corrective actions tend to be expensive [Boehm 1981]. The IEEE standard [IEEE 1990] for software engineering terminology defines the waterfall software development cycle as "a model of the software development process in which the constituent activities, typically a concept phase, requirements phase, design phase, implementation phase, test phase, and installation and checkout phase, are performed in that order, possibly with overlap but with little or no iteration." During the development cycle, different metrics can be collected that can be related to product quality. The goal is to use such metrics to make estimates of post-release failures early in the software development cycle, during the implementation and testing phases. For example, such estimates can help focus testing and code and design reviews and affordably guide corrective actions.

The selection of metrics is dependent on using empirical techniques such as the G-Q-M principle [Basili et al. 1994] to objectively assess the importance of selecting the metrics for analysis. An *internal metric* (measure), such as cyclomatic complexity [McCabe 1976], is a measure derived from the product itself. An *external metric* is a measure of a product derived from the external assessment of the behavior of the system. For example, the number of failures found in the field is an external metric. The ISO/IEC standard [ISO/IEC 1996] states that an internal metric is of little value unless there is evidence that it is related to an externally visible attribute. Internal metrics have been shown to be useful as early indicators of externally visible product quality when they are related in a statistically significant and stable way to the field quality/reliability of the product. The validation of internal metrics requires a convincing demonstration that (1) the metric measures what it purports to measure and (2) the metric is associated with important external metrics such as field reliability, maintainability, or fault-proneness [El Emam 2000].

In this chapter we discuss six different sets of metrics for failure prediction. Each set of metrics is described, and its importance to failure prediction is illustrated. Results of published industrial case studies at Microsoft are provided with references for future reading. We then provide a summary of failure prediction and discuss future areas of importance. We discuss six different sets of internal metrics to predict failures:

1. Code coverage

2. Code churn

3. Code complexity

4. Code dependencies

5. People and organizational metrics

6. Integrated/combined approach

Executable binaries are the level of measurement we use in reference to the Windows case studies. Binaries are the result of compiling source files to form an *.exe*, *.dll*, or *.sys* file. Our choice of binaries was governed by the facts that: (1) binaries are the lowest level at which field failures are mapped back to; (2) fixes usually involve changes to several files, most of which are compiled into one binary; (3) binaries are the lowest level at which code ownership is maintained, thereby making our results more actionable. Historically, Microsoft has used binaries as the unit of measurement due to the ability to map back customer failures accurately.

For each of the six sets of metrics, we provide evidence from a case study at Microsoft predicting failures in Windows Vista and/or Windows Server 2003. For each of the predictions, we provide the related precision and recall values or accuracy values. *Precision* measures the false-negative rate, which is the ratio of failure-prone binaries that were classified as not-failure-prone. *Recall* measures the false-positive rate, which denotes the ratio of not-failure-prone binaries that were classified as failure-prone. We focus here on the metrics for failure prediction rather than on the statistical or machine-learning techniques for which standard techniques such as logistic regression, decision trees, support vector machines, etc., can be used [Han and Kamber 2006].

As with all research on empirical evidence on software engineering, drawing general conclusions from empirical studies in software engineering is difficult because any process depends to a large degree on a potentially large number of relevant context variables [Basili et al. 1999]. For this reason, we cannot assume a priori that the results of a study generalize beyond the specific environment in which it was conducted [Basili et al. 1999]. Researchers become more confident in a theory when similar findings emerge in different contexts [Basili et al. 1999]. We encourage readers to investigate and, if possible, replicate the studies in their specific environments to draw conclusions. We hope this chapter serves as a documentation of the metrics and feature sets that have been shown to be successful (or not) at predicting failures at Microsoft.

Code Coverage

Code coverage is an important metric by which the extent of testing is often quantified. The main assumption behind coverage is that if a branch or a statement contains a flaw, it cannot be detected unless a test at least executes that statement or branch (and obtains an output contrary to the normal expectation). It can be argued that higher coverage should lead to detection of more flaws in the code and, if they are fixed, to better release quality. Although this assumption is widely believed, there is little evidence to show that higher code coverage results in fewer failures.

There are a number of potential flaws with the argument that higher code coverage leads to better quality. First, the coverage measure reflects the percent of statements covered but does not consider whether these statements are likely to contain a flaw. Therefore, it is possible to create two test sets with the same coverage measure but a markedly distinct ability to detect post-release defects. Second, the fact that a statement or a branch was executed does not imply that all possible data values have been exercised by the test. The customer/usage scenario could be totally different from what the tester perceives it to be. This is of particular concern for systems with simple control flow that can be easily covered with a few test cases. In our study on code coverage, based on qualitative interviews with engineers, the reasons for observing such a trend was attributed to several factors [Mockus et al. 2009]:

- Code covered is not correct code.

- Developers inherently know that certain binaries are complex and will tend to get very high coverage in those binaries. But these binaries may be the ones most used in the system, which can lead to more failures being found in them, i.e., code coverage and usage profiles might not match.

- Complexity should tie into code coverage. For example, obtaining a code coverage of 80% on a binary with cyclomatic complexity 1000 is more difficult than getting a coverage of 80% on a binary with cyclomatic complexity 10. The complexity values tied into the code coverage helps exploit the efficacy of the code coverage measures.

Despite these flaws, coverage appears to be a promising measure due to its wide use in practice. However, there has been little published about the relationship between code coverage and quality. Most studies performed to date on this relationship suffer from issues of internal validity (studies of 100-line programs). In order to find evidence of the relationship between code coverage and quality, we mapped the branch and block coverage values for Windows Vista (40+ million lines of code and several thousand binaries and engineers) and field failures for Windows Vista six months after release. We observe a weak positive correlation between coverage and quality and a low prediction precision and recall (precision 83.8% and recall 54.8%; for further reading, please refer to [Mockus et al. 2009]). Our investigation of this straightforward and simple hypothesis leads us to believe that code coverage is not best used in isolation, but instead needs to be combined with other metrics, such as code churn, complexity, etc.

Code Churn

Software systems evolve over time due to changes in requirements, optimization of code, fixes for security and reliability bugs, etc. Code churn measures the changes made to a component over a period of time and quantifies the extent of this change. It is easily extracted from a system's change history, as recorded automatically by a version control system. Most version control systems use a file comparison utility (such as *diff*) to automatically estimate how many lines were added, deleted, and changed by a programmer to create a new version of a file from an old version. These differences are the basis of churn measures.

Relative churn measures are normalized values of the various churn measures. Some of the normalization parameters are total lines of code, file churn, file count, etc. In an evolving system it is highly beneficial to use a relative approach to quantify the change in a system. As we show, these relative measures can be devised to cross-check each other so that the metrics do not provide conflicting information. Our basic hypothesis is that code that changes many times pre-release will likely have more post-release defects than code that changes less over the same period of time.

In our analysis, we used the code churn between the release of Windows Server 2003 (W2k3) and the release of the W2k3 Service Pack 1 (W2k3-SP1) to predict the defect density in W2k3-SP1. Using the directly collected churn metrics such as added, modified, and deleted lines of code (LOC), we also collected the time and file count measures to compute a set of relative churn measures [Nagappan and Ball 2005]:

METRIC1: Churned LOC / Total LOC

We expect the larger the proportion of churned (added + changed) code to the LOC of the new binary, the larger the magnitude of the defect density for that binary.

METRIC2: Deleted LOC / Total LOC

We expect the larger the proportion of deleted code to the LOC of the new binary, the larger the magnitude of the defect density for that binary.

METRIC3: Files churned / File count

We expect the greater the proportion of files in a binary that get churned, the greater the probability of these files introducing defects. For example, suppose binaries A and B contain 20 files each. If binary A has five churned files and binary B has two churned files, we expect binary A to have a higher defect density.

METRIC4: Churn count / Files churned

Suppose binaries A and B have twenty files each and also have five churned files each. If the five files in binary A are churned 20 times and the five files in binary B are churned 10 times, then we expect binary A to have a higher defect density. METRIC4 acts as a cross check on METRIC3.

METRIC5: Weeks of churn / File count

METRIC5 is used to account for the temporal extent of churn. A higher value of METRIC5 indicates that it took a longer time to fix a smaller number of files. This may indicate that the binary contains complex files that may be hard to modify correctly. Thus, we expect that an increase in METRIC5 would be accompanied by an increase in the defect density of the related binary.

METRIC6: Lines worked on / Weeks of churn

> The measure "Lines worked on" is the sum of the churned LOC and the deleted LOC. METRIC6 measures the extent of code churn over time in order to cross check on METRIC5. Weeks of churn does not necessarily indicate the amount of churn. METRIC6 reflects our expectation that the more lines are worked on, the longer the weeks of churn should be. A high value of METRIC6 cross checks on METRIC5 and should predict a higher defect density.

METRIC7: Churned LOC / Deleted LOC

> METRIC7 is used in order to quantify new development. All churn is not due to bug fixes. In feature development the lines churned is much greater than the lines deleted, so a high value of METRIC7 indicates new feature development. METRIC7 acts as a cross check on METRIC1 and METRIC2, neither of which accurately predicts new feature development.

METRIC8: Lines worked on / Churn count

> We expect that the larger a change (lines worked on) relative to the number of changes (churn count), the greater the defect density will be. METRIC8 acts as a cross check on METRIC3 and METRIC4, as well as METRIC5 and METRIC6. With respect to METRIC3 and METRIC4, METRIC8 measures the amount of actual change that took place. METRIC8 cross checks to account for the fact that files are not getting churned repeatedly for small fixes. METRIC8 also cross checks on METRIC5 and METRIC6 to account for the fact that the higher the value of METRIC8 (more lines per churn), the higher the time (METRIC5) and lines worked on per week (METRIC6). If this is not so, then a large amount of churn might have been performed in a small amount of time, which can cause an increased defect density.

Using the relative code churn metrics identified about a prediction model identifies with random splitting an accuracy of 89% the failure-prone and non-failure-prone binaries in W2K3-SP1. Further, the defect density of W2k3-SP1 is also predicted with a high degree of accuracy (shown in Figure 23-1). (The axes are normalized to protect confidential data). The spikes above the solid line indicate overestimations and below the solid line indicate underestimations. The correlation between actual and estimated defect density is strong, positive, and statistically significant—indicating that with the increase in actual defect density there is an increase in estimated defect density.

These results, along with results from prior published research studies (for example, [Ostrand et al. 2004] and [Nagappan and Ball 2005] have a more detailed list), indicate that code churn and code quality are highly and positively correlated. That is, the higher the code churn, the more the failures in a system. Because code churn is an essential part of new software development (say, new product features), we introduced the relative code churn measures to alleviate this problem by cross-checking the metrics. However, our results show that it is clear that code churn measures need to be used in conjunction with other internal metrics.

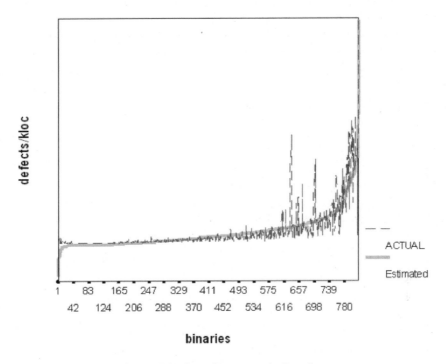

FIGURE 23-1. Actual versus estimated system defect density [Nagappan and Ball 2005]

Code Complexity

Following code churn, we analyzed code complexity. That is, how does the complexity of a piece of code influence the ability to predict failures? Complexity can be quantified using several metrics, more suited toward object-oriented and non-object-oriented metrics ranging from the more traditional metrics such as fan-in and fan-out to the more recent CK metrics [Chidamber and Kemerer 1994]. The CK metric suite consists of six metrics (designed primarily as object-oriented design measures): weighted methods per class (WMC), coupling between objects (CBO), depth of inheritance (DIT), number of children (NOC), response for a class (RFC), and lack of cohesion among methods (LCOM). The typical object-oriented and non-object-oriented complexity metrics used at Microsoft based on prior published metrics (for example, [Chidamber and Kemerer 1994]) are:

Lines
    Executable noncommented lines of code.

Cyclomatic complexity
    The Cyclomatic complexity metric [McCabe 1976] measures the number of linearly independent paths through a program unit.

Fan-in

Fan-in is the number of other functions calling a given function in a module.

Fan-out

Fan-out is the number of other functions being called from a given function in a module.

Methods

Number of methods in a class, including public, private, and protected methods.

Inheritance depth

Inheritance depth is the maximum depth of inheritance for a given class.

Coupling

This signifies coupling to other classes through (a) class member variables, (b) function parameters, and (c) classes defined locally in class member function bodies, as well as (d) coupling through immediate base classes and (e) coupling through return type.

Subclasses

This metric indicates the number of classes directly inheriting from a given parent class in a module.

The overall efficacy of using these metrics for predicting failures is with a precision of 79.3% and a recall of 66% in Windows Vista. The measures indicate that though complexity measures are fair predictors of code quality, they are not as good as code churn. In related work, Khoshgoftaar et al. studied two consecutive releases of a large legacy system (containing over 38,000 procedures in 171 modules) for telecommunications and identified fault-prone modules based on 16 static software product metrics [Khoshgoftaar et al. 1996]. Their model, when used on the second release, showed an overall misclassification rate of 21.0%. El Emam et al. studied the effect of class size on fault-proneness by using a large telecommunications application [El Emam et al. 2001]. Class size was found to confound the effect of all the metrics on fault-proneness. The CK metrics have also been investigated in the context of fault-proneness. Basili et al. studied the fault-proneness in software programs using eight student projects [Basili et al. 1996]. They observed that the WMC, CBO, DIT, NOC, and RFC were correlated with defects, whereas the LCOM was not correlated with defects. Briand et al. performed an industrial case study and observed the CBO, RFC, and LCOM to be associated with the fault-proneness of a class [Briand et al. 1999]. Tang et al. studied three real-time systems for testing and maintenance defects [Tang et al. 1999]. Higher WMC and RFC were found to be associated with fault-proneness. For further reading, refer to [Nagappan et al. 2006a], [Briand et al. 1999], and [Bhat and Nagappan 2006].

Code Dependencies

We have seen that code churn and complexity are good predictors of failures. This led us to look at tying together these two pieces of information to effectively quantify the relationship between different pieces of code. In general, in any large-scale software development effort, a good software architecture enables teams to work independently on different components in the architecture. A software dependency is a relationship between two pieces of code, such as a data dependency (component A uses a variable defined by component B) or call dependency (component A calls a function defined by component B). Suppose that component A has many dependencies on component B. If the code of component B changes (churns) a lot between versions, we may expect that component A will need to undergo a certain amount of churn in order to keep it in sync with component B. That is, churn often will propagate across dependencies. Together, a high degree of dependence plus churn can cause errors that will propagate through a system, reducing its reliability.

In order to study the effectiveness of dependencies to predict failures, we studied the dependencies between binaries in Windows Vista. The dependencies are computed at the function level, including caller-callee dependencies, imports, exports, RPC, COM, Registry access, etc. The system-wide dependency graph can be viewed as the low-level architecture of Windows Vista. Dependencies are classified into incoming and outgoing dependencies with the binaries. Further classifications include the total number of dependencies between binaries and the span of binaries across different components. The prediction models built using the dependency metrics to predict failures in Windows Vista have a precision and recall of 74.4% and 69.9%, respectively. This is as good as the precision and recall results obtained from code complexity metrics but does not compare to the results obtained from code churn. Further reading on the ability of dependencies and code churn to predict failures on the Microsoft case study can be found in [Nagappan and Ball 2007].

In related work, Schröter et al. showed that import dependencies can predict defects [Schröter et al. 2006]. They proposed an alternate way of predicting failures for Java classes. Rather than looking at the complexity of a class, they looked exclusively at the components that a class uses. For Eclipse, an open source IDE, they found that using compiler packages results in a significantly higher failure-proneness (71%) than using GUI packages (14%). Von Mayrhauser et al. investigated the relationship of the decay of software architectures with faults using a bottom-up approach of constructing a fault-architecture model [von Mayrhauser et al. 1999]. A fault-architecture model was constructed incorporating the degree of fault-coupling between components and how often these two components are involved in a defect fix. Their results indicated the most fault-prone relationships for each release and showed that the same relationships between components are repeatedly fault-prone, indicating underlying architectural problems.

People and Organizational Measures

Conway's Law states that "organizations that design systems are constrained to produce systems which are copies of the communication structures of these organizations" [Conway 1968]. Similarly, Fred Brooks argues in *The Mythical Man-Month* that the product quality is strongly affected by organizational structure [Brooks 1995]. Software engineering is a complex engineering activity. It involves interactions between people, processes, and tools to develop a complete product. In practice, commercial software development is performed by teams consisting of a number of individuals, ranging from the tens to the thousands. Often these people work via an organizational structure reporting to a manager or set of managers. Often failure predictions are obtained from measures such as code churn, code complexity, code coverage, code dependencies, etc. But these studies often ignore one of the most influential factors in software development: specifically, "people and organizational structure."

With the advent of global software development where teams are distributed across the world, the impact of organization structure on Conway's Law and its implications on quality are significant. In this section, we investigate the relationship between organizational structure and software quality via a set of eight measures that quantify organizational complexity [Nagappan et al. 2008]. For the organizational metrics, the metrics capture issues such as organizational distance of the developers; the number of developers working on a component; the amount of multitasking developers are doing across organizations; and the amount of change to a component within the context of that organization. Using these measures, we predict failure-prone binaries in Windows Vista. Some of the organizational measures are the following (for a more detailed list, refer to [Nagappan et al. 2008]):

Number of Engineers (NOE)
> This is the absolute number of unique engineers who have touched a binary and are still employed by the company.

Number of Ex-Engineers (NOEE)
> This is the total number of unique engineers who have touched a binary and have left the organizations as of the release date of the software system.

Edit Frequency (EF)
> This is the total number times the source code that makes up the binary was edited. An edit is when an engineer checks code out of the version control system, alters it, and checks it back in again. This is independent of the number of lines of code altered during the edit.

Depth of Master Ownership (DMO)
> This metric determines the level of ownership of the binary depending on the number of edits done. The organizational level of the person whose reporting engineers perform more than X% of the rolled-up edits is deemed as the DMO. The DMO metric determines the binary owner based on activity on that binary. We used 75% as the X%, based on prior historical information on Windows to quantify ownership.

Percentage of Org contributing to development (PO)
> The ratio of the number of people reporting to the DMO-level owner relative to the DMO overall org size.

Level of Organizational Code Ownership (OCO)
> The percent of edits from the organization that contains the binary owner, or if there is no owner, then the organization that made the majority of the edits to that binary.

Overall Organization Ownership (OOW)
> This is the ratio of the percentage of people at the DMO level making edits to a binary relative to total engineers editing the binary. A high value is desired.

Organization Intersection Factor (OIF)
> A measure of the number of different organizations that contribute greater than 10% of edits, as measured at the level of the overall org owners.

The measures proposed here attempt to balance the various hypotheses about how organizational structure can influence the quality of the binary, some of which seem to represent opposing positions. A high-level summary of the hypotheses and the measures that purport to quantify these hypotheses is presented in Table 23-1.

TABLE 23-1. Summary of organizational measures [Nagappan et al. 2008]

Hypothesis	Metric
The more people who touch the code, the lower the quality.	NOE
A large loss of team members affects the knowledge retention and thus quality.	NOEE
The more edits to components, the higher the instability and lower the quality.	EF
The lower the level of ownership, the better the quality.	DMO
The more cohesive are the contributors (organizationally), the higher the quality.	PO
The more cohesive the contributions (edits), the higher the quality.	OCO
The more diffused the contribution to a binary, the lower the quality.	OOW
The more diffused the different organizations contributing code, the lower the quality.	OIF

Using random splitting on the entire Vista code base for 50 random splits, we obtained the precision and recall values as shown in Figure 23-2. The figure indicates the uniformity and consistency of the predictions of precision and recall. The values show little variance, explaining the overall efficacy of the models built and the ability of organizational metrics to effectively act as predictors of software quality. The precision and recall values were 86.2% and 84%, respectively. This is, as from our prior studies, the highest precision and recall in terms of predicting failures. This provided evidence that understanding the team structure in the organization is a crucial factor in predicting and understanding software quality. The interpretation lies in the fact that the organizational metrics were much better indicators of code quality, more than actual code metrics. This stresses the importance of getting the organization and team right for doing software development. These results also illustrate the impact of organizational structure on quality and the importance of planning for reorganization of teams to minimize the impact on software quality.

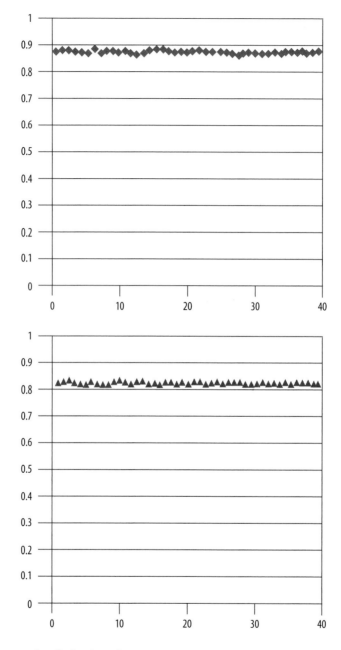

FIGURE 23-2. Precision and recall values for predictions using organization structure [Nagappan et al. 2008]

Integrated Approach for Prediction of Failures

So far we have analyzed sets of metrics—complexity metrics, code churn, code coverage, etc.—in isolation. In this section we address how the metrics may be combined to form stronger predictors of failures.

In Figure 23-3 a simple network of engineering working together in different binaries is shown. Similarly, Figure 23-3 shows the code dependencies between various networks. Figure 23-3 shows combining both pieces of information to integrate people, churn (in terms of edits/contributions), and dependencies together into one network.

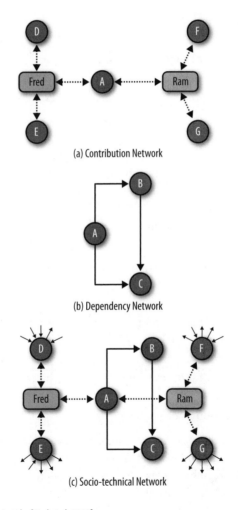

(a) Contribution Network

(b) Dependency Network

(c) Socio-technical Network

FIGURE 23-3. Socio-technical networks [Bird et al. 2009]

For Windows Vista we generate such a network integrating the people, churn contribution, and dependency information. Several social-network measures [Bird et al. 2009], detailed next, are computed for the Windows Vista social network (similar to the network in Figure 23-3).

Ego network measures [Borgatti et al. 2002] are based on the neighborhood for any particular node. The node being evaluated is denoted ego, and the neighborhood includes ego, the set of nodes connected to an ego, and the complete set of edges between this set of nodes.

Size
> The number of nodes in the ego network

Ties
> Number of edges in the ego network

Pairs
> Number of possible directed edges in the ego network

Density
> Proportion of possible ties that actually are present (Ties/Pairs)

Weak Components
> Number of weakly connected components

Normalized Weak Components
> Number of weakly connected components normalized by size, i.e., (Weak Components/ Size)

Two Step Reach
> The proportion of nodes that are within two hops of ego

Reach Efficiency
> Two Step Reach normalized by size of the network (higher reach efficiency indicates that the ego's primary contacts are influential in the network)

Brokerage
> Number of pairs of nodes that are connected only by ego (thus ego acts as the sole broker for the pair)

Normalized Brokerage
> Brokerage normalized by number of pairs

Ego Betweenness
> Betweenness of ego within its ego network

The preceding social network measures are computed for the complete Vista network (which includes the developers, contributions, and dependencies). Using these social network measures as input, prediction models are built. We observe that precision and recall of the built models are much higher when also using the dependency network for prediction. Similar results were also observed for multiple versions of IBM Eclipse (the open source IDE from IBM) [Bird et al. 2009]. Table 23-2 shows the precision and recall values with the model fit F-scores, which also indicate the increased ability of the socio-technical approach to predict failures. The "combined" model in Table 23-2 denotes a model purely built by just adding both the "Contribution" network (people working together) and the "Dependency" network (between various pieces of code), which provides a contrast to the socio-technical network. Further readings in which code complexity, churn, and coverage metrics are combined to predict failures can be found in [Nagappan et al. 2006b].

TABLE 23-2. Overall socio-technical network model efficacy using different release of Eclipse [Bird et al. 2009]

Release	Network	Precision	Recall	F-score	Nagel.
2.0	Dependency	0.667	0.779	0.705	0.532
	Contribution	0.808	0.854	0.824	0.702
	Combined	0.826	0.814	0.813	0.909
	Socio-technical	0.755	0.859	0.800	0.747
2.1	Dependency	0.693	0.753	0.710	0.626
	Contribution	0.675	0.780	0.719	0.607
	Combined	0.755	0.777	0.758	0.805
	Socio-technical	0.747	0.809	0.770	0.689
3.0	Dependency	0.631	0.737	0.673	0.494
	Contribution	0.681	0.683	0.673	0.353
	Combined	0.745	0.756	0.743	0.616
	Socio-technical	0.767	0.777	0.769	0.600
3.1	Dependency	0.579	0.718	0.634	0.391
	Contribution	0.639	0.646	0.629	0.295
	Combined	0.693	0.796	0.735	0.689
	Socio-technical	0.820	0.800	0.806	0.668
3.2	Dependency	0.698	0.780	0.731	0.495
	Contribution	0.614	0.720	0.654	0.371
	Combined	0.835	0.866	0.846	0.816
	Socio-technical	0.793	0.784	0.785	0.572
3.3	Dependency	0.693	0.743	0.711	0.433
	Contribution	0.725	0.669	0.688	0.356
	Combined	0.742	0.780	0.754	0.686
	Socio-technical	0.820	0.831	0.823	0.727

Summary

In the preceding sections we have described various metrics that have been used to predict failures from the Windows experience. To summarize, Table 23-3 summarizes the precision and recall of using these sets of metrics to predict failures in Windows Vista.

TABLE 23-3. Overall model accuracy using different software measures

Model	Precision	Recall
Organizational structure	86.2%	84.0%
Code churn	78.6%	79.9%
Code complexity	79.3%	66.0%
Social network/combination measures	76.9%	70.5%
Dependencies	74.4%	69.9%
Code coverage	83.8%	54.4%

In addition, social network measures developed by integrating several of the measures also provides accurate predictions of failures. As stated earlier, as with all empirical studies, the evidence provided here is based only upon empirical results obtained at Microsoft, and more specifically in Windows. It is possible that these results might not hold for other software products or environments. We become more confident in results when similar studies are done in different software domains to show or disprove generality of the evidence provided for failure prediction. A step-by-step guide to building predictors is illustrated in the sidebar "Building Quality Predictors: A Step-by-Step Guide" [Nagappan et al. 2006a]. The primary purpose and goal of this chapter is to share experiences of results learned at Microsoft using various metrics and to describe the metrics, to encourage repetition in different domains by researchers and software engineers and thereby determine the efficacy of the applied metrics for other projects on a case-by-case basis.

BUILDING QUALITY PREDICTORS: A STEP-BY-STEP GUIDE

1. Determine a software E from which to learn. E can be an earlier release of the software at hand or a similar project.

2. Decompose E into entities (subsystems, modules, files, classes...) $E = \{e_1, e_2, ...\}$ for which you can determine the individual quality (for example, binaries/modules).

3. Build a function $quality: E \rightarrow \mathbb{R}$, which assigns to each entity $e \in E$ a quality. This typically requires mining version and bug histories.

4. Have a set of *metric functions* $M = \{m_1, m_2, \ldots\}$ such that each $m \in M$ is a mapping $m: E \rightarrow R$, which assigns a metric to an entity $e \in E$. The set of metrics M should be adapted for the project and programming language at hand.

5. For each metric $m \in M$ and each entity $e \in E$, determine $m(e)$.

6. Determine the correlations between all $m(e)$ and *defects*(e), as well as the inter-correlations between all $m(e)$.

7. If needed, using principal component analysis, extract a set of principal components $PC = \{pc_1, pc_2, \ldots\}$, where each component $pc_i \in PC$ has the form $pc_i = \langle c_1, c_2, \ldots c_{|M|} \rangle$.

8. You can now use the principal components PC to build a predictor for new entities $E' = \{e'_1, e'_2, \ldots\}$ with $E' \cap E = \varnothing$. Be sure to evaluate the explanative and predictive power.

The collection of the metrics discussed in this chapter is fully automated and most users can automatically collect these metrics for their projects using tools available in commercial and open source IDEs. Example screenshots from the Microsoft Visual Studio™ and IBM Eclipse plug-ins are shown in Figures 23-4[*] and 23-5.[†]

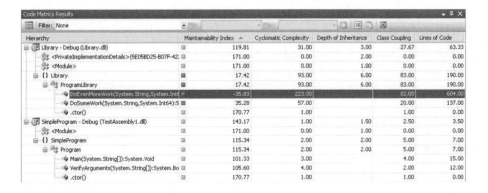

FIGURE 23-4. Metrics report in Microsoft Visual Studio™

---

[*] From: *http://blogs.msdn.com/b/codeanalysis/archive/2007/02/28/announcing-visual-studio-code-metrics.aspx*. Retrieved on June 13, 2010.

[†] From: *http://metrics.sourceforge.net/*. Retrieved on June 13, 2010.

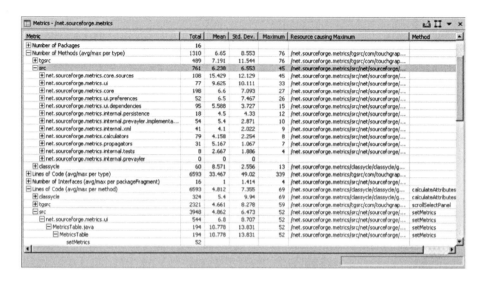

FIGURE 23-5. Metrics plug in for IBM Eclipse

Acknowledgments

We would like to thank all our colleagues at Microsoft Corporation and Windows for their help with these studies. We would also like to thank all our coauthors, more specifically, Thomas Zimmermann, Brendan Murphy, Vic Basili, Andreas Zeller, Audris Mockus, Prem Devanbu, and Chris Bird.

References

[Basili et al. 1994] Basili, V., G. Caldiera, and D.H. Rombach. 1994. The Goal Question Metric Paradigm. In *Encyclopedia of Software Engineering*, ed. J. Marciniak, 528–532. Hoboken, NJ: John Wiley & Sons, Inc.

[Basili et al. 1996] Basili, V., L. Briand, and W. Melo. 1996. A Validation of Object Oriented Design Metrics as Quality Indicators. *IEEE Transactions on Software Engineering* 22(10): 751–761.

[Basili et al. 1999] Basili, V., F. Shull, and F. Lanubile. 1999. Building Knowledge through Families of Experiments. *IEEE Transactions on Software Engineering* 25(4): 456–473.

[Bhat and Nagappan 2006] Bhat, T., and N. Nagappan. 2006. Building Scalable Failure-proneness Models Using Complexity Metrics for Large Scale Software Systems. *Proceedings of the XIII Asia Pacific Software Engineering Conference*: 361–366.

[Bird et al. 2009] Bird, C., et al. 2009. Putting It All Together: Using Socio-technical Networks to Predict Failures. *Proceedings of the 20th IEEE international conference on software reliability engineering*: 109–119.

[Boehm 1981] Boehm, B.W. 1981. *Software Engineering Economics*. Englewood Cliffs, NJ: Prentice-Hall, Inc.

[Borgatti et al. 2002] Borgatti, S., M.G. Everett, and L.C. Freeman. 2002. *UCINET 6 for Windows: Software for Social Network Analysis*. Harvard, MA: Analytic Technologies.

[Briand et al. 1999] Briand, L.C., J. Wuest, S. Ikonomovski, and H. Lounis. 1999. Investigating quality factors in object-oriented designs: an industrial case study. *Proceedings of the 21st international conference on software engineering*: 345–354.

[Brooks 1995] Brooks, F.P. 1995. *The Mythical Man-Month*, Anniversary Edition. Boston: Addison-Wesley.

[Chidamber and Kemerer 1994] Chidamber, S.R., and C.F. Kemerer. 1994. A Metrics Suite for Object Oriented Design. *IEEE Transactions on Software Engineering* 20(6): 476–493.

[Conway 1968] Conway, M.E. 1968. How Do Committees Invent? *Datamation* 14(4): 28–31.

[El Emam 2000] El Emam, K. 2000. *A Methodology for Validating Software Product Metrics*. Ottawa, Ontario, Canada: National Research Council of Canada.

[El Emam et al. 2001] El Emam, K., S. Benlarbi, N. Goel, and S.N. Rai. 2001. The Confounding Effect of Class Size on the Validity of Object-Oriented Metrics. *IEEE Transactions on Software Engineering* 27(7): 630–650.

[Han and Kamber 2006] Han, J., and M. Kamber. 2006. *Data Mining: Concepts and Techniques*, Second Edition. San Francisco: Elsevier.

[Herbsleb and Grinter 1999] Herbsleb, J.D., and R.E. Grinter. 1999. Architectures, coordination, and distance: Conway's Law and beyond. *IEEE Software* 16(5): 63–70.

[IEEE 1990] IEEE. 1990. *IEEE Std 610.12-1990, IEEE Standard Glossary of Software Engineering Terminology*. New York: The Institute of Electrical and Electronics Engineers.

[ISO/IEC 1996] ISO/IEC. 1996. *DIS 14598-1 Information Technology—Software Product Evaluation*. International Organization for Standardization.

[Khoshgoftaar et al. 1996] Khoshgoftaar, T.M., E.B. Allen, N. Goel, A. Nandi, and J. McMullan. 1996. Detection of Software Modules with High Debug Code Churn in a Very Large Legacy System. *Proceedings of the Seventh International Symposium on Software Reliability Engineering*: 364.

[McCabe 1976] McCabe, T.J. 1976. A Complexity Measure. *IEEE Transactions on Software Engineering* 2(4): 308–320.

[Mockus et al. 2009] Mockus, A., N. Nagappan, and T.T. Dinh-Trong. 2009. Test Coverage and Post-verification Defects: A Multiple Case Study. *Proceedings of the 2009 3rd International Symposium on Empirical Software Engineering and Measurement*: 291–301.

[Nagappan and Ball 2005] Nagappan, N., and T. Ball. 2005. Use of Relative Code Churn Measures to Predict System Defect Density. *Proceedings of the 27th international conference on software engineering*: 284–292.

[Nagappan and Ball 2007] Nagappan, N., and T. Ball. 2007. Using Software Dependencies and Churn Metrics to Predict Field Failures: An Empirical Case Study. *Proceedings of the First International Symposium on Empirical Software Engineering and Measurement*: 364–373.

[Nagappan et al. 2006a] Nagappan, N., T. Ball, and A. Zeller. 2006. Mining metrics to predict component failures. *Proceedings of the 28th international conference on software engineering*: 452–461.

[Nagappan et al. 2006b] Nagappan, N., T. Ball, and B. Murphy. 2006. Using Historical In-Process and Product Metrics for Early Estimation of Software Failures. *Proceedings of the 17th International Symposium on Software Reliability Engineering*: 62–74.

[Nagappan et al. 2008] Nagappan, N., B. Murphy, and V. Basili. 2008. The Influence of Organizational Structure on Software Quality: An Empirical Case Study. *Proceedings of the 30th international conference on software engineering*: 521–530.

[Ostrand et al. 2004] Ostrand, T.J., E.J. Weyuker, and R.M. Bell. 2004. Where the Bugs Are. *Proceedings of the 2004 ACM SIGSOFT international symposium on software testing and analysis*: 86–96.

[Schröter et al. 2006] Schröter, A., T. Zimmermann, and A. Zeller. 2006. Predicting Component Failures at Design Time. *Proceedings of the 2006 ACM/IEEE international symposium on empirical software engineering*: 18–27.

[Tang et al. 1999] Tang, M.-H., M.-H. Kao, and M.-H. Chen. 1999. An empirical study on object-oriented metrics. *Proceedings of the 6th International Symposium on Software Metrics*: 242.

[von Mayrhauser et al. 1999] von Mayrhauser, A., J. Wang, M.C. Ohlsson, and C. Wohlin. 1999. Deriving a fault architecture from defect history. *Proceedings of the 10th International Symposium on Software Reliability Engineering*: 295.

CHAPTER TWENTY-FOUR

The Art of Collecting Bug Reports

Rahul Premraj
Thomas Zimmermann

Kids love bugs, and some kids even collect bugs and keep them in precious "kill jars." Over a period of time, bug collectors can amass a large number of different species of bugs. Some kids study the bugs they collected and label them based on such characteristics as shape, size, color, number of legs, whether it can fly, and so on. The bugs may be valued differently depending upon how rare they are or how difficult they are to catch. The collection may have some duplicate bugs. But duplicates are rarely identical, as characteristics such as appearance and size can differ widely.

But we software developers do not like bugs. We hope to have none in our software, and when they are found, we squash them! Unfortunately, squashing bugs, or more politely, responding to software change requests, is rarely easy. Developers have to study the information about the bug in detail, conduct a thorough investigation on how to resolve the bug, examine its side effects, and eventually decide on and take a course of action. This is a difficult task because, like earthly bugs, software bugs differ widely. Often software bugs that are collected in bug databases of projects are studied in isolation because they are different from the other bugs in their effects on the software system, their cause and location, and their severity. Over time, a project will accumulate duplicate bugs, just as a live-bug collector may have multiple bugs of the same species. And finally, nearly every project knows about more bug reports than it can fix, just as there are too many live bugs to be collected by a single person.

So the study of software bugs is a valuable pastime. The starting point for the study of software bugs is the information filed in bug reports by those who report them. In this chapter, we discuss the characteristics of good bug reports and implications for the practice of collecting bug reports.

Good and Bad Bug Reports

When some users of a software system encounter a bug, they report it to developers with the hope that the bug will be fixed. The information in a bug report gives the developers a detailed description of the failure and occasionally hints at the cause.

But the quality and level of detail of information can vary a lot from one bug report to another. Take for example the following bug report (#31021) from the Eclipse project:

```
I20030205

Run the following example. Double click on a tree item and notice that
it does not expand.

Comment out the Selection listener and now double click on any tree
item and notice that it expands.

public static void main(String[] args){
    Display display = new Display();
    Shell shell = new Shell(display);
    [. . . ] (21 lines of code removed)
    display.dispose();
}
```

The reporter provides a code example and concise steps on how to run it in order to reproduce the bug. Once a developer can reproduce and observe the bug, it is likely to make the process of investigating the cause of the bug comparatively easier.

On the other hand, the following bug report (#175222), again from the Eclipse project, is not in fact a bug at all and has been misfiled as one:

```
I wand to create a new plugin in Eclipse using CDT. Shall it possible.
I had made a RD in eclipse documentation. I had get an idea about
create a plugin using Java. But i wand to create a new plugin ( user
defined plugin ) using CDT. After that I wand to impliment it in my
programe. If it possible?. Any one can help me please...
```

The quality of information in bug reports can crucially influence the resolution of a bug as well as its resolution time. Reports that contain all the necessary information can make resolving the bug somewhat easier. In contrast, reports with inadequate information may lead to avoidable delays when developers find themselves filling the gaps in information or contacting reporters to request more information.

It's clear that high-quality information in bug reports would be in the interest of everyone involved. Developers might be able to resolve more and more bugs in shorter periods of time, and reporters would have their bugs fixed quickly. But what information in a bug report enhances its quality? We describe our search for the answer in this chapter.

What Makes a Good Bug Report?

Through an online survey, we asked over 150 developers from three large and successful open source projects—Apache, Eclipse, and Mozilla—what information in bug reports they consider valuable and helpful when resolving bugs. We also contacted bug reporters from the same projects to find out what information they provide and what information is most difficult to provide.

Our online survey is presented in Table 24-1. The survey sent out to developers comprised four questions in two categories:

Contents of bug reports

- (D1) Which items have developers previously used when fixing bugs?
- (D2) Which three items helped the most?

Insight into this issue can help develop guides or tools for reporters to provide information in bug reports that focuses on the details that are most important to developers. We provided the developers with 16 items to choose from, some selected from the Mozilla bug-writing guidelines* and others found as standard fields in the Bugzilla database. Developers were free to check as many items as they liked for the first question (D1), but at most three for the second question (D2), thus indicating the importance of the choices in their perspectives.

Problems with bug reports

- (D3) Which problems have developers encountered when fixing bugs?
- (D4) Which three problems caused the most delay in fixing bugs?

Our motivation for these questions was to find the prominent obstacles faced by developers that can be tackled in the future by more cautious, and perhaps even automated, bug reporting. Typical problems include reporters accidentally providing incorrect information, such as the wrong operating system.

---

* The Mozilla bug-writing guidelines describe principles of effective bug reporting (e.g., be precise and clear, one bug per report) and list information that is essential to every bug report, such as steps to reproduce it, actual results, and expected results [Goldberg 2010].

Other problems in bug reports include poor use of language (ambiguity), bug duplicates, and incomplete information. Spam recently has become a problem, especially for the TRAC issue tracking system. We decided not to include the problem of incorrect assignments to developers, because bug reporters have little influence on the triaging of bugs. In total, we provided 21 problems that developers could select. Again, they were free to check as many items for the third question (D3), but at most three for the fourth question (D4). For a complete list of items, see Table 24-1.

We asked bug reporters the following three questions, divided into two categories (again, see Table 24-1):

Contents of bug reports

- (R1) Which items have reporters previously provided?
- (R2) Which three items were most difficult to provide?

We offered the same 16 items to reporters that we offered to developers. This allowed us to check whether the information provided by reporters is in line with what developers frequently use or consider to be important (by comparing the responses for R1 with D1 and D2). The second question helped us to identify items that are difficult to collect and for which better tools might support reporters in this task. Reporters were free to check as many items as they wanted for the first question (R1), but at most three for the second question (R2).

Contents considered to be relevant

- (R3) Which three items do reporters consider to be most relevant for developers?

Again we listed the same items to see how much reporters agree with developers (comparing R3 with D2). For this question (R3), reporters were free to check at most three items, but could choose any item, regardless of whether they selected it for question R1.

Additionally, we asked both developers and reporters about their thoughts and experiences with respect to bug reports (D5 and R4).

TABLE 24-1. The questionnaire presented to Apache, Eclipse, and Mozilla developers (Dx) and reporters (Rx)

Contents of bug reports.	D1: Which of the following items have you previously used when fixing bugs?			
	D2: Which three items helped you the most?			
	R1: Which of the following items have you previously provided when reporting bugs?			
	R2: Which three items were the most difficult to provide?			
	R3: In your opinion, which three items are most relevant for developers when fixing bugs?			
	☐ product	☐ hardware	☐ observed behaviour	☐ screenshots
	☐ component	☐ operating system	☐ expected behaviour	☐ code examples
	☐ version	☐ summary	☐ steps to reproduce	☐ error reports
	☐ severity	☐ build information	☐ stack traces	☐ testcases

| Problems with bug reports. | D3: Which of the following problems have you encountered when fixing bugs? |
| | D4: Which three problems caused you most delay in fixing bugs? |

You were given:	There were errors in:	The reporter used:	Others:
▢ product name	▢ code examples	▢ bad grammar	▢ duplicates
▢ component name	▢ steps to reproduce	▢ unstructured text	▢ spam
▢ version number	▢ test cases	▢ prose text	▢ incomplete information
▢ hardware	▢ stack traces	▢ too long text	▢ viruses/worms
▢ operating system		▢ non-technical language	
▢ observed behaviour		▢ no spell check	
▢ expected behaviour			

| Comments. | D5/R4: Please feel free to share any interesting thoughts or experiences. |

Survey Results

The results of our survey are summarized in Figure 24-1 (for developers) and Figure 24-2 (for reporters).

In the figures, responses for each item are annotated as bars (■■▭) , which can be interpreted as follows (explained with D1 and D2 as examples):

- The colored part (■■+▭) denotes the count of responses for an item in question D1.
- The black part (■■) of the bar denotes the count of responses for the item in both question D1 and D2.

The larger the black bar is in proportion to the gray bar, the higher is the corresponding item's importance in the developers' perspective. The importance of every item is also listed in parentheses. For example, Figure 24-1 shows that developers consider steps to reproduce (■■■▭ , 83%) to be more important than build information (■▭▭ , 8%).

Contents of Bug Reports (Developers)

Figure 24-1 shows that the most widely used items across projects are steps to reproduce the bug, observed and expected behavior, stack traces, and test cases. Information rarely used by developers include hardware and severity. Eclipse and Mozilla developers liked screenshots, whereas Apache and Eclipse developers more often used code examples and stack traces.

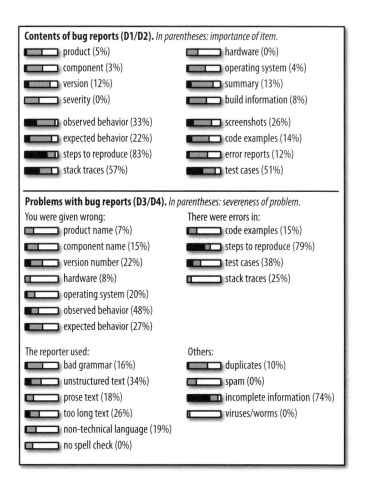

Contents of bug reports (D1/D2). *In parentheses: importance of item.*

product (5%)   hardware (0%)
component (3%)   operating system (4%)
version (12%)   summary (13%)
severity (0%)   build information (8%)

observed behavior (33%)   screenshots (26%)
expected behavior (22%)   code examples (14%)
steps to reproduce (83%)   error reports (12%)
stack traces (57%)   test cases (51%)

Problems with bug reports (D3/D4). *In parentheses: severeness of problem.*

You were given wrong: There were errors in:
product name (7%)   code examples (15%)
component name (15%)   steps to reproduce (79%)
version number (22%)   test cases (38%)
hardware (8%)   stack traces (25%)
operating system (20%)
observed behavior (48%)
expected behavior (27%)

The reporter used: Others:
bad grammar (16%)   duplicates (10%)
unstructured text (34%)   spam (0%)
prose text (18%)   incomplete information (74%)
too long text (26%)   viruses/worms (0%)
non-technical language (19%)
no spell check (0%)

FIGURE 24-1. Results from the survey among developers (130 consistent responses by Apache, Eclipse, and Mozilla developers)

For the importance of items, steps to reproduce the bug stand out clearly as most important. Next in line are stack traces and test cases, both of which help to narrow down the search space for defects. Observed behavior mimics, albeit weakly, steps to reproduce the bug, which is why it may be rated as important. Screenshots were rated as high, but often are helpful only for a subset of bugs, e.g., GUI errors.

Smaller surprises in the results include the relative low importance of items such as expected behavior, code examples, summary, and mandatory fields such as version, operating system, product, and hardware. As pointed out by a Mozilla developer, not all projects need the information that is provided by mandatory fields:

> "That's why product and usually even component information is irrelevant to me and that hardware and to some degree [OS] fields are rarely needed as most our bugs are usually found in all platforms."

In any case, we advise caution when interpreting these results. Items with low importance in our survey are not totally irrelevant, because they still might be needed to understand, reproduce, or triage bugs.

Contents of Bug Reports (Reporters)

The items provided by most reporters are listed in the first part of Figure 24-2. As expected, observed and expected behavior and steps to reproduce the bug rank highest. Only a few users added stack traces, code examples, and test cases to their bug reports. An explanation might be the difficulty of providing these items, which we measured by the percentage of people who selected an item as difficult to provide in bug reports; the difficulty is listed in parentheses. All three items rank among the more difficult items, with test cases being the most difficult item. Surprisingly, steps to reproduce the bug are considered difficult as well, as is the component. For the latter, reporters revealed in their comments that often it is impossible for them to locate the component in which a bug occurs.

Among the items considered to be most helpful to developers, reporters ranked steps to reproduce the bug and test cases highest. Comparing the results for test cases among all three questions reveals that most reporters consider them to be helpful, but only a few provide them because they are most difficult to provide. This suggests that capture/replay tools that record test cases should be integrated into bug tracking systems. A similar but weaker observation can be made for stack traces, which are often hidden in logfiles and difficult to find. On the other hand, both developers and reporters consider the component to be only marginally important; furthermore, as already mentioned, it is rather difficult to provide.

Evidence for an Information Mismatch

We compared the results from the developer and reporter surveys to find out whether they agree on what is important in bug reports.

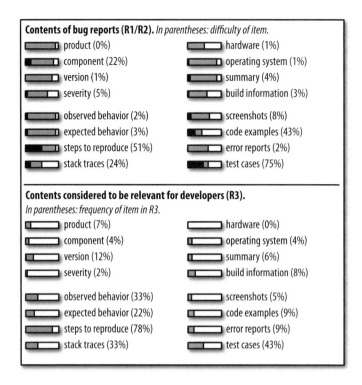

FIGURE 24-2. Results from the survey among reporters (215 consistent responses by Apache, Eclipse, and Mozilla reporters)

First, we compared the information developers use to resolve bugs (question D1) and the information reporters provide (R1). In Figure 24-3, items in the left column are sorted decreasingly by the percentage of developers who have used them, and items in the right column are sorted decreasingly by the percentage of reporters who have provided them. Lines connect the same items across columns and indicate the agreement (or disagreement) between developers and reporters on that particular item. Figure 24-3 shows that the results match only for the top three items and the last one. In between there are many disagreements, and the most notable ones are for stack traces, test cases, code examples, product, and operating system. Overall, the Spearman correlation[†] between what developers use and what reporters provide was 0.321, far from ideal.

† Spearman correlation is a measure of strength of the association between two variables. Its value ranges from -1 to +1. Values closer to -1 or +1 indicate a strong relationship, while 0 suggests there is no relationship between the variables. The sign indicates whether the association is in the same (+) or opposite (-) directions.

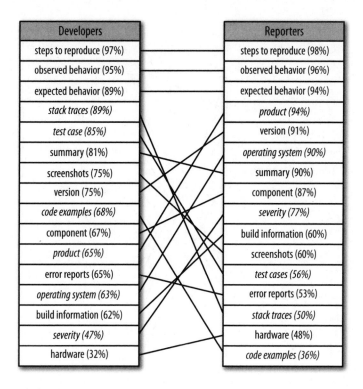

Developers	Reporters
steps to reproduce (97%)	steps to reproduce (98%)
observed behavior (95%)	observed behavior (96%)
expected behavior (89%)	expected behavior (94%)
stack traces (89%)	product (94%)
test case (85%)	version (91%)
summary (81%)	operating system (90%)
screenshots (75%)	summary (90%)
version (75%)	component (87%)
code examples (68%)	severity (77%)
component (67%)	build information (60%)
product (65%)	screenshots (60%)
error reports (65%)	test cases (56%)
operating system (63%)	error reports (53%)
build information (62%)	stack traces (50%)
severity (47%)	hardware (48%)
hardware (32%)	code examples (36%)

FIGURE 24-3. Used by developers versus provided by reporters

Next, we checked whether reporters provide the information that is most important for developers. In Figure 24-4, the left column corresponds to the importance of an item for developers (measured by questions D2 and D1), and the right column to the percentage of reporters who provided an item (R1). Developers and reporters still agree on the first and last item, but overall the disagreement increased. The Spearman correlation of -0.035 between what developers consider as important and what reporters provide shows a huge gap. In particular, it indicates that reporters do not focus on the information important for developers.

Interestingly, Figure 24-5 shows that most reporters know which information developers need. In other words, ignorance among reporters cannot be blamed for the aforementioned information mismatch. As before, the left column corresponds to the importance of items for developers; the right column now shows what reporters expect to be most relevant (question R3). Overall there is a strong agreement; the only notable disagreement is for screenshots. This is confirmed by the Spearman correlation of 0.839, indicating a very strong relation between what developers and reporters consider as important.

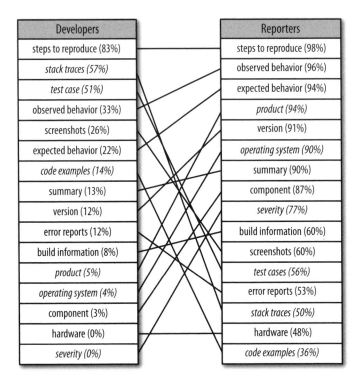

Developers	Reporters
steps to reproduce (83%)	steps to reproduce (98%)
stack traces (57%)	observed behavior (96%)
test case (51%)	expected behavior (94%)
observed behavior (33%)	product (94%)
screenshots (26%)	version (91%)
expected behavior (22%)	operating system (90%)
code examples (14%)	summary (90%)
summary (13%)	component (87%)
version (12%)	severity (77%)
error reports (12%)	build information (60%)
build information (8%)	screenshots (60%)
product (5%)	test cases (56%)
operating system (4%)	error reports (53%)
component (3%)	stack traces (50%)
hardware (0%)	hardware (48%)
severity (0%)	code examples (36%)

FIGURE 24-4. Most helpful for developers versus most often provided by reporters

To sum up, to improve bug reporting systems, one could tell users while they are reporting a bug what information is important (e.g., screenshots). At the same time, systems should provide better tools to collect important information, because often this information is difficult to obtain for users.

Problems with Bug Reports

Among the problems experienced by developers, incomplete information was, by far, most commonly encountered. Other common problems include errors in steps to reproduce the bug, errors in test cases, bug duplicates, incorrect version numbers, and incorrect observed and expected behavior. Another issue that often challenges developers is the reporter's language fluency. These problems can easily lead developers astray when fixing bugs.

The most severe problems were errors in the steps to reproduce the bug and incomplete information. In fact, in question D5 many developers commented on being plagued by bug reports with incomplete information. As one developer commented:

> "The biggest causes of delay are not wrong information, but absent information."

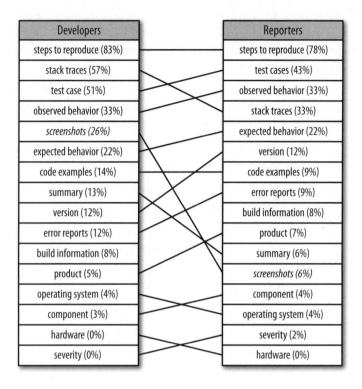

Developers	Reporters
steps to reproduce (83%)	steps to reproduce (78%)
stack traces (57%)	test cases (43%)
test case (51%)	observed behavior (33%)
observed behavior (33%)	stack traces (33%)
screenshots (26%)	expected behavior (22%)
expected behavior (22%)	version (12%)
code examples (14%)	code examples (9%)
summary (13%)	error reports (9%)
version (12%)	build information (8%)
error reports (12%)	product (7%)
build information (8%)	summary (6%)
product (5%)	*screenshots (6%)*
operating system (4%)	component (4%)
component (3%)	operating system (4%)
hardware (0%)	severity (2%)
severity (0%)	hardware (0%)

FIGURE 24-5. Most helpful for developers versus expected by reporters to be helpful

The low occurrence of spam is not surprising, because in Bugzilla and Jira, reporters have to register before they can submit bug reports, and this registration successfully prevents spam. Finally, errors in stack traces are highly unlikely because they are copy-pasted into bug reports, but when they do happen they can be a severe problem.

Other major problems included errors in test cases and observed behavior. A very interesting observation is that developers do not suffer too much from bug duplicates, although earlier research considered this to be a problem [Anvik et al. 2005]. Perhaps developers can easily recognize duplicates, and sometimes even benefit from a different bug description. The following section provides an extensive study of the value of duplicate bug reports.

The Value of Duplicate Bug Reports

A common argument against duplicate bug reports is that they strain bug tracking systems and demand more effort from quality assurance teams—effort that could instead be spent to improve the product. In this section, we provide empirical evidence for the contrary: duplicate bug reports actually contain additional information that may be useful to resolve bugs.

When a bug report is identified as a duplicate, a common practice is to simply close the bug and discard the information, which in the long term discourages users from submitting bug reports. They become reluctant to provide additional information, once they see that a bug report has already been filed:

> "Typically bugs I have reported are already reported but by much less savvy people who make horrible reports that lack important details. It is frustrating to have spent lots of time making an exceptionally detailed bug report to only have it marked as a duplicate..."

Not everyone agrees that bug duplicates are bad. In our survey, several developers pointed out the value of bug duplicates for resolving bugs:

> "Duplicates are not really problems. They often add useful information. That this information were filed under a new report is not ideal though."

> "It would be better to somehow mend the reports instead of just writing off the good report simply because it was posted after the bad report. This would probably help software engineers much more."

Alan Page, a test architect at Microsoft, makes a similar argument and summarizes three reasons why "worrying about [duplicates] is bad" [Page et al. 2008]:

- Often there are negative consequences for users who enter duplicates. As a result, *they might err on the side of not entering a bug*, even though it is not filed yet.
- *Triagers are more skilled in detecting duplicates* than users, and they also know the system better. Whereas a user will need a considerable amount of time to browse through similar bugs, triagers can often decide within minutes whether a bug report is a duplicate.
- *Bug duplicates can provide valuable information* that helps diagnose the actual problem.

Do bug duplicates really provide extra information, and if so, how much? We found out with an empirical study. First, we built a tool to detect and quantify information items such as patches, screenshots, and stack traces in bug reports. Next, we compared the amount of information found in the original bug report (called the *master report*), and the *extended report*, which combines the original master bug report with its duplicates.

Table 24-2 summarizes our findings for the Eclipse project. The first column, "Information item," presents all the pieces of information that we commonly found and extracted from bug reports. The items fall in four categories: predefined fields such as product and component, patches, screenshots, and stack traces. The second column, "Master," lists the average count of each information item in the original bug reports. For example, every master report contains exactly one operating system, as indicated by the 1.000 value in the "Master" column. This count corresponds to a practice that is found in many projects: once duplicates are detected, they are simply closed and all information that they provided is discarded.

The third column, "Extended," lists the average count of each information item in the extended bug reports. When merged with their duplicates, the average number of unique operating systems in extended bug reports increases to 1.631. This count would correspond to a practice where duplicates are merged with master reports and all information is retained. The fourth column, "Change," calculates the increase from "Master" to "Extended" and quantifies the amount of information added by bug duplicates per master report. For example, duplicates could add on average 0.631 operating systems to existing bugs as long as duplicates are not just discarded.

TABLE 24-2. Average amount of information added by duplicates per master report in Eclipse

| Information item | Average count per master report | | |
	Master	Extended	Change[a]
Predefined fields			
Product	1.000	1.127	+0.127 (12.7%)
Component	1.000	1.287	+0.287 (28.7%)
Operating system	1.000	1.631	+0.631 (63.1%)
Reported platform	1.000	1.241	+0.241 (24.1%)
Version	0.927	1.413	+0.486 (52.4%)
Reporter	1.000	2.412	+1.412 (41.2%)
Priority	1.000	1.291	+0.291 (29.1%)
Target milestone	0.654	0.794	+0.140 (21.4%)
Patches			
Total	1.828	1.942	+0.113 (6.2%)
Unique: patched files	1.061	1.124	+0.062 (5.9%)
Screenshots			
Total	0.139	0.285	+0.145 (105.0%)
Stacktraces			
Total	0.504	1.422	+0.918 (182.1%)
Unique: exception	0.195	0.314	+0.118 (61.0%)
Unique: exception, top frame	0.223	0.431	+0.207 (93.3%)
Unique: exception, top 2 frames	0.229	0.458	+0.229 (100.0%)
Unique: exception, top 3 frames	0.234	0.483	+0.248 (106.4%)
Unique: exception, top 4 frames	0.239	0.504	+0.265 (110.9%)
Unique: exception, top 5 frames	0.244	0.525	+0.281 (115.2%)

[a] For all information items, the increase is significant at p < .001.

Table 24-2 shows that most duplicates are filed by different users from those who filed the original master report, which explains the large increase in the number of unique reporters.

We found that duplicates add on average only 0.113 patches and 0.062 patched files per master report. This is a rather small relative increase of about 6% and suggests that most patches are filed against the master report. However, bug duplicates add on average 0.145 screenshots, which doubles the number of screenshots. Duplicates also provide substantial additional information for version, priority, and component.

We compared stack traces by considering the exception that triggered them and the first five stack frames. For Eclipse on average, 0.918 additional stack traces were found in the duplicate bug reports (an increase of 182%). Within these, we found on average 0.118 occurrences (61%) of additional exceptions in duplicates and 0.281 stack traces (115.2%) that contained code locations (in the top five frames) that had not been reported before.

These findings show that duplicates are likely to provide different perspectives and additional pointers to the origins of bugs and thus can help developers correct them. For example, having more stack traces reveals more active methods during a crash, which helps to narrow down the suspects. These findings make a case for reevaluating the treatment and presentation of duplicates in bug tracking systems.

Not All Bug Reports Get Fixed

Most projects have more bug reports that can be fixed given limited resources and time. To characterize how the quality of bug reports increases the chances of bugs getting fixed, we sampled 150,000 bugs from Apache, Eclipse, and Mozilla (50,000 per project). These bugs had various resolutions, such as FIXED, DUPLICATE, MOVED, WONTFIX, and WORKSFORME. We divided the bug reports into two groups, successful and not successful, and then used statistical tests such as Chi-Square and Kruskal-Wallis ($p<.05$) to check for relationships between the success of bug reports and the presence of information items (code samples, stack traces, patches, screenshots). Our comparisons were:

Resolution of bug reports
> We compared bug reports resolved as FIXED against bug reports with other resolutions, such as WONTFIX and WORKSFORME. We treated duplicate bug reports as a separate group because for some the master report is fixed, whereas for others the master report is not fixed.

Lifetime of bug reports
> We compared bug reports with a short lifetime against bug reports with a long lifetime. A fast turnaround for bug reports is desirable, especially for users, but also for developers.

We also checked for the influence of readability on the success of bug reports. To measure the readability of bug reports, we used the *Style* tool, which "analyses the surface characteristics of the writing style of a document" [Cherry and Vesterman 1981]. The readability of a text is measured by the number of syllables per word and the length of sentences. Readability measures are used by Amazon.com to inform customers about the difficulty of books and by the U.S. Navy to ensure readability of technical documents. For our experiments we used the following seven readability measures: Kincaid, Automated Readability Index (ARI), Coleman-Liau, Flesh, Fog, Lix, and SMOG Grade.

Our findings from this experiment are:

- Bug reports with stack traces get fixed sooner. (Apache, Eclipse, and Mozilla)
- Bug reports that are easier to read get fixed sooner. (Apache, Eclipse, and Mozilla)
- Including code samples in a bug report increases the chances of it getting fixed. (Mozilla)

Independently from us, Hooimeijer and Weimer observed for Firefox that bug reports with attachments get fixed later, and bug reports with many comments get fixed sooner [Hooimeijer and Weimer 2007]. They also confirmed our results that easy-to-read reports are fixed faster. Panjer observed for Eclipse that comment count and activity as well as severity have the most effect on bugs' lifetimes [Panjer 2007]. Schröter et al. validated our finding that bugs with stack traces get fixed sooner and further emphasized the importance of adding stack traces to bug reports [Schröter et al. 2010]. A study conducted by Guo et al. at Microsoft for Windows Vista and Windows 7 [Guo et al. 2010] found that number of reassignments, organizational and geographical distribution, and reputation of bug opener influence the chances of bug reports getting fixed.

The findings in this section show that well-written bug reports help in comprehending the problem better, consequently increasing the likelihood of the bug getting fixed in a shorter time.

Conclusions

Bug reports are central to maintaining the quality of software systems. Their information contents help developers identify the cause of the failure and resolve it. But for this to happen, it is important that the information in the bug reports be reliable and complete.

But what makes a good bug report? In this chapter, we have presented the findings from a survey of developers and bug reporters from three large open source software products to identify which contents contribute to the information quality of bug reports from the perspective of those surveyed. Responses to our survey sent to developers indicated the importance of stack traces, steps to reproduce the bug, and expected and observed behavior in resolving bugs. Reporters indicated a similar set of important items as useful to help resolve bugs, but interestingly their responses also showed that they frequently don't provide such information, i.e., there is a mismatch between what information developers expect and what reporters provide.

Bug tracking systems can be enhanced to mitigate such information mismatch between developers and reporters. Several automations can be built in for data collection (such as stack traces from crashes), and the interfaces can be improved to remind reporters to add certain information. Our extensive study on bug duplicates has shown that duplicate bug reports often contain additional and useful information, so perhaps such new information should be automatically merged with the original bug reports. Offering incentives, such as listing the advantages of including certain types of information ("Bug reports with stack traces get fixed sooner"), may encourage bug reporters to go the extra mile to improve their reports.

All in all, the better the quality of bug reports, the more likely the bug will get fixed soon. Meanwhile, happy bug reporting and fixing!

Acknowledgments

This chapter is based on research work conducted by us jointly with Nicolas Bettenburg, Sascha Just, Sunghun Kim, Adrian Schröter, and Cathrin Weiss.

References

[Anvik et al. 2005] Anvik, John, Lyndon Hiew, and Gail C. Murphy. 2005. Coping with an open bug repository. *Proceedings of the 2005 OOPSLA workshop on Eclipse technology eXchange*: 35-39.

[Bettenburg et al. 2008a] Bettenburg, Nicolas, Sascha Just, Adrian Schröter, Cathrin Weiss, Rahul Premraj, and Thomas Zimmermann. 2008. What Makes a Good Bug Report?. *Proceedings of the 16th ACM SIGSOFT International Symposium on Foundations of Software Engineering: 308-318.*

[Bettenburg et al. 2008b] Bettenburg, Nicolas, Rahul Premraj, Thomas Zimmermann, and Sunghun Kim. 2008. Duplicate Bug Reports Considered Harmful...Really?. *Proceedings of the 24th International Conference on Software Maintenance.*

[Breu et al. 2010] Breu, Silvia, Rahul Premraj, Jonathan Sillito, and Thomas Zimmermann. 2010. Information Needs in Bug Reports: Improving Cooperation Between Developers and Users. *Proceedings of the 2010 ACM Conference on Computer Supported Cooperative Work:* 301-310.

[Cherry and Vesterman 1981] Cherry, L.L., and W. Vesterman. 1981. Writing Tools—The STYLE and DICTION Programs. Computer Science Technical Report No. 91, Bell Laboratories, Murray Hill, NJ.

[Goldberg 2010] Markham, Gervase, and Eli Goldberg. 2010. Bug Writing Guidelines. *https://developer.mozilla.org/en/Bug_writing_guidelines.*

[Guo et al. 2010] Guo, Philip J., Thomas Zimmermann, Nachiappan Nagappan, and Brendan Murphy. 2010. Characterizing and Predicting Which Bugs Get Fixed: An Empirical Study of Microsoft Windows. *Proceedings of the 32nd ACM/IEEE International Conference on Software Engineering* 1: 496-504.

[Hooimeijer and Weimer 2007] Hooimeijer, Peter, and Westley Weimer. 2007. Modeling bug report quality. *Proceedings of the 22nd IEEE/ACM International Conference on Automated Software Engineering*: 34-43.

[Page et al. 2008] Page, Alan, Ken Johnston, and B.J. Rollison. 2008. *How We Test Software at Microsoft*. Bellevue, WA: Microsoft Press.

[Panjer 2007] Panjer, Lucas D. 2007. Predicting Eclipse Bug Lifetimes. *Proceedings of the Fourth International Workshop on Mining Software Repositories*: 29.

[Schröter et al. 2010] Schröter, Adrian, Nicolas Bettenburg, and Rahul Premraj. 2010. Do Stack Traces Help Developers Fix Bugs?. *Proceedings of the 7th International Working Conference on Mining Software Repositories*: 118-121.

## CHAPTER TWENTY-FIVE

Where Do Most Software Flaws Come From?

Dewayne Perry

The holy grail of software development management is "cheaper, faster, and better." Unfortunately, a lot of poor management decisions are made in pursuit of this grail. While "cheaper and faster" are often very important, "better" clearly is the most important in a wide variety of software systems where reliability or safety is of paramount importance.

There are a variety of different ways in which a product can be made better, ranging from more clearly understanding customer needs to minimizing faults in the software system. It is the latter that is the focus of this chapter. Only by understanding the mistakes we make can we determine what remedies need to be applied to improve either the products or the processes. Monitoring faults is a relatively simple matter, either as they are found or in project retrospectives (often referred to as "project post-mortems").

A fundamental aspect in minimizing faults in software systems is the managing of complexity, the most critical of essential characteristics of software systems [Brooks 1995]. One of the most useful techniques in managing that complexity is that of separating the interfaces of components from their implementations. It is because of this critical technique that the difference between interface and implementation faults is an important distinction that is addressed in this chapter.

Studying Software Flaws

On the one hand, it is frustrating that so few studies of software faults have been published to guide researchers in finding ways of detecting, ameliorating, or preventing these faults from happening. On the other hand, it is not at all surprising that projects are reluctant to make such sensitive data public because of internal politics or external competitiveness in software-intensive businesses.

Despite this paucity of studies and the reluctance of companies to make data available, there is a set of landmark studies about software faults that provide useful foundations for product and process improvements. Endres [Endres 1975], Schneidewind and Hoffmann [Schneidewind and Hoffmann 1979], and Glass [Glass 1981] reported on various fault analyses of software development. A weakness in their work is that they do not delineate interface faults as a specific category.

Thayer, Lipow, and Nelson [Thayer et al. 1978] and Bowen [Bowen 1980] provide extensive categorization of faults, but with a relatively narrow view of interface faults. Basili and Perricone [Basili and Perricone 1984] offer the most comprehensive study of problems encountered in the development phase of a medium-scale system, reporting data on the fault, the number of components affected, the type of the fault, and the effort required to correct the fault. Interface faults were the largest class of faults (39% of the faults).

We note, however, that none of these studies address the kinds of problems that arise in very large-scale software developments, nor do they address the evolutionary phase of developments. Perry and Evangelist [Perry and Evangelist 1985], [Perry and Evangelist 1987] were the first to address fault studies in the evolution of a large real-time system. An extremely important factor in this study is the fact that interface faults were by far the overwhelming and dominant faults (68% of the faults). An important question that was left unanswered was whether these interface faults were the easy or the hard ones to find and fix.

The distinction between an evolutionary software system release and an initial development release is a critical one. In the latter case, the design and implementation choices are much less constrained than in evolutionary development. In the former, you have to make changes to an existing system, and so the choices are far more constrained and there are many more difficulties in understanding the implications of changes. As the evolutionary development part of a system's life cycle is far greater than its initial development, so too are studies of the faults in that evolutionary part much more important.

In this study, we take a detailed look at one specific release of one ultra-reliable, ultra-large-scale, real-time system rather than a more superficial look at several more moderately sized systems in several domains. The advantage of this approach is that we gain a deeper understanding of the system and its problems. The disadvantage is that we are less able to generalize our results compared to the latter course. This type of trade-off is often encountered in empirical studies.

As we will see, however, this deeper look provides us with a number of practical and useful insights. For example, it is commonly accepted wisdom that "once a bug is found, it is easy to fix." Unfortunately, our data contradicts this "common wisdom." Or, in the case of the unanswered question about interface faults, our data supports our original but unsubstantiated intuition that interface faults are harder to fix than implementation faults.

Context of the Study

The system discussed in this chapter is a very large-scale (that is, a million lines or more), distributed, real-time system written in the C programming language (with additional domain-specific languages as needed) in a Unix-based, multiple machine, multiple location environment.

The organizational structure is typical with respect to projects for systems of this size and for the number of people in each organization. Not surprisingly, different organizations are responsible for various parts of the system development: requirements specification; architecture, design, coding and capability testing; system and system stability testing; and alpha testing.

The process of development is also typical with respect to projects of this size. Systems engineers prepare informal and structured documents defining the requirements for the changes to be made to the system. Designers prepare informal design documents that are subjected to formal reviews by 3 to 15 peers, depending on the size of the unit under consideration. The design is then broken into design units for low-level design and coding. The products of this phase are subjected both to formal code reviews by three to five reviewers and to low-level unit testing. As components are available, integration and system testing is performed until the system is completely integrated.

The release considered here is a "non-initial" release—one that can be viewed as an arbitrary point in the evolution of this class of systems. Because of the size of the system, the system evolution process consists of multiple, concurrent releases—that is, while the release dates are sequential, a number of releases proceed concurrently in differing phases. This concurrency accentuates the inter-release dependencies and their associated problems. The magnitude of the changes (approximately 15–20% new code for each release) and the general make up of the changes (bug fixes, improvements, new functionality, etc.) are generally uniform across releases. It is because of these two facts that we consider this study to provide a representative sample in the life of the project.

Faults discovered during testing phases are reported and monitored by a modification request (MR) tracking system (such as, for example, CMS [Rowland et al. 1983]). Access to source files for modification is possible only through the tracking system. Thus all change activity (whether fixing faults, adding new functionality, or improving existing functionality—that is, whether they are corrective, adaptive, or perfective changes) is automatically tracked by the system. This activity includes not only repairs, but enhancements and new functionality as well. It should be kept in mind, however, that this fault tracking activity occurs only during the testing and released phases of the project, not during the architecture, design, and coding phases. Problems encountered during these earlier phases are resolved informally without being tracked by the MR system.

The goal of this study was to gain insight into the current process of system evolution by concentrating on one release of a particular system. The approach we used is that of surveying, by means of a prepared questionnaire, those developers who "owned" the fault MR at the time it was closed, surveying first the complete set of faults and then concentrating on the largest set of faults in more depth. This survey was the first of its type, although there have been some smaller studies using random selections. The CMS MR database was used to determine the initial set of fault MRs to survey and the developers who were responsible for closing those fault MRs. The survey identifying the fault MR was then sent to the identified developer to complete.

For a variety of reasons (schedule pressure among them), there were significant constraints placed on the study by project management: first, the study had to be completely non-intrusive; second, it had to be strictly voluntary; and third, it had to be completely anonymous. We will see in the later discussion about validity issues that these mandates were the source of some study weaknesses.

It is with this background that we present our surveys, analyses, and results.

Phase 1: Overall Survey

There were three specific purposes in the original overall survey:

- To determine, generally, what kinds of problems were found (which we report here), as well as, specifically, what kinds of application-specific problems arose during the preparation of this release (which we do not report, because of their lack of generality)
- To determine how the problem was found (that is, in which testing phase)
- To determine when the problem was found

One of the problems encountered in any empirical survey study is ensuring that the survey is in the "language" of those being surveyed. By this "language" we mean both the company- or project-specific jargon that is used but also the process that is being used. You want the developer surveyed to clearly understand what is being asked in terms of his own context. Failing to understand this results in questions about the validity of the survey results. To this end, we used developers to help us design the survey, and we used the project jargon and process to provide a familiar context.

Summary of Questionnaire

The first phase of the survey questionnaire had two main components: the determination of the category of the fault reported in the MR and the testing phase in which the fault was found. In determining the fault, two aspects were of importance: first, the development phase in which the fault was introduced, and second, the particular type of the fault. Since the particular type of fault reported at this stage of the survey tended to be application or methodology specific, we have emphasized the phase-origin nature of the fault categorization. The general fault categories are as follows:

Previous
> Residual problems left over from previous releases

Requirements
> Problems originating during the requirements specification phase of development

Design
> Problems originating during the architectural and design phases of development

Coding
> Problems originating during the coding phases of development

Testing environment
> Problems originating in the construction or provision of the testing environment (for example, faults in the system configuration, static data, etc.)

Testing
> Problems in testing (for example, pilot faults, etc.)

Duplicates
> Problems that have already been reported

No problems
> Problems due to misunderstandings about interfaces, functionality, etc., on the part of the user

Other
> Various problems that do not fit neatly in the preceding categories, such as hardware problems, etc.

The other main component of the survey concerned the phase of testing that uncovered the fault. The following are the different testing phases:

Capability Test (CT)
> Testing isolated portions of the system to ensure proper capabilities of that portion

System Test (ST)
> Testing the entire system to ensure proper execution of the system as a whole in the laboratory environment

System Stability Test (SS)

Testing with simulated load conditions in the laboratory environment for extended periods of time

Alpha Test (AT)

Live use of the release in a friendly user environment

Released (RE)

Live use. However, in this study, this data refers not to this release, but the previous release. Our expectation is that this provides a projection of the fault results for this release

The time interval during which the faults were found (that is, when the fault MRs were initiated and when they were closed) was retrieved from the MR tracking system database.

Ideally, the testing phases occur sequentially. In practice, however, due to the size and complexity of the system, various phases overlap. The overlap is due to several specific factors. First, various parts of the system are modified in parallel. This means that the various parts of the system are in different states at any one time. Second, the iterative nature of evolution results in recycling back through previous phases for various parts of the system. Third, various testing phases are begun as early as possible, even though it is known that that component may be incomplete. Looked at in one way, testing proceeds in a hierarchical manner: testing is begun with various pieces, then subsystems, and finally integrating those parts into the complete system. It is a judgment call as to when different parts of the system move from one phase to the next, determined primarily by the percentage of capabilities incorporated and the number of tests executed. Looked at in a slightly different way, testing proceeds by increasing the size and complexity of the system, while at the same time increasing its load and stress.

Summary of the Data

Table 25-1 summarizes the fault MRs by fault category. The fault MRs representing the earlier part of the development or evolution process (that is, those representing requirements, design, and coding) are the most significant, accounting for approximately 33.7% of the fault MRs. Given that the distinction between a design fault and a coding fault required a "judgment call" on the part of the respondent, we decided to merge the results of those two categories into one: design/coding faults account for 28.8% of the MRs. However, in the process structure used in the project, the distinction between requirements and design/coding is much clearer. Requirements specifications are produced by systems engineers, whereas the design and coding are done by developers.

TABLE 25-1. Summary of faults

MR category	Proportion
Previous	4.0%
Requirements	4.9%
Design	10.6%
Coding	18.2%
Testing environment	19.1%
Testing	5.7%
Duplicates	13.9%
No problems	15.9%
Other	7.8%

The next most significant subset of MRs were those that concern testing (the testing environment and testing categories)—24.8% of the MRs. On the one hand, it is not surprising that a significant number of problems are encountered in testing a large and complex real-time system where conditions have to be simulated to represent the "real world" in a laboratory environment. First, the testing environment itself is a large and complex system that must be tested. Second, as the real-time system evolves, so must the laboratory test environment evolve. On the other hand, this general problem is clearly one that needs to be addressed by further study.

"Duplicate" and "no problem" MRs account for another significant subset of the data—29.8%. Historically, these have been considered to be part of the overhead. Certainly the "duplicate" MRs are in large part due to the inherent concurrency of activities in a large-scale project and, as such, are difficult to eliminate. The "no problem" MRs, however, are in large part due to the lack of understanding that comes from informal and out-of-date documentation. Obviously, measures taken to reduce these kinds of problems will have beneficial effects on other categories as well. In either case, reduction of administrative overhead will improve the cost effectiveness of the project.

"Previous" MRs indicate the level of difficulty in finding some of the faults in a large, real-time system. These problems may have been impossible to find in the previous releases and have only now been exposed because of changes in the use of the system.

Figure 25-1 charts the requirements, design, and coding MRs by testing phase. We have focused on this early part of the software development process because that is where the most MRs occurred and, accordingly, where closer attention should yield the most results.

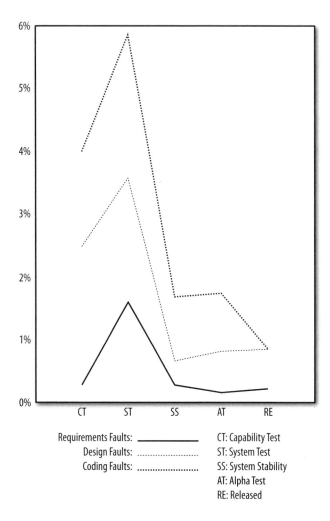

Requirements Faults: ——————— CT: Capability Test
Design Faults: .... ST: System Test
Coding Faults: .... SS: System Stability
                                  AT: Alpha Test
                                  RE: Released

FIGURE 25-1. Fault categories found by phase

Please note that the percentages used in Figures 25-1 and 25-2 are the percentages of those faults relative to all the faults, not the percentages relative to just the charted faults. The phases in Figure 25-1 appear as sequential when in actual fact (as is almost always the case in software systems' development) there is a lot of parallelism, with phases overlapping significantly. With hundreds of software engineers developing hundreds of features concurrently, the actual project life cycle is nothing like the sequential waterfall model, even though software development proceeds through a set of, often iterative, phases. That is the reason for Figure 25-2, which shows the same data relative to a fixed timeline.

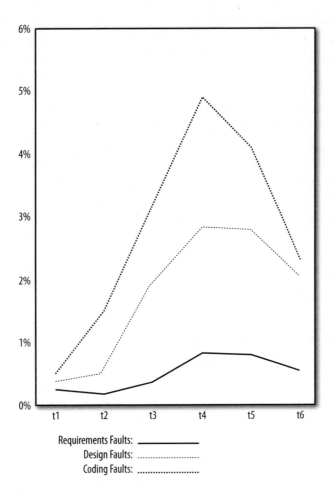

FIGURE 25-2. Fault categories found over time

There are two important observations. First, system test (ST) was the source of most of the MRs in each category; capability testing (CT) was the next largest source. This is not particularly surprising, since that is when we were looking the hardest for, and expecting the most, faults. System test is where the various components are first integrated and is the most likely place to encounter the mismatches and misassumptions among components. So while all testing is looking for faults, system test is where we look the hardest. Capability testing is akin to unit testing in an appropriate context—internal and initial interaction faults are looked for. The capability test context limits the kinds of faults that can be exposed.

Second, all testing phases found MRs of each fault category. It is also not surprising that coding faults are found over the entire set of testing phases. One obvious reason for this phenomena is that changes are continually made to correct the faults that are found in the various earlier testing phases. Moreover, while it is disturbing to note that both design and requirements faults continue to be found throughout the entire testing process, we feel that this is due to the lack of precision and completeness in requirements and design documentation and is a general problem in the current state-of-practice rather than a project-specific problem.

The time values in Figure 25-2 are fixed intervals. From the shape of the data, it is clear that System Testing overlaps interval t4. It is unfortunate that we have only the calendar data (that is, the time boundaries on the MRs), as a correlation with effort data [Musa et al. 1987] (that is, the actual amount of time spent in that time period) would be extremely valuable.

For the requirements, design, and coding fault categories over time, Figure 25-2 shows that all fault types peaked at time t4 and held through time t5, except for the coding faults, which decreased.

Summary of the Phase 1 Study

The following general observations may be drawn from this general survey of the problems encountered in evolving a large-scale, real-time system:

- Implementation, testing, and administrative overhead faults occurred in roughly equal proportions
- Requirements problems, while not overwhelmingly numerous, are still significant (especially since the majority were found late in the testing process)
- All types of faults continued to be found in all the testing phases
- The most faults were found when the level of testing effort was the highest (that is, at system test)
- The majority of faults were found late in the testing cycle

These observations are limited by the fact that the tracking of fault MRs is primarily a testing activity. It would be extremely useful to observe the kinds and frequencies of faults that exist in the earlier phases of the project. Moreover, it would be beneficial to incorporate ways of detecting requirements and design faults into the existing development process.

Phase 2: Design/Code Fault Survey

As a result of the general survey, we decided to survey the design and coding MRs in depth. The following were the goals we wanted to achieve in this part of the study:

- Determine the kinds of faults that occurred in design and coding
- Determine the difficulty both in finding or reproducing these faults and in fixing them

- Determine the underlying causes of the faults

- Determine how the faults might have been prevented

- Compare the difficulty in finding and fixing interface and implementation faults

There were two reasons for choosing this part of the general set of MRs. First, it seemed to be exceedingly difficult to separate the two kinds of faults. Second, catching these kinds of faults earlier in the process would provide a significant reduction in overall fault cost; that is, the cost of finding faults before system integration is significantly less than finding them in the laboratory testing environment. Our internal cost data is consistent with Boehm's [Boehm 1981] (see also Chapter 10 by Barry Boehm). Thus, gaining insight into these problems will yield significant (and cost beneficial) results.

In the two subsections that follow, we summarize the survey questionnaire, present the results of our statistical analysis, and summarize our findings with regard to interface and implementation faults.

The Questionnaire

The respondents were asked to indicate the difficulty of finding and fixing the problem, determine the actual and underlying causes, indicate the best means of either preventing or avoiding the problem, and give their level of confidence in their responses. It should be kept in mind that the people surveyed were those who owned the MR at the time it was closed (i.e., completed).

- For each MR, rank it according to how difficult it was to reproduce the failure and locate the fault.

    1. *Easy*—could produce at will.

    2. *Moderate*—happened some of the time (intermittent).

    3. *Difficult*—needed theories to figure out how to reproduce the error.

    4. *Very Difficult*—exceedingly hard to reproduce.

- For each MR, how much time was needed to design and code the fix, and document and test it. (Note that what would be an easy fix in a single-programmer system takes considerably more time in a large, multiperson project with a complex laboratory test environment.)

    1. *Easy*—less than one day

    2. *Moderate*—1 to 5 days

    3. *Difficult*—6 to 30 days

    4. *Very difficult*—greater than 30 days

- For each MR, consider the following 22 possible types and select the one that most closely applies to the immediate cause (that is, the fault type).

    1. *Language pitfalls*—for example, pointer problems, or the use of "=" instead of "= =".
    2. *Protocol*—violated rules about interprocess communication.
    3. *Low-level logic*—for example, loop termination problems, pointer initialization, etc.
    4. *CMS complexity*—for example, due to software change management system complexity.
    5. *Internal functionality*—either inadequate functionality or changes and/or additions were needed to existing functionality within the module or subsystem.
    6. *External functionality*—either inadequate functionality or changes and/or additions were needed to existing functionality outside the module or subsystem.
    7. *Primitives misused*—the design or code depended on primitives that were not *used* correctly.
    8. *Primitives unsupported*—the design or code depended on primitives that were not adequately developed (that is, the primitives do not work correctly).
    9. *Change coordination*—either did not know about previous changes or depended on concurrent changes.
    10. *Interface complexity*—interfaces were badly structured or incomprehensible.
    11. *Design/code complexity*—the implementation was badly structured or incomprehensible.
    12. *Error handling*—incorrect handling of, or recovery from, exceptions.
    13. *Race conditions*—incorrect coordination in the sharing of data.
    14. *Performance*—for example, real-time constraints, resource access, or response-time constraints.
    15. *Resource allocation*—incorrect resource allocation and deallocation.
    16. *Dynamic data design*—incorrect design of dynamic data resources or structures.
    17. *Dynamic data use*—incorrect *use* of dynamic data structures (for example, initialization, maintaining constraints, etc.).
    18. *Static data design*—incorrect design of static data structures (for example, their location, partitioning, redundancy, etc.).
    19. *Unknown interactions*—unknowingly involved other functionality or parts of the system.
    20. *Unexpected dependencies*—unexpected interactions or dependencies on other parts of the system.
    21. *Concurrent work*—unexpected dependencies on concurrent work in other releases.
    22. *Other*—describe the fault.

- Because the fault may be only a symptom, provide what you regard to be the underlying root cause for each problem.

  1. *None given*—no underlying causes given.

  2. *Incomplete/omitted requirements*—the source of the fault stemmed from either incomplete or unstated requirements.

  3. *Ambiguous requirements*—the requirements were (informally) stated, but they were open to more than one interpretation. The interpretation selected was evidently incorrect.

  4. *Incomplete/omitted design*—the source of the fault stemmed from either incomplete or unstated design specifications.

  5. *Ambiguous design*—the design was (informally) given, but was open to more than one interpretation. The interpretation selected was evidently incorrect.

  6. *Earlier incorrect fix*—the fault was induced by an earlier, incorrect fix (that is, the fault was not the result of new development).

  7. *Lack of knowledge*—there was something that I needed to know, but did not know that I needed to know it.

  8. *Incorrect modification*—I suspected that the solution was incorrect, but could not determine how to correctly solve the problem.

  9. *Submitted under duress*—the solution was submitted under duress, knowing that it was incorrect (generally due to schedule pressure, etc.).

  10. *Other*—describe the underlying cause.

- For this fault, consider possible ways to prevent or avoid it, and select the most useful or appropriate choice for preventing, avoiding, or detecting the fault.

  1. *Formal requirements*—use precise, unambiguous requirements (or design) in a formal notation (which may be either graphical or textual).

  2. *Requirements/design templates*—provide more specific requirements (or design) document templates.

  3. *Formal interface specifications*—use a formal notation for describing the module interfaces.

  4. *Training*—provide discussions, training seminars, and formal courses.

  5. *Application walk-throughs*—determine, informally, the interactions among the various application-specific processes and data objects.

  6. *Expert person/documentation*—provide an "expert" person or clear documentation when needed.

  7. *Design/code currency*—keep design documents up to date with code changes.

  8. *Guideline enforcement*—enforce code inspections guidelines and the use of static analysis tools such as lint.

9. *Better test planning*—provide better test planning and/or execution (for example, automatic regression testing).

10. *Others*—describe the means of prevention.

Confidence levels requested of the respondents were: *very high, high, moderate, low,* and *very low.* We discarded the small number of responses that had a confidence level of either low or very low.

Statistical Analysis

Out of all the questionnaires, 68% were returned. Of those, we dropped the responses that were either low or very low in confidence (6%). The remainder of the questionnaires were then subjected to Chi-Square analysis [Siegel et al. 1988] to test for independence (and for interdependence) of various paired sets of data. In Chi-Square analysis, the lower the total chi-square value, the more independent the two sets of data; the higher the value, the more interdependent the two sets of data. The p-value indicates the significance of the analysis: the lower the number, the less likely the relationships are due to chance. In Table 25-2, the prevention data and the find data are the most independent (the total chi-square is the lowest), and that lack of relationship is significant (the p-value is less than the standard .05 and indicates that the odds are less than 1 in 20 that the relationship happened by chance). The fault-cause, fault-prevention, and cause-prevention pairs are the most interdependent, as their total chi-square values are the largest three of the entire set and the significance of these relationships is very high (the odds are less than 1 in 10,000 of being by chance).

The fact that the relationships between the faults and their underlying causes, faults and means of prevention, and means of prevention and the underlying causes are the most significantly interdependent is a good thing: 1) faults should be strongly related to their underlying causes, and 2) both faults and their underlying causes should be strongly related to their means of prevention. This indicates that the respondents were consistent in their responses and the data aligns with what one would logically expect.

TABLE 25-2. Chi-Square analysis summary

Variables	Degrees of freedom	Total Chi-Square	p
Find, Fix	6	51.489	.0001
Fault, Find	63	174.269	.0001
Fault, Fix	63	204.252	.0001
Cause, Find	27	94.493	.0001
Cause, Fix	27	55.232	.0011
Fault, Cause	189	403.136	.0001
Prevention, Find	27	41.021	.041

Variables	Degrees of freedom	Total Chi-Square	p
Prevention, Fix	27	97.886	.0001
Fault, Prevention	189	492.826	.0001
Cause, Prevention	81	641.417	.0001

Finding and fixing faults

Table 25-3 provides a cross-tabulation of the difficulty in finding and fixing the design and coding faults. Of these faults, 78% took five days or less to fix. In general, the easier-to-find faults were easier to fix; the more difficult-to-find faults were more difficult to fix.

TABLE 25-3. Find versus fix comparison

Find/fix		<1 day	1-5 days	6-30 days	>30 days
		30.1%	48.8%	18.0%	3.6%
easy	**67.5%**	23.7%	32.1%	10.0%	1.7%
moderate	**23.4%**	4.2%	12.5%	5.6%	1.1%
difficult	**7.7%**	1.7%	3.4%	2.1%	.5%
very difficult	**1.4%**	.5%	.3%	.3%	.3%

One of the interesting things about Chi-Square analysis is that it is based on the difference between expected and observed values of the paired data. The expected value in this case is the product of the observed find value and the observed fix value. If the two sets of data are independent of each other, the expected percentages will match or be very close to the observed percentages; otherwise, the two sets of data are not independent.

The first row of data is the observed percentages of how long it took to fix the MR; the first column is the observed percentages of how hard it was to find/duplicate the problem. The expected value of easy to find and fixable in a day or less is 67.1% × 30.1% = 20.2%, whereas the actually observed value of 23.7% is 17% more than that expected value.

There were more faults that were easy to find and took less than one day to fix than were expected by the Chi-Square analysis. Interestingly, there were fewer than expected easy to find faults (expected: 12%) that took 6 to 30 days to fix (observed: 10%).

Although the coordinates of the effort to find and fix the faults are non-comparable, we note that the following relationship is suggestive. Collapsing the previous table yields an interesting insight in Table 25-4 that seems counter to the common wisdom that says "once you have found the problem, it is easy to fix it." There is a significant number of "easy/moderate to find" faults that require a relatively long time to fix.

TABLE 25-4. Summary of find/fix

Find/fix effort	≤ 5 days	≥ 6 days
easy/moderate	72.5%	18.4%
difficult/very difficult	5.9%	3.2%

Faults

Table 25-5 shows the fault types of the MRs as ordered by their frequency in the survey independent of any other factors. For the sake of brevity in the subsequent tables, we use the fault type number to represent the fault types.

The first five fault types account for 60% of the faults. That "internal functionality" is the leading fault by such a large margin is somewhat surprising; that "interface complexity" is such a significant problem is not surprising at all. However, that the first five fault types are leading faults is consistent with the nature of the evolution of the system. Adding significant amounts of new functionality to a system easily accounts for problems with "internal functionality," "low-level logic," and "external functionality."

The fact that the system is a very large, complicated real-time system easily accounts for the fact that there are problems with "interface complexity," "unexpected dependencies" and design/code complexity," "change coordination," and "concurrent work."

C has well-known "language pitfalls" that account for the rank of that fault in the middle of the set. Similarly, "race conditions" are a reasonably significant problem because of the lack of suitable language facilities in C.

That "performance" faults are relatively insignificant is probably due to the fact that this is not an early release of the system, and performance was always a significant concern of code inspections.

Fault Frequency Adjusted by Effort

There are two interesting relationships to consider in the ordering of the various faults: the effect that the difficulty in *finding* the faults has on the ordering and the effect that the difficulty of *fixing* the faults has on the ordering. The purpose of weighting is to provide an adjustment to the observed frequency by how easy or hard the faults are to find or to fix. From the standpoint of "getting the most bang for the buck," the frequency of a fault is a good prima facie indicator of the importance of one fault relative to another. Table 25-5 shows the fault types ordered by frequency.

TABLE 25-5. Fault types ordered by frequency

Fault type	Observed %	Fault type description
5	25.0%	internal functionality
10	11.4%	interface complexity
20	8.0%	unexpected dependencies
3	7.9%	low-level logic
11	7.7%	design/code complexity
22	5.8%	other
9	4.9%	change coordination
21	4.4%	concurrent work
13	4.3%	race conditions
6	3.6%	external functionality
1	3.5%	language pitfalls
12	3.3%	error handling
7	2.4%	primitives misused
17	2.1%	dynamic data use
15	1.5%	resource allocation
18	1.0%	static data design
14	.9%	performance
19	.7%	unknown interactions
8	.6%	primitives unsupported
2	.4%	protocol
4	.3%	CMS complexity
16	.3%	dynamic data design

Table 25-6 is an attempt to capture the weighted difficulty of finding the various faults. The weighting is done by multiplying the proportion of observed values for each fault with multiplicative weights of 1, 2, 3, and 4 for each find category, respectively, and summing the results.

Obviously it would have been better to have had some duration assigned to the effort to find faults and then correlated the weighting with those durations, as we do subsequently in weighting by effort to fix faults. The weights used are intended to be suggestive, not definitive.

We experimented with several different weightings, and the results were pretty much the same. Thus we used the simplest approach.

Better yet would have been effort data associated with each MR that could be used to get a more realistic picture of actual difficulty. But this type of data is seldom available, and an approximation is needed instead.

For example, if a fault was easy to find in 66% of the cases, moderate in 23%, difficult in 11%, and very difficult in 0%, the weight is 145 = (66 * 1) + (23 * 2) + (11 * 3) + (0 * 4). Table 25-6 shows the fault types weighted by difficulty to find, from easiest to most difficult.

TABLE 25-6. Determining the find weighting

Fault type	Find proportion e/m/d/vd	Weight	Fault type description
4	100/0/0/0	100	CMS complexity
18	100/0/0/0	100	static data design
7	88/8/4/0	120	primitives misused
2	75/25/0/0	125	protocol
20	78/16/5/1	129	unexpected dependencies
21	70/23/2/4	130	concurrent work
3	73/22/5/0	132	low-level logic
22	82/12/2/5	132	other
5	74/19/6/1	134	internal functionality
6	67/31/3/0	139	external functionality
1	68/26/2/2	141	language pitfalls
10	66/23/11/0	145	interface complexity
9	65/20/12/2	149	change coordination
8	67/17/17/0	152	primitives unsupported
19	88/8/4/0	157	unknown interactions
16	67/0/33/0	157	dynamic data design
17	52/38/10/0	158	dynamic data use
15	47/47/7/0	162	resource allocation
12	55/30/12/3	163	error handling
11	55/29/16/1	165	code complexity
14	56/11/11/22	199	performance
13	12/67/21/0	209	race conditions

Typically, performance faults and race conditions are very difficult to isolate and reproduce. We would expect that "code complexity" and "error handling" faults also would be difficult to find and reproduce. Not surprisingly, "language pitfalls" and "interface complexity" are reasonably hard to detect.

In the Chi-Square analysis, "internal functionality," "unexpected dependencies," and "other" tended to be easier to find than expected. "Code complexity" and "performance" tended to be harder to find than expected. There tended to be more significant deviations where the population was larger.

If we weight the proportions by multiplying the number of occurrences of each fault by its weight from Table 25-5 and dividing by the total weighted number of occurrences, we get only a slight change in the ordering of the faults, with "internal functionality," "code complexity," and "race conditions" (faults 5, 11, and 13) changing slightly more than the rest of the faults.

Table 25-7 represents the results of weighting the difficulty of fixing the various faults by factoring in the actual time needed to fix the faults. The multiplicative scheme uses the values 1, 3, 15, and 30 for the four average times in fixing a fault. The calculations are performed as in the example of weighting the difficulty of finding the faults.

The weighting according to the difficulty in fixing the fault causes some interesting shifts in the ordering. "Language pitfalls," "low-level logic," and "internal functionality" (faults 1, 3, and 5) drop significantly in their relative importance. This coincides with one's intuition about these kinds of faults. "Design/code complexity," "resource allocation," and "unexpected dependencies" (faults 11, 15, and 20) rise significantly in their relative importance; "interface complexity," "race conditions," and "performance" (faults 10, 13, 14) also rise, but not significantly so.

TABLE 25-7. Determining the fix weighting

Fault type	Proportion e/m/d/vd	Weight	Fault type description
16	67/33/0/0	166	dynamic data design
4	67/33/0/0	166	CMS complexity
8	50/50/0/0	200	primitives unsupported
18	50/50/0/0	200	static data design
1	63/31/6/0	244	language pitfalls
3	59/37/3/1	245	low-level logic
2	25/75/0/0	250	protocol
17	38/48/14/0	392	dynamic data use
9	37/49/14/0	394	change coordination
5	27/59/14/0	414	internal functionality

Fault type	Proportion e/m/d/vd	Weight	Fault type description
22	40/43/12/5	496	other
7	46/37/8/8	497	primitives misused
10	17/57/26/1	608	interface complexity
21	25/43/30/2	661	concurrent work
6	22/50/22/6	682	external functionality
13	16/56/21/7	709	race conditions
12	21/52/18/9	717	error handling
19	29/43/14/14	785	unknown interactions
20	24/39/33/5	786	unexpected dependencies
11	22/39/27/12	904	design/code complexity
14	11/22/44/22	1397	performance
15	0/47/27/27	1356	resource allocation

Table 25-8 shows the top fix-weighted faults. According to our weighting schemes, these four faults account for 55.2% of the effort expended to fix all the faults and 51% of the effort to find them, but represent 52.1% of the faults by frequency count. Collectively, they are somewhat harder to fix than rest of the faults and slightly easier to find. We again note that although the two scales are not strictly comparable, the comparison is an interesting one nonetheless.

TABLE 25-8. Faults weighted by fix difficulty

Fault type	Weighted %	Brief description
5	18.7%	internal functionality
10	12.6%	interface complexity
11	12.6%	code complexity
20	11.3%	unexpected dependencies

In the Chi-Square analysis, "language pitfalls" and "low-level logic" took fewer days to fix than expected. "Interface complexity" and "internal functionality" took 1 to 6 days to fix more often than expected, and "design/code complexity" and "unexpected dependencies" took longer to fix (that is, 6 to over 30 days) than expected. These deviations reinforce our weighted assessment of the effort to fix the faults.

Underlying causes

In Table 25-9, we show the underlying causes of the MRs as ordered by their frequency in the survey, independent of any other factors.

TABLE 25-9. Underlying causes of faults

Underlying causes	Observed %	Brief description
4	25.2%	incomplete/omitted design
1	20.5%	none given
7	17.8%	lack of knowledge
5	9.8%	ambiguous design
6	7.3%	earlier incorrect fix
9	6.8%	submitted under duress
2	5.4%	incomplete/omitted requirements
10	4.1%	other
3	2.0%	ambiguous requirements
8	1.1%	incorrect modification

The high proportion of "none given" as an underlying cause requires some explanation. One of the reasons for this is that faults such as "language pitfalls," "low-level logic," "race conditions," and "change coordination" tend to be both the fault and the underlying cause (7.8%—or 33% of the faults in the "none given" underlying cause category in Table 25-12 below). In addition, one could easily imagine that some of the faults, such as "interface complexity" and "design/code complexity," could also be considered both the fault and the underlying cause (3.4%—or 16% of the faults in the "none given" underlying cause category in Table 25-12). On the other hand, we were surprised that no cause was given for a substantial part of the "internal functionality" faults (3.3%—or 16% of the faults in the "none given" category in Table 25-12). One would expect there to be some underlying cause for that particular fault.

Table 25-10 shows the relative difficulty in finding the faults associated with the underlying causes. The resulting ordering is particularly nonintuitive: the MRs with no underlying cause are the second most difficult to find; those submitted under duress are the most difficult to find.

TABLE 25-10. Weighting of the underlying causes by find effort

Underlying causes	Proportion	Weight	Brief description
8	91/9/0/0	109	incorrect modification
7	74/18/7/1	135	lack of knowledge
3	60/40/0/0	140	ambiguous requirements
5	66/27/7/0	141	ambiguous design
2	70/17/13/0	143	incomplete/omitted requirements
4	68/25/7/1	143	incomplete/omitted design
6	73/12/10/5	147	earlier incorrect fix
10	76/12/0/12	148	other
1	63/25/11/1	150	none given
9	50/46/4/0	158	submitted under duress

In the Chi-Square analysis of finding underlying causes, faults caused by "lack of knowledge" tended to be easier to find than expected, whereas faults caused by "submitted under duress" tended to be moderately hard to find more often than expected. This latter finding is interesting, as we know very little about faults "submitted under duress."

In Table 25-11, we weight the underlying causes by the effort to fix the faults represented by the underlying causes. This yields a few shifts in the proportion of effort: "incomplete/omitted design" increased significantly; "unclear requirements" and "incomplete/omitted requirements" increased less significantly; "none" decreased significantly; and "unclear design" and "other" decreased less significantly. However, the relative ordering of the various underlying causes is unchanged.

TABLE 25-11. Weighting of the underlying causes by fix effort

Underlying causes	Proportion	Weight	Brief description
10	37/42/12/10	340	other
1	43/43/12/2	412	none given
5	29/55/14/2	464	ambiguous design
7	30/50/17/3	525	lack of knowledge
6	34/45/17/4	544	earlier incorrect fix
9	18/57/25/0	564	submitted under duress
8	18/55/27/0	588	incorrect modification
4	23/50/22/5	653	incomplete/omitted design

Underlying causes	Proportion	Weight	Brief description
2	26/44/24/6	698	incomplete/omitted requirements
3	25/30/24/6	940	ambiguous requirements

The relative weighting of the effort to fix these kinds of underlying causes seems to coincide with one's intuition very nicely.

In the Chi-Square analysis of fixing underlying causes, faults caused by "none given" tended to take less time to fix than expected, whereas faults caused by "incomplete/omitted design" and "submitted under duress" tended to take more time to fix than expected.

In Table 25-12, we present the cross-tabulation of faults and their underlying causes. Faults are represented by the rows, underlying causes by the columns. The numbers in the matrix are the percentages of the total population of faults. Thus, 1.5% of the total faults were fault 1 with the underlying cause 1. The expected number of faults for fault 1 and underlying cause 1 can be computed by multiplying the total faults for each of those categories: 20.5% * 3.5% = .7%. In this example, the actual number of faults was higher than expected.

TABLE 25-12. Cross-tabulating fault types and underlying causes

		1	2	3	4	5	6	7	8	9	10
		20.5%	5.4%	2.0%	25.2%	9.8%	7.3%	17.8%	1.1%	6.8%	4.1%
1 language pitfalls	3.5%	1.5	.0	.0	.2	.1	.2	.8	.1	.5	.1
2 protocol	.4%	.0	.0	.1	.2	.0	.0	.1	.0	.0	.0
3 low-level logic	7.9%	3.7	.3	.1	.6	.3	1.2	.7	.0	.6	.4
4 CMS complexity	.3%	.1	.0	.0	.0	.0	.1	.1	.0	.0	.0
5 internal functionality	25.0%	3.3	1.3	.6	7.7	2.8	2.0	5.2	.3	1.2	.6
6 external functionality	3.6%	.7	.3	.1	.4	.5	.6	.7	.0	.3	.0
7 primitives misused	2.4%	.4	.0	.0	.5	.0	.1	.8	.0	.0	.6
8 primitives unsupported	.6%	.0	.2	.0	.1	.0	.1	.1	.0	.1	.0
9 change coordination	4.9%	1.1	.0	.0	.8	1.0	.6	.8	.1	.3	.2

		1	2	3	4	5	6	7	8	9	10
		20.5%	5.4%	2.0%	25.2%	9.8%	7.3%	17.8%	1.1%	6.8%	4.1%
10 interface complexity	11.4%	2.1	.6	.2	4.1	1.4	1.1	1.4	.2	.0	.3
11 design/ code complexity	7.7%	1.3	.0	.3	3.0	1.6	.2	1.0	.0	.0	.3
12 error handling	3.3%	.9	.3	.0	.8	.0	.1	.7	.0	.4	.1
13 race conditions	4.3%	1.4	.2	.0	1.3	.5	.1	.3	.0	.4	.1
14 performance	.9%	.2	.0	.1	.2	.0	.0	.3	.0	.0	.1
15 resource allocation	1.5%	.5	.0	.0	.3	.1	.0	.4	.1	.0	.1
16 dynamic data design	.3%	.0	.0	.0	.1	.0	.0	.1	.0	.1	.0
17 dynamic data use	2.1%	.7	.1	.0	.2	.1	.0	.6	.0	.4	.0
18 static data design	1.0%	.3	.1	.1	.2	.1	.0	.1	.0	.1	.0
19 unknown interactions	.7%	.0	.1	.1	.0	.2	.0	.2	.0	.1	.0
20 unexpected dependencies	8.0%	.5	.8	.3	2.7	.5	.1	1.4	.0	1.7	.0
21 concurrent work	4.4%	.6	.3	.0	1.2	.2	.4	.9	.2	.4	.2
22 other	5.8%	1.2	.8	.0	.6	.4	.4	1.1	.1	.2	1.0

For the sake of brevity, we consider only the most frequently occurring faults and their major underlying causes. "Incomplete/omitted design" (cause 4) is the primary underlying cause in all of these major faults. "Ambiguous design" (cause 5), "lack of knowledge" (cause 7), and "none given" (cause 1) were also significant contributors to the presence of these faults.

internal functionality (fault 5)

"Incomplete/omitted design" (cause 4) was felt to have been the cause of 31% (that is, 7.7% / 25%) of the occurrences of this fault, a percentage higher than expected; "lack of knowledge" (cause 7) was thought to have caused 21% of the occurrences of this fault, higher than expected; and "none given" was listed as the third underlying cause, representing 13% of the occurrences.

interface complexity (fault 10)

Again, "incomplete/omitted design" was seen to be the primary cause in the occurrence of this fault (36%), higher than expected; "lack of knowledge" and "ambiguous design" were seen as the second and third primary causes of this fault (13% and 12%, respectively).

unexpected dependencies (fault 20)

Not surprisingly, "incomplete/omitted design" was felt to have been the primary cause of this fault (in 34% of the cases); "submitted under duress" (cause 9) contributed to 21% of the occurrences, a percentage higher than expected; and "lack of knowledge" was the tertiary cause of this fault, representing 18% of the occurrences.

design/code complexity (fault 11)

Again, "incomplete/omitted design" was felt to have been the primary cause in 39% of the occurrences of this fault, a percentage higher than expected; "ambiguous design" was the second most frequent underlying cause of this fault, causing 21% of the faults (also a higher percentage than expected); and "none given" was listed as the third underlying cause, representing 17% of the occurrences.

Again, for the sake of brevity, we consider only the most frequently occurring underlying causes and the faults to which they were most applicable.

incomplete/omitted design (cause 4)

As we noted previously, "internal functionality," "interface complexity," "code/design complexity," and "unexpected dependencies" were the major applicable faults (31%, 12%, 12%, and 11%, respectively), with the first three occurring with higher than expected frequency.

none given (cause 1)

"Low-level logic" (fault 3) was the leading fault, representing 18% of the occurrences (a percentage higher than expected); "internal functionality" (fault 5) was the second major fault, representing 16% of the occurrences (a percentage lower than expected); "interface complexity" (fault 10) was the third leading fault, representing 10% of the occurrences; and "language pitfalls" was the fourth leading fault, representing 8% of the occurrences (a percentage higher than expected).

lack of knowledge (cause 7)

"Internal functionality" was the leading fault, representing 29% of the occurrences (a percentage higher than expected); "interface complexity" was next with 8% of the occurrences (a percentage lower than expected); "unexpected dependencies" was third with 8% of the occurrences; and "other" (fault 22) was the fourth with 6%.

ambiguous design (cause 5)

"Internal functionality" represented 29% of the occurrences; "code/design complexity" (fault 11) was second fault, representing 16% of the occurrences (a percentage higher than expected); "interface complexity" was third with 14%; and "change coordination" (fault 9) was fourth, representing 10% of the occurrences (a percentage higher than expected).

Means of prevention

Table 25-13 shows the means of prevention of the MRs, as ordered by their occurrence independent of any other factors. We note that the means selected may well reflect a particular approach of the responder in selecting one means over another (for example, see the discussion later in this section about formal versus informal means of prevention).

TABLE 25-13. Means of error prevention

Means of prevention	Observed %	Brief description
5	24.5%	application walk-throughs
6	15.7%	expert person/documentation
8	13.3%	guideline enforcement
2	10.0%	requirements/design templates
9	9.9%	better test planning
1	8.8%	formal requirements
3	7.2%	formal interface specifications
10	6.9%	other
4	2.2%	training
7	1.5%	design/code currency

It is interesting to note that the application-specific means of prevention ("application walk-throughs") is considered the most effective. This selection of application walk-throughs as the most useful means of error prevention appears to confirm the observation of Curtis, Krasner, and Iscoe [Curtis et al. 1988] that a thin spread of application knowledge is the most significant problem in building large systems.

Further, it is worth noting that informal means of prevention rank higher than formal ones. On the one hand, this may reflect the general bias in the United States against formal methods. On the other hand, the informal means are a nontechnical solution to providing the information that may be supplied by formal representations (and which provide a more technical solution with perhaps higher attendant adoption costs).

The level of effort to find the faults for which these are the means of prevention does not change the order found in Table 25-13, with the exception of "requirements/design templates," which seems to apply to the easier-to-find faults, and "guideline enforcement," which seems to apply more to the harder-to-find faults.

In the Chi-Square analysis, the relationship between finding faults and preventing them is the most independent of the relationships, reported here with p=.041. "Application walk-throughs" applied to faults that were marginally easier to find than expected, whereas "guideline enforcement" applied to faults that were less easy to find than expected.

In Table 25-14, the means of prevention is weighted by the effort to fix the associated faults.

TABLE 25-14. Means of prevention weighted by fix effort

Prevention	Proportion	Weight	Brief description
8	38/52/7/3	389	guideline enforcement
9	35/52/12/1	401	better test planning
7	40/40/20/0	460	design/code currency
5	33/50/17/1	468	application walk-throughs
10	49/36/6/9	517	other
2	10/52/30/1	654	requirements/design templates
3	26/43/26/4	675	formal interface specifications
6	22/48/24/6	706	expert person/documentation
1	20/50/22/8	740	formal requirements
4	23/36/23/18	1016	training

It is interesting to note that the faults considered to be prevented by training are the hardest to fix. The formal methods also apply to classes of faults that take a long time to fix.

Weighting the means of prevention by effort to fix their corresponding faults yields a few shifts in proportion: "application walk-throughs," "better test planning," and "guideline enforcement" decreased in proportion; "expert person/documentation" and "formal requirements" increased in proportion; and "formal interface specifications" and "other" less so. As a result, the ordering changes slightly to 5, 6, 2, 1, 8, 10, 3, 9, 4, 7: "expert person/documentation" and "formal requirements" (numbers 6 and 1) are weighted significantly higher; "requirements/design templates," "formal interface specifications," "training," and "other" (numbers 2, 3, 4, and 10) are less significantly higher; and "guideline enforcement" and "better test planning" (numbers 8 and 9) are significantly lower.

In the Chi-Square analysis, faults prevented by "application walk-throughs," "guideline enforcement," and "other" tended to take fewer days to fix than expected, whereas faults prevented by "formal requirements," "requirements/design templates," and "expert person/ documentation" took longer to fix than expected.

In Table 25-15, we present the cross-tabulation of faults and their means of prevention. Again, the faults are represented by the rows, and the means of prevention are represented by the columns. The data is analogous to the preceding cross-tabulation of faults and underlying causes.

For the sake of brevity, we consider only the most frequently occurring faults and their major means of prevention. "Application walk-throughs" were felt to be an effective means of preventing these most significant faults. "Expert person/documentation," "formal requirements," and "formal interface specifications" were also significant means of preventing these faults.

internal functionality (fault 5)

"Application walk-throughs" (prevention 5) were thought to be the most effective means of prevention, applicable to 27% of the occurrences of this fault; "expert person/ documentation" (prevention 6) was felt to be the second most effective means, applicable to 18% of the fault occurrences; and "requirements/design templates" were thought to be applicable to 14% of the fault occurrences, a percentage higher than expected.

TABLE 25-15. Cross-tabulating faults and means of prevention

		1	2	3	4	5	6	7	8	9	10
		8.8%	10.0%	7.2%	2.2%	24.5%	15.7%	1.5%	13.3%	9.9%	6.9%
1 language pitfalls	3.5%	.0	.1	.1	.0	1.0	.3	.1	1.3	.4	.2
2 protocol	.4%	.1	.2	.0	.0	.1	.0	.0	.0	.0	.0
3 low-level logic	7.9%	.1	.0	.1	.2	2.3	.3	.2	3.2	.8	.7
4 CMS complexity	.3%	.0	.0	.0	.0	.0	.1	.0	.1	.1	.0
5 internal functionality	25.0%	1.9	3.5	1.5	.4	6.6	4.4	.2	3.3	3.1	.1
6 external functionality	3.6%	.6	.3	.4	.0	.1	.7	.0	.5	.9	.1
7 primitives misused	2.4%	.1	.1	.2	.0	.8	.3	.0	.1	.2	.6

		1	2	3	4	5	6	7	8	9	10
		8.8%	10.0%	7.2%	2.2%	24.5%	15.7%	1.5%	13.3%	9.9%	6.9%
8 primitives unsupported	.6%	.1	.0	.0	.0	.3	.0	.0	.0	.1	.1
9 change coordination	4.9%	.4	.9	.3	.4	.8	.3	.3	.3	.7	.5
10 interface complexity	11.4%	2.1	.3	2.1	.0	3.0	1.7	.1	1.2	.7	.2
11 design/ code complexity	7.7%	.8	.5	.1	.4	2.2	2.4	.2	.3	.4	.4
12 error handling	3.3%	.2	.2	.3	.1	.6	.6	.0	.4	.5	.4
13 race conditions	4.3%	.8	.0	.4	.0	1.2	.4	.2	.4	.2	.7
14 performance	.9%	.0	.0	.0	.2	.2	.3	.0	.0	.0	.2
15 resource allocation	1.5%	.1	.1	.1	.0	.3	.3	.0	.3	.3	.0
16 dynamic data design	.3%	.0	.0	.0	.0	.1	.0	.0	.1	.0	.1
17 dynamic data use	2.1%	.0	.0	.2	.0	.8	.5	.0	.5	.0	.1
18 static data design	1.0%	.1	.1	.0	.0	.2	.2	.0	.0	.3	.1
19 unknown interactions	.7%	.1	.0	.2	.0	.0	.2	.0	.0	.2	.0
20 unexpected dependencies	8.0%	.6	2.2	1.1	.1	2.3	.6	.0	.4	.6	.1
21 concurrent work	4.4%	.4	.7	.0	.2	1.2	1.1	.1	.3	.0	.4
22 other	5.8%	.3	.8	.1	.2	.4	1.0	.1	.6	.4	1.9

interface complexity (fault 10)

Again, "application walk-throughs" were considered to be the most effective, applicable to 26% of the cases; "formal requirements" (prevention 1) and "formal interface specifications" were felt to be equally effective, with each preventing 18% of the fault occurrences (in both cases, a percentage higher than expected).

unexpected dependencies (fault 20)

"Application walk-throughs" were felt to be the most effective means of preventing this fault, applicable to 29% of the occurrences; "requirements/design templates" were considered the second most effective and applicable to 28% of the fault occurrences (a percentage higher than expected); and "formal interface specifications" were considered applicable to 14% of the fault occurrences, a percentage higher than expected.

design/code complexity (fault 11)

"Expert person/documentation" was felt to be the most effective means of preventing this fault, applicable to 31% of the cases (higher than expected); "application walk-throughs" were the second most effective means, applicable to 29% of the occurrences; and "formal requirements" was third, applicable to 10% of the fault occurrences.

Again, for the sake of brevity, we consider only the most frequently occurring means of prevention and the faults to which they were most applicable. Not surprisingly, these means were most applicable to "internal functionality" and "interface complexity," the most prevalent faults. Counterintuitively, they are also strongly recommended as applicable to "low-level logic."

application walk-throughs (prevention 5)

"Internal functionality" (fault 5) was considered as the primary target in 27% of the uses of this means of prevention; "interface complexity" (fault 10) was felt to be the secondary target, representing 12% of the uses of this means; and "low-level logic" (fault 3) and "unexpected dependencies" (fault 20) were next with 9% each.

expert person/documentation (prevention 6)

Again, "internal functionality" is the dominant target for this means, representing 29% of the possible applications; "design/code complexity" is the second most applicable target, representing 15% of the possible applications (a percentage higher than expected); and "interface complexity" represented 11% of the uses (higher than expected).

guideline enforcement (prevention 8)

"Internal functionality" and "low-level logic" were the dominant targets for this means of prevention, representing 25% and 24%, respectively (the latter being higher than expected); "language pitfalls" (fault 1) was seen as the third most relevant fault, representing 10% of the possible applications (higher than expected); and "interface complexity" was the fourth with 9% of the possible applications of this means of prevention.

Underlying causes and means of prevention

In Table 25-16, it is interesting to note that in the Chi-Square analysis there are lots of deviations (that is, there is a wider variance between the actual values and the expected values in correlating underlying causes and means of prevention). This indicates that there are strong dependencies between the underlying causes and their means of prevention. Intuitively, this type of relationship is just what we would expect.

TABLE 25-16. Cross-tabulating means of prevention and underlying causes

		1	2	3	4	5	6	7	8	9	10
		20.5%	5.4%	2.0%	25.2%	9.8%	7.3%	17.8%	1.1%	6.8%	4.1%
1 formal requirements	8.8%	.4	2.3	.9	3.5	.8	.3	.5	.1	.0	.0
2 reqs/design templates	10.0%	.4	1.7	.1	3.7	1.9	.1	.8	.0	1.3	.0
3 formal interface specs	7.2%	.8	.3	.1	2.7	.8	.3	2.0	.0	.2	.0
4 training	2.2%	.4	.0	.1	.7	.1	.3	.6	.0	.0	.0
5 application walk-thrus	24.5%	7.5	.2	.3	7.3	3.1	1.8	3.1	.0	.5	.7
6 expert person/doc	15.7%	1.5	.4	.4	3.5	1.8	1.0	5.8	.6	.3	.4
7 design/code currency	1.5%	.4	.0	.0	.6	.2	.1	.2	.0	.0	.0
8 guideline enforcement	13.3%	4.0	.1	.0	.6	.2	1.6	2.5	.0	3.7	.6
9 better test planning	9.90%	2.8	.2	.0	1.7	.8	1.6	1.9	.3	.2	.4
10 others	6.9%	2.3	.2	.1	.9	.1	.2	.4	.1	.6	2.0

We first summarize the means of prevention associated with the major underlying causes. "Application walk-throughs," "expert person/documentation," and "guideline enforcement" were considered important in addressing these major underlying causes.

incomplete/omitted design (cause 4)

> "Application walk-throughs" (prevention 5) was thought to be applicable to 28% of the faults with this underlying cause (a percentage higher than expected); "requirements/ design templates" (prevention 2) and "expert person/documentation" (prevention 6) were

next in importance with 14% each (the first being higher than expected); and "formal requirements" (prevention 1) was felt to be applicable to 12% of the faults with this underlying cause (a percentage higher than expected).

none given (cause 1)

Again, "application walk-throughs" was thought to be applicable to 37% of the faults with these underlying causes; "guideline enforcement" (prevention 8), "better test planning" (prevention 9), and "other" (prevention 10) were felt to be applicable to 19%, 14%, and 10% of the faults, respectively. In all four of these cases, the percentages were higher than expected.

lack of knowledge (cause 7)

"Expert person/documentation" was thought to be applicable to 32% of the faults with this underlying cause, a percentage higher than expected; "application walk-throughs," "guideline enforcement," and "formal interface specifications" were felt to be applicable to 17%, 14%, and 11% of the faults with this underlying cause, respectively, though "application walk-throughs" had a lower percentage than expected, whereas "formal interface specifications" had a higher percentage than expected.

The following summarizes the major underlying causes addressed by the most frequently considered means of prevention. "Lack of knowledge," "none given," "incomplete/omitted design," and "ambiguous design" were the major underlying causes for which these means of prevention were considered important. It is somewhat non-intuitive that the "none given" underlying cause category is so prominent as an appropriate target for these primary means of prevention.

application walk-throughs (prevention 5)

"None given" (cause 1) and "incomplete/omitted design" (cause 4) were thought to be the appropriate for this means of prevention for 31% and 30% of the cases, respectively (higher than expected); "ambiguous design" (cause 5) and "lack of knowledge" (cause 7) both were felt to apply to 13% of the cases (though the first was higher than expected and the second lower).

expert person/documentation (prevention 6)

"Lack of knowledge" was considered the major target for this means of prevention, accounting for 37% of the cases (a higher than expected value); "incomplete/omitted design" and "ambiguous design" were thought to be appropriate in 23% and 11% of the cases, respectively; and "none given" was thought appropriate in 10% of the cases (lower than expected).

guideline enforcement (prevention 8)

"None given" and "incorrect modification" were felt to be the most appropriate for this means of prevention for 30% and 28% of the cases, respectively (both higher than expected); "lack of knowledge" and "incorrect earlier fix" were appropriate in 19% and 12% of the cases, respectively (the latter was higher than expected).

Interface Faults Versus Implementation Faults

The definition of an interface fault that we use here is that of Basili and Perricone [Basili and Perricone 1984] and Perry and Evangelist [Perry and Evangelist 1985], [Perry and Evangelist 1987]: interface faults are "those that are associated with structures existing outside the module's local environment but which the module used." Using this definition, we roughly characterize "language pitfalls" (1), "low-level logic" (3), "internal functionality" (5), "design/code complexity" (11), "performance" (14), and "other" (22) as implementation faults. The remainder are considered interface faults. We say "roughly" because there are some cases where the implementation categories may contain some interface problems; remember that some of the "design/code complexity" faults were considered preventable by formal interface specifications. Table 25-17 shows our interface versus implementation fault comparison.

TABLE 25-17. Interface/implementation fault comparison

	Interface	Implementation
Frequency	49%	51%
Find weighted	50%	50%
Fix weighted	56%	44%

Interface faults occur with slightly less frequency than implementation faults, but require about the same effort to find them and more effort to fix them.

Table 25-18 compares interface and implementation faults with respect to their underlying causes. Underlying causes "other," "ambiguous requirements," "none given," "earlier incorrect fix," and "ambiguous design" tended to be the underlying causes more for implementation faults than for interface faults. Underlying causes "incomplete/omitted requirements," "incorrect modification," and "submitted under duress" tended to be the causes more for interface faults than for implementation faults.

Note that underlying causes that involved ambiguity tended to result more in implementation faults than in interface faults, whereas underlying causes involving incompleteness or omission of information tended to result more in interface faults than in implementation faults.

TABLE 25-18. Interface/implementation faults and underlying causes

		Interface	Implementation
		49%	**51%**
1	none given	45.2%	54.8%
2	incomplete/omitted requirements	79.6%	20.4%
3	ambiguous requirements	44.5%	55.5%
4	incomplete/omitted design	50.8%	49.2%

		Interface	Implementation
		49%	**51%**
5	ambiguous design	47.0%	53.0%
6	earlier incorrect fix	45.1%	54.9%
7	lack of knowledge	49.2%	50.8%
8	incorrect modification	54.5%	45.5%
9	submitted under duress	63.1%	36.9%
10	other	39.1%	60.1%

Table 25-19 compares interface and implementation faults with respect to the means of prevention. Not surprisingly, means 1 and 3 were more applicable to interface faults than to implementation faults. Means of prevention 8, 4, and 6 were considered more applicable to implementation faults than to interface faults.

TABLE 25-19. Interface/implementation faults and means of prevention

		Interface	Implementation
		49%	**51%**
1	formal requirements	64.8%	35.2%
2	requirements/design templates	51.5%	48.5%
3	formal interface specifications	73.6%	26.4%
4	training	36.4%	63.6%
5	application walk-throughs	48.0%	52.0%
6	expert person/documentation	44.3%	55.7%
7	design/code currency	46.7%	53.3%
8	guideline enforcement	33.1%	66.9%
9	better test planning	48.0%	52.0%
10	others	49.3%	50.7%

What Should You Believe About These Results?

Designing empirical studies is just like designing software systems: it is impossible to create a bug-free system, and we often make design mistakes and create systems with flaws and weaknesses. The main question in both cases is: do the problems negate the usefulness of the software systems or the empirical studies?

There are three main questions we need to address in order to determine how good our study is and whether you can justifiably use our results: 1) are we measuring the right things, 2) are there other things that might be the explanations for what we see (i.e., did we do it right?), and 3) what do our results apply to (i.e., what can we do with the results)?

Are We Measuring the Right Things?

We believe that we have a very strong argument to support our claim that we have addressed the critical issues in understanding software development faults and their implications. We address the fundamental issues in fault studies: the faults that occur, how hard it is to find and fix them, their underlying causes, and how might we prevent them, detect them, or ameliorate them. In addition, we addressed a question raised in response to the interface fault studies we had done earlier: which are harder to find and/or fix, interface or implementation faults? Strong support for this comes from the consistency and mutual support provided by the Chi-Square analysis, in which there are very strong relationships between the faults detected, their underlying causes, and their means of prevention. These strong relationships indicate a consistent understanding of the various parts of the survey and their interrelationships.

There are, however, several weaknesses that need to be addressed. First, the fault categories are poorly constructed. Second, the find and fix scales are not identical, with the fix scale being much better than the find scale. Third, the line between interface and implementation faults is not cleanly drawn.

The primary strength of the fault type list is that it was drawn up by the developers themselves, not the researchers. The weakness is that the list is basically unstructured and too long. There may be a tendency to pick the first thing that comes close rather than search the list exhaustively to find the best match.

In a subsequent study [Leszak et al. 2000], [Leszak et al. 2002], we corrected the fault type problem by partitioning the fault list into three categories: implementation, interface, and external faults (which also solved the third weakness mentioned above). Under each of these three fault categories were then between six and eight fault subcategories appropriate for each fault category (see page 177 of [Leszak et al. 2002]).

The scales used for finding and fixing faults was again the choice of the software developers, but had more serious consequences than poor structuring. The scale used for fixing faults is intuitively one that can be used easily, as it is easy to remember if something took less than a day, week, or month, which makes this measure much less likely to be misclassified. The scale for finding a fault, on the other hand, was qualitative rather than quantitative and much more likely to be subjective with individual variance (which we were not able to determine, because of management restrictions). Our recommendation is to use the quantitative scale for effort in terms of time for both scales. Indeed we did do that as well in subsequent studies [Leszak et al. 2000], [Leszak et al. 2002].

The separation of faults into interface and implementation faults was not a completely clean one, as some of the fault categories counted as interface may have included some implementation faults as well (and vice versa). So our distinction between the two is approximate at best. As mentioned earlier, we later solved that problem by structuring the separation of faults into implementation, interface, and external [Leszak et al. 2000], [Leszak et al. 2002].

Did We Do It Right?

In both phases, approximately 68% of questionnaires were returned—that is, we have data on about two-thirds of the MRs in both the overall survey and in the design/coding survey. Given the circumstances under which the survey was taken, this level of response exceeded our best expectations. Indeed, this factor of a large number of responses alone provides an argument for having data that can be relied upon.

As we cannot give the hard numbers as part of our report, we have tried to indicate the level of responses via the precision we used in discussing the results. Given the amount of data, we could have easily justified using two decimal places in reporting the data instead of the one decimal place we used for ease of understanding the data.

As with all surveys, there is the unanswerable question of how those who did not respond would have affected the results. Fortunately, we know of no existent factors (such as reporting only the hard or easy problems, receiving reports from only junior or senior programmers, etc.) that would have skewed the results in any way [Basili and Hutchens 1983].

We mentioned earlier that there were significant constraints placed on the study by project management: first, the study had to be completely nonintrusive; second, it had to be strictly voluntary; and third, it had to be completely anonymous. Because of these management mandates, we were unable to validate the results [Basili and Weiss 1984] and are unable to assess the accuracy of the responses. Mitigating the lack of validation are two facts: first, the questionnaire was created by the authors working with a group of developers; second, the questionnaire was reviewed by an independent group of developers. Since the purpose of the post-survey validation is understanding the level at which those surveyed understood the survey properly, we believe that our pre-survey efforts provide a useful and valid alternative because 1) we ensured that the survey was the language used by the developers themselves by their participation in its development, and 2) we pretested the survey successfully with a small group of developers, and no misunderstandings arose in the pretests.

The remaining problem is raised by the fact that there was a lapse time of up to a year between closing the MR and filling out the survey. Thus, there is a possibility of information loss due to the time lapse between solving the problem and describing it. However, having the person who was in charge of the problem at time of closure is still much better than having someone who had no involvement in the problem interpreting the MR for the survey. This lack of "freshness" could of course be resolved by making the fault survey part of the normal process of closing an MR.

One remaining caveat: the overall proportions of the faults may be affected by the fact that data is kept only during the testing phase of evolution. MRs for the entire process from the receipt of the requirements to the release of the system would, of course, give a much more accurate picture. We note, however, that this approach of keeping track of faults only once testing has begun is pretty much standard for most software developments and therefore only a very minor issue.

On the whole, we believe that the few problems with our empirical design are significantly outweighed by the evidence supporting our claim that our data is valid and that there are no other factors responsible for our results.

What Can You Do with the Results?

The main question for any empirical study is: "what do these results mean for me in the context of my work as a software developer?" Part of that answer depends on how representative the study is, and there are two different ways of answering that question.

The first way is to ask the question: "how representative is this release in the context of all the releases for this system that has been studied?" If it is not representative of the system and its various releases, then its general usefulness is not clear. In this case, we claim that it is representative because the mix of fault fixes, new features, and improvements was the same as for previous releases. For the first few releases after this one, however, there was an increased emphasis on removing faults before the previous mix of corrective, adaptive, and perfective changes was resumed.

Given a positive answer to the first question, then the second way to answer this question is to ask: "how representative is this release of this system of other software systems?" With respect to other large-scale, highly fault-tolerant, ultra-reliable real-time systems, this release would represent this small class of systems in that it is built and evolved in the context of a commonly used Unix Development Environment using a commonly used programming language such as C. One would expect to see similar kinds of problems in such systems.

How relevant is it to the development of other types of software systems? We would claim that it is highly relevant. Look at the top five fault types. There is nothing there that would lead one to believe that the main problems were domain specific. Indeed the entire list of faults, with a few exceptions, would be the kinds of things found in pretty much any software system development, whatever the domain or size of the project. We would further claim that there is nothing in the list of underlying causes that would preclude the vast variety of other types of software developments. We would make a similar claim for the means of prevention. The primary differences would be in the observed frequencies of the various faults, causes, and means of preventions.

The design of the study is certainly applicable, no matter what the size or domain of the software system being developed. The data itself is also applicable if you find you have the same frequently observed problems. There is an internal consistency to the data and their interrelationships that supports this claim.

What Have We Learned?

The results of the two studies are summarized as follows:

- Problems with requirements, design, and coding accounted for 34% of the total MRs. Requirements account for about 5% of the total MRs and, although not extremely numerous, are particularly important because they have been found so late in the development process, a period during which they are particularly expensive to fix.

- Testing large, complex real-time systems often requires elaborate test laboratories that are themselves large, complex real-time systems. In the development of this release, testing-related MRs accounted for 25% of the total MRs.

- The fact that 16% of the total MRs are "no problems" and the presence of a significant set of design and coding faults such as "unexpected dependencies" and "interface and design/code complexity" indicate that *lack of system knowledge* is a significant problem in the development of this release.

- Of the design and coding faults, 78% took five days or less to fix; 22% took six or more days to fix. We note that there is a certain overhead factor that is imposed on the fixing of each fault that includes getting consensus, building the relevant pieces of the system, and using the system test laboratory to validate the repairs. Unfortunately, we do not have data on those overhead factors.

- Five fault categories account for 60% of the design and coding faults: internal functionality, interface complexity, unexpected dependencies, low-level logic, and design/code complexity. With the exception of "low-level logic," this set of faults is what we expect would be significant in evolving a large, complex real-time system.

- Weighting the fault categories by the effort to find and to fix them yielded results that coincide with our intuition of which faults are easy and hard to find and fix.

- "Incomplete/omitted design," "lack of knowledge," and "none given" (which we interpret to mean that sometimes we just make a mistake with no deeper, hidden underlying cause) account for the underlying causes for 64% of design and coding faults. The weighting of the effort to fix these underlying causes coincides very nicely with our intuition: faults caused by requirements problems require the most effort to fix, whereas faults caused by ambiguous design and lack of knowledge were among those that required the least effort to fix.

- "Application walk-throughs," "expert person/documentation," "guideline enforcement," and "requirements/design templates" represent 64% of the suggested means of preventing design and coding faults. As application walk-throughs accounted for 25% of the suggested means of prevention, we believe that this supports Curtis, Krasner, and Iscoe's claim [Curtis et al. 1988] that lack of application knowledge is a significant problem.

- Although informal means of prevention were preferred over formal means, it was the case that informal means of prevention tended to be suggested for faults that required less effort to fix and formal means tended to be suggested for faults that required more effort to fix.

- In Perry and Evangelist [Perry and Evangelist 1985], [Perry and Evangelist 1987], interface faults were seen to be a significant portion of the entire set of faults (68%). However, there was no weighting of these faults versus implementation faults. We found in this study that interface faults were roughly 49% of the entire set of design and coding faults and that they were harder to fix than the implementation faults (see the previous discussion). Not surprisingly, formal requirements and formal interface specifications were suggested as significant means of preventing interface faults.

The system reported here was developed and evolved using the current "best practice" techniques and tools with well-qualified practitioners. Because of this fact, we feel that the data point is generalizable to other large-scale real-time systems. With this in mind, we offer the following recommendations to improve the current "best practice":

- Obtain fault data throughout the entire development/evolution cycle (not just in the testing cycle), and use it monitor the progress of the process.

- Incorporate the fault survey as an integral part of MR closure and gather the fault-related information while it is fresh in the developer's mind. This data provides the basis for measurement-based process improvement where the current most frequent or most costly faults are remedied.

- Incorporate the informal, people-intensive means of prevention into the current process (such as application walk-throughs, expert person or documentation, guideline enforcement, etc.). As our survey has shown, this will yield benefits for the majority of the faults reported here.

- Introduce techniques and tools to increase the precision and completeness of requirements, architecture, and design documents. This will yield benefits for those faults that were generally harder to fix and will help to detect the requirements, architecture, and design problems earlier in the life cycle.

We close with several lessons learned that may go a long way toward the improvement of future system developments:

- The fastest way to product improvement as measured by reduced faults is to hire people who are knowledgeable about the domain of the product. Remember, lack of knowledge tended to dominate the underlying causes. The fastest way to increase the knowledge needed to reduce faults is to hire knowledgeable people.

- One of the least important ways to improve software developments is to use a "better" programming language. We found relatively few problems that would have been solved by the use of better programming languages.
- Techniques and tools that help to understand the system and the implications of change should be emphasized in improving a development environment. Remember that knowledge-intensive activities tended to dominate the means of prevention.

Acknowledgments

My special thanks to Carol Steig for her earlier work with me on this project. David Rosik contributed significantly to the general MR survey; Steve Bruun produced the cross-tabulated statistical analysis for the design/coding survey and contributed, along with Carolyn Larson, Julie Federico, H. C. Wei, and Tony Lenard, to the analysis of the design/coding survey; and Clive Loader increased our understanding of the Chi-Square analysis. We especially thank Marjory P. Yuhas and Lew G. Anderson for their unflagging support of this work. And finally, we thank all those who participated in the survey.

References

[Basili and Hutchens 1983] Basili, Victor R., and David H. Hutchens. 1983. An Empirical Study of a Syntactic Complexity Family. *IEEE Transactions on Software Engineering* SE-9(6): 664–672.

[Basili and Perricone 1984] Basili, Victor R., and Barry T. Perricone. 1984. Software Errors and Complexity: An Empirical Investigation. *Communications of the ACM* 27(1): 42–52.

[Basili and Weiss 1984] Basili, Victor R., and David M. Weiss. 1984. A Methodology for Collecting Valid Software Engineering Data. *IEEE Transactions on Software Engineering* SE-10(6): 728–738.

[Boehm 1981] Boehm, Barry W. 1981. *Software Engineering Economics*. Englewood Cliffs, NJ: Prentice-Hall.

[Bowen 1980] Bowen, John B. 1980. Standard Error Classification to Support Software Reliability Assessment. *Proceedings of the AFIPS Joint Computer Conferences, 1980 National Computer Conference*: 697–705.

[Brooks 1995] Brooks, Frederick P., Jr. 1995. *The Mythical Man-Month: Essays on Software Engineering*, Anniversary Edition. Addison-Wesley.

[Curtis et al. 1988] Curtis, Bill, Herb Krasner, and Neil Iscoe. 1988. A Field Study of the Software Design Process for Large Systems. *Communications of the ACM* 31(11): 1268–1287.

[Endres 1975] Endres, Albert. 1975. An Analysis of Errors and Their Causes in System Programs. *IEEE Transactions on Software Engineering* SE-1(2): 140–149.

[Fenton and Ohlsson 2000] Fenton, N.E., and N. Ohlsson. 2000. Quantitative Analysis of Faults and Failures in a Complex Software System. *IEEE Transactions on Software Engineering* SE-26(8): 797–814.

[Glass 1981] Glass, Robert L. 1981. Persistent Software Errors. *IEEE Transactions on Software Engineering* SE-7(2): 162–168.

[Graves et al. 2000] Graves, T.L., A.F. Karr, J.S. Marron, and H. Siy. 2000. Predicting Fault Incidence Using Software Change History. *IEEE Transactions on Software Engineering* SE-26(7): 653–661.

[Lehman and Belady 1985] Lehman, M.M., and L.A. Belady. 1985. *Program Evolution: Processes of Software Change*. London: Academic Press.

[Leszak et al. 2000] Leszak, Marek, Dewayne E. Perry, and Dieter Stoll. 2000. A Case Study in Root Cause Defect Analysis. *Proceedings of the 22nd International Conference on Software Engineering*: 428–437.

[Leszak et al. 2002] Leszak, Marek, Dewayne E. Perry, and Dieter Stoll. 2002. Classification and Evaluation of Defects in a Project Retrospective. *Journal of Systems and Software* 61(3): 173–187.

[Musa et al. 1987] Musa, J.D., A. Jannino, and K. Okumoto. 1987. *Software Reliability*. New York: McGraw-Hill.

[Ostrand and Weyuker 1984] Ostrand, Thomas J., and Elaine J. Weyuker. 1984. Collecting and Categorizing Software Error Data in an Industrial Environment. *The Journal of Systems and Software*, 4(4): 289–300.

[Ostrand and Weyuker 2002] Ostrand, Thomas J., and Elaine J. Weyuker. 2002. The Distribution of Faults in a Large Industrial Software System. *Proceedings of the 2002 ACM SIGSOFT International Symposium on Software Testing and Analysis*: 55–64.

[Ostrand et al. 2005] Ostrand, T.J., E.J. Weyuker, and R.M. Bell. 2005. Predicting the Location and Number of Faults in Large Software Systems. *IEEE Transactions on Software Engineering* SE-31(4): 340–355.

[Perry and Evangelist 1985] Perry, Dewayne E., and W. Michael Evangelist. 1985. An Empirical Study of Software Interface Errors. *Proceedings of the International Symposium on New Directions in Computing*: 32–38.

[Perry and Evangelist 1987] Perry, Dewayne E., and W. Michael Evangelist. 1987. An Empirical Study of Software Interface Faults—An Update. *Proceedings of the Twentieth Annual Hawaii International Conference on Systems Sciences* II: 113–126.

[Perry and Steig 1993] Perry, Dewayne E., and Carol S. Steig. 1993. Software Faults in Evolving a Large, Real-Time System: A Case Study. In *Lecture Notes in Computer Science, Volume 717: Proceedings of the 4th European Software Engineering Conference*, ed. I. Sommerville and M. Paul, 48–67.

[Perry and Wolf 1992] Perry, Dewayne E., and Alexander L. Wolf. 1992. Foundations for the Study of Software Architecture. *ACM SIGSOFT Software Engineering Notes* 17(4): 40–52.

[Perry et al. 2001] Perry, Dewayne E., Harvey P. Siy, and Lawrence G. Votta. 2001. Parallel Changes in Large Scale Software Development: An Observational Case Study. *Transactions on Software Engineering and Methodology* 10(3): 308–337.

[Purushothaman and Perry 2005] Purushothaman, Ranjith, and Dewayne E. Perry. 2005. Toward Understanding the Rhetoric of Small Source Code Changes. *IEEE Transactions on Software Engineering* SE-31(6): 511–526.

[Rowland et al. 1983] Rowland, B.R., R.E. Anderson, and P. S. McCabe. 1983. The 3B20D Processor & DMERT Operating System: Software Development System. *The Bell System Technical Journal* 62(1/2): 275–290.

[Schneidewind and Hoffmann 1979] Schneidewind, N.F., and Heinz-Michael Hoffmann. 1979. An Experiment in Software Error Data Collection and Analysis. *IEEE Transactions on Software Engineering* SE-5(3): 276–286.

[Shao et al. 2007] Shao, D., S. Khurshid, and D. Perry. 2007. Evaluation of Semantic Interference Detection in Parallel Changes: An Exploratory Experiment. *Proceedings of the 23rd IEEE International Conference on Software Maintenance*: 74–83.

[Siegel et al. 1988] Siegel, Sidney, and N. John Castellan, Jr. 1988. *Nonparametric Statistics for the Behavioral Sciences*, Second Edition. New York: McGraw-Hill.

[Thayer et al. 1978] Thayer, Thomas A., Myron Lipow, and Eldred C. Nelson. 1978. Software Reliability—A Study of Large Project Reality. In *TRW Series of Software Technology*, Volume 2. Amsterdam: North-Holland.

[Thione and Perry 2005] Thione, G. Lorenzo, and Dewayne E. Perry. 2005. Parallel Changes: Detecting Semantic Interferences. *Proceedings of the 29th Annual International Computer Software and Applications Conference*: 47–56.

## CHAPTER TWENTY-SIX

Novice Professionals: Recent Graduates in a First Software Engineering Job

Andrew Begel
Beth Simon

Much is written about software engineering education: how to teach novice computer scientists the programming, design, and testing skills they need to become professional software engineers. However, computer science students are not done with their education at graduation; it is really just the beginning. Newly hired engineers must learn to edit, debug, and create code on a deadline while learning to communicate and interact appropriately with a large team of colleagues. In this chapter, we explore the similarities and differences between these two educational experiences, by providing a detailed view of the novice experience of software developers in their first industry job.

Universities try to prepare students for industry by teaching them core computing concepts that will allow them to become lifelong learners and keep pace with innovations in the discipline. Approaches to teaching these "hard" skills have been driven by advances in industry, such as through new programming paradigms (OO) and new development methodologies (Agile, Extreme Programming). Academic settings offer less support for "soft" skills, or human factors in software engineering, such as the ability to create and debug specifications, to document code and its rationale and history, to follow a software methodology, to manage a large project, and to work and communicate with others on a software team.

Students who enter the professional software engineering workforce have to learn new skills, techniques, and procedures, effectively becoming novices all over again. What they may be surprised to find is that the soft skills are a major component of their new jobs [Curtis et al. 1988], [Perkins et al. 1989]. Employers recognize that students entering the workforce directly from university training often do not have the complete set of software development skills that they will need to be productive, especially in large, independent software development companies. An article in eWeek.com interviewed several industry software developers who said that new college graduates lack communication and teamwork skills, and are unprepared for complex development processes, legacy code, deadlines, and working with limited resources [Taft 2007].

Schein proposed that there were three main aspects to introducing newcomers to organizations: function, hierarchy, and social networking [Schein 1971].

Function

> This represents the tasks and technical requirements of a position. This is very well addressed through university courses that teach general knowledge such as programming, data structures, and software engineering, and domain knowledge such as graphics, artificial intelligence, and operating systems.

Hierarchy

> This is the organizational command structure. This is not covered as well. For example, in many courses where students work in groups, everyone in the group shares equal power, and often equal experience, which is very unlike a newcomer in an industrial job.

Social networking

> This is the movement of the newcomer from the periphery of the network toward the center as new personal connections are made. Unfortunately, this is all too often left completely up to the students, with the only message from the faculty being reminders not to cheat or collaborate too closely on homework assignments.

Due to limitations of the instruction they receive in university, we believe that many students are inadequately prepared for software development jobs in industry. We came to this belief after conducting a study of eight college graduates starting jobs as software developers at Microsoft. We observed these new developers in their daily work over a two-month period within the first six months of their employment. After analyzing our data around novice software developers' tasks, activities, social interactions, and outcomes, we found that although new developers were functionally and technically competent, they lacked preparation and training in the social and communication interactions they encountered on a daily basis. We believe that their initial naïveté caused extra stress, anxiety, low performance, and poor productivity during their formative months at the company.

The lessons from the newcomer socialization research and our data on software developers teach us that the mastery of function, hierarchy, and social networking is critical to the productivity, effectiveness, and satisfaction of new professional software developers. This mastery may be more easily acquired when new software developers are prepared through a variety of pedagogical approaches such as pair programming, legitimate peripheral participation, and mentoring programs. We hope that this chapter's detailed information on new software developers will enable a better discussion and evaluation of new programs designed to improve undergraduate education. We encourage the reader to think about experimenting with educational programs and interventions while looking at our data.

Study Methodology

We conducted a direct observation case study and analyzed the data using grounded theory. Direct observation involves one of the researchers sitting in the same office as the participant, watching everything that the participant does and writing it down in a log. We often prefer direct observation to interviews or surveys because, as nonparticipant observers, we can be impartial and record every detail of the action, which gives us an exact view of events as they occurred. This contrasts with an interview or a survey, where subjects suffer from several biases. Typical are generalization bias, where they tell us generally how their day goes instead of giving us specific events, and memory bias, where they remember more recent events better than older ones. In qualitative studies like ours, the goal is not to eliminate all bias (which is impossible), but to choose the biases that will have the least influence on the results we uncover.

The case study aspect of our approach was to choose a small number of participants to observe. Participants were selected to be as different from one another as possible, so that we might observe a diverse set of activities, behaviors, and phenomena. Direct observation is an expensive way to gather data due to the time commitment of following someone around for many hours of the day. This limits the number of people we can include in the study, so we try to make sure that we see as much phenomena as we can from a small number of participants.

To analyze our data, we used grounded theory [Strauss 1987]. Grounded theory is a qualitative research methodology that enables researchers to create theories about what they see solely from their data, and not from any prior assumptions about how people behave. This methodology is useful when we are not sure what kind of data we will get and do not yet know which aspects will be most important. Grounded theories analyze their data in three phases:

1. *Open coding*

    In this phase, every artifact in the log is tagged with a label (or multiple labels) that describes what it is about.

2. *Axial coding*

    In this phase, the labels created in open coding are related to one another, to show cause and effect, moderators to effects, or actions that take place because of some behavior.

3. *Selective coding*

> In this phase, all of the labels and their relationships are organized into a coherent storyline. This often forms the basis of a theory about the data that was gathered.

In this section, we describe our observation and analysis techniques, and present several examples of our raw data.

Subjects

We selected eight developers newly hired by Microsoft between one and seven months before the start of the study. We identified 25 available subjects (based on manager approval and schedule consideration) and selected 8 (seven men and one woman), balancing years of schooling and division within the company. Four had BS degrees, one had an MS, and three had PhDs, all in computer science or software engineering. Of the BS recipients, two were educated in the U.S., two in China, one in Mexico, one in Pakistan, one in Kuwait, and one in Australia. All PhDs were earned in U.S. universities. We also selected for the least amount of previous software development experience (none outside of limited internships), with the exception of the subject from Australia, who had two years of development experience outside of Microsoft. Subjects were compensated weekly (USD $50) for their participation.

Each developer was observed for 6–11 hours over 2 two-week periods, with a one-month break in between. We observed the developers in their own work environment without interrupting them, followed them to meetings, and watched them as they interacted with their colleagues and friends. We recorded our observations in time-stamped logs, which were the basis for our subsequent analyses. Similar to what you might see on reality TV, developers were asked to record a video diary entry at the end of each day that they were not observed. They were asked to talk about the most interesting thing that happened that day, followed by a question asking them to reflect on some aspect of their college education or new hire experience.

Task Analysis

In the open coding phase of our grounded theory analysis, we identified the tasks that novices perform by reviewing the observation log entries of what subjects were doing, and tagged each with one or two task and subtask types. The task types we coded are arranged in the taxonomy presented in Table 26-1. For example, an entry might be tagged Coding/Searching and also Communication/Asking Questions if the developer asked a colleague where an API call was defined in the code.

TABLE 26-1. Tasks performed by novices, listed in the order of their frequency

Programming	Reading, Writing, Commenting, Proofreading, Code Review
Working on Bugs	Reproduction, Reporting, Triage, Debugging
Testing	Writing, Running

Project Management	Check in, Check out, Revert
Documentation	Reading, Writing, Search
Specifications	Reading, Writing
Tools	Discovering, Finding, Installing, Using, Building
Communication	Asking Questions, Persuasion, Coordination, Email, Meetings, Meeting Prep, Finding People, Interacting with Managers, Teaching, Learning, Mentoring

Task Sample

In this section we give a flavor of the observation of one of our participants along with a section of its associated activity log (shown in Table 26-2). Timothy was assigned to fix a bug. After reading the five bug reproduction steps, he attempted but failed to successfully execute the first step. He spent 45 minutes trying to debug the problem by swapping various software libraries on his computer, including swapping computers, to no avail. He went across the hall to a colleague, Abdul, and asked him for help. Timothy explained what he had tried, but Abdul disagreed with his assessment of the problem. Abdul returned with him to the office, noticed that Timothy had copied incorrect libraries to his computer, told him where to find the proper binaries, and then went back to his office.

The incorrect binaries were a consequence of Timothy's debugging strategy, however, and not the original problem. Timothy tried to reproduce the bug for another 12 minutes before going back to Abdul to tell him that things were still not working. Abdul explained more about the libraries he copied, causing Timothy to realize that he had the wrong mental model of the libraries and the directories in which they were meant to be placed. Abdul taught him the proper model, recounting stories of his own debugging prowess from years back, and sent Timothy on his way with another few generic debugging strategies, both of which Timothy had already tried. Timothy did not press his colleague for more help until he could prove that he had tried these strategies with the corrected mental model, though he knew they would not work. After another 25 minutes of debugging and testing on his own, Timothy had still not successfully executed the first reproduction step, and appeared to have made no progress at all.

Reflection Methodology

On each day that we did not observe them, the subjects in the study recorded a 3–5 minute video diary entry using a webcam we gave to them to use. We created 40 questions, of which most subjects recorded answers to the first 20. One made it to 35. The numbers vary due to absence, lack of free time, and number of observations we made. We listened to the videos and transcribed the answers to 13 of the questions that related to learning and the college experience.

Threats to Validity

Empirical qualitative studies like ours see all the complexities of real life. Naturally, with so many multifaceted experiences spread over just a few subjects, it is difficult to ascertain with 100% certainty what caused the effects we saw. Some aspects of our study and its participants may have caused biased results.

Our study subjects came from a range of educational backgrounds, and were at different stages of personal and professional development at the start of the study. In addition, each changed and learned a different amount over the course of the two months we watched them. Although this makes it hard to compare participants with one another, this learning effect is the focus of the study.

An unavoidable bias in our study is the *Hawthorne effect*, where the observer's mere presence influences the subject to change his behavior. We believe our continuous and lengthy observations helped put them more at ease. At the end of the study, we asked the subjects if they noticed any change in their own behavior, but most remarked only that they took fewer breaks while we were around. To avoid a hierarchy bias, we made it clear to the newcomers and their managers that all data collected would be private and would never be available to anyone, including management. In addition, we took steps to ensure that our subjects were not coerced to participate by their managers. At any point, even after the study had finished, subjects could withdraw and erase all their data. None did.

When reading our findings, one must keep in mind that a developer's expression of a need for information does not tell the entire story about what developers really need to do their jobs. In particular, due to the nonintrusive, observational approach of our study, it was possible to observe that novices do not always recognize that they need some information. That is, they may flail, stop making progress, task switch, or do any number of things when, in the eyes of the observer, seeking out some information could allow them to make progress. In particular, we observed many cases in which a novice did not recognize that they should seek information from a colleague in order to make progress on the current task. Our data indicate what novices actually do, but not, perhaps, what they should be doing.

TABLE 26-2. An activity log from Timothy shown with tagged task types and subtypes

Timestamp	Description	Task type/subtask type
11:45:43 AM	Reruns copy script.	Working on Bugs/ Reproduction
11:46:18 AM	Script done. Checks over script output to make sure it looks right. Says that the script is complaining that the files aren't signed. Email with source directory says that they *are* signed. Weird. Copied successfully, but binaries aren't signed.	Working on Bugs/ Reproduction

Timestamp	Description	Task type/subtask type
11:47:26 AM	Shakes head. Timothy is confused. Team lead says they're signed. But empirical evidence says they're not.	Working on Bugs/ Reproduction
11:48:11 AM	Timothy says maybe he wants to sign the binaries himself.	
11:48:36 AM	Timothy mutters to himself "bad bad very bad."	
11:56:23 AM	Timothy goes to Abdul across the hall to ask what's going on.	Communication/Asking Questions
11:56:35 AM	After explaining problem, Abdul disagrees with Timothy's assessment, comes to Timothy's office and notices that Timothy is copying the wrong architecture binaries to computer. Unsigned binaries are a red herring. Now he copies the right binaries (still said unsigned) and no need to reboot.	Communication/Learning
11:57:27 AM	[Application] now launches just fine.	Working on Bugs/ Reproduction
11:57:49 AM	Attempts to repro the bug again. URL works success. Repro fails. Timothy expresses confusion—how can I repro this bug? Debug binaries and non-debug binaries eliminate repro.	Working on Bugs/ Reproduction

Software Development Task

In this section, we provide some low-level details about the specific software tasks in which novices engage, summarize the distribution of the amount of time they spend on them, and show exemplars of the types of things they did during those tasks. Those tasks that they spend the most time on are worthy candidates for analysis to determine whether they are supported by computer science pedagogy.

Figure 26-1 shows the percentage time spent on various tasks by our novice subjects over all of their observations normalized by the length of time that we observed the subject. The bars in the graph may be directly visually compared with one another within and between subjects, so we can see, for instance, from the length of the bars that Timothy spent the most time doing communication tasks.

Task Breakdown

Most of our novices spend a large portion of their time in communication tasks. This covers meetings (both organized and spontaneous, and with varying numbers of colleagues), seeking awareness of team members (and their code and tasks), requesting help, receiving help, helping others, working with others, persuading others, coordinating with others, getting feedback (such as on code), and finding people.

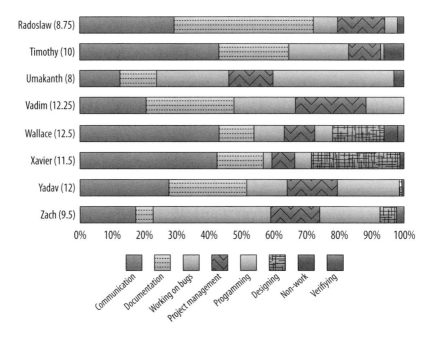

FIGURE 26-1. Tasks by time for each subject, normalized by the total time + time where events overlapped in each observation. Total observation time in hours is listed in parentheses after each subject's name.

Communication

Wallace, Xavier, and Timothy spent an overwhelming amount of their time in communication tasks. Both attended several meetings and got help from others in dealing with bugs. Wallace had particularly high levels of communication due to the low cost of communicating with his team—he worked in a "bull pen" arrangement with four other developers, where it was customary for them to casually request help by spoken means, or offer to provide it in case of sudden outbursts of frustration.

Xavier and Yadav also spent the largest amount of their time on communication tasks compared to any others, but both also have strong representation in a second task. Xavier spent a large number of hours in design meetings with his team's feature lead and a team from another product that was involved in his design process. He also frequently engaged in pair-programming and pair-debugging exercises with other novices in his team. Yadav also spent time communicating in bug triage meetings, but spent a good deal of time coding, which often included utilizing documentation to figure out how to code. In addition, Yadav frequently used instant messaging (IM) to ask and answer coding questions with experienced members of his team.

Much of Radoslaw's communication was about coordination. Radoslaw's tasks required him to work with several other teammates to analyze and coordinate test runs of a benchmark, and collect and present test results in a report. The test computers were a limited resource, which required a great deal of coordination, as did the development of the shared test results reports.

Overall, communication was a critical and common activity for novices. They communicated in order to get help and to develop and confirm their understanding of how to do their job in relation to their team. Additionally, our tally of tasks novices do may even underestimate the importance of communication. If novices had spent *more* time in communication with their colleagues, they might have been able to gather information more productively than they did.

Documentation

The next most common task for Radoslaw, Timothy, Vadim, and Yadav was documentation. Documentation occurred in conjunction with programming and debugging by searching for documentation and understanding it (often of APIs on the Web) in order to comprehend or create code. Novices would also write documentation in the form of bug reports and specification plans. Finally, novices often kept personal documentation to record project management and tool knowledge or to record information that they would need to present at meetings. Several of the subjects made comments to the researchers that they struggled to keep these personal notes organized and accessible. They had no structure for them and desired some help or scaffolding for managing their personal documentation.

Radoslaw and Vadim spent more time on documentation than anything else. In both cases, their time was spent reading documentation (in a variety of sources: textual documents, on MSDN, on the Web, and in emails) to try to understand their team's code. This was as a result of flailing in other efforts, either to code something or to install/set up their development environment. Vadim thought this extensive reading was not the best use of his time, but as a very new hire, he felt he had no other resources.

Working on bugs

The next most common activities were working on bugs and programming. The frequency of bug fixing varied greatly from one subject to another because it depended on the stage of their development cycle during observation. Yadav and Timothy were observed in bug triage meetings, and Wallace's team had virtual and physical triage meetings, though none were observed. All subjects were observed reproducing bugs (sometimes their own) and understanding why they occurred. Zach was very focused on debugging, often correlating success with a reduction in bug count. At one time, he was resolving hundreds of bugs a day through pattern-matched changes. Other debugging tasks we observed included testing, navigating, and searching.

Programming

Three of our novices spent time implementing features (Umakanth, Yadav, and Zach), an activity that combined programming, specifications, and debugging. Subjects observed writing or understanding code often were jointly engaged in a documentation task (to understand how code or APIs worked or by mimicking online code samples). Especially when programming in support of the debugging process, we observed novices navigating and searching through code—a process often difficult for them to manage effectively. Finally, we observed very conscientious code commenting by novices. Sometimes they commented code that they were reading for a debugging fix, even if they were not changing those exact lines of code. In their struggles to understand and become conversant with a code base, they were in a position to appreciate code comments, and seemed willing to add them.

Umakanth's first project was to design and implement a wizard dialog box using APIs he had never used before. He spent the majority of his time programming, but mostly because of an inefficient technique of learning a new language by trying everything on his own. He might have been more productive and perhaps less stressed if he had spent more time seeking help and less time flailing on his code alone.

Xavier's work required recoding a project written the previous summer by an intern who was no longer available to answer questions. Wallace worked on a web service whose development life cycle involved writing many small features and fixing bugs on an ongoing basis. As Wallace was new to the code base, he had many questions for his colleagues to answer. In addition, Wallace worked in the bullpen with four other, more experienced developers all working on similar projects. They would answer questions that Wallace had (and vice versa), even if Wallace had not directly addressed his questions to anyone in particular.

Project management and tools

We saw novices doing a wide range of project management and tools tasks, such as using revision control systems, building their project, setting up their project or development environment, running auxiliary tools, and creating tools that they needed to support project management tasks and procedures. Project management and tools seemed to occupy an inordinate amount of the novices' time. In particular, these tasks tended to interrupt their progress. In the extreme, the newest of our subjects (Vadim) was completely blocked in getting set up in his development environment by project management issues. Zach's team was in an active bug-fixing phase, and he had been assigned the job of eliminating 1,300 new compiler warnings. He separated each batch of removed warnings into a separate check-in, each requiring coordination with colleagues for code review and submission to the revision control system.

Design specifications and testing

Time spent on design depended heavily on the phase of development that a subject's team was currently in. Both Xavier and Wallace spent significant time both understanding and writing specifications. Testing came up most notably in specific projects for Zach, but was also seen in small instances across a number of subjects.

Strengths and Weaknesses of Novice Software Developers

Our observations revealed that novice software developers demonstrate a wide variety of abilities as well as deficiencies. Among their strengths are:

- Programming
- Reading and writing specifications
- Debugging (persistence and hypothesis generation)

Weaknesses include:

- Communications
- Cognition
- Orientation (engaging with a large code base and preexisting software team)

Strengths

From our observations, we could see that novice software developers were very well prepared by their universities for programming, design, and debugging. They were capable of using IDEs to code, command-line tools to analyze files, and online documentation to learn about unfamiliar APIs. They tried not just to complete their tasks, but to understand why the code change was the right one to make. Several of them practiced copy-paste coding, either from documentation or from other sections of their team's codebase. When debugging, all of the novices demonstrated prolific hypothesis generation (e.g., see the previous section "Task Sample" on page 499) and persistence in trying all possibilities before contemplating giving up if nothing worked. Most took these incremental failures to solve problems in stride, and though complaints about unfamiliar and undocumented tools pervaded their self-commentary, they seldom reported this to others.

One subject had to review design specifications for two software features. This led to frequent discussions with the head of the team, leading to further clarifications of the design and outlining specific use cases to be considered. This experience led to his relative comfort in his second month, during which he wrote his own structured, lengthy development specification document. Notable here was the team lead's skill in mentoring, being very open in asking for and guiding his subordinate's input, sprinkling in background information on the code and design decisions that stemmed from his historical knowledge, and in providing advice about appropriate level of detail for the current design stage.

Weaknesses

The novices in our study experienced numerous problems with communication, collaboration, cognition, and orientation.

An overarching theme of new developers' communication problems is knowing how and when to ask questions of others. In general, novices do not ask questions soon enough, and often struggle to ask questions at an appropriate level. Sometimes they would go into too much detail in design meetings. At other times, they would not provide enough detail, nor push for enough detail in a response from others, which often led to miscommunication.

The social issues we observed focused on working in large teams, working in conjunction with multiple teams, and working with a large preexisting code base. Many times, novices were explicitly told that there was little written documentation on a feature, and that the original developers had left the team or the company. This was often stated with the emphasis "you are on your own here [with regard to documentation]" and "life will be more difficult because there is no one to go ask about this."

Understanding how team norms differ from those in academic settings confused some subjects. Timothy learned about his team's software process the hard way. He had fixed a bug and submitted it for check-in. However, his bug fix was rejected and omitted from the shipped product, not due to code quality, as he had expected, but instead because managers (in other groups) had not yet had time to approve it. Timothy believed he had addressed the customer's bug, but obediently accepted the decision of the managers so as "not to rock the boat." He learned that developers are not just programmers, but in some situations, must be their own best advocates at moving their code and ideas through the software development process. A month later, Timothy faced this issue again, but was better prepared. In the bug triage meeting, he described his bug's status efficiently and spoke in great detail about his efforts to get another group to approve it.

Novices struggled to collect, organize, and document the wide range of information that they needed to absorb. One subject reflected that he usually takes notes in a paper notebook, but "it's always very scattered, I can't usually understand them. I wish I had a better way to take notes." Often, an impromptu teaching session on revision control or the bug database was not necessarily well organized or stated in terms or in a context with which the developer was familiar. In these cases, the developer may not always interrupt for full information, out of concern for using the time of the experienced developer or because the "teacher" barrels through the instruction without stopping. As such, some of their knowledge is built haphazardly in an unstructured and piecemeal fashion.

Novices had difficulty orienting themselves in the low-information environments presented by their project team, code base, and resources. However, this was sometimes coupled with confusing and poorly organized documentation, which was difficult for a novice to navigate or engage with effectively. Novices also struggle to know "when they don't know" something. Because there is so much new infrastructure to learn, it becomes the norm to have only partial knowledge of a tool or some code. While this is their reality, it also leads many novices to fail to recognize when they are truly stuck and should ask for help. The most recently hired subject exhibited this on a frequent basis. Even after asking for help on some code and getting a very specific answer that the specification was ambiguous, he kept on trying to reason through it.

Some novices felt woefully isolated from their teams, sometimes not even knowing all the members of their team, and rarely knowing who to talk to about certain issues (or where that person's office was). This impacted both their productivity and frustration greatly. There was a large variation among subjects in their degree of isolation. One subject chose to seek other forms of information and (somewhat fruitlessly) spent much time reading high-level documents in an attempt to gather any information on his team's work. Another learned early on that all knowledge was most easily discovered through people. Instead of searching for specifications online, he would roam the hallway looking for colleagues to ask. If the first person was not there or did not know the answer, he moved on to the next person down the hall. Only when the person who knew the answer was out of office did he fall back to less efficient forms of knowledge acquisition, such as reading code and debugging through test cases.

Reflections

While observation log analysis summarizes the tasks that novices could be objectively seen *doing*, it does not capture all aspects of their experience. In particular, investigating how novices feel about what they do and why they do it may also be instructive. In this section, we organize and classify some of the reflections made by novices in video diary entries about their experiences. These reflections help round out the picture of the social and hierarchical newcomer issues that define the novice software developer experience.

Scaffolding the diary questions proved helpful in getting the subjects to think about their own learning experiences in university and industry. Particularly fruitful questions are listed here:

- How did your university experience prepare you for your job at Microsoft?
- What things would best prepare a college student for their first year at Microsoft?
- If a "future you" came back to advise you now, what words of wisdom would he offer?
- If you could go back to the past and give yourself advice at the end of your third week at Microsoft, what advice or warnings would you give?
- How do you know when you are stuck? What do you do when that happens?

In the following sections we characterize and summarize the responses given by our subjects to these questions.

Managing Getting Engaged

When employees first arrive at a company, they face an immediate quandary. They feel the need to prove to their managers that they are smart, productive, and infallible, but they do not know any of the functional aspects of their role yet. Thus, stress and anxiety increase as new employees attempt to master immense amounts of material in a short amount of time, all the while trying to take on tasks that have an impact on the team. Our subjects reflected on this and often regretted their speedy ramp-up. Timothy said, "You don't need a very deep understanding of one component, but you need a broad knowledge of everything—you don't want to go deeply in one hole. It will take you longer time and it will delay your progress." Vadim remarked that he should have spent more time learning: "Put up some extra time and effort (apart from work time) to learn some new technologies, to learn about the product in much more depth...the very first year." Wallace reflected on his high stress: "I would probably tell myself to not get so stressed about things and take things in stride because it's no use getting yourself stressed about something. You're learning, I'm learning, I don't want to get myself stressed out over these little things...." Xavier mentioned a strategy that most felt reluctant to engage in at the beginning of their careers: "Ask questions of the other devs." "You can figure out something in five minutes by asking someone instead of spending a day of looking through code and design docs," said Vadim. Asking questions, however, reveals to your coworkers and managers that you are not knowledgeable, an exposure that most new developers felt might cause their manager to reevaluate why they were hired in the first place.

Persistence, Uncertainty, and Noviceness

Perkins et al. classified novice programmers into "stoppers" and "movers" [Perkins et al. 1989]. Stoppers get stuck easily and give up. Movers experiment, tinker, and keep going until a problem is solved. All of our subjects noted the importance of persistence, likely making them movers. Wallace, in particular, noted "the attitude of not giving up here at MS...if I am given a problem I am expected to solve it. There's no going to my supervisor and saying, 'I can't figure this out'.... Ultimately it's my responsibility."

Perkins proposed uncertainty and a lack of self-efficacy as the reasons why students became stoppers. However, we see these uncertainty and self-efficacy issues in our movers' observation logs, even though they are very persistent. When asked, our subjects never admitted to having stopper characteristics: Wallace admitted, "I often don't know when I am stuck. [But] I try to persevere and find a solution no matter what." Apparently, being a mover does not imply success, nor is it an attitude that always leads to success, as evidenced by Xavier's quote on being stuck: "I know I'm stuck when I've exhausted the known ways of solving the problem." A better strategy for getting oneself unstuck is to ask someone else, a strategy hindered by the power inequality and social anxiety of newcomers. Some of our subjects did, in fact, ask others questions. Timothy said, "[When] I am stuck, I go to a more senior teammate and see if they have encountered this kind of problem or situation before." Often, however, this was only after flailing for a long time and spending many hours ineffectually trying to solve a problem.

Consequently, one might propose that these traits of uncertainty and lack of self-efficacy are more applicable to the notion of "noviceness" than to the task of learning to program. Indeed, the organizational management literature finds that uncertainty and lack of self-efficacy are characteristic of any newcomer to an organization [Bauer et al. 2007].

Large-Scale Software Team Setting

The subjects' reflections indicate that their technical/functional preparation for their software development jobs was adequate: Zach said, "I don't think I need a lot more technical skills." However, subjects indicated they were ill-prepared for the degree of social interaction required: Vadim said that "in university you are focusing on individual projects or 2–3 man team projects. The first thing that anyone is not prepared for and I was not prepared for is collaborating in a team of 75 people, which was 35 developers and similar amount of testers, and [having to] collaborate with all of them." The consequences of poor interactions are dire (continuing with the same quote): "In [the] fashion that you don't break any of the part of the core or affect anyone else." Xavier remarked: "Even if you think something is simple, it's not. If you think something is a minor change, it's probably not. There's lots of interesting consequences, side effects, things that you didn't think about when you are working on something." Working closely with teammates was one way to improve the likelihood of success: Wallace said, "What I think I need to improve on is being a team player....When my teammates have a success, or when they need help, I want to be more willing to make their goals my goals as well. Because their success is the success of the team and I want to help the team to be successful." Finally, regardless of whether it was possible in his university, Xavier expressed a desire to have worked on larger projects with more people. "[I should] get a lot of experience working on a team project with people...not just some stupid homework assignment that only lasts one week."

Misconceptions That Hinder Learning

Many times during our observations, we noticed some misconceptions among novices that affected their actions and interactions with their colleagues:

I must do everything myself so that I look good to my manager.
> This misconception is particularly dangerous, especially in large, complex development environments. We saw it mostly in new hires from outside the U.S. The perceived need to "perform" and not "reveal deficiencies" makes for much wasted time. It also seems to contribute to poor communication and a longer acclimatization. Communication suffered both by waiting too long to seek help and by trying to cover up issues that the novice perhaps felt he "should know." Additionally, novice developers were occasionally seen to continue to work on issues deemed (by teammates) either not worth solving or someone else's problem. Though our sample size is extremely small, it's worth noting that this misconception was not evidenced in new hires native to the US.

Over the two months of observation, the subjects in our study became more self-confident, less stressed-out, and gained self-esteem. At the final exit interview, many participants revealed that their early worries and expectations had been unrealistic.

I must be the one to fix any bug I see—and I should fix it the "right" way, even if I do not have time for it. This is one of the most ubiquitous misconceptions, likely driven by the lack of team-based development and the deadline-driven grading system in academia. Novice developers had the perception that *anything* they found that was "not working" *had* to be fixed immediately. Even though they had been made aware of established procedures for reporting, triaging, and dealing with bugs, they often sought to work around them. Some novices were chastised when "caught out" in this respect, but it appears to be a very ingrained belief and one that would require time to drill out of them.

If there were only more documentation... Not so much a misconception as a daily plea, the desire for accurate and findable documentation was pervasive. Even though some of the more experienced novices accompanied these pleas with recognition that such documentation becomes stale quickly, they still wished that more existed. More experienced novices desired information about people in their environment, i.e., whom to go talk to about specific issues or code. They recognized that the complexity and timelines of software development limit documentation, and that people are considered the most valuable documentation resource.

I know when I am stuck when solving a problem. Based on explicit statements made by subjects (Umakanth, Timothy, Vadim, Zach) and contrary to explicit observations, it is clear that novices almost always waste time, effort, and money by flailing—and do not recognize that they are stuck. This may not be a surprising result, as explicit instruction in meta-cognitive skills for programming is not common. Although greatly frustrated at these times, novices seem to lack the resources for either recognizing they are stuck or, perhaps more likely, the resources to do something about it. Notably, despite a greater propensity for reflection on their own progress, PhD graduates were just as likely to get stuck and flail when trying to solve a problem as the BS graduates.

Reflecting on Pedagogy

In this section, we review various computer science curricula and pedagogical approaches through the lens of newcomer socialization. The software development tasks we listed earlier—programming, working on bugs, testing, project management, documentation, specifications, tools and communications—are addressed to various degrees in university courses. Within each task, we can find Schein's three components of belonging to an organization: function, hierarchy, and social networking. Three relatively recent and uncommon pedagogical approaches—pair programming, legitimate peripheral participation, and mentoring—address the hierarchical and social aspects of newcomer socialization in a university setting. We urge that these practices be more universally adopted.

Pair Programming

Our participants were surprised at the degree of communication with their colleagues required for the software development process. Some aspects of this communication can be found in pair programming exercises. Two students are paired together, both acting as developers, creating, editing, and rationalizing the code in concert. Pair programming, whose impact in the workplace is explored by Laurie Williams in Chapter 17 of this book, has been shown to increase student performance and self-efficacy [McDowell et al. 2006]. It is less stressful and frustrating because of an increase in brainstorming, number of solutions explored, and the ability to defer to the partner to solve a problem when one's brain is tired. Pair programming also builds a community of people of whom the students feel comfortable asking questions.

Pair programming does not, however, address the issues of hierarchy. Both students have the same experience and similar backgrounds, and both are striving to achieve a grade. Contrast this situation with a typical newcomer in an industrial job. Similar to the student situation, there is a manager who is evaluating the newcomer's performance, and who, like a college professor, endeavors to give the newcomer time to acquire knowledge and skills before applying harsh grading metrics. However, a new college graduate does not really know who is on his team, nor in what knowledge each member of the team is expert, and is the least knowledgeable member of his team.

Legitimate Peripheral Participation

One issue faced by university pedagogy is the inauthenticity of the experience. Industry practices change much faster than pedagogy, making this a persistent problem. This inauthenticity can be ameliorated in a course such as Mark Guzdial's Media Computation [Guzdial and Tew 2006], which strives to convince students that they are part of a community of practice.

Lave and Wenger discuss how people join a community of practice by learning from others in apprentice positions [Lave and Wenger 1991]. Through legitimate peripheral participation, doctors learn by observing more experienced doctors conduct procedures and are mentored by them when performing these procedures for their first time, and then become mentors to other newcomers. In their Media Computation course, Guzdial and Tew reported that retention increased, especially of women, a group that had been more likely to drop out of computer science. The course also altered the expectations of its students to fit better with how experimentation with computers is actually practiced in the community to which the students were introduced. This realignment of expectations has a large effect on newcomers' self-efficacy and increases their commitment to remain part of the community.

Hazzan and Tomayko's Human Aspects of Software Engineering course specifically simulates the social dynamics of software teams [Tomayko and Hazzan 2004]. Their software engineering course teaches students about handling difficult social situations on software teams, ethics, processes and techniques for learning on the job, how incentive structures are conceived, and values that affect team performance and cohesiveness.

Mentoring

Newcomer socialization research shows the importance of mentoring to the newcomer's success [Ostroff and Kozlowski 1993]. Mentors introduce newcomers to people in their social network and help them build relationships with the people who can best answer their questions and support opportunistic learning situations. Mentors explain design rationales, help find information that is difficult for novices to locate, and provide advice on procedures and processes. Basically, mentors teach newcomers how to fit in both technically and socially.

Peer mentoring was an important source of learning and information for two of the subjects in our study. These two joined Microsoft at the same time as a friend. Every time they learned something new, they would tell their friend (and vice versa). This was much more fluid than knowledge transfer from a mentor or manager to the new hire. Peer mentors are at similar levels of experience, and feel more comfortable exchanging information about these basic tasks without feeling insecure about revealing their lack of knowledge. Many universities use mentoring as an approach to improve retention of women and underrepresented minorities in computer science education [Margolis and Fisher 2003], [Payton and White 2003]. Mentoring increases the sense of belonging by enabling mentor and protégé to relate on culture, diversity, and values, which may not be reflected in daily work practice. This helps move the novice from the periphery of the social network toward the center.

Implications for Change

We see that many of the problems suffered by novice software developers have a root cause in poor communication skills and social naïveté. After analyzing our observations through the lens of newcomer socialization, we suggest possible changes to new hire "onboarding"* programs and university computer science curricula. We believe our suggestions can better prepare new college graduates for the ways that new developers work before they become experts, and hopefully speed them along in the process of gaining expertise.

---

* The term *onboarding* is the Microsoft term for the orientation process by which new hires adjust to and become effective software developers within the corporation.

New Developer Onboarding

Many new hires at Microsoft are assigned a mentor for their first few months on the job; we believe that the best outcomes are associated with intensive mentoring in the first month. A good mentor does not simply provide pointers to extant information on tools, processes, and people, but also models proper behavior and actions. For example, when Vadim came to someone in his team (incidentally, not his official mentor) with a bug reproduction problem, this person mentored him by looking at the bug report with him, figured out that it was inherently ambiguous (which was causing the new developer his reproduction problems), looked up the people who had written the bug report, and composed, with Vadim, an email to the bug report author asking about the ambiguity. He then looked up the author in the corporate address book, found out that he was in the building, and asked Vadim if he wanted to go visit the author in person. This process viscerally demonstrated to the new hire how the social norms of Microsoft worked, in a way that merely telling him would not have done. In contrast, Vadim's official mentor was quite busy, which limited his availability. He often simply pointed Vadim at resources and documentation—sometimes incorrectly.

In addition to training managers and mentors and giving them time and permission to increasing their effectiveness and proactivity, we should do the same for the new developers themselves. Helping newcomers find others with similar experiences of whom they can ask questions—for example, on a new hire mailing list and/or chat room, per software team— could alleviate anxiety and foster a community of questions and answers about topics deemed too "simple" to ask a more experienced colleague. A similar practice to this kind of cohort mentoring is to have slightly more experienced colleagues mentor new hires. They have a similar outlook on their job since they are still beginners, and have additional related experience with which to offer advice and career mentoring in a way that much more experienced colleagues cannot relate.

Learning who team members are and how their projects are structured is an important activity often left to new hires to figure out for themselves. We propose *feature interviews* to make the process more explicit. A new developer will make appointments each week with a different developer on their team; in this appointment, she will interview the developer to learn about the features that the developer owns, the features' overall architecture and place within the larger system, the design and implementation challenges faced, the developer's job philosophy, and what the developer finds personally interesting or meaningful about his work. Hopefully, this would teach the new developer about the software system as it exists (rather than as its specification presents it) slowly, over time, giving the novice time to assimilate the information. It should also help to spread the value system and culture of the workplace more deliberately than now, which would help novices identify which values are held by all and which should not be held by anyone.

How do managers measure the performance of new developers? They will not be as productive as experienced developers, and their learning process is an important aspect of their development. We feel that the right set of metrics would judge new hires on time spent learning, risk-taking, and cooperation with others. Additionally, mentors would be judged on how fast the new hire came up to speed, rather than being assigned a novice as an unvalued side project. Many of the new hires we spoke to mentioned that they wished they had taken more time in the first few months to simply learn the system in breadth and depth, rather than jumping straight into a project and trying to work like an experienced developer. They said their managers did not expect them to be productive from day one, but later in their tenure, they had too much "real work" to do to spend much time learning. We are developing a framework for teams and mentors to create a set of benchmark guidelines that list a series of personal development milestones, e.g., when to write one's first feature, or review someone else's code, or be assigned a bug, or write one's first bug report. Each procedure can be written down and made part of a "curriculum" for new developers, so that their progress can be monitored. This monitoring would also enable companies to measure the effects of any changes they make to the onboarding process, in order to see whether it improves the status quo.

Personal software processes can be used to help novices reflect on their progress through a task, and provide an artifact to share with mentors, managers, and other helpful colleagues early on to illustrate process mistakes and potential for improvement. New developers should be encouraged to think about how to figure out what to do next at any moment, when they should ask for help, and when they are stuck or making progress. One could adapt performance-monitoring techniques from intelligent tutoring systems to understand developer activities and help notify novice developers to get up and ask someone for help at the moment they really need it.

Educational Curricula

In many universities, "greenfield" software engineering capstone courses expose students to a full design, implementation, and test cycle, and in doing so teach students how to work on a team of many people on a relatively large piece of software while remaining in a pedagogically supportive setting. These students take on roles such as requirements engineer, developer, tester, and documenter, and work together to deliver software to a customer, usually in an egalitarian fashion. The de facto leader of most of these teams is the teaching assistant or course instructor. But our study reveals realistic work situations that differ considerably from the artificial experience provided by greenfield courses. Many of the social and communication problems we found, especially with Xavier and Wallace, were rooted in the anxieties of working on a large team with a large legacy code base. The anxiety of being the most junior member of a team incurs the need to impress everyone. The anxiety of not knowing the code at all requires "wasting" time to learn it. They feel anxiety in taking too long to solve problems. Courses that incorporate teamwork typically do not address these insecurities.

Instead of a greenfield project, a more constructive experience might provide students a large preexisting code base for which they must fix bugs (injected or real) and write additional features. Incorporating a management component would be valuable, where students must interact with more experienced colleagues (students who have taken the class previously, who can act as mentors) or project managers (teaching assistants) who teach them about the code base or challenge them to solve bugs several times until the "right" fix is found. During the development process, students could be asked to log bugs in a bug database, develop bug reproduction steps, and/or triage the importance of the bugs given some planned release schedule.

In large software projects, bug fixes are not just code changes. There are many possible fixes for any particular bug, and each proposed fix has to pass a social bar in addition to a technical one. Simulate some possibilities: how "big" is the bug fix? How many lines of code does it touch? The more lines of code changed, the more likely you have introduced a new bug. Does the fix touch code that is frozen at this point in the development cycle? If so, find another fix that masks the bug in unfrozen code. Instead of grading students on fixing all bugs in their assignments, have them document the bugs and prioritize just the 25% that are most worth fixing, and have them justify their reasoning.

Instructors should take time in class to model meta-cognitive skills for students. How do you know if you are making progress? How should you organize your thoughts when asking a colleague a question or bringing them up to speed? How do you get the most out of interactions with a teacher or mentor? How do you take notes when the person giving you instruction is ill-trained as a teacher (and may be your manager)? Students who are well-trained in these arts will make better peer mentors for a new class of software engineers in future software development positions.

References

[Bauer et al. 2007] Bauer, T., T. Bodner, B. Erdogan, D. Truxillo, and J. Tucker. 2007. Newcomer adjustment during organizational socialization: A meta-analytic review of antecedents, outcomes, and methods. *Journal of Applied Psychology* 92: 707–721.

[Curtis et al. 1988] Curtis, B., H. Krasner, and N. Iscoe. 1988. A field study of the software design process for large systems. *Communications of the ACM* 31(11): 1268–1287.

[Guzdial and Tew 2006] Guzdial, M., and A.E. Tew. 2006. Imagineering inauthentic legitimate peripheral participation: An instructional design approach for motivating computing education. *Proceedings of the second international workshop on computing education research*: 51–58.

[Lave and Wenger 1991] Lave, J., and E. Wenger. 1991. *Situated Learning: Legitimate Peripheral Participation*. Cambridge, UK: Cambridge University Press.

[Margolis and Fisher 2003] Margolis, J., and A. Fisher. 2003. *Unlocking the Clubhouse: Women in Computing*. Cambridge, MA: MIT Press.

[McDowell et al. 2006] McDowell, C., L. Werner, H.E. Bullock, and J. Fernald. 2006. Pair programming improves student retention, confidence, and program quality. *Communications of the ACM* 49(8): 90–95.

[Ostroff and Kozlowski 1993] Ostroff, C., and S. Kozlowski. 1993. The role of mentoring in the information gathering processes of newcomers during early organizational socialization. *Journal of Vocational Behavior* 42: 170–183.

[Payton and White 2003] Payton, F.C., and S.D. White. 2003. Views from the field on mentoring and roles of effective networks for minority IT doctoral students. *Proceedings of the 2003 SIGMIS conference on computer personnel research: Freedom in Philadelphia—leveraging differences and diversity in the IT workforce*: 123–129.

[Perkins et al. 1989] Perkins D.N., C. Hancock, R. Hobbs, F. Martin, and R. Simmons. 1989. Conditions of learning in novice programmers. In *Studying the Novice Programmer*, ed. E. Soloway and J. C. Spohrer, 261–280. Hillsdale, NJ: Lawrence Erlbaum Associates.

[Schein 1971] Schein, E.H. 1971. The individual, the organization and the career. *Journal of Applied Behavior Science* 7: 401–426.

[Strauss 1987] Strauss, A.L. 1987. *Qualitative Analysis for Social Scientists*. Cambridge, UK: Cambridge University Press.

[Taft 2007] Taft, D.K. 2007. Programming Grads Meet a Skills Gap in the Real World. *eWeek.com*, Sept 3.

[Tomayko and Hazzan 2004] Tomayko, J.E., and O. Hazzan. 2004. *Human Aspects of Software Engineering*. Hingham, MA: Charles River Media.

## CHAPTER TWENTY-SEVEN

Mining Your Own Evidence

Kim Sebastian Herzig
Andreas Zeller

Throughout this book, you will find examples of how to gather *evidence*—evidence on the effectiveness of testing, the quality of bug reports, the role of complexity metrics, and so on. But do these findings actually apply to *your* project? The definite way to find this out is to repeat the appropriate study on your data, in your environment. This way, you will not only gather lots of insight into your own project; you will also experience the joys of experimental research. Unfortunately, you may also encounter the downside: empirical studies can be very expensive, in particular if they involve experiments with developers.

Fortunately, there is a relatively inexpensive way to gather lots of evidence about your project. *Software archives,* such as version or bug repositories, record much of the activity around your product, in terms of problems occurring, changes made, and problems fixed. By *mining* these archives automatically, you can obtain lots of initial evidence about your product—evidence that already is worthy in itself, but which may also pave the path toward further experiments and further insights. In this chapter, we give a hands-on tutorial into mining software archives, covering both the basic technical steps and possible pitfalls that you may encounter on the way.

What Is There to Mine?

During software development, programmers routinely produce and collect lots of data, all of which can be accessed and analyzed automatically:

- The *source code* for your product. This is the most important input to your analysis, as it provides you with *locations* (files, units, classes, components, etc.) that can be associated with various product or process factors.

- Collecting data on the execution of the software provides you with *profiles*, telling you which parts are frequently used and which parts are not.

- Your product may come with additional documentation, such as *design documents* or *requirements documents*; these may also provide important features that explain why code looks the way it does.

- The resulting software can be analyzed statically, providing features such as *complexity metrics* or *dependencies*.

- *Version archives* record the changes made to the product, including who, when, where, and why. Version archives can tell a lot about a project's history, if the stored changes are all logically separated and if the stored *rationales* are used in a systematic and consistent manner.

- To map problems to locations, it is important to have a *problem database* that describes all the problems that ever occurred and tracks their life cycles.

- Finally, you may have *social data*: a partitioning of developers into projects or groups, emails or other messages between developers, and even billing or effort data. With such data, you can, for instance, determine how effort maps to individual tasks or locations, or how individual groups contribute to changes—and to errors. Before you rank groups by their error density, though, keep in mind that the most difficult tasks produce the most errors. Making mistakes might be just a side effect of being assigned the most difficult tasks—which developers get by being the most experienced and trusted programmers.

From a researcher's standpoint, the advantage of accessing these data sources is that they are *unbiased*—they record changes, problems, and other events at the moment they happen and with a realistic perspective that directly reflects the activities of the developers dealing with them. On the other hand, the data also may be *noisy* and *incomplete*, which is why special steps are required before analysis.

Designing a Study

Once you have decided which data to leverage, you have to choose a *methodology*—that is, a plan on how to conduct your investigation. This very book collects a number of successful approaches and gives plenty of ideas on the investigations to pursue.

There is a caveat, though. Even though many mining and research projects follow the same basic principles, projects experience many small differences that might lead your mining efforts into a dead end. Two of these factors include the *nature of the project* and the underlying *development process*. A good example is the differences between open source software (e.g., Eclipse) and industrial software (e.g., Microsoft or SAP projects). Differences in the environments (physical and organizational) that surround the software projects engender fundamental difference in development processes. For example, in open source projects that tend to draw developers from around the world, none of them sharing the same office, pair programming or group code reviews become difficult if not impossible. Even a quick face-to-face chat about a problem requires advanced technology and must respect different time zones.

Differences in development environments and processes will have a fundamental impact on the project history and thus must be considered when mining that history. Recent research projects and replication studies mining data sets from both distributed open source projects and industry projects showed that some mining activities succeed on one type, and some on the other type [Bird et al. 2009b], [Zimmerman et al. 2009]. Many process-related metrics, such as *socio-technical network metrics* [Bird et al. 2009b] or metrics related to *organizational structure* [Nagappan et al. 2008], depend heavily on the software development process in place, and show very different results on open source software.

Thus we recommend that before designing your own study, your first task should be to *replicate* a study that has already shown valid results. If you come up with good or even better results, all is fine. But if your results are different, you need to investigate what makes them different—and this difference will also impact the design of your own studies.

A Mining Primer

Let us now describe how to retrieve actual historic data. Each software repository is different, and so are the mining steps necessary to extract the relevant data points. But most mining tools and setups share a common procedure. Here we give a step-by-step guide to mining a software repository on a real-world example: the IBM Eclipse project. Eclipse is open source software and has been a subject of many empirical software engineering research projects.

Thus, Eclipse is an ideal candidate for a hands-on example. But even though it is an open source project that exposes all the data about bugs and their fixes, the unstructured ways in which this information was collected makes it an interesting and challenging case study.

Historic data for a software project is preserved through many different activities in many different systems (e.g., version control, bug tracking systems, email messages, etc.). In order to extract and learn from the history of a software project, you have to access these resources. For many open source systems such as Eclipse, most of these resources are publicly available and can be accessed easily.

Following the steps detailed in the following sections, we will extract and link Eclipse history, process data, and bug data that can be used for various kinds of defect prediction or process analysis. Normally, the results get stored in persistent data storage systems (e.g., relational databases) that allow further analysis steps and manual inspection. In the end, you will have a data set that identifies bug-inducing code changes and allows you to see how many bugs were fixed and in which source code file.

Step 1: Determining Which Data to Use

Eclipse stores useful information about coding problems and fixes in its version control system (CVS) and bug tracking system (Bugzilla). A wealth of related information is probably buried in email archives, but its lack of structure leaves it unfeasible for statistical analysis. As we'll see, there are plenty of difficulties just mining the version control and bug tracking systems.

In our Eclipse example, we'll store the source code change history and the bug reports in a MySQL database. To do so, we have to decide which information from each resource is relevant for your purposes and how we want to link information extracted from both repositories to each other. Our goal is to identify bug-inducing source code changes and map defects to files. For this purpose, we need all the information we can get about source code transactions (especially their commit messages) and all the information about bug reports that can help us identify 1) in which source code transaction this bug was fixed and 2) which files were changed. Figure 27-1 shows an example database table layout that allows you to link source code change transactions (`rcs_transaction`) to source code file revisions (`rcs_revision`) as well as bug reports (`bts_report`).

In order to map bugs to files, we need to find a way of linking bug reports to source code transactions. Since the two Eclipse data sources are not connected to each other (unlike more modern programming environments, such as IBM's Jazz [Frost 2007], which do connect the bug report system and version control system), we have to rely on developer input. The only two locations that allow developer input are *commit messages* (messages that can be attached to a transaction when checking in source code changes) and the description/discussion body of the bug reports. Both types of data must be extracted.

To map defects to files, we have to keep track of which files were changed in which transactions. Combining this information with the bug-to-transaction mapping allows you to map bugs to files.

Version repositories maintain *change logs* for each set of simultaneously applied source code changes (*transactions*). These change logs contain information about the author, the time of the change, the files that changed, how these files changed, and the commit messages of the transaction. Thus, parsing these change logs will provide the information we need about all source code changes ever applied to the project.

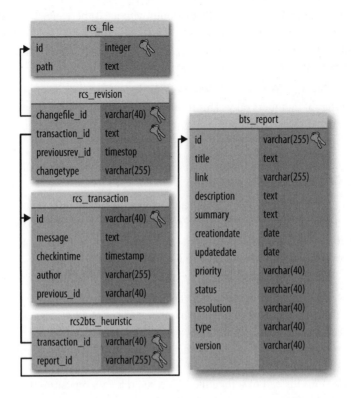

FIGURE 27-1. Database layout for bug, transaction, and file data. The arrows indicate foreign keys and join points.

Step 2: Data Retrieval

To ensure the continued availability of the version control and bug tracking information, and to allow fast access to the data, you should make local copies.

A prepared dump of the version control system can be downloaded from the Eclipse website.* This dump can be used to create a local copy of the complete version control system, including all source code files and all source code changes ever applied to Eclipse.

Getting a local copy of the bug tracking system is more complicated. Parsing the bug reports requires a machine-readable and well-defined data format. Bugzilla meets these requirements by allowing you to export each bug report as an XML document. Triggering this functionality using a simple script, you can download all bug reports as XML documents to the local hard disk for later processing.

* http://archive.eclipse.org/arch/

The following Bash script downloads all Eclipse bugs with an ID between 1 and 300,000 as XML documents to a temporary directory:

```
for i in {0..300000}; do curl -o /tmp/eclipse_bug_${i}.xml
"https://bugs.eclipse.org/bugs/show_bug.cgi?ctype=xml&id=${i}"; done
```

One caveat: Some bug IDs are not valid, because some bug reports got deleted while other bug reports are for internal members only. This means some of the downloaded XML documents will contain an error message instead of a bug report. Keep this in mind when parsing the bug reports.

Step 3: Data Conversion (Optional)

Data mining requires you not only to download and process that data, but also to understand many of its characteristics in advance. Whenever you mine a repository, keep in mind the goal: extracting project and process data. So the data you are about to process should fit your prerequisites and conform to your assumptions.

In our case, the CVS version control system used by Eclipse does not have the same information basis as Bugzilla bug reports. A bug report encapsulates all information relevant for a single transaction (fixing a bug). CVS, on the other hand, maintains change logs corresponding to source files instead of transactions. So in the case of Eclipse, it makes sense to transform one of the two data resources to match the other's data representation. For this purpose, you should convert the CVS repository to a repository format such as Subversion (SVN) that maintains logfiles for transactions instead of source files. To convert a CVS repository to an SVN repository, you can use the *cvs2svn* tool,[†] which converts large CVS repositories into SVN repositories with 100% data preservation (including repositories for GCC, Mozilla, FreeBSD, KDE, GNOME, and other projects).

The following command will turn the Eclipse CVS into an SVN repository:

```
cvs2svn --svnrepos path_to_new_svn_repo --include-empty-directories --no-prune
--no-cross-branch-commits --retain-conflict-attic-files --verbose
```

Be aware that this conversion step takes some time (depending on the size of the CVS repository you are converting). To ensure that the process will actually succeed without errors, it is highly recommended to run *cvs2svn* with the --dry-run option before doing the actual conversion. This option will not convert any data but instead will simulate the conversion process and show you what a real run would do.

---

† *http://cvs2svn.tigris.org/*

Step 4: Data Extraction

Now that you have the data resources ready at your local hard disk and in a shape that fits your process prerequisites, you can process the data. Processing involves extracting, filtering, and storing the resources' contents in a persistent and human-readable format.

In this step we create XML files containing the data from the version control system and bug database. As we explained earlier, logs in the Eclipse version control system contain information on transactions. Use a native SVN command to extract change logs as XML documents:

```
svn log --xml --verbose
```

You can parse these XML documents, along with the bug reports we downloaded in Step 2, using your preferred XML parsing framework. Then, store the information in the appropriate fields of your database (see Figure 27-1).

Step 5: Parsing the Bug Reports

The next step is to parse the bug reports saved to the local hard disk in Step 2: Data Retrieval. It is important to fill all the fields of the bts_report table, especially ID, title, description, creationDate, status, resolution, and version. These fields can be used to link bug reports to version control transactions.

Step 6: Linking Data Sets

Now that you have extracted all information from your data resources, you can start linking these data sets together. So far, all data sources have been collected independently and without any cross-references to other data sources.

To map bugs to transactions, you have to rely on user input identifying or mentioning cross-reference candidates to other data sources. In our Eclipse example, there are two possibilities:

- When committing code changes to the version repository, the developer specified the bug number that was fixed with these changes (e.g., "Fixed bug 88352: Operation supports leaks contexts...").

- When closing a bug report, the developer mentioned the transaction ID that fixed the bug (e.g., "Fixed for Windows, svn revision 6800. Would someone double ...").

To handle these situations, you have to search for potential cross-reference candidates in both the transaction commit messages and the bug report comments.

Expect to find many false positive links between bug reports and commit messages, and be prepared to keep updating your regular expressions and heuristics. Perform the searches iteratively so that you can inspect each data set manually and use the classification problems you find to refine the next iteration.

Linking code changes to bug reports

The most common situation we've found is when a developer writes the ID of the fixed bug report into the commit message. Fischer et al. [Fischer et al. 2003] and Cubranic and Murphy [Cubranic and Murphy 2003] were among the first to search for references to bug databases in commit messages and to use these references to infer links from CVS archives to bug databases. Later, Sliwerski et al. refined both approaches to identify fix-inducing changes—changes that subsequently were reflected in successful closings of bug reports [Sliwerski et al. 2005]. Following their approach, we have to perform the following steps:

1. Select all commit messages that might contain keywords (such as fix, issue, bug, solved, etc.) indicating that the transaction actually fixed a bug. Such messages are likely to contain cross-references.

2. In all keyword-matching commit messages, search for each of the following regular expressions:[‡]

   - bug[# \t]*[0-9]+
   - pr[# \t]*[0-9]+
   - show_bug\.cgi\?id=[0-9]+ or \[[0-9]+\]

Every match is a potential link to a bug. This approach, however, might give you a lot of false positives (e.g., "Updated copyrights to 2004"). To validate a link, you have to consider information from the linked bug reports. Since you are interested only in fix-inducing changes, you can concentrate on links to bug reports with all of the following characteristics:

- A status marked as "closed"
- A resolution field set to "fixed"
- A resolution date close to the commit date of the commit message candidate (for instance, a time difference of less than five days)

More link validation criteria can be checked, but these criteria typically depend on the development process of the software project and have to be adapted for each project. Also keep in mind that code changes applied within the same transactions can fix more than one bug.

Linking bug reports to code changes (optional)

Although scanning commit messages to find reference candidates suffices for many projects, others require an additional or different step. Cubranic and Murphy were among the first to infer links in the other direction, from Bugzilla to CVS archives, by relating bug activities to changes [Cubranic and Murphy 2003].

If necessary, reverse the process described in the previous step, searching for possible revision IDs and keywords (e.g., revision, transaction, patch, etc.) in comments and descriptions of bugs

---

[‡] This list is just illustrative. It is not complete.

marked as "closed" and "fixed." Then, try to map these IDs to transaction IDs. Again, filter out false positives by deleting references from bug reports to revisions applied after the bug was marked as fixed. Keep in mind that a bug report might reference multiple transactions. Some of them might be earlier, incomplete fixes. Other transactions might have been reverted again. The temporal order in which these references were added might matter.

Step 6: Checking for Missing Links

When you link bug reports to changes and vice versa, you will find that a number of bug reports and changes remain unlinked—that is, you have bug reports that were fixed without your finding any associated change, and you have transactions in the version control repository without a recorded associated problem. Having such missing links is part of the noise you get during mining. You can be sure you've missed some links, but that's hard to fix without lots of manual classification. Be aware, though, that missing links might not be random, but actually correlated with some confounding factor. For instance, experienced developers may have more discipline in associating changes with bug reports, so the subset of changes you are looking at may be biased with respect to developer experience.

Recently, Bird et al. showed that biased data sets lead to serious problems, especially for bug prediction models and hypothesis tests regarding bug data [Bird et al. 2009a]. Manual inspection of the data sets does not solve this issue, but can be used to detect coarse-grained bias.

Step 7: Mapping Bugs to Files

So far you have mapped bugs to revision control transactions. Next, you have to assign bugs to source code files. Luckily, this step is easy. Using our database layout (see Figure 27-1), you can identify which source code files have been changed in which transaction. Zimmermann et al. used a similar technique to count the distinct number of bug IDs per source code location (file) [Zimmermann et al. 2007].

Now your resulting data set contains a count of bugs fixed in each source code file as a quality measurement for that file. This data can now be related to other factors, such as the number of changes in the file or its code complexity metrics.

Figure 27-2 for instance, shows the distribution of fixed bugs in Eclipse 3.1 files with more than 300 lines changed, established from the Eclipse repositories using the steps described in this chapter.§ Each square in the figure represents a source file shipped within Eclipse 3.1. All files within the same package are grouped together. The larger a file's square, the more lines were changed since the previous release. The more white the square, the more bugs had to be fixed in the corresponding source file of Eclipse 3.1. Data like this raises lots of questions: why

§ The figure was generated using the Treemap program developed by the University of Maryland, *http://www.cs.umd.edu/hcil/treemap/*.

is it that some classes are so much more error-prone than others? Finding out the common factors, making predictions for where future bugs will be, and checking the quality of these predictors brings a lot of intriguing insights. Applying these techniques on your own project is the most exciting of all—giving you all the data at your fingertips that you need for making your next decision.

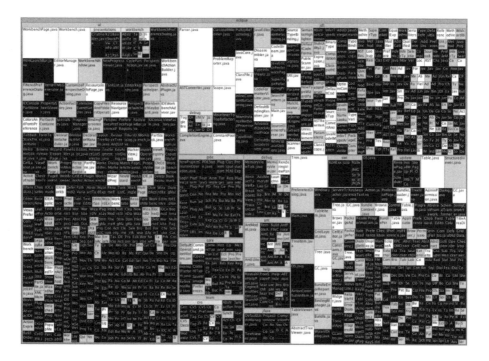

FIGURE 27-2. Changes and bugs in Eclipse packages. The bigger the rectangle (a package), the more lines were changed; the brighter a package, the more bugs occurred.

Where to Go from Here

A distribution of bugs and changes like the one in Figure 27-2 is already worthy in itself: you literally see where most activity takes place and where the most problems occur. The next interesting question is the *cause* of this distribution. As a manager, you will be able to explain many of the effects you see, particularly when it comes to extremes, such as the modules with the most bugs or the highest amount of change. You may also be surprised, though, at some effects that did not make it into the headlines: effects distributed all across your project and possibly related to some recurring causes.

In our experience so far, the problems on every project have their own specific causes that are related to changes and bugs (which of course motivates the need for mining project histories). Typical starting points for investigation include:

The problem domain of the component

Analyzing the APIs that components use, Schröter et al. showed that Eclipse internal compiler code is seven times as error-prone as Eclipse GUI components [Schröter et al. 2006]. Evidence like this can help not only to identify critical areas of your application but can also be used to predict the quality of new components without any history, just by looking at their used APIs.

The complexity of the source code

Complicated tasks increase the likelihood of mistakes. The more complex source code is, the more difficult it is to make changes that are defect-free. There are many ways to define code complexity and many research studies showing that code complexity can indeed be an excellent defect predictor [Nagappan et al. 2006b], [Zimmermann et al. 2007].

The change history of the component

Components that were recently (or massively) changed carry a higher risk of bugs. Hassan and Holt introduced a caching algorithm for fault-prone modules that highlight the 10 most susceptible subsystems to contain a bug [Hassan and Hold 2005]. To build this top-10 list, the authors use only history information that reveals the modules that were most frequently modified, most recently modified, most frequently fixed, and most recently fixed. As a manager or developer, you can use tools like the "top-10 list" to focus your testing resources on particular modules that are most likely to fail.

The test history of the component

The more tested a program, the less likely its risk to contain a bug. Hutchins et al. showed that test sets with high coverage levels (more than 90%) show better fault detection than randomly chosen test sets of the same size [Hutchins et al. 1994]. Later, Nagappan et al. used coverage data sets to build successful defect prediction models [Nagappan et al. 2006a]. So mining test data sets and system health information in your software project can certainly help to detect risky but not yet well-tested parts of your source code.

The people involved in component development

Humans write software, and humans tend to err. Therefore, the authors of source code are a consideration in determining the quality of a component. At Microsoft, Nagappan et al. investigated whether components written by distributed development teams are more risky than local developed components [Nagappan et al. 2008]. Surprisingly, it does not make a significant difference. But as Ekanayake et al. showed, the number of authors editing the same source code file and the number of defects they fixed influence the defect prediction quality [Ekanayake et al. 2009].

By combining these data sources, you will find correlations, but not all of these translate into causations. As we tried to relate the bug density in Eclipse to individual developers, for instance, we found that Erich Gamma, the head architect, appeared among the developers with the highest bug density overall. As we asked him how this could be, Gamma replied: "There are always problems that you cannot solve, so you pass them on to your supervisor, who is supposed to be better than you. Some problems go up the entire hierarchy—to the group leader, to the department head, and so on, and nobody wants to touch them, until they end up on my desk. And as I have no one to delegate them to, I have to take care of them. In fact, most of what I do all day is really risky."

With this in mind, you are now ready to mine for correlations—and to turn these into causations by providing a theory on how specific effects in your product come to be. Be aware, though, that every bit of evidence thus gained raises more questions—and the need for more evidence. An infrastructure for automated mining will make it easy for you to obtain this evidence and to support your decisions with real information.

Acknowledgments

Many of the essential mining techniques described in this chapter were pioneered together with Peter Weißgerber and Thomas Zimmermann [Zimmermann et al. 2004], who deserve our eternal gratitude. Yana Mileva, Nadja Altabari, and Clemens Hammacher provided helpful comments on earlier revisions of this chapter.

References

[Bird et al. 2009a] Bird, C., A. Bachmann, E. Aune, J. Duffy, A. Bernstein, V. Filkov, and P. Devanbu. 2009. Fair and Balanced? Bias in Bug-Fix Datasets. *Proceedings of the Seventh Joint Meeting of the European Software Engineering Conference and the ACM SIGSOFT Symposium on the Foundations of Software Engineering*: 121–130.

[Bird et al. 2009b] Bird, C., N. Nagappan, H. Gall, B. Murphy, and P. Devanbu. 2009. Putting it all together: Using socio-technical networks to predict failures. *Proceedings of the 20th International Symposium on Software Reliability Engineering*: 109–119.

[Cubranic and Murphy 2003] Cubranic, D., and G. C. Murphy. 2003. Hipikat: Recommending pertinent software development artifacts. *Proceedings of the 25th International Conference on Software Engineering*: 408–418.

[Ekanayake et al. 2009] Ekanayake, J., J. Tappolet, H. Gall, and A. Bernstein. 2009. Tracking concept drift of software projects using defect prediction quality. *Proceedings of the 2009 6th IEEE International Working Conference on Mining Software Repositories*: 51–60.

[Fischer et al. 2003] Fischer, M., M. Pinzger, and H. Gall. 2003. Populating a release history database from version control and bug tracking systems. *Proceedings of the International Conference on Software Maintenance*: 23.

[Frost 2007] Frost, R. 2007. Jazz and the Eclipse Way of Collaboration. *IEEE Software* 24(6): 114–117.

[Hassan and Hold 2005] Hassan, A., and R. Hold. 2005. The Top Ten List: Dynamic Fault Prediction. *Proceedings of the 21st IEEE International Conference on Software Maintenance*: 263–272.

[Hutchins et al. 1994] Hutchins, M., H. Forster, T. Goradia, and T. Ostrand. 1994. Experiments of the effectiveness of dataflow- and control flow-based test adequacy criteria. *Proceedings of International Conference on Software Engineering*: 191–200.

[Nagappan et al. 2006a] Nagappan, N., T. Ball, and B. Murphy. 2006. Using Historical In-Process and Product Metrics for Early Estimation of Software Failures. *Proceedings of the 17th International Symposium on Software Reliability Engineering*: 62–74.

[Nagappan et al. 2006b] Nagappan, N., T. Ball, and A. Zeller. 2006. Mining metrics to predict component failures. *Proceedings of the 28th International Conference on Software Engineering*: 452–461.

[Nagappan et al. 2008] Nagappan, N., B. Murphy, and V. Basili. 2008. The influence of organizational structure on software quality: An empirical case study. *Proceedings of the 30th International Conference on Software Engineering*: 521–530.

[Schröter et al. 2006] Schröter, A., T. Zimmermann, and Andreas Zeller. 2006. Predicting component failures at design time. *Proceedings of the 2006 ACM/IEEE International Symposium on Empirical Software Engineering*: 18–27.

[Sliwerski et al. 2005] Sliwerski, J., T. Zimmermann, and A. Zeller. 2005. When do changes induce fixes? *Proceedings of the 2005 International Workshop on Mining Software Repositories*: 1–5.

[Zimmermann et al. 2004] Zimmermann, T., and P. Weißgerber. 2004. Preprocessing CVS Data for Fine-Grained Analysis. *Proceedings of the First International Workshop on Mining Software Repositories*: 2–6.

[Zimmermann et al. 2007] Zimmermann, T., R. Premraj, and A. Zeller. 2007. Predicting defects for Eclipse. *Proceedings of the Third International Workshop on Predictor Models in Software Engineering*: 9.

[Zimmerman et al. 2009] Zimmermann, T., N. Nagappan, H. Gall, E. Giger, and B. Murphy. 2009. Cross-project defect prediction: A large scale experiment on data vs. domain vs. process. *Proceedings of the 7th joint meeting of the European software engineering conference and the ACM SIGSOFT symposium on the foundations of software engineering*: 91–100.

## CHAPTER TWENTY-EIGHT

Copy-Paste as a Principled Engineering Tool

Michael Godfrey
Cory Kapser

⟨*Ctrl-C*⟩ ⟨*Ctrl-V*⟩ Every software developer knows that copy-paste—aka *code cloning*—is a bad habit, yet we all do it. We might wince, knowing that we're being a little lazy, but we usually manage to convince ourselves that the programmatic ends justify the means. After all, a lot of the time it's simply quicker to copy and paste a piece of existing code that does something similar to what we want, and then carefully clean things up afterwards.

Yet the act often makes us feel uneasy. We know that good intentions don't always manifest themselves as concrete actions and, like the proverbial potato chip, we know that it can be hard to stop after just one. And we suspect that by taking the easy way out, we've perched our project on a slippery slope that can lead to decaying design and inconsistent maintenance. Certainly, most of the expert advice out there says that code cloning is bad news, full stop. But how bad is it? And how do we know?

So we may pause to reflect, and perhaps ask ourselves some questions: just how harmful a practice is code duplication anyway? Does it lead to demonstrable maintenance problems in the long run? What motivates its use in the first place? Are there different reasons that developers duplicate code, and might some uses be more defensible than others? Is code duplication ever a good idea? Can code duplication be managed successfully, and if so at what cost?

These are good questions, worthy of some study. As software engineering researchers, we had noticed that almost every talk we attended on this topic began with the stated premise that code cloning was uniformly a bad practice. But we were pretty sure, based on our own anecdotal experiences, that this wasn't the case. So we decided to investigate using state of the art software clone detection tools and perform some qualitative and quantitative studies on large open source systems—and we were surprised by what we found out.

An Example of Code Cloning

Before we go further, we should probably explore the problem space a little. To that end, let's consider the following two functions that are taken from version 1.6.3 of the Gnumeric source code base:

```
// Both functions are from the file py-gnumeric.c, version 1.6.3
static PyObject *
py_new_Range_object (GnmRange const *range) {
        py_Range_object *self;
        self = PyObject_NEW (py_Range_object, &py_Range_object_type);
        if (self == NULL) {
                return NULL;
        }
        self->range = *range;
        return (PyObject *) self;
}

static PyObject *
py_new_RangeRef_object (const GnmRangeRef *range_ref){
        py_RangeRef_object *self;
        self = PyObject_NEW py_RangeRef_object, &py_RangeRef_object_type);
        if (self == NULL) {
                return NULL;
        }
        self->range_ref = *range_ref;
        return (PyObject *) self;
}
```

At first glance, it seems pretty obvious that one of these functions has been cloned from the other (or that both have been cloned from a third source), as they are almost token-for-token identical. Indeed, a little investigation reveals that these are boilerplate designs for dealing with the instantiation of Python objects from within the main C codebase. The functions differ in two ways, one obvious and one more subtle. The obvious difference is that some of the identifiers are slight variations on each other: each identifier that has the suffix Range in the first function has the suffix RangeRef in the second. The more subtle difference concerns the parameters: in the first function, the parameter is a constant pointer to an object (here, an instance of a C struct), whereas in the second it is a pointer to a constant object. The latter is a common programming idiom when an object is being passed around, but we want to be sure that it will not be changed by anyone who sees it. The former, on the other hand, promises that the pointer parameter will not be changed, but makes no guarantees about the object it points to. To an experienced C programmer, this seems like a mistake; changes to parameters do not percolate back to the calling environment anyway, so there is little point in making the parameter a const. Probably the const is in the wrong place in the parameter declaration.

So what happened here? Our guess is that the first function is the original and the second is a clone, based on the assumption that developers are more likely to add a suffix to an identifier than to delete one. Furthermore, we suspect that the parameter bug was noticed and fixed in the clone but wasn't backported to the original. If this is indeed what has happened, then it's an example of what's called *inconsistent maintenance*: bugs are fixed in some clones, but not in others. It's one of the main perceived problems with the use of code cloning.

The other major objection to the use of cloning is that it degrades the design of the system over time. Awkward, verbose designs lead to the accumulation of cruft and obscure the original intent of the code, right? Wouldn't it be better to abstract the commonalities to a single place in the codebase and use parameterization? Or in the case of object-oriented languages, wouldn't it be better to use some combination of inheritance and generics to achieve a more elegant design?

In the previous example, it's hard to be sure what the "right" design is without a more detailed understanding of the full codebase. It certainly looks a little awkward as it is, but would a parameterized solution look any better? Can over-abstraction lead to hard-to-understand code and subsequent maintenance problems? These are more good questions.

Detecting Clones in Software

The problem of detecting code clones is an interesting one technically; if an existing code fragment is duplicated and then changed to fit a new purpose, how can you recognize this with an automated tool? If all code clones were verbatim copies that were never subsequently altered—and some clones do fit this description—then code clone detection would be pretty easy. However, usually clones are adapted for new uses: existing lines are changed or removed, and new code may be added. Thus, it's probably a good idea to pause at this point and ask the question: just what is a software clone?

Well, first we should note that almost all clone detection techniques actually measure *similarity* of code chunks. That is, we typically don't have access to logs that record actual copy-paste edit events; we just infer they happened if the similarity measures are within a given threshold.

Second, there is no consensus on what similarity means concretely or what thresholds are reasonable. (Ira Baxter, a researcher in the community, likes to say, "Software clones are segments of code that are similar…according to some definition of similarity.") Detection tools use a wide variety of techniques. Some tools treat programs as a sequence of character strings, and perform textual comparisons. Other tools compare token streams, abstract syntax trees (ASTs), and program dependence graphs (PDGs). Some compute metrics or compare lightweight semantic models of program components. And more and more tools use hybrid approaches, combining computationally cheap techniques applied widely with more expensive techniques applied narrowly.

Although having a wide range of techniques to attack this problem makes for an interesting research field, in practice the working definition of what exactly a clone is depends strongly on the tool that is used. For example, simple string comparisons are unable to account for a change in identifier names. Consequently, two code segments that are considered to be clones by one tool may not be by a different tool. And even when experts sit together in the same room and examine code manually, there's often no clear consensus as to how similar code segments must be to be considered as clones [Kapser et al. 2007]. Needless to say, this lack of agreement hinders progress because there's no "gold standard" or accepted benchmark, and so it is hard to know just how good your results are or to evaluate tools against each other.

That said, there has been some progress in clarifying the problem domain. Bellon et al. have created a categorization scheme for software clones that has been widely embraced by the community [Bellon 2007]:

Type 1
> Two chunks of code have identical text (possibly ignoring differences in comments and white space formatting).

Type 2
> Two chunks of code have identical text, except that identifiers and explicit constant values may differ.

Type 3
> Two chunks of code have segments that are Type 2 clones, but may also have "gaps" where they do not agree.

As mentioned earlier, detecting Type 1 clones is fairly easy. All that is needed is simple lexical processing to normalize the input, after which any number of algorithms can be used to perform sequence analysis on the remaining lines of text.

Detecting Type 2 clones is not much harder. A lexical analyzer can perform simple rewriting (for example, mapping all identifiers to "id" and all string constants to "foo"), after which the resulting token stream can be analyzed as lines of plain text or using programming-language-aware analyses.

Type 3 clones—the interesting ones—are harder because they require sensible threshold values: how long must the matching contiguous chunks be, and how long can the gaps between them be? Given suitably loose thresholds, any two chunks of code can be considered to be Type 3 clones!

And not all clone detection tools map neatly to Bellon et al.'s definition. Metrics-based detection, for example, does not explicitly model program structure, but rather blends structural and semantic information of program fragments into sets of numbers and compares the numbers.

So let's take for granted that, at least for the moment, there's no authoritative answer to the question, "Just how much cloning is there in my software system?" This doesn't mean we have to pack up and go home. Our previous experience made us pretty confident that we were finding a good percentage of the clones that were out there. So we decided to use a "best effort" approach with state-of-the-art detection techniques, and see where that led us.

Investigating the Practice of Code Cloning

The unspoken and largely unchallenged presumption among software engineers is that code cloning is a bad thing. Always. OK, maybe you can cheat a little in the short term, but in the long term, it's a bad idea. In fact, Kent Beck says precisely this in his chapter on "code smells" in Fowler's *Refactoring*:

> Number one in the stink parade is duplicated code. If you see the same code structure in more than one place, you can be sure that your program will be better if you find a way to unify them.

Our experience and intuition said this was too simplistic a view. For example, our colleague Jim Cordy reminded us that the engineering view of using existing solutions was pretty different: in languages such as FORTRAN and COBOL, where the syntax is awkward and the ability to form high-level abstractions is limited, existing solutions are often treated as tools to be reused and adapted for new situations. (This sounds like what a library is for, but often these kinds of solutions can't be packaged up so neatly to make a library.)

So we decided to go in a different direction: what are the characteristics of code cloning in industrial software systems? What patterns exist? Can we identify them using static analysis? Can we make judgment calls about when cloning might be a reasonable, and even advantageous, design decision? Armed with knowledge and empirical studies, can we use code duplication as a principled engineering tool?

We set out to create a catalog of cloning patterns that would be informed by the work of our colleagues as well as our own previous explorations in code clone detection and analysis. We devised a template listing for the patterns that included:

- The *name* of the pattern
- A description of the perceived *motivation* of the programmers to create the clone in the first place

- A list of the *advantages* and *disadvantages*

- A description of the *management and long-term maintenance issues* that might need to be addressed subsequently by developers

- A description of the *structural manifestations* of the clone pattern with a code base (e.g., how it might be recognized by a tool)

- A set of *known examples* of the pattern

We ended up identifying three broad but distinct categories of cloning: *forking, templating,* and *customizing*. Within each, we further identified several cloning patterns. We'll now give you an overview of these categories and patterns, but for more details, you might want to read our paper on the subject [Kapser and Godfrey 2008].

Forking

Forking occurs when developers want to springboard the development of similar solutions within different contexts. The original code is typically copied to new source files, and then the variants are maintained independently, although probably with some coordination between the development teams. Forking helps to protect the stability of the system by forcing variation points to the fringes, away from the core components. In this way, hardware or platform variants interact with the rest of the system through a kind of virtualization layer, and experimental features can be tested with relatively little risk to the main system. Forking is a good strategy when variants need to evolve independently, especially if the long-term evolution of the variants is unclear.

We identified three cloning patterns that fit into the category of forking:

Hardware variation

This can occur when a new piece of hardware is released that bears a strong semantic resemblance to a previous version, yet is different enough to require special handling. For example, a single device driver in the Linux operating system may combine support for several different hardware versions of a SCSI card. When a new card is released that is similar enough to be able to take advantage of some of the functionality in an existing driver, a new driver may be created by cloning some of the existing code. Since the drivers are maintained independently, new code is isolated from older, working code, minimizing risk to backward compatibility for users of the older cards and drivers. Additionally, drivers are usually managed and installed as single units, so it is difficult to refactor common sub-pieces into components that can be shared.

Platform variation

This is closely related to hardware variation, and occurs when there is a natural abstraction layer for certain kinds of tasks that may be implemented differently by different target platforms or operating systems (OSes). The Apache Portable Runtime (APR) is a good example: programs use a universal API provided by the APR to access low-level services such as memory allocation and file I/O. The universal API is implemented differently—but often very similarly at the code level—by the various supported OSes. Much of the APR implementation is divided into OS-specific directories, and there is a lot of high-level cloning between the various implementation files. This allows the variants to be maintained separately, which is advantageous because subsequent changes are often OS-specific. However, there is also clearly a good deal of communication between the APR developers of the different platforms, which minimizes the risks of design drift and inconsistent maintenance.

Experimental variation

This is often employed when a system has a stable branch with many users, but developers wish to try out new features that might negatively impact either the performance or the reliability of the system. So the developers create a safe sandbox for experimenting by cloning the existing system and playing around with the new ideas there. Features that seem like good ideas can then in time be backported to the main codebase, and the clone itself may eventually be abandoned or even adopted as the new baseline. The Apache project, the Linux kernel, and many other well-known open source systems have used experimental variation extensively.

Templating

Templating is a way to directly copy behavior of existing code in the absence of appropriate abstraction mechanisms such as inheritance or generics. Templating is used when clones share a similar set of requirements, such as behavioral requirements or the use of a particular library. When these requirements change, all clones must be maintained together. For example, consider the following code from the Gnumeric version 1.6.3 codebase:

```
gnumeric_oct2bin (FunctionEvalInfo *ei, GnmValue const * const *argv)
{
        return val_to_base (ei, argv[0], argv[1],
                8, 2,
                0, GNM_const(7777777777.0),
                V2B_STRINGS_MAXLEN | V2B_STRINGS_BLANK_ZERO);
}

gnumeric_hex2bin (FunctionEvalInfo *ei, GnmValue const * const *argv)
{
        return val_to_base (ei, argv[0], argv[1],
                16, 2,
                0, GNM_const(9999999999.0),
                V2B_STRINGS_MAXLEN | V2B_STRINGS_BLANK_ZERO);
}
```

The differences between these cloned functions are in the function names and the explicit numeric constants used. Experienced C programmers will recognize this as an idiom for performing simple conversions from one data format to another. In an object-oriented programming language, inheritance and genericity can often greatly simplify the implementation of tasks like these; on the other hand, procedural languages such as C generally require the creation of a large set of these routines. This phenomenon often results in a lot of small clones: if there are m input formats and n output formats, then $m*n$ virtually identical functions must be created and maintained. Although this approach may seem mathematically inelegant and a bit of a pain to deal with, the inexpressiveness of the language may simply demand it. In such cases, the clones are an unfortunate necessity. We identified four templating patterns:

Parameterized code

This pattern is characterized by a simple and precise mapping between variants, such as in the previous code. Given a more powerful and expressive programming language, the clones could be easily merged into a single function using features such as inheritance and generics. Sometimes parameterized code is generated automatically by special-purpose tools to avoid accidental errors; this technique was used in the early days of Java's JDK, before generics had been added to the language.

Boilerplating

This pattern is related to parameterized code but is a little more general, relaxing the requirement for a precise mapping between the variants. It is particularly common in systems written in older procedural languages such as COBOL and FORTRAN. In such cases, a programmatic solution may be seen as an intellectual asset worthy of study, reuse, and emulation in other contexts. The lack of language support for user-defined abstractions often means that a solution to a relatively straightforward problem may be lengthy, complicated, and awkward. When a developer has to solve a similar problem later on, he may choose to copy and then tweak a known working solution rather than develop a new one from scratch, and in so doing avoid the mistakes of those who have gone before. Boilerplating differs from parameterized code in that the differences between clones usually cannot be easily mapped to a single solution.

API protocols

This pattern is a variation on boilerplating, where programmers invoke a library or framework with a recommended protocol for use. For example, when creating a button in a GUI using the Java SWING API, a common order of activities is to create the button, add it to a container, and assign the action listeners. Similarly, setting up a network socket in a C program within Unix requires an established set of function calls to a particular library. Documentation for libraries, and especially for frameworks, often take the form of "cookbooks," giving code exemplars that demonstrate how various common tasks can be implemented. Users are encouraged to copy these exemplars into their code and adapt them for their own needs.

Programming idioms

This pattern employs language-specific programming idioms systematically throughout a codebase to perform certain kinds of low-level tasks. For example, within the Apache codebase, there is an explicit idiom for how a pointer to a platform-specific data structure should be set in the memory pool. First, the code checks whether the data structure containing the pointer exists in the memory pool. If not, space is allocated for it and then the platform-specific pointer is assigned. This idiom exists because the APR library uses similarly defined data structures to point to platform-specific constructs such as *pthreads*. These data structures also store platform-specific data that is relevant to the concept, such as the exit status of the thread. In a slight variation on this idiom, code often checks whether a memory pool exists, and returns an error if it does not. We found at least 15 occurrences of this particular idiom within the APR subsystem.

Customizing

Customizing arises when existing code is found that solves a problem that's pretty similar to the one under consideration, but not similar enough to use the same code. Sometimes customization clones arise from pressures that are more managerial than directly technical, such as code ownership or the desire to isolate fresh code from well-tested code. In such cases, the existing code can't be modified "in place" to achieve the desired new functionality, so it is copied and adapted elsewhere within the system.

Customizing differs from forking and templating in several ways. In customization, cloning is often a starting point for a new design idea that diverges from the original over time; there may be little or no coordination between the clones in the long term. In forking, although variants tend to evolve more or less independently in the details, there is usually communication between the development groups when common external requirements change. In templating, the relationship between clones is even stronger, as it is mostly the inexpressiveness of the language or design of the system that prevents the clones being combined into a single abstraction. While templating and forking typically have the goal of maintaining the original behavior to a high degree, customization is a *reuse* of behavior, often without the requirement that the behaviors must remain strongly similar over time. The uncoordinated evolution that occurs in customization clones sets them apart from other clones in important ways: their differences can be harder to spot, the effects of the changes on behavior may be harder to understand, and the code clones may be harder to detect.

We identified two customization patterns:

Bug workarounds
> These are used when a developer finds a bug in code that she doesn't have permission to change, perhaps in a third-party library or framework. Since she can't change the original code, the developer may choose to copy and paste the offending function into a module or class that she can modify, and apply the fix there, perhaps with a guard to ensure that it is being applied correctly. In object-oriented programs, this has a particularly neat solution: it may be possible to create an inheritance descendant of the class and override the buggy method.

Replicate and specialize

This is used when a developer has found a piece of functionality that he wants to adapt to a new purpose elsewhere in the system. The duplication might be small in size and narrow in context or large and wide-ranging. LaToza et al. noted the latter case as a practice within Microsoft, which they call "clone and own" [LaToza et al. 2006]: when a product group wants specialized functionality added to code that is owned by another development group, they may decide simply to create a copy of the original for use within their system and then adapt for their own purposes. However, the implicit understanding is that they will also be responsible for its future maintenance and evolution; that is, they now own this clone (see also [Al-Ekram 2005] and [German 2009] for more on this topic).

Our Study

The categorization we have presented here came out of our experiences analyzing code clones that we found in several open source software systems, including the Linux kernel, the Apache *httpd* web server, the PostgreSQL relational database system, the Gnumeric spreadsheet application, the Columba email client, nine text editors, including vim and emacs, and eight X11 window managers. Since we had spotted each of these patterns multiple times across several systems, we were pretty confident that the patterns were "real" and not peculiar to a particular system or application domain. And although we were also pretty sure that cloning was often used as a principled practice, we lacked any concrete quantitative evidence. So we set out to examine two large open source systems from different domains, and tried to measure just how commonly cloning is used as a principled design tool, at least in those systems.

To crawl and categorize these large systems, we used our own clone detection tool, called CLICS (CLoning Interpretation and Categorization System). CLICS tokenizes the source code input and then employs suffix arrays to perform parameterized string matching; this is similar to the approach of other tools such as CCfinder. In order to detect clones where variable names might have been changed, this technique maps all identifiers to a single proxy token; that is, all identifiers will match each other, and the remaining tokens in the input stream—keywords, operators, and separators—play an enhanced role in identifying cloned segments of code. However, this approach also leads to a lot of false positives, since we lose information by ignoring the actual identifiers. Because of this, we performed aggressive filtering on the initial results to remove likely false positives. For example, `switch` statements in C-like languages often look similar at this level, even when they are doing tasks that are pretty different. In such cases where we felt that false positives were more likely, we used stronger matching criteria for the candidates to be considered clones.

If two chunks of code passed our matching criteria and automated filtering, we considered them to be a clone pair. We then looked at regions of code within source files to make better sense of the results. The precise definition of what we did can be found in our paper, but a simplified explanation goes that we broke up files into function boundaries and other "regions," such as struct definitions, and then considered the cloning relationships between code regions. We broke the previously found clones at region boundaries, and looked for regions that had cloning relationships between them; we called these Regional Groups of Clones (RGCs). The RGCs represent a coarser view of cloning within a software system, at a level that is likely to make more sense to developers. We have done most of our studies using RGCs, as they seem more intuitive to us as a measure of significant cloning. Thus, for each system, we report both the number of clone pairs found and the number of RGCs.

For our case study, we decided to use minimum thresholds of 30 and 60 consecutive matching tokens for candidates to be considered clones of each other, thresholds that were suggested by our previous work in the area.

We picked two large open source systems that we had studied before: Apache and Gnumeric. We thought they were good choices because they were both successful, long-lived systems of similar size but from different application domains. In particular, we looked at Apache version 2.2.4, which has more than 300,000 lines of code across 783 files, and Gnumeric version 1.6.3, which has more than 300,000 lines of code across 530 files.

Using the settings we described, CLICS identified 21,270 clones comprising 1,580 RGCs for Apache, and 11,400 clones comprising 3,437 RGCs for Gnumeric. That sounds like a lot, doesn't it? It *is* a lot, yet it's not at all atypical of the systems we have examined. That is, cloning is pretty common in big systems, and probably a lot more common than you might have imagined.

We randomly selected 100 RGCs from each of the systems. Then, we manually examined each one and asked the question: is this use of cloning a good idea, a bad idea, or simply unavoidable? Good clones, in our estimation, were those that represented an improvement over any alternative design that might reasonably have been picked. Bad clones were those for which we could see an obviously better design, and were likely due to developer laziness, design drift, or some other unfortunate circumstance. Unavoidable clones were those that were either too trivial to bother refactoring, or for which there was no reasonable alternative; API protocols were most commonly considered unavoidable, as they are hard to abstract and the client typically does not "own" the code anyway. We also found some false positives: 7% of the Apache RGCs and 29% of the Gnumeric RGCs that we examined manually were judged to not be real clones; consequently, the totals in the following tables don't sum to 100 for each system.

The following table summarizes what we found. We show only the 60-token results, since longer clones are more likely to be interesting and less likely to be false positives. In general, we judged about 35-40% of the clones to be good, a little less than that to be bad clones, and 15-20% to be simply unavoidable. To us, this was pretty good evidence that open source developers often use cloning as a principled development tool.

Category	Pattern	Apache: Good	Apache: Unavoidable	Apache: Harmful	Gnumeric: Good	Gnumeric: Unavoidable	Gnumeric: Harmful
Forking	Hardware variation	0	0	0	0	0	0
Forking	Platform variation	10	0	0	0	0	0
Forking	Experimental variation	4	0	0	0	0	0
Templating	Boilerplating	5	0	0	6	0	1
Templating	API protocols	0	17	0	0	8	1
Templating	Programming idioms	0	0	12	1	0	0
Templating	Parameterized code	5	1	12	10	0	24
Customizing	Bug workarounds	0	0	0	0	0	0
Customizing	Replicate and specialize	12	0	4	15	0	1
Other		3	0	8	1	0	3
Total		39	18	36	33	8	30

To be clear, we certainly don't think that this is the last word on the relative harmfulness of cloning. Our categorization is our current best effort, but certainly other categories and even organizing principles are possible. Furthermore, no empirical study is perfect. For one thing, we designed and executed the study ourselves; employing a neutral third party to make the judgment calls about harmfulness of clones would have reduced the risk of bias, but at the cost of less expertise in the decision-making process. Also, we studied only two systems, which is neither statistically significant nor representative of the innumerable possible application domains in the known universe. And both systems were open source, which may bias the results further. Finally, we have no data on, say, how cloning affects long-term code quality or if the risks of inconsistent maintenance are significant, although some studies are now beginning to appear [Krinke 2007]. But we think that the evidence that cloning can be used as a principled development tool is pretty strong.

Although you can see our paper for details about our results, it's probably worth pointing out here a couple of the interesting differences we found between the two systems. For one thing, we found that Apache made significant (and principled, in our opinion) use of forking, whereas Gnumeric did not. We didn't find this too surprising, since Apache provides a large set of fairly low-level services; it's meant to run directly on top of a variety of platforms, so the kind of virtualization provided by the Apache Portable Runtime, which we knew uses the platform variation pattern, makes good sense. Gnumeric, on the other hand, achieves portability largely by relying on the GTK widget set, which is not actually part of the Gnumeric codebase. We also noticed that Gnumeric appeared to make more use of the parameterized code pattern than

Apache; manual inspection suggested that many of the features implemented as GUI-based operations were indeed highly similar to each other, hence the cloning. Finally, it's worth pointing out that these numbers represent a random sample of 100 RGCs from each system, which amounts to only about 6% of the Apache RGCs, and about 3% of the Gnumeric RGCs.

Conclusions

We started out asking a simple question: is code cloning really such a bad idea as some people claim? Our previous experience in studying code cloning in large open source software systems led us to believe that it wasn't always a bad idea, and that indeed sometimes it was the right and proper thing to do! Inspired by some thought experiments and supported by empirical studies, we're now pretty sure that we're right. Of course, as any interesting study is wont to do, this work opens up a lot more questions than it answers: What other cloning patterns are there? What is the relative risk of one kind of cloning over another? How does the application domain affect the risks of cloning? What happens when clones migrate across application boundaries? And what kind of tool or language support might help to ease the maintenance and mitigate the risk of cloning? Well, these are certainly good questions, but we'll be happy to address them another day.

References

[Al-Ekram 2005] Al-Ekram, R., C.J. Kapser, R.C. Holt, and M.W. Godfrey. 2005. Cloning by Accident: An Empirical Study of Source Code Cloning Across Software Systems. *Proceedings of the 2005 International Symposium on Empirical Software Engineering* (ISESE-05).

[Bellon 2007] Bellon, S., R. Koschke, G. Antoniol, J. Krinke, and E. Merlo. 2007. Comparison and evaluation of clone detection tools. *IEEE Transactions on Software Engineering*, 33(9): 577-591.

[Cordy 2003] Cordy, J.R. 2003. Comprehending reality—Practical barriers to industrial adoption of software maintenance automation. *Proceedings of the 11th IEEE International Workshop on Program Comprehension*: 196-206.

[German 2009] German D.M., M. Di Penta, Y.-G. Gueheneuc, and G. Antoniol. 2009. Code siblings: Technical and legal implications of copying code between applications. *Proceedings of the 6th IEEE International Working Conference on Mining Software Repositories*: 81-90.

[Kapser and Godfrey 2008] Kapser, C.J., and M.W. Godfrey. 2008. 'Cloning considered harmful' considered harmful: Patterns of cloning in software. *Empirical Software Engineering*, 13(6).

[Kapser et al. 2007] Kapser, C.J., P. Anderson, M.W. Godfrey, R. Koschke, M. Rieger, F. van Rysselberghe, and P. Weißgerber. 2007. Subjectivity in clone judgment: Can we ever agree? *Proceedings of Dagstuhl Seminar #06301*.

[Krinke 2007] Krinke, J. 2007. A study of consistent and inconsistent changes to code clones. *Proceedings of the 14th Working Conference on Reverse Engineering.*

[LaToza et al. 2006] LaToza, T., G. Venolia, and R. DeLine. 2006. Maintaining mental models: A study of developer work habits. *Proceedings of the 28th International Conference on Software Engineering:* 492–501.

CHAPTER TWENTY-NINE

How Usable Are Your APIs?

Steven Clarke

In November 1999, I started working as a user experience researcher on the user experience team for Visual Studio. I was excited to be part of a team that designed the product I had used in my previous job. While working as a software developer at Motorola, I had always wanted to be able to make big improvements to the user experience of Visual Studio, and now I had my chance. But, although it seems obvious now, it took me almost a year to figure out that the way to improve the developer's user experience wasn't necessarily to focus exclusively on the development tools.

When I joined the team, I focused exclusively on achieving a deep understanding of the way that developers used Visual Studio. Together with my colleagues, we spent countless hours observing the experiences developers had creating new projects in Visual Studio, adding new classes to existing C++ projects, debugging web services, and many other experiences. We learned a great deal of useful information that enabled us to better understand our customers and how to apply that understanding to designing and building a great development tool.

But there was something missing. Although the developers' experience with the development tool was getting better all the time, the overall developer experience wasn't improving to the same extent. We needed to change focus. Instead of focusing on things that developers rarely do (how often do you create a new project compared to everything else that you do?), we needed to focus on the things that developers often do. And that is reading, writing, and debugging code that uses many different APIs. So we started the long journey of measuring and improving the user experience of the class libraries and APIs that developers use.

We didn't get it right on the first try. But through perseverance and a strong desire to improve, we managed to achieve a good understanding of what it means for an API to be considered usable. We learned many lessons along the way, some of which fundamentally questioned our assumptions about how developers write code. In this chapter I share those stories and the journey we took.

Why Is It Important to Study API Usability?

Unlike graphical user interfaces, developers don't interact with APIs in a direct manipulation style through widgets or UI controls. Instead, the developer types some text into a text editor and then, some time later, compiles and runs the program. The developers don't interact directly with the API, but rather interact directly with the tools they use to write and run the code. Obviously the usability of these tools will have a great impact on the developer's ability to write and run code that uses the API.

But is it OK to stop there? What if, in an ideal world, the tools were the perfect tools for a developer? Would the experience that the developer has writing and running code that uses an API also be perfect? Let's consider the impact a badly designed API has on a developer trying to use it, even with the ideal set of tools.

APIs are supposed to increase a developer's productivity by providing components that perform common tasks. Indeed, many times a developer must use an API to accomplish some task because doing so is the only way to access encapsulated system functionality that can't be implemented from scratch. Even when the operations can be executed without the special privileges to reach into hidden parts of the system, using the API saves the developers the time and effort required to create their own implementations of these components. Unfortunately, when an API is badly designed, it can be difficult to determine whether the time saved in using the API is worth the investment of effort in using it.

Alan Blackwell presented a model for describing how to determine whether the investment in programming a custom solution instead of using a predefined API is worth the effort [Blackwell 2002]. In the model, the developer estimates the cognitive cost of using the API as well as the cost of figuring out how to use the API. He then weighs these costs against the payoff, the potential savings in time and effort that he will accrue by using the API. The model takes into account the possibility that no such payoff will result.

To perform such an analysis, the developer uses cues in the API design such as class names, method names, and documentation to estimate the cost involved. Particular design patterns employed in the API might be recognized by the developer, and these might help him better understand how to use the API. The developer may have had experience with other parts of the API, which might suggest a particular approach to take. Additionally, the developer's own understanding of the domain in which he is working provides another perspective on the API. The combination of API cues, design patterns, prior experience with the API, and domain understanding helps the developer estimate the effort involved to implement a solution. From this, he can decide whether or not to use the API.

However, many things can prevent the developer from making an accurate estimate of the effort required:

- Class names and documentation obviously can be misleading and inaccurate. They can suggest that the API behaves in one way, even if it actually behaves in another. Martin Robillard indicated that one of the biggest obstacles to learning an API is the lack of good resources that describe the API and how it works [Robillard 2009].

- Another common problem with names is that they can have multiple meanings. Determining the specific meaning often requires an understanding first of the conceptual model underlying the design of the API.

- Prior experience with other parts of the API might not indicate how other parts of the API will work, particularly if design guidelines have not been followed consistently throughout the design.

- The way that the developer thinks about the domain may well be very different from the way that the API represents the domain.

Unfortunately, the developer can rarely tell right away that an API is inconsistent, has poorly named classes and methods, or represents the domain differently from the way he expects. A big problem in estimating the costs involved in using an API is that the developer often has to go through the effort of creating and running a small program that uses the API before he can estimate the costs involved in creating and running a larger program that uses the API. Only once he has started writing some code that uses the API do all the idiosyncrasies and quirks in the API's design become apparent.

Crucially, this effort is an added burden to the effort the developer had already estimated he would spend in using the API, and can quickly exceed the estimated costs of implementing a custom solution. Thus, developers may feel that instead of increasing their productivity, the API has actually made them less productive.

Hence the explosion of online forums, websites, and blogs devoted to helping developers understand the costs involved in using an API. Sites such as StackOverflow.com allow the developer to post questions and read answers about performing specific tasks with an API.

The end result is that developers often can't figure out how to use the API, and instead of writing code and being productive, they end up spending their time browsing online forums, posting questions and reading answers. Their self-esteem takes a hit. The developer feels that all she is doing is repeatedly crafting search queries for online forums and copying and pasting code she finds online. It doesn't really feel like she is "programming" anymore.

Even perfect tools can't compensate for a badly designed API. Tools can help developers write and run code, but a lot of the effort in using a badly designed API is cognitive effort. The developers have to think about the best way to translate their intentions into a particular incantation of different classes and methods. Debuggers and other such analysis tools can help the developers recognize more quickly that there is a mismatch between the way that they understood or expected the API to work and the way that it actually works. But the developers still need to process the information from the tools. And the more mismatches that occur between the API and the developers' expectations, the more mental processing the developers need to do to overcome them.

In contrast, a well-designed API allows developers to make accurate estimates of the investment required to use the API. The names used in the API effectively communicate the purpose of the classes and methods to the developers. The classes and methods in the API map well to the classes and methods that the developers expect to find in the API. The way that these classes and methods work is consistent with the way that other parts of the API work. The developers are able to get into "the zone," and the code that they write flows naturally from their thoughts to the screen. Even if the tools that the developers use aren't optimal, they can still have a great experience with the API because the developers don't depend as much on the tools as they do when working with a badly designed API. In an ideal world, the tools really just let the developer type in and run their programs.

First Attempts at Studying API Usability

It seems obvious now that the usability of an API plays a critical part in the overall developer experience. But at the time that I joined the Visual Studio user experience team, it simply didn't occur to me.

As a developer who had used Visual Studio before joining the Visual Studio team, I was often frustrated by the tools I used. Compiler settings were difficult to find and set. Configuring library paths seemed cumbersome. These were the types of usability issues that I wanted to fix when I joined the Visual Studio user experience team.

It's not that I hadn't experienced any difficulties with the Microsoft APIs. On the contrary, some of the biggest difficulties I had faced were related to understanding how the Microsoft Foundation Classes (MFC) APIs worked. But in stark contrast to the way I responded to the tools when they didn't work as I expected them to, I blamed myself for not being able to figure out how to use MFC. Not once did I think that the problem could have been with the design of the API.

This reaction to a badly designed API can be quite common. Many developers explain away the difficulties they are having with an API by putting it down to their lack of experience with the API. If they only had enough time, they could work it out. I have heard many developers say that the problem is with them, that they aren't smart enough to figure out how to use an API.

So, even though I was part of the Visual Studio user experience team, the insight that we can study the usability of an API didn't come from me. Instead, it came from a team I was working with that was developing a brand-new API called ATL Server.

ATL Server was a C++ API for building web applications. Many of the developers, testers, and program managers working on the ATL Server API team had also worked on creating the MFC API. They had learned from their experience working on MFC that they didn't always know the best way to design the API. They knew there were some usability issues in the API that were related to design decisions they had made during the development of the API. But now that the MFC API had shipped and was being used by customers, it was too late to make significant changes, since these would run the risk of breaking customers' code. Now that the team was working on a brand-new API, the team had the opportunity to find out whether they were making the right design decisions before shipping it.

Since I was the usability engineer assigned to their team, they asked me for help. I set about trying to figure out how to study the usability of an API.

My first thought was: how could I possibly study the many different ways that the API can be used? There are many tasks that a developer could perform with this API. How could I possibly hope to study each of these? Instead, the approach I took in designing the study was to focus on the architecture of the whole API. I thought it would be important to learn whether the classes' organization made sense to developers. This would help me address the issue of scale and would allow me to measure how closely the developers' domain model for ATL Server mapped to the API model. My hope was that I would be able to identify the areas where mismatches occurred so that the ATL Server team would be able to correct the design of the API.

To that end, I set about running a card sort study on the API. In a card sort study, participants are given a stack of physical cards. A description of some concept or the name of some object (e.g., a web page, product, method) is written on each card, one name per card. Participants read each card one by one and group the cards into piles that they think are most similar. Participants can group cards according to any criteria they choose. Once all participants have created their groups, a cluster analysis is performed over the collection of groupings to measure similarities between pairs of cards. The end result of the analysis is a graph known as a *dendogram* that shows the most common groupings for each card. A card sort study seemed the most appropriate way to gather data about the developers' conceptual model.

Study Design

Fourteen experienced C++ developers participated in this study. All participants said that they developed C++ code for more than 20 hours per week at work, using Visual C++ v6.0 (the study was performed in March 2000). None of the participants had extensive experience developing for the Web. One of the objectives for ATL Server was to make it appropriate for developers who did not have significant prior experience building web applications. So the participants' lack of web development experience was fine for the purposes of this study.

Twenty-four classes were identified as being core to ATL Server and were the focus of this study. These classes are listed in Table 29-1.

TABLE 29-1. Core ATL Server classes

CStencil	CMultiPartFormParser	CWriteStreamHelper	CHtmlStencil
CISAPIExtension	CHttpRequestParams	CValidateObject	CStencilCache
CValidateContext	CHttpRequestFile	CDBSessionDataSource	CHttpResponse
TServerContext	CPersistSessionDB	CHttpRequest	CCookie
CSessionNameGenerator	CDefaultErrorProvider	CHtmlTagreplacer	CSessionStateService
CSessionState	CRequestHandlerT	CPersistSessionMem	CDllCache

Short, succinct descriptions of the functionality exposed by these classes were created by the technical writers on the team. These descriptions were typically one or two sentences long. Each description was printed onto an index card, one description per card. For example, put and get methods for setting and retrieving class member variables would map to one card containing the description "Manage variable." Common methods shared by all classes, such as constructors and destructors, were not listed.

Fifty-nine cards were prepared describing the functionality implemented by these classes. None of the cards contained the name of the class that exposed the functionality described on the card.

As an example, the CHttpRequest class exposes four main pieces of functionality. Descriptions of each of these were written onto four cards:

- Get the request data (name-value pairs, form fields) from the HTTP query.
- Initialize object with information about the current request.
- Maintain the request buffer.
- Retrieve request and server variables.

Finally, a short document presenting an overview of the ATL Server framework was provided to participants as reference material throughout the study.

Participants were given 90 minutes to use their own judgment and understanding of the framework to sort the 59 description cards into what they felt would be appropriate classes, or groups. The minimum number of groups created by any participant was eight, and the maximum was fourteen. The participant's groupings were recorded in a spreadsheet, and we performed a cluster analysis of the data.

Summary of Findings from the First Study

The cluster analysis showed that responses fell into three common groups. One group contained two descriptions, the second group contained eight descriptions, and the third contained the rest (minus two that were ungrouped).

The descriptions contained in each group had very little in common. The research team expended a good deal of time trying to determine what, if anything, could be learned from the groupings, but without success. Because the cluster analysis showed three distinct groups among the participants, we concluded that they had no conceptual model in common.

At first, the results were very disappointing. The three groups that the analysis had created weren't at all meaningful and could not be used by the team to determine any specific corrective action. It seemed like the effort involved in designing, running, and analyzing the study had been for nothing.

However, in the long run, the study taught us a very valuable lesson, totally apart from its formal outcome. The experience that we gained designing, running, and analyzing this study taught us that API usability isn't a function of the whole API. Studying the architectural design of an API doesn't tell you everything you need to know about its usability.

I had been attracted to a card sort study because I had been concerned with the issue of scale: how could I account for the many different ways that the same set of classes and methods in an API can be used together to accomplish different tasks? But after running the study, I realized that was the wrong thing to focus on. In real usage, very few developers ever concern themselves with the whole API. They concern themselves with the task they are trying to perform.

Many people can have different experiences with an API due to the different tasks that they are performing, the different backgrounds that they have, and the different work styles that they follow. Attempting to determine the usability of an API without taking all of that into account will likely end up with the inconclusive result that we reached in the card sort study.

Even if the card sort study had been able to identify a common grouping, it would not be clear what to do with such a result. If the API design had been altered so that the classes more closely mapped onto such a fictional grouping, how would we measure the impact of changing the design on the ability of developers to use the API? We would know that the API now mapped to the conceptual model that participants had, but would that be a good thing? Is it really the case that we should map the API design to the conceptual model of developers who have not used the API?

Effectively, that is the argument I had been making in designing and running the card sort study, but in retrospect the argument lacks credibility. The card sort study convinced me that if we really want to understand API usability, we need to try to study the API when it is being used by real developers solving real tasks.

Thankfully, the culture at Microsoft is such that, even having produced no useful result from my first API study, I was encouraged to continue exploring ways to measure and describe API usability.

If At First You Don't Succeed...

The next opportunity to study API usability came 18 months later. With my colleagues in the Visual Studio user experience team, I worked on a study that investigated whether experienced Visual Basic 6 developers could write .NET applications using the Visual Basic .NET language.

Visual Basic .NET is the latest version of the Visual Basic programming language, and it departs radically from earlier versions of Visual Basic, such as Visual Basic 6. Most notably, the .NET framework used to write programs in Visual Basic .NET provides similar functionality to Visual Basic 6 frameworks, but is composed of a completely different set of classes and namespaces. There are other differences as well. For example, in Visual Basic .NET, the default lower bound of every dimension of an array cannot be changed from 0 to 1 as it can be in Visual Basic 6.

Our team wanted to evaluate the experience of developers using Visual Basic .NET for the first time to perform common tasks such as writing to and reading from text files on disk. Having learned our lesson from the card sort study on the ATL Server API, we decided that in this study, we would provide participants with a specific task and observe them in our usability labs performing those tasks. We would videotape each participant and ask them to talk out loud as they were performing the task. We would then analyze each video to look for common patterns of behavior, interesting highlights, and any evidence that could help us better understand the experience that participants had with both Visual Basic .NET and the .NET framework.

Design of the Second Study

We recruited eight developers, all of whom said that they spent at least 20 hours per week writing Visual Basic 6 code at work. We asked them to use Visual Basic .NET and the .NET framework to write a program that would write to and read from text files on disk. Each participant was given two hours to complete the task. While working on the task, they were free to browse the documentation available for any of the classes in the .NET framework. Each participant tackled the task individually in the usability labs on our campus in Redmond, WA. A usability engineer was behind the one-way mirror in the usability lab to operate the video cameras and to take notes. Other than helping the participant recover from any bugs or crashes that came up with the pre-release version of Visual Studio, the usability engineer did not help the participant with any of the tasks.

Summary of Findings from the Second Study

In contrast to the results from the ATL Server card sort study, the results from this study were very enlightening. The headline result was that not one participant could complete any of the tasks successfully in the two hours given.

This was quite unexpected. We didn't think every participant would be completely successful, but we also hadn't expected such a complete bust. Our first reaction was that the participants simply had not satisfied the study recruiting profile and were in fact not experienced programmers at all. But it was clear from the video recording of each session that this was not the case. Each participant was clearly an experienced programmer who was not daunted at the prospect of picking up and using a new programming language and environment.

So what was the reason for the poor success rate? We reviewed the videos from each session in detail soon after the study. We had already reviewed each session to create highlight video clips that we distributed internally around the Visual Studio product team almost immediately after the last session had ended. These highlights showed the difficulties that participants had performing each of these tasks, so we had a few hypotheses about the reason for the difficulties.

The first hypothesis we tested was whether the documentation was to blame. This hypothesis was inspired by watching all of the participants spend most of their time in the usability lab searching and hunting through the documentation, looking for some class or method that would help them write to or read from a file on disk. At the time we ran the study (summer 2002), the documentation did not contain any code snippets for common tasks such as writing to or reading from a file on disk.

For example, the transcript of one participant browsing the documentation for the System.IO namespace is typical:

PARTICIPANT:

[Reading names of classes]

Binary reader. Buffered stream. Reads and writes....

[Pauses. Scrolls through list of classes].

So let me just...stream writer. Implements a text writer for writing characters to a stream in a particular encoding. Umm...stores an underlying string. String builder. Text...hmmm. Text reader, text writer. Represents a writer that can write a sequential series of characters. This class is abstract.

[Pause]

Ummm....

[scrolls up and down through list of classes]

So it, you know, it sounds to me like it's, you know, it's more low-level kind of stuff. Whereas I just want to create a text file. Umm.

[Points at the description of one of the classes]

Characters to a stream in a particular encoding. I'm not sure what...obviously a text writer for writing characters to a stream.

[Clicks on the link to view more details about the TextWriter class. Then looks at list of classes that derive from TextWriter]

System dot IO dot StringWriter. This seems too low-level to me to be a text writer thing but maybe I am wrong. Umm....

[scrolls through description of the TextWriter class]

Text writer is designed for character output, whereas the stream class is designed for byte input and output.

[Sigh. Clicks on link to view TextWriter members]

Probably going where no man should have gone before here.

The associated video clip is very compelling and is the one we used extensively to publicize the results of the study throughout the Visual Studio product team. Along with other critical video clips, it generated huge empathy for the customer on the part of the product team and a massive desire to figure out what was broken and how to fix it.

In another video clip, a participant is struggling with a compiler error:

PARTICIPANT:

OK. We are back to one error.

[Reads the compiler error message]

Value of system. Value of type system dot io dot filestream cannot be converted to system dot io dot streamwriter. No clue....

[pause]

Are you gonna make me suffer through this?

Since a large proportion of each participant's time was spent browsing the documentation, many people in the product team latched onto that and believed that the best way to improve the experience would be to modify the documentation. If the documentation could provide clear pointers to sample code and code snippets, developers could copy and paste those snippets into their own code.

However, we wanted to be sure that the lack of code snippets truly was the underlying cause of the problems we observed in the usability lab. Although modifying the documentation at this stage (three-quarters of the way through the project life cycle) would be a less costly fix than modifying the APIs, it would be wasted energy if it turned out to have no relationship to the underlying cause.

In order to be confident in our analysis of the problems, we needed a framework or a language upon which to base our analysis. Without such a framework, we would have difficulties explaining and justifying our analysis to a product team that was already convinced by the video clips that the problem was the documentation. We ended up using the Cognitive Dimensions framework [Green and Petre 1996].

Cognitive Dimensions

The Cognitive Dimensions framework is an approach to analyzing the usability of programming languages and, more generally, any kind of notation, such as an API. The framework consists of 13 different dimensions, each describing and measuring a specific attribute that contributes to the usability of the notation.

Each dimension is effectively a probe into the design of the notation, measuring one attribute of its usability. Each measurement can be compared to a baseline (for example, the preferences of a set of developers), and the results of the measurements and comparisons can then be used to determine any corrective action that needs to be taken to ensure that the notation maps well to the baseline.

The measurements that result from this kind of analysis aren't numerical or even necessarily absolute measurements, but are instead more like ratings on a scale, defined by each dimension. Although this may introduce some uncertainty about the accuracy of each measurement, the beauty of the framework overall is that it identifies and provides a vocabulary with which to discuss the detailed attributes of the usability of a notation. Without such a detailed vocabulary, any analysis of the usability of a notation is fraught with difficulty, because the lack of labels and definitions for each of the different attributes of the usability of a notation makes it close to impossible to reach a shared understanding of what important attributes need to be considered.

We made some modifications to the names to make the framework more relevant to API usability [Clarke and Becker 2003]. A short description of each dimension follows:

Abstraction level
> The minimum and maximum levels of abstraction exposed by the API, and the minimum and maximum levels usable by a targeted developer

Learning style
> The learning requirements posed by the API, and the learning styles available to a targeted developer

Working framework
> The size of the conceptual chunk (developer working set) needed to work effectively

Work-step unit
> How much of a programming task must or can be completed in a single step

Progressive evaluation
> To what extent partially completed code can be executed to obtain feedback on code behavior

Premature commitment
> The number of decisions that developers have to make when writing code for a given scenario and the consequences of those decisions

Penetrability
> How the API facilitates exploration, analysis, and understanding of its components, and how the targeted developers go about retrieving what is needed

API elaboration
> The extent to which the API must be adapted to meet the needs of targeted developers

API viscosity
> The barriers to change inherent in the API, and how much effort a targeted developer needs to expend to make a change

Consistency
> How much of the rest of an API can be inferred once part of it is learned

Role expressiveness
> How apparent the relationship is between each component exposed by an API and the program as a whole

Domain correspondence
> How clearly the API components map to the domain, and any special tricks that the developer needs to be aware of to accomplish some functionality

We were attracted to the framework based on claims about its ease of use. Green and Petre claim that the Cognitive Dimensions framework can be used by people without any formal training or background in cognitive psychology [Green and Petre 1996]. We believed that it was vital for the development team reviewing the results of our study to view those results in the context of a framework or language that made sense to them.

We used the framework to help describe the experience that participants had in each task. We reviewed the video recordings of each session and made video clips for each interesting event we observed. We then tagged each event with the set of specific cognitive dimensions that we believed were relevant, and reviewed the video clips in the context of the dimensions associated with them. Thus, we reviewed all the abstraction level clips together, all of the viscosity clips together, etc. This approach gave us a different perspective on the video recordings of each session. We used that perspective to develop and articulate a clearer explanation for the difficulties observed.

Crucially, we were able to use the Cognitive Dimensions framework to convince the product team that fixing the documentation alone would not suffice. Although it was necessary, our analysis told us it would not be sufficient.

The Cognitive Dimensions analysis suggested that the critical underlying problem was related to the abstraction level of the APIs used. To explain this explanation in more detail, let's consider the code snippet that a participant had to write in order to read code from a text file:

```
Imports System
Imports System.IO

Class Test
    Public Shared Sub Main()
        Try
            ' Create an instance of StreamReader to read from a file.
            Dim sr As StreamReader = New StreamReader("TestFile.txt")
            Dim line As String
            ' Read and display the lines from the file until the end
            ' of the file is reached.
            Do
                line = sr.ReadLine()
                Console.WriteLine(Line)
            Loop Until line Is Nothing
            sr.Close()
        Catch E As FileNotFoundException
            ' Let the user know what went wrong.
            Console.WriteLine("The file could not be found:")
            Console.WriteLine(E.Message)
        End Try
    End Sub
End Class
```

Writing to a file is very similar:

```
Imports System
Imports System.IO

Class Test
    Public Shared Sub Main()
        ' Create an instance of StreamWriter to write text to a file.
        Dim sw As StreamWriter = New StreamWriter("TestFile.txt")
        ' Add some text to the file.
        sw.Write("This is the ")
        sw.WriteLine("header for the file.")
        sw.WriteLine("-------------------")
        ' Arbitrary objects can also be written to the file.
        sw.Write("The date is: ")
        sw.WriteLine(DateTime.Now)
        sw.Close()
    End Sub
End Class
```

This code doesn't appear particularly complex. The `StreamReader` or `StreamWriter` constructor takes a string representing a path to a file. Then, the reader or writer is used to read from or write to the disk accordingly.

If you already know the solution to these tasks, and you watch the videos of participants struggling to write this code, it is natural to leap to the conclusion that the problem lies with the documentation not showing a code snippet for this task. After all, how could this code be made any simpler?

However, when we analyzed the video clips and the associated talking commentary provided by each participant, we knew that the problem is not the lack of code snippets. For example, reread a portion of the transcript that I quoted previously:

> PARTICIPANT:
>
> System dot IO dot StringWriter. This seems too low-level to me to be a text writer thing but maybe I am wrong. Umm....
>
> *[scrolls through description of the TextWriter class]*
>
> Text writer is designed for character output whereas the stream class is designed for byte input and output.
>
> *[Sigh. Clicks on link to view TextWriter members]*
>
> Probably going where no man should have gone before here.

When the participant says that this seems too low-level, he is referring to the abstraction level of the classes he is browsing. Instead of a very flexible, but somewhat abstract, stream-based implementation, participants expected something less abstract and more concrete. The representation of the task in the API was far removed from the way participants expected the task to be represented. Instead, participants had to change the way they thought about text files in order to recognize that the `StreamWriter` and `StreamReader` classes were the correct classes to use.

We made this same observation among the majority of the participants. Even when they were browsing the documentation for the class that would allow them to complete the task (`StreamReader` or `StreamWriter`) they would dismiss it, because it didn't map to the way they expected reading and writing to work.

So the problem wasn't so much that the documentation lacked appropriate code snippets. It was more that participants were searching for something in the documentation that didn't exist. They expected to find a concrete representation of a text file, but found only representations of file streams.

The Cognitive Dimensions framework gave us a language with which to analyze and better understand the problems we observed in the study. With this analysis, we convinced the team that the best way to fix the problem, in addition to addressing the need for better documentation, would be to design and create a new class that concretely represented the filesystem and files on disk.

Six months later, the team had designed and implemented a prototype version of this new class. The code required to complete the same tasks using this new class (FileObject) follows:

```
Dim f As New FileObject
f.Open(OpenMode.Write, "testfile.txt")
f.WriteLine("A line of text")
f.Close()
```

In this case, a file is represented by an instance of the FileObject class. The FileObject class can exist in different modes (in this case, OpenMode.Write opens the file for writing). This contrasts starkly with the earlier code examples that use different classes to represent the different modes (StreamWriter and StreamReader).

We ran a study like our previous one on the new FileObject API, using the same tasks and the same profile of participants (although not the same participants). This time the results were markedly different. Within 20 minutes and without browsing any documentation, all participants were able to complete each task.

Adapting to Different Work Styles

Our study not only helped us add useful new classes to a single (albeit important) API, but also led to a new respect and zeal for studies throughout Microsoft. The API review process that every API had to go through in order to ship with the .NET framework was updated to include an API usability process.

Although we found it very encouraging to see the increased level of interest in our way of generating usability information, it wasn't clear at the time if API usability meant something different to different developers or if it was a universally agreed upon quantity. The developers who had participated in our file I/O studies all shared the same profile: experienced Visual Basic developers who used Visual Basic at work for more than 20 hours per week. But would developers with a different profile have responded the same way?

We had a hunch that they wouldn't. The developers who had participated in the studies were representative of one of the three developer personas that we used at the time to design the Visual Studio IDE:*

Opportunistic developers
> Characterized by a habit for rapid experimentation, a task-focused approach, and extensive use of high-level, concrete components

Pragmatic developers
> Characterized by a code-focused approach and use of tools that help them focus on the robustness and correctness of the code that they write (refactoring tools, unit testing tools, etc.)

---

* For a description of how we developed these personas, see [Clarke 2007].

Systematic developers

> Characterized by a defensive approach to development and their need for a deep understanding of any technology before they start working with it

The developers who had participated in the file I/O studies were very much in the opportunistic camp. The way they used the `FileObject` class in the second study was almost a perfect example of opportunistic programming. The contrast with the more abstract classes they had to use in the first study was stark. Indeed, one of the main findings from the file I/O studies was that without such high-level concrete components, opportunistic developers are unlikely to be successful.

With the raised levels of interest in API usability, we now needed to determine what made an API usable for pragmatic and systematic developers as well.

Having developed the three personas through observations of developers during many studies that had taken place earlier, we had a large body of data we could return to. A colleague and I reviewed that data and used the cognitive dimensions to define API usability relative to each persona.

To begin with, we defined a scale for each dimension in the framework. For example, for the abstraction level, we defined a scale ranging from "Primitives" to "Aggregates."

APIs that have a primitive abstraction level expose a collection of low-level components. In order to complete a task with a primitive API, developers select a subset of these primitive components and use them together to achieve some effect.

For example, a primitive file I/O API might represent a file as a stream. To read data from the stream, the API might expose a `StreamReader` class. The developer needs to combine these classes together in order to read data from the file. For example:

```
File f = new File();
StreamReader sr = f.OpenFile("C:\test.txt");
Byte b = sr.Read();
string s = b.ToString();
f.CloseFile();
```

In such an API, developers need to figure out how to combine the primitives to achieve the effect they desire (in this case, reading from a text file).

In contrast, an aggregate API might contain a class that represents a text file and exposes all of the operations that can be performed on a text file. For example:

```
TextFile tf = new TextFile("C:\text.txt");
string s = tf.Read();
tf.Close();
```

Having defined the endpoints for each of the dimensions, we then used the evidence from our usability studies to determine the preferences of each persona with respect to each dimension.

After this determination, we reviewed the videotapes from each study and watched participants use different APIs. We knew the persona of each participant because we matched participants to our personas during our recruitment interviews. Thus, we were able to estimate persona preferences for each dimension. Although we didn't do any quantitative analysis of the events we observed in each study, we were confident that our subjective assessments of persona preferences would be reasonably accurate, given the large number of studies we were able to review. And we would often be helped by the participant's verbal commentary recorded during each session, which often made their preferences *very* clear.

As an example of the preferences we observed, we noted that most opportunistic developers seem to prefer an API with an aggregate abstraction level. Systematic developers, on the other hand, prefer the flexibility that primitive components offer. Pragmatic developers favor what we call *factored components*, which are effectively aggregate components with all the "modes" of operation factored out into different components.

We performed this analysis for each dimension until we had a profile for each persona. We then graphed out the profiles as shown in Figure 29-1.

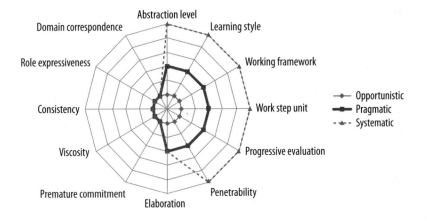

FIGURE 29-1. *Cognitive dimensions profile for each persona*

The graph makes it clear that each persona has a different view of API usability. The abstraction level preferences of opportunistic and systematic developers differ along the same lines as their learning styles, working frameworks, etc.

The graph was immediately useful at Microsoft in making clear that it would be very difficult, if not impossible, to design and build a usable API that targeted all three developer personas. This posed quite a challenge, however. Most of the teams designing and building APIs believed, correctly, that they *should* be targeting all three of the personas. If they wanted each persona to have a great experience with their API, what should they do? Should they build three versions of the API, one for each persona? The final piece of the jigsaw puzzle, scenario-based design, needed to be fit into place.

Scenario-Based Design

When we refer to an API, sometimes we mean the complete set of classes that form the interface between the application and the programmer. In other words, every class that the developer could possibly use, regardless of whether she actually uses them, is considered part of the API. When the API design teams said that they were building an API that all three personas would use, it was in this sense that they were using the term.

The experience we learned from the ATL Server card sort study was that API usability is not determined by analyzing all of the classes in an API. The complete set of classes is what the API team thinks about, but the developers think about the scenarios in which they will use the API and the experience they have during those scenarios.

We saw this in action during the file I/O study. In that study, the participants didn't concern themselves with every single class in the .NET framework. Instead, they focused on the classes that would help them complete the task. Furthermore, we observed them dismiss certain classes that weren't at the expected abstraction level. The combination of the scenario and developer expectations served to filter out which classes they considered using.

So one way to deal with the problem of designing an API for all personas is to focus on the scenarios in which the API is expected to be used and the type of developer who will perform those scenarios. In many cases, the scenario will determine the type of developer and thus the type of API that should be designed for that scenario.

For illustrative purposes only, consider a general I/O API. Some of the scenarios the API supports might be:

- Reading a line of text from a text file
- Writing binary data to a file
- Performing memory-mapped I/O

It is unlikely that each of the three personas would perform all these scenarios. For example, opportunistic developers might be more likely than systematic developers to interact with text files because text files allow for rapid prototyping and experimentation (text files are quick and easy to create and modify in a text editor, so test cases, sample data, etc., can be created easily).

Pragmatic developers, on the other hand, may be more likely to work with binary data, since the mapping between the code that they write and the representation of data on disk is more direct. Being more code focused, pragmatic developers are attracted to frameworks that reduce the number of representations of data they need to work with.

Finally, systematic developers might be more likely to use memory-mapped file I/O, due to the flexibility that such an abstraction offers. With memory-mapped I/O, they can share memory between multiple processes and exercise full control over who has access to the memory.

In this simplistic example, the I/O API is indeed used by each of the three personas—but crucially, different parts of the API. Those different parts can be designed according to the persona that uses them. The text file component might expose aggregate components, for example, whereas the memory mapped component might expose primitives.

In scenario-based design, the API designers write out the code that they would expect a developer to write to accomplish each scenario. The designers take into account the preferences of the developer, in terms of the cognitive dimensions, as they write the sample code. In effect, they step into the shoes of the developer and try to behave as that developer would. At each step of the way, the API design team can use the cognitive dimensions framework as a checklist for what they are designing. They can review each code sample they have written and ensure that it truly meets the preferences of the developer to whom the scenario is targeted. Only when the design team is happy with the scenario do they start to design and build the API to enable the scenario.

Of course, once implementation begins, unanticipated questions arise about the design. On such occasions, the team refers to the set of scenarios they are building and considers the impact that the design question might have on the scenario. In doing so, the design team focuses on the *user experience* of the multiple APIs instead of the *architecture* of the total API. By striving to deliver a great set of experiences around the scenarios, design decisions can be made throughout the development of the API that are grounded in a good understanding of what it means for an API to be usable.

A scenario-based design approach to API design focuses the API designers' minds on what the API is for instead of what the API is. It makes it clear that designers are designing experiences that a developer has with a set of classes, rather than the architecture of the API. When considering API design decisions, the designers can focus on the scenarios in which the API is used and the type of developer using it.

Conclusion

When we started looking at API usability, we didn't know how to do it or whether the effort would be worthwhile. We can now unreservedly state that it is absolutely possible and absolutely vital. We have learned a lot about how different developers approach APIs and the different expectations they have of those APIs. We have been able to utilize that understanding both to design new APIs and to discover and fix usability issues in existing APIs.

For example, the scenario-based design approach has been used at Microsoft for a few years now. Our design guidelines and API review process reinforce the need to do scenario-based design [Cwalina and Abrams 2005] and usability studies on APIs.

But this is only the beginning. There is much work still to be done. Given how critical it is to find and address API usability issues before the API ships, we need to develop additional techniques that can be used as early in the API development process as possible. For example, Farooq et al. describe a method for evaluating the usability of an API that does not require a usability study [Farooq and Zirkler 2010].

It's also important to understand how trends in application development impact the usability of APIs. For example, there is a trend toward the use of design patterns such as dependency injection [Fowler 2004]. There are very clear and sound architectural reasons for such patterns, but how do they affect usability? Jeff Stylos has investigated these issues and learned that there can be surprising usability consequences associated with some popular design patterns [Stylos and Clarke 2007], [Ellis et al. 2007].

Being in a position to ask and answer these questions is very satisfying. Now, over 10 years since I joined the Visual Studio User Experience team, I can appreciate how much we have learned about how best to create a positive impact on the developer user experience. I look forward to seeing similar advances in the future.

References

[Blackwell 2002] Blackwell, A. F. 2002. First Steps in Programming: A Rationale for Attention Investment Models. *Proceedings of the IEEE 2002 Symposia on Human Centric Computing Languages and Environments (HCC'02)*: 2.

[Clarke 2007] Clarke, S. 2007. What Is an End-User Software Engineer? Paper presented at the End-User Software Engineering Dagstuhl Seminar, February 18–23, in Dagstuhl, Germany.

[Clarke and Becker 2003] Clarke, S., and C. Becker. 2003. Using the cognitive dimensions framework to measure the usability of a class library. *Proceedings of the First Joint Conference of EASE & PPIG (PPIG 15)*: 359–366.

[Cwalina and Abrams 2005] Cwalina, K., and B. Abrams. 2005. *Framework Design Guidelines: Conventions, Idioms, and Patterns for Reusable .NET Libraries*. Upper Saddle River, NJ: Addison-Wesley Professional.

[Ellis et al. 2007] Ellis, B., J. Stylos, and B. Myers. 2007. The Factory Pattern in API Design: A Usability Evaluation. *Proceedings of the 29th International Conference on Software Engineering*: 302–312.

[Farooq and Zirkler 2010] Farooq, U., and D. Zirkler. 2010. API peer reviews: A method for evaluating usability of application programming interfaces. *Proceedings of the 2010 ACM Conference on Computer Supported Cooperative Work*: 207–210.

[Fowler 2004] Fowler, M. 2004. Module Assembly. *IEEE Software* 21(2): 65–67.

[Green and Petre 1996] Green, T.R.G., and M. Petre. 1996. Usability Analysis of Visual Programming Environments: A "Cognitive Dimensions" Framework. *Journal of Visual Languages and Computing* 7(2): 131–174.

[Robillard 2009] Robillard, M. 2009. What Makes APIs Hard to Learn? Answers from Developers. *IEEE Software* 26(6): 27–34.

[Stylos and Clarke 2007] Stylos, J., and S. Clarke. 2007. Usability Implications of Requiring Parameters in Objects' Constructors. *Proceedings of the 29th International Conference on Software Engineering*: 529–539.

## CHAPTER THIRTY

What Does 10x Mean? Measuring Variations in Programmer Productivity

Steve McConnell

One of the most replicated results in software engineering research is the 10-fold difference in productivity and quality between different programmers with the same levels of experience. Researchers have also found that this difference applies at the team level, even to different teams working within the same industries.

Individual Productivity Variation in Software Development

The original study that found huge variations in individual programming productivity was conducted in the late 1960s by Sackman, Erikson, and Grant [Sackman et al. 1968]. They studied professional programmers with an average of 7 years' experience and found that the ratio of initial coding time between the best and worst programmers was about 20 to 1; the ratio of debugging times over 25 to 1; of program size 5 to 1; and of program execution speed about 10 to 1. They found no relationship between a programmer's amount of experience and code quality or productivity.

Detailed examination of Sackman, Erickson, and Grant's findings shows some flaws in their methodology (including combining results from programmers working in low-level programming languages with those working in high-level programming languages). However, even after accounting for the flaws, their data still shows more than a 10-fold difference between the best programmers and the worst.

In the years since the original study, the general finding that "There are order-of-magnitude differences among programmers" has been confirmed by many other studies of professional programmers [Curtis 1981], [Mills 1983], [DeMarco and Lister 1985], [Curtis et al. 1986], [Card 1987], [Boehm and Papaccio 1988], [Valett and McGarry 1989], [Boehm et al. 2000].

There is also lots of anecdotal support for the large variation between programmers. When I was working at the Boeing Company in the mid-1980s, one project with about 80 programmers was at risk of missing a critical deadline. The project was critical to Boeing, and so they moved most of the 80 people off that project and brought in *one guy* who finished all the coding and delivered the software on time. I didn't work on that project, and I didn't know the guy, but I heard the story from someone I trusted, and it struck me as credible.

This degree of variation isn't unique to software. A study by Norm Augustine found that in a variety of professions—writing, football, invention, police work, and other occupations—the top 20% of the people produced about 50% of the output, whether the output is touchdowns, patents, solved cases, or software [Augustine 1979]. When you think about it, this just makes sense. We've all known people who are exceptional students, exceptional athletes, exceptional artists, exceptional parents. These differences are just part of the human experience, and why would we expect software development to be any different?

Extremes in Individual Variation on the Bad Side

Augustine's study observed that, since some people make no tangible contribution whatsoever (quarterbacks who make no touchdowns, inventors who own no patents, detectives who don't close cases, and so on), the data probably understates the actual variation in productivity.

This appears to be true in software. In several of the published studies on software productivity, about 10% of the subjects in the experiments weren't able to complete the experimental assignment. The studies' write-ups say, "Therefore those experimental subjects' results were excluded from our data set." But in real life, if someone "doesn't complete the assignment," you can't just "exclude their results from the data set." You have to wait for them to finish, assign someone else to do their work, and so on. The interesting (and frightening) implication of this is that something like 10% of the people working in the software field might actually be contributing *negative* productivity to their projects.

Again, this lines up well with real-world experience. I think many of us can think of specific people we've worked with who fit that description.

What Makes a Real 10x Programmer

Some people have objected to the "10x" label, making an argument like, "We had a super programmer on our team once. He was so obnoxious he alienated the whole team, and overall productivity was actually better without him."

In general, any practical definition of a real 10x programmer has to include the effect the programmer has on the rest of the team. I have known super programmers who were obnoxious. More often, a supposed super programmer with an obnoxious personality was really an average programmer, or worse than average, using an obnoxious personality to hide a lack of performance. The true super programmers I've worked with have generally also been cooperative team players, although of course there are always exceptions.

Issues in Measuring Productivity of Individual Programmers

The general research finding of 10x differences in programmer productivity have led some people to want to measure the productivity of individual programmers in their organizations. For better or worse, the issues involved in measuring "live" programmers are quite different from the issues in measuring productivity for research purposes.

Software engineering studies normally measure productivity in terms of time to complete a specific task, or sometimes in terms of lines of code per effort-hour, staff-month, or some other measure of effort. When you try to measure productivity in any of these ways in a commercial setting, you'll run into complications.

Productivity in Lines of Code per Staff Month

Software design is a nondeterministic activity, and different designers/developers will produce significantly different designs in response to a particular problem specification. Measuring productivity in lines of code per staff month (or equivalent) implicitly assumes that writing 10 times as much code to solve a particular problem means a programmer is 10 times more productive. That clearly is not always true. One programmer might have had a brilliant design insight that allowed him to satisfy the problem using only 10% as much code as a less capable programmer.

Some commentators have asserted that great programmers always write less code. Indeed, there probably is some correlation between programming excellence and code compactness, but I wouldn't make that statement so broadly. I would say that great programmers strive to write clear code, and that usually translates to less code. Sometimes, however, the clearest, simplest, and most obvious design takes a little more code than a design that's more "clever"— and in those cases I think the great programmer will write more code to avoid an overly clever design solution. One way or the other, the idea that productivity can be measured cleanly as "lines of code per staff month" is subject to problems.

The problem with measuring productivity in terms of lines of code per staff month is encapsulated by the old Dilbert joke about Wally coding himself a minivan. If you measure productivity in terms of volume of code generated, some people will optimize for that measure, i.e., they will find ways to write more lines of code, even if more lines of code aren't needed. The problem here isn't really with the specific "lines of code" measurement per se, but rather is an instance of the old management chestnut that "what gets measured gets done." You need to be careful what you measure.

Productivity in Function Points

Some of the problems created by using "lines of code per staff month" can be avoided by measuring program size in function points. Function points are a "synthetic" measure of program size in which inputs, outputs, queries, and files are counted to determine program size. An inefficient design/coding style won't generate more function points, so function points aren't subject to the same issues as lines of code. They are, however, subject to more practical issues, namely that to get an accurate count of function points you need the services of a certified function point counter (which most organizations don't have available), and the mapping between how function points are counted and individual work packages is rough enough that it becomes impractical to use them to ascertain the productivity of individual programmers.

What About Complexity?

Managers frequently say, "I always give my best programmer the most difficult/most complex sections of code to work on. His productivity on any measured basis might very well be low compared to programmers who get easier assignments, but my other programmers would take twice as long." That's also a legitimate phenomenon that does affect the attempt to define and measure productivity.

Is There Any Way to Measure Individual Productivity?

Difficulties like these have led many people to conclude that measuring individual productivity is so fraught with problems that no one should even try. I think it is possible to measure individual productivity meaningfully, as long as you keep several key factors in mind:

Don't expect any single dimensional measure of productivity to give you a very good picture of individual productivity.

> Think about all the statistics that are collected in sports. We can't even use a single measure to determine how good a hitter in baseball is. We consider batting average, home runs, runs batted in, on-base percentage, and other factors—and then we still argue about what the numbers mean. If we can't measure a "good hitter" using a simple measure, why would we expect a simple measure to capture something as complex as individual programming productivity? What we need to do instead is use a combination of measures, which collectively will give us insights into individual productivities. (Measures could include on-time task completion percentage, manager evaluation on a scale of 1–10, peer evaluation on a scale of 1–10, lines of code per staff month, defects reported per line of code, defects fixed per line of code, bad fix injection rate, and so on.)

Don't expect any measures—whether single measures or a combination—to support fine-grain discriminations in productivity among individuals.

A good principle to keep in mind is that measures of individual productivity give you questions to ask but not the answers. Using measures of performance for, say, individual performance reviews is both bad management and bad statistics.

Trends are usually more important than single-point measures.

Measures of individual productivity tend to be far less useful in comparing one individual to another than they are in seeing how one individual is progressing over time.

Ask why you need to measure individual productivity at all.

In a research setting, researchers need to measure productivity to assess the relative effectiveness of different techniques, and their use of these measures is subject to far fewer problems than measuring individual productivity on real projects. In a real project environment, what do you want to use the measures for? Performance reviews? Not a good idea, for the reasons mentioned earlier. Task assignments? Most managers I talk with say they know who their star contributors are without measuring, and I believe them. Estimation? No, the variations caused by different design approaches, different task difficulty, and related factors make that an ineffective way to build up project estimates.

On real projects it's hard to find a use for individual productivity measures that is both useful and statistically valid. In my experience, aside from research settings, the attempt to measure individual performance arises most often from a desire to do something with the measurements that isn't statistically valid. So while I see the value of measuring individual performance in research settings, I think it's difficult to find cases in which the measurement effort is justified on real projects.

Team Productivity Variation in Software Development

Software experts have long observed that team productivity varies about as much as individual productivity does—by an order of magnitude [Mills 1983]. Part of the reason is that good programmers tend to cluster in some organizations and bad programmers in others, an observation that has been confirmed by a study of 166 professional programmers from 18 organizations [Demarco and Lister 1999].

In one study of seven identical projects, expended effort varied by a factor of 3.4 to 1 and program sizes by a factor of 3 to 1 [Boehm et al. 1984]. In spite of the productivity range, the programmers in this study were not a diverse group. They were all professional programmers with several years of experience who were enrolled in a computer-science graduate program. It's reasonable to assume that a study of a less homogeneous group would turn up even greater differences. An earlier study of programming teams observed a 5-to-1 difference in program size and a 2.6-to-1 variation in the time required for a team to complete the same project [Weinberg and Schulman 1974].

After reviewing more than 20 years of data in constructing the COCOMO II estimation model, Barry Boehm and other researchers concluded that developing a program with a team in the 15th percentile of programmers ranked by ability typically requires about 3.5 times as many staff-months as developing a program with a team in the 90th percentile [Boehm et al. 2000]. The difference will be much greater if one team is more experienced than the other in the programming language, in the application area, or in both.

One specific data point is the difference in productivity between Lotus 123 version 3 and Microsoft Excel 3.0. Both were desktop spreadsheet applications completed in the 1989–1990 timeframe. Finding cases in which two companies publish data on such similar projects is rare, which makes this head-to-head comparison especially interesting. The results of these two projects were as follows: Excel took 50 staff years to produce 649,000 lines of code [Cusumano and Selby 1995]. Lotus 123 took 260 staff years to produce 400,000 lines of code [Schlender 1989]. Excel's team produced about 13,000 lines of code per staff year. Lotus's team produced 1,500 lines of code per staff year. The difference in productivity between the two teams was more than a factor of eight, which supports the general claim of order-of-magnitude differences—not just between different individuals, but also between different project teams.

Interestingly, the quantitative results very closely match the layperson's perceptions of those projects. Lotus 123 v3 was famously late, shipping at least two years after its initially announced release date. Excel was heralded within Microsoft as one of the best projects Microsoft had ever done. This is as pure an apples-to-apples comparison as it's possible to get with "live" projects from real companies.

Having said that, this example illustrates the numerous sources of productivity variations. Both Lotus and Microsoft were in a position to recruit top talent for their projects. I doubt that the difference in team productivity was as much a result of differences in individual talent as it was a result of numerous organizational factors, such as how good the organization was about defining a clear product vision, defining unambiguous requirements, coordinating efforts of team members, and so on.

Organizational influences define the productivity envelope within which a team performs. A team comprised of individuals of average capability in an exceptional organization can outperform a team of exceptional capability working in a mediocre organization. Of course there are also teams made up of exceptional individuals in exceptional organizations, as well as teams comprised of mediocre individuals in mediocre organizations. Consequently, team productivity (aka organizational productivity) varies by a factor of 10 just as individual productivity does.

References

[Augustine 1979] Augustine, N.R. 1979. Augustine's Laws and Major System Development Programs. *Defense Systems Management Review*: 50–76.

[Boehm and Papaccio 1988] Boehm, Barry W., and Philip N. Papaccio. 1988. Understanding and Controlling Software Costs. *IEEE Transactions on Software Engineering* 14(10): 1462–1477.

[Boehm et al. 1984] Boehm, Barry W., T.E. Gray, and T. Seewaldt. 1984. Prototyping Versus Specifying: A Multiproject Experiment. *IEEE Transactions on Software Engineering* 10(3): 290–303.

[Boehm et al. 2000] Boehm, Barry, et al. 2000. *Software Cost Estimation with Cocomo II*. Boston: Addison-Wesley.

[Card 1987] Card, David N. 1987. A Software Technology Evaluation Program. *Information and Software Technology* 29(6): 291–300.

[Curtis 1981] Curtis, Bill. 1981. Substantiating Programmer Variability. *Proceedings of the IEEE* 69(7): 846.

[Curtis et al. 1986] Curtis, Bill, et al. 1986. Software Psychology: The Need for an Interdisciplinary Program. *Proceedings of the IEEE* 74(8): 1092–1106.

[Cusumano and Selby 1995] Cusumano, Michael, and Richard W. Selby. 1995. *Microsoft Secrets*. New York: The Free Press.

[DeMarco and Lister 1985] DeMarco, Tom, and Timothy Lister. 1985. Programmer Performance and the Effects of the Workplace. *Proceedings of the 8th International Conference on Software Engineering*: 268–272.

[DeMarco and Lister 1999] DeMarco, Tom, and Timothy Lister. 1999. *Peopleware: Productive Projects and Teams*, Second Edition. New York: Dorset House.

[Mills 1983] Mills, Harlan D. 1983. *Software Productivity*. Boston: Little, Brown.

[Sackman et al. 1968] Sackman, H., W.J. Erikson, and E.E. Grant. 1968. Exploratory Experimental Studies Comparing Online and Offline Programming Performance. *Communications of the ACM* 11(1): 3–11.

[Schlender 1989] Schlender, Brenton. 1989. How to Break the Software Logjam. *Fortune*, September 25.

[Valett and McGarry 1989] Valett, J., and F.E. McGarry. 1989. A Summary of Software Measurement Experiences in the Software Engineering Laboratory. *Journal of Systems and Software* 9(2): 137–148.

[Weinberg and Schulman 1974] Weinberg, Gerald M., and Edward L. Schulman. 1974. Goals and Performance in Computer Programming. *Human Factors* 16(1): 70–77.

Contributors

Jorge Aranda is a Postdoctoral Fellow at the University of Victoria, working with the SEGAL and CHISEL Labs. He obtained his doctoral degree from the University of Toronto, after performing empirical studies, observations, and interviews with hundreds of professionals at dozens of software organizations. These studies, along with his previous experience as a software consultant and developer, convinced him that team coordination and communication are the greatest problems in our field, and his research aims to help fix them. Jorge is a Mexican who now lives in Victoria, B.C., Canada, with his wife and their cat. He likes board games, books, movies, cooking, jogging, and juggling.

Thomas Ball is Principal Researcher at Microsoft Research where he manages the Software Reliability Research group (*http://research.microsoft.com/srr/*). Tom received a PhD from the University of Wisconsin-Madison in 1993, was with Bell Labs from 1993-1999, and has been at Microsoft Research since 1999. He is one of the originators of the SLAM project, a software model checking engine for C that forms the basis of the Static Driver Verifier tool. Tom's interests range from program analysis, model checking, testing and automated theorem proving to the problems of defining and measuring software quality.

Dr. Victor R. Basili is Professor of Computer Science at the University of Maryland. He was founding director of the Fraunhofer Center for Experimental Software Engineering, where he currently serves as Senior Research Fellow and one of the founders and principals in the Software Engineering Laboratory (SEL) at NASA/GSFC. For over 35 years he has worked on measuring, evaluating, and improving the software development process and product via mechanisms for observing and evolving knowledge through empirical research, e.g., the Goal/Question /Metric Approach, the Quality Improvement Paradigm, and the Experience Factory.

Dr. Basili received his PhD in computer science from the University of Texas and is the recipient of two honorary degrees. He has received awards from ACM SIGSOFT, the IEEE Computer Society, and NASA among others, and in 2005 the 27th International Conference on Software Engineering held a Symposium in his honor. In 2007 he was awarded the Fraunhofer Medal. He served as editor-in-chief of the *IEEE Transactions on Software Engineering* and is founding co-editor-in-chief of the *Journal of Empirical Software Engineering*.

ANDREW BEGEL is a researcher in Microsoft Research's Human Interactions in Programming group in Redmond, Washington, USA. He studies software engineers at Microsoft to understand how they communicate, collaborate, and coordinate, and the impact of these activities on their effectiveness in collocated and distributed development. After conducting studies, he builds tools to help mitigate the coordination issues that have been discovered.

Andrew has led workshops on human aspects of software engineering, kinesthetic learning activities for computer science education, and teaching teachers about computer science education and complex systems science. He has served on the program committees of many Computer Science and Computer Science Education–related conferences and workshops.

CHRISTIAN BIRD is a postdoctoral researcher at Microsoft Research in the Empirical Software Engineering group. He is primarily interested in the relationship between software design and social dynamics in large development projects, and the effects of these issues on productivity and software quality. In an effort to empirically answer questions in that area, Dr. Bird has pioneered a number of software mining techniques. He has studied software development teams at Microsoft, IBM, and in the Open Source realm, examining the effects of distributed development, ownership policies, and the ways in which teams complete software tasks.

Dr. Bird is the recipient of the ACM SIGSOFT distinguished paper award and the "Best Graduate Student Researcher" at U.C. Davis, where he received his PhD under Prem Devanbu. He has published in the top academic software engineering venues, has a Research Highlight in *CACM*, and was a National Merit Scholar at BYU, where he received his BS in computer science.

DR. BARRY BOEHM is the TRW Professor in the Computer Sciences and Industrial and Systems Engineering Departments at the University of Southern California. He is also the Director of Research of the DoD-Stevens-USC Systems Engineering Research Center and the founding Director Emeritus of the USC Center for Systems and Software Engineering. He was director of DARPA-ISTO 1989-92, at TRW 1973-89, at Rand Corporation 1959-73, and at General Dynamics 1955-59. His contributions include the COCOMO family of cost models and the Spiral family of process models. He is a Fellow of the primary professional societies in computing (ACM), aerospace (AIAA), electronics (IEEE), and systems engineering (INCOSE), a member of the U.S. National Academy of Engineering, and the 2010 recipient of the IEEE Simon Ramo Medal for exceptional achievement in systems engineering and systems science.

MARCELO CATALDO is a Researcher in the Institute for Software Research at Carnegie Mellon University. His research interests focus on understanding the relationship between the structure of large-scale software systems and the ability of development organizations to realize those systems. Specific areas of inquiry include (a) the development and analysis of software architectures suitable for distributed software development; and (b) the assessment of the impact that technical factors, socio-organizational factors and the interplay among them have on development productivity and software quality in geographically distributed projects.

Dr. Cataldo received MS and PhD degrees in Computation, Organizations and Society from the School of Computer Science at Carnegie Mellon University in 2007. He also holds a BS in Information Systems from Universidad Tecnológica Nacional (Buenos Aires, Argentina) and a MS in Information Networking from Carnegie Mellon University.

STEVEN CLARKE is a Senior User Experience Researcher in the Developer Division at Microsoft. He received both BSc and PhD degrees from the University of Glasgow, Scotland, in 1993 and 1997 respectively. He was a software developer at Motorola from 1997 until 1999, building development tools for smartcard operating systems. He has been working in his present position since 1999. With colleagues in the Visual Studio team and in Microsoft Research, he uses results from studies into developer behaviors and work styles to identify ways to significantly improve the experience that developers have building applications with Microsoft tools and platforms.

JASON COHEN has started four companies, including Smart Bear Software, which makes Code Collaborator, the most popular peer code review tool. He's also the author of *Best Kept Secrets of Peer Code Review*, which includes the largest case study ever recorded of code review. Currently, Jason writes about startups for geeks at *http://blog.ASmartBear.com* and runs his latest startup, *WPEngine.com*.

ROBERT DELINE is a principal researcher at Microsoft Research (*http://research.microsoft.com/ ~rdeline*), working at the intersection of software engineering and human-computer interaction. His research group designs development tools in a user-centered fashion: they conduct studies of development teams to understand their work practice and prototype tools to improve that practice. He received his PhD from Carnegie Mellon University in 1999 and his BS/MS from the University of Virginia in 1993.

MADELINE M. DIEP is a research scientist at the Fraunhofer Center for Experimental Software Engineering. Her research interests include software quality assurance, software analysis, and empirical evaluation. She received a PhD in computer science from the University of Nebraska–Lincoln.

HAKAN ERDOGMUS is an independent consultant based in Ottawa, Canada, an adjunct faculty member at University of Calgary's Department of Computer Science, and Editor in Chief of *IEEE Software*. He specializes in software process, software development practices, and the economics of software development. From 1995 to 2009, he worked as a research scientist at the Canadian National Research Council's Institute for Information Technology. Hakan holds a doctorate degree in Telecommunications from INRS, Université du Québec, Montreal (1994), an MSc degree from McGill University's School of Computer Science, Montreal (1989), and a BSc degree from Boğaziçi University's Computer Engineering Department, Istanbul (1986). He is a senior member of IEEE and IEEE Computer Society and a member of ACM and Agile Alliance.

MICHAEL W. GODFREY is an Associate Professor in the David R. Cheriton School of Computer Science at the University of Waterloo (Canada), where he is also a member of SWAG, the Software Architecture Group. After finishing his PhD in computer science at the University of Toronto, he was a faculty member at Cornell University for two years before joining the University of Waterloo in 1998. Between 2001 and 2006, he held an Associate Industrial Research Chair in telecommunications software engineering sponsored by Nortel Networks and the National Sciences and Engineering Research Council of Canada (NSERC).

His main research interests concern software evolution: understanding how and why software changes over time. In particular, he is interested in evidence-based software engineering, software clone analysis, mining software repositories, software tool design, reverse engineering, and program comprehension.

MARK GUZDIAL is a professor in the School of Interactive Computing at Georgia Institute of Technology. He is a leading researcher in computing education, and has helped change the discourse towards addressing the computer science education needs across campus, not just among CS majors. He recently wrote a series of textbooks called *Media Computation* to introduce computing through manipulation of digital media.

JO E. HANNAY holds a PhD in formal specification, type theory, and logic from the Laboratory for Foundations of Computer Science at the University of Edinburgh. Currently a researcher at Simula Research Laboratory in Norway, he has worked as a programmer in the insurance industry and has been an associate professor at the University of Oslo. His research includes defining software engineering expertise and tasks, developing and combining scientific and practitioners' theories, and understanding what goes on in large agile development projects. He used to be a violinist.

AHMED E. HASSAN is the NSERC/RIM Industrial Research Chair in Software Engineering for Ultra Large Scale systems at Queen's University in Kingston, Ontario, Canada. Dr. Hassan spearheaded the organization and creation of the Mining Software Repositories (MSR) conference and its research community. The MSR community seeks to support decision-making processes through empirical data about software projects and their evolution. Dr. Hassan co-edited special issues on the MSR topic for the *IEEE Transactions on Software Engineering* and the *Journal of Empirical Software Engineering*.

Early tools and techniques developed by Dr. Hassan and his team are already integrated into products used by millions of users worldwide. Dr. Hassan's industrial experience includes helping architect the Blackberry wireless platform at RIM, and working for IBM Research at the Almaden Research Lab and for Nortel Networks at the Computer Research Lab. Dr. Hassan is the named inventor of patents at several jurisdictions around the world, including the United States, Europe, India, Canada, and Japan.

ISRAEL HERRAIZ teaches and conducts research at the Universidad Alfonso X el Sabio in Madrid, Spain. He obtained a PhD from Universidad Rey Juan Carlos, while working at the GSyC/Libresoft research group. His research interests lie in the intersection between software evolution, mining software repositories, and empirical software engineering, with an emphasis on large scale studies and statistical analysis of software projects. He is also an active contributor to several free/open source software projects.

KIM SEBASTIAN HERZIG is a graduate student in the Software Engineering Lab of Professor Andreas Zeller at Saarland University, Germany. The focus of his current research activities lies in empirical software engineering and mining software repositories. He is currently exploring and analyzing version archives and bug databases to create tools and techniques to help software developers code reliable software and estimate the risk of source code changes.

CORY KAPSER has published numerous papers on coding practices, notably concerning code cloning. He won Best Paper Award at the 13th IEEE Working Conference on Reverse Engineering in 2006.

BARBARA KITCHENHAM is Professor of Quantitative Software Engineering at Keele University in the UK. She has worked in software engineering for over 30 years, both in industry and academia. Her main research interest is software measurement and its application to project management, quality control, risk management, and evaluation of software technologies. Her most recent research has focused on the application of evidence-based practice to software engineering. She is a Chartered Mathematician and Fellow of the Institute of Mathematics and Its Applications, a Fellow of the Royal Statistical Society, and a member of the IEEE Computer Society.

ANDREW KO is an Assistant Professor at the Information School at the University of Washington. His research interests include human and cooperative aspects of software development and design, and more broadly, the fields of human-computer interaction and software engineering. He has published articles in all of these areas, receiving best paper awards at top conferences such as the International Conference on Software Engineering (ICSE) and the ACM Conference on Human Factors in Computing (CHI), as well as extensive press on the Whyline, a debugging tool that lets users ask "why" questions about problematic output. In 2004, he was also awarded both NSF and NDSEG research fellowships in support of his PhD research. He received his PhD at the Human–Computer Interaction Institute at Carnegie Mellon University, advised by Brad Myers. He received Honors Bachelors of Science degrees in Computer Science and Psychology from Oregon State University in 2002.

Lucas Layman is Research Scientist at the Fraunhofer Center for Experimental Software Engineering. His areas of expertise include the application of measurement and metrics to evaluate and improve software development processes and products, agile methods, and software reliability. He has performed empirical studies and technology transfer with a number of organizations, including NASA, Microsoft, the Department of Defense, IBM, and Sabre Airline Solutions. In addition to empirical evaluations of process and process improvement, Dr. Layman has investigated human factors in software development and authored a number of papers on computer science education. He received his PhD in Computer Science from North Carolina State University in 2009 and his BS in Computer Science from Loyola College in 2002. He has previously worked at Microsoft Research and the National Research Council of Canada.

Steve McConnell is CEO and Chief Software Engineer at Construx Software, where he consults to a broad range of industries, teaches seminars, and oversees Construx's software engineering practices. He is the author of *Software Estimation: Demystifying the Black Art* (2006), *Code Complete* (1993, 2004), *Rapid Development* (1996), *Software Project Survival Guide* (1998), and *Professional Software Development* (2004), as well as numerous technical articles. His books have won numerous awards for "Best Book of the Year" from *Software Development* magazine, *Game Developer* magazine, Amazon.com's editors, and other sources.

Steve serves as Editor-in-Chief Emeritus of *IEEE Software* magazine, is on the Panel of Experts of the SWEBOK project, and is past Chair of the IEEE Computer Society's Professional Practices Committee. In 1998, readers of *Software Development* magazine named him one of the three most influential people in the software industry along with Bill Gates and Linus Torvalds.

Tim Menzies, an Associate Professor in CS at West Virginia University, researches data mining algorithms for software engineering. His algorithms find patterns in software engineering data that predict for aspects of software quality (defects, construction time, etc). A repeated conclusion for that work is "less is more," propelling AI tools that can quickly and automatically learn the least number of constraints that most effect critical decisions.

A former research chair for NASA, Dr. Menzies holds a PhD from the University of New South Wales, Australia (1995) in artificial intelligence. He is the author of over 190 referred papers and the co-founder of the PROMISE series conference on repeatable experiments in software engineering (see http://promisedata.org/data). Recently, he was ranked in the top 1% of over 26,000 SE researchers (see *http://academic.research.microsoft.com/CSDirectory/author_category_4 _last5.htm*). His website is *http://menzies.us*.

Gail Murphy is a Professor in the Department of Computer Science at the University of British Columbia. She joined UBC in 1996 after completing PhD and MS degrees at the University of Washington. Before returning to graduate school, she worked as a software developer at a telecommunications company for five years. She also holds a BSc degree from the University of Alberta.

Dr. Murphy works primarily on building simpler and more effective tools to help developers manage software evolution tasks. In 2005 she held a UBC Killam Research Fellowship, and she received the AITO Dahl-Nygaard Junior Prize for her work in software evolution. In 2006, she received an NSERC Steacie Fellowship and the CRA-W Anita Borg Early Career Award. In 2007, she helped co-found and is currently Chair of the Board and CFO of Tasktop Technologies Inc. In 2008, she served as the program committee chair for the ACM SIGSOFT FSE conference and received the University of Washington College of Engineering Diamond Early Career Award. In 2012, she will be a Program Co-Chair for the International Conference on Software Engineering. She is currently an associate editor for *ACM Transactions on Software Engineering* journal and on the editorial board of *Communications of the ACM*. One of the most rewarding parts of her career has been collaborating with many very talented graduate and undergraduate students.

NACHIAPPAN NAGAPPAN is a Senior Researcher at Microsoft Research in the Software Reliability Research group. His primary area of interest is empirical software engineering. He has collaborated with several product teams at Microsoft to apply his ideas to practice. He earned his PhD degree from North Carolina State University.

ANDY ORAM is an editor at O'Reilly Media. His work for O'Reilly includes the 2005 groundbreaking book *Running Linux*, the influential 2001 title *Peer-to-Peer*, and the 2007 bestseller *Beautiful Code*. Andy also writes often for the O'Reilly Network and other publications on policy issues related to the Internet and on trends affecting technical innovation and its effects on society. Print publications where his work has appeared include *The Economist*, *Communications of the ACM*, *Copyright World*, and *Internet Law and Business*.

THOMAS OSTRAND is a Principal Member of Technical Staff in the Information and Software Systems Research department of AT&T Labs in Florham Park, NJ. His current research interests include software test generation and evaluation, defect analysis and prediction, and tools for software development and testing.

Prior to joining AT&T, Dr Ostrand was with Siemens Corporate Research, Sperry Univac, and the Computer Science Department of Rutgers University. He is a senior member of the ACM, and has been a Member-at-Large of the ACM/SIGSOFT Executive Committee. He has served as Program Chair and Steering Committee member of the International Symposium on Software Testing and Analysis, and of the PROMISE Conference on Predictive Models in Software Engineering. He is currently an associate editor of the *Empirical Software Engineering* journal, and is a past associate editor of *IEEE Transactions on Software Engineering*.

DEWAYNE E. PERRY is currently the Motorola Regents Chair of Software Engineering at The University of Texas at Austin. The first third of his software engineering career was spent as a professional software developer, with the latter part combining both research (as a visiting faculty member in Computer Science at Carnegie-Mellon University) and consulting in software architecture and design. The next 16 years were spent doing software engineering research at Bell Laboratories in Murray Hill NJ. His appointment at UT Austin began January 2000.

He has done seminal research in empirical studies, formal models of the software processes, process and product support environments, software architecture, and the practical use of formal specifications and techniques. He is particularly interested in the role architecture plays in the coordination of multi-site software development as well as its role in capitalizing on company software assets in the context of product lines.

He is a member of ACM SIGSOFT and IEEE Computer Society; and has served as organizing chair, program chair, and program committee member on various software engineering conferences. He has been a co-Editor in Chief of Wiley's *Software Process: Improvement & Practice*, and a former associate editor of *IEEE Transactions on Software Engineering*.

MARIAN PETRE is a Professor of Computing and the Director of the Centre for Research in Computing (CRC) at the Open University in the UK. She holds a Royal Society Wolfson Research Merit Award in recognition of her empirical research into software design. Her research focuses on expert reasoning and representation in professional software design. She is also an innovative educator in empirical research methods and has co-authored several books, including *The Unwritten Rules of PhD Research* (now in its second edition) and *A Gentle Guide to Research Methods*.

LUTZ PRECHELT is professor of software engineering at Freie Universität Berlin. He started his research career in artificial intelligence, neural network learning, compiler construction, and parallel computing before moving to empirical software engineering. He has also worked as a software developer and as a software development manager. Today, his research interests focus on qualitative and quantitative studies of software processes, in particular agile ones, and on research methodology and research quality.

RAHUL PREMRAJ is an Assistant Professor in the Computer Science Department of VU University Amsterdam. He received his Masters in Information Systems from the Robert Gordon University, UK in 2002 and his PhD from Bournemouth University, UK in 2007. His research interests include empirical software engineering, mining software archives, software quality assurance, distributed software development, and software process improvement.

DR. FORREST SHULL is a division director at the Fraunhofer Center for Experimental Software Engineering in Maryland (FC-MD), a nonprofit research and tech transfer organization, where he leads the Measurement and Knowledge Management Division. He is also associate adjunct professor at the University of Maryland College Park.

At FC-MD, he has been a lead researcher on projects for NASA's Office of Safety and Mission Assurance, the NASA Safety Center, the U.S. Department of Defense, the National Science Foundation, the Defense Advanced Research Projects Agency (DARPA), and companies such as Motorola and Fujitsu Labs of America. He has also developed and delivered several courses on software measurement and inspections for NASA engineers.

Since 2007, Forrest has served as IEEE Software's associate editor-in-chief for empirical results and editor of its popular Voice of Evidence department. He will be taking over as Editor in

Chief of IEEE Software in January 2011. He also serves on the editorial board of *Journal of Empirical Software Engineering*.

BETH SIMON is a faculty member in the Computer Science and Engineering Department at the University of California, San Diego. Her research interests focus on Computer Science education, with specific interests in novices in computing (both in university and industry), peer instruction, and assessment. Dr. Simon earned her bachelor's degree in Computer Science at the University of Dayton, and her master's and PhD in Computer Science and Engineering at the University of California, San Diego.

DIOMIDIS SPINELLIS is a Professor in the Department of Management Science and Technology at the Athens University of Economics and Business, Greece. His research interests include software engineering, computer security, and programming languages. He has written the two award-winning *Open Source Perspective* books, *Code Reading* and *Code Quality*, as well as dozens of scientific papers.

Dr. Spinellis is a member of the IEEE Software editorial board, authoring the regular "Tools of the Trade" column. He is also a FreeBSD committer and the developer of UMLGraph and other open source software packages, libraries, and tools. He holds an MEng in Software Engineering and a PhD in Computer Science, both from Imperial College London. Dr. Spinellis is senior member of the ACM and the IEEE and a member of the Usenix association.

NEIL THOMAS is a Software Engineer at Google. His work on HTML5 mobile web applications, including Gmail and Google Buzz, continues to push the mobile web forward and redefine what is possible in a web browser. He is named as a co-inventor on multiple patents in this area. He has also contributed to internal tools at Google for improving programmer productivity.

Mr. Thomas graduated from UBC in 2010 with a BSc in Computer Science. In his senior year, he had the pleasure of working with Gail Murphy in the Software Practices Lab. His research explored how developers understand and reason about the modularity of complex systems.

WALTER F. TICHY has been professor of Computer Science at the Karlsruhe Institute of Technology (formerly University Karlsruhe), Germany, since 1986, and was dean of the faculty of computer science from 2002 to 2004. He is also a director of FZI, a technology transfer center in Karlsruhe. His primary research interests are software engineering and parallelism. In the 1980s, he created the Revision Control System (RCS), a version management system that is the basis of CVS and is still used worldwide. Dr. Tichy had his first exposure to parallel programming as a student, when C.mmp, a parallel computer consisting of 16 PDP-11 computers, was built at CMU. He has also worked on the Connection Machine and a number of parallel computers in the 1980s, and along with students developed Parastation, which runs a machine that is ranked 10th on the Top 500 list as of June 2009.

Dr. Tichy earned his PhD in Computer Science in 1980 from Carnegie Mellon University. His dissertation was one of the first to discuss software architecture. He has created controversy by insisting that software researchers need to test their claims with empirical studies rather than rely on intuition. He has conducted controlled experiments testing the influence of type-checking, inheritance depth, design patterns, testing methods, and agile methods on programmer productivity.

BURAK TURHAN is a postdoctoral researcher in the Department of Information Processing Science at the University of Oulu in Northern Finland. Before moving to Finland, he was a Research Associate in the Institute for Information Technology at the National Research Council of Canada. He holds a PhD in Computer Engineering from Bogazici University in Istanbul. His research interests include empirical studies on software quality, application of machine learning and data mining methods in software engineering for defect and cost modeling, and agile/lean software development with a special focus on test-driven development.

ELAINE WEYUKER is an AT&T Fellow doing software engineering research. Prior to moving to AT&T, she was a professor of computer science at NYU's Courant Institute of Mathematical Sciences. Her research interests currently focus on software fault prediction, software testing, and software metrics and measurement. In an earlier life, Elaine did research in Theory of Computation and is the co-author of a book *Computability, Complexity, and Languages* with Martin Davis and Ron Sigal.

Elaine is the recipient of the 2010 ACM President's Award, the ACM SIGSOFT Retrospective Impact Paper Awards in 2009, the 2008 Anita Borg Institute Technical Leadership Award, and 2007 ACM/SIGSOFT Outstanding Research Award. She is also a member of the US National Academy of Engineering, an IEEE Fellow, and an ACM Fellow and has received IEEE's Harlan Mills Award for outstanding software engineering research, Rutgers University 50th Anniversary Outstanding Alumni Award, and the AT&T Chairman's Diversity Award as well has having been named a Woman of Achievement by the YWCA. She is the chair of the ACM Women's Council (ACM-W) and a member of the Executive Committee of the Coalition to Diversify Computing.

MICHELE WHITECRAFT is a dynamic teacher, lecturer, and researcher. She takes a holistic, interdisciplinary approach to education and is actively involved in advancing women in science. She has been the recipient of the Presidential Award for Excellence in Secondary Science Education, the Tandy Scholar Teacher Award, and the Governor's Award for Excellence in Education. From her unique research and consulting experiences with the Department of Energy, National Science Foundation, National Institutes for Environmental Health Science, National Institutes of Health, and National Aeronautics Space Association, Michele has designed science curricula with real world experiments ranging from her work on the International Experimental Thermonuclear Reactor at Princeton to the artificial transmutation of the transuranium elements at UC Berkeley. With more than 25 years' experience in teaching high school and college chemistry, she has authored several monographs to enhance science education nation-wide and presented at several national conferences. She has publications in *BioScience*, *Journal of Nuclear Materials*, *Human Ecology*, and the *Encyclopedia of Ethics*.

Michele's experiences with these national organizations and research projects have inspired her desire to help advance women in all scientific endeavors in an effort to realize NSF's goal of 50-50 gender participation in science by 2020. Michele has been a member of the American Chemical Society, American Association for the Advancement of Science, Society of Women Engineers, American Association of University Women, Association for Supervision and Curriculum Development, and National Association of Research in Science Teaching. Michele has her master's degree in curriculum and instruction and is currently a doctoral student in Learning, Teaching and Social Policy at Cornell.

DR. LAURIE WILLIAMS is an Associate Professor at North Carolina State University. She received her undergraduate degree in Industrial Engineering from Lehigh University, an MBA from Duke University, and a PhD in Computer Science from the University of Utah. Prior to returning to academia to obtain her PhD, she worked at IBM for nine years. Laurie is the lead author of *Pair Programming Illuminated* and a co-editor of *Extreme Programming Perspectives*. She was a founder of the XP Universe conference, which has now evolved to the Agile Software Development conference. She has conducted several empirical studies on Extreme Programming and other agile development practices.

WENDY M. WILLIAMS, PHD is a Professor in the Department of Human Development at Cornell University, where she studies the development, assessment, training, and societal implications of intelligence in its many forms. She has authored nine books, edited five volumes, and written dozens of articles, including the 2007 edited volume *Why Aren't More Women in Science?* (APA Books; winner of a 2007 Independent Publisher Book Award) and the 2010 coauthored book *The Mathematics of Sex: How Biology and Society Conspire to Limit Talented Women and Girls* (Oxford; both with Stephen Ceci).

Dr. Williams holds two Early Career awards from the American Psychological Association and three Senior Investigator Awards from the Mensa Research Foundation, and is a Fellow of various professional societies. Her research has been featured in *Nature*, *Newsweek*, *Business Week*, *Science*, *Scientific American*, *The New York Times*, *The Washington Post*, *USA Today*, *The Philadelphia Inquirer*, *The Chronicle of Higher Education*, and *Child Magazine*, among other media outlets. In 2009, she launched the National Institutes of Health–funded Cornell Institute for Women in Science, a research and outreach center that studies and promotes the careers of women scientists.

GREG WILSON is the project lead for Software Carpentry, a crash course in basic software development skills for scientists and engineers. In previous lives, he has been a programmer, an author, and a professor. Greg has a PhD in Computer Science from the University of Edinburgh, and is a proud Canadian.

Andreas Zeller is professor for software engineering at Saarland University, Saarbrücken, Germany. His research is concerned with the analysis of large software systems, in particular their execution and their development history. He is one of the pioneers in automated debugging ("Why does my program fail?") and mining software archives ("Where do most bugs occur?").

Thomas Zimmermann received his Diploma degree in Computer Science from the University of Passau, and his PhD degree from Saarland University, Germany. He is a researcher in the Software Reliability Research Group at Microsoft Research, and an adjunct assistant professor in the Department of Computer Science at the University of Calgary. His research interests include empirical software engineering, mining software repositories, software reliability, development tools, and social networking. Notable research includes the systematic mining of version archives and bug databases to conduct empirical studies and to build tools to support developers and managers.

Dr. Zimmermann co-organized an ICSM working session on Myths in Software Engineering (MythSE '07) as well as workshops on software defects (DEFECTS '08 and '09) and recommendation systems in software engineering (RSSE '08 and '10). He received two ACM SIGSOFT Distinguished Paper Awards for his work published at the ICSE '07 and FSE '08 conferences. He has served on a variety of program committees, including ICSE, MSR, PROMISE, ICSM, and the ACM Conference on Recommender Systems (RecSys). He is co-chair of the program committee for MSR '10 and '11. His home page is *http://thomas-zimmermann.com*.

INDEX

We'd like to hear your suggestions for improving our indexes. Send email to *index@oreilly.com*.

K

Kafura, D., 270, 276
Kan, S. H., 131
Kapser, Cory, 531–544
Kim, Sunghun, 450
Kit pattern, 395
Kitchenham, Barbara
    evidence-based software engineering, 7, 8, 18
    on meta-study, 117
    result replicability and, 6
    systematic reviews, 22, 35–54, 208
KLOC metric, 147
Knuth, Donald, 58–60
Ko, Andrew, 55–63, 340
Kochan, Thomas A., 230, 231
Koru, Gunes, 9
Krasner, Herb, 478, 491
Kruskal-Wallis test, 448

L

Labor Statistics, Bureau of, 111, 228
Labor, Department of, 228
Larson, Carolyn, 492
LaToza, T., 540
Lave, J., 511
Layman, Lucas, 207–217
Lean software development, 46, 47
learning to program
    contextualizing for motivation, 118–121
    improving tools, 117, 118
    Lister Working Group, 114
    McCracken Working Group, 113
    natural language and, 114–116
    Rainfall Problem, 112
Lenard, Tony, 492
Libresoft tools, 128
linking data sets, 523–525
Linux operating system
    code structure, 270–276, 287
    code style, 276–282, 287
    data organization, 284–286, 288
    file organization, 266–270, 287
    historical background, 262
    key study metrics, 265
    preprocessing, 282–284, 288
    study background, 261
    study outcome, 286–289
Lipow, Myron, 454
Lister Working Group, 114
Lister, Raymond, 114
Lister, Timothy, 306, 341, 342
Loader, Clive, 492
LOC (lines of code) metric
    about, 130

AT&T study, 151
    measuring productivity via, 569
    sample analysis, 134
logical dependencies
    defined, 354
    productivity and, 356
    socio-technical dimension, 361
    software quality and, 356
logistic regression, 197
Louridas, Panos, 289
Lubinski, D., 225

M

maintainability index measure, 261
Malone, T. W., 350
management structure (see organizational
       structure)
Mann-Whitney test, 5
Mannix, E., 229, 230
Mantis tool, 363
mapping studies, 38
March, J. G., 350
Margolis, J., 224, 225
master report, 446
mathematical abilities, gender differences, 222–
      224
MBT (Model-Based Testing), 6
McCabe's cyclomatic complexity
    about, 130, 131
       Halstead's comparison, 132
       sample analysis, 134–137
       selection considerations, 416
McConnell, Steve, 567–573
McCracken Working Group, 113
McCracken, Mike, 113
McGrath Cohoon, J., 226
measurement (see metrics/measurement)
Media Computation course, 119–121, 511
memory
    chunking theory on, 397, 398
    comparing consumption, 243
Menlo Innovations, 315
mentoring novice developers, 512
Menzies, Tim, 3–16
meta-study, defined, 117
metrics/measurement, 133
    (see also statistical analysis)
    AT&T study warnings, 159
    CK suite, 421, 422
    code churn, 418–420
    code complexity, 421, 422
    code coverage, 417, 418
    code dependencies, 422, 423
    for congruence, 190
    of expertise, 92

female mathematical-spatial abilities, 222–224
integrated approach, 427–429
of intelligence, 88–89
measuring source code, 127
mining software archives, 518, 519
operating system studies, 261, 265
of organizational structure, 194–200, 194–200
OS code structure, 270–276, 287
OS code style, 276–282, 287
OS data organization, 284–286, 288
OS file organization, 266–270, 287
OS preprocessing, 282–284, 288
OS study outcome, 286–289
people and organizational measures, 423–425
of personality, 85
programmer productivity, 567–573
programming performance, 91
readability, 449
sample tools, 128–133
selection considerations, 416, 417
of skills, 90, 95
software faults study, 487
surveying software, 126
TDD study, 209–211–214
MFC (Microsoft Foundation Classes) APIs, 548
Microsoft Corporation
API usability study, 545–565
failure prediction study, 415–434
office layout study, 340
onboarding concept, 512–514
organizational complexity, 194–200
pair programming and, 315, 316, 321
productivity studies, 572
SE education study, 498
software developer study, 298–307
Visual Studio, 363
Microsoft Foundation Classes (MFC) APIs, 548
Mileva, Yana, 528
Miller, F., 224, 225
Miller, George A., 397
Miller, L. A., 115
mining software archives
about, 517
checking for missing links, 525
data conversion, 522
data extraction, 523
data retrieval, 521
data sources for, 518, 520
designing studies, 518
linking data sets, 523–525
mapping bugs to files, 525
mining primer, 519–526
parsing bug reports, 523
typical starting points, 526–528
MIT, 231

Mockus, Audris, 432
Model-Based Testing (MBT), 6
modification requests, 455
(see also software faults study)
about, 148
work dependencies and, 189–194
modularity
analyzing changes, 376–381
defined, 202
historical background, 373, 374
programming languages and, 373, 381–383
study results, 383–389
systems analyzed, 374–375
threats to study validity, 389
Moher, Tom, 117
Moløkken-Østvold, K. J., 45
Motorola, 315, 367, 545
Mozilla Firefox browser
about, 375
analyzing changes, 376–381
bug-writing guidelines, 437
modularity and, 381–383
study results, 383–389
threats to study validity, 389
multicolinearity, 200
multitasking, 300
Murphy, Brendan, 432
organizational structure study, 194–200
Murphy, Gail C., 373–391, 524
Mylyn framework
about, 375
analyzing changes, 376–381
modularity and, 381–383
study results, 383–389
threats to study validity, 389
MySQL database, 520
The Mythical Man-Month (Brooks), 187, 312, 342,
423

N

Nagappan, Nachiappan
evidence-based failure prediction, 415–434
organizational structure study, 194–200
risk study, 527
syntactic dependencies and, 355
Nambiar, S., 356, 361, 364
NASA
IV&V standards, 6
Software Engineering Laboratory, 9, 67–68
National Academy of Engineering, 231
National Association of Colleges and Employers,
228
National Science Foundation (NSF), 9, 163, 322
natural language, 114–116
Navy (U.S.), 449

NBR (negative binomial regression)
  additional information, 156
  Bayesian additive regression trees and, 156
  defined, 150
  model replication/variations, 152
  random forests and, 155
  recursive partitioning and, 155
  role of developers, 152
Neale, M., 229, 230
Nelson, Eldred C., 454
Neto, A., 6
Nosek, John, 313
novice dominance, 408
Nowell, A., 223
NSF (National Science Foundation), 9, 163, 322

O

object-oriented (OO) design
  inspection methods and, 49
  modularity and, 373
Observer pattern
  about, 393, 394
  comparing solutions, 405
  testing documentation, 400
OECD (Organization for Economic Cooperation
        and Development), 232
office layout
  communal workshops, 342–345
  doors that close, 339–342
  work patterns and, 345–346
Olson, Gary M., 343
Olson, Judith S., 343
ombudsperson, 61
onboarding, 512–514
open source software, 259
  (see also operating system studies)
  ArchLinux software distribution, 127
  bug report survey, 437–441
  Conway's Law and, 189, 201–204
  efficacy comparison, 259
  sample measurement, 128–133
  statistical analysis, 133–139
  study background, 261–265
  surveying, 126
OpenSolaris operating system
  code structure, 270–276, 287
  code style, 276–282, 287
  data organization, 284–286, 288
  file organization, 266–270, 287
  historical background, 261, 262
  key study metrics, 265
  preprocessing, 282–284, 288
  study outcome, 286–289
operating system studies
  background, 260, 261

code structure, 270–276, 287
code style, 276–282, 287
data organization, 284–286, 288
file organization, 266–270, 287
key metrics, 265
preprocessing, 282–284, 288
study background, 261–265
study outcome, 286–289
optimization algorithms, 10
Organization for Economic Cooperation and
        Development (OECD), 232
organizational structure
  collaboration and, 357
  complexity study, 194–200
  Conway's Law on, 423–425
  coordination and, 353, 357
  dependencies and, 357, 359
  mining software archives and, 519
  in software faults study, 455
OSGi technology, 373
OSS (see open source software)
Ostrand, Thomas J., 145–160, 362
outsourcing (see GSD)

P

Pace University, 319
Page, Alan, 446
Page, S., 229
pair programming
  challenges, 320, 321
  collaboration and, 96, 312
  defined, 311
  distributed, 319, 320
  education study on, 511
  in educational setting, 317–319
  historical background, 312–314
  improving code production, 96
  in industrial settings, 314–317
  lessons learned, 321
  primary studies, 47
Pane, John, 115
Panjer, Lucas D., 449
Pareto distribution, 146–150
Parnas, David L., 350, 393
Pasteur project, 312
Pauling, Linus, 37
Paulson, J. W., 261
PBR (perspective-based reading), 49
PDGs (program dependence graphs), 533
PDR (Preliminary Design Review), 168
Pearson correlation coefficient, 134, 389
PeopleWare (DeMarco and Lister), 306, 341
Perkins, D. N., 508
Perl language (web development study), 248–257
Perricone, Barry T., 454, 485

result considerations, 486–490
statistical analysis, 466–484
study background, 453, 454
study context, 455, 456
underlying causes of MRs, 473–478, 483–484
Software Psychology (Shneiderman), 82
software quality, 261
(see also operating systems study)
dependencies and, 355, 356, 358, 359
design patterns and, 397
external quality, 210, 212, 259
internal quality, 209, 212, 259
operating system studies, 260
organizational structure and, 194–200, 425
study background, 261–265
TDD and, 209–211
software releases, distinctions in, 454
software testing
AT&T study, 146–150
design pattern documentation, 398–403
education study observations, 505
identifying problems, 145
TDD considerations, 214
Software-artifact Infrastructure Research (SIR), 8
Soloway, Eliot, 112
source code, 329
(see also code review)
accessing via tracking systems, 455
code churn metric, 418–420
code cloning, 531–544
code complexity metric, 421, 422
code coverage metric, 417, 418
code dependencies metric, 422, 423
distributions and, 127
leveraging repository data, 362
measuring aspects of, 127
measuring quality, 209
mining software archives, 518, 520
operating systems study, 270–276–282, 287
search for rationale, 300
statistical analysis, 133–139
Spangler, W. D., 88
spatial abilities, gender differences, 222–224
Spearman correlation, 442, 443
Spearman, C., 90
SPEC CPU benchmark, 24
Spinellis, Diomidis, 259–289
Spohrer, Jim, 113
Spolsky, Joel, 80
SQO-OSS, 289
SSL (Secure Sockets Layer), 204
StackOverflow.com, 547
The Standish Group, 45
Stasko, John, 117
statistical analysis, 466

(see also metrics/measurement)
about, 30
challenges to, 5, 139
design pattern experiments, 411
software faults study, 466–484
source code files, 133–139
Staudenmayer, Nancy A., 296–298
STC (socio-technical congruence)
about, 349
dependencies and, 351–361
future directions, 368
socio-organizational dimension, 356–360
socio-technical dimension, 360–361
technical dimension, 353–356
STDD (Story-Test-Driven Development), 208
Steig, Carol, 492
STEM fields, 222, 225
Sternberg, Robert, 100, 101
Story-Test-Driven Development (STDD), 208
Stroggylos, Konstantinos, 289
structural congruence, 190, 192
Style tool, 448
Stylos, Jeff, 564
Subversion tool, 363, 522
surveys
credibility and, 26, 27
defined, 26
relevance and, 27
for software faults study, 456–462–486
syntactic dependencies, 353–356
systematic reviews
advantages of, 37
Agile methods, 46–48
author's conclusions, 49
background, 35
bias and, 43
conducting, 40, 42–44
cost estimation studies, 44, 45
evidence-based software engineering and, 36
inspection methods, 48
Kitchenham and, 22
mapping studies and, 38
overview, 36–38
planning, 39
problems associated with, 42–44
process overview, 39–41
reporting, 41
strengths and weaknesses, 39–44
TDD research, 207–217

T

Tanenbaum, A. S., 262
Tang, M.-H., 422
task congruence, 191
TAT (Thematic Apperception Test), 88

Williams, Laurie, 96, 311–328, 511
Williams, Wendy M., 221–238
Windows Meeting Space, 319
Windows operating system, failure prediction study, 415–434
Windows Research Kernel (see WRK)
WMC (Working Memory Capacity), 92
women in computer science
    ability deficits and, 222–224
    benefits of, 227–234
    cross-national data on, 232–234
    cultural biases and, 224, 225–227
    preferences and, 224, 225
    reversing the trend, 232
    statistics, 221, 222
    STEM fields and, 222, 225
    stereotypes and, 225–227
work dependencies (see dependencies)
work-sample tests, 90
workflow patterns, 345–346
Working Memory Capacity (WMC), 92
Wright, Bill, 312
WRK (Windows Research Kernel)
    code structure, 270–276, 287
    code style, 276–282, 287
    data organization, 284–286, 288
    file organization, 266–270, 287
    historical background, 262
    key study metrics, 265
    preprocessing, 282–284, 288
    study background, 265
    study outcome, 286–289
Wulf, W. A., 231

X

XP (extreme programming)
    about, 46
    cost-to-fix considerations, 162, 164
    Dybå and Dingsøyr study, 47
    pair programming and, 311, 313
    ThoughtWorks lease management project, 165
xpairtise tool, 320

Y

Yale University, 112
Yuhas, Marjory P., 492

Z

Zannier, C., 6
Zarnett, B., 82
Zeller, Andreas, 432, 517–529
Zimmermann, Thomas
    acknowledgments, 432, 528
    collecting bug reports, 435–450

mapping bugs to files, 525
result replicability and, 6
syntactic dependencies and, 355

COLOPHON

The image on the cover of *Making Software* is the Arthur Ravenel Jr. Bridge, in South Carolina.

The cover image is from Getty Images. The cover font is Adobe ITC Garamond. The text font is Linotype Birka; the heading font is Adobe Myriad Condensed; and the code font is LucasFont's TheSansMonoCondensed.

Related Titles from O'Reilly

Software Development

97 Things Every Software Architect Should Know

Algorithms in a Nutshell

Applied Software Project Management

Beautiful Architecture

Beautiful Code

Beautiful Teams

CJKV Information Processing

Coding4Fun

Designing Interfaces

Essential Business Process Modeling

Enterprise Service Bus

Getting Started with Arduino

Head First Design Patterns

Head First Object-Oriented Analysis and Design

Head First PMP

Head First Software Development

Java SOA Cookbook

Learning UML 2.0

Making Things Happen

Masterminds of Programming

Practical Development Environments

Prefactoring

Process Improvement Essentials

Real World Haskell

SOA in Practice

The Art of Agile Development

The Art of Application Performance Testing

The Art of Capacity Planning

The Art of Lean Software Development

The Productive Programmer

UML 2.0 in a Nutshell

UML 2.0 Pocket Reference

Our books are available at most retail and online bookstores.
To order direct: 1-800-998-9938 • *order@oreilly.com* • *www.oreilly.com*
Online editions of most O'Reilly titles are available by subscription at *safari.oreilly.com*